SHORT STORIES
for Students

Advisors

Jayne M. Burton is a teacher of English, a member of the Delta Kappa Gamma International Society for Key Women Educators, and currently a master's degree candidate in the Interdisciplinary Study of Curriculum and Instruction and English at Angelo State University.

Mary Beth Maggio teaches seventh grade language arts in Schaumburg, Illinois.

Tom Shilts is the youth librarian at the Okemos branch of Capital Area District Library in Okemos, Michigan. He holds an MSLS degree from Clarion University of Pennsylvania and an MA in U.S. History from the University of North Dakota.

Amy Spade Silverman has taught at independent schools in California, Texas, Michigan, and New York. She holds a bachelor of arts degree from the University of Michigan and a master of fine arts degree from the University of Houston. She is a member of the National Council of Teachers of English and Teachers and Writers. She is an exam reader for Advanced Placement Literature and Composition. She is also a poet, published in *North American Review, Nimrod,* and *Michigan Quarterly Review,* among others.

Mary Turner holds a BS in Secondary Education from East Texas State University and a Master of Education from Western Kentucky University. She teaches English 7 and AP English 12 literature and composition at SBEC in Southaven, Mississippi.

Brian Woerner teaches English at Troy High School in Troy, Ohio. He is also a Program Associate of the Ohio Writing Project at Miami University.

SHORT STORIES

for Students

Presenting Analysis, Context, and Criticism on Commonly Studied Short Stories

VOLUME 38

Matthew Derda, Project Editor

Foreword by Thomas E. Barden

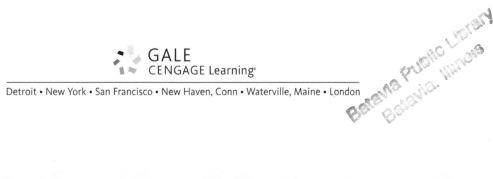

GALE
CENGAGE Learning®

Detroit • New York • San Francisco • New Haven, Conn • Waterville, Maine • London

GALE
CENGAGE Learning

Short Stories for Students, Volume 38

Project Editor: Matthew Derda

Rights Acquisition and Management: Sheila Spencer

Composition: Evi Abou-El-Seoud

Manufacturing: Rhonda A. Dover

Imaging: John Watkins

Product Design: Pamela A. E. Galbreath, Jennifer Wahi

Digital Content Production: Kevin Duffy

Product Manager: Meggin Condino

For product information and technology assistance, contact us at
Gale Customer Support, 1-800-877-4253.
For permission to use material from this text or product,
submit all requests online at **www.cengage.com/permissions.**
Further permissions questions can be emailed to
permissionrequest@cengage.com

Gale
27500 Drake Rd.
Farmington Hills, MI, 48331-3535

ISBN13:-978-1-4144-9525-5
ISBN10:1-4144-9525-0
ISSN 1092-7735

This title is also available as an e-book.
ISBN-13: 978-1-4144-9282-7
ISBN-10: 1-4144-9282-0
Contact your Gale, a part of Cengage Learning sales representative for ordering information.

Printed in Mexico
1 2 3 4 5 6 7 17 16 15 14 13

Table of Contents

Why Study Literature At All?

Short Stories for Students is designed to provide readers with information and discussion about a wide range of important contemporary and historical works of short fiction, and it does that job very well. However, I want to use this guest foreword to address a question that it does *not* take up. It is a fundamental question that is often ignored in high school and college English classes as well as research texts, and one that causes frustration among students at all levels, namely why study literature at all? Isn't it enough to read a story, enjoy it, and go about one's business? My answer (to be expected from a literary professional, I suppose) is no. It is not enough. It is a start; but it is not enough. Here's why.

First, literature is the only part of the educational curriculum that deals directly with the actual world of lived experience. The philosopher Edmund Husserl used the apt German term *die Lebenswelt*, "the living world," to denote this realm. All the other content areas of the modern American educational system avoid the subjective, present reality of everyday life. Science (both the natural and the social varieties) objectifies, the fine arts create and/or perform, history reconstructs. Only literary study persists in posing those questions we all asked before our schooling taught us to give up on them. Only literature gives credibility to personal perceptions, feelings, dreams, and the "stream of consciousness" that is our inner voice. Literature wonders about infinity, wonders why God permits evil, wonders what will happen to us after we die. Literature admits that we get our hearts broken, that people sometimes cheat and get away with it, that the world is a strange and probably incomprehensible place. Literature, in other words, takes on all the big and small issues of what it means to be human. So my first answer is that of the humanist we should read literature and study it and take it seriously because it enriches us as human beings. We develop our moral imagination, our capacity to sympathize with other people, and our ability to understand our existence through the experience of fiction.

My second answer is more practical. By studying literature we can learn how to explore and analyze texts. Fiction may be about *die Lebenswelt*, but it is a construct of words put together in a certain order by an artist using the medium of language. By examining and studying those constructions, we can learn about language as a medium. We can become more sophisticated about word associations and connotations, about the manipulation of symbols, and about style and atmosphere. We can grasp how ambiguous language is and how important context and texture is to meaning. In our first encounter with a work of literature, of course, we are not supposed to catch all of these things. We are spellbound, just as the writer wanted us to be. It is as serious students of the writer's art that we begin to see how the tricks are done.

Seeing the tricks, which is another way of saying "developing analytical and close reading skills," is important above and beyond its intrinsic literary educational value. These skills transfer to other fields and enhance critical thinking of any kind. Understanding how language is used to construct texts is powerful knowledge. It makes engineers better problem solvers, lawyers better advocates and courtroom practitioners, politicians better rhetoricians, marketing and advertising agents better sellers, and citizens more aware consumers as well as better participants in democracy. This last point is especially important, because rhetorical skill works both ways when we learn how language is manipulated in the making of texts the result is that we become less susceptible when language is used to manipulate us.

My third reason is related to the second. When we begin to see literature as created artifacts of language, we become more sensitive to good writing in general. We get a stronger sense of the importance of individual words, even the sounds of words and word combinations. We begin to understand Mark Twain's delicious proverb "The difference between the right word and the almost right word is the difference between lightning and a lightning bug." Getting beyond the "enjoyment only" stage of literature gets us closer to becoming makers of word art ourselves. I am not saying that studying fiction will turn every student into a Faulkner or a Shakespeare. But it will make us more adaptable and effective writers, even if our art form ends up being the office memo or the corporate annual report.

Studying short stories, then, can help students become better readers, better writers, and even better human beings. But I want to close with a warning. If your study and exploration of the craft, history, context, symbolism, or anything else about a story starts to rob it of the magic you felt when you first read it, it is time to stop. Take a break, study another subject, shoot some hoops, or go for a run. Love of reading is too important to be ruined by school. The early twentieth century writer Willa Cather, in her novel *My Antonia*, has her narrator Jack Burden tell a story that he and Antonia heard from two old Russian immigrants when they were teenagers. These immigrants, Pavel and Peter, told about an incident from their youth back in Russia that the narrator could recall in vivid detail thirty years later. It was a harrowing story of a wedding party starting home in sleds and being chased by starving wolves. Hundreds of wolves attacked the group's sleds one by one as they sped across the snow trying to reach their village. In a horrible revelation, the old Russians revealed that the groom eventually threw his own bride to the wolves to save himself. There was even a hint that one of the old immigrants might have been the groom mentioned in the story. Cather has her narrator conclude with his feelings about the story. "We did not tell Pavel's secret to anyone, but guarded it jealously as if the wolves of the Ukraine had gathered that night long ago, and the wedding party had been sacrificed, just to give us a painful and peculiar pleasure." That feeling, that painful and peculiar pleasure, is the most important thing about literature. Study and research should enhance that feeling and never be allowed to overwhelm it.

Thomas E. Barden
Professor of English and Director of
Graduate English Studies, The
University of Toledo

Introduction

Purpose of the Book

The purpose of *Short Stories for Students* (*SSfS*) is to provide readers with a guide to understanding, enjoying, and studying short stories by giving them easy access to information about the work. Part of Gale's "For Students" Literature line, *SSfS* is specifically designed to meet the curricular needs of high school and undergraduate college students and their teachers, as well as the interests of general readers and researchers considering specific short fiction. While each volume contains entries on "classic" stories frequently studied in classrooms, there are also entries containing hard-to-find information on contemporary stories, including works by multicultural, international, and women writers.

The information covered in each entry includes an introduction to the story and the story's author; a plot summary, to help readers unravel and understand the events in the work; descriptions of important characters, including explanation of a given character's role in the narrative as well as discussion about that character's relationship to other characters in the story; analysis of important themes in the story; and an explanation of important literary techniques and movements as they are demonstrated in the work.

In addition to this material, which helps the readers analyze the story itself, students are also provided with important information on the literary and historical background informing each work. This includes a historical context essay, a box comparing the time or place the story was written to modern Western culture, a critical overview essay, and excerpts from critical essays on the story or author. A unique feature of *SSfS* is a specially commissioned critical essay on each story, targeted toward the student reader.

To further help today's student in studying and enjoying each story, information on audiobooks and other media adaptations is provided (if available), as well as reading suggestions for works of fiction and nonfiction on similar themes and topics. Classroom aids include ideas for research papers and lists of critical and reference sources that provide additional material on the work.

Selection Criteria

The titles for each volume of *SSfS* were selected by surveying numerous sources on teaching literature and analyzing course curricula for various school districts. Some of the sources surveyed include: literature anthologies, *Reading Lists for College-Bound Students: The Books Most Recommended by America's Top Colleges; Teaching the Short Story: A Guide to Using Stories from around the World*, by the National Council of Teachers of English (NCTE); and "A Study of High School Literature Anthologies," conducted by Arthur Applebee at the Center for the Learning and Teaching of Literature and sponsored by the National Endowment for the

Arts and the Office of Educational Research and Improvement.

Input was also solicited from our advisory board, as well as educators from various areas. From these discussions, it was determined that each volume should have a mix of "classic" stories (those works commonly taught in literature classes) and contemporary stories for which information is often hard to find. Because of the interest in expanding the canon of literature, an emphasis was also placed on including works by international, multicultural, and women authors. Our advisory board members—educational professionals—helped pare down the list for each volume. Works not selected for the present volume were noted as possibilities for future volumes. As always, the editor welcomes suggestions for titles to be included in future volumes.

How Each Entry Is Organized

Each entry, or chapter, in *SSfS* focuses on one story. Each entry heading lists the title of the story, the author's name, and the date of the story's publication. The following elements are contained in each entry:

Introduction: a brief overview of the story which provides information about its first appearance, its literary standing, any controversies surrounding the work, and major conflicts or themes within the work.

Author Biography: this section includes basic facts about the author's life, and focuses on events and times in the author's life that may have inspired the story in question.

Plot Summary: a description of the events in the story. Lengthy summaries are broken down with subheads.

Characters: an alphabetical listing of the characters who appear in the story. Each character name is followed by a brief to an extensive description of the character's role in the story, as well as discussion of the character's actions, relationships, and possible motivation.

Characters are listed alphabetically by last name. If a character is unnamed—for instance, the narrator in "The Eatonville Anthology"—the character is listed as "The Narrator" and alphabetized as "Narrator." If a character's first name is the only one given, the name will appear alphabetically by that name.

Themes: a thorough overview of how the topics, themes, and issues are addressed within the story. Each theme discussed appears in a separate subhead.

Style: this section addresses important style elements of the story, such as setting, point of view, and narration; important literary devices used, such as imagery, foreshadowing, symbolism; and, if applicable, genres to which the work might have belonged, such as Gothicism or Romanticism. Literary terms are explained within the entry, but can also be found in the Glossary.

Historical Context: this section outlines the social, political, and cultural climate in which the author lived and the work was created. This section may include descriptions of related historical events, pertinent aspects of daily life in the culture, and the artistic and literary sensibilities of the time in which the work was written. If the story is historical in nature, information regarding the time in which the story is set is also included. Long sections are broken down with helpful subheads.

Critical Overview: this section provides background on the critical reputation of the author and the story, including bannings or any other public controversies surrounding the work. For older works, this section may include a history of how the story was first received and how perceptions of it may have changed over the years; for more recent works, direct quotes from early reviews may also be included.

Criticism: an essay commissioned by *SSfS* which specifically deals with the story and is written specifically for the student audience, as well as excerpts from previously published criticism on the work (if available).

Sources: an alphabetical list of critical material used in compiling the entry, with bibliographical information.

Further Reading: an alphabetical list of other critical sources which may prove useful for the student. Includes full bibliographical information and a brief annotation.

Suggested Search Terms: a list of search terms and phrases to jumpstart students' further information seeking. Terms include not just titles and author names but also terms and topics related to the historical and literary context of the works.

In addition, each entry contains the following highlighted sections, set apart from the main text as sidebars:

Media Adaptations: if available, a list of audio-books and important film and television adaptations of the story, including source information. The list also includes stage adaptations, musical adaptations, etc.

Topics for Further Study: a list of potential study questions or research topics dealing with the story. This section includes questions related to other disciplines the student may be studying, such as American history, world history, science, math, government, business, geography, economics, psychology, etc.

Compare and Contrast: an "at-a-glance" comparison of the cultural and historical differences between the author's time and culture and late twentieth century or early twenty-first century Western culture. This box includes pertinent parallels between the major scientific, political, and cultural movements of the time or place the story was written, the time or place the story was set (if a historical work), and modern Western culture. Works written after 1990 may not have this box.

What Do I Read Next?: a list of works that might give a reader points of entry into a classic work (e.g., YA or multicultural titles) and/or complement the featured story or serve as a contrast to it. This includes works by the same author and others, works from various genres, YA works, and works from various cultures and eras.

Other Features

SSfS includes "Why Study Literature At All?," a foreword by Thomas E. Barden, Professor of English and Director of Graduate English Studies at the University of Toledo. This essay provides a number of very fundamental reasons for studying literature and, therefore, reasons why a book such as *SSfS*, designed to facilitate the study of literature, is useful.

A Cumulative Author/Title Index lists the authors and titles covered in each volume of the *SSfS* series.

A Cumulative Nationality/Ethnicity Index breaks down the authors and titles covered in each volume of the *SSfS* series by nationality and ethnicity.

A Subject/Theme Index, specific to each volume, provides easy reference for users who may be studying a particular subject or theme rather than a single work. Significant subjects from events to broad themes are included.

Each entry may include illustrations, including photo of the author, stills from film adaptations (if available), maps, and/or photos of key historical events.

Citing Short Stories for Students

When writing papers, students who quote directly from any volume of *SSfS* may use the following general forms to document their source. These examples are based on MLA style; teachers may request that students adhere to a different style, thus, the following examples may be adapted as needed.

When citing text from *SSfS* that is not attributed to a particular author (for example, the Themes, Style, Historical Context sections, etc.), the following format may be used:

> "How I Met My Husband." *Short Stories for Students.* Ed. Sara Constantakis. Vol. 36. Detroit: Gale, Cengage Learning, 2013. 73–95. Print.

When quoting the specially commissioned essay from *SSfS* (usually the first essay under the Criticism subhead), the following format may be used:

> Dominic, Catherine. Critical Essay on "How I Met My Husband." *Short Stories for Students.* Ed. Sara Constantakis. Vol. 36. Detroit: Gale, Cengage Learning, 2013. 84–87. Print.

When quoting a journal or newspaper essay that is reprinted in a volume of *SSfS*, the following form may be used:

> Ditsky, John. "The Figure in the Linoleum: The Fictions of Alice Munro." *Hollins Critic* 22.3 (1985): 1–10. Rpt. in *Short Stories for Students.* Vol. 36. Ed. Sara Constantakis. Detroit: Gale, Cengage Learning, 2013. 92–94. Print.

When quoting material from a book that is reprinted in a volume of *SSfS,* the following form may be used:

> Cooke, John. "Alice Munro." *The Influence of Painting on Five Canadian Writers.* Lewiston, NY: Edwin Mellen Press, 1996. 69–85. Rpt. in

Short Stories for Students. Vol. 36. Ed. Sara Constantakis. Detroit: Gale, Cengage Learning, 2013. 89–92. Print.

We Welcome Your Suggestions

The editorial staff of *Short Stories for Students* welcomes your comments and ideas. Readers who wish to suggest short stories to appear in future volumes, or who have other suggestions, are cordially invited to contact the editor. You may contact the editor via E-mail at: **ForStudentsEditors@cengage.com.** Or write to the editor at:

Editor, *Short Stories for Students*
Gale
27500 Drake Road
Farmington Hills, MI 48331-3535

Literary Chronology

1860: Anton Chekhov is born on January 17 in Taganrog, Russia.

1862: Mori Ōgai is born on February 17 in Tsuwano, Japan.

1871: Stephen Crane is born on November 1 in Newark, New Jersey.

1877: Anton Chekhov's "The Kiss" is published.

1899: Stephen Crane's "An Episode of War" is published in *Gentlewoman*.

1900: Stephen Crane dies of tuberculosis on June 5 in Badenweiler, Germany.

1904: Anton Chekhov dies of tuberculosis on July 15 in Badenweiler, Germany.

1910: Mori Ōgai's "Under Reconstruction" is published.

1914: Bernard Malamud is born on April 26 in New York City, New York.

1917: (Lula) Carson Smith McCullers is born on February 19 in Columbus, Georgia.

1922: Mori Ōgai dies of tuberculosis on July 8 in Tokyo, Japan.

1924: Joan Aiken is born on September 4 in Rye, Sussex, England.

1930: Ted Hughes is born on August 17 in Mytholmroyd, England.

1937: Rudolfo Anaya is born on October 30 in Pastura, New Mexico.

1942: Carson McCullers's "A Tree. A Rock. A Cloud." is published.

1947: Charles Baxter is born on May 13 in Minneapolis, Minnesota.

1950: Diana García is born in the San Joaquin Valley, California.

1952: Alice Hoffman is born on March 16 in New York City, New York.

1954: Mary Gaitskill is born on November 11 in Lexington, Kentucky.

1955: Barbara Ellen Kingsolver is born on April 8 in Annapolis, Maryland.

1955: Gish Jen is born in Scarsdale, New York.

1960: Ted Hughes's "The Rain Horse" is published in *Harper's*.

1961: Bernard Malamud's "Idiots First" is first published in *Commentary*.

1967: Bernard Malamud is awarded the Pulitzer Prize for Fiction for *The Fixer*.

1967: Carson McCullers dies of stroke on September 29 in Nyack, New York.

1981: Joan Aiken's "Lob' Girl" is published.

1985: Charles Baxter's "Gryphon" is published in *Through the Safety Net*.

1986: Bernard Malamud dies of heart failure on March 18 in New York City, New York.

1987: Rudolfo Anaya's "In Search of Epifano" is published.

1987: Barbara Kingsolver's "Rose-Johnny" is published.

1990: Gish Jen's "What Means Switch" is published.

1993: Diana García's "The Flat of the Land" is published in *Pieces of the Heart: New Chicano Fiction*.

1997: Mary Gaitskill's "Tiny, Smiling Daddy" is published in her collection *Because They Wanted To*.

1998: Ted Hughes dies of cancer on October 28 in London, England.

2004: Joan Aiken dies on January 4 in Petworth, West Sussex, England.

2005: Alice Hoffman's "Saint Helene" is published in *Ploughshares*.

Acknowledgements

The editors wish to thank the copyright holders of the excerpted criticism included in this volume and the permissions managers of many book and magazine publishing companies for assisting us in securing reproduction rights. We are also grateful to the staffs of the Detroit Public Library, the Library of Congress, the University of Detroit Mercy Library, Wayne State University Purdy/Kresge Library Complex, and the University of Michigan Libraries for making their resources available to us. Following is a list of the copyright holders who have granted us permission to reproduce material in this volume of *SSfS*. Every effort has been made to trace copyright, but if omissions have been made, please let us know.

COPYRIGHTED EXCERPTS IN *SSfS*, VOLUME 38, WERE REPRODUCED FROM THE FOLLOWING SOURCES:

Aiken, Joan. From *The Way to Write for Children*. St. Martin's Press, 1982. Copyright © 1982, St. Martin's Press. Reproduced by permission of the publisher.—Bassnett, Susan. From *Ted Hughes*. Northcote House Publishers, 2009. Copyright © 2009, Northcote House Publishers. Reproduced by permission of the publisher.—Baxter, Charles. From *The Art of Subtext: Beyond Plot*. Graywolf Press, 2007. Copyright © 2007, Graywolf Press. Reproduced by permission of the publisher.—Carr, Virginia Spencer. From *Understanding Carson McCullers*. University of South Carolina Press, 1989. Copyright © 1989, University of South Carolina Press. Reproduced by permission of the publisher.—*Commonweal*, 124.19, November 7, 1997. Copyright © 1997 by *Commonweal*. Reproduced by permission of the publisher.—Conrad, Joseph L. From *Critical Essays on Anton Chekhov*. Edited by Thomas A. Eekman. G. K. Hall, 1989. Copyright © 1989, G. K. Hall. Reproduced by permission of the publisher.—DeMarr, Mary Jean. From *Barbara Kingsolver: A Critical Companion*. Greenwood Press, 1999. Copyright © 1999, Greenwood Press. Reproduced by permission of the publisher.—Fernández Olmos, Margarite. From *Rudolpho A. Anaya: A Critical Companion*. Edited by Kathleen Gregory Klein. Greenwood Press, 1999. Copyright © 1999, Greenwood Press. Reproduced by permission of the publisher.—Friedman, Alan Warren. From *Bernard Malamud and the Critics*. Edited by Leslie A. Field and Joyce W. Field. New York University Press, 1970. Copyright © 1970, New York University Press. Reproduced by permission of the publisher.—García, Diana. From *Placing the Academy: Essays on Landscape, Work, and Identity*. Edited by Jennifer Sinor and Rona Kaufman. Utah State University Press, 2007. Copyright © 2007, Utah State University Press. Reproduced by permission of the publisher.—Herrerra, Juan Felipe. From *Reading U.S. Latina Writers: Remapping American Literature*. Edited by Alvina E. Quintana. Palgrave Macmillan,

2003. Copyright © 2003, Palgrave Macmillan. Reproduced by permission of the publisher.—*Interactions*, 15.2, fall, 2006. Copyright © 2006 by *Interactions*. Reproduced by permission of the publisher.—Johnson, Ronald L. From *Anton Chekhov: A Study of the Short Fiction*. Edited by Gordon Weaver. Twayne Publishers, 1993. Copyright © 1993, Cengage Learning. Reproduced by permission of Gale, a part of Cengage Learning.—Johnson, Sarah Anne. From *The Very Telling: Conversations with American Writers*. University Press of New England, 2006. Copyright © 2006, University Press of New England. Reproduced by permission of the publisher.—*Kirkus Reviews*, October 15, 2010. Copyright © 2010 by *Kirkus Reviews*. Reproduced by permission of the publisher.—*Library Journal*, 135.17, October 15, 2010. Copyright © 2010 by *Library Journal*. Reproduced by permission of the publisher.—*MELUS*, 25.1, spring, 2000. Copyright © 2000 by *MELUS*. Reproduced by permission of the publisher.—Ozick, Cynthia. From *The Magic Worlds of Bernard Malamud*. Edited by Evelyn Avery. State University of New York Press, 2001. Copyright © 2001, State University of New York Press. Reproduced by permission of the publisher.—Phillips, Robert. From *Critical Essays on Carson McCullers*. Edited by Beverly Lyon Clark and Melvin J. Friedman. G. K. Hall, 1996. Copyright © 1996, G. K. Hall. Reproduced by permission of the publisher.—*Ploughshares*, 26.2-3, fall, 2000; 29.2-3, fall, 2003. Copyright © 2000, 2003 by *Ploughshares*. Reproduced by permission of the publisher.—*Review of Contemporary Fiction*, 31.3, fall, 2011. Copyright © 2011 by *Review of Contemporary Fiction*. Reproduced by permission of the publisher.—Rimer, J. Thomas. From *The Historical Fiction of Mori Ogai*. Edited by David A. Dilworth and J. Thomas Rimer. University of Hawaii Press, 1991. Copyright © 1991, University of Hawaii Press. Reproduced by permission of the publisher.—Robertson, Michael. From *Stephen Crane, Journalism, and the Making of Modern American Literature*. Columbia University Press, 1997. Copyright © 1997, Columbia University Press. Reproduced by permission of the publisher.—Schaefer, Michael W. From *A Reader's Guide to the Short Stories of Stephen Crane*. G. K. Hall, 1996. Copyright © 1996, G. K. Hall. Reproduced by permission of the publisher.—Schapiro, Barbara Ann. From *Literature and the Relational Self*. Edited by Jeffrey Berman. New York University Press, 1994. Copyright © 1994, New York University Press. Reproduced by permission of the publisher.—Shechner, Mark. From *Critical Essays on Bernard Malamud*. Edited by Joel Salzberg. G. K. Hall, 1987. Copyright © 1987, G. K. Hall. Reproduced by permission of the publisher.—Snodgrass, Mary Ellen. From *Barbara Kingsolver: A Literary Companion*. McFarland, 2004. Copyright © 2004, McFarland. Reproduced by permission of the publisher.—Solotaroff, Robert. From *Bernard Malamud: A Study of the Short Fiction*. Twayne Publishers, 1989. Copyright © 1989, Cengage Learning. Reproduced by Gale, a part of Cengage Learning.—Townsend, John Rowe. From *A Sense of Story: Essays on Contemporary Writers for Children*. J.B. Lippincott, 1971. Copyright © 1971, J.P. Lippincott. Reproduced by permission of the publisher.—Whitt, Jan. From *Reflections in a Critical Eye: Essays on Carson McCullers*. University Press of America, 2008. Copyright © 2008, University Press of America. Reproduced by permission of the publisher.—*Women's Review of Books*, 14.8, May, 1997. Copyright © 1997 by *Women's Review of Books*. Reproduced by permission of the publisher.—*World Literature Today*, 69.1, winter, 1995; 70.2, spring, 1996. Copyright © 1995, 1996 by *World Literature Today*. Reproduced by permission of the publisher.

Contributors

Susan K. Andersen: Andersen holds a PhD in literature. Entry on "Rose-Johnny." Original essay on "Rose-Johnny."

Bryan Aubrey: Aubrey holds a PhD in English. Entries on "In Search of Epifano" and "The Kiss." Original essays on "In Search of Epifano" and "The Kiss."

Andrea Betts: Betts is a freelance writer specializing in literature. Entry on "Saint Helene." Original essay on "Saint Helene."

Cynthia A. Bily: Bily teaches English at Macomb Community College in Michigan. Entry on "A Tree. A Rock. A Cloud." Original essay on "A Tree. A Rock. A Cloud."

Catherine Dominic: Dominic is a novelist and a freelance writer and editor. Entries on "An Episode of War" and "Gryphon." Original essays on "An Episode of War" and "Gryphon."

Kristen Sarlin Greenberg: Greenberg is a freelance writer and editor with a background in literature and philosophy. Entry on "What Means Switch." Original essay on "What Means Switch."

Michael Allen Holmes: Holmes is a writer with existential interests. Entries on "The Flat of the Land" and "The Rain Horse." Original essays on "The Flat of the Land" and "The Rain Horse."

David Kelly: Kelly is an instructor of literature and creative writing. Entry on "Tiny, Smiling Daddy." Original essay on "Tiny, Smiling Daddy."

Amy Lynn Miller: Miller attended the University of Cincinnati and now resides in New Orleans, Louisiana. Entry on "Under Reconstruction." Original essay on "Under Reconstruction."

Michael J. O'Neal: O'Neal holds a PhD in English. Entry on "Idiots First." Original essay on "Idiots First."

Laura Pryor: Pryor has a master's degree in English and over twenty-five years' experience as a professional writer. Entry on "Lob's Girl." Original essay on "Lob's Girl."

An Episode of War

STEPHEN CRANE

1899

Stephen Crane is perhaps best known for *The Red Badge of Courage* (1895), a novel depicting the horrors of the American Civil War. Like this novel, a number of Crane's works of short fiction explore a variety of aspects of warfare. "An Episode of War" takes place during the Civil War and focuses on one soldier's loss of his arm. Ironically, he is not injured during combat but is shot by a stray bullet off of the battlefield. The brief story describes the soldier's short journey past the battlefield, from which he is now isolated, to the makeshift hospital comprising tents grouped around an old schoolhouse.

In this tale, Crane focuses on capturing the way war and injury isolate the soldier both from his fellow soldiers and from his family. Crane additionally demonstrates the fear experienced by the man and explores the way his injury shapes his perceptions. "An Episode of War" was originally published in England in 1899 in the magazine the *Gentlewoman* and was reprinted in 1902 in the collection *Last Words*. It is included in *The Complete Short Stories & Sketches of Stephen Crane* (1963) and *Great Short Works of Stephen Crane* (2004).

AUTHOR BIOGRAPHY

Crane was born in Newark, New Jersey, on November 1, 1871, the last of fourteen children born to the Reverend Dr. Jonathan Townley

STEPHEN CRANE.

Stephen Crane (© *Mary Evans Picture Library / Alamy*)

printed. Appearing in 1893 under the pseudonym Johnston Smith, the grimly realistic work depicts the life of a girl forced to turn to prostitution in the slums of New York. The work was rejected by several publishers, who felt the realities explored would be too shocking to readers. *The Red Badge of Courage*, Crane's second novel, was published in full in 1895. The internationally acclaimed work presents, in a series of vignettes, the wartime experiences of a young soldier during the Civil War. Roughly two years later, Crane met Cora Taylor, who ran a brothel. The pair considered themselves common-law husband and wife, and they subsequently moved to England.

Crane reported on the Greco-Turkish War in 1897 and the Spanish-American War in 1898 for the *New York World*. After returning to England, he continued to write short fiction, including such works as "The Monster" and "The Blue Hotel" in 1898. "An Episode of War" was published in 1899 by the British magazine the *Gentlewoman*. Crane suffered from tuberculosis after returning to England. Cora eventually borrowed money from friends to take Crane to Germany for rest and treatment. He died in Badenweiler, Germany, on June 5, 1900.

Crane and Mary Helen Crane. Crane's father was a Methodist minister, and owing to Dr. Crane's various ecclesiastical positions, the large family moved about during Crane's youth. In 1876 the family settled in Paterson, New Jersey, and just two years later they moved to Port Jervis, New York. When Dr. Crane died in 1880, Mrs. Crane moved her family to Asbury Park, New Jersey.

From 1888 to 1890, Crane attended the Hudson River Institute. In the fall of 1890, he began studying at Lafayette College, intending to pursue a degree in mining engineering. Crane abandoned this goal, and the college itself, before the end of the first semester. In 1891, he enrolled at Syracuse University but completed only one semester. During this time, Crane had begun writing for the *New York Tribune* but was fired a year later for a satirical piece he had penned.

In December 1891, Crane wrote the novella *Maggie: A Girl of the Streets*. With financing provided by his brothers, Crane had the work

PLOT SUMMARY

"An Episode of War" opens with a lieutenant dividing coffee for the various squadrons in his company. As the coffee is divided, the lieutenant suddenly cries out. His companions echo his shock when they see blood pouring out on the officer's sleeve. The gathered men gaze about, noticing the smoke arising from beyond the bulwark surrounding the encampment. It becomes apparent that a stray bullet from the forest across the field has struck the lieutenant.

The lieutenant finds that he must move his sword from his limp right hand to his left. Stunned by his wound, he performs this maneuver awkwardly, and the narrator describes the way the lieutenant grips the sword in the middle of the blade and tries to sheathe it. As he struggles to "sheathe a sword held by the left hand, at the middle of the blade, in a scabbard hung at the left hip," the other soldiers finally wake from their own stupor and help their comrade to sheathe his sword.

MEDIA ADAPTATIONS

- In 2007, Audible Audio published a 10-minute MP3 recording of Crane's "An Episode of War," read by Christopher Graybill.

The lieutenant then holds his right wrist with his left hand and begins to walk away, passing the battery and the line of battle as he does so. He observes details of the scene, noticing the actions of a bugler, several orderlies, the movement of the horses, and a general on horseback. The lieutenant witnesses the smoke from the gunfire and is directed by "stragglers" from the battlefield to the hospital.

An officer whom he encounters along the way sees the lieutenant's wound and begins to reprimand him for the way he is holding his arm and for his lack of attention to his wound. The officer cuts away the sleeve and binds the bullet wound with a handkerchief. As the lieutenant approaches the tents surrounding the school that has become the base of the hospital unit, he sees a chaotic scene. Two ambulances are stuck wheel-to-wheel in the mud while the drivers argue over who is to blame. Meanwhile, the cries of the wounded within the horse-drawn vehicles can be heard. Innumerable wounded men mill about around the facility.

As the lieutenant crosses paths with a surgeon, the surgeon sees the lieutenant's arm. He notes angrily how improperly it has been treated to this point. Examining the wound, the surgeon instructs the lieutenant to come with him. Worriedly, the lieutenant searches the doctor's face, and states, "I guess I won't have it amputated." The doctor assures him such a measure will not be necessary, further admonishing the lieutenant, "Don't be a baby." The lieutenant resists the grip of the surgeon and looks fearfully at the schoolhouse door.

In the final paragraph of the story, the lieutenant, who has in fact lost his arm, returns home. The women in his family—his wife, mother, and sisters—sob at the sight of the empty sleeve. In response, the lieutenant attempts to shrug off their grief, stating that he supposes the loss of the arm does not matter that much.

CHARACTERS

Lieutenant

The unnamed lieutenant is the protagonist of "An Episode of War." The lieutenant's story quickly progresses from the mundane to the tragic as he is wounded while rationing coffee for his company. The narrative traces his progression past the battlefield to the field hospital, where his arm is amputated. At the story's conclusion, the lieutenant returns home to his family.

Crane details the emotions the lieutenant experiences throughout the story and further delineates the reactions of the other soldiers to him after he is wounded. The lieutenant and his comrades are equally shocked when they realize he has been shot. Crane notes that the other soldiers now treat the lieutenant with a combination of reverence and awe, yet the lieutenant feels victimized, diseased, and helpless. Journeying toward the hospital tents, the lieutenant becomes almost hyperaware of the elements of the battle that is being played out just beyond the bulwarks. When he is later scolded for not binding his wound, he hangs his head, feeling as though "he did not know how to be correctly wounded." When approached by the surgeon who studies his wound, the lieutenant grows full of fear and dread at the thought of a possible amputation. His fears are in fact realized, and although he attempts to minimize the significance of the injury to his female family members, he feels shame at being regarded as less than whole.

Lieutenant's Family

The lieutenant's family members, including his wife, mother, and sisters, weep when the lieutenant returns home and they see that his arm has been amputated. Their grief causes the lieutenant to feel a sense of shame.

Officer

One of several officers who are members of a roadside brigade and whom the lieutenant passes on his way to the hospital intercepts the wounded man. The officer examines the lieutenant's wound and binds it with a handkerchief, all the while scolding the lieutenant. He is depicted as having a knowing, nonchalant attitude about the lieutenant's wound, suggesting that he has seen many soldiers who have been maimed over the course of the war.

Orderly Sergeant

The orderly sergeant helps the wounded lieutenant by taking his sword and sheathing it for him. He is careful not to touch the lieutenant directly and leans away from the lieutenant in a nervous manner.

Surgeon

The surgeon passes near the lieutenant by the hospital tents. The warmth of his friendly greeting evaporates when he sees the lieutenant's wounded arm. Despite his apparent battle fatigue, he is compelled by a sense of duty to examine the wound. Crane describes his demeanor: "He seemed possessed suddenly with a great contempt for the lieutenant." He instructs the lieutenant to come with him in a tone that seems to the lieutenant to be disapproving. Presumably, the surgeon now knows what must be done and is disgruntled and dismayed by the prospect of having to perform yet another amputation. Nevertheless, he assures the lieutenant that an amputation will not be necessary, in an effort to prevent the obviously fearful lieutenant from panicking. Chastising the lieutenant, he instructs him to not "be a baby."

THEMES

United States Civil War, 1861–1865

As in *The Red Badge of Courage*, Crane depicts the Civil War in grim detail in "An Episode of War." However brief the story, in it Crane captures wartime realities, although the incident he details is not one that occurs on the battlefield. Rather, Crane features an injury caused by a stray bullet and focuses his narrative on the man who, enduring the injury, journeys toward the hospital for the treatment that ends up being an amputation. The war as Crane depicts it is not characterized by fervency of belief in the justice of a cause or marked by battlefield glory. Rather, war lurks like a beast in the woods, mysterious and attacking at random. A lieutenant rationing coffee is struck in the arm by a stray bullet as the story opens. Crane emphasizes

the confusion of the moment by not directly relating the detail of the bullet's striking the lieutenant. Instead, the lieutenant suddenly cries out "and looked quickly at a man near him as if he suspected it was a case of personal assault." The other soldiers respond similarly at the sight of blood on the lieutenant's sleeve. They see "puffs of white smoke" beyond the bulwark, and they contemplate the "catastrophe." Further, they gaze at "the distant forest, as if their minds were fixed upon the mystery of a bullet's journey." It is only in this hazy manner that Crane hints at what has happened.

Other details are suggestive of the pain the lieutenant endures. He awkwardly shifts his sword from one hand to the other and attempts to sheathe the weapon. The lieutenant later holds "his right wrist tenderly in his left hand as if the wounded arm was made of very brittle glass." As the lieutenant journeys to the hospital area, consisting of a series of tents surrounding an old schoolhouse, he witnesses the battlefield scenes before him—a general on horseback, other soldiers riding horses and trying to hold their ground against enemy fire, and the intermittent shooting at the front lines. In these details, the reader witnesses the chaos of the battle, but as an echo. The enemy is not directly shown, nor does Crane depict battlefield gore. The images of warfare, as described by the wounded lieutenant, are alternately focused and sweeping so that they, like the sounds the lieutenant hears, blur into a "war-chorus."

The next portion of the story features the treatment the lieutenant receives for his wound, first from the officer who binds it with a handkerchief and then from the surgeon who amputates the arm. The lieutenant endures the examination of the officer. The officer "cut the sleeve and laid bare the arm, every nerve of which softly fluttered under his touch." Not long after, the lieutenant's terror of the impending amputation is conveyed when he begs the surgeon, "Let go of me." The lieutenant then glances at the schoolhouse door, which seems "as sinister to him as the portals of death." Finally, the lieutenant returns home. There he receives the grief of his family and feels shame in response. In this brief episode, Crane identifies a series of war-related horrors endured by the lieutenant. It is not a grand, sweeping, blood-soaked battlefield that Crane portrays, but rather the quiet and painful journey of a newly broken soldier.

TOPICS FOR FURTHER STUDY

- "An Episode of War" takes place during the Civil War. Research this time period in American history and create a research project in which you outline the causes of the war, the major battles, the political issues that contributed to and were shaped by the war, the key players including politicians and generals, and the events surrounding the end of the war. Your project may take the form of an interactive web-based time line, a poster, a PowerPoint presentation, or another print or electronic visual presentation. Be sure to cite your sources.

- Originally published in 1891, S. Alice Callahan's novel *Wynema: A Child of the Forest* is among the first-known written works by a Native American woman. Like Crane, Callahan lived during the later half of the nineteenth century. Her work examines what life in America was like for Native Americans during this time period. Read *Wynema* and write an essay in which you begin by providing a summary of the story's plot and characters. Consider what Callahan reveals about the time in which she lived. What themes did she choose to write about in this novel? How do her tone and style differ from those elements of Crane's fiction?

- In the 1990 young-adult novel *The Slopes of War*, by Norah Perez, the author focuses on the Battle of Gettysburg, describing this battle from the viewpoint of teenagers fighting as soldiers on both sides of the battle lines. With a small group, read Perez's novel. How do Perez's descriptions of war compare with those of Crane? Does Perez attempt to realistically capture the grim realities of battle? How do the characters change over the course of the novel? How does the battle transform them? Create an online blog in which you discuss these issues as well as other matters of plot, characterization, and theme.

- "An Episode of War" ends abruptly with the lieutenant's return home to his crying family. What do you think would happen next had the story not ended there? Write the next scene of the story in two ways. In the first, re-create to the best of your ability Crane's style. Continue the convention of leaving the characters unnamed and focus on the lieutenant's impression of himself as isolated from his family. Additionally, write the scene as you imagine it in a more modern tone, giving the lieutenant and his family members names and including more dialogue but retaining the lieutenant's feeling of alienation. Present both versions to your class and discuss which ending was easier to write and why.

Isolation

In "An Episode of War," Crane highlights the isolating effect of the lieutenant's injury. After he is shot in the arm, the lieutenant feels an almost instantaneous sense of disconnection from his comrades and from everything that once seemed ordinary. He looks at his once-familiar sword as a suddenly "strange thing." It is utterly foreign to him, and he considers it in a confused manner, "as if he had been endowed with a trident, a scepter, or a spade." Unable to successfully sheathe the sword with his left hand into a scabbard on his left hip, the lieutenant is aided by another soldier. Although the lieutenant's fellow soldiers are described as sympathetic in their attitude toward the wounded lieutenant, they are also hesitant, awestruck, and newly reverent. The orderly sergeant assisting the lieutenant with his sword "leaned nervously backward, and did not allow even his finger to brush the body of the lieutenant." Crane goes on to insist, "A wound gives strange dignity to him who bears it." The lieutenant feel isolated from his fellow soldiers by his wound, and they now

Civil War hospital tents, 1864 (*Library of Congress*)

regard him differently as well. He is possessed of this "strange dignity," but they fear touching him, as if "the weight of a finger upon him might send him headlong, precipitate the tragedy, hurl him at once into the dim, grey unknown." They fear touching him because they fear *for* him, not knowing if his contact with their whole, uninjured selves might intensify the lieutenant's feeling of brokenness and thereby send him into madness.

As much as the soldiers fear touching the lieutenant, he also recoils from their touch. He waves off their help "mournfully" and bears "the look of one who knows he is the victim of a terrible disease and understands his helplessness." He has been indelibly marked as different, as "other," and the lieutenant knows it as well as his fellows. The lieutenant's solitary journey to the hospital underscores his sense of isolation; he views the battle but is not a part of it. Once

his arm has been amputated and he returns home to his family, the lieutenant's alienation from his family is highlighted. His wife, mother, and sisters sob at the sight of his "flat sleeve." The lieutenant, enduring their grieving response to his injury, stands "shamefaced amid these tears." Their sorrow and his shame stand out despite the lieutenant's words about the injury's not really mattering so much. Crane depicts the lieutenant as a figure who feels intensely alienated from others and who is keenly aware of the ways in which his fellow soldiers and his family feel isolated from him.

STYLE

Realism

Crane is known as one of the forerunners of literary realism in America at the end of the nineteenth century, but he is also associated with literary naturalism and impressionism. Like real-ism, naturalism is focused on the depiction of everyday life and the social conditions of the world in a truthful manner. Yet naturalism, even more than realism, is stripped of emotional interpretation and typically views human beings as similar to any other animal on earth, soulless and subject to the laws of science and nature. Literary impressionism borrows from the French painting style known as impressionism in that it evokes episodic scenes that make use of imagery and emotion as vital components in the narrative. In "An Episode of War," Crane combines a jour-nalistic sensibility in the reporting of war-related details with an attempt to capture the psycholog-ical state of the protagonist. This fidelity to the truth of warfare, to everyday life as a soldier, is the hallmark of Crane's realism in the story. Fur-ther, he incorporates another layer of realism, that of psychological realism, in his portrayal of the lieutenant's state of mind as he journeys from a state of wholeness to one of fracture.

Crane opens the story with an almost domestic scene, with the soldiers waiting for the lieutenant to provide them with their rations of coffee. When the lieutenant is injured by the stray bullet, he winces and sways but does not fall. Crane combines such details as the sound of the lieutenant's "hoarse breathing" with an indi-cation of the lieutenant's emotional state, noting that he "looked sadly, mystically, over the breast-work at the green face of a wood." (The *breastwork* referred to is the partition, or bul-wark, that serves as a protective barrier enclos-ing the army camp.) Such exterior and interior details commingle throughout the story. Crane portrays the lieutenant's feeble attempt to sheathe his sword, followed by an examination of the awe with which the other soldiers now regard the wounded lieutenant. The lieutenant observes a vast array of details related to the army camp and the battlefield as he makes his way to the hospital, noticing, for example, the artillery battery and the mobile unit of guns and cannons. He sees it as an "aggregation of wheels, levers, motors" that is marked by a "beautiful unity." The lieutenant's thoughts grow increas-ingly poetic as he contemplates the noise of the battery. "The sound of it," he thinks, "was a war-chorus that reached into the depths of man's emotion." Crane details the way the officer tears the fabric of the lieutenant's sleeve, reveal-ing the wounded flesh it concealed. These phys-ical details of war and wounds are followed by a revelation of the lieutenant's feelings of inad-equacy, as if "he did not know how to be cor-rectly wounded."

After the amputation, the lieutenant returns home. The detail of his "flat sleeve" is juxtaposed with the shame the lieutenant feels. His "shame-faced" stance is further contrasted with the words that belie his feelings of emptiness and brokenness when he states, "I don't suppose it matters so much as all that." This sentiment is often taken to indicate that the lieutenant has stoically embraced an understanding that he, or any other individual for that matter, is an insig-nificant part of the universe. While he may be indicating that his injury is rather insignificant in the broader scope of things, it remains a perti-nent part of his own identity and shapes the way he views himself and the way he is regarded by society. His attempt to minimize the impact of the injury for the sake of his grieving family exemplifies Crane's effort to craft a realistic emotional response on the part of the lieutenant to his injury.

Nature Imagery

Crane incorporates into the lieutenant's story several images rooted in the natural world. He repeatedly references the "green face of a wood" that stands beyond the bulwark. The wood, or forest, is mentioned first when the lieutenant is shot. He gazes at the wood "sadly, mystically." Moments later, the other soldiers also turn, seek-ing the source of the lieutenant's injury and try-ing to ascertain "the mystery of a bullet's journey." As the lieutenant makes his journey away from the scene of his injury and toward the hospital, his comrades watch him leave. Crane describes the scene: "And the men in silence stared at the wood, then at the departing lieutenant; then at the wood, then at the lieuten-ant." The wood continues to draw their atten-tion; it is a source of mystery as well as dread. Surveying the battle scene before him, the lieu-tenant notices a general on horseback, "gazing over the lines of blue infantry at the green woods which veiled his problems."

Crane noticeably does not call attention to the enemy soldiers. Rather, he repeatedly draws the reader's gaze toward the wood where the enemy clearly hides. The woods themselves are characterized as a source of mystery as well as power. The movements of the enemy are cloaked by the cover the trees provide. The woods veil the problems of the general in that they disguise the enemy soldiers. For the comrades of the lieutenant, the woods are similarly inscrutable. In the way their collective gaze fluctuates from the lieutenant to the wood and back repeatedly as the lieutenant leaves their midst, Crane underscores a subtle sense not only of disbelief but almost of betrayal. The wood becomes a symbol of the unknown, with all its danger and power to destroy. The moments of their disbelief are prolonged, as when, staring at the wood, the men "gazed statue-like and silent, astonished and awed by this catastrophe which happened when catastrophes were not expected—when they had leisure to observe it."

HISTORICAL CONTEXT

US Civil War, 1861–1865

Although Crane was born several years after the Civil War ended, it was a time period to which he was drawn, as seen in works such as "An Episode of War" and *The Red Badge of Courage*. The Civil War began in 1861 and ended in 1865. Tensions leading to the war were rooted not only in the debate over slavery but also in the disagreements between northern and southern states over which powers could be exercised by the federal government and which belonged to the states. As new states entered the Union in the early to mid-1800s, the arguments over states' rights intensified. The states of the South sought to protect their slave-driven economy and culture and opposed the idea that new states would enter the Union as nonslave states. By the 1850s, the southern states had begun to raise the prospect of secession, by which they would leave the United States. When Abraham Lincoln was elected president in 1860, the Southern states feared that the North would increasingly limit states' rights while giving more power to the federal government and that consequently slavery would be abolished and the southern economy would be devastated. Lincoln's administration and the northern states did not regard secession as a legitimate or legal action.

Nonetheless, South Carolina and then Mississippi, Florida, Alabama, Georgia, Louisiana, and Texas all declared their secession from the United States in January 1861. In February, the seven states that had seceded created the Confederate Constitution and elected Jefferson Davis as their president. Later that month, the seceded states seized several southern forts. Lincoln was inaugurated in March. He attempted to assure the Southern states that he did not intend to end slavery where it already existed, and he insisted that he did not accept the secession of the seven states. On April 12, 1861, the Confederate army opened fire on the US fort in Charleston Bay, Fort Sumter. These were the first shots fired in the Civil War, and the US forces at Fort Sumter surrendered to the Confederates. More southern states then left the Union and joined the Confederacy. Four slaveholding states—Delaware, Kentucky, Maryland, and Missouri—did not wish to secede and maintained their status as states of the Union.

On July 21, the first full-scale battle of the Civil War, the Battle of Bull Run, was fought in Virginia when Union troops unsuccessfully attacked Confederate troops. The war continued, with fighting centralized largely in the South along the states that bordered the Union. In January 1863, Lincoln, who continued to resist the complete abolition of slavery, as he hoped to appease the border states that still held slaves, passed the Emancipation Proclamation. This act declared that slaves owned by men fighting for the Confederacy were free. The war spread increasingly northward, with the infamous Battle of Gettysburg, in Pennsylvania, taking place in 1863. Lincoln was reelected president in 1864. The Union's use of blockades was one factor that contributed to the defeat of the South, as it resulted in extreme shortages of food and supplies in the South by the beginning of 1865. In February 1865, the Confederate president Jefferson Davis sought a peace conference with Lincoln but insisted on Southern independence as a prerequisite. However, on April 2, 1865, the Southern capital, Richmond, Virginia, fell to Union forces, and it became clear that a Union victory was imminent. On April 9, 1865, the Confederate general Robert E. Lee and the Union general Ulysses S. Grant met at Appomattox Court House, in Virginia. Lee surrendered. Just days later, on April 14, 1865, President Lincoln was assassinated.

Late Nineteenth-Century Literary Movements

In the years following the Civil War, a number of literary movements arose. In the mid-nineteenth century, romanticism characterized American fiction. Romanticism features

COMPARE
&
CONTRAST

- **1861–1865:** The Civil War rages as the rebelling Southern states, having seceded from the United States, fight for the right to hold slaves and the right for states to be free of interference from the federal government. An estimated 750,000 people are killed during the war.

  1899: The United States has just emerged from the Spanish-American War, which was fought over governance rights to islands including Cuba, Puerto Rico, the Philippines, and Guam. At the conclusion of the war in December 1898, Cuba gains independence. Spain cedes Puerto Rico and Guam to the United States as territories and allows the United States to purchase the Philippines. Approximately three thousand Americans are killed during this war, largely owing to infectious diseases.

  Today: The United States is emerging from long-standing war efforts in Iraq and Afghanistan, Operation Iraqi Freedom and Operation Enduring Freedom. The wars, fought ostensibly to protect US security and to free Iraqis and the Afghan people from oppressive regimes, result in a combined total of 6,630 US service member casualties.

- **1861–1865:** Fiction during this time period is a mixture of styles; romanticism is prevalent, but new modes of narration focused on realistic portrayals of people, places, and society are emerging.

1899: Realism has begun to dominate American literary fiction. There are a number of styles of realism prevailing in fiction at this time, including naturalism and impressionism.

Today: Realism holds its position as the characteristic narrative mode of literary fiction, but it is increasingly challenged or blurred by experimental forms of narration and those that incorporate elements of fantasy, magic, or science fiction.

- **1861–1865:** On the Civil War battlefield, medical procedures are brutal. Surgeons are referred to as "sawbones," as amputation is often regarded as the best possible solution to saving lives. Approximately thirty thousand amputations are performed during the Civil War.

  1899: Friends and relatives grieve for the three thousand Americans who lost their lives during the Spanish-American War, which just ended at the close of 1898. Most of those killed died from infectious diseases such as yellow fever.

  Today: Battlefield medicine has changed dramatically since the nineteenth century. Penicillin and new antibiotics have been used for troops since World War II. Survival rates for marines injured in theaters such as Iraq and Afghanistan range from 95 to 98 percent.

---

idealized places and characters and is typically sentimental. Increasingly in the years following the Civil War, American fiction became more focused on realism, although elements of romanticism remained as well. Authors of realist works sought to capture the world around them accurately and truthfully; there was a direct correspondence between the words on the pages of their books and the world they viewed outside their windows. Under the umbrella of realism existed naturalism and regionalism. Regionalist authors, including Mark Twain in his novel *Adventures of Huckleberry Finn* (1884) and Kate Chopin in short-story collections such as *Bayou Folk* (1894), sought to incorporate, as an element of their realistic portrayal of their world, the dialects particular to the regions they were writing about, such as the American South or the bayou. Naturalists, like realists, eschewed sentimentality. Naturalists of the era viewed the world in a scientific manner and regarded the behavior of individuals as dictated by the circumstances into which they were born. People, like other animals, were seen as subject to the mechanizations of the natural world.

G. R. Thompson, in *Reading the American Novel, 1865–1914*, emphasizes the fact that romanticism overlapped the realist movement; the romantic novel did not wither and die while realism took root and sprouted. Thompson explains, "Most of the great realist works … have various forms of romanticism and romance embedded deep within their realist fabric." He goes on to point out that the same is true of the relationship between naturalism and romanticism. Thompson points to Crane's *Maggie: A Girl of the Streets*, published in 1983 and revised and reissued in 1896, and Jack London's 1903 novel *Call of the Wild* as examples of naturalist fiction in this time period. Keith Newlin, in *The Oxford Handbook of American Literary Naturalism*, explains that there existed during the late nineteenth century an affinity between naturalists and melodramatists. Newlin explains that "the didactic conceptual paradigm underlying melodrama—the belief that nature's laws are comprehendible and inevitable—also extends to the naturalistic novel." Newlin further underscores the point that while realistic authors observed life and portrayed it as faithfully as possible, naturalist writers sought to "demonstrate a particular thesis."

Notable realists of the 1880s and 1890s included Henry James in *The Bostonians* (1886), for example, and William Dean Howells in *The Rise of Silas Lapham* (1885), along with Stephen Crane in *The Red Badge of Courage* (1895). Crane's work has been described as realistic, naturalistic, and impressionistic. Impressionism is another mode of realistic narration, involving the capturing of the protagonist's or narrator's impressions of the world around him. In this way, literary impressionism is related to the notion of psychological realism, or realism that explores in detail the thoughts, emotions, and motivations of its characters. Newlin cautions that "the impact of impressionism upon Crane is still unclear" but notes that he is often associated with impressionism. Newlin

This portrait of an army lieutenant was taken during the Civil War. (Library of Congress)

points to Crane's association with young artists in New York, along with the fact that Crane's literary mentor Hamlin Garland "was a staunch proponent of impressionism in painting," as possible reasons for the connection of Crane with impressionism. Newlin further comments on "Crane's extraordinary color sense—color both as metaphor and as literal rendering," suggestive of "a direct link between his work and an art movement which revolutionized painting by emphasizing color as the principal vehicle of pictorial representation." In *Facing Facts: Realism in American Thought and Culture, 1850–1920*, David E. Shi also emphasizes the association between Crane and impressionism by observing that Crane's "objective was not to produce an *imitation* of life but to offer a vivid *impression* of life as he saw and experienced it." The work of Henry James has similarly been associated with impressionism.

CRITICAL OVERVIEW

"An Episode of War" is now regarded by many critics as one of Crane's best works of short fiction. Published just before his death by a British magazine, it did not receive a great deal of critical attention in 1899. Richard M. Weatherford, in *Stephen Crane: The Critical Heritage*, observes that at the time of Crane's death, "he was one of the best known writers of the time, even though his books had been selling poorly." Weatherford goes on, explaining that "within months of his death, Crane was almost totally forgotten. The obvious implication to be drawn is that Crane himself and not his works appealed to the public." Critics such as Sara J. Triller, in *Companion to Literature: The Facts on File Companion to the American Short Story*, count "An Episode of War," along with works such as Crane's "Death and the Child" (1898), as "among the best of his later war stories." Triller states that Crane's "characteristic use of sensory details" is a powerful feature of these works. Many other critics focus on the ending of the short story, insisting that it speaks to the transformation the lieutenant undergoes in terms of his understanding of his place within the world. As Donald B. Gibson claims in *The Fiction of Stephen Crane*,

> The stoical indifference manifest in the last line of the story stems from the lieutenant's undistorted view of himself in relation to the world, and stands in sharp contrast to the view he has when he is first wounded, when the wound matters a great deal.

Critics such as Stanley Wertheim concur. Wertheim, in *A Stephen Crane Encyclopedia*, maintains that the lieutenant's "awareness of the insignificance of the individual in the universal scheme" is underscored in his response to his family about his injury not mattering. Paul M. Sorrentino, in the *Student Companion to Stephen Crane*, reiterates the notion that the lieutenant's words at the story's conclusion speak to his acceptance of the insignificant role of the individual within the universe.

CRITICISM

Catherine Dominic

Dominic is a novelist and a freelance writer and editor. In the following essay, she examines the transformation the lieutenant in "An Episode of War" undergoes after his injury and maintains

> THE LIEUTENANT WITNESSES WAR DIFFERENTLY, ALMOST PHILOSOPHICALLY, AFTER HIS INJURY. DISCONNECTED FROM THE BATTLE, HE REGARDS THE SCOPE OF THE BATTLE IN A WAY THAT IS BOTH TERRIFYING AND MOVING."

that he attains a broader understanding of the universe rather than simply accepting his insignificant role in it.

Often, critics offer cursory summaries and analyses of Stephen Crane's story "An Episode of War" and conclude that the lieutenant's final words indicate his resigned recognition of his insignificance—or any individual's insignificance—within the universe. Such assessments attribute to the lieutenant a transformation of sorts, in that his understanding of the world has broadened to incorporate the knowledge of his own inconsequentiality. What these analyses overlook is the extent to which the lieutenant's perspective and knowledge shift and are reshaped. While he may now recognize the ways in which he is essentially powerless or irrelevant within the larger world, he gains a deeper understanding of the universe, painful though this knowledge may at times be.

Confusion reigns when the lieutenant is first shot. Neither he nor his companions are fully aware of what has happened, yet they all look toward the forest. They gradually become aware that a shot has been fired from that direction. The wood is at first regarded in benign terms. The lieutenant, though he glances "sadly, mystically" toward the forest, sees only "the green face of a wood." The "green face" does not seem like a source of harm. Yet the confused lieutenant nevertheless feels a commingled sense of sorrow and spirituality when he gazes upon it. As he experiences a growing realization of what has happened, the lieutenant has a new understanding of the wood as "hostile."

Now that the lieutenant is wounded and he and his comrades are beginning to grasp what has occurred, everything about the way he views them and they him changes. The orderly sergeant

WHAT DO I READ NEXT?

- Crane's well-known Civil War novel *The Red Badge of Courage* was originally published in book form in 1895. (It appeared in a condensed and serialized version in newspapers in 1894.) The work is a fuller portrait of the war than that which Crane drew for the short story "An Episode of War."

- "The Blue Hotel," by Crane, is a highly praised work that was originally published in 1898. Often described in terms of its impressionism and realism, the story focuses on a man's death in a Nebraska hotel.

- Crane's contemporary and fellow realist William Dean Howells published *The Rise of Silas Lapham* in 1885. A work of domestic rather than war fiction, it exemplifies elements of the realist style prevalent during that time period.

- Henry James, like Crane, was considered a realist who employed elements of literary impressionism, a mode which can be observed in his 1881 novel *Portrait of a Lady*.

- Linda Beatrice Brown's 2009 young-adult novel *Black Angels* explores the Civil War experience from the viewpoints of three young children—one a runaway joining the Union army, one the son of a plantation owner, and one a former slave whose master has set her free only to let the nine-year-old girl fend for herself.

- Sook Nyul Choi, in the 1993 young-adult novel *Year of Impossible Goodbyes*, explores life in Japanese-occupied Korea at the close of World War II. The author explores the family bonds that are tested by the challenges of life in an occupied nation.

- In the 2009 title *Stephen Crane*, part of the Bloom's Classic Critical Views series, scholar Harold Bloom gathers a collection of critical essays, written during Crane's life or just after his death, on Crane's life and major works.

"leaned nervously backward" while moving to help the lieutenant sheathe his sword. Moments later, the lieutenant recoils noticeably as another soldier attempts to help brace him with his shoulder. The other soldiers are afraid to touch the lieutenant, and he hesitates to be touched. Crane details this mutual resistance to touch by describing a wounded man as endowed with a "strange dignity" that other, well men respond to by shying away from. "It is as if the wounded man's hand is upon the curtain which hangs before the revelations of all existence," Crane explains, listing examples of such revelations: "the meaning of ants, potentates, wars, cities, sunshine, snow, a feather dropped from a bird's wing." The power of this knowledge can be perceived in those who are wounded by those who are not, and such power "makes the other men understand sometimes that they are little." The men who have not been injured subsequently fear that if they touch the wounded man, the contact might "precipitate the tragedy, hurl him at once into the dim, grey unknown." It is as if the wounded man stands on the border between life and death, between the mortal world and a spiritual world where all knowledge of the universe is within reach. This state of existence inspires awe and terror in the soldiers surrounding the lieutenant, and the lieutenant senses this. Rather than feel the power of the knowledge just beyond that "curtain," however, the lieutenant feels as though he is "the victim of a terrible disease." He has become alienated from his fellows, and he turns away from them.

The lieutenant does not pull back the curtain and step into another realm, of madness or death, but instead remains with the living as a wounded man. He nevertheless has been transformed by his shift in perspective. He has knowledge and perceptive abilities that he previously lacked. As he passes the front lines of battle, the lieutenant "was enabled to see many things which as a participant in the fight were unknown to him." He witnesses the scope of the battle and particular details in a manner previously hidden from him. Surveying the line of battle in a sweeping gaze, the lieutenant takes in a scene characterized by the fluidity and power of action—a galloping horse, the riding soldier who pulls him suddenly to a stop, and the soldier's salute to a general are frozen for the lieutenant in an instant: "It was, for a wonder, precisely like a historical painting." The lieutenant has begun to *see* differently.

This new way of viewing and understanding the world is further depicted in the next paragraph of the story. As the lieutenant surveys the movement of the artillery battery, the mobile, horse-drawn unit of guns and cannons, he takes in the scene, seeing and hearing the "wild thud of hoofs, the cries of the riders shouting blame and praise, menace and encouragement, and, last, the roar of the wheels, the slant of the glistening guns." All of this chaotic movement brings the lieutenant "to an intent pause." He considers the way the motion of the battery as a unit "swept in curves that stirred the heart." The halting of the unit sounds like the "crash of a wave on the rocks," while its forward charges are seen by the lieutenant as an "aggregation of wheels, levers, motors." The lieutenant alternately sees a unity that is breathtaking and notices the intricate working of the various parts of the machinery. He hears the sounds of battle as echoes of nature. His injury has allowed him to witness the war as he has not previously been able to as a participant.

As the lieutenant walks on, he approaches a brigade along the road. One of the officers speaks to him and makes inquiries "concerning things of which he knew nothing." Despite his new observations and knowledge, the lieutenant does not know how to answer the officer's questions. He knows nothing of the aspects of the battle that the officer seeks to ascertain. His new knowledge now seems transcendent—he sees the affinity between nature and the warfare of man, his vision encompasses both grand scope and fine details. Yet of the practical matters of the battle he is ignorant, despite the fact that "he was enabled to see many things which as a participant in the fight were unknown to him." The new type of knowledge the officer possesses is further highlighted as he approaches the hospital. He notices a man seated beneath a tree. His face is "as grey as a new army blanket," while he smokes a pipe "serenely." The lieutenant is alarmed. He "wished to rush forward and inform him he was dying." The lieutenant here seems attuned to things he had not been previously. The grey face of the man appears to signal that his circumstances are dire, and to the lieutenant, his serenity is unseemly. The lieutenant wishes to startle the man out of this serene state, perhaps to urge him to fight for his life. In his urgency, in his desire to "rush" to the man, the certainty of his knowledge is underscored.

At the close of the story, the lieutenant seems aware of the disconnection between words and truth, another component perhaps of the new knowledge he possess. He instinctively senses what is about to happen. Although he states, "I guess I won't have it amputated," his demeanor transforms. Once "very meek," his face now flushes, sensing what must happen though dreading it. The surgeon insists amputation will not be necessary, and he scolds the lieutenant for acting like a "baby." Yet the lieutenant knows the truth. He demands the doctor let him go, he pulls away "wrathfully," and he sees the door to the schoolhouse-turned-hospital as the "portals of death."

Returning home to his grieving family, the lieutenant states, "I don't suppose it matters so much as all that." Paul Sorrentino echoes the sentiments of many critics when he assesses this, stating in the *Student Companion to Stephen Crane*, "The lieutenant's stoic resignation at the end of the story reveals an acceptance of his—or anyone else's—insignificance in the universe." Although through his experience of being wounded the lieutenant may in fact have gained an understanding of one's limited relevance in the world, as critics such as Sorrentino have indicated, this assessment is itself limited. The lieutenant has also gained other new understandings of his world. He sees a connection between the world of man and the natural world as he observes the war. There is an affinity between the roar of the battle and the sounds of crashing waves on rocks. There is a "beautiful unity" in the mechanisms of war that humans have created. He hears an almost musical quality—a "war-chorus" on the battlefield, and it reaches "into the depths of man's emotion." The lieutenant witnesses war differently, almost philosophically, after his injury. Disconnected from the battle, he regards the scope of the battle in a way that is both terrifying and moving. He regards the power of man as an extension or an echo of nature. He knows nature to be both beautiful and dangerous, as evidenced by the "green face of a wood" that is soon recognized as "hostile" as well. The lieutenant may feel powerless or insignificant, but he is also more attuned to the connection of humanity, in all its beauty and brutality, to the natural world and the universe as a whole.

Source: Catherine Dominic, Critical Essay on "An Episode of War," in *Short Stories for Students*, Gale, Cengage Learning, 2014.

This drawing shows a soldier's homecoming that is happier than that of Crane's protagonist. (Library of Congress)

Michael Robertson

In the following excerpt, Robertson explains how working as a war correspondent affected the writing of Crane, who had never witnessed combat before writing The Red Badge of Courage.

The hardcover publication of *The Red Badge of Courage* in 1895 turned Stephen Crane into an anomaly: an internationally famous writer on war who had never witnessed combat. Journalism gave Crane the means to resolve that contradiction. Within a year after *Red Badge* appeared, he attempted to become a war correspondent, a role that would engage him for much of the short time remaining in his life.

Crane's first efforts to report on war, late in 1896, led to his thirty hours in an open boat, an experience that did not dampen his ardor for war correspondence. He tried for weeks after his shipwreck to find another boat to Cuba in

order to report on the rebellion there. When that effort was unsuccessful, he signed on with William Randolph Hearst's *New York Journal* to cover the short-lived Greco-Turkish War of 1897. That war over, he waited only a few weeks before making attempts to serve as correspondent in another war—any war. In quick succession he made and discarded plans to cover conflicts in India, South Africa, and the Sudan. When the U.S. battleship *Maine* sank in Havana harbor early the next year, drawing the United States into a war with Spain, Crane was gleeful. Joseph Conrad, Crane's closest friend in England, described how Crane, "white-faced" with excitement at the imminent declaration of war, careened around London one day that spring searching for money to pay his passage to the United States. He had "to find È60 that day . . . at once, that instant," Conrad wrote, "lest peace should be declared and the opportunity of

THE IMPORTANT THING TO CRANE WAS THE OPPORTUNITY TO WITNESS WAR, TO TEST HIS IMAGINATION AGAINST ACTUALITY."

seeing a war be missed." Conrad eventually pledged his future work as security for a loan. In his memoir of the episode Conrad mused about his responsibility for sending Crane to a war that undoubtedly hastened the young writer's death. However, Conrad concluded that any aid he gave was insignificant in Crane's decision. "Nothing could have held him back," Conrad wrote. "He was ready to swim the ocean." Once in Cuba, Crane zealously sought out combat. He spent weeks aboard a hired tugboat covering the naval campaign, was the only correspondent to witness every land battle in Cuba, and remained in the Caribbean for months after Spain surrendered, covering the peace negotiations. He wrote, all together, fifty Spanish-American War dispatches for Hearst's *New York Journal* and Pulitzer's *New York World*, in addition to completing *Wounds in the Rain* (1900), a book of short stories and sketches about the war.

Crane's war correspondence fills a volume of his collected works, but critics have virtually ignored it. H. G. Wells established the dominant view of the war reporting in an essay he wrote shortly after Crane's death. Wells constructed a mythic narrative of Crane's post–*Red Badge* career that still shapes Crane criticism. In the life of Crane according to Wells, a young novelist who writes a brilliant imaginative account of the Civil War is lured from fiction into journalism by newspaper publishers eager to capitalize on his reputation. However, he is a complete failure as a war correspondent. Moreover, while traveling in foreign climes he contracts tropical diseases that bring on his lamentably early death. In a heavily ironic passage of his essay Wells writes,

> Since Crane had demonstrated, beyond all cavil, that he could sit at home and, with nothing but his wonderful brain and his wonderful induction from recorded things, build up the truest and most convincing picture of war..., it was clearly the most reasonable thing in the

world to propose, it was received with the applause of two hemispheres as a most right and proper thing, that he should go as a war correspondent, first to Greece and then to Cuba. Thereby, and for nothing but disappointment and bitterness, he utterly wrecked his health...; and I read even in the most punctual of his obituary notices the admission of his journalistic failure.

Wells thought Crane's journalism beneath notice; the few critics who have given any attention to his war correspondence generally examine it for clues to his fiction.

It is possible to take a different approach to Crane's war journalism. Instead of viewing Crane's interest in war reporting purely as a response to commercial pressures, we can locate Crane within the cultural forces of the 1890s that promoted both masculine ideals of the strenuous life and the war against Spain. Rather than using the journalism to throw light on the fiction, we can examine it on its own terms. If we can free ourselves of preconceptions about journalism's lower status within a hierarchy of literary value, we can take a fresh look at a body of work that deserves more than its reputation as a footnote to *The Red Badge of Courage*.

Crane wrote almost all his war correspondence for Joseph Pulitzer's *World* or William Randolph Hearst's *Journal*. These ambitious publishers frequently reminded readers of their celebrated writer's Civil War novel in the headlines that they attached to his dispatches. A typical example, published in the *World* during the Spanish-American War, reads, "*The Red Badge of Courage* Was His Wig-Wag Flag. Sergeant of Marines Signalling the Dolphin the Central Figure in Stephen Crane's Story of the First Fight at Guantanamo Bay." Crane's publishers primed readers to expect connections between the famous writer's best-selling novel and his war journalism, and the correspondences between *Red Badge* and the war dispatches are many: a focus on individual acts of heroism, an impressionistic detailing of the process of perception, and frequent use of irony. However, the differences between *Red Badge* and the war journalism are even more striking. The war correspondence frequently romanticizes war and fighting men in a way that the more consistently ironic *Red Badge* does not. During the Spanish-American War this romanticizing led Crane to join in the jingoistic trumpeting of U.S. superiority common in 1898. However, in his final piece of war journalism, written a year after the Spanish-American War's conclusion, Crane rejected jingoism and produced one of his greatest works, an extraordinary autobiographical essay marked by daring stylistic experiments and by an avant-garde attention to the limits of language.

* * *

H. G. Wells was convinced that Crane became a war correspondent only in response to newspaper publishers' entreaties. John Berryman, who correctly noted Crane's eagerness to witness combat, developed a complex, highly speculative Freudian interpretation that located Crane's fascination with war in his family's psychological dynamics and in a violent incident he may have witnessed as a child. More recently, Christopher Benfey has traced Crane's desire to go to war after completing *Red Badge* to a repeated pattern within the author's life in which he first wrote about an experience, then attempted to live it.

Another way to think about Crane's drive to experience warfare is to turn from his personal life to larger forces within American culture. For example, although Philip Rahv never mentions Crane in his famous essay "The Cult of Experience in American Writing," it would be easy enough to insert Crane into Rahv's line of writers from Whitman to Hemingway who placed a premium on "bare experience" rather than on ideas or values. Rahv's broad-brush analysis, however, is largely ahistorical. It is possible to analyze Stephen Crane's urge for experience, and particularly experience of war, specifically within the conditions of the late nineteenth century.

If we focus on the 1890s, we can substitute for the general term "the cult of experience" the more historically specific notion of the cult of "the strenuous life." Theodore Roosevelt did not make his famous speech of that title until 1899, but the concept of the strenuous life permeated the United States of the 1890s. Vast numbers of middle- and upper-class males felt uneasy in the increasingly urbanized, mechanized, rationalized post–Civil War culture. In a culture where "personal meaning had dissolved in comfort and complacency," in T. J. Jackson Lears's phrase, people sought intense and "authentic" experience. Men reacted against a genteel Victorian culture that they saw as soft and flaccid by turning for recreation to athletics, the outdoors, and heroic fiction. Football, boxing, camping, hunting, and romantic action novels all experienced a tremendous surge of popularity in the 1890s.

The ultimate expression of the strenuous life and the highest test for the male's heroic capacities was war. A generation removed from the horrors of the Civil War, many American men viewed that conflict nostalgically, as a testing ground for manhood denied to the veterans' children and grandchildren. T. J. Jackson Lears writes of this period, "As the rationalization of culture increasingly . . . reduced more and more existence to banal routine, life at war . . . sometimes seemed to promise authentic experiences no longer available in everyday life: the opportunity for moral and physical testing, the sheer excitement of life amid danger and death."

Stephen Crane serves as exemplar of the quest for meaning and for masculine identity through the strenuous life and through war. His career from adolescence on can be seen as a reaction against genteel Victorian propriety, as embodied by his highly religious parents. When he was sixteen, Crane convinced his mother to allow him to transfer from Pennington Seminary, a Methodist institution formerly directed by his father, to a military school—an early sign of his lifelong interest in war and the strenuous life. Despite his small size—full grown, he was under 5'8" and 125 pounds—Crane was an enthusiastic outdoorsman and athlete. He spent long periods camping and hunting and was a highly regarded baseball player.

His fascination with war rivaled his enthusiasm for baseball. Crane's entire generation was absorbed with the Civil War. Young men during the 1890s commonly measured themselves against the earlier generation of soldiers. Crane's contemporary Carl Sandburg wrote of the 1890s, "Over all of us . . . was the shadow of the Civil War and the men who fought it to the end." *Battles and Leaders of the Civil War* (1888), which Crane used as background for *The Red Badge of Courage*, was a phenomenal best-seller, although it was surpassed by *The Personal Memoirs of U. S. Grant* (1885), which became one of the best-selling American books of the nineteenth century.

Crane, who wrote a best-seller on the Civil War before he had any personal experience of combat, presumably felt a need to authenticate his novel. If so sensitive a person as Joseph Conrad asked Crane at their first meeting if it was true that the young novelist had never witnessed combat, the question must have been repeated by dozens of others whom Crane encountered. His response to Conrad shows a certain testiness: "No. But the 'Red Badge' is all right." When Conrad asked his question in the fall of 1897, Crane was able to assert his war novel's fidelity to truth with some authority, because he had just returned from his first experience as a war correspondent in the Greco-Turkish War. On his way to the war, he had told a London reporter that "he was off to Crete because, having written so much about war, he thought it high time he should see a little fighting." Note that Crane did not say it was high time to fight but rather to *see* some fighting. It was the relatively new role of war correspondent that enabled Crane to see whether *Red Badge* was all right.

Reports of war have always been a journalistic staple, but until the mid-nineteenth century newspapers obtained their accounts of battles from participants. The Civil War produced the first American war correspondents. The role quickly became institutionalized. By 1897, when Crane set off to cover the war in Greece, he was able to join an entire cadre of U.S. correspondents.

The Greco-Turkish War of 1897 lasted only one month, but the newspapers had ample opportunity to assemble correspondents in Greece before the formal declaration of war in April. The previous year had seen a rebellion in Crete against Turkish rule. Although Greece had achieved independence from the Ottoman Empire seventy years earlier, Crete was still under Turkish control. Early in 1897 an ambitious Greek prime minister sent ships and troops to Crete; once the troops were mobilized, war between Greece and Turkey was inevitable.

Crane read about the incipient war in Greece while he was in Jacksonville, Florida, trying to get passage to the guerrilla war in Cuba after his rescue from the open boat. In March 1897 he abandoned the attempt, writing to his brother, "I have been for over a month among the swamps further south wading miserably to and fro in an attempt to avoid our derned U.S. Navy. And it cant be done. I am through trying. I have changed all my plans and am going to Crete." In New York on his way to Europe he acknowledged to an acquaintance, "Greece means nothing to me, nor does Turkey." The important thing to Crane was the opportunity to witness war, to test his imagination against actuality....

Source: Michael Robertson, "After *The Red Badge*: War Journalism," in *Stephen Crane, Journalism, and the Making of Modern American Literature*, Columbia University Press, 1997, pp. 138–42.

Michael W. Schaefer

In the following excerpt, Schaefer places "An Episode of War" in context with Crane's other works.

. . . Wounded men feature prominently in a number of Crane's war stories besides "Episode," most notably *The Red Badge*, but the story's closest connection in terms of plot, as Stallman points out, is to the Spanish-American War story "The Price of the Harness." In both of these pieces a character is wounded in the arm, feels disoriented as a result, moves away from the battle line in an increasingly confused state, and winds up being intimidated by a surgeon whose crushing workload causes him to react to the wounded man with exasperation rather than compassion (*Stephen Crane*). More broadly, in terms of theme, several critics have included this story in groupings of Crane's works in which suffering leads to increased insight. Stallman sees "Episode" as one of three war stories, the other two being *The Red Badge* and "A Mystery of Heroism," in which the protagonist has his vision of battle altered by his painful experiences with it. He also notes structural parallels between "Episode" and *The Red Badge*, pointing out that despite their differences in length both are composed of "alternations of moods: perspectives of motion and change shifting into picture-postcard impressions where everything is felt as fixed and static" (*Houses*). Marston LaFrance implicitly agrees but does not limit this theme of altered vision to Crane's war stories; he says that the lieutenant belongs to a small cadre of Crane protagonists of various stripes—the others being Henry Fleming, the correspondent in "The Open Boat," Manolo Prat in "The Clan of No-Name," and Dr. Trescott in "The Monster"—who possess both imagination and conscience. Taken together, these qualities can lead to self-knowledge and a concomitant understanding of one's small place in the universe, which is "the only 'salvation' that Crane ever offers." Similarly, Wolford says that "Episode" is one of a group of stories in which the main character "discovers a small measure of reality relating to the unknown—specifically death," but he notes further that these pieces are also linked by their protagonists' "corresponding inability to make [their discovery] known." He identifies the others in this group as *The Red Badge*, "A Mystery of Heroism," and "The Monster."

Wertheim groups "Episode" with "The Open Boat" and "The Monster" as Crane's most potent meditations on "the pervasive theme of American literature [:] . . . Human isolation in its physical, emotional, or ideological manifestations"—a theme Crane was drawn to because of his own revolt against and subsequent feelings of isolation from his respectable, religious family. When the lieutenant finds himself estranged from his men because his wound puts them too much in mind of their own mortality, Wertheim says, he becomes, like the correspondent and Dr. Trescott, one of Crane's "autobiographical . . . isolatoes," men locked in "an unsuccessful struggle to integrate their lives with that of society and yet preserve separate identities" ("Wrath").

Milne Holton sees "Episode" as belonging to several groups with different characteristics. Like Stallman, LaFrance, and Wolford, he points out its close connection to *The Red Badge* through the emphasis in both on "the process of gaining an apprehension," of seeing the nature of the universe and one's place in it more clearly as a result of hardship. He also links it to the Spitzbergen tales in that these, like "Episode," deal with "the paradox of apprehension and love"—that is, with the tension between forming a meaningful relationship with another person and the terrifying awareness of death which that person's being killed or wounded produces. And finally, he views it as one of a set of stories, also including "The Five White Mice," "Flanagan and His Short Filibustering Adventure," and "War Memories," which have ironic endings that "deny the very [stories] they conclude." . . .

Source: Michael W. Schaefer, "'An Episode of War,'" in *A Reader's Guide to the Short Stories of Stephen Crane*, G. K. Hall, 1996, pp. 117–18.

SOURCES

Crane, Stephen, "An Episode of War," in *Great Short Works of Stephen Crane*, Perennial Classics, 2004, pp. 268–72.

"Faces of the Fallen," in *Washington Post*, February 25, 2013, http://apps.washingtonpost.com/national/fallen/ (accessed February 25, 2013).

Gibson, Donald B., "Some Other Tales of War: Heroism Re-examined," in *The Fiction of Stephen Crane*, Southern Illinois University Press, 1968, pp. 90–105.

Gugliotta, Guy, "New Estimate Raises Civil War Death Toll," in *New York Times*, April 2, 2012, http://www.nytimes.com/2012/04/03/science/civil-war-toll-up-by-20-percent-in-new-estimate.html?_r=0 (accessed February 25, 2013).

Kovatch, Gretel C., "Advances in Battlefield Medicine," in *UT San Diego*, December 18, 2011, http://www.utsandiego.com/news/2011/dec/18/advances-battlefield-medicine-and-casualty-care/ (accessed February 25, 2013).

McPherson, James, "A Brief Overview of the American Civil War," Civilwar.org, http://www.civilwar.org/education/history/civil-war-overview/overview.html (accessed February 25, 2013).

Newlin, Keith, ed., "Introduction: The Naturalistic Imagination and the Aesthetics of Excess," in *The Oxford Handbook of American Literary Naturalism*, Oxford University Press, 2011, pp. 3–20.

Pizer, Donald, "Naturalism and the Visual Arts," in *The Oxford Handbook of American Literary Naturalism*, edited by Keith Newlin, Oxford University Press, 2011, pp. 463–82.

"Selected Civil War Photographs," American Memory, Library of Congress website, http://memory.loc.gov/ammem/cwphtml/ (accessed February 25, 2013).

Shi, David E., "A World Full of Fists," in *Facing Facts: Realism in American Thought and Culture, 1850–1920*, Oxford University Press, 1995, pp. 223–50.

Sorrentino, Paul M., "Other War Stories," in *Student Companion to Steven Crane*, Greenwood Press, 2006, pp. 77–96.

"Introduction," The World of 1898: The Spanish-American War, Library of Congress website, http://www.loc.gov/rr/hispanic/1898/intro.html (accessed February 25, 2013).

"Stephen Crane," Poetry Foundation website, http://www.poetryfoundation.org/bio/stephen-crane (accessed February 25, 2013).

"Stephen Crane: Biography," Pearson Literature website, http://wps.ablongman.com/long_kennedy_lfpd_9/0,9130,1489982-,00.html (accessed February 25, 2013).

Thompson, G. R., Introduction to *Reading the American Novel, 1865–1914*, Wiley-Blackwell, 2012, pp. 1–8.

Triller, Sara J., "Stephen Crane," in *The Facts on File Companion to the American Short Story*, 2nd ed., edited by Abby H. P. Werlock, Facts on File, 2010, pp. 157–59.

Weatherford, Richard M., ed., Introduction to *Stephen Crane: The Critical Heritage*, Routledge, 1997, pp. 1–34.

Wertheim, Stanley, "'An Episode of War,'" in *A Stephen Crane Encyclopedia*, Greenwood Press, 1997, pp. 96–97.

FURTHER READING

Barryman, John, *Stephen Crane: A Critical Biography*, Cooper Square Press, 2001.

Barryman provides a detailed examination of Crane's life and works, discussing as well the rise and fall of the popularity of his fiction in the years after his death.

Bierce, Ambrose, *The Civil War Short Stories of Ambrose Bierce*, edited by Ernest Jerome Hopkins, Bison Books, 1988.

Bierce was a Civil War veteran, journalist, and author. This collection of his short fiction reveals the brutal nature of warfare in a way designed to warn rather than glorify, and serves as an example of postbellum realism.

Pizer, Donald, *Realism and Naturalism in Nineteenth-Century American Literature*, rev. ed., Southern Illinois University Press, 1984.

Originally written in 1966 and updated and expanded in 1984, this text remains a standard source of analysis and criticism of works of American nineteenth-century realist and naturalist fiction.

Robertson, James, *The Untold Civil War: Exploring the Human Side of War*, edited by Neil Kagan, National Geographic, 2011.

Robertson examines the day-to-day life of soldiers and civilians during the Civil War, providing an array of archival images along with his study. Robertson discusses the impact of the seemingly mundane on the war and also analyzes the impact of such trends as the increasing number of female workers that arose during the war.

SUGGESTED SEARCH TERMS

Stephen Crane AND An Episode of War

The Red Badge of Courage AND An Episode of War

Stephen Crane AND Civil War fiction

nineteenth-century American literary realism

nineteenth-century American literary naturalism

nineteenth-century American literary impressionism

Stephen Crane AND the short story

Stephen Crane AND William Dean Howells

Stephen Crane AND Henry James

fin de siècle American expatriates in England

The Flat of the Land

DIANA GARCÍA

1993

"The Flat of the Land" is a story by Diana García about what an isolated Mexican American woman experiences when the land around her house begins taking on a life of its own, in the form of spreading mud of mysterious origin. García, who was born and reared in a migrant labor camp in California, is best known as a poet whose debut collection, *When Living Was a Labor Camp* (2000), won an American Book Award from the Before Columbus Foundation. García drew on autobiographical experiences for the poems of that collection, which pay tribute to the lives of her many family members who endured—and in some instances fell victim to—the tribulations of Mexican American farmworkers.

Though García's experiences may have informed the perspective in "The Flat of the Land," the story is above all a work of imagination in which the protagonist, Amparo, is a cryptic individual. The details of the story solidify Amparo's identity as Chicana, but her past remains a mystery, while for the present she has withdrawn from the broader cultural experience not only of Mexican Americans but of all Americans: she is living alone in a modern, adobe-walled model house in the midst of an abandoned development. As an interesting bubble of mud nearby spreads into a crevice, then a pond, then more, Amparo's solitary life becomes stranger and stranger. "The Flat of the Land" can be found in the collection *Pieces of the Heart: New Chicano Fiction* (1993), edited by Gary Soto.

García's parents were farm workers in the San Joaquin Valley. © *Richard Thornton / ShutterStock.com*

AUTHOR BIOGRAPHY

Karen Diana García was born in 1950 in a migrant labor camp in the San Joaquin Valley, California, to parents Manuel and Tomasa García. The camp was owned by the California Packing Corporation. Although the camps and farms were notoriously hard on the migrant laborers employed in the region, the young García—who went by Diana (pronounced "thee-ah-nah")—did not find the setting without its charms, as she told the *Monterey Herald*: "As a child it was idyllic. There was a sense of constant companionships and a swirl of family and friends and culture in the camp." Everyone she knew, including her two brothers, spoke Spanish. They lived in cabins on the banks of Bear Creek, fostering a sense of closeness to the land.

By the time García turned five, her parents had moved off the camp to a home in Merced, close to their daughter's new grammar school, and they instructed her to go by her first name, Karen, because it sounded like an ordinary Anglo name. But García associated her middle name with the encircling nature and family of the labor camp—"Diana, redolent of sage cracking through dirt in August," she wrote in her essay "Valley Language." As such, the name change came to define the dissonance she felt in trying to suppress her Chicana labor-camp self in favor of a refined American one. When García was nearly placed in a remedial sub-first-grade class, her parents decided that the family would speak only English at home, intensifying her sense of internal conflict. To cope with this, she escaped into books, indulging her habit so constantly that her parents became worried and started ordering her outside—where she would climb an apricot tree and read there. García excelled in school, from fifth grade onward getting bused across the tracks to the predominantly white side of town to attend a gifted program.

Upon graduating from high school, García—now calling herself Diana again—attended Fresno State College for a year, but she then became pregnant, began raising a son as a single mother, and went on welfare. In time, she moved to San Diego; worked variously as a secretary, a consultant for defense attorneys, and a personnel manager; and after some sixteen years, in 1989, earned a BA from San Diego State University. When, in her mid-thirties, a composition teacher highly commended her writing, she enrolled in a creative writing course and gained further encouragement. García earned a master of fine arts degree from San Diego State University in 1993, the year in which her story "The Flat of the Land" was published in Gary Soto's anthology *Pieces of the Heart*. She then moved to New England and taught for four years at Central Connecticut State University.

García returned west and was eventually named associate professor at California State University, Monterey Bay, where she would also become the codirector of the Creative Writing and Social Action Program. Her 2000 poetry collection *When Living Was a Labor Camp* won an American Book Award, and her poems have been included in several anthologies. She has engaged in a number of programs—such as the San Diego/Tijuana Border Voices Project—promoting poetry in the schools, including those of juvenile halls, and in recent years her primary focuses have been social action and her teaching. Her family includes a husband, her son, and grandsons.

PLOT SUMMARY

In the opening scene of "The Flat of the Land," Amparo, the protagonist, is surveying the local scene from her rooftop: she figures that the nearby tilting Pixley water tower may be visible for just a couple more weeks; the text implies that flowing mud will soon topple and bury it. Throughout the story, the text follows Amparo's mental processes so closely that the narration can often be understood as the direct communication of her thoughts. She imagines that few would notice the missing tower in this isolated location off Highway 99, in California. A reference to how Amparo would perhaps be missed by the women at the local store and restaurant suggests that her circumstances, too, are threatened by the mud.

The story rolls back in time to when Amparo first noticed the mud, six months ago, in April, when it was just a bubble near the clothesline by her house. Expanding to a pond and then following a dried-up riverbed, the mud spread eastward across a flat expanse of land

toward the Sequoia foothills (that is, those of the Sierra Nevada in Sequoia National Park).

Surrounding Amparo's house, portions of the land are carved out for the foundations of other long-unbuilt houses. The development was never finished. It seems the spreading mud might be due to a leak from the water tower or is perhaps a natural feature of the area. As the mud becomes a widening crevice, Amparo realizes that both her clothesline and her shelter, "her hideaway," are in danger. Living off of disability income, she has been tricking her family—meaning her brothers and parents, as her ex-husband and son are evidently now forgotten—into thinking she is living in Fresno.

Amparo begins talking to the mud, trying to coax it away from her house. She listens to Mexican radio stations and talks with the coyotes. The house is not really a secret; she imagines someone else, a laborer, must have once lived there to get away from relations and the world. Now claiming the house, which has a solar generator, Amparo washes clothes with a wringer, while the stairs provide exercise and the plumbing is excellent. For food, she favors oatmeal, seasonal produce from roadside stands, and tortillas, beans, and rice—along with a greasy burger and fries from the Pixley store's lunch counter every few weeks.

When the mud reaches Amparo's old station wagon, she drives to Pixley and chats with the women who work the counter, a mother and grandmother, asking whether there used to be any local mud baths. As the mother notes, there are only dried-up hot springs; the region is a desert, and the creeks have been dry for a decade. But the grandmother remembers that the Chocolate River—the riverbed by the development—was running seventy years ago, and when her own great-great-grandmother first arrived, the area was marshland.

The mud indeed devours the clothesline and a manzanita bush. By the Fourth of July, Amparo is inclined to honor the mud, lighting sparklers and playing games on the banks of the foot-wide crevice. It reaches fifty yards in length and three to four feet in depth. She notices that the mud is especially clean, and she wonders what it might want—perhaps to consume more flowery bushes and serve as fertilizer. Lugging buckets of mud up to her tub, she takes a warm mud bath, then returns outside to first let the mud harden soothingly and then

MEDIA ADAPTATIONS

- A video titled *U Stories: Diana Garcia on Writing Poetry*, was produced in 2007 by Silvia Turchin for California State University, Monterey Bay. This 4-minute video presents the author discussing her creative process, her life, her sources of inspiration, and her approach to teaching. It is available at http://www.youtube.comwatch?v=2LG 7OcLDlME.

peel it off. She feeds the mud her leftover rice and beans.

As the mud begins branching around the house, Amparo figures it is heading for the foothills. By October, the flow eastward is unmistakable. She is especially fond of the rooftop escape offered by her house and is accustomed to eating breakfast while enjoying the view. The roof becomes her "lookout post," from which she offers the mud guidance. She talks to the coyotes more and leaves them grilled chicken.

With the full moon of mid-autumn, she buys some special vegetables and arranges an offering on her roof. She shares with the mud an appreciation for solitude and independence. She also talks to the house, assuring it that they will ride out the mudflow together. That night, she dreams of the house bobbing submerged in the mud out over the flatlands.

Meanwhile, the mud caresses and cajoles the house, and the mud and house share their inspiring perspectives of the natural world with each other. The house and mud also appreciate each other aesthetically.

Just before dawn, the house lurches off its foundation and settles into the mud river. Amparo rushes up to the roof and accustoms herself to the rocking motion of the floating house as it turns away from the highway and toward the foothills. The house surges forward with increasing speed, the mud splashing ten or fifteen feet in the air. Amparo shouts to the hills as she approaches them. She asks the sun to give its light, and she urges the house and mud onward. At the foothills, an opening in the hills appears, leading upward to a meadow laced with trees. Through the opening, the air is clear, the passage is smooth, and the flow of the mud is somehow free of friction.

CHARACTERS

Amparo

The character at the heart of García's story, Amparo, is something of a mystery. Beyond the implication that she is Chicana—her name is Spanish, and she listens to Mexican music—the reader is given only the vaguest hints about her background: She is said to have living brothers and parents, but details such as where they live, what they do, and what they are like are not provided. Amparo started her own family, but "she never talked about her son or her former husband" anymore, signaling to her brothers and parents that she "had laid those memories to rest." She later recalls something her ex-husband, Sammy, once told her about her hair, suggesting that she does not completely avoid memories of him, but specifics such as whether they fought and what about go unstated. While cutting off contact with an ex-spouse would not be unnatural, Amparo's distance from her son is less easy to explain. Did the son side with the father in a great dispute, or did son and mother have their own falling out, or has the son perhaps died? Even the slightest details in these familial regards would go a long way in helping the reader grasp Amparo's character, but García withholds them.

Significantly, the forty-five-year-old Amparo is said to be living off of disability income, though it is not specified whether she has a chronic illness or a heart condition or, perhaps, a psychological disorder. García may mean to suggest the last possibility: Amparo's mental state seems to meander as she lives alone in the isolated house. Ultimately, the reader is shown a portrait of Amparo in her immediate present—the unique life she is leading in the circumstances she has fostered. Seemingly without friends beyond the family she was raised with, Amparo sees fit to express herself and satisfy her need for communication by befriending the objects and animals around her. The Spanish word *amparo* can translate as "protection" or "shelter," meanings that highlight Amparo's ultimate identification with her closest companion, the house—in effect, the woman and house ride off into the sunset together—while also suggesting the notion that this imaginatively self-sufficient woman is herself her own protection, her own shelter.

Amparo's Son
Apparently Amparo's son, whether alive or dead, is no longer a part of her life.

Girl
A girl with blonde hair and freckles—an Anglo girl—works at the combination store and restaurant in the nearby town of Pixley. She does not appear in the story.

Sammy
Like her son, Amparo's ex-husband appears to now be no more than a memory to her.

Woman
The mother of the blonde girl covers her hair at work with either a torn net or rollers. With a voice like a record player on slow speed, the woman seems to have an indifferent, by-the-book demeanor, giving Amparo just the facts about water and mud in the area.

Woman's Mother
The mother of the woman at the Pixley lunch counter—the girl's grandmother—is spurred to recall the distant past by Amparo's questions about local mud. The grandmother's comments enable Amparo to envision a dramatically altered version of the landscape around her. The grandmother's own great-great-grandmother came to California from Illinois.

THEMES

Abandonment
Between the protagonist and the setting, the reader of García's story is confronted early on with a powerful sense of abandonment. The notion of abandonment is most explicitly connected with the development where Amparo is staying, with the one house erected as a model surrounded by empty excavations for other houses that were never built. The

reader may assume that the threat of mudflows rendered the development too risky, but the narration connects the aborted project with a different concern: that it was all simply too expensive, uniting classic pueblo walls, surfaced with adobe, or clay, with modern amenities like solar generators. In other words, the modernization of Native home design was found to be unfeasible—perhaps metaphorically suggesting that the modernization of an indigenously minded Chicana like Amparo is also unfeasible, which would explain why she has ended up where she has. That is, perhaps her spirit rejected the dislocated, disconnected urban American life that she was subjected to, leading her to effectively opt out of the American dream; she seems no longer concerned with building or rebuilding a family, acquiring wealth, immersing herself in a community, and being swept along in mainstream culture. Rather, she wishes only to live from day to day, eat nourishing food, and (with monetary assistance from the government) independently support herself.

It is clear, at least, that Amparo has abandoned American culture; what is unclear is the extent to which in Amparo's experience the culture has abandoned her. The reader is given the freedom to imagine an array of backstories that might explain Amparo's present circumstances. Her husband may have cheated on her, or abused her, leaving her psychically scarred and romantically disillusioned; her son may have rebelled against the traditional values she tried to instill in him, joining a gang and getting jailed or killed; an indifferent medical establishment may have labeled her bipolar or psychotic after an episode of instability caused by the compounded stresses of living in poverty. While none of these conjectures can be identified as reflecting the backstory García had in mind—if she had a specific one in mind—imagining how the blanks of Amparo's life story might be filled in reveals a likelihood, as almost any plausible life story involves not just one-sided but mutual abandonment: Amparo abandoned and was abandoned by the family and American culture to which she once belonged.

Solitude
Consistent with her overall sense of abandonment—of being both abandoned and abandoner—Amparo seems content with

TOPICS FOR FURTHER STUDY

- Write a short story in the third or first person in which the protagonist settles into a place of relative solitude, such as a cabin in the woods, a mountaintop camp, or a tropical island—or even a city apartment or an empty metro train—and from there departs on a magic-realist journey that suggests some sort of spiritual awakening or transcendence. If you like, share your story on a blog and allow your classmates to comment.

- Consult two or three sources on the meaning of dreams—such as Sigmund Freud's *The Interpretation of Dreams* (1900), Lucy Goodison's *Dreams of Women: Exploring and Interpreting Women's Dreams* (1995), or Kay Stone's *The Golden Woman: Dreaming as Art* (2004)—to analyze Amparo's fantastic experience with the mud as if it were all a dream. In a paper, relate what each source says about what the mud, the journey, and other elements of the story might represent. Conclude by discussing how and why the sources offer contrasting interpretations and whether or not analyzing Amparo's experience as a dream is useful for understanding the story.

- Read Rosalie Otero's short story "The Closet," also found in Gary Soto's anthology *Pieces of the Heart*, about a thirteen-year-old girl named Lucy who is forced to share a room with her brother when an aunt moves in. (The story includes a number of Spanish words, so your comprehension will increase if you know Spanish and/or use a dictionary or online translation.) Write an essay comparing Lucy's personality, perspective, and circumstances with those of Amparo in "The Flat of the Land," discussing how the two protagonists are similar and different as reflected in their comments, actions, and decisions. Also address the role that Chicano culture plays for Lucy and Amparo and the extent to which their circumstances are universal.

- Research the building of traditional adobe houses in the American Southwest as practiced by Native Americans. Create a presentation that explains and demonstrates the process of how such a house is built by composing an oral report to accompany either a three-dimensional model of such a structure, poster board charting the process with hand-drawn or borrowed illustrations, or a PowerPoint slide show.

---

extraordinary solitude. Once or twice a month she sees her brothers and parents, and once or twice a month she drops by the lunch counter in Pixley. She must also interact with people at the farm stands from which she buys produce, but otherwise Amparo evidently interacts with no one at all. She appears to have no phone, no neighbors to speak of, and even no friends; if she had any friends, the opening paragraph would probably have mentioned them missing her if the mud overtook the house, whereas instead it mentions only the lunch-counter women. Her lack of people to converse with is further suggested by her tendency to talk to the objects and creatures around her: the mud (which in spreading indeed gains a sort of personality), the coyotes, the hills, and the sun. The reader who shies away from solitude may find Amparo's one-sided conversations to be evidence of mental instability, but by and large Amparo is content with her solitude, and these interactions can be read differently, as suggesting that in her solitude she has reverted to a more primal sense of compassion, directed not only toward other people but toward every creature and creation around her.

Nature

In her solitude, Amparo's inherent compassion is mainly directed toward facets of nature. At first feeling threatened by the mud, she eventually welcomes and sympathizes with it, wondering what it wants out of life and whispering, when she finally understands the mud's direction, "Ahh, you want the foothills." With the coyotes, she demonstrates not mere animal fear but instead an acquired understanding of what coyotes need in the world, such as good cover (like manzanita bushes), flea remedies, and knowledge of how to avoid getting killed. As for her own needs, Amparo persists and might even be said to flourish in her unique circumstances, squatting in a model house on an unfinished development where the land is pockmarked by excavations. But the story gradually reveals that Amparo craves a stronger connection with the natural world. Her favorite part of her house is the skylight escape, where she enjoys "watching the day take hold," as García notes in understated text; the view of the sky there would surely be magnificent. Amparo takes her mud bath on her birthday "when the sun was at its highest," and the full harvest moon inspires a ceremonial offering; she is clearly attuned to the natural rhythms of the days and the seasons. Especially revealing is how Amparo's voice drops to a whisper when she realizes that the mud is heading for the foothills—as if the mud has hit upon her own most secret desire. She gladly takes up the task of offering the mud guidance toward those foothills. When, as the story closes, the mud romances the house and sweeps it off its foundation, so to speak, sending house and Amparo alike rushing toward the foothills, the excitement is palpable. Amparo is finally heading back into nature.

Escape

Posed as a problem, the primary theme of "The Flat of the Land" is abandonment; posed as a solution, the primary theme is escape. What does Amparo do when American culture rejects her and/or she rejects the culture? She escapes, to the secluded hideaway of a house caught halfway between tradition and modernity. But this can only be a temporary escape, a holding cell or purgatory—to truly escape, she must somehow go farther. Given that this woman has no one to live with, has no connections beyond her family, craves connections with nature, listens to

Amparo hears coyotes in the night and occasionally talks to them. © *outdoorsman / ShutterStock.com*

Mexican radio stations, and eats traditional Mexican food, the reader may wonder why she does not find her way down to a quiet village in Mexico. The fact that she does not may be seen as indicating that she is indeed not Mexican but Chicana, an American of Mexican descent. Amparo was perhaps (like García herself) born in California, such that she has little connection with modern-day Mexico even if she retains traditional culture and attitudes. Amparo's ultimate escape, then, must be conducted on another level—not a geographic level but an existential level, a spiritual level. Her fondness for her skylight escape signals that her desire for a greater degree of liberation is simmering within her and need only be fired by circumstances to lead to action. To her evident delight, such circumstances are provided by the river of mud. Bending the reader's conception of what is possible in reality, the closing scene of the book demands to be read on more than just a literal level. The passage of mud, house, and Amparo through the cleft in the foothills is like an act of spiritual elevation or transcendence; she is being carried off to the natural heaven of "the tree-laced meadow above" where her spirit belongs.

STYLE

Magic Realism

A stylistic approach often associated with Latin American writers owing to its remarkable use by the likes of Gabriel García Márquez and Isabel Allende, magic realism has been recognized as an especially apt literary response to the often-surreal colonial and postcolonial circumstances faced in the various regions of Latin America (where some Spanish conquistadors were mistaken for gods). García Márquez's works at times juxtapose apparently incompatible things, placing modern-day technological wonders brought to provincial Colombia next to mythical wonders like a person suddenly rising up into the sky. Such juxtapositions highlight the ways that science can be viewed as magic, magic as science, and how a mythical story revolving around a miraculous occurrence can be a more powerful representation of truth than the truth itself. The style is not without its detractors, who may be impatient with the introduction of fantastic elements that can be seen to disrupt the realism of the narrative and thus not enhance but lessen its impact. But the response ultimately falls to the individual reader.

"The Flat of the Land" contains only hints of magic realism in the course of the story. The spreading mud at first seems reasonable and explainable. The manner in which it slowly spreads is detailed precisely, while the region's history as marshland offers a potential explanation for the presence of underground water. And yet the narration points out that this desert region has been experiencing drought conditions for three years, making the sudden development of a river-like mudflow especially improbable. Still, it is only in the closing paragraphs that the fantastic or magical occurs, in quite a gradual manner. That the mud might loosen the house from the solid earth is not inconceivable; that the mud might become a fairly raging river, kicking up wash a story high, is less believable; that the foothills might part to somehow send house, mud, and woman uphill toward a tree-lined meadow is, essentially, impossible.

Arguably, García's approach is masterful: All along the mud has been gaining a sense of character, reinforced by Amparo's interactions with it as well as the metaphorical descriptions of mud and house romancing each other, justifying the mud's seeming to take independent action in

heading for the foothills. As for Amparo, her state of mind is cast into doubt by her circumstances—living on disability income while apparently free of physical ailment, inhabiting a void of solitude, talking to the objects and creatures around her as if they truly speak to her. For whatever reason, Amparo and mainstream American culture have abandoned each other, and when a person is set adrift, one might end up anywhere, both circumstantially and psychologically. Indeed, one reading of this story's fantastic ending would be as a representation of Amparo's going crazy: in her solitude, she begins hallucinating the movement of the mud, and her passage into the foothills atop the house via the mudflow could be a departure from the ordinary world in terms of sanity. But it seems more likely that García is suggesting psychological movement in the opposite direction: like a hermit in search of enlightenment, Amparo has distilled all of the unnecessary parts of life out of her existence, and in the daily purity that remains, she inclines toward a transcendent spiritual experience. The trip to the foothills is indeed an *ascent*, not a *descent*, and whether considered a holy land, heaven, or pure land, the "tree-laced meadow above" is without doubt a higher plane. The reader who approaches this magically real experience of Amparo's with an open mind is apt to be swept along as well.

Chicana Literature

While only a scattering of details speak to the identification of García's story as a work of Chicana literature, the themes attest to various concerns often addressed by Chicana writers of fiction. García herself is a Mexican American who was born and raised in California, and "The Flat of the Land" suggests a similar background for Amparo: her name is Spanish, she listens to Mexican radio stations, and her immediate family is likewise in California, while she is acculturated enough to be speaking English even in her solitude (there is no suggestion that her dialogue should be understood as taking place in Spanish). In sum, like many descendants of Mexican American immigrants—or indeed immigrants of any ethnicity—Amparo is caught between the culture of her ancestors and the culture in which she is immersed.

Thus, on the one hand, a degree of American-style feminism can be detected in Amparo's utter independence from any masculine counterpart—she has escaped her former husband

and seems in no hurry to find a new one—and yet this feminism does not manifest itself in a drive for success and achievement on par with men, a significant aim of Anglo feminism. As Deborah L. Madsen suggests in *Understanding Contemporary Chicana Literature*, Chicana distaste for white feminism can be traced to that feminism's inherent support of the existing unbalanced socioeconomic structure in America, in which impoverished minorities by default remain impoverished minorities. More broadly, Madsen notes that since collective Chicana identity has come to be defined in contrast not only to white identity but also to (male) Chicano identity, subjective Chicana experiences are typically at the heart of Chicana literature. "The Flat of the Land" follows a single Chicana protagonist, Amparo, whose experiences are very much presented subjectively, as seen through her eyes. Even in the absence of a detailed backstory, the reader is led to sympathize with Amparo in the stark isolation that mainstream culture has washed her out into. And through this one example of the unique direction taken by a marginalized Chicana life, the reader is advanced toward a greater awareness and understanding of the collective Chicana experience.

HISTORICAL CONTEXT

Late Twentieth-Century Chicano Culture and Literature

In "The Flat of the Land," the grandmother at the Pixley lunch counter refers to seventy years ago being "right after the war," likely World War I, suggesting that the story takes place sometime around 1990, the time period when it was written. Mexican American culture had been thriving in California especially since the late 1960s and the Chicano civil rights movement, spearheaded by legendary labor organizer César Chávez. In the realm of literature, José Antonio Villareal's *Pocho* (1959) is celebrated as the first Chicano novel, while Luis Valdez became the father of Chicano theater through his *actos*, one-act plays staged by his Teatro Campesino to inspire farmworkers. Rodolfo Gonzales's social action organization Crusade for Justice brought about the 1969 publication of "El Plan Espiritual de Aztlán," which is recognized as the Chicano civil rights

manifesto. This document declares Chicano independence from European domination and reclaims in spirit the mythohistorical Chicano homeland of Aztlán—the southwestern region that was inhabited by mestizos of Native American and Spanish descent before it was annexed by the United States and infiltrated by Anglos.

Much of the early Chicano literary recognition was bestowed on male writers, including Rudolfo Anaya, Rolando Hinojosa, Alejandro Morales, and Tomás Rivera. But from the mid-1970s onward, as a sort of coming-together of the preceding Chicano and (white) feminist movements, increasing numbers of Chicana voices gained attention and entered the Mexican American literary canon. Chicana concerns had been addressed only partially by those feminists who pushed for women to gain equality with men in the mainstream American cultural and commercial spheres, and by those Chicanos who strove to assert a valid (masculine) Mexican American identity in the face of disregard and discrimination by whites. As Madsen notes in *Understanding Contemporary Chicana Literature*, "white feminists and macho Chicanos provide poor alternatives for women laboring under a triple burden of sexism, racism, and economic deprivation."

The Chicanas who emerged in this period remain well known in the twenty-first century. Poet Bernice Zamora's first significant publication was the 1976 collection *Restless Serpents*, which was praised as a feminist Chicana manifesto. She followed this up with *Releasing Serpents* in 1994. Sandra Cisneros is best known for her universally admired collection of vignettes *The House on Mango Street* (1984), and she has also gained recognition for *Woman Hollering Creek and Other Stories* (1991) and poetry collections with titles such as *My Wicked, Wicked Ways* (1987). Also working in multiple genres, Ana Castillo would publish poetry collections such as *Women Are Not Roses* (1984), novels such as *The Mixquiahuala Letters* (1986), and the nonfiction collection *Massacre of the Dreamers: Essays on Xicanisma* (1995). Other Chicana authors of note include Gloria Anzaldúa, Lorna Dee Cervantes, Denise Chávez, Alma Luz Villanueva, and Helena María Viramontes. Although García's output has not elevated her to the level of these foremost Chicana authors,

COMPARE
&
CONTRAST

- **1990:** There are some 13.5 million Mexican Americans in the United States, or 5.4 percent of the total population of nearly 249 million. Over 83 percent of Mexican Americans live in the Southwest.

  Today: Numbering 31.8 million in 2010, Mexican Americans account for 10.3 percent of the US population of almost 309 million. They account for more than half of the total US Hispanic population, and some 10 percent of native-born Mexicans are living in the United States.

- **1990:** With Sandra Cisneros having emerged on the scene in the mid-1980s, a flood of literature by Chicanas and Mexican women continues with works such as Laura Esquivel's *Like Water for Chocolate* (1989), a magic-realist novel about a woman caught in the cultural expectations placed on her by her mother, and Ana Castillo's *Sapogonia* (1990), about the tragic objectification of the female protagonist Pastora.

  Today: Among the most recent Chicana novels are Emma Pérez's *Forgetting the Alamo; or, Blood Memory* (2009), a revisionist Chicana lesbian western, and Cisneros's illustrated novel *Have You Seen Marie?* (2012).

- **1990:** As the decade opens, the nation experiences an economic recession that involves a bust in the housing market, with homes in California losing 26 percent of their value by 1996, when median prices drop to a low of $250,000.

  Today: After California home prices peak at a median of nearly $600,000 in the course of a precarious real-estate bubble in 2006, the Great Recession sees prices lose 53 percent of their value, reaching a median of around $280,000 by 2009. Photographs of empty and unfinished housing developments are common.

---

her 1993 story "The Flat of the Land" strongly connects with the emerging Chicana tradition of the era. In portraying Amparo as a willful, independent Mexican American woman who has distanced herself from both (white) Anglo and (male) Chicano concerns, the story presents a sort of foundational Chicana ideal, a woman who thrives physically, reconnects with nature, and achieves a degree of spiritual transcendence in affirming an essential life and worldview for herself.

CRITICAL OVERVIEW

García's works have not received a great deal of critical attention, in part because of their limited number and variety of genres. Her poetry collection *When Living Was a Labor Camp* (2000) won a 2001 American Book Award, but nonetheless, few publications had reviewed the debut title. In a *Publishers Weekly* review, a contributor praised García for rendering "three generations worth of detached anger and small pleasures with an unerring eye"—a comment that speaks to the detachment from emotion and appreciation for small pleasures embodied by Amparo in "The Flat of the Land."

The anthology in which "The Flat of the Land" appeared, *Pieces of the Heart: New Chicano Fiction*, edited by accomplished author Gary Soto, was also reviewed by *Publishers Weekly*, where the stories are said to be united "by their examination of family relationships and cultural identity," both of which are subterranean concerns of García's story. Reviewing *Pieces of the Heart* in the *Nation*, Ray Gonzalez affirms that in this "kaleidoscopic anthology"

The crack in the mud grows to a threatening crevice. © *Dalibor Sevaljevic | ShutterStock.com*

Soto has assembled an admirably varied selection of stories. In phrasing that speaks to García's contribution, Gonzalez notes that the stories "reinforce the notion that successful Chicano literature has to interweave the traditional with the new."

With Frances Payne Adler and Debra Busman, García coedited the 2009 volume *Fire and Ink: An Anthology of Social Action Writing.* In *Tikkun* magazine, a reviewer hails "this rich and important collection" for presenting "a perspective on contemporary experiences that is rarely reflected in the popular media or in public policy." In *Publishers Weekly*, a reviewer observes that the "passionate pieces" presented elevate the collection to "a meditation on the sanctity and wonder of each life"—a description that may equally apply to "The Flat of the Land." What Amparo seems to be responding to through her solitary existence might be summed up in a phrase quoted by the reviewer in reference to García's own labor camp poems included in *Fire and Ink*, which illuminate "the trauma of being different."

CRITICISM

Michael Allen Holmes

Holmes is a writer with existential interests. In the following essay, he explores whether or not the reader of "The Flat of the Land" should question Amparo's sanity.

A single detail in Diana García's short story "The Flat of the Land" adds a fair amount of mystery regarding the circumstances of the protagonist, Amparo. Certain aspects of her circumstances are made clear: the reader is straightforwardly shown that Amparo, living alone, talks sometimes to the coyotes that prowl the environs as well as to the mud besieging her house—much as one might talk to one's pets and even one's houseplants. In the present day, many people occasionally talk to their computers. In and of itself, Amparo's habit of sharing her thoughts with nonhuman entities is not so extraordinary. The reader might find the extent of her solitude troubling, but in any given month she will have at least a couple of visits to family and to the lunch counter in Pixley; she is not completely cut off from the outside

WHAT DO I READ NEXT?

- The one book-length work authored by García is her award-winning poetry collection *When Living Was a Labor Camp* (2000), which includes an introduction peppered with reminiscences and a glossary of the Spanish words used in the poems.

- García has expressed admiration for a number of Latin American and Chicana authors, including Mexican poet and novelist Carmen Boullosa. Among Boullosa's works translated into English is the novel *Cleopatra Dismounts* (2003), which imagines a pair of alternate lives for the famous Egyptian queen, one in which she joins up with pirates, and another in which she is taken by a magical bull to live among the Amazons.

- García has also cited as a literary model Chilean author María Luisa Bombal, whose collection *New Islands and Other Stories* (1982), translated by Richard Cunningham, includes several tales from the late 1930s, such as "The Tree," that address the oppressive circumstances endured by women expected to fulfill passive feminine roles.

- In her collection *Nepantla: Essays from the Land in the Middle* (1993), Latina author Pat Mora considers such topics as women, family, bilingualism, and education in view of the US-Mexican borderland.

- The anthology *Riding Low on the Streets of Gold: Latino Literature for Young Adults* (2003), edited by Judith Ortiz Cofer, includes short stories as well as poetry focusing on Latino experiences marked by love, courage, and acceptance.

- *Infinite Divisions: An Anthology of Chicana Literature* (1993), edited by Tey Diana Rebolledo and Eliana S. Rivero, includes some fifty stories by well- and lesser-known Chicana authors, including Anzaldúa, Castillo, Cervantes, Chávez, Cisneros, Mora, and Viramontes.

- Egyptian physician, psychiatrist, and author Nawal el Sa'adawi is known for her feminist activism. Having been incarcerated at Qanatir Women's Prison, she produced both a novel based on the life of a fellow inmate, *Woman at Point Zero* (1975), translated by Sherif Hetata, and an autobiographical work, *Memoirs from the Women's Prison* (1986), translated by Marilyn Booth.

world, and there is no suggestion that the lunch-counter women perceive her as unsettled in any way. Yet the reader is pointedly told that Amparo is living not off of alimony or welfare—narrative options that García could have employed without substantially altering the reader's perception of the story—but off of disability income. This detail may force the reader to reexamine the way Amparo is portrayed.

One must read between the lines to recognize the potential significance of the fact of Amparo's disability income, which is easily glanced over. Perhaps the first explanation to arise in the reader's mind is that she was injured

on a job. Given that García is a Chicana author with firsthand knowledge of the risks of migrant farmwork in California—one of her uncles died after being poisoned by pesticides sprayed on a field of tomatoes he picked—the reader may imagine that Amparo has been disabled by some farming accident or the conditions in the fields. Yet if this were García's intent, it stands to reason that she would have also included a more specific allusion to the resulting disability; in order to actually draw attention to the risks of inadequately regulated migrant farmwork, she would have to give the reader some further detail pointing in that

> ALTHOUGH AMPARO DOES NOT USE HER OWN LUMBER, BRICKS, AND MORTAR, SHE IS VERY MUCH IN THE MIDST OF CLAIMING AND DEFINING A SPACE FOR HERSELF OUTSIDE THE BOUNDS OF HISTORICAL PRECEDENT AND LIMITATIONS."

direction. To the contrary, the story provides no further hints at any sort of physical disability. Amparo manages to wash her own laundry with a wringer (more manually demanding than a washing machine), hang the clothes up outside to dry, cook her own food, and even get aerobic exercise by running up and down the stairs, during which she is not said to experience any particular pain. That is, her physical abilities do not appear to be limited in any way. She could have a chronic condition, but again, no details are provided to suggest that she is, say, coping with a disease caused by pesticide exposure. She does not appear to be overtired or debilitated at all in the course of her days. She gets along fine.

Behind such considerations, the reader may conclude that the only disability Amparo could have must be psychological. In this light, her habit of talking to the forces around her takes on a shifted significance. Should the reader understand that Amparo is mentally or emotionally unstable—in a colloquial word, crazy? García's depiction in itself is inconclusive; given the range of behaviors shown, Amparo might be crazy, or she might not be. To address the question, more reading between the lines is necessary.

It is worth noting that in various ways, Amparo's circumstances speak to García's own onetime circumstances in life as well as her persisting outlook on the world. Some critics steer clear of the so-called biographical fallacy—the notion, generally held to be false, that a work of literature can be interpreted through the life story of the author. Surely to equate a fictional character with the author, or to assume that the words spoken by such a character represent the author's thoughts, would be going too far. But if an author's experiences and comments speak to the fictional circumstances she has created, those

experiences and comments merit critical consideration. This may be especially true in the present case, since García has not fully exercised her talents in the short-story genre; she has produced no collections and otherwise has almost exclusively published poetry. An author with little ambition to make a name for herself in the realm of fiction may be more likely to craft a story not out of purely artistic motivation but out of personal inspiration as well.

One of the uncommon aspects of Amparo's life is that she appears to be somehow liberated from the desire to have an immediate family. She remains close with her brothers and parents, but her ex-husband and son—whether resented, disowned, convicted, or dead—have apparently been dismissed from her mind. Though at forty-five she perhaps considers herself beyond her childbearing years, Amparo could be dating occasionally or seeing someone, but there is no suggestion that such is the case. Those who prefer companionship may be inclined to pity those who live alone—as if they could not be choosing to do so but have only failed to find a companion—but García has noted, in her essay "Valley Language," that as a young woman (a perspective she inhabits retrospectively) she herself was disinclined to seek a permanent union:

> The dream I do not have is that of marrying and having children. I am aware that, unlike my friends, I do not write "Mrs. Juan Mendoza" in my binder. I do not talk about weddings or how many children I will have. Instead, in my dreams I travel to distant continents where no one speaks English or Spanish. Too bad my dreams don't indicate how I will pay for all this travel.

This passage appears relevant to "The Flat of the Land" for several reasons. To begin with, it indicates García's support of Amparo's indifference toward companionship. Amparo did once have a companion and bear a child, but this does not preclude her preferring solitude later in life. As it happens, García became pregnant and bore a son soon after beginning college, but the father would not remain a part of her life—allowing her the joy of a child without the burden, as she saw it, of a male companion. (García did eventually marry happily.) As a second point of relevance, the passage from "Valley Language" conjures, with positive connotations, the notion of escaping to a faraway place where nobody speaks the languages one knows. In "The Flat of the Land," Amparo has not attained a distant continent, but she has definitely found a home where nobody speaks intelligible words to her; the coyotes and the mud speak in nonverbal ways, but otherwise her own thoughts go undisturbed and unregulated by the bounds of conventional human interaction. Finally, García closes the above passage with a lament that she dreams of traveling but has not conceived of how she will pay for this travel; one might venture to suggest that she vicariously fulfills her dream through the magic-realist voyage undertaken by Amparo.

Other comments that García has made likewise speak to her sympathy for Amparo's circumstances. In particular, she has expressed an appreciation for nature that echoes the appreciation for nature shown by Amparo. As she relates in "Valley Language," she was raised for the first five years of her life in a farm labor camp consisting of cabins on the banks of a creek, such that "it was hard not to feel a strong connectedness to soil and water" (the two ingredients, of course, of mud). Later, when she was living in urban San Diego, she at times needed to reconnect with the countryside: "When hunger for soil and brindled cows overwhelms me, I will drive an hour east to the Cuyamaca Mountains, take deep breaths of meadow and sage." Thus is the meadow framed as an idyllic place of escape, a sacred destination. More broadly, in an interview for Pat Mora's website *Bookjoy*, García noted, "I have always trusted my response to the natural world, that sense of self that is best reflected by moments in nature." In view of these words, it is fitting that she created in her protagonist Amparo a woman who likewise seems to best get in touch with herself by getting in touch with the aspects of nature surrounding her. And it is perhaps no coincidence that García characterized herself in that interview as having been "reclusive, and living in a world of my imagination."

Altogether, in establishing García's sympathy for and similarities to Amparo, such quotes support the contention that the author does not intend for the reader to view Amparo as mentally unstable or psychologically "disabled." Indeed, the use of the word *disability* in the story should be taken with a grain of salt. This is not the narrator's judgment of Amparo but only a classification explaining why Amparo is granted a certain income by the government. In other words, someone within the medical

establishment has labeled her "disabled," but as García knows, again from firsthand experience, American institutions do not always apply the most appropriate labels to people being classified within their systems. In "Valley Language," she recalls a friend she made as a schoolchild, Victoria, who, because she spoke inadequate English and had been raised to embody feminine passivity, rode the same crosstown bus as García but to attend a remedial program. García was attending a program for students considered gifted; officially, Victoria and the other primarily Spanish-speaking children were considered "mentally retarded." García recognized how difficult the experience was for Victoria, whose shoulders slumped as soon as the two friends separated, as "the taunts and humiliations shamed her." Sometime during the eighth grade, Victoria disappeared from the academic sphere, and García never saw her again. As this anecdote shows, García knows how little reason can lie behind labels like "retarded" or "disabled." García may have even had Victoria in mind when she wrote "The Flat of the Land"; as she states in "Valley Language," she imagined for Victoria a direction reminiscent of Amparo's direction: "I imagine her in class, lifting her head to study the shape and silence of fog, study how she might disappear into it."

The author's background, then, if considered alongside her fictional story, strongly suggests that even if Amparo has been judged psychologically "disabled" (perhaps owing to a unique response to unbearable circumstances) and awarded income for it, she remains in perfectly adequate mental health. There is also a recent critical construct that offers support for the validity of Amparo's mode of living in the world. In her book *Spiritual Mestizaje: Religion, Gender, Race, and Nation in Contemporary Chicana Narrative*, Theresa Delgadillo elaborates on a concept prominently discussed before her by Chicana scholar Gloria Anzaldúa, namely, the concept of spiritual mestizaje. From the root word *mestiza*, which is Spanish for "mixed" and more specifically refers to women of mixed European and American Indian ancestry, the term *mestizaje* denotes the state of being mixed as such. Going beyond the concept of racial mixture, *spiritual mestizaje* as used by Anzaldúa has a more expansive meaning, with feminist and individualist overtones.

In Delgadillo's words, spiritual mestizaje "is the transformative renewal of one's relationship to the sacred through a radical and sustained multimodal and self-reflexive critique of oppression in all its manifestations and a creative and engaged participation in shaping life that honors the sacred." In other words, if an individual—especially a mestiza—reflects upon the ways in which oppression has shaped the circumstances of one's life, whether this be due to race, gender, sexuality, or religion, one may realize that the truest way of countering that oppression is by creating for oneself an original spiritual relationship with the world, one that bypasses faulty institutions—such as the Roman Catholic Church, which up to the present day actively frames the lives of women in limiting ways (such as by denying access to contraception). In simpler terms, Delgadillo calls spiritual mestizaje "the critical and conscious process of transformation in all aspects of being," and elsewhere, "a process directed toward the creation of new ways of being in the world." Delgadillo quotes Anzaldúa presenting a very personal and provocative affirmation of such a process of transformation and creation:

> What I want is an accounting with all three cultures—white, Mexican, Indian. I want the freedom to carve and chisel my own face, to staunch the bleeding with ashes, to fashion my own gods out of my entrails. And if going home is denied me then I will have to stand and claim my space, making a new culture—*una cultura mestiza*—with my own lumber, my own bricks and mortar and my own feminist architecture.

Although Amparo does not use her own lumber, bricks, and mortar, she is very much in the midst of claiming and defining a space for herself outside the bounds of historical precedent and limitations. She is certainly concerned with regard for the sacred, as evidenced in her leaving offerings for the coyotes and for the mud. It is likely that there have been at least some manifestations of oppression in Amparo's past, whether at the hands of employers, doctors, her husband, other Chicanos, or white people generally. Disregarding all of these cultures, she has now embarked on a journey of spiritual mestizaje, one that evolves into a physical journey of magic-realist proportions.

Amparo's journey is readily seen as symbolic of an experience of spiritual transcendence—perhaps akin to the night journey undertaken by Muhammad, the founder of Islam. Consisting of the Isra, in which he miraculously traveled to distant Jerusalem, and the Miraj, in which he was taken by God up to heaven, Muhammad's journey has been framed as being at the same time both a spiritual and a physical journey. Perhaps Amparo's journey should be viewed likewise. In this light, one might look more closely at the symbolic value of the journey and of the mud that propels her house across the flatlands. Amparo's relation to the mud is most strongly evoked in the scene of her mud bath, taken "when the sun was at its highest"—a ritualistic time—on her birthday. The terms used to describe the sensation of being submerged in the mud—"like that of someone holding her without making contact," producing "an unnatural buoyancy"—tend to connote not just a physical but a spiritual experience. That Amparo enjoys a feeling of deep communion with the confluence of the sacred elements of soil and water is reflected in her comment to the mud then, "How perfectly you've caught me," and in how the dried and peeled mud is "stamped with the lines of her body." In a sense, the mud, gaining the woman's curves, is explicitly feminized. In contrast, the expanse of flatlands adjoining the development has a masculine character, being not fluid but firm, unyielding, unchanging. What Amparo and the mud both seem to yearn to do is bypass the flat of the land to gain the foothills beyond, where the curvature and fertility of the terrain again suggest alliance with femininity. Along these lines, Amparo's final journey, in which "a cleft in the foothills parted," can be read as suggesting a return to a place of female origination, namely, the womb, metaphorically a place of traditional, nature-aligned consciousness. The journey is unmistakably fantastic, and the reader is left to decide whether it should be read literally or surreally or spiritually or miraculously. At the very least, with due consideration, the reader is apt to conclude that García's protagonist is by no means insane and rather should be seen as more like a saint.

Source: Michael Allen Holmes, Critical Essay on "The Flat of the Land," in *Short Stories for Students*, Gale, Cengage Learning, 2014.

Diana García

In the following excerpt, García describes some of her childhood, including her early love of reading and her interest in becoming a writer.

. . . Return to an earlier time when I spoke Spanish. In the farm labor camp where my parents lived and worked when I was born, my aunts and uncles, my godparents, my cousins, everyone I knew spoke Spanish. Consigned to small cabins perched on the banks of the Bear Creek, it was hard not to feel a strong connectedness to soil and water. Ripening peach orchards on one side and tomato fields on the other, guitars strumming in the background, I knew who I was—*mija*, beloved daughter. That language of familial love was the litany of daily life, the sounds of the creek, the scent of ripening fruit, all part of the valley's own liturgy.

But that life, that sense of connectedness to valley and community, changed at age five when I became Karen, not Diana. Having experienced their own share of racial discrimination when they were in school, at my birth my parents had given me a first name they hoped would spare me some of the humiliations their own first names— Manuel and Tomasa—had engendered. At home, my family called me by my middle name, Diana, pronounced "Thee-ah-nah," accent over the first *a*. Sometime before my first day in kindergarten, my mother must have explained to me that when I started school, I would become Karen. She must have told me something like, "When the teacher calls the name 'Karen Garcia,' raise your hand and answer 'here.'" Dutiful child, I'm sure that's exactly what I did.

Years later, when I ask my mother why they gave me the first name Karen but always called me Diana, she explains that they thought Karen sounded more American, more professional. At age five, I must have pondered these changes. No longer surrounded by family at the labor camp, we had moved to Merced, to a house not far from my grammar school. Nestled in a swing I'd make by twisting together lengths of branches from the weeping willow in our backyard, I'd shoot up, lean back to study an expanse of sky, clouds I could transform into specific shapes even as I contemplated my own transformation. I did not know why I needed to become Karen to start school, but even at such a young age, I must have realized there was something not right about being Diana, something you did not want to be. I must have sensed that being Karen was better. Of such small but critical moments do we develop initial perceptions of a self. Instead of feeling self-confident and comfortable entering school, I must have felt a dissonance between my home life and my school life, between being my parents' daughter

> HEADS BOWED, EYES LOWERED, THEIR BODY SPEAKS OF RESPECT FOR THOSE IN AUTHORITY. AUTHORITY DOES NOT RECOGNIZE THEIR PRIMAL LANGUAGE OF SURVIVAL."

and becoming a student, between living in the labor camp and moving into town.

As if it weren't enough that I had to leave the comfort of the camp, then change to fit the name Karen, I also had to undergo the transformation of speaking English instead of Spanish. I had learned English well enough to make friends on the monkey bars my first day of kindergarten, but I was raised a proper Mexican American child; I answered in the language in which I was addressed, and at home, this was in Spanish. As a result, my conversational Spanish was better than my conversational English. Also, I had been raised to be respectful to my elders, to cast my eyes down and not speak unless directly addressed. My kindergarten teacher had feared that my silence and timidity during class discussions was a symptom of deeper learning problems. At the beginning of first grade, I was shocked to learn I had been placed in junior first, a half step between kindergarten and first grade. When my mother learned what had happened, she marched me back to school and made me read aloud in English. I was reinstated to a proper first grade, but my parents never let us speak Spanish at home again. Although my father was more comfortable, more articulate, more poetic in Spanish, we became an English-speaking family.

Again, I cannot explain the process that occurred. I barely remember the moment I became Karen at school—Karen, a name centered somewhere north of Scandinavia; not Diana, redolent of sage cracking through dirt in August. I've lost the memory of a time when I spoke Spanish and English both at home and in my neighborhood but then switched to an English-only life beginning in first grade.

To understand what happened during those early grammar school years, I draw on my relationship to the San Joaquin Valley. In summer, the valley stretches endlessly, bordered by coastal hills to the west and the Sierra Nevada foothills to the east. Standing motionless in the middle of a cotton or a tomato field, I must have felt what the French scientist and philosopher Gaston Bachelard describes as that "[i]mmensity ... within ourselves" in his book, *The Poetics of Space* (184). That "inner immensity" allowed me to focus on the smallest details of a fig orchard canopy, how it loomed above and around me, yet spit me out to that expansive valley at the end of the day (185). At another level, I drew on my experience of tule fogs—how, if I walked three feet in any direction, I lost all sense of where I had been. The valley cocooned me and obscured me, swallowed me and challenged my imagination.

Not surprisingly, in a region of such cultural and geographic extremes, reading became my crutch and my escape. By third grade I was a classic bookworm. When I read, I became one of the characters in the book. I was present. I could visualize each scene, hear the accents and intonations each character used, breathe the scents of a world of foods coming from each kitchen.

My first experience with a library was the small stone building next to the Merced County Fairgrounds. I fell in love with the smell of books lining old bookshelves and the odor of furniture polish lifting from the checkout counter. The children's section was in back, two steps up from the rest of the building. Two small windows offered a pale light blocked in part by a mature pine to one side of the yard. The adult section was in front, the first section I saw as I walked through the door. That was the section I yearned for, with books over a half-inch thick and no pictures to get in the way of the ideas and images. One of the first books I read from the adult section was Pearl S. Buck's *The Good Earth*. I can still smell the steam rising from the rice bowls, feel the shape of the bowl in my hands. From John Steinbeck's *Cannery Row*, I learned to envy a life spent collecting marine samples from Monterey Bay, marine life as diverse and interconnected as those of the local residents whose stories he also told. The scent of seaweed and drying mollusks filled my nostrils.

I checked out three, four, five, six books at a time, the numbers increasing as the librarian became familiar with my passion for reading. I was voracious. I read before and after school, before bed, after lights out. My parents refused to let me read during meals. In fact, my reading

became a worry for them. They began throwing me out of the house, ordering me outside into the sun and fresh air. I learned to sneak a book under my shirt, then climb the apricot tree in the backyard where I could read without interruption. From my perch, I selected the ripest, rosiest apricots, their perfume thundering up my nose and mouth. I had a bird's-eye view of the comings and goings in the alley behind our house and in our neighbors' yards. Or, at least I might have if I had had better vision. Instead, I guessed by size and shape who was coming out of Helen's back door, who was coming to Sammy's house, which brother was chasing which sister directly next door. The neighborhood goings-on became the backdrop for my growing relationship to writers and their books.

All that reading, all those disparate bits of information that filtered through these books quickly paid off. Beginning in fifth grade, I was bused east of the first set of tracks to attend a program for gifted children. Ostracized by my brothers, cousins, and old elementary school friends for leaving our side of town, I rode the bus with my grammar school friend, Victoria. We collected at the bus stop each morning, relishing the crisp October air and despairing in January's damp fog. This passage from the west side to the east side of town delivered me to an almost-all-white class. All the other children on the bus, including Victoria, were going to the MR class—that's what my friends and busmates were called, mentally retarded.

From that bus, we filed past the talented jeers of students, some my new classmates. I veered right, into the gifted classroom. I was protected from the longer walk my busmates took, a walk the length of the school to the portable classrooms parked on the former basketball court. I remember my sense of relief at the spared embarrassment from the vicious humiliations. It was bad enough that the larger student body considered those of us in the gifted program a bunch of brains, that my own brothers and cousins ostracized me. It was bad enough that my new classmates tolerated my presence but never invited me into their social circles. After all, I was not a member of their Brownie (later, Girl Scouts) troops; I did not attend any of the grammar schools they attended on the good side of town. Thank goodness, I thought, I was not one of the mentally retarded students as well.

That first year on the bus, Victoria and I whispered about our catechism class, about the nuns who directed us in choir. She told me who got her first kiss behind the parish hall, who climbed the water tower and panicked halfway up. I remember her descriptions of ghosts shaped by fog—this one a boy looking for a dog, that one a dog hiding from a boy. Hers was delicious gossip, frightening stories, possible endings that unnerved me in brightest daylight. I admired her sharp dissection of some of the students who lined the sidewalk. She kept her head up, her back straight, as we walked from the bus, hand in hand. When the time came to separate, I'd watch as her shoulders slumped. The contrast pained me. She was the most beautiful girl in my grade.

Now I'll tell you two facts: Victoria, my friend and bus companion, was not dumb. She was smarter than I was at math. Next, her family spoke Spanish. Hers was a formal and hierarchical tongue: the *Ud.* for parents, elders, anyone in authority; *tu* for the rest of us. Victoria was raised to stay silent when spoken to unless commanded to speak. She was raised to keep her head bowed, to keep her voice low, her eyes averted, not to appear challenging or aggressive when confronted by adults. Unlike Victoria, at my parents' insistence, I had learned the language of parity: there was no formal *you* in English. I did not know how to teach her what I had learned. Years later, the first time I saw an oystercatcher, its glossy black feathers reminded me of Victoria's hair. What was not to admire? Her Indian features, her dark skin, her slight build, hinted at ancestors older than mine.

The classmates in my gifted class knew nothing about Victoria. Their fathers were dentists, mayors, judges. They would graduate, move away to college, marry well (or not), and succeed (or not). Sometime in eighth grade, Victoria disappeared. She left school, and I never saw her again. The taunts and humiliations shamed her. At home, she was a good girl, respectful, honest, hardworking. At school, she was the girl whose accent and diction proclaimed her dumb, not worthy of more than the barest attention. I imagine her in class, lifting her head to study the shape and silence of fog, study how she might disappear into it.

Children of those who walk in heat and soil, offspring of those with little or no education, have no connection to a language that speaks to them from radio and television, from the mouths of those who stand in front of a classroom or behind the counter at a bank. Heads bowed, eyes lowered, their body speaks of respect for those in authority. Authority does not recognize their primal language of survival.

Victoria disappeared. I almost disappeared, too. A teenage pregnancy, welfare, single motherhood ahead of me, I was little different. What gifted me was the importance of hard work, modeled by both my parents. What inspired me were the memories of books I'd read, universes I'd devoured, information to be learned. What saved me was knowledge of tomatoes ripe on the vine, how fine bristles prickle when you lift them, unlock those last fruits steamed in heat, soil, rot. The message of meadowlarks and red-winged blackbirds nurtured me, the beauty of a valley's sunrise, the sharp sting of snowmelt as I drifted the Merced River, waves of lightning hitting Half Dome in the distance. This valley and the sierra to the east taught me a focused gaze and close attention to detail. I learned to raise my head, look teachers in the eye, pattern the cadence of my voice to theirs, read and write in precise, calculated words. I could imagine a world beyond the valley, peopled with characters as complex as any I had savored in a book....

Source: Diana García, "Valley Language," in *Placing the Academy: Essays on Landscape, Work, and Identity*, edited by Jennifer Sinor and Rona Kaufman, Utah State University Press, 2007, pp. 53–58.

Juan Felipe Herrera

In the following excerpted analysis of When Living Was a Labor Camp, Herrera discusses García's place in the context of Chicana literature as well as some of the major themes of her work.

TEXTUAL OVERVIEW

Diana García is a fiery *campesina* speaker from the San Joaquin Valley. She is a solar poet who ignites her heart and casts her sparkle-words into the original fields from where she came—the farm worker *campesino* labor camp. Inside the "camp" of her poetry, housing is created from past experiences that have by extension framed the possibilities of her voice, the prisms of her existence. Because the camp also dissolves and disrupts life, García's words and language move and break across regions, producing bordered voices, styles, and textures—her "snake-skins."

> IN A SENSE GARCÍA'S POETRY IS DOUBLE
> SKINNED; IT CROSSES NATIONS, SELVES, WOMEN'S
> LIVES AND YET REMAINS OSCILLATING AND
> DISPLACED IN *EL VALLE*."

In many ways, Diana García's award-winning *When Living Was a Labor Camp* props up a stark set of questions that may illuminate the ways through which we can read Chicana poetry today. These questions have to do with what in large part Chicana critics have elaborated in the last three decades—the formation of a new way of speaking about the Chicana text. What is salient? García's book seems to say, "the serpentine transformations of consciousness."

This is a book of skin-spiral—voices, selves, and awarenesses going back and forth as they progress in forward motion. In the sixty-one poems sectioned into six vineyard-like chapters, we go from familiar observations to inscrutable mediations. We cross one row to the other, smelling, touching, tasting, and pruning local lives, peering into personal day-to-day encounters and the shifting auras of vast landscapes and intimate seasons. In this narrative flare, cultural relationships, familial memoirs, and the intimate flickering of the self blur, fade, and condense. The speaker transforms and channels hybrid figures: a farmworkers' daughter, a *curandera* casting spells, a lover, and a cast of "other Marías." Within the poems themselves we find multiple voices, other lives and other "undocumented and documented workers" at play—Barbie, women's magazines, Mexican radio fifties classics, even old cassette tape speakers—singing, announcing, presenting, blooming.

The voices also cross over as the seasons and *campesinas* flow in between Mexico and "El Norte." At times the poems in the middle section are as formal, careful, and lyrical as most of the pieces in the first and last sections. At other moments, the speaker's tenor loosens and speaks out bilingually and loudly or fractures into itself, as in "The Love Affairs" and "The Girlfriends" in the third section.

Power, connection, discontinuity, hybridity, and borderlessness are key valences in Diana García's first poetry collection. These inner- and outer-directed narratives are also developed through García's line and stanza work. Most of the time, the poet utilizes a medium-length narrative line; the conversation is personal and seems to be attentive to the "listener." What varies is the stanza, its breath size and architecture. This is how García makes room for stories, how she casts moments and twines in the templates of time, self, and consciousness.

HISTORICAL CONTEXT

During and particularly after the male-centered *"Floricanto* Generation" of the late sixties and early seventies, Chicana writers and poets produced, performed, and powered a woman text and a new paradigm of Latina literary practices. These new creative charters of feminist and social concerns are surveyed in groundbreaking critical works such as *Chicana Poetry, Beyond Stereotypes, Borderlands, Women Singing in the Snow, Infinite Divisions,* and *Homegirls: Chicana Literary Voices.* Diana García's new volume reinvigorates these feminist investigations within the position of a California Chicana poetics.

To begin with, García's work is from an "interior" California—from the inner spaces of a woman from the San Joaquín Valley. Naturally, we miss the point to say that *el valle* is well represented by male writers such as José Montoya, Omar Salinas, and Gary Soto. *When Living Was a Labor Camp* is not only one of the most recent collections by a poet from this region but, more significantly, it may be one of only two written by a Latina; the other is Margarita Luna Robles's *Typtich: Dreams, Lust and Other Performances.*

García's California Chicana literary mentors as seen through her work seem to be Gloria Anzaldúa, Lorna Dee Cervantes, and Bernice Zamora. Although Anzaldúa and Zamora are not native to the state, they both have spent many years writing major works and establishing a complex and enduring project in the area. It is possible that García is calling out from and into this site. However, to cast García's poems as merely regional is to discard her various contributions.

In a sense García's poetry is double skinned; it crosses nations, selves, women's lives and yet remains oscillating and displaced in *el valle.* And when she does leave *el Valle de San Joaquín*, she migrates to another "valley"—Brawley, Salinas, or deserts-of-sorts in the inner zones of New York, San Diego, and Kansas.

BIOGRAPHICAL BACKGROUND

As her book states, "A native of California's San Joaquín Valley, Diana García was born in Camp CPC, a migrant farmworker labor camp owned by the California Packing Corporation." During a visit to my Chicano Artistic Expression Class at Cal State Fresno, a few years ago, Diana made it a point to let the students know about her roots, that she had been a "single mother on welfare" while she attended the very same university from 1968 to 1973. She dismantled tired notions regarding "welfare mothers" when she spoke of participating in student protests that demanded the formation of a La Raza studies program on campus, holding a series of odd jobs and spending considerable time as a sentencing consultant to criminal defense attorneys. Years later, she received both her B.A. and her M.F.A. from San Diego State University and went on to teach creative writing at Central Connecticut State University. García currently teaches at California State University, Monterey Bay, where she coordinates the Institute for Human Communication's Reading, Writing and Critical Thinking Program.

RECEPTION OF THE TEXT

Since *When Living Was a Labor Camp* is García's first collection (2000), it is not surprising to note that there has been little time to produce a body of critical response to her offerings. Nevertheless, it is important to note that the book won the 2001 Before Columbus American Book Award. It also became one of the California Council of the Humanities' recommended books for its state-wide John Steinbeck Commemoration campaign in 2002. Given the unique "rural" and mid-California position of the book as well as its multiple recastings of previous Chicana and Latina concerns, ways of seeing, and investigations, this material will no doubt be well reviewed and discussed for years to come. On the road, in terms of community and audience reception, Diana is invited frequently to visit campuses in states like Ohio and North Carolina, where Mexicano working-class populations are on the rise. As these demographic figures increase so does the thirst for the socially

powered poem and García's migrant illuminations.

MAJOR THEMES AND CRITICAL ISSUES

At first glance, reading through García's book and also noting the concatenation of themes in her vineyard of chapters, a key set of concerns appears to be encapsulated in the phrase "Woman Observer of the Senses and the Local." This can be seen as merging a trinity of clustered themes: feminist concerns, daily life/work, and space.

The speakers in the poems chart their moments, minds, personas, and environments as Chicanas, women, girlfriends, Marías, daughters, healer women, and partners with husbands and lovers to evoke a number of feminist questions:

Who are the Marías?

Why are these gendered speakers so careful with detail?

Why are they so busy documenting voices, locations, stories, families, and even "how best to clean tomatoes from twice-picked fields?"

How do gender and cultural identity and class converge?

Which is more central to García's poetic—gender, class, color, or culture?

Where, when, and why do these gender figures change?

These questions are all encouraged by the gender perspective of the work. García's *campesina* camp is thus not as pastoral, static, and monolithic as seemingly portrayed by the image on the cover. The shifting and fluid flux of gender positioning is a major key to García's project.

García's feminist vision also focuses on the issue of the body. This focus begins with her corporeal frame within a variety of poems that address the physical aspect. This body lens also gives us the opportunity to talk about the interests in permeating landscapes and relationships as well as the body of women's voices in each chapter. We can also talk of the cultural body, the herstories within the collective text of ninety-seven pieces. These may include issues of language, dialect, and the use of Caló. And perhaps more significant and radically subtle is the body-in-between. This is the speaker that wants to "return" to camp, to remember it, to feverishly document it with a "practical" air that conveys the smell, touch, and sounds of the site. Despite this insider perspective the speaker remains locked outside, in the "wild zone" as Chicana critics say, in the "Nepantla" space, in between two time spaces and time places. No matter how hard she tries to sense the "camp," the speaker is elsewhere. One of the primary activities in this in-between zone is the myriad of photographic documentary operations and intimate relationships of daily life, power relations, and work.

From the initial poem, almost as a camp birthing ritual, the collection begins with "we cradled hoes." And in an ironic gesture, after we labor through the complexities and shifts of the progressive chapters, the last page ends with the migrant family "claiming the floor," an act somewhere in between work and pleasure, showing the young Diana (as narrator) how to dance. Indeed, labor is one of the central macrothemes throughout the book, whether it is by hand, the mind at work, or performed by the various agents that animate García's writing. However, there is another kind of "work" represented by García's book, something we might call *curandera* practice even though García seems to categorize it as "Serpentine."

In the third chapter, García opens with "Serpentine Voices," a poem that asks the question that indirectly and directly flows throughout the entire book and consequently may be Diana's Ars Poetica: "How many voices can I plumb in this poem?" Readers thus move from hoeing cotton to crafting voices. It is this literary shaman behavior, the extracting of selves, the words of other Marías, taken from the writing body of these poems, that suggests the conjurer poet working as a healer-woman, a poetry *curandera*.

The next major thematic element of woman as observer of the senses and the local has to do with "migrant space"—the ways time and place shift, intermingle, and change frames. The "camp" that Diana yearns for and seeks to map has a seemingly fixed location—Montgomery, California—and to further contain its boundaries we can imagine, almost by occupational definition, that it is a dwelling place for a loose-knit collective of migrant farm worker families. García's text moves beyond a single locale, representing the camp as more of a blurred foreground that loses its lines of demarcation as soon as the poem begins to spiral between that distant place

in the past and the speaker's present space. This interplay of time, space, and voice creatively portrays the significant "camp," the one that is inhabited by numerous counterpoints, conflicts, wavy memory fragments. And because of its migratory and peripheral nature, it is brimming with power, creativity, and the possibility for transformation—"serpentine" consciousness. . . .

Source: Juan Felipe Herrera, "Diana García, *When Living Was a Labor Camp*," in *Reading U.S. Latina Writers: Remapping American Literature*, edited by Alvina E. Quintana, Palgrave Macmillan, 2003, pp. 103–108.

SOURCES

Adler, Frances Payne, Debra Busman, and Diana García, eds., *Fire and Ink: An Anthology of Social Action Writing*, University of Arizona Press, 2009, p. 440.

Caravantes, Ernesto R., *The Mexican-American Mind*, Hamilton Books, 2008, pp. xv–xxi, 35–41.

Delgadillo, Theresa, *Spiritual Mestizaje: Religion, Gender, Race, and Nation in Contemporary Chicana Narrative*, Duke University Press, 2011, pp. 1–16.

"Diana Garcia," California State University–Monterey Bay website, http://hcom.csumb.edu/diana-garc%-C3%AD (accessed February 10, 2013).

"Diana García," Poetry Foundation website, http://www.poetryfoundation.org/bio/diana-garcaa (accessed February 10, 2013).

García, Diana, "The Flat of the Land," in *Pieces of the Heart: New Chicano Fiction*, edited by Gary Soto, Chronicle Books, 1993, pp. 163–71.

———, "Valley Language," in *Placing the Academy: Essays on Landscape, Work, and Identity*, edited by Jennifer Sinor and Rona Kaufman, Utah State University Press, 2007, pp. 52–64.

———, *When Living Was a Labor Camp*, University of Arizona Press, 2000, pp. xi–xiv.

Gonzalez, Ray, Review of *Pieces of the Heart: New Chicano Fiction*, edited by Gary Soto, in *Nation*, Vol. 256, No. 22, June 7, 1993, p. 772.

Madsen, Deborah L., *Understanding Contemporary Chicana Literature*, University of South Carolina Press, 2000, pp. 1–40.

Mermann-Jozwiak, Elisabeth, *Postmodern Vernaculars: Chicana Literature and Postmodern Rhetoric*, Peter Lang, 2005, pp. 1–22.

"The Mexican-American Boom: Births Overtake Immigration," Pew Research Hispanic Center website, July 14, 2011, http://www.pewhispanic.org/2011/07/14/the-mexican-american-boom-brbirths-overtake-immigration/ (accessed February 13, 2013).

Mora, Pat, "Creativity Salon: An Interview with Poet Diana Garcia," in *Bookjoy*, September 30, 2012, http://sharebookjoy.blogspot.com/2012/09/creativity-salon-interview-with-poet.html (accessed February 10, 2013).

Myers, Dowell, Ray Calnan, Anna Jacobsen, and Josh Wheeler, "California Roller Coaster: Income and Housing in Boom and Bust, 1990–2010," University of Southern California website, April 2011, http://www.usc.edu/schools/price/research/popdynamics/pdf/2011_Myersetal_California-Roller-Coaster.pdf (accessed February 13, 2013).

Petruccelli, Kathryn, "CSUMB Poet Diana Garcia Gives Voice to the Voiceless," in *Monterey County Weekly*, May 1, 2003, http://www.montereycountyweekly.com/news/2003/may/01/fighting-words/ (accessed February 10, 2013).

Review of *Fire and Ink: An Anthology of Social Action Writing*, edited by Frances Payne Adler, Debra Busman, and Diana García, in *Publishers Weekly*, Vol. 256, No. 32, August 10, 2009, p. 47.

Review of *Fire and Ink: An Anthology of Social Action Writing*, edited by Frances Payne Adler, Debra Busman, and Diana García, in *Tikkun*, Vol. 24, No. 6, November–December 2009, p. 81.

Review of *Pieces of the Heart: New Chicano Fiction*, edited by Gary Soto, in *Publishers Weekly*, Vol. 240, No. 14, April 5, 1993, p. 70.

Review of *When Living Was a Labor Camp*, in *Publishers Weekly*, Vol. 247, No. 44, October 30, 2000, p. 73.

Saenz, Rogelio, Maria Cristina Morales, and Janie Filoteo, "The Demography of Mexicans in the United States," in *Chicanas and Chicanos in Contemporary Society*, 2nd ed., edited by Robert M. De Anda, Rowman & Littlefield, 2004, pp. 3–20.

"Written Word Speaks Volumes for Diana Garcia," California State University website, March 22, 2004, http://www.calstate.edu/pa/clips2004/march/22march/diana.shtml (accessed February 10, 2013); originally published in *Monterey Herald*, March 21, 2004.

FURTHER READING

Blackwell, Maylei, *Chicana Power: Contested Histories of Feminism in the Chicano Movement*, University of Texas Press, 2011.

Hailed as the first history to focus on women's roles in the Chicano movement of the 1960s and 1970s, Blackwell's volume tells of how women's involvement through student and community organizations evolved to produce a feminist agenda in response to subjugation by Chicano leaders.

Feldon, Barbara, *Living Alone and Loving It: A Guide to Relishing the Solo Life*, Simon & Schuster, 2007.

Drawing on her own experiences after a dead-end relationship, Feldon seeks to enlighten the reader about how life alone can be as enriching as life with a partner, if not more so. She addresses such topics as coping with feelings of loneliness, maintaining self-esteem, and tapping into creative potential.

Serros, Michele, *How to Be a Chicana Role Model*, Riverhead Books, 2000.

This nonfiction volume by a Chicana writer of poetry and fiction relates the author's experiences in trying to represent her community and remain in touch with herself while functioning within the dominant Anglo culture.

Woods, Michael, and Mary B. Woods, *Mudflows and Landslides*, Lerner Publications, 2007.

For the reader interested in the facts about how mudflows originate and evolve, this volume aimed at young adults, part of the Disasters Up Close series, addresses the relevant science as well as how humans can respond.

SUGGESTED SEARCH TERMS

Diana Garcia AND poet

Diana Garcia AND The Flat of the Land

Diana Garcia AND Chicana literature

Chicana literature AND history

Chicano movement

California AND migrant labor camps

California AND Chicanos

Mexican Americans AND history

Gryphon

CHARLES BAXTER

1985

Novelist and short story writer Charles Baxter often incorporates elements of the supernatural, spiritual, or simply out-of-the-ordinary into otherwise realistic fiction. He has infused the short story "Gryphon" with mystery and a hint of supernaturalism. In Baxter's tale, a class of fourth-grade students is introduced to a substitute teacher who suggests to the children that there are secret truths in the universe that can be uncovered, truths that are magical, delightful, and sometimes frightening. The story is narrated by one of the fourth graders, who becomes increasingly awed by Miss Ferenczi and her tales of wonder. Miss Ferenczi also makes declarations that seem bizarre and fantastical to her students.

In this story, Baxter explores the importance of imagination in the way one learns and perceives the world, and at the same time he reflects on the relative openness of the mind during childhood. Through the character of Tommy, the narrator, Baxter emphasizes the importance of the imagination and maintaining one's youthful open-mindedness throughout life. "Gryphon" was originally published in Baxter's 1985 short-story collection *Through the Safety Net* and is also included in his 2011 collection *Gryphon: New and Selected Stories.*

AUTHOR BIOGRAPHY

Baxter was born in Minneapolis, Minnesota, on May 13, 1947, to John Baxter, an insurance salesman, and Mary Eaton Baxter. The youngest

Charles Baxter (© *ZUMA Wire Service | Alamy*)

of three boys, Baxter was raised in Excelsior, Minnesota, on a large estate. His schooling included private secondary education and four years at Macalester College in Saint Paul, where he earned a bachelor of arts degree. After working as a high-school teacher for a year in Pinconning, Michigan, Baxter entered graduate school at the State University of New York at Buffalo, from which he graduated with a PhD in 1974. That same year, he began teaching English at Wayne State University, in Detroit, Michigan, where he taught for fifteen years.

Baxter published a collection of poetry, *Chameleon*, in 1970. His first published fiction was the short-story collection *Harmony of the World*, which appeared in 1984. A year later, he published another short-story collection, *Through the Safety Net*, a work containing the much-anthologized story "Gryphon." This was followed in 1987 by the publication of his first novel, *First Light*. In 1989, Baxter accepted a professorship in the English Department at the University of Michigan, in Ann Arbor. His 2000

novel *The Feast of Love* was a finalist for the National Book Award and was later adapted as a film.

In 2003, Baxter began teaching at the University of Minnesota. His recent work includes the 2008 novel *The Soul Thief* and the 2011 collection *Gryphon: New and Selected Stories*. In 2012, Baxter was awarded the prestigious Rea Award for the Short Story, a major literary prize that is accompanied by a $30,000 honorarium.

PLOT SUMMARY

"Gryphon" begins in a fourth-grade classroom in the fictional town of Five Oaks, Michigan. The narrator of the story is a fourth-grade boy in Mr. Hibler's class; he is later identified as Tommy. Through Tommy's perspective, the reader is introduced to the other students in the class as Mr. Hibler takes the children through their lessons. Throughout this particular

MEDIA ADAPTATIONS

- "Gryphon" was adapted into a television movie in 1990 by Max Mabru Films for PBS Wonderworks. The movie was directed by Mark Cullingham, and writers Manuel Arce and Carl Haber adapted the story. Notably, the setting was changed for the movie, which features an inner-city rather than a rural school.

Wednesday, Mr. Hibler develops a cough, which Carol Peterson rightly suspects will keep Mr. Hibler home from school the next day.

The next morning, a new substitute teacher arrives in Mr. Hibler's stead. Tommy reflects that there was typically only a small pool of substitute teachers from which the rural school could draw. The usual substitute would have been one of four community-college-educated mothers, but instead, a stranger, Miss Ferenczi, appears. Before she introduces herself, Miss Ferenczi insists that the classroom needs a tree, and she proceeds to draw one on the chalkboard. She then begins to tell the children about her background: her grandfather had been Hungarian royalty, and her mother had been a pianist who gave concerts to kings and queens in Europe.

Miss Ferenczi proceeds to follow the lesson plan Mr. Hibler has left, although she makes her boredom apparent to the students. As the class begins its arithmetic lesson, Miss Ferenczi appears not to notice one student's computational error: John Wazny recites multiplication tables and states that six times eleven is sixty-eight. Miss Ferenczi does not correct him. Rather, after John has finished his recitation, Miss Ferenczi praises his efforts. Another student points out the error, but Miss Ferenczi is unfazed, observing that occasionally, six times eleven is in fact sixty-eight. The students are confused by the explanation Miss Ferenczi then provides, which involves the "fluid" nature of "higher mathematics." Miss Ferenczi goes on

to suggest to the students that, "it would be better for you to think that six times eleven is sixty-eight only when I am in the room." When another student questions why this is so only when Miss Ferenczi is in the room, she replies, "Because it's more interesting that way." Miss Ferenczi seems to express disappointment when students like Janice Weber insist upon the wrongness of permitting six times eleven to be sixty-eight even some of the time.

The teacher then redirects the students to their spelling test. Tommy is confused by the way Miss Ferenczi pronounces some of the words and is frustrated by his inability to spell them correctly. Miss Ferenczi confidentially empathizes with him, telling him she believes that people should not have to use words they do not like.

At lunch recess, Miss Ferenczi chooses to eat in the classroom with the children despite the fact that a lunch monitor remains in the class during this time. The children ask Miss Ferenczi questions about a lunch that seems unusual to them. She consumes a stuffed fig, smoked sturgeon, and raw spinach. After lunch, the class is to study ancient Egyptian civilization. Rather than following the textbook as a means of instruction, Miss Ferenczi begins to talk to the class about the cosmic forces of the pyramids. She tells the children about Egyptian explorers and identifies Genghis Khan as the greatest of conquerors. Miss Ferenczi goes on to tell a story about her own visit to Egypt, when an old man who worked for a circus showed her an animal in a cage. The animal, called a gryphon, was half lion and half bird.

Tommy and another boy discuss Miss Ferenczi on the bus ride home from school. Although Carl Whiteside insists the teacher lied, Tommy defends her. When Tommy arrives home, he tries to discuss the day with his mother. She is washing vegetables in the kitchen while Tommy's baby brother bellows from the playpen. Tommy's mother appears distracted by her task and insists that Tommy complete his own chores. She suggests that he relate his tale later, after his father has arrived home. Tommy looks up *gryphon* in the dictionary, learning that Miss Ferenczi described the animal properly and that it is a "fabulous" creature.

At school the next day, Miss Ferenczi has returned. Tommy observes that today, "there seemed to be less connection between her ideas, but the ideas themselves were, as the dictionary would say, fabulous." She speaks directly of magic, specifically of the magic that women possess but men lack. She talks about trees that eat meat and about the flat creatures that live at the bottom of the sea. Miss Ferenczi goes on to talk about the angels she believes live under the clouds on Venus, fires burning under the earth's surface in Ohio, and how babies conceived during a solar eclipse would have webbed feet. After stating that she understands that the children enjoy being told such secrets, she affirms that there is no death, but rather, transformation into different elements.

Once again, Carl and Tommy discuss Miss Ferenczi on the way home from school. Carl is conflicted; he knows that meat-eating plants exist but believes that Miss Ferenczi lied about the angels. Tommy attempts to construct a fantastic tale about a tree, but Carl interrupts, telling his friend, "Don't you try to do it.... You'll just sound like a jerk." At home, Tommy's mother asks him about school and about Miss Ferenczi, but Tommy now seems disinclined to discuss his mysterious teacher. His mother is concerned about him, telling him he looks pale, but Tommy insists he is fine.

The next day, Mr. Hibler is back at school. For a couple of months, daily life in the classroom passes as it always has. Then, Miss Ferenczi returns. She tells the students she is going to reward them, because she has enjoyed their company in the past. Taking out a Tarot pack, Miss Ferenczi begins to tell the children's fortunes. When the Death card appears during Wayne Razmer's reading, along with the nine of swords and the ten of wands, Miss Ferenczi tells Wayne that he will endure "suffering and desolation" and bear "a heavy load," and further, that he will soon die. She assures him that he should not be fearful, that he will only change out of his "earthly shape." Abruptly, Miss Ferenczi then announces that they will turn to arithmetic.

By lunch, Wayne has reported the incident to Mr. Faegre, the principal. At recess, the children see Miss Ferenczi drive away. Wayne approaches the other children in the class and brags of how he told on Miss Ferenczi. Tommy expresses his outrage, taunting Wayne and accusing him of being afraid. Wayne begins to punch Tommy, and Tommy responds in kind. Later in the afternoon, the children join a sixth-grade class for a science lesson.

CHARACTERS

Edith Atwater

Edith Atwater is a fourth grader in Mr. Hibler's class. After Mr. Hibler returns to school following his illness, Edith explains that their substitute teacher did not faithfully follow his lesson plan. When Miss Ferenczi returns to school about two months later, during Mr. Hibler's next absence, Edith questions Miss Ferenczi about the Tarot cards she has produced.

Mr. Bodine

Mr. Bodine is a fourth-grade teacher at Tommy's school. He is only referred to briefly, when Tommy describes the way his fourth-grade class was merged with the sixth-grade class for a science lesson. Mr. Bodine helped move the desks into Mrs. Mantei's room.

Joyce Eddy

Joyce Eddy is regarded by Tommy as interchangeable with her twin, Judy. They are referred to in the story as the Eddy twins. At one point, Tommy mentions how "one of the Eddy twins" pointed out to Miss Ferenczi the inaccuracy of John Wazny's multiplication.

Judy Eddy

Judy Eddy is regarded by Tommy as interchangeable with her twin, Joyce. The girls are referred to in the story as the Eddy twins. At one point, Tommy discusses the way "one of the Eddy twins" points out to Miss Ferenczi the inaccuracy of John Wazny's multiplication.

Mrs. Eddy

Mrs. Eddy is the mother of fourth-grade twins Joyce and Judy. She knits wordlessly in the back of the classroom while serving as a lunchtime room monitor.

Mr. Faegre

Mr. Faegre is the principal of the school. He does not directly appear but is referred to by the narrator as the authority figure to whom Wayne reports Miss Ferenczi's disturbing fortune-telling. Tommy also is sent to Mr. Faegre after fighting with Wayne.

Miss Ferenczi

Miss Ferenczi is the substitute teacher who replaces Mr. Hibler when he is out sick. She is instantly perceived as unusual by the students in the fourth-grade class. Described as being of "no special age—an adult is an adult," she is distinguished by the vertical, marionette-like lines on her face and by the story she tells of her background. She identifies herself as descended from Hungarian royalty on her father's side and from a musically gifted mother who played piano professionally throughout Europe. Skipping the Pledge of Allegiance, Miss Ferenczi proceeds with the morning's lessons in an ordinary manner until one student incorrectly recites a multiplication table. While she simply praises the boy, another student points out the inaccuracy, which provides Miss Ferenczi the opportunity to launch into a speech about the fluidity of facts.

During the afternoon geography lesson, Miss Ferenczi begins to truly astonish the children with her bizarre stories and views. She tells them of the time she spent in Egypt and about being shown a beast that was half lion and half bird. The next day, she expounds on such topics as the magical nature of women and the angels who live under the clouds on Venus. The children debate her veracity. When she returns about two months later, Miss Ferenczi performs Tarot readings, telling the children their future. Their responses to her convey a combination of apprehension and anxiety. When she predicts the death of a student, she is sent home after the student tells the principal.

Throughout the story, Miss Ferenczi is depicted by the narrator as a source of fascination. As no adults interact with Miss Ferenczi during the story, the reader only witnesses the way she behaves with children, and her character is filtered through the voice of an intrigued Tommy. Consequently, whether or not Miss Ferenczi is to be regarded as an effective, if eccentric, teacher is left to the reader. She embodies the notions of imagination and creativity, and through the specialized knowledge she claims to hold, she is linked to the supernatural world. Miss Ferenczi claims she has been kissed by God in a dream, and she infers that this experience has given her special powers.

Mr. Hibler

Mr. Hibler is a fourth-grade teacher. It is his absence, due to a cough, that leads to the arrival of the substitute teacher Miss Ferenczi. His presence in the story is minimal, but his bland personality contrasts sharply with Miss Ferenczi's odd and quirky nature.

Harold Knardahl

Harold Knardahl, another fourth grader, jokes about Miss Ferenczi's strange appearance and mannerisms, suggesting she is from Mars.

Bobby Kryzanowicz

Bobby Kryzanowicz is a fourth-grade student described by the narrator as a "faultless brown-noser" who wishes Mr. Hibler a speedy recovery. Later, Bobby asks Miss Ferenczi what she means when she states that she intends to tell the children their fortunes with her Tarot cards.

Mrs. Mantei

Mrs. Mantei is mentioned only briefly in the story. She is the teacher of a sixth-grade class with whom Tommy's fourth-grade class pairs for a science unit. Tommy knows where Mrs. Mantei lives. His description of her home in the trailer park emphasizes a mundane existence and serves as a point of contrast with Miss Ferenczi. As Tommy points out, Mrs. Mantei "was no mystery."

Kelly Munger

Kelly Munger is another fourth-grade boy in Mr. Hibler's class. Kelly has difficulty finding his geography book in his desk. He is scolded by Miss Ferenczi. Bobby Kryzanowicz informs the substitute teacher that Kelly can never find his things.

Carol Peterson

Carol Peterson is a fourth grader who is described by the narrator as a "bad person" due to habits such as blowing her nose into notebook paper. Yet it is also noted that "at times of crisis she spoke the truth." In this instance, the truth is that the class will have a substitute the next day due to Mr. Hibler's cough. Carol is the first student to raise her hand when Miss Ferenczi asks for volunteers to have their fortune told. Miss Ferenczi describes Carol's future as "bleak and dreary" and appears bored by the results of the reading.

Mark Poole

Mark Poole, a fourth grader, questions Miss Ferenczi when she states that the children should think of six times eleven as equaling sixty-eight only when she is in the room.

Wayne Razmer

Wayne Razmer is a fourth grader who asks Miss Ferenczi why she does not want to eat with the other teachers in the lounge. Wayne is the last of the students to have his fortune told by Miss Ferenczi. The reading is a serious one, in which Miss Ferenczi foretells the "suffering and desolation" that will be a part of Wayne's life. She describes a "great metamorphosis" that he will endure before he becomes an adult. Moments later, as Wayne points to the Death card he has turned up, Miss Ferenczi tells him that he will die, that is, change out of his "earthly shape." Although Miss Ferenczi does not elaborate further, the connection between the "metamorphosis" and the fact that Wayne will undergo a change "out of his earthly shape," as the Death card indicates, is implied. Whether or not Miss Ferenczi means to suggest that Wayne will die before he becomes an adult is not relevant. The reader, and perhaps the other students, possibly make that assumption in the absence of further explanation. Wayne is clearly troubled by what has occurred. At lunch, he informs the principal about what happened, and Miss Ferenczi is dismissed. Tommy then accuses Wayne of having been afraid of the Tarot card that indicated his death. The two boys fight briefly before being sent to the principal's office.

Ray Schontzeler

Ray Schontzeler is a fourth-grade student who once punches Tommy at the end of noon recess.

Maxine Sylvester

Maxine Sylvester, a fourth-grade student, asks Miss Ferenczi about her lunch, not recognizing the stuffed figs, raw spinach, and smoked sturgeon as edible items.

Tommy

Tommy is the narrator of the story, although the reader does not learn his name until he arrives home from school and is addressed by his mother. A fourth-grade student in Mr. Hibler's class, Tommy has strong opinions about his classmates, such as the "brownnoser" Bobby and Carol, who is a "bad person" with an "evil giggle." He observes the way his classmates question Miss Ferenczi when she behaves in an unorthodox fashion and when she makes peculiar announcements. When Tommy has trouble with a spelling test, Miss Ferenczi seems sympathetic. Watching him struggle with the word *balcony*, Miss Ferenczi whispers to Tommy that she does not care for that word either. Not long after this, Miss Ferenczi relates a story about visiting Egypt and seeing a gryphon, and Tommy's fascination with Miss Ferenczi intensifies. He defends her when another student riding the bus accuses Miss Ferenczi of lying. Although Tommy is not a vocal character throughout much of the story, he reacts strongly when Miss Ferenczi is asked to leave after the Tarot reading. Tommy fights with the boy who told on Miss Ferenczi, accusing him of being scared.

Tommy's Brother

Tommy's brother is a baby. He is described as yelling from within his playpen when Tommy comes home from school.

Tommy's Father

Tommy's father does not appear in the story but is referred to by Tommy's mother, who asks Tommy to wait until his father gets home to tell them about his substitute teacher.

Tommy's Mother

Tommy's mother is the only member of Tommy's family who has a direct role in the story. She is depicted initially as preoccupied with household duties and has little time or inclination to hear Tommy describe his substitute teacher. Later in the story, she seems more interested and asks questions of her son, but he does not discuss his teacher with her further.

Jeannie Vermeesch

Jeannie Vermeesch is a student in Tommy's fourth-grade class. When she points out to Miss Ferenczi that the class usually says the Pledge of Allegiance, Miss Ferenczi dismisses the idea.

John Wazny

John Wazny is a fourth grader who is instructed by Miss Ferenczi to recite his multiplication tables. He announces that six times eleven is sixty-eight, but Miss Ferenczi does not correct him.

Janice Weber

Janice Weber is a fourth-grade student who is clearly perturbed by Miss Ferenczi's insistence that sixty-eight may sometimes be viewed as the product of six times eleven.

Carl Whiteside

Carl Whiteside is a boy in Mr. Hibler's fourth-grade classroom. He sits by Tommy on the bus, where the two boys discuss the strangeness of Miss Ferenczi. Carl is skeptical about her so-called knowledge and insists that she has lied to the class about various things, although he cannot quite pinpoint what it is she has been untruthful about. Carl is the second child in the class to have his fortune told by Miss Ferenczi. She seems more engaged in the reading she does for Carl than in the "dreary" one she does for Carol. Miss Ferenczi even giggles during Carl's reading and informs him that his future will be happy.

THEMES

Imagination

"Gryphon" centers in many ways on the theme of imagination. Miss Ferenczi advocates an imaginative view of the world that is not rooted in facts or preconceived notions of the way things are or should be. She challenges the children's understanding of the world and of the knowledge that is the object of their quest as students. Miss Ferenczi responds to their questioning natures and skeptical attitudes by presenting them with an ever-broadening view of the world. Miss Ferenczi inspires the children's imagination from her first introduction to them. Tommy notes that "she didn't look usual," while his classmate Harold suggests there is something otherworldly about her when he simply whispers the word "Mars." When Miss Ferenczi describes her background, her tale has a distinctly fictive and fairy-tale quality about it, with her grandfather having been a Hungarian prince and her mother a pianist who played for "crowned heads." Miss Ferenczi begins to share her unconventional view of the world when she suggests that mathematical facts may be characterized by fluidity; they may be thought of as *sometimes* true. This is a confusing concept for the children, and she defers to their insistence on the notions of "right" and "wrong" in reminding them that when Mr. Hibler returns, "six times eleven will be sixty-six again, you can rest assured."

Later, Miss Ferenczi opens the children's minds to the possibility that the fantastical and the magical exist in the world. She describes having seen firsthand the mythical creature known as the gryphon, half lion, half bird. She speaks of the magic women possess and of the angels she believes live under the clouds on Venus. Miss Ferenczi further expresses her conviction that she knows such things to be true because God kissed her in a dream. Miss Ferenczi goes on to tell the fortunes of the children, further pushing the boundaries of what they regard as known reality. In the end, however, her imaginative worldview is rejected. Significantly, it is a child, not an adult, whose complaint results in Miss Ferenczi's dismissal from the school. After an uncomfortable Tarot card reading in which his death is predicted, one of the students, Wayne, tells the principal about Miss Ferenczi's fortune-telling. She is subsequently asked to leave.

Baxter in this way seems to frown upon society's unwillingness to be open to the spiritual, the supernatural in the world. If a child cannot face these realms—made stark by the prospect of his own death—without fear, the likelihood of imaginative, magical convictions persisting into adulthood seems doomed. Through the character of Tommy, however, Baxter suggests a sense of hopefulness that unconventional beliefs, imaginative views, and the conviction that the supernatural can exist within an otherwise rational and realistic world, can persist into adulthood.

Youth

In "Gryphon," Baxter explores the notion of youth, focusing on the way children view their world, other children, and adults. The young people in the story are not, however, depicted as a uniform group who may be contrasted as a whole with adults. They are individuals, distinct from one another in opinions and attitudes, but often reduced by the narrating Tommy to character types, associated with one particular trait. Carol is described as a truth teller, but she is otherwise "a bad person." Bobby is perpetually trying to be the teacher's pet. Jeannie likes routine and points out to Miss Ferenczi when the substitute teacher is not behaving in the way Mr. Hibler would have. Some of the children, including one of the Eddy twins and Janice Weber, are put off by Miss Ferenczi's insistence that some facts are "fluid." Tommy repeatedly refers to Bobby as "the faultless brownnoser," while Bobby stresses the fact that Kelly Munger "can't ever find his stuff. He always does that." Carl is the skeptic, pointing out to Tommy his

TOPICS FOR FURTHER STUDY

- Jean Kwok's *Girl in Translation*, published in 2010, is the semiautobiographical tale of a young Chinese girl who moves to Brooklyn with her family and must navigate the challenging English-speaking world in which she now finds herself. At age eleven, the protagonist is not much older than the characters in Baxter's "Gryphon." Read Kwok's novel with a small group. What obstacles does Kimberly Chang, the protagonist, face? How is her experience as a student different from that of her classmates due to her foreign-born status? What types of struggles are universal, faced by most schoolchildren of this age regardless of their ethnicity or birthplace? Create an online blog that you and the members of your group use as a discussion forum. Consider these questions, and also discuss elements of plot, style, theme, and characterization. Are there any similarities you can draw between this story and Baxter's? Compile your blog exchanges and submit them as a group paper.

- In "Gryphon," Miss Ferenczi believes that she can see the future and tell the children's fortunes using Tarot cards. Research the history of Tarot cards and their popularity in America as a fortune-telling method. Where did the use of Tarot cards originate? How are they regarded by believers and non-believers in the occult? What is the origin of the pictures on the cards? Create a poster, a PowerPoint production, or an interactive web-based presentation in which you share your findings.

- "Gryphon" takes place in a small town in rural Michigan. Research the geography, demographics, and industrial profile of Michigan. What are its largest and smallest cities in terms of population, and where are they located? In what areas of the state is agriculture the primary industry? What parts of the state are considered rural? What types of agricultural goods does the state produce? Do two short reports on this topic, one as if you were in a class conducted by Mr. Hibler or any of the conventional teachers in the story. The second report would be a report on the same topic, but for Miss Ferenczi.

- Jose Cruz Gonzalez, born in California to Mexican migrant workers, has written plays aimed at mature young-adult audiences. The works, collected by editor Coleman A. Jennings in the 2008 volume *Nine Plays by Jose Cruz Gonzales*, are considered to have been written in the magical-realist mode, as they incorporate elements of the magical, supernatural, or fantastic into an otherwise realistic setting. Read one of the plays in this collection. As you read, consider the way the playwright incorporates the imaginative, magical elements into the realistic play. How are these elements used to advance the plot? How do the characters in the play react to them? Write an essay in which you discuss these points. Also provide a summary of the plot and the play's main themes, and consider performing the play or a section of it with other students for the rest of your class.

---

sense that Miss Ferenczi has lied to them. While most of the children's characters are portrayed as fixed and unchanging, the skeptical Carl does volunteer to have his fortune read, which suggests that perhaps he is willing to believe in Miss Ferenczi in a different way than he has before,

as someone with powers or knowledge he cannot understand.

Tommy views the children as having a wide variety of personality traits among them, despite the fact that they seem fixedly associated with the traits Tommy assigns them, or that they assign

The story takes place in an average fourth grade class. (© Olesya Feketa / ShutterStock.com)

each other. The adults in the story, however, except for Miss Ferenczi, are presented as similar to one another in terms of their dull natures and in their lack of interest in the children in their lives. Mr. Hibler is not shown as engaging with the children in any particular way, and likewise, Tommy's mother is more focused on her household tasks than on Tommy's description of Miss Ferenczi. At the conclusion of the story, the other teachers mentioned are as unremarkable as Mr. Hibler. As the adult Tommy who narrates the story is focused on his younger self and his fourth-grade experience, the exploration of youth is shaped more by the youthful Tommy's thoughts than the elder Tommy's recollections. In this way, Baxter provides an examination of youth that translates as authentic rather than as wistful or sentimentalized.

STYLE

Realism

In "Gryphon," Baxter writes in a realistic style. Realism is a style of narration in which the author conveys a sense of authenticity, a fidelity

to the real world. Details are related with accuracy, and the author attempts to place the reader within a setting that, while fictional, mirrors the real world. Yet through the character of Miss Ferenczi, Baxter pushes the boundaries of his realistic tale. The extent to which the border between realism and the literary style known as magical realism blurs in "Gryphon" depends upon the way the reader interprets the character of Miss Ferenczi. In works of magical realism, supernatural, fantastic, or absurd characters or situations interrupt what is otherwise a straightforwardly realistic narrative. Miss Ferenczi does not actually perform any supernatural feats, but rather relates stories of fantastic creatures, such as angels and gryphons, and tells the children their fortunes, using Tarot cards. The narrator, Tommy, seems awestruck by Miss Ferenczi's presence and her tales of otherworldly creatures.

As an adult narrator recollecting this period of his youth, the grown Tommy does not pass judgment on Miss Ferenczi, nor does he retrospectively question her soundness of mind. The reader is therefore left to consider whether the substitute teacher is deliberately deceiving the children, or if she believes that she has seen a gryphon and can tell the future. If Miss Ferenczi believes she has seen such things, the reader is forced to wonder whether Baxter is suggesting that Miss Ferenczi be taken as somewhat unstable or rather as a being with some supernatural abilities. In asserting that there is no death, only transformation, Miss Ferenczi insists, "I have seen this truth with these eyes. I know it because in a dream God kissed me." This experience with God, she suggests, has bestowed on her the ability to understand things other people cannot grasp. In other, longer works of Baxter's, the author similarly surprises the reader by incorporating possibly supernatural events into an otherwise solidly realistic narrative.

First-Person Narration

Baxter utilizes a first-person narrator in "Gryphon." That is, the narrator is a character within the story who refers to himself as "I." The events in the story are related entirely from his perspective. In telling the story from the fourth grader's point of view, Baxter fluctuates between relating Tommy's fourth-grade thoughts and casting the narration as the recollections of an adult Tommy. In doing so, Baxter offers the reader both a firsthand account of the events that take place during Miss Ferenczi's stint as substitute teacher and a view of these events filtered by time. As the fourth-grade Tommy interacts with his classmates and thinks about Miss Ferenczi's words and actions, the reader is provided with an intimate understanding of the impact Miss Ferenczi makes on young, imaginative children's minds. At the same time, as the adult Tommy remembers his youthful experience, he layers into his narration a more mature sensibility, but one that nevertheless remains infused with the awe he felt in response to Miss Ferenczi. This firsthand, first-person narration, however, is not characterized by complete access to Tommy's thoughts and experiences. Although Tommy conveys his opinions about other characters in the story, he does not reveal what Miss Ferenczi told him about his own future; his Tarot reading is mentioned in passing but not described. By withholding such information, Baxter maintains the aura of mystery that surrounds Miss Ferenczi. The use of the first-person narration is controlled and deliberate, with Baxter divulging precisely what he wishes to relate of Tommy's thoughts as a child and perceptions as an adult.

HISTORICAL CONTEXT

Literary Realism in the 1980s

Realism as a literary mode evolved during the nineteenth century and focuses on the accurate portrayal of people, daily life, and social conditions. Over time, the term was broadened to encompass other modes of writing, all of which possess a similar aim of representing reality in a truthful manner, but which shift the focus in varying ways. Literary impressionism, for example, seeks to capture a character's, or an author's, impression of the reality surrounding him or her, and it is sometimes linked to psychological realism in the way it reveals one person's consciousness and his or her impressions of reality. Naturalism is another narrative mode linked to realism, and it focuses on the way humans are related to the natural world, subject to scientific laws, and motivated like other animals by instinct.

During the 1980s, realism in American fiction was influenced by several movements. As some authors rejected straightforward realism and moved toward fiction that was distinctly experimental in terms of structure or style, others sought to incorporate new narrative techniques or modes into their realist fiction. During the last years of the 1970s and the early 1980s, a type of realist fiction appeared that became known as "dirty realism." Dirty realism typically focuses on working-class characters, and it explores their environment in grim, unadorned detail. Robert Rebein explains in an essay for *The Cambridge Companion to American Fiction after 1945*, "Dirty Realism focused on the small rather than the large," telling "spare" stories about segments of American society and the cultures and moral conditions of those populations.

Another narrative style, magical realism, can be described as an offshoot of realism. As Dana Gioia states in an essay originally published in *Sniper Logic*, magical realism existed in various forms for decades, but it began to be seen as a narrative mode or style when the term was applied to the work of Latin American fiction writers in the 1970s, beginning with Gabriel García Márquez. Magical realism

COMPARE & CONTRAST

- **1985:** Literary realism is a popular mode of writing that has come to include a number of subgenres or related modes, including dirty realism and magical realism. Some authors incorporate elements of more than one of these modes into their realistic fiction. Raymond Carver and Tobias Wolff are noted authors of dirty-realist fiction. Magical realism is largely associated with Latin American authors such as Gabriel García Márquez and Isabel Allende but has influenced other writers, such as Charles Baxter, the Canadian Jack Hodgins, and English author Angela Carter.

  Today: A new trend in literary realism builds on the magical realism of the past, incorporating creatures of fantasy—zombies and vampires, for example—into literature that is otherwise rooted in realism. Literary novelists who have incorporated elements of supernaturalism, fantasy, or science fiction into their works include Colson Whitehead, in *Zone One* (2012), and Cormac McCarthy, in the 2006 postapocalyptic tale *The Road*.

- **1985:** Rural communities see populations dwindling, and as a result of migrations from rural to urban areas, school enrollment numbers are declining. Some schools must close or be consolidated.

  Today: Rural communities still face challenges in terms of educational opportunities. The National Center for Education Statistics reports that in 2003 to 2004, one-third of all public schools were in rural areas. However, only one-fifth of all public school students were enrolled in these rural schools. Rural schools are disproportionately small, with more students in rural areas compared to urban areas attending schools with fewer than two hundred students.

- **1985:** Short fiction as a literary form thrives; it is published in small literary journals as well as in collections. Some scholars insist that the vigorous debate over the defining characteristics and traits of the form indicate its status as an important and vital literary form.

  Today: Literary journals continue to publish short fiction, and short-fiction collections continue to be an avenue of publication for established authors. Susan Lohafer, in *The Cambridge Companion to American Fiction after 1945*, points to "the undeniable proliferation of short fiction in the 1990s and the twenty-first century" as evidence of the continued vitality of short fiction.

---

incorporates elements of the fantastic, absurd, or supernatural into a narrative that is otherwise strictly realistic. In an introduction to *A Companion to Magical Realism*, Stephen M. Hart describes the way Latin American magical realism has influenced the work of many authors. The mode became prevalent enough for some writers to be accused of imitating a formula rather than having a more comprehensive understanding of the narrative style. In *Literary Luxuries: American Writing at the End of the Millennium*, Joe David Bellamy characterizes the developments in American realism from 1960 to 1990 as "a movement from middlebrow realism or modernist realism to superfiction...followed by a return to a different sort of realism, minimalist realism or dirty realism or designer realism or lifestyle fiction."

Rural Education in the 1980s

In "Gryphon," Baxter presents the fictional town of Five Oaks as a rural midwestern community. The narrator observes, "the supply of substitute teachers was limited to the town's unemployed community college graduates, a pool of about four mothers." In this statement, and in others where the narrator references the bleakness of the landscape (the "rusted cars piled in a small heap behind a clump of sumac," for example), Baxter highlights the educational and economic struggles of rural, midwestern communities during the 1980s. Demographic studies have documented the departure rates of people from rural communities. Kenneth Johnson, in *Demographic Trends in Rural and Small Town America*, observes, "For much of the 20th century, most rural communities experienced population loss as millions of rural residents left for the opportunities in booming cities." Johnson further explains that the volume of this flow varied over the years, but "the direction of the flows did not." Some gains made in the 1970s had leveled off by the 1980s. Johnson notes,

> By the late 1970s, growth in rural America was lagging and this slowdown became more pronounced in the 1980s. Between 1980 and 1990, the number of rural counties gaining population sharply declined and overall rural population gains slowed.

The decline in agricultural employment opportunities and the increase in urban employment opportunities are cited as part of the impetus for the shifts in demographics. The exodus of college-educated populations from rural communities during the 1980s was also a feature of the population shift out of rural communities and into urban areas. A US Department of Agriculture (USDA) report, *Understanding Rural America*, describes a brief period of economic turnaround in the 1970s in rural communities, as industries moved to rural locations, mining activities increased, recreation and retirement opportunities were explored, and urban workers fatigued by city life returned to the rural areas. The report indicates, however, "In the 1980s, this trend reversed under the weight of the lengthy general business recession, foreign industrial competition, the farm crisis, and fewer retirees moving to rural areas." Describing the effect of this stagnation in the 1980s, the USDA report asserts, "The loss of well-educated young adults (a continuation of a long-term trend) was indicative of the poorer prospects that people saw for rural communities."

Other researchers pointed to the effects on education of the economic-driven migration

The substitute teacher makes Tommy think of the marionette Pinocchio, who is known for telling lies. (© *Daniele Pietrobelli | ShutterStock.com*)

out of rural communities. Patrick J. Carr and Maria J. Kefalas, in *Hollowing Out the Middle: The Rural Brain Drain and What It Means for America*, argue that the "final death knell" for rural communities that have experienced the migration of young adults "sounds when there are no longer enough children to keep the doors of the area school open." The National Center for Education Statistics underscores this point in the report *Characteristics of Small and Rural School Districts*, stating, "While the majority of public elementary and secondary schools experienced declining enrollments during the 1970s and early 1980s, rural schools, already serving small numbers of pupils, experienced the greatest percentage reduction of enrollment." Some schools were forced to close or to consolidate as a result, and in the latter half of the 1980s, population and enrollment in rural districts continued declining.

CRITICAL OVERVIEW

Although Baxter's "Gryphon" was published in his 1985 collection *Through the Safety Net* and was often included in anthologies thereafter, it has received more critical attention as the title story of the more recent publication *Gryphon: New and Collected Stories* (2011). In a review for the *Washington Post*, Jeff Turrentine describes the way the characters in the stories in the 2011 collection are transformed. He praises the way Baxter "lovingly teases anguish, humor and heart-rending beauty out of clear, unaffected sentences describing the gray-clouded interior worlds inhabited by his cast of (largely) Midwestern melancholics." In discussing "Gryphon" in particular, Turrentine focuses on Miss Ferenczi, describing her as a "fantastic creature" who instructs the children "in the hows, whys and wherefores of her own altered reality." Turrentine views Miss Ferenczi's role in the story in relation to the warning she seems to be conveying to the children, that after fourth grade, they will be "subjects of the cold, empirical world, where whimsy and imagination have been smothered to death by science and data."

In a review for National Public Radio, Jane Ciabattari summarizes the story in terms of Tommy's transformation, stating that "a palpably normal fourth-grader describes how a substitute teacher introduces him to the wonders of the imagination." Although critics like Turrentine characterize the story's ending as dire, emphasizing that reality and empiricism are threats to imagination, Susan Salter Reynolds, in a *Los Angeles Times* review, insists that the science lesson at the end of the tale "turns out to be pretty darn amazing. Regular life, even in the suburbs, is full of foolish joys and uncharted mysteries."

Claire Messud, in the *New York Review of Books*, likens Miss Ferenczi to similar advocates of imaginative learning, such as Miss Frizzle of *The Magic School Bus* fame, or Willy Wonka, the character in Roald Dahl's 1964 children's novel *Charlie and the Chocolate Factory*. Messud applauds Baxter's achievement in the story, claiming, "In its exuberance and wistfulness, this is one of the most joyous of Baxter's random encounters, the cracking open of Tommy's childhood world to embrace the exotic, the magical and the new." Writing for the *Winnipeg Review*, Richard Cumyn finds much to laud in the collection as a whole. He praises in particular the

"remarkable consistency of the prose." However, Cumyn is dismissive of the title piece of *Gryphon: New and Selected Stories*, stating that the "quirkiness" of the tale "might be its undoing."

CRITICISM

Catherine Dominic

Dominic is a novelist and a freelance writer and editor. In the following essay, she focuses on the characters of Tommy and Miss Ferenczi in "Gryphon," demonstrating the extent to which Miss Ferenczi influences Tommy and shapes his worldview.

In "Gryphon," Charles Baxter explores the intertwined themes of youth and imagination, using the character of Miss Ferenczi as the embodiment of imaginative power, and as a source of inspiration to the fourth grader Tommy, who serves as the story's narrator. Close scrutiny of Tommy's recollection of the events in the story underscores the ways in which he is transformed by his acquaintance with Miss Ferenczi. Not only do the fourth-grade Tommy's actions indicate the extent to which his character changes, but the ways in which the adult Tommy includes and omits various details further emphasizes that the changes Miss Ferenczi inspired in Tommy have lasted a lifetime. Throughout the story, Baxter juxtaposes the adult Tommy's interpretation of the past with the fourth-grade Tommy's thoughts and actions. Although these are presented as immediate occurrences, happening in the "present" of the story, they are obviously recollections, too. The fourth-grade Tommy and the adult Tommy sometimes seem like two distinct presences in the story, but they form a unified persona, one who is awestruck by Miss Ferenczi.

As the story begins, the narrator speaks in the first person but is yet unidentified as Tommy. He reports on the progression of his teacher's cough, and the way his classmate rightly assumes that the class will have a substitute teacher the next day. From Miss Ferenczi's first appearance, Tommy notices the completely unordinary nature the teacher possesses, stating that she "didn't look usual." While Harold jokingly suggests Miss Ferenczi hails from Mars, Tommy nods, "savoring the imminent weirdness of the day." He eagerly

WHAT DO I READ NEXT?

- The short-story collection *Through the Safety Net*, published in 1985, is Baxter's second collection and contains "Gryphon," among other works.

- Published in 1997, Baxter's *Believers: A Novella and Short Stories* exemplifies his particular brand of realism.

- *The Feast of Love*, Baxter's 2000 novel, was a finalist for the National Book Award. It was later adapted for the screen and is noted for its unusual narrative structure, in which a first-person narrative is woven into what appear to be unrelated vignettes. The connections between the characters and the stories are gradually revealed as the story progresses.

- The 2002 young-adult novel *Gina. Jamie. Father. Bear.*, by George Ella Lyon, incorporates elements of the fantastic into a contemporary novel set alternately in rural Ohio and in Cleveland. In this work, coming-of-age themes intertwine with family drama.

- *Dreaming in Cuban*, a 1993 novel by Cuban novelist Cristina García, combines superstitions and surreal elements into an episodic narrative set in the 1970s and 1980s in Cuba and New York.

- Baxter's fellow realist author Tobias Wolff's *Our Story Begins: New and Selected Stories*, published in 2008, includes short fiction that spans the same time period as Baxter's recent collection *Gryphon: New and Selected Stories*. Like Baxter, Wolff focuses on the experiences and relationships of ordinary people in their everyday lives.

- The 1992 volume *Neo-realism in Contemporary American Fiction*, edited by Kristiaan Versluys, includes a number of essays that explore trends in American realist literature during the 1980s and early 1990s.

> BY DESCRIBING OTHER PEOPLE'S FORTUNE-TELLING SESSIONS, AND BY COMMENTING ONLY THAT HIS READING WAS DONE AS WELL, THE ADULT TOMMY EMPHASIZES THAT WHAT WAS AND REMAINS IMPORTANT TO HIM IS THE NOTION THAT FORTUNE-TELLING IS POSSIBLE, THAT PEOPLE WHO SEEM TO HAVE SUCH POWERS EXIST."

anticipates strange things to come, indicating his appetite for the unusual. Tommy's youthful observations are underscored by the way Miss Ferenczi's appearance in the story is prefaced. The narrating adult Tommy notes, "the supply of substitute teachers was limited to the town's unemployed community college graduates, a pool of about four mothers." Miss Ferenczi is obviously none of these women.

After Miss Ferenczi's introduction—a bizarre tale involving her being descended from Hungarian royalty—and following a dull language arts lesson, Miss Ferenczi surprises the children with her views on mathematics. An incorrect fact is recited, yet Miss Ferenczi does not comment on it until another child points out her classmate's error. Miss Ferenczi explains that in some instances, math facts are only sometimes true. While some children seem disturbed by her insistence and her explanations, Tommy simply reports this exchange; he does not comment on it. Possibly, the fact that he does not join in this debate verbally with his classmates and Miss Ferenczi indicates his quiet agreement with Miss Ferenczi's view, or, alternatively, that he has not yet made up his mind about his substitute teacher and her unorthodox views. As the school day continues, however, Tommy's own opinions become more apparent. During the spelling test, Tommy struggles. Listening to Miss Ferenczi's pronunciation of the spelling words, Tommy thinks, "Somehow, the way she said those words, they seemed foreign, mis-voweled and mis-consonanted." As he misspells *balcony*, Miss Ferenczi leans over his shoulder, telling him that she does not like the word and finds it "ugly." She insists that if a person dislikes a word, he or she should not have to use it.

After this incident, Tommy tries to help Miss Ferenczi, directing her to the lounge where the other teachers eat. She demurs, however, deciding to eat with the children in the classroom. In relating her explanation, the narrating Tommy underscores Miss Ferenczi's difference from the other adults in the story, particularly the other teachers. She insists that she does not enjoy their sense of humor. When the geography lesson begins after lunch, Miss Ferenczi eagerly begins to discuss Egypt with the class. Tommy relates this portion of the narrative by listing the strange variety of comments and pronouncements Miss Ferenczi makes about Egypt and Egyptian culture and society. He repeats the phrase "she said" a number of times as he recalls the odd things she conveys as facts: "She said that the Egyptians were great explorers and conquerors. She said that the greatest of all the conquerors, Genghis Khan, had had forty horses and forty young women killed on the site of his grave." Tommy goes on, stating, "We listened. No one tried to stop her." Miss Ferenczi then describes her own experiences in Egypt, insisting that she has seen "an animal in a cage, a monster, half bird and half lion. She said that this monster was called a gryphon."

Later, on the bus ride home, Carl Whiteside proclaims, "She lies." Having been absolved of his troubles on the spelling test, and having been treated to the tales of Egypt, the Tommy who had eagerly anticipated the "imminent weirdness of the day" now defends Miss Ferenczi. He presses Carl to identify something he is certain Miss Ferenczi lied about. Carl is unable to. He fumbles. "I don't know" is all he can manage, followed by the generic "stuff." Tommy goes on to describe another creature as fantastic as the gryphon, one he saw in a newspaper, the *National Enquirer*. Tommy delights in convincing Carl of the journalistic evidence for the "humster," a creature that is half hamster, half human. When Tommy arrives home, he attempts to tell his mother about his unusual substitute teacher. Although his mother is uninterested in hearing about Miss Ferenczi, Tommy's enthusiasm is undeterred. He looks up *gryphon* in the dictionary. Finding it described as half lion, half eagle, he takes the definition of it as a "fabulous beast" as vindication. He does not realize that the word "fabulous" in this instance does not mean wonderful or marvelous but refers to something that is based on a fable, that is, a fiction. So

Tommy believes the dictionary has confirmed Miss Ferenczi's veracity.

At school the next day, Miss Ferenczi speaks rapidly. To Tommy, her ideas seem unconnected, "but the ideas themselves were, as the dictionary would say, fabulous." Tommy recounts how Miss Ferenczi rambles about diamonds. She describes them as magic, "and this is why women wear them on their fingers, as a sign of the magic of womanhood. Men have strength, Miss Ferenczi said, but no true magic." Miss Ferenczi goes on to discuss a variety of topics, all involving something magical or fantastic or bizarre, such as the angels who live under the clouds on Venus. After telling the children about the way the "planets control behavior, and anyone conceived during a solar eclipse would be born with webbed feet," Miss Ferenczi informs the class that she is saying all these things because children "like to hear these things . . . these secrets."

During recess the children do not play but gather in small groups to talk about Miss Ferenczi. Tommy and his classmates cannot figure out "if she was crazy, or what." Looking across the landscape, Tommy thinks, "I wanted to see shapes there, approaching me." He has become infused with the notion that magical things lurk everywhere, just waiting to be noticed. On the bus ride home, he and Carl discuss some of the things Miss Ferenczi has mentioned, identifying items that might actually be true. Despite the fact that Tommy acknowledges to himself his familiarity with every aspect of the landscape of Five Oaks, he attempts a Miss Ferenczi–like observation, stating, "There's a tree that' . . . that I've seen. . . ." Carl interrupts, telling him not to bother: "Don't you try to do it." Carl goes on to tell Tommy that he will only sound "like a jerk." In this exchange, an understanding passes between the boys that some, perhaps much but not all, of what Miss Ferenczi says is complete fiction. Yet there is a desire to believe in something extraordinary. For Carl, this desire is focused on the elements of Miss Ferenczi's stories that sound like they could actually be true. He references the meat-eating plants that she has discussed. "I know it's true. I saw it on television," he explains. For Tommy, though, this desire to believe is not forced to confront factual evidence, as it is for Carl. Tommy wants to *see* the way Miss Ferenczi sees. Truth and reality are secondary to this desire to view the world *differently*.

When Tommy arrives home, his mother attempts to ask him about his substitute teacher. Tommy is now less inclined to discuss the matter with his mother than he was the previous day. Looking at her son, Tommy's mother tells him he looks pale. The adult Tommy recalls, "She touched the back of her hand to my forehead and I felt her diamond ring against my skin." The detail Baxter includes here, the diamond ring, is significant. Although the fourth-grade Tommy does not react to the diamond, despite the fact that Miss Ferenczi has told him about the magic of women and their connection to diamonds, the adult narrating Tommy recalls this detail. Its inclusion in the narrative underscores the extent to which the adult Tommy still clings to the desire to believe in extraordinary things. When Tommy's mother asks if he feels okay, his response is affirmative. Although the narrator does not suggest that the mother's act of stroking her son's forehead with the ring cures or aids him in any way, to the reader attuned to the diamond as the symbol of the power of women, this act seems deliberate, like a warding off of illness.

Miss Ferenczi does not appear again at school until two months later. Tommy's heart pounds. Miss Ferenczi does not even pretend to be concerned with Mr. Hibler's lesson plan this time. She commences with Tarot card readings immediately. The adult narrator describes the fortunes of Carol and Carl before noting that he had raised his hand that day as well to have his fortune told. Yet that fortune is not revealed to the reader. After Wayne's reading, in which Miss Ferenczi predicts the student's death, Wayne tells the principal about what the substitute teacher has been up to, and she is asked to leave by midday. The reader can only wonder what Tommy's future was revealed to be. Perhaps the adult narrator did not depict the telling of his own fortune because he did not want to comment on whether or not it had come true. By describing other people's fortune-telling sessions, and by commenting only that his reading was done as well, the adult Tommy emphasizes that what was and remains important to him is the notion that fortune-telling is possible, that people who seem to have such powers exist. Whether or not the fortunes are true is not relevant to Tommy. Although initially he sought to verify the truth about the gryphon, as the story progresses, truth becomes less important than possibility, as evidenced by Tommy's second conversation with Carl on the bus. Carl tries to find the parts of Miss Ferenczi's story that are true, while Tommy tries to emulate Miss Ferenczi's storytelling techniques. Essentially, what comes to matter most to Tommy is the power of fiction.

In narrating his altercation with Wayne after Wayne has divulged to the principal Miss Ferenczi's fortune-telling, Tommy describes the way he accuses Wayne. First, he insists to Wayne that Miss Ferenczi was "just kidding." He calls Wayne a "chicken," saying he was "scared of a little card." Wayne then begins pummeling Tommy. Tommy fights back, with his fists and with words. He tells Wayne that Miss Ferenczi was in fact right: "She was always right! She told the truth!" Here, Tommy alternates between two versions of Miss Ferenczi—that she told stories to entertain them, and that she told the truth. Although these versions seem distinct, Tommy uses these notions alternately to defend Miss Ferenczi and to frighten Wayne. Quite possibly, Tommy regards them both as true. The element of truth runs through fiction, which is what makes fiction so powerful. It can contain imaginative possibilities alongside grim truths, like the death Miss Ferenczi predicts for Wayne.

The final images of the story are stark. Tommy's bloody nose and swollen lip are described. The sixth-grade teacher who is conducting the science lesson is "no mystery." The combined classes learn about a variety of insects, and Tommy provides a listing of the creatures they studied that day, and how they learned about the parts of their bodies, their life cycles. The adult narrator then describes the way the students proceeded to make lists, "on lined white pieces of paper." They listed "insects we might actually see, then a list of insects too small to be clearly visible." The sixth-grade teacher then instructs the students to memorize the lists. All of these activities are presented as dull and methodical. They serve as stark contrast to the stimulation inspired by Miss Ferenczi's "instruction." In a way, the conclusion of the story seems to remind the reader that life went back to "normal" for the students of the Five Oaks school. Yet Tommy's description of the events of this time period suggests that for him, Miss Ferenczi created a spark that did not dim over time.

Source: Catherine Dominic, Critical Essay on "Gryphon," in *Short Stories for Students*, Gale, Cengage Learning, 2014.

The gryphon is a mythical creature — part eagle and part lion. *(© Morphart Creation | ShutterStock.com)*

Kirkus Reviews

In the following review, the latest collection in which "Gryphon" appears is described as having stories of varying quality.

This is the fifth story collection from novelist Baxter (*The Soul Thief*, 2008, etc.); its 23 stories (seven of them new) range from mediocre to memorable to mesmerizing.

How well do you know your other half? The question haunts some of the relationship stories. As Dennis and Emily are splitting up after eight years, they learn new things about each other ("Poor Devil"). Janet (in "Flood Show") has a lesson for husband Conor, still obsessed with his first wife. Our ultimate unknowability is driven home most strongly in "Kiss Away." In this radiant love story, Jodie and Walton are head over heels. Then Jodie meets his ex, who tells her Walton is abusive. Is she lying? Is Jodie ready to make that leap of faith into marriage? With its cliffhanger ending, this is one for the anthologies. Sometimes it's parents and children who don't

know each other. Jaynee, a troubled teenager, is threatening to shoot a lion in the Detroit zoo ("Westland"). Her propensity for violence shocks Earl, her harried parent, but not as much as her diary revelations. Borderline crazies figure prominently: A guilty liberal tries to help three of them, all homeless ("Shelter"). Melissa tells an intruder he's a devil, though a really minor one, before sleeping with him ("Ghosts"). That's pure Baxter—he's forthright but unpredictable, a sweet combination. "Royal Blue" is not a 9/11 story, as first appears: It's the coming-of-age of a pretty boy after his girlfriend's miscarriage. The encounter of a desperate recovering alcoholic and a paroled murderer, next-door neighbors, should read grim, but "The Old Murderer" is so fast-paced it's oddly buoyant.

The uncanny power of Baxter's work derives from his knowledge of our secret selves as well as our surface ones.

Source: Review of *Gryphon: New and Selected Stories*, in *Kirkus Reviews*, October 15, 2010.

Joshua Finnell

In the following review, Finnell explains how the stories in the collection Gryphon: New and Selected Stories *fit into a thematic whole.*

This collected work reminds us that Baxter shines in the short story form. Whereas his novels (e.g., *The Feast of Love*) are cinematic in tone, his stories read like unfinished journal entries from a secret diary. By allowing the reader only a glimpse into the lives of each character, Baxter weaves together seemingly mundane activities into complex examples of love, fear, and anxiety. This collection is officially touted as a best of, with a few new additions, but, thematically, each of the 23 stories is a piece of a larger puzzle that cannot be put together. Whether his characters are standing on their head to relieve stress, writing fake horoscopes to instill confidence in their children, or teaching children to tell their fortune with a tarot deck, each action serves as a lens to focus Baxter's illumination of the mystery of life. VERDICT: Readers who enjoy the simple prose of John Irving and the imagination of Michael Chabon will be delighted by this collection.

Source: Joshua Finnell, Review of *Gryphon: New and Selected Stories*, in *Library Journal*, Vol. 135, No. 17, October 15, 2010, p. 71.

Charles Baxter

In the following excerpt, Baxter discusses some aspects of his writing process and explains why some kind of conflict is needed to create a good story.

Proposition A: In fiction we want to have characters create scenes that in life we would, in all likelihood, avoid. This contrasting attraction-and-avoidance turns out to be a terrible spiritual problem for young writers. In daily life, a writer may practice conflict-avoidance, but in fiction a writer must welcome conflict and walk straight into it. The writer may be aided in creating a narrative by having a repellant character around in the story, who in some significant way has lost control and who gets the entire narrative engine up and running.

Proposition B: When writers avoid conflict in an effort to keep up an appearance of control and placidity, they have confused the realms of life and of fiction: it is as if they are claiming that dramatic conflict has an element of vulgarity and that life, even as it is lived in fiction, is best conducted through a series of avoidance procedures. Such a course of action betrays a feeling of

> EVERYTHING I HAD EVER BEEN TAUGHT AS A CHILD ABOUT SELF-CONTROL STOOD AGAINST EVERY INSTINCT THAT I EVENTUALLY ACKNOWLEDGED OR ACQUIRED AS A WRITER OF DRAMATIC NARRATIVE."

shame about the inner life and the sorts of resonance that the inner life can create in fiction—a shame that has not been successfully overcome, as it must be—spiritually and dramatically.

Some years ago, a friend of mine told me the story of how she came to be married. When I had first known her, she had been dating a rather quiet, undemonstrative graduate student in political science, a somewhat shy though physically rather large man and certainly aggressive whenever he played touch football, which he did on weekends, returning dirtied and bruised from his outings. This man's character had an attractive mix of qualities, she thought, both nurturing and fierce, and after a few months of seeing him socially she thought she was in love with him. She herself was a graduate student in biology.

After several months, this boyfriend had suggested that they go out to dinner in one of the more expensive restaurants in Baltimore. When he picked her up at her apartment—they were not yet living together—he was wearing a threadbare coat and tie. A small and almost invisible food stain discolored the tie near the knot, but instead of being dismayed, my friend was charmed by her boyfriend's inattentiveness to appearances, and in any case she was used to it.

At dinner, in the waterfront restaurant where he had made the reservation, she had ordered scallops when she noticed that her boyfriend was blushing. "You're blushing," she said. "How come?"

"There's something I have to do," he told her. The restaurant, which had a good local reputation, was rather crowded and noisy. As if she hadn't heard him, he repeated, more loudly, "There's something I have to do." It seemed that he was working up his courage. He reached into his pocket and drew out a little box and opened it. In it was an engagement ring. Then he pulled back his chair and got down on one knee beside her.

"M—," he asked, "will you marry me?"

My friend remembers this moment and likes to tell this story not because she was pleased by the proposal, but because everyone in the restaurant was looking at them. She was embarrassed and amused by her own embarrassment. She examined the engagement ring and the stain on his tie. What she remembers saying in response was, "Yes, I'll marry you, if you'll please stop making a scene."

If you were raised in the genteel tradition, as I was, you avoid scenes, even when people say they love you. This is not the best preparation in the world for writing stories.

I live in a part of Minneapolis where several bookstores vie for my attention. One of them, an independent bookstore, has a fine selection of Native American literature, fiction and nonfiction, and wisdom literature shelved close to philosophy. In the gigantic Barnes and Noble two miles away in the strip mall, by contrast, you can find large selections of almost every printed book that could be considered mainstream, including a large selection on writing. The books on writing, that is, books on the craft of writing, are shelved next to the self-help books, which have a section all to themselves. After you look at these selections for a minute or two, you start to notice that the books in the two sections have been commingling. Some of the writing books include pep talks, and some of the self-help books include the activity of writing as a means of self-improvement.

It's doubtful whether a lifetime's dedication to the writing of fiction has cured anyone of anything. Keats noted that writers spend most of their time trying to figure out if they're the healer or the patient. But as it happens, among these self-help writing books is one by a woman I happened to know when I was in my teens and early twenties, Brenda Ueland. At that time, thirty years ago, Brenda was in her eighties. She encouraged me, as she encouraged many others, to follow their particular ambitions. She urged me to be a writer, since I had claimed I wanted to be one. "'Better to kill a babe in its cradle than to nurse unacted desires,'" Brenda used to say, quoting William Blake. When she was in her eighties, no one could still match Brenda's fearlessness. Someone I knew said,

"Brenda is always picking people up." I think this phrase was meant in both senses. She encouraged everyone to do what they wanted to do and to do it sooner rather than later. Her book on the craft of writing is called *If You Want to Write*, and it consists of a series of pep talks, and in my local Barnes and Noble, this book is shelved under self-help.

In a materialist society, to devote oneself to non-material ends requires quite a bit of energy and resolve, and Brenda Ueland knew all about the difficulties in finding such resources, with the result that her book is a kind of exclamatory spirit-lifter. *If You Want to Write* is actually full of good sense about writing and life because Brenda Ueland could see through the hypocrisy of gentility quickly and easily. In one chapter, she wrote she had two rules she followed absolutely: to tell the truth, and not to do anything she didn't want to do. This is sensible advice if you have never been poor or unemployed.

If You Want to Write is aimed at the sort of person who wants to break out of the spiritual doldrums into the practice of an art and who has to get free of smug middle-class values to do it. Such a person needs strength of will to face up to failure and interrogations from practical-minded friends, who, in an effort to appear concerned, will ask, "How will you make any money?" or "How will you raise your children?"

In the short term, writing may indeed do some of the work of self-improvement and therapy, particularly for those who have been forced to confront what has been done to them and what they themselves have done to others. For all those who are working with people in prisons and in halfway houses and various shelters and affinity groups, I say, "Good luck and blessings on you," without ever doubting that literature and therapy are two different enterprises, and that their outcomes may be at war with each other.

The particular dark reflecting pool that literature presents to us quite possibly has no purpose at all, any more than great music does. The pointlessness of art is not an argument against it. It is simply a proposition that pragmatists worry over. Consequently, as a way to stave off pointlessness and the specter of a profitless activity, we—Americans particularly—tend to moralize and pragmatize the practice of literature. We sometimes try to avoid in our own writing and reading what we may find troubling in our lives.

But what is good when encountered in life is often not good for literature, and the reverse: what's good for fiction is not always good when instrumentalized in life.

The distorting effect of wishes in the writing of fiction can hardly be overestimated. In fiction the force of a wish can result in the formal characteristics of fantasy writing. The story becomes the stage, not for truth, but self-actualization. We try to imagine the person as we would like ourselves to be and as a result write a banal and lifelessly idealistic story. Stories of this type commit a number of sins against literature, among them, first, the distortion of events in the service of a positive self-image, and, second, the habit of making people out to be better than they actually are.

In fiction we want to have characters create scenes that in real life we would typically avoid. Writers might want to have happy lives, but they fear the revenge of the genteel community if their writings are too lively. If they do, they give up their writerly badge of honor. Stories often require sparkplug characters—radically unpleasant type—as focusing agents. The refusal of a story to grant a wish, its refusal to be polite, genteel, or *useful*, offers manifold opportunities for the messy self-reproaches and grotesqueries characteristic of fiction.

The household of my childhood was one of prolonged silences. My stepfather was a learned, witty, irascible man who, as the years passed, enthusiastically developed a curmudgeon side. Every time he saw a highway under construction, for example, he called it a make-work project meant to keep the riffraff employed. He was also affronted by the slow speed limits posted near elementary schools. My mother, by contrast, had a strong will, but a Protestant and Midwestern middle-class reluctance to display it directly. When I had the nerve to give way to the angers of that house, particularly in adolescence, my mother would upbraid me by saying, "Now, Charlie, don't make a scene."

Where I came from, making a scene was considered vulgar. The lower classes created scenes: they shouted at each other and threw dishes and plates. Their lack of control indicated clearly why they should not be put in charge of things. We were certainly not supposed to follow their model. Whenever my stepfather saw a drama on television or in the movies in which people raised their voices in passion or anger, he would say, "Life isn't like that." He meant that people like us were not like that, or at least we weren't supposed to be like that, and above all we weren't supposed to create scenes of that sort. We were supposed to button it up, whatever "it" was, as a sign of our habitation in the professional-managerial classes. And the lives we led were the definition of what "life" was. What other definition could there be?

We ourselves were not supposed to be dramatic. Drama was for others, or for the purposes of entertainment. Along with being told not to create scenes, I was told not to tattle on people, which was worded as, "Charlie, don't tell tales." It is interesting to me now how the construction of a narrative—any narrative—was frowned upon in that household.

All this suppression was a product of my stepfather's latent Anglophilia and his ideas about self-control. Foreign customs and habits were all right in their place far across the Atlantic, where you had to have a passport to witness them, but when imported to America, these strange bohemian behaviors, beliefs, and their associated food groups—Catholicism! confessionals! pasta!—were merely comical.

But of course our family did create scenes, eventually. We shouted and misbehaved just as they did everywhere else. In order to recognize my own anger for what it was, I had to struggle through the layered insulations of our family's mock-gentility, just as I had to struggle through that same gentility to get at any passions I could claim as my own. Everything I had ever been taught as a child about self-control stood against every instinct that I eventually acknowledged or acquired as a writer of dramatic narrative.

What I had to learn—the lesson of bad behavior—was to honor the most profound desires I had, no matter how unpresentable or unsavory they might be, and to do it by creating scenes, on paper. First I created scenes in life, and then I put them into stories.

One curiosity of writers' workshops is that, when confronted with a highly dramatic scene in which the writer has probably gone for broke in the presentation of a crucial conflict, the workshop participants will habitually call the result "melodramatic." This is a way of saying that drama makes them uneasy and that the characters who create scenes are often unpleasant and unlikable. (It is of course true that freshman write fiction full of hideously overdramatized conflict, but they get over it once they try to become respectable and obtain jobs.) Overt anger and straightforward conflicts still strike many genteel readers as unrefined. There is nothing more vulgar than a fistfight in the country club. . . .

Source: Charles Baxter, "Creating a Scene," in *The Art of Subtext: Beyond Plot*, Graywolf Press, 2007, pp. 115–24.

Molly Winans

In the following excerpt, Winans describes how Baxter explores the extraordinary and mysterious through ordinary characters.

. . . If Baxter comes bearing one gift, it is this central understanding: the world keeps proving itself bigger than the people who think about it. His characters mess up a lot; they stumble, sway, and sink as often as they stride or swim. They are weird, but quiet about it, daily about it. Many of them, in fact, bring to mind what Irish writer Frank O'Connor in his study of the short story, *The Lonely Voice*, called "the Little Man." They live in the flat Midwest. They sell insurance or make minor decisions in city bureaucracies. They don't finish their dissertations. They cut hair, teach high school, sell cars, get married, get dumped. They are small-town priests and ministers, foundlings and runts, recent college graduates waiting for the moment when they'll know what to do. They are full of wonder and violence, struggling to believe in all sorts of things. If they have resigned themselves to failure, as many of them have, they have done so without giving up their claims on grace.

Baxter's career took wing in 1984 with the publication of his first collection of short stories, *Harmony of the World*. Since that time, he has published reliably every two to three years: three more collections of stories (*Through the Safety Net, A Relative Stranger, Believers*); two novels (*First Light, Shadow Play*); a poetry collection (*Imaginary Paintings*); and a collection of essays (*Burning Dozen the House*). A prize-winner whose stories have twice appeared in Best American Short Stories, a recipient of NEA and Guggenheim grants, director of the writing program at the University of Michigan, Baxter has still somehow remained a hidden treasure. He is a "writer's writer"—he has earned consistently glowing praise from critics and little popular name recognition. As Francine Prose announces in her recent review of *Believers* in the *New York Times Book Review*, "there are some writers so gifted that even their colleagues agree: really, they should be better known, their books should be best sellers."

Baxter is first and foremost a short-story writer; it is the perfect vehicle for what he does best, unveiling but not unraveling the tight knot of mystery that lies at the heart of every insight. "Strangeness of behavior," Frank O'Connor wrote, "is the very lifeblood of the short story." Baxter's fiction illustrates that true strangeness, the extra-ordinary, is arrived at only through the ordinary.

. . . Baxter understands the importance of glimpses. His characters are constantly turning themselves—or finding themselves turned—toward mystery. Conclusive insight, Baxter maintains in the essay "Against Epiphanies," is the real illusion; a fiction writer's fealty should be to giving events the "dignity of their own complexity." As a writer, he is unfailingly true to this mission. In the story "Flood Show," a kindhearted family man discovers after fourteen years that he has never gotten over his first wife, who left him suddenly. In "A Relative Stranger" a man adopted as a baby gets a call from someone claiming to be his brother and receives the man with a rich mix of skepticism, anger, anxiety, and reluctant hope. "I don't like people watching me when they think they're going to get a skeleton key to my character," he explains. "I'm not a door and I won't be opened that easily."

Flannery O'Connor, in her 1969 collection of essays, *Mystery and Manners*, wrote that "the sharper the light of faith, the more glaring are apt to be the distortions the writer sees in the life around him." Baxter is keenly aware of distortions, always mindful not to exaggerate them but to observe them with care and precision. His fictional worlds are perfectly familiar yet a little odd. His characters shoot at nuclear reactors, spend the night at the zoo, sit on benches in blizzards. In "Gryphon," probably Baxter's best-known story, a substitute fourth-grade teacher named Miss Ferenczi, a strange woman who carries a checkerboard lunch box and accuses a group of boys of forming a "cabal" before she has even introduced herself, announces to a class of slightly stunned students that sometimes six multiplied by eleven equals sixty-eight—a "substitute fact," as she calls it. Baxter finds first the humor then the eeriness in the moment, the creepy ease with which, as class proceeds, she manipulates the children's minds. Her secret is to find a strange truth around which to coil her elaborate, wild "facts." Venus flytraps lead her to the cloud cover around Venus, which houses angels, who sometimes travel to Earth to attend concerts, where they sit in the aisles and no one pays attention to them. Baxter has said in an interview that he thinks of Miss Ferenczi as "half miracle, half monster." We understand the miracle part of the equation through the story's unnamed narrator, who finds joy in the substitute teacher's hyper-reality and defends her against detractors; Miss Ferenczi's world, where the facts of science are mysterious enough to keep good company with zany inanities like angels in the aisles of concert halls, is a miracle.

But mystery can be monstrous as well; "the unexpected," writes Baxter elsewhere, "is seldom beautiful." When Miss Ferenczi, using Tarot cards, tells a boy named Wayne he will soon die, the story delivers a moment of shocking cruelty. But Baxter doesn't stop there. When Wayne tells the principal what Miss Ferenczi has done, the youthful narrator attacks him for a coward. Boyhood alliance against adults dissolves—the undertow of the fabulous has pulled the narrator out to sea.

Miss Ferenczi presents an extreme case—a mystic, a charlatan, a woman determined to be weird. Usually, Baxter's characters seem unlikely bearers of mystery, plunged into it by accident. Baxter's fiction is rife with accident; without ever seeming merely random, it manages to remain true to the way things happen to happen. In "Snow," a bored twelve-year-old tags along with his older brother and girlfriend to see the two-door Impala that went through the ice on the lake, and learns a lesson in the "desperate and beautiful." In "The Next Building I Plan to Bomb," a man comes upon those ominous words on a windblown scrap of paper, an accident which ultimately propels him into angry uncertainty about the worth of his life. In "Winter Journey," Harrelson, described with typical rueful acuity as a "perpetual Ph.D. student, poverty-stricken dissertation non-finisher, academic man of all work, gourmand," drives drunk in a snowstorm to rescue a soon-to-be-ex-fiancée and manages to hit two parked cars and run over a rat-sized dog without running it down. Accidents are dream-like curiosities to Harrelson, part of a universe run by "his familiars in the spirit world," a kind but bumbling crew.

Still, accident reveals mystery only to those willing to look. Some refuse, clinging to a false innocence. For Baxter, spiritual life demands a capacity for grace, a willingness to be open to what you don't understand. Baxter wrestles with innocence, that state we Americans romanticize so fervently. He sees innocence as complicated—as is the fall from it. The fall is not always one dramatic moment; characters fall and fall and fall from innocence, in moments that parcel themselves out over time. Wisdom, when it is to be had, lies not in the discovery of answers but in the will to struggle for them; to join what Flannery O'Connor calls "our slow participation in the Redemption." Wisdom relies on faith; and faith, as O'Connor insists, "is a walking in darkness and not a theological solution to mystery." . . .

Source: Molly Winans, "Bigger Than We Think: The World Revealed in Charles Baxter's Fiction," in *Commonweal*, Vol. 124, No. 19, November 7, 1997, p. 12.

SOURCES

Baxter, Charles, "Gryphon," in *Gryphon: New and Selected Stories*, Pantheon, 2011, pp. 103–19.

Bellamy, Joe David, "Muscular Fiction: A Postscript," in *Literary Luxuries: American Writing at the End of the Millennium*, University of Missouri Press, 1995, pp. 83–86.

Caesar, Terry, "Charles Baxter," in *Dictionary of Literary Biography*, Vol. 130, *American Short Story Writers since World War II*, edited by Patrick Meanor, Gale Research, 1993, pp. 35–38.

Carr, Patrick J., and Maria J. Kefalas, "The Heartland and the Rural Youth Exodus," in *Hollowing Out the Middle: The Rural Brain Drain and What It Means for America*, Beacon Press, 2009, pp. 1–26.

Ciabattari, Jane, "*Gryphon*: Beautiful Stories for a Snowy Afternoon," National Public Radio website, January 13, 2011, http://www.npr.org/2011/01/13/132870103/gryphon-beautiful-stories-for-a-snowy-afternoon (accessed February 25, 2013).

Cumyn, Richard, Review of *Gryphon: New and Selected Stories*, in *Winnipeg Review*, March 18, 2011, http://www.winnipegreview.com/wp/2011/03/gryphon-stories-charles-baxter/ (accessed February 25, 2013).

Gioia, Dana, "Gabriel García Márquez and Magical Realism," in *Dana Gioia: Essays*, 2009, http://www.danagioia.net/essays/emarquez.htm (accessed February 25, 2013); originally published in *Sniper Logic*, 1998.

Hart, Stephen M., "Magical Realism: Style and Substance," in *A Companion to Magical Realism*, edited by Stephen M. Hart and Wen Chin Ouyang, Tamesis, 2005, pp. 1–12.

Johnson, Kenneth, "Executive Summary" and "Historical and Demographic Trends," in *Demographic Trends in Rural and Small Town America*, Carsey Institute, University of New Hampshire, 2006, pp. 1–5, 8–9, http://www.carseyinstitute.unh.edu/publications/Report_Demographics.pdf (accessed February 25, 2013).

Lohafer, Susan, "The Short Story," in *The Cambridge Companion to American Fiction after 1945*, edited by John S. Duvall, Cambridge University Press, 2012, pp. 68–84.

Messud, Claire, "An Experiment with Wonder," in *New York Review of Books*, April 28, 2011, http://www.nybooks.com/articles/archives/2011/apr/28/experiment-wonder/?pagination = false (accessed February 25, 2013).

Rebein, Robert, "Contemporary Realism," in *The Cambridge Companion to American Fiction after 1945*, edited by John S. Duvall, Cambridge University Press, 2012, pp. 30–43.

Reynolds, Susan Salter, Review of *Gryphon: New and Selected Stories*, in *Los Angeles Times*, January 23, 2011, http://articles.latimes.com/2011/jan/23/entertainment/la-ca-charles-baxter-20110123 (accessed February 25, 2013).

"Small Public School Districts in America's Rural Locales," in *Characteristics of Small Rural School Districts*, National Center for Education Statistics, May 1997, pp. 7–20, http://nces.ed.gov/pubs97/97529.pdf (accessed February 25, 2013).

"Status of Education in Rural America: Demographics," National Center for Education Statistics website, http://nces.ed.gov/pubs2007/ruraled/hl_demographics.asp (accessed February 25, 2013).

Turrentine, Jeff, Review of *Gryphon: New and Selected Stories*, in *Washington Post*, February 24, 2011, http://www.washingtonpost.com/wp-dyn/content/article/2011/02/23/AR2011022306402_pf.html (accessed February 25, 2013).

"Understanding Rural America," US Department of Agriculture website, February 1995, http://www.nal.usda.gov/ric/ricpubs/understd.htm (accessed February 25, 2013).

Werlock, Abby H. P., ed., Introduction to *The Facts on File Companion to the American Short Story*, 2nd ed., Facts on File, 2010, pp. ix–xv.

FURTHER READING

Baxter, Charles, *Burning Down the House: Essays on Fiction*, Graywolf Press, 2008.

> Baxter's essays both examine the condition of contemporary fiction and explain elements of the craft from a writer's perspective.

Hemingway, Ernest, *The Short Stories: The First Forty-Nine Stories*, Scribner, 1995.

> Hemingway, considered one of the American masters of short fiction, wrote in the realist mode and set several of his stories in Michigan, where he, like Baxter, periodically lived.

Rebein, Robert, *Hicks, Tribes, and Dirty Realism: American Fiction after Postmodernism*, University of Kentucky Press, 2001.

> Rebein explores the evolution of realism from the 1980s and beyond, studying such trends as the return to the early realists' emphasis on setting and the individual's place in and response to it.

Schafft, Kai A., and Alecia Youngblood Jackson, eds., *Rural Education for the Twenty-First Century: Identity, Place, and Community in a Global World*, Pennsylvania State University Press, 2010.

> This collection of essays explores the history of and challenges faced by schools in rural portions of the United States and abroad. The essays investigate the impact on rural education of such issues as local economies, agriculture, racism, and immigration.

SUGGESTED SEARCH TERMS

Charles Baxter AND magical realism

Charles Baxter AND Gryphon

literary realism AND magical realism

Charles Baxter AND rural Michigan

1980s short fiction AND literary realism

Charles Baxter AND realist fiction

Charles Baxter AND University of Michigan

Charles Baxter AND Five Oaks

Charles Baxter AND Tobias Wolff

dirty realism

Idiots First

BERNARD MALAMUD
1961

Bernard Malamud, a Pulitzer Prize–winning short-story writer and novelist, is the author of "Idiots First," a story first published in *Commentary* magazine in December 1961. It was then the lead story in Malamud's 1963 collection also titled *Idiots First*. "Idiots First" depicts the plight of Mendel, a poor widower who has struggled with life for years and is now facing death, personified by a bearded man named Ginzburg who pursues him. Before he dies, Mendel wants to scrape together enough money to ensure that his mentally disabled son, Isaac, can take a train from New York to California to find a home with a relative.

"Idiots First" is in many ways representative of the author's work. Malamud, a Jewish American, is best known for capturing the pathos of the Jewish experience, often in fable-like stories and novels that have pronounced allegorical and mythological elements. That he would personify death in his depiction of his character's struggle with life is characteristic of his creative vision. "Idiots First" is available in *A Malamud Reader*, published in 1967, and online at the Southeast Missouri State University website at http://cstl-cla.semo.edu/hhecht/Readings/Idiots%20First.htm.

AUTHOR BIOGRAPHY

Malamud was born on April 26, 1914, in Brooklyn, New York, the elder of the two sons of Russian Jewish immigrants. His father, Max,

Bernard Malamud (© *Nancy R. Schiff | Archive Photos | Getty Images*)

was a grocer; Malamud's schizophrenic mother, Bertha, also worked in the family grocery store before dying—probably by her own hand—when Malamud was in his teens. Malamud remembered his parents as gentle, kindly people who managed to make a living but remained relatively poor. He also remembered the cultural deprivation of his early life. The family owned no books or records; they did not even have any pictures on the walls. Only after Malamud became ill when he was nine years old did his father procure any books for him: a twenty-volume set titled *The Book of Knowledge.*

As a child, Malamud entertained himself by going to the movies; he especially enjoyed Charlie Chaplin films. He also read dime novels (that is, sensationalized mass-market fiction) and watched the Brooklyn Dodgers baseball team at Ebbets Field. Occasionally, the family saw a play in the Yiddish theater, where relatives were actors. It was not until Malamud was in high school that his father bought a radio. He told an interviewer for the *Paris Review*:

Around the neighborhood the kids played Chase the White Horse, Ringolevio, Buck-Buck, punchball, and one o'cat. Occasionally we stole tomatoes from the Italian dirt farmers, gypped the El to ride to Coney Island, smoked in cellars, and played blackjack. I wore sneakers every summer. My education at home derived mostly from the presence and example of good, feelingful, hard-working people.

Malamud attended Erasmus Hall High School in Brooklyn from 1928 to 1932. After a stint as a teacher in training, he attended City College of New York, earning a bachelor's degree in 1936. He then completed a master's degree at Columbia University in 1942. In 1945, against the wishes of his father, he married an Italian American Catholic, Ann DeChiara, and in time the couple had two children. Malamud would later say that his marriage to a Gentile caused him to question his Jewish identity and impelled him to begin reading and writing about Jewish history and traditions. After working briefly for the Bureau of the Census in Washington, DC, he returned to New York City to teach English primarily to adults at Erasmus

Hall Evening High School. In 1949, he took a position teaching English composition at Oregon State University, where he launched his writing career in earnest. In 1952, he published the novel for which he is perhaps best remembered, *The Natural*, a baseball fable turned into a major motion picture in 1984. His 1957 novel *The Assistant* is in many ways autobiographical. During the 1950s he began publishing short stories in such publications as *Harper's Bazaar*, *Partisan Review*, and *Commentary*. His 1958 short-story collection *The Magic Barrel* won the National Book Award.

In 1961, Malamud accepted a position teaching creative writing at Bennington College, in Vermont, where he remained until his retirement. His novel *A New Life* (1961) explores the efforts of a transplanted English professor to create a new life at a fictional university in the West. In 1963, he published the short-story collection *Idiots First*, a title derived from the collection's lead story. His 1966 novel *The Fixer*, which examines the plight of Russian Jews, won both the National Book Award and the Pulitzer Prize for Fiction in 1967. This novel was followed by the short-story collection *Pictures of Fidelman* (1969); *The Tenants* (1971), a novel about racial tensions and the emergence of African American literature; and *Dubin's Lives* (1979), a novel about an aging writer. In 1974, he published the short-story collection *Rembrandt's Hat*. His final novel, a fable about the sole survivor of a nuclear war, was *God's Grace* (1982). Malamud died of heart failure on March 18, 1986, at his home in Manhattan, New York.

PLOT SUMMARY

As "Idiots First" opens, Mendel, an aging Jewish man, is dozing in his New York City apartment on a Friday evening around dinnertime. He wakens in fright as his clock stops ticking. His son, Isaac, is in the apartment with him; as the story unfolds, the reader learns that Isaac is thirty-nine years old and mentally disabled. Isaac urges his father to sleep, but Mendel instead gathers his gold watch and winds it, retrieves a bag of crumpled one- and five-dollar bills from a drawer, and leaves the apartment with Isaac in tow. As they leave, Mendel makes an enigmatic reference to Ginzburg, although at this point it is unclear who Ginzburg is and why he came to see Mendel the day before.

MEDIA ADAPTATIONS

- "Idiots First" was turned into a one-act opera begun by Marc Blitzstein and completed by Leonard Lehrman. It was first presented in concert by the Ithaca Opera Association in 1974. It premiered in performance with the Marc Blitzstein Opera Company in Bloomington, Indiana, in 1976. Its New York City premiere by the Bel Canto Opera Company took place in 1978. The opera can be seen on the Internet at http://ljlehrman.artists-in-residence.com/IdiotsFirst.html and the running time is one hour and seven minutes.

Mendel and his son go to a pawnshop where the pawnbroker offers Mendel eight dollars for his watch. Mendel is disappointed, telling the pawnbroker that he needs thirty-five dollars, which, with the money he already has, will be enough to buy a train ticket for Isaac to California, where Mendel's eighty-one-year-old uncle Leo lives. He offers the pawnbroker his coat and hat, but the pawnbroker declines. Mendel accepts the eight dollars and leaves, telling Isaac they will eat after they go to the home of the wealthy Mr. and Mrs. Fishbein. They ride the train to Upper Manhattan and then walk several blocks to the Fishbein home. At first, a servant, Levinson, refuses them entrance, but after Mendel pleads for admittance, the servant relents, and the two enter the foyer. Mr. Fishbein appears and asks the nature of their business with him. Mendel explains again that he wants to send Isaac to his great-uncle Leo in California. Mendel indicates that he is gravely ill, making it imperative that Isaac depart that night. The hard-hearted Fishbein refuses to give Mendel the thirty-five dollars he needs, although he offers his visitors food. Mendel and Isaac depart into the windy November evening.

Mendel and Isaac rest on a park bench. A bearded stranger appears, greets them, and disappears into the bushes. A policeman arrives and beats the bushes with his nightstick, but he does not find the stranger. Mendel and Isaac take a trolley to the home of a former friend, but they discover that the friend has died. They then stop at a cafeteria to get Isaac something to eat. They return to the pawnbroker's shop to talk with him about pawning Mendel's furniture, but the shop is closed.

The two take refuge in a doorway as Mendel ponders their plight. He dreams momentarily of life in warm and sunny California, until he spots a synagogue across the street. He and Isaac cross the street, and Mendel pounds on the door of the synagogue. A sexton answers, but he refuses to allow Mendel to see the rabbi, saying that the rabbi and his wife are in bed. Mendel makes clear to the sexton that he is dying and cannot return at a later time. The sexton relents and directs Mendel to a nearby house. Once again, he is rebuffed, this time by the rabbi's wife, but the rabbi appears and agrees to see Mendel and Isaac. The rabbi listens to Mendel's story, and while he is too poor to give Mendel money, he does give Mendel a fur-lined caftan (a loose, usually long-sleeved garment, similar to a cape, worn primarily in Middle Eastern countries). The rabbi's wife objects and grabs the caftan, but Mendel wrestles it away from her and, at the urging of the rabbi, runs from the house. As he and Isaac run through the streets, they are pursued by Ginzburg.

Mendel and Isaac arrive at a train station, where Mendel buys a ticket for Isaac. Isaac, however, is unable to board the train because the gate to the platform is closed. Mendel begs a ticket collector to allow Isaac to pass, but the ticket collector refuses, noting that it is past midnight. Mendel realizes that the ticket collector is Ginzburg. Ginzburg, a personification of death, has come to "collect" Mendel, who was scheduled to die at midnight, which has now passed. He and Mendel quarrel: Mendel asks Ginzburg to have pity on Isaac, but Ginzburg cites "cosmic universal law" in refusing to take any responsibility for what will happen to Isaac after his father's death. Mendel cites the many hardships of his life, including poor health, but Ginzburg responds that others have worse lives. Mendel, now angry, lunges at Ginzburg's throat, but Ginzburg laughs and threatens to freeze Mendel, who begins to shiver with extreme cold.

As Ginzburg grasps Mendel, the two stare into each other's eyes. Ginzburg sees in Mendel's eyes a "blinding light that produced darkness." Ginzburg releases his grip on Mendel and lets him slump to the ground. He then directs a guard to let Mendel and Isaac pass. Isaac helps his father to his feet, and the two walk down the platform to the waiting train. Mendel helps Isaac to a seat, then waits on the platform as the train departs. After the train is gone, Mendel ascends the stairs to learn what became of Ginzburg.

CHARACTERS

Mr. Fishbein

Mendel, accompanied by Isaac, takes the train to Upper Manhattan and Fishbein's house to ask for the money he needs, but the story does not make clear precisely who Fishbein is. The dialogue suggests that he is a philanthropist, or at least a man known for his wealth, in the New York City Jewish community. The reader knows he is wealthy from the description of his home: "The foyer was a vast high-ceilinged room with many oil paintings on the walls, voluminous silken draperies, a thick flowered rug at foot, and a marble staircase." Fishbein himself, wearing a tuxedo at dinner, is described as "a paunchy bald-headed man with hairy nostrils and small patent leather feet." Fishbein indicates that he does not give money to individuals, only to organizations, and he is dismissive of both Mendel and Isaac.

Mrs. Fishbein

Mrs. Fishbein is the wife of Mr. Fishbein. She appears briefly in the story when Mendel and his son visit the Fishbein home, but she plays no real role in the story.

Ginzburg

Ginzburg is a burly, bearded figure who represents death; he functions in the story as a kind of grim reaper who has come to collect the ill and dying Mendel but also as a representation of the implacability of an indifferent universe. He pursues Mendel and his son until they arrive at a train station, where he has a confrontation with Mendel. In response to Mendel's pleas for pity, especially for Isaac, Ginzburg says that he is accountable only to the "cosmic universal law" of death and that he is not responsible for what happens to Isaac. He relents when he sees his own anger reflected in Mendel's eyes. He then allows Mendel to take Isaac aboard the train and get him settled.

Isaac

Isaac, Mendel's thirty-nine-year-old son, has been mentally disabled his entire life. He accompanies his father on his journey through New York City in an effort to procure money for a train ticket to California. He says little, usually uttering single words to indicate, for example, that he is hungry or that his father should sleep. He carries with him a handful of peanuts.

Levinson

Levinson is a servant in the Fishbein home. He is identified by his long sideburns. At first he denies Mendel and Isaac entrance, but he relents when he sees that Mendel is ill.

Mendel

Mendel is an aging Jewish widower who lives in New York City; his physical condition is indicated at the pawnshop, where the narration states that "the dying man wet his cracked lips." He cares for his son, Isaac, who is mentally disabled—one of many hardships he has endured throughout his life. He knows that he is dying, and his goal before death is to procure enough money to put Isaac on a train to California, where he can live with his great-uncle Leo. His need to visit a pawnshop to pawn the only object of value he owns, a gold watch, indicates his poverty. He literally begs for money from Mr. Fishbein and finally from a rabbi. The rabbi gives him a valuable coat, enabling Mendel to buy the train ticket for his son. At the train station, he encounters Ginzburg, a personification of death. At first, Ginzburg refuses to allow Mendel and his son onto the platform so that Isaac can board the train. He finally relents, allowing Mendel to put Isaac into a seat on the train. At the end of the story, Mendel climbs the stairs at the train station to have what promises to be his final encounter with Ginzburg.

Pawnbroker

Mendel and Isaac visit the shop of a mercenary pawnbroker, described as "a red-bearded man with black horn-rimmed glasses ... eating a whitefish at the rear of the store." At first, the pawnbroker ignores Mendel, emerging from the back of the shop after several minutes. After examining the gold watch Mendel wants to pawn, he offers him eight dollars. The implication is that this amount is unfairly low, at least in the estimation of Mendel.

Rabbi

The rabbi, called Yascha by his wife, is described as "an old skinny man with bent shoulders and a wisp of white beard." He listens to Mendel's story, and while he is unable to give Mendel money, he is able to give him a valuable fur-lined caftan, over the objections of his wife. The rabbi is the only character in the story who treats Mendel and his son with kindness and compassion.

Rabbi's Wife

The rabbi's wife is greedy and reluctant to have anything to do with Mendel and his son. When her husband offers Mendel his fur-lined caftan, she objects and tries to wrestle the caftan away from Mendel.

Sexton

When Mendel pounds on the door of a synagogue, a sexton answers. At first, the sexton refuses to allow Mendel and Isaac to see the rabbi and tries to send them away, but he relents and directs them to the rabbi's nearby house. A *sexton* is a church or synagogue employee who looks after the grounds and is often responsible for digging graves. The sexton character adds to the theme of death, particularly Mendel's impending death, that runs throughout the story.

Yascha

See Rabbi

THEMES

Death

At the center of "Idiots First" is Mendel, who is depicted as aging (he is described as an "old man") and in ill health, at least according to his own testimony—although his exhaustion as he reaches the pawnshop, for example, also suggests that his health is poor. As the story unfolds, the reader learns that Mendel is being pursued by death as personified by the character of Ginzburg. Mendel, too, knows that he is about to die, for the day before he received a visit from Ginzburg, who most likely announced his plans for Mendel. At the beginning of the story, however, this sense of impending death is unclear. The reader's first hint that Ginzburg represents death for Mendel is when Mendel tells his son, "Young people he don't bother so much." It is only after Mendel arrives at the pawnbroker's shop that the narration refers to him as "the

TOPICS FOR FURTHER STUDY

- Malamud claimed that he owed a significant debt in his fiction to the movies of Charlie Chaplin, particularly their blend of comedy and sadness, and to the quick cutting of scenes that was coming to be a commonly used film technique when Malamud was a boy. Locate a Charlie Chaplin film; twenty-three of them are available on the Open Culture website at http://www.openculture.com/2011/12/free_charlie_chaplin_films_on_the_web.html. After viewing one or more of his films, write a report in which you trace any broad similarities you see between Chaplin's work and "Idiots First."

- Another prominent Jewish American writer in the twentieth century was Polish-born Isaac Bashevis Singer (not to be confused with the Isaac Singer who invented the sewing machine). Singer wrote numerous short stories, among them the frequently anthologized "Gimpel the Fool." Locate and read the story "Gimpel the Fool," then prepare an oral report in which you discuss similarities and differences in tone, style, and theme with Malamud's "Idiots First."

- A third major figure in Jewish American literature is Canadian-born Saul Bellow. One of Bellow's earliest novels, published in 1953, is *The Adventures of Augie March*, a picaresque novel in which the title character tries to make sense out of an alien world, one that seems to be ruled by an indifferent fate. Read Bellow's novel, then write a brief essay in which you compare and contrast Bellow's version of fate with Malamud's vision of the "cosmic universal law."

- Conduct research on Yiddish. Where did it originate? What languages is it related to? What has been the language's history? Present the results of your findings in an oral report with examples. As part of your efforts, prepare a chart listing a dozen or so Yiddish words that have entered American English and invite your classmates to provide a definition of each. Be sure to let them know whether their definitions are correct or not.

- Conduct research on the experience of Jews in America, particularly during the period ranging from World War I through the Great Depression and World War II. Where did American Jews come from? What kind of reception did they meet within the United States? How might the Jewish experience in America have influenced a writer like Malamud? Organize the results of your research in a PowerPoint presentation for your classmates, and include any images you find on the Internet. A place to begin your research might be this PBS website: http://www.pbs.org/jewishamericans/jewish_life/holocaust.html.

- For some readers, the ending of "Idiots First" may be ambiguous: "When the train was gone, Mendel ascended the stairs to see what had become of Ginzburg." Imagine that the story continues and that you have been given the task of writing the remainder, or perhaps a sequel. Write your version of what happens after this point. Post your version on a blog and invite your classmates to comment.

- "Idiots First" is in part a portrait of the New York City Jewish community. Locate a young-adult work about another ethnic community—for example, Sandra Cisneros's *The House on Mango Street*, about the Hispanic community—and prepare a chart that lists similarities and differences in the authors' treatment of their ethnic communities. Share your chart with your classmates.

Hoping to get help from the rabbi, Mendel goes to the local synagogue. *(© sarkao / ShutterStock.com)*

dying man." The thrust of the story is that Mendel wants to accomplish one more task—providing for his son's care—before he dies.

Suffering

Connected with the theme of aging and death is the suffering that Mendel has endured throughout his life, suffering that can perhaps be thought of as reflecting the historical suffering of the Jewish people. It is clear from the beginning of the story that Mendel is poor. His "embittered" clothing is not quite adequate to keep him warm. He has little money, and the money he does have he keeps in a paper bag to be used to buy a train ticket for his son. The only object of value he owns is his gold watch. Later, the reader learns that his wife died when she was young. Throughout his life, Mendel often had to work hard, but there were times when he was apparently unable to work, probably, the reader imagines, because of poor health. Through it all he had to care for a mentally disabled son. Now, he is being pursued by death in the form of Ginzburg, and while he might seem to be at a stage in life when he would welcome death as a means of ending his suffering, he desperately wants to carry out one final task: ensuring that his son will be cared for.

Love

When Mendel and Isaac visit Mr. Fishbein, the latter refers to Isaac as a "halfwit" and urges Mendel to provide for his son by putting him in an institution. Fishbein's cold indifference (his name means "whalebone" in German, suggesting perhaps hardness and inflexibility) is in contrast to the love Mendel has for his son. Mendel indicates that his heart was broken by his son's inability to grow up, but at no point does he complain or lament his fate as a parent. Rather, he has unconditional love for his son and is determined to provide for his son's welfare before he dies. This determination enables him to stave off death at the train station and complete his errand. He is able to do so in part because of the love exhibited by the rabbi, who, over the objections of his wife, gives Mendel his valuable fur-lined caftan.

STYLE

Dialogue

Malamud captures the Jewish American experience in part through dialogue, much of it reflecting the influence of Yiddish (a Germanic language of Jewish origin). The story contains a few examples of Yiddish words. Isaac, for example, tells his father to *schlaf*, a German-Yiddish word (often spelled *shlaf*) meaning "sleep." Later, a bearded stranger—Ginzburg—greets Mendel with the expression *gut yuntif*, usually spelled *gut yontif* in English, an expression that means "good holiday." (It is not clear what holiday Ginzburg might be referring to, but the story takes place on a Friday evening into the first minutes of Saturday and thus is taking place on the Shabbat, or the Jewish sabbath.)

For the most part, though, the Yiddish influence is reflected in syntax, word order, and grammatical constructions that would be considered unusual in standard English. One example is the use of what appear to be superfluous relative pronouns. Thus, Mendel tells Isaac, "Ginzburg, that he came to see me yesterday"; the more standard phrasing would be "Ginzburg came to see me yesterday." Another example occurs when Mendel tells the pawnbroker, "Isaac must go to my uncle that he lives in California." A common feature of Yiddish dialect is to move the direct object to the head of a sentence. Thus, Mendel says "Young people he don't bother so much" rather than "He don't bother young people so much." Adverbs are moved about freely, so that Mendel at one point says "I have already the rest" rather than "I have the rest already" or "I already have the rest." Perhaps one of the most striking Yiddish-influenced sentences comes from Fishbein, who asks, "Who comes on Friday night to a man that he has guests, to spoil him his supper?" These and numerous other examples of the Yiddish influence on the characters' language help to create a portrait of the twentieth-century American Jewish community.

Symbolism

A key symbol in "Idiots First" is time and the passage of time. The story begins with the words "The thick ticking of the tin clock stopped," anticipating the end of Mendel's life. (The opening sentence is also a striking example of consonance—the repeated *t* and *k* sounds—and assonance—the repeated *i* and *o* sounds.) Mendel in effect tries to "buy time" by pawning his gold watch. Throughout the story, the reader is kept aware of the passage of time; at one point, for example, the narration says, "Then a bell chimed and it was only ten." Near the story's conclusion, the reader learns that midnight has passed and Ginzburg is on hand to collect Mendel.

Another symbol is the "leafless two-branched tree" in a park where Mendel and Isaac pause to rest. When they arrive, "the thick right branch was raised, the thin left one hung down." But after the appearance of Ginzburg, who is following Mendel, Mendel glances back at the tree, which "had its thin arm raised, the thick one down." This type of symbolism adds a note of mysticism to the story, for the natural world is conspiring to remind Mendel that his time is running out; the alternation of the thick, robust "hand" of the tree and the thin, weaker "hand," like the hands of a clock, suggests that death is imminent for the character.

Setting

Setting plays a key role in "Idiots First." The setting appears in many ways to be realistic, even commonplace. Mendel and his son live in a New York City apartment. They leave the apartment to travel about the city in their quest for funds that will enable Mendel to buy a train ticket for Isaac. At various points they board a trolley. At one point they rest in a park. They encounter a pawnbroker in his shop, Mr. Fishbein in his Upper Manhattan mansion, and the rabbi and his wife at their home near a synagogue. But the setting of the story also has symbolic significance. The atmosphere is bleak, cold, and windy. The characters move about largely in darkness and shadows, a darkness punctuated by small points of light. The wind is said to blow "mournfully," and the characters are "buffeted by winds." The streets appear to be deserted. The suggestion is that the characters are on a diasporic journey through a hostile, alien, uncaring universe. However, the sky is clear, and Mendel and Isaac are able to see myriad stars and the moon. These points of light prefigure the blinding illumination that takes place at the end of the story, when Mendel is able to stave off death and complete his errand by wrestling with Ginzburg in the train station.

HISTORICAL CONTEXT

Jews in New York City

"Idiots First" embodies virtually nothing in the way of historical context. The details of the story indicate that it takes place sometime in the twentieth century. The existence of trolleys in the story suggests a time predating the mid-1950s, when the transit authority in New York City, the story's setting, was discontinuing its trolley lines. The poverty of the main character gives the story the feel of taking place during the Great Depression of the 1930s, but none of the details of the story confirm that supposition. The pawnbroker suggests that Mendel acquired his gold watch in 1905, and if the reader imagines that he acquired the watch in early adulthood, and that he fathered his thirty-nine-year-old son at roughly the same time, a time period in the 1940s might be inferred. But again, the story offers no firm evidence to support this kind of inference. Like many of Malamud's stories, this one takes the form of a fable, so it is likely that the author wanted to make it as timeless as possible.

The story, however, is fully rooted in the history of American Judaism. Perhaps a testimony to the impact that Jewish immigration had on the American experience is the Statue of Liberty and "The New Colossus," a sonnet engraved on a plaque mounted inside the statue's lower level. The sonnet includes the well-known words "Give me your tired, your poor, / Your huddled masses yearning to breathe free." The poem was written by Emma Lazarus, the daughter of Sephardic Jews from Portugal who had settled in the United States during the colonial period.

At the beginning of the twentieth century, the US Jewish population, at about one million, was the world's third largest. Fully half lived in New York City, and in fact, New York City's Jewish population was twice that of the world's second-place Jewish city, Warsaw, Poland. Fueling the continued growth of the US Jewish population during the twentieth century was immigration. From 1900 to 1924, some 1.75 million Jews immigrated to the United States, many of them, like Malamud's parents, from eastern Europe. This mass immigration slowed with the end of World War I, and after the mid-1920s, for the first time, the majority of American Jews who lived in the United States were born in the United States rather than overseas. During the interwar period, anti-Semitism became common, with Jews blatantly denied employment, educational opportunities, and access to public spaces, forcing them to carve out space for themselves in finance (including less-reputable forms of finance such as pawnbroking), publishing, manufacturing, and entertainment; Malamud likely expected that the reader would imagine that Mr. Fishbein in "Idiots First" made his fortune in one of these ways.

Although many eastern European Jews came from shtetls, or small towns and villages with a largely agricultural flavor, most settled in big cities along the nation's East Coast. They were able to preserve their identity through the neighborhood, the New World version of the shtetl, where first- and second-generation Jews could preserve a sense of identity and community without being absorbed into the larger urban experience. In this way, Jews, and Jewish writers, were able to stake out a turf that sheltered them from the chaos of urban life, and Jewish literature embodied a peculiar blend of outer experience reflected in the city and an inner experience that protected the Jew *from* the city.

That urban experience was nowhere more evident than in New York City. In an essay titled "New York City, the Jews, and 'The Urban Experience,'" Eli Lederhendler quotes numerous midcentury authors who commented on the vitality and sheer size of the New York Jewish community. He notes that New York City reminded Isaac Bashevis Singer of Warsaw because of its large Jewish population. He quotes David Bazelon, a writer and social critic, who recalled, "To the kid from Chicago, New York was an astoundingly bright new world, filled with Jews of marvelous variety." He further quotes political scientist Hans Morgenthau, who wrote:

> There is so much that is specifically Jewish here. You expect to run into Jews continuously: you always expect to be touched by the emanations of Jewish life. How else could it be in a city one of whose main ethnic characteristics is Jewishness?

Lederhendler then concludes that "New York became the model upon which many postwar urban Jewish writers based their image of 'the city.'" He continues:

COMPARE
&
CONTRAST

- **1961:** The Upper East Side of Manhattan enjoys the nickname "Millionaire's Row" because of the area's large number of opulent mansions built by wealthy New Yorkers earlier in the century.

  Today: The Friends of the Upper East Side Historic Districts (founded in 1982) functions as an independent, nonprofit organization dedicated to preserving the architectural legacy of the Upper East Side.

- **1961:** Jews form a major ethnic group in New York City. As of 1960, the Jewish population of New York City is estimated to be about 1.9 million.

  Today: After decades of decline, the Jewish population of New York City has risen to about 1.54 million, or about 18 to 19 percent of the city's population.

- **1961:** At the start of the decade, New York City discontinues its last trolley line, bringing a seventy-year history of electric trolleys to a close.

  Today: New Yorkers depend on a fully integrated bus and subway system for their transportation needs.

Identifying themselves fully with the gritty, abrasive, brittle unquietness of it, they also imagined that "Jewishness" (*not* Judaism) and urban-ness were inherently overlapping qualities, thus doing for the Big Apple what their Yiddish and Hebrew predecessors had done for the shtetl.

It is this vision of Jewish ethnic identity in big-city America that underpins Malamud's "Idiots First."

CRITICAL OVERVIEW

Malamud's reputation with critics was high during his lifetime. Alfred Kazin, in a 1958 essay titled "Bernard Malamud: The Magic and the Dread," states, "There seems to me no writer of his background who comes so close to the bone of human feeling, who makes one feel so keenly the enigmatic quality of life." In his 1961 book *Radical Innocence: Studies in the Contemporary American Novel*, Ihab Hassan praises Malamud in this way:

> In Bernard Malamud we find . . . testimony that the urban Jewish writer, like the Southern novelist, has emerged from the tragic underground of culture as a true spokesman of mid-century America. . . . His finest work shows an order of excellence no critic . . . can justly deny.

Critics have often focused on the fable-like quality of Malamud's work. Jonathan Baumbach, in *Moderns and Contemporaries: Nine Masters of the Short Story*, notes that "even Malamud's most realistic stories leap at times into fantasy. His world is magical, metaphoric." Baumbach continues: "A moral fabler and [fantasist], Malamud writes of the conflicting demands of the inner and outer worlds of his heroes, who move uncertainly, often looking the other way, toward self-knowledge." Marcia B. Gealy picks up this theme in a comment on "Idiots First" in an essay titled "Malamud's Short Stories: A Reshaping of Hasidic Tradition":

> The power of "Idiots First" lies in its masterful tension between terror and hope and the artfulness with which we are suspended between the real and the supernatural. . . . We see here Malamud's gift in creating a dream-like landscape, for, while the setting is New York, the deserted streets and the reappearance of the bearded stranger transport us to somewhere beyond.

Many critics have focused on Malamud's style. Alan Lelchuk, in a review titled "Malamud's Dark Fable," mentions "Idiots First" when he remarks:

Mendel sells his watch to get money for his son's train ticket. (© Pshenichka / ShutterStock.com)

Constructing fables, we should remember, is nothing new for Malamud.... Malamud has always had a fondness for telling tales arranged for the purpose of a specific moral lesson; for a story surface deceptively simple, a prose style artfully direct; for an atmosphere marked by the childlike and pristine, even the religious.

Similarly, David Remnick, in "The Voice of a Natural: Bernard Malamud and His Miraculous Tales," comments, "His prose was direct, clear and swift. At his best he had the ear of a poet." Remnick quotes the first four sentences of "Idiots First," remarking, "The iambic accents of that first sentence, the clarity of the image, the choice of 'embittered' to describe a man's clothing: a master is at work." Finally, Fred Lutz, in "Malamud's Art Celebrated Life," written the

same year as Malamud's death, comments on "Idiots First":

> After some pitifully realistic begging that has gone before, this mortal meeting [between Mendel and death at the train station] seems a breathtaking leap into sheer imaginative genius, with Malamud making his point in a kind of emotional explosion: If we care enough about those we love, our own well-being is only of secondary importance.

Cheryl Miller, in a 2008 essay in *Commentary* (the magazine in which "Idiots First" was first published), notes that Malamud's reputation with critics tended to decline in later years, even before his death. "From the mid-1950's through the late 60's," Miller notes, "he was considered a master of the American short story, and taken with the utmost seriousness as a novelist." But, contended Miller, "Malamud is regarded today, if he is regarded at all, as a chronicler of a time long past." Miller summarizes the reason for this decline:

> And here is the clue to the cause of Malamud's eclipse. He fell from literary grace because his entire sense of the world was powerfully antithetical to the cultural ethos of the times [i.e., the 1970s]. What could have been more out of step with a belief in liberating the demands of appetite and desire than Malamud's embrace of the need for renunciation, of forgoing the demands of appetite and liberating the demands of conscience?

CRITICISM

Michael J. O'Neal

O'Neal holds a PhD in English. In the following essay, he examines "Idiots First" as a biblical fable of Jewish experience.

To try to encapsulate the history of a major religious and ethnic community—in this case, the Jewish community—in the space of a brief essay is an exercise in futility, one that cannot do justice to that community. But at the risk of oversimplification, the history of Judaism might be characterized as one of rejection, expulsion, and diasporic wandering throughout a world indifferent to people's suffering. This history took on a new and more horrifying reality during the World War II–era Holocaust, when Bernard Malamud was in his late twenties and early thirties and just beginning his career as a writer. As Jewish writers tried to distill something essential about the Jewish diaspora, they often turned to fable and mysticism as the only way to put into words the nature of the Jewish encounter with the rest of the world. Malamud's "Idiots First" conforms to this tendency, for the story captures the Jewish experience in the form of a modern biblical fable, one that reaffirms the redemptive power of love.

Most readers will recognize the term *fable* from the stories of Aesop, the legendary Greek figure who wrote brief stories intended to teach a moral lesson. In the modern world, the tradition of the fable, often complete with talking animals, continues to be used, but more realistic fiction writers tend to introduce "fabulous" elements in more subtle ways. Such is the case with Malamud in "Idiots First." The story takes

> **THE READER IS LEFT TO FEEL THAT ANYONE WHO FEELS LOVE, DEVOTION, AND LOYALTY WITH THE SAME INTENSITY AS MENDEL DOES CAN STAVE OFF DESPAIR, DARKNESS, AND NOTHINGNESS."**

place in a forbidding and foreboding atmosphere, a chilly, windy Friday evening in November, the first hours of the sabbath. The story emphasizes darkness: "Isaac looked at one dark window, then at the other.... They went slowly down the darkly lit stairs.... The November night was cold and bleak." Further, the cityscape appears to be almost abandoned, as though an apocalypse has taken place. Throughout the story, Mendel and Isaac wander through a cold, dismal, indifferent landscape, enacting their own version in miniature of a diaspora.

The indifference of their urban world is reinforced by the reactions of most of the other characters to their needs. After they leave their New York City apartment, Mendel and his son arrive at a pawnshop. There, Mendel hopes to pawn his gold watch for enough money to supplement his savings (contained in a paper bag he carries with him) so that he can buy a train ticket to California for Isaac; it seems no accident that Mendel is forced to send his son about as far away as it would be possible for him to go, emphasizing again the diasporic nature of the Jewish experience. The symbolic significance of a man pawning a timepiece when he is marked for death is apparent. Mendel's hope is that he can exchange the limited amount of time he has left for an act of filial love—his effort to provide for Isaac in the best way that he can after his own death. (*Mendel*, incidentally, is a Yiddish variant of the Hebrew name *Menachem*, meaning "one who comforts.") The pawnbroker, however, is mercenary. He is indifferent to Mendel's plight. He violates the Old Testament Mosaic law as it pertains to moneylending by apparently taking advantage of Mendel. When Mendel protests, the pawnbroker sarcastically advises him to see "Rothschild," the name of a prominent Jewish banking dynasty, whose

WHAT DO I READ NEXT?

- One of Malamud's most frequently anthologized short stories is "The Magic Barrel," first published in 1954 and included in his 1958 collection of the same title. It tells the story of a rabbinical student, Leo Finkle, who decides he needs a wife. He meets a matchmaker who may (or may not) have supernatural powers.

- Malamud's 1952 novel *The Natural* is unique among the author's works in that it does not focus on Jewish characters or themes. It tells the story of baseball phenomenon Roy Hobbs, who is shot by a mysterious woman, leaves baseball because of his injury, and then makes a dramatic comeback with the struggling New York Knights. The story is highly mythologized, and many critics see similarities between the novel and the Perceval legend of the twelfth century, one of the chief stories in the legends of King Arthur and the Knights of the Round Table.

- Markus Zusak's young-adult novel *The Book Thief* (2005) is set in Nazi Germany during World War II. The story is narrated by Death, who relates the story of Liesel, a young German girl who steals books and tells stories to keep up the spirits of her foster family, her neighbors, and a Jewish man her family is hiding.

- Philip Roth is a prominent Jewish American novelist whose 2006 novel *Everyman* (for which he became the only writer ever to win a third PEN/Faulkner Award) is a meditation on aging, illness, and death.

- In "The Masque of the Red Death" (1842), a short story by American author Edgar Allan Poe, an allegorical figure of death (perhaps representing the bubonic plague, or Black Death) confronts people at a ball. A great ebony clock rings out the hours of

life, just as "Idiots First" frequently marks the passage of time.

- Yoel Hoffmann is the editor and compiler of a volume titled *Japanese Death Poems: Written by Zen Monks and Haiku Poets on the Verge of Death* (1998). The book collects *jisei*, or death poems, a major poetic genre in Japanese literature, providing a different cultural view of the immanence of death in comparison with that of "Idiots First."

- Tzvi C. Marx's *Disability in Jewish Law* (2002), part of Routledge's Jewish Law in Context series, examines the treatment of disabilities in halakha, or Jewish law, tracing the obligations of the Jewish community to people like Isaac with disabilities.

- Readers interested in the history of pawnbrokers and anti-Semitic stereotypes of Jewish moneylenders as predatory will find Wendy A. Woloson's *In Hock: Pawning in America from Independence through the Great Depression* (2009) informative.

- Langston Hughes's "Ballad of the Pawnbroker" (1942), in which the speaker tries to pawn his father's gold watch (just as Mendel pawns a watch), offers insight into the relationship between the Jewish and African American communities during the mid-twentieth century.

- Samuel C. Heilman's *Portrait of American Jews: The Last Half of the Twentieth Century* (1995) is a sociological examination of what it has meant to be Jewish in America. The author emphasizes that, in many ways, Jewish identity is being eroded and that a shrinking number of American Jews know and adhere to the values, beliefs, and traditions of earlier generations of Jews.

---

wealth would reduce people such as Mendel to insignificance. In the face of the pawnbroker's indifference, Mendel and Isaac resume their diaspora through the cold night of the city, in much the same way as the Jews of the Hebrew Bible faced rejection and exile.

Their next stop is Upper Manhattan and the home of the Fishbeins. Upper Manhattan is a vaguely defined area of the borough of Manhattan, generally referring to Manhattan's more northerly stretches. The story does not specify whether the travelers are on the Upper East Side or Upper West Side. The Upper West Side historically has been seen as home to the city's cultural and artistic elite, while the Upper East Side is where prominent business and commercial leaders reputedly lived, so Malamud perhaps envisioned his characters traveling to the Upper East Side to visit Mr. Fishbein. In either case, they would be in an affluent section of the city, one dotted at the time with elaborate mansions.

Once again, however, the wanderers meet with rejection. The servant, Levinson, treats them with disdain. After he relents and grants them admission to the home's foyer, Fishbein appears. He appears to be a wealthy philanthropist, but he holds his philanthropy at arm's length, telling Mendel that he donates his money only to organized charities, not to individuals in need. He offers food to Mendel and his son, but the gesture seems cold after he tells them that they can go downstairs to eat; some readers may detect an echo of the biblical parable of Lazarus begging for crumbs from the table of the rich man. (This parable is found in the Christian New Testament, but it had parallels in the midrashim of Jewish tradition.) When Mendel falls to his knees to beg, Fishbein calls the servant to expel the visitors. Throughout he is indifferent to Isaac, calling him a "halfwit" and recommending that Mendel send his son to an institution for care—an attitude in marked contrast to Mendel's willingness to assume care for his son.

The diaspora resumes. The next stop is the synagogue, but even here, Mendel and his son meet with rejection, in this case from the sexton. Once again, however, Mendel's persistence in the face of desperate odds allows him to get his foot in the door, as the sexton directs Mendel to the nearby home of the rabbi and his wife. The greedy wife refuses to have anything to do with Mendel, but the rabbi, reflecting the power of divine love, reassures Mendel that "God will give you" the money needed. The rabbi himself is unable to give Mendel money, but he gives him instead a valuable fur-lined caftan, which enables Mendel to purchase the train ticket for Isaac (although the story is unclear how this comes about). As he struggles with the rabbi's wife

over the caftan, Mendel directs what amounts to an anti-Semitic slur at her, calling her Shylock. Shylock, a central character in Shakespeare's play *The Merchant of Venice*, is a Jewish moneylender whose name has become synonymous with stereotypes of avarice and greed. Note that the incident involving the caftan echoes the biblical verse from the book of Luke (3:11 in the New International Version): "John answered, 'The man with two tunics should share with him who has none, and the one who has food should do the same.'" This New Testament precept has parallels in the Hebrew Bible, particularly the book of Isaiah (58:7).

Throughout "Idiots First," the reader learns that Mendel's life has been difficult, putting the reader in mind of the story of Job and his many tribulations in the biblical book of Job. Mendel's health has not been good, he had to work hard, and he is poor. Lacking even enough money to buy a train ticket for his son, he has to pawn his watch and then has to beg on his knees. Mendel has also had to care for a mentally disabled son for thirty-nine years. Now, in the final hours of his life, he is being pursued by death in the figure of the bearded and burly Ginzburg, who also gives expression to the notion of an indifferent universe. When Mendel worries about what will happen to Isaac, Ginzburg responds, "What will happen happens. This isn't my responsibility." When Mendel asks him what his responsibility is, he replies, "To create conditions. To make happen what happens." He goes on to say that pity "ain't my commodity. The law is the law." Mendel asks him what law he is referring to. Ginzburg replies, "The cosmic universal law." The suggestion is that the suffering, poverty, rejection, expulsion, and ultimately death that form the warp and woof of Mendel's life, and by extension the life of Jews, are part of an implacable and inevitable cosmic scheme.

And yet, for all its cold and dark, its bleakness and despair, "Idiots First" is ultimately a hopeful story. Throughout, references to the number of stars that dot the sky and to the moon help to counterbalance the dark mournfulness of the setting. Most important, however, is the single-minded persistence of Mendel. In spite of all his hardships, including ill health, the death of his wife, the mental disability of his son, and his own impending death, Mendel trudges on. His sole goal, born entirely of filial

Mendel is able to buy his son a train ticket by the end of the story and knows that he is on his way to a safe new home. *(© Tatiana Morozova | ShutterStock.com)*

devotion, is to provide for the care of his son, whose name puts the reader in mind of the Isaac in the Hebrew Bible, the valued son born to the long-awaiting Abraham and Sarah. At no point does Mendel lament his fate or curse his God. He explains his need to the characters he encounters matter-of-factly, without bitterness or rancor.

Only at the end, in his struggle with death in the person of Ginzburg, does Mendel refer to himself. But even then, he does so in the context of a "father's heart." Because of his sheer tenacity, he is able to make even death back down, at least for the moment. As death stares into Mendel's eyes, he "beheld a shimmering, starry, blinding light that produced darkness." At this point, the reader begins to see that the heavens and the stars, points of light in an otherwise bleak universe, reaffirm the existence of God. (And the reader should note that the Jewish sabbath traditionally ends when stars appear in the sky on Saturday evening.) The reader is left to feel that anyone who feels love, devotion, and loyalty with the same intensity as Mendel does can stave off despair, darkness, and nothingness.

Source: Michael J. O'Neal, Critical Essay on "Idiots First," in *Short Stories for Students*, Gale, Cengage Learning, 2014.

Cynthia Ozick

In the following essay, Ozick recalls her acquaintance with Malamud and discusses his reluctance to be labeled a Jewish writer.

In 1976 I answered the telephone and heard privately an instantly recognizable public voice. I knew this voice with the intimacy of passionate reverence. I had listened to it in the auditorium of the 92nd Street Y reading an as yet unpublished tale called "The Silver Crown," a story so electrifying that I wished with all my heart that it was mine. Since it was not, I stole it. In my version, I described the author of the stolen story as "very famous, so famous that it was startling to see he was a real man. He wore a conventional suit and tie, a conventional haircut and conventional eyeglasses. His whitening mustache made him look conventionally distinguished. He was not at all as I had expected him to be—small and astonished, like his heroes."

His voice on the telephone was also not what I had expected. Instead of bawling me out for usurping his story, he was calling me with something else in mind. He had noticed that the dedication to a collection containing the stolen story was to my daughter, who was then ten years old. "Joy of my life," I had written. "I have to tell you," he said, "that I understand just how you feel." And he spoke of his own joy in being the father of his own children—but in such a way that it was clear he understood love as something both particularized and capacious, belonging to everyone. The more you have of it yourself, the more you see it everywhere. A magic barrel. When after a while we hung up, I recognized that I had been visited through this awkward instrument by an angel. I had been blessed, anointed, by an illumination of generosity fetched up out of the marrow of human continuity. Malamundian annunciations are not overly fussy, and are sometimes willing to materialize as birds or talking horses or even on the telephone.

After that, it became possible to say hello on occasion, face to face. But I always found this difficult. His largeness afflicted my courage. This, after all, was the very writer who had brought into being a new American idiom of his own idiosyncratic invention; this was the writer who had introduced the idea of blessing—a virtue as insight, virtue as crucible—into the literature of a generation mainly sunk in aestheticism or nihilism or solipsism. The last time I saw him on a public platform—he was standing before the historic lectern at Cooper Union—he was reading from a work in progress, and since this was not so long ago, I imagine a grieving table upon which an unfinished chapter liturgically murmurs its loss. That meticulous and original hand will not come again. The reading at Cooper Union: a straight back, a straightforward voice, tricky cadences hidden in it, an audience intensely alert to the significance of its own memory, taking in Presence and sending back the hunger of its homage. Afterward, there was, as always, the knot of admirers at his margins. But I fled him, afraid of so much light.

Consequently, I never learned, or never dared, to say "Bern." So I settled on "Maestro," and it seemed just right, not merely because it reflected the stories with Italian landscapes but because he is, and always will be, one of our Masters.

Is he an American Master? Of course. He not only wrote in the American language, he augmented it with fresh plasticity, he shaped our English into startling new configurations. Is he a Jewish Master? Of course. Some people appear to be confused by why he resisted being called a Jewish writer. I think I have this figured out, and it may be simple enough. It troubled him, and he was right to be troubled, that the term *Jewish writer* sometimes carries with it the smudge of so-called ethnicity, a cataloguing of traits or vulnerabilities in place of meaning. *Jewish writer* is a usage that often enough smacks of parochialism. And when it is put to that purpose it is a plain lie. The Jewish spirit is the opposite of ethnicity or parochialism, and this cry out of Sinai is all over the Maestro's work. It is everywhere.

"The important thing," Morris Bober says to Frank Alpine, "is the Torah. This is the Law—a Jew must believe in the Law...This means to do what is right, to be honest, to be good, this means to other people. Our life is hard enough. Why should we want to hurt somebody else? For everybody should be the best, not only for you and me. We ain't animals. This is why we need the Law. This is what a Jew believes." Artists are never equivalent to their own characters, this goes without saying; but it is also true that to separate certain characterological strains from the blood and lungs of their maker is to do violence to the force of authorial conscience. Morris Bober is the whole soul of Malamud's sacral knowledge; no one can gainsay that. And in his own language, in the preface of *The Stories of Bernard Malamud*, he wrote: "And let me say this. Literature, since it values man by describing him, tends to morality in the same way that Robert Frost's poems are 'a momentary stay against confusion.' Art celebrates life and gives us our measure." So if this Maestro of humanity protested the phrase *Jewish writer*, it was the imputation of parochialism he was, with furious justice, repudiating. Whoever thinks of Jewish writers as "ethnic" has long ago lost the origin, intent, and meaning of our civilization; or, worse yet, believes that conscience and mercy are ethnic traits.

I danced with him once. We linked arms— wasn't this in Donald Barthelme's living room in the Village?—and twirled together. It was a wedding party, and the only music available was in the strong throat of the Israeli writer Matti

Megged, who sang in Yiddish, a song about a frolicsome rabbi with certain affinities to Old King Cole. The Rabbi Eli Melech calls for his fiddlers, his drummers, his cymbal-players; his phylacteries fly from him, his robes; he goes rollicking with the sexton, he cavorts, he carouses, he drinks! To this tune the Maestro and I danced, arm in arm, and will do it again, I trust, when the International PEN Congress meets at last in the Garden of Eden, in Paradise.

He wrote about suffering Jews, about poor Jews, about grocers and fixers and birds and horses and angels in Harlem and matchmakers and salesmen and rabbis and landlords and tenants and egg candlers and writers and chimpanzees; he wrote about the plentitude and unity of the world. And that is why, in his memory and for his sake, I want to recite the Shi'ma, which calls us to listen to the indivisible voice of Unity, of Allness—that Unity and Allness in whose image all mankind is made, well-worn words that are found on the living and dying lips of every Jew

> . . . [Hear, O Israel, the Lord our God, the Lord is One]

—that comprehensive vision of mercy under whose wings we stand. May the memory of this great and humane Master be blessed and forever green. As it will be, as long as there are readers. . . .

Source: Cynthia Ozick, "Remembrances: Bernard Malamud," in *The Magic Worlds of Bernard Malamud*, edited by Evelyn Avery, State University of New York Press, 2001, pp. 25–27.

Robert Solotaroff

In the following excerpt, Solotaroff looks at Mendel's journey in "Idiots First" as a spiritual quest.

By the late 1950s Malamud likely felt that the characteristic strategies of the fiction of the folk ghetto would serve more to imprison his imagination than release it, and it was time to move on. On the whole he moved into more realistic modes. Unlike his first two novels, *A New Life*, which he wrote between 1958 and late 1960 or early 1961, is set in a particular time, and in a particular political climate. When the novel's protagonist, S. Levin, steps off a train on the last Sunday in August 1950, he has to add to his own "backlog of personal insecurity his portion of the fear that presently overwhelmed America. The country was frightened silly of Alger Hiss and Whittaker

> **MENDEL IS PITTED AGAINST NATURAL LAW, THE PHYSICAL WORLD, AND CONTEMPORARY MANNERS."**

Chambers, Communist spies and Congressional committees, flying saucers and fellow travelers, their friends and associates, and those who asked them for a match or the time of day." The setting is neither the surreal product of the collision between the contemporary mythology of baseball and past mythologies (as in *The Natural*) or the folk ghetto of *The Assistant*. Even if we did not know from Malamud's life or the geographic and academic details that Eastchester, Cascadia, *is* Corvallis, Oregon, we can recognize the setting easily enough: a mediocre English department of the state agricultural college, in an attractive small town, in beautiful natural surroundings. In short, Malamud tried for the first time to dramatize his abiding moral concerns against the manners and relative affluence of a representative slice of post–World War II America.

The novel completed, Malamud turned again to writing stories. In the first of these, "Idiots First," which was published in *Commentary* in December 1961, he temporarily retreated from realism and set the tale in a New York that is even more expressionistically abstracted than the stylized New Yorks of the earlier stories of the folk ghetto or of *The Assistant*. But "Idiots First" proved to be the last fictional work set in a folk New York. Later stories, like "The Jewbird" (1963) and "The Silver Crown" (1972), contain Jews (one of them a talking bird) who do—or seem to do—amazing things in New York, but the setting is very much a recognizable, contemporary New York, with Jewish leading characters who have assimilated into vocations like teaching high school or selling frozen foods.

When Malamud's second collection of stories, *Idiots First*, came out in 1963, the degree to which he was setting his moral fables in the here and now was somewhat obscured by the fact that he included two stories of suffering Jewish shopkeepers—"The Cost of Living" and "The Death of Me"—that he had published in the early 1950s. But Malamud's tendency to write in a more realistic mode than he employed in the fifties makes itself felt in all of the other stories save "Idiots First." "Black Is My Favorite Color" deals with interactions between New York Jews and blacks, as does "Angel Levine," but no softening gauzes of fantasy and dialect humor are laid over the hard realities of their interactions. "The German Refugee" once again recounts the grim consequences of not extending enough credit, but in a context of precisely noted historical and cultural dislocation. In "A Choice of Profession" the protagonist seeks a new life in the same profession and in the same general locale as the protagonist of Malamud's most recent novel.

As for the four stories in the collection that are set in Italy, Malamud used Italian life somewhat differently than he did in the Italian stories of *The Magic Barrel*. In each of the three earlier stories a relatively young American male must confront the moral consequences of his Jewish or American identity. "Still Life" and "Naked Nude," which I discuss in the next chapter, do not particularly deal with moral concerns. In "The Maid's Shoes" an American law professor is, like Carl Schneider of "Behold the Key," unwillingly pulled into the complexities of Italian life, but no moral revelations surface for him. He is sixty and seems to have had a good sense of the limitations of his sympathies before he arrived in Rome. No American appears in the fourth story, "Life Is Better Than Death."

Though the characters of "Idiots First" uncharacteristically roam through the city, the story culminates some of the earlier strategies of the fiction of the folk ghetto. More than all of the earlier protagonists save Manischevitz of "Angel Levine," Mendel is driven by an immediate need for an ironically qualified end, and it is this need that propels the story's feverish physical movement. The old, wasted man must on the last night of his life raise the thirty-five dollars he still needs to send Isaac, his thirty-nine-year-old idiot son, to the improbable care of an eighty-one-year-old uncle in California. But the minute that he needs to put his son on the train is denied him in the name of "the cosmic universal law, goddamit, the one I got to follow myself" (*IF*). The speaker is Ginzburg, the angel of death, at that moment in the uniform of a ticket collector in Pennsylvania Station. Unmoved by Mendel's pleas that his lifetime of suffering has earned him the minute's respite, Ginzburg refuses to open the iron gate. "You bastard, don't you understand what it means human?" Mendel incongruously cries as he tries to choke the angel of death.

Like Hawthorne, Malamud often uses visual or reflecting images to signal that a particular degree of realism is swerving further into fantasy or allegory. At this point, as Ginzburg is blasting the old man with his icy, killing gaze, Malamud pushes a story that is already fantastic into one of his most extended reaches:

> Clinging to Ginzburg in his last agony, Mendel saw . . . that Ginzburg, staring at himself in Mendel's eyes, saw mirrored in them the extent of his own awful wrath. He beheld a shimmering, starry, blinding light that produced darkness. . . .
>
> His grip on the squirming old man slowly loosened, and Mendel, his heart barely beating, slumped to the ground.
>
> "Go." Ginzburg muttered, "take him to the train." (*IF*)

Who is the "he" who beholds the starry blinding light? The story works best if it is Ginzburg, particularly since Malamud brilliantly relates the many light-dark images in the story to the angel of death. But have we for the only time in the story moved into someone else's mind besides Mendel's? Or are we to believe that the old man has seen what Ginzburg is seeing (as well as his own reflected image in the angel of death's eyes)? The *reality* of the moment becomes as evasive as the color we see when we close our eyes. It is during this breakdown of our resolutely binary, either-or mode of thinking that Malamud, like the nineteenth-century Russian and Yiddish writers he loved, seems to be asking us to believe, for an instant, that even ahuman, inhuman universal law must for an instant bend and recognize "what it means human" if the petitioner has suffered enough and is desperately enough committed to his just cause. Manischevitz lunges into irrationality, Mendel into violence; but each release is actually a clinging, a heightened commitment to otherness—for Malamud the glue that holds together the moral world.

The spiritual quests of some of his characters have caused some critics to place Malamud in the Kafka tradition. For me Malamud is most Kafkaesque when, as in "Idiots First," he transforms the external world so that it mirrors his characters' troubled inner lives and, above all, when he creates a fictional world that emphasizes the human animal's radical homelessness in the world. Two of the authors' aphorisms—Kafka's

"In the fight between you and the world bet on the world" and Malamud's "Der oilem iz a goilem (The world is a monster)" (*TA*)—have a good deal in common. But we must be aware of a crucial difference. For all of his pessimism, Malamud possessed a humanist streak that the Czech genius lacked. Either Malamud's spiritual strugglers never seek supernatural comfort and validation or they eventually realize that the ethical and spiritual exist only through human efforts.

"Idiots First" strikes me as Malamud's most heightened plea for human possibility. Mendel is pitted against natural law, the physical world, and contemporary manners. Even the idiot son he is trying to help symbolically opposes his father, yet Mendel "wins." The primary adversary is, of course, Ginzburg, but Malamud also bestows various attributes of the angel of death to all but one of the other humans Mendel meets during the three main encounters that precede the climactic one with Ginzburg: with a pawnbroker, with the philanthropist Fishbein and his servant, and with an aged rabbi, his sexton, and his wife. The exception is the rabbi, who donates the coat that Mendel pawns for the rest of the money he needs for Isaac's ticket. The rabbi shares what we know of Mendel's appearance: Mendel has wasted arms, the rabbi is skinny; both are old and have weak hearts. Apart from his arms, we only know that Mendel's lips are cracked. Since the story is so clearly an allegory, with the party of humane concern (Mendel and the rabbi) pitted against the party of indifference (Ginzburg and all other characters in the story), the stripping from Mendel of physical attributes—save a few details that emphasize his vulnerability—achieves several purposes. First, the strategy asserts the force of his inner life, best expressed by his commitment to place his son before he dies. Second, it allies all others, with their more detailed physical attributes, with Ginzburg and places them in the party of death, of annihilation of the moral urge.

In his guise as a ticket collector, Ginzburg is "a bulky, bearded man with hairy nostrils and a fishy smell" (*IF*). His beard is black, his eyes glitter, and he cynically disclaims responsibility, usually by uttering clichés: "The law is the law.. .. You ain't the only one[;] . . . some got it worse than you. That's how it goes in this country" (*IF*). He is associated with food, both by the fish smell and by the fact that Mendel and Isaac are

driven from a cafeteria by the sight of him eating as he sits.

His black beard is echoed by the red one of the pawnbroker, who will give Mendel only eight dollars for his gold watch, his hairy nostrils by Fishbein's. In fact, enough is made of the black hair of Ginzburg's beard and nostrils to associate with him all possessors of hair: Fishbein's servant with his long sideburns; the rabbi's gray-haired wife who fights with Mendel for the coat. She also shares Ginzburg's bulkiness and glittering eyes. The pawnbroker also eats fish. Apart from Fishbein's name, his concern with his dinner, his "fixed policy" (*IF*) of denying individual requests for charity, and his paunch also ally him with Ginzburg.

Even Isaac is of the party of resistance. His concern about eating, the references to his eyes and thick hair, his idiot's ignorance of what his father has done for him ally him more with Ginzburg than with his father. Much of the moral grandeur of Mendel's commitment follows from the absurdity of expecting any gratitude from his son. The dying man's last two statements in the story are to tell Isaac to remember his mother and father, and to tell the conductor "Be nice to him, . . . Show him where everything is." But as the train leaves, Isaac does not even turn to say good-bye to his father; his face is "strained in the direction of his journey" (*IF*). All Mendel has left is Ginzburg, whom he seeks in the last sentence of the story.

What is nonhuman in the story seems icily or malevolently resistant to Mendel's attempt to assert the humane in the inhuman world we inhabit. The clock that stops in the first sentence of the story, the "cold embittered clothing" (*IF*) the old man puts on, the remote stars and moon, the uncanny tree whose surrealistically altered branches serve to shorten the amount of time Mendel has left, the gates over the pawnbroker's windows—all these point toward the iron gates of Pennsylvania Station that block Isaac's way to the train. My discussion of this great story gives little sense of its visionary intensity, and the wonderfully apt gradations of tone and image within its rush toward the moment of Mendel and Ginzburg locked in each others' arms before the closed gates. . . .

Source: Robert Solotaroff, "*Idiots First*," in *Bernard Malamud: A Study of the Short Fiction*, Twayne Publishers, 1989, pp. 67–71.

Mark Shechner

In the following excerpt, Shechner reviews The Stories of Bernard Malamud and defines Malamud as a specifically Jewish writer.

. . . Any doubts we may have had about Bernard Malamud's stature as a modern master should be dispelled by this collection of his stories. This personal selection of twenty-five stories presents Malamud at his best—as a writer of eloquent and poignant vignettes. Though Malamud has published seven novels, each one touched with his distinctive laconic grace, the short story remains the purest distillation of his abiding leitmotif: the still, sad music of humanity. Typically, the Malamud story is an epiphany of disappointment and failure, a document of the half-life—the shabby region of mediocre existence just a notch above pure disaster— bathed in the melodies of despair, in the taut, concise adagios of woe. By and large, however, Malamud's range of characters and situations has been too narrow to sustain longer constructions. Lacking variety and any feel for the architecture of sustained fiction, his novels hold the note of sorrow too long, until what had begun as a lamentation ends as a *kvetch*. But in the short story, Malamud achieves an almost psalmlike compression. He has been called the Jewish Hawthorne, but he might just as well be thought a Jewish Chopin, a prose composer of preludes and nocturnes.

The Malamud character is one we've long since come to recognize: the underground man transposed into a small merchant or retiree or pensioner. He is commonly alone, or beset by family, creditors, or customers (he seldom has friends). He runs a grocery, a deli, a candy store where the cash register is always empty and the accounts receivable book full. His sons, if he has sons, avoid him; his daughters, like Lear's, are ungrateful, and there is no Cordelia to love him in spite of himself. He may have a heart condition, like Mendel in "Idiot's First," or Marcus the tailor in "The Death of Me," or Mr. Panessa in "The Loan," or he may take his own life, like Rosen the ex-coffee salesman in "Take Pity," or Oskar Gassner in "The Jewish Refugee." At his most wretched he is a Jewbird, black as a caftan, fishy as a herring, and cursed/blessed with the powers of flight, though he longs only for the comforts of a home. With few exceptions, he is miserable, without hope, and waiting for death. Indeed, not only does the typical Malamud story end with death, but the keynote story in this collection, "Take Pity," begins with death, one that releases the character into a chamber of heaven that looks remarkably like a furnished room. Even death, it seems, brings no elevation.

This makes for anything but happy reading, and we might well ask why anyone would bother with a writer so insistently depressive, who peoples his stories with characters who exist for most of us only in memory and nightmare. That is not a simple question to answer, but we might begin with Malamud's own words. In one of the stories in this collection, "Man in the Drawer," Levitansky, a Russian-Jewish writer whose work cannot be published in the Soviet Union, entices an American journalist, Howard Harvitz, who is touring Russia, to read some of his stories. Harvitz, after much shilly-shallying, reads them and renders an approving judgment: "I like the primary, close-to-the-bone quality of the writing. The stories impress me as strong if simply wrought; I appreciate your feeling for the people and at the same time the objectivity with which you render them. It's sort of Chekhovian in quality, but more compressed, sinewy, direct, if you know what I mean." Levitansky, it appears, is a portrait of what Malamud himself might have been and have suffered had fate seen fit to send his grandparents east to Russia rather than west to America, and these terms of praise are Malamud's own terms for what is strong in his art.

. . . The initial impression Malamud gave in the 1950s, with his early stories in *The Magic Barrel* and the novels *The Natural* and *The Assistant*, was that of being a purveyor of Jewish admonitions. The novels in particular cast long, didactic shadows and ask us to judge some of their characters as deserving of their trials. Moreover, *The Natural* and *The Assistant*, as well as stories like "The Lady of the Lake," "Girl of My Dreams," and "The Magic Barrel," broadcast suggestions of a sexual moralism as well, though its exact nature is never spelled out. The sexual moralist in Malamud has been largely excluded from this collection, and where sex turns up in a moral equation, as it does in "God's Wrath" and "The Magic Barrel," it posits mysteries rather than precepts.

And yet Malamud *is* a moralist and an insistent one, though the law to which he binds his characters has little in it of noticeably Jewish content. It is the law of simple charity and compassion. Most of his characters either earn their misery through hardheartedness or are the victims of others'. Kessler, the former egg candler of "The Mourners," is quarrelsome and a troublemaker and is self-isolated in his tenement apartment. Rosen, the ex-coffee salesman in "Take Pity," has been driven to the grave by a widow who, out of misplaced pride, rejects his charity. Glasser, the retired shamus in "God's Wrath," has had poor luck with his children, and we may guess without being told that they had had no better luck with him. In story after story coldness is returned for love, a warm heart is battered by a cold one. The word "no" is the most powerful and bitter word in all of Malamud.

Malamud is quintessentially a Jewish writer, though there is nothing of religious belief and only the shards of ritual to be found in his writing and only *shmatas* of Jewish culture or history. Yet, for all that, his writing is so impregnated with Jewishness—as distinct from Judaism—that there can be no mistaking it. Sometimes it is the spectral Jewishness of Singer and Chagall, but more commonly it is the melancholy Jewishness of Roman Vishniac's photos of the old country in its last hours. In his modest and laconic style of narrative, Malamud has found the exact prose equivalent of the dull light and gray tones of Vishniac's world, a world exhausted by siege and conscious of its defeat.

Perhaps Malamud's Jewishness is best understood in terms of Matthew Arnold's definition of Hebraism, "strictness of conscience." By such a definition, Malamud is our leading Hebraist of letters, for strictness of conscience is as much his abiding theme as sorrow is his abiding disposition. But though Malamud treats it as a requirement of civilized existence, he often renders it as a curse, a habit of withholding that interdicts the normal flow of human feelings. Many of Malamud's characters treat others with a rabbinical harshness, though one detached from any conception of a sacramental life or, for that matter, a clear moral intention. They habitually ward off intimacy and often give the appearance of performing archaic rites that they have long since ceased to understand. A textbook approach to their "problem" might call them compulsive-neurotics, for they are case studies of conscience gone haywire....

Source: Mark Shechner, "Sad Music," in *Critical Essays on Bernard Malamud*, edited by Joel Salzberg, G. K. Hall, 1987, pp. 68–72.

Alan Warren Friedman

In the following excerpt, Friedman cites "Idiots First" as an example of Malamud's naturalism and humanism.

... Unlike both the theater of the absurd and the experimental novel of forty or so years ago, the contemporary novel of the antihero is not noticeably marked by distinctive style; its writers are more "realists" than are such technical innovators as Joyce and Virginia Woolf, even Conrad and Faulkner. But Malamud is of special interest for at least two reasons. First, his Jewish victims are not simply realistic, they are naturalistic almost to the point of predetermined misery. *The Fixer* is the *reductio ad absurdum* Naturalistic novel; Yakov Bok, the title character, is a Naturalistic victim-hero with a vengeance, and he not only inhabits but becomes a symbol for the lowest of "lower depths." Macbeth says, "I dare do all that may become a man; who dares do more is none." At the other end of the spectrum, Yakov Bok is stripped seemingly of all that separates man from the beasts below him: in his case, "who dares do less is none."

In addition, Malamud's superb understanding of the endlessly enduring Jewish spirit—simultaneously despairing and comic—best reveals itself in a masterful stylistic and thematic device I call "Talmudic tautology." It is a term easier to illustrate than to define. For example, in one of the short stories, a recent suicide named Rosen, in limbo awaiting judgment, is being questioned by Davidov the census taker about the death of a poor refugee grocer, the husband of the woman Rosen secretly loved:

> "How did he die?" Davidov spoke impatiently. "Say in one word."
> "From what he died?—he died that's all."
> "Answer, please this question."
> "Broke in him something. That's how."
> "Broke what?"
> "Broke what breaks. He was talking to me how bitter was his life...but the next minute his face got small and he fell down dead....I am myself a sick man and when I saw him laying on the floor, I said to myself, 'Rosen, say goodbye, this guy is finished.' So I said it."

Talmudic tautology, then, has the wit of a pun, the quiet bitterness of stoic resignation, the force of sudden truth; it accepts and expresses both the transcendence of God's ways and the essential crumminess of this world. "'What happened then?' [Davidov] asked. 'What happened?' mocked Rosen. 'Happened what happens.'"

Both *The Assistant* and *The Fixer* are founded on this note, this attitude; the universe, the given, is impossibly antithetical to human dignity and worth, and its impoverished creatures struggle gamely to make a go of things. And usually, as a consequence, out of the dungheap seemingly conducive only to despair, glimmers of values begin to assert and affirm themselves. The short story "Idiots First," for example, is a successful allegory of man's feeble, hopeless existence and the irrelevance of his death. Mendel, who knows he is to die this night, spends his last few hours scrounging for money to get his thirty-nine-year-old idiot son, Isaac, a train ticket to California—where eighty-one-year-old Uncle Leo, drinking tea with lemon under a warm sky, presumably waits to care for him. Mendel's steps are dogged by death in the person of Ginzburg, "a bulky, bearded man with hairy nostrils and a fishy smell," who turns out to be the ticket collector at the station and who refuses them access to the still-waiting train because it is after midnight—after, that is, the time when the train was *supposed* to leave and Mendel was *supposed* to be dead. As he has throughout the evening, Mendel, in anguish, once again cries out for compassion, for human relevance—and again receives rules for an answer. The millionaire he had earlier appealed to had told him, "I never give to unorganized charity," and now Ginzburg disclaims any responsibility for Isaac's helplessness.

> "What then is your responsibility?" [Mendel asks.]
>
> "To create conditions. To make happen what happens. I ain't in the anthropomorphic business."

But Mendel persists:

> "Whatever business you in, where is your pity?"
>
> "This ain't my commodity. The law is the law."
>
> "Which law is this?"
>
> "The cosmic universal law, goddamit, the one I got to follow myself."

But Mendel goes Job one better, for after having laid bare the essence of his misery, he refuses to accept inscrutability and power as a valid response. In desperation, he "lunged at Ginzburg's throat and began to choke. 'You bastard, don't you understand what it means human?'" And Ginzburg, though he laughs at Mendel at first, is as astounded as Mendel himself at the dying man's "awful wrath," and he accedes, allowing Mendel to put Isaac on the train and see the train depart. Only afterwards, "when the train was gone, [did] Mendel ascend . . . the stairs to see what had become of Ginzburg."

Scratch a naturalist then and you find a humanist. For Malamud, man has nothing but the misery and intensity of his suffering—but the point is that it *is* intense; he is committed to it because it defines his uniqueness, his humanness. As a consequence, he can—at least at odd moments—impose meaning where God has not. He can make the universe take notice of him and pay some attention to his claims. . . .

Source: Alan Warren Friedman, "The Hero as Schnook," in *Bernard Malamud and the Critics*, edited by Leslie A. Field and Joyce W. Field, New York University Press, 1970, pp. 289–91.

SOURCES

"Ann DeChiara Malamud, Helpmate to Writer, 89, Dies," in *New York Times*, March 22, 2007, http://www.nytimes.com/2007/03/22/obituaries/22malamud.html?_r=0 (accessed December 31, 2012).

Baumbach, Jonathan, "Bernard Malamud," in *Moderns and Contemporaries: Nine Masters of the Short Story*, edited by Jonathan Baumbach and Arthur Edelstein, Random House, 1968, pp. 305–306.

Berger, Joseph, "Aided by Orthodox, City's Jewish Population Is Growing Again," in *New York Times*, June 11, 2012, http://www.nytimes.com/2012/06/12/nyregion/new-yorks-jewish-population-is-growing-again.html?_r=0 (accessed January 3, 2013).

"Bernard Malamud Biography," in *Encyclopedia of World Biography* website, http://www.notablebiographies.com/Lo-Ma/Malamud-Bernard.html (accessed December 21, 2012).

Gealy, Marcia B., "Malamud's Short Stories: A Reshaping of Hasidic Tradition," in *Judaism*, Vol. 28, No. 1, 1979, pp. 51–61.

Hassan, Ihab, *Radical Innocence: Studies in the Contemporary American Novel*, Princeton University Press, 1961, pp. 161–62.

Jacobs, Louis, "Halakha," in *Jewish Virtual Library*, http://www.jewishvirtuallibrary.org/jsource/judaica/ejud_0002_0008_0_08206.html (accessed December 24, 2012).

"Jewish Population in the United States, 1960," North American Jewish Data Bank website, http://www.jewishdatabank.org/AJYB/AJY-1961.pdf (accessed May 20, 2013).

Kazin, Alfred, "Bernard Malamud: The Magic and the Dread," in *Contemporaries*, Atlantic–Little, Brown, 1962, pp. 202–207.

Lederhendler, Eli, "New York City, the Jews, and 'The Urban Experience,'" in *Studies in Contemporary Jewry*, Vol. 15, *People of the City*, edited by Ezra Mendelsohn, Oxford University Press, 1999, pp. 49–67, http://www.policyarchive.org/handle/10207/bitstreams/15008.pdf (accessed January 3, 2013).

Lelchuk, Alan, "Malamud's Dark Fable," in *New York Times Book Review*, August 29, 1982, pp. 1, 14–15.

Lutz, Fred, "Malamud's Art Celebrated Life," in *Blade*, April 13, 1986, pp. 1, 4.

Malamud, Bernard, "Idiots First," in *A Malamud Reader*, edited by Philip Rahv, Farrar, Straus and Giroux, 1967, pp. 403–13.

McMichael, George, ed., "Bernard Malamud," in *Anthology of American Literature*, 2nd ed., Vol. 2, *Realism to the Present*, Macmillan, 1980, pp. 1875–76.

Miller, Cheryl, "Why Malamud Faded," in *Commentary*, June 2008, http://www.commentarymagazine.com/article/why-malamud-faded/ (accessed December 30, 2012).

"New York Architecture Images," New York Architecture website, http://www.nyc-architecture.com/walks-ues.htm (accessed January 3, 2013).

"New York City Transit: History and Chronology," MTA.info, http://www.mta.info/nyct/facts/ffhist.htm (accessed January 3, 2013).

Remnick, David, "The Voice of a Natural: Bernard Malamud and His Miraculous Tales," in *Washington Post*, March 20, 1986, pp. D1, D8.

Rothstein, Mervyn, "Bernard Malamud Dies at 71," in *New York Times*, March 19, 1986, http://www.nytimes.com/1986/03/19/books/malamud-obit.html (accessed December 21, 2012).

Sarna, Jonathan D., and Jonathan Golden, "The American Jewish Experience in the Twentieth Century: Antisemitism and Assimilation," National Humanities Center website, http://www.nationalhumanitiescenter.org/tserve/twenty/tkeyinfo/jewishexpb.htm (accessed January 3, 2013).

"Statue of Liberty National Monument," Statue of Liberty and Ellis Island website, http://www.libertystatepark.com/emma.htm (accessed January 3, 2013).

Stern, Daniel, "Bernard Malamud, the Art of Fiction No. 52," in *Paris Review*, No. 61, Spring 1975, http://www.theparisreview.org/interviews/3869/the-art-of-fiction-no-52-bernard-malamud (accessed December 21, 2012).

Thompson, Bob, "For Roth, a 3rd PEN/Faulkner Win," in *Washington Post*, February 26, 2007, http://www.washingtonpost.com/wp-dyn/content/article/2007/02/25/AR2007022501608.html (accessed December 31, 2012).

FURTHER READING

Avery, Evelyn Gross, ed., *The Magic Worlds of Bernard Malamud*, SUNY Press, 2001.

This volume is a collection of essays by various Malamud scholars. It is part of the SUNY Series in Modern Jewish Literature and Culture.

Bloom, Harold, ed., *Bernard Malamud*, Chelsea House, 2000.

This volume is part of the Bloom's Modern Critical Views series. It contains critical essays that examine Malamud's major works. The volume also includes a biography of Malamud, a chronology of his life, and an introductory essay written by Bloom.

Chametzky, Jules, John Felstiner, Hilene Flanzbaum, and Kathryn Hellerstein, eds., *Jewish American Literature: A Norton Anthology*, Norton, 2000.

This volume is a comprehensive anthology of work by 145 Jewish American authors dating back to 1645. It includes fiction, poetry, drama, essays, letters, editorials, journals, autobiographies, cartoons, song lyrics, and jokes. Among the writers represented, along with Malamud, are Emma Lazarus, Nathanael West, Clifford Odets, Tillie Olsen, Saul Bellow, Grace Paley, Philip Roth, Allen Ginsberg, and Harold Bloom. More recent authors include Melvin Jules Bukiet, Jacqueline Osherow, Art Spiegelman, Steve Stern, and Allegra Goodman.

Davis, Philip, *Bernard Malamud: A Writer's Life*, Oxford University Press, 2010.

This is the first full-length biography of Malamud. Davis compiled it through exclusive interviews with colleagues, friends, and family. He also examined the author's private journals and letters and analyzed the author's working habits through detailed examination of previously unexamined manuscripts.

Lasher, Lawrence M., *Conversations with Bernard Malamud*, University Press of Mississippi, 1991.

This volume collects twenty-eight interviews Malamud gave to journalists, critics, and academic scholars. Included are comments on each of his novels and many of his short stories.

Sachar, Howard M., *A History of the Jews in America*, Vintage, 1993.

Sachar examines 350 years of Jewish experience in the United States. He chronicles the experiences of Marranos—Iberian Jews forced to convert to Christianity in the fifteenth century—

Russian revolutionaries, philanthropists, and Hollywood magnates. Sachar also explores major themes, including bigotry at the hands of the Christian majority, conflicts between Jewish communities of different origins and beliefs, and the Jewish struggle for acceptance in American life.

Smith, Janna Malamud, *My Father Is a Book: A Memoir of Bernard Malamud*, Houghton Mifflin Harcourt, 2006. The author, Malamud's daughter, published this memoir on the twentieth anniversary of her father's death. She opens up her father's unpublished letters and journals to focus on the key events in his life, the anguish he felt due to insecurity about his writing ability, and his sadness and even shame about his family upbringing.

SUGGESTED SEARCH TERMS

allegory

Bernard Malamud

fable AND Jewish literature

halakha

Isaac Bashevis Singer

Jewish American AND literature

Malamud AND Idiots First

Philip Roth

Saul Bellow

Yiddish

In Search of Epifano

"In Search of Epifano," by American writer Rudolfo Anaya, is about an old woman who drives from Southern California into the Mexican desert to find out what is left of the large ranch her great-grandfather Epifano built in the state of Chihuahua. Her life has been an unfulfilled one, and she journeys in search of her familial, ethnic, and spiritual roots in the Mexican desert. "In Search of Epifano" is an excellent example of Anaya's frequent subject matter, the rediscovery by Mexican Americans of their ethnic Mexican heritage, and demonstrates his use of mythical and symbolic elements to convey his themes.

Anaya's story was first published in *Voces: An Anthology of Nuevo Mexicano Writers* in 1987. It was reprinted in *Iguana Dreams: New Latino Fiction* (1992), *The Anaya Reader* (1995), and Anaya's collection of short stories *The Man Who Could Fly and Other Stories* (2006).

RUDOLFO ANAYA

1987

AUTHOR BIOGRAPHY

Novelist, short-story writer, poet, and essayist Rudolfo Alfonso Anaya was born to Martin and Rafaelita (Mares) Anaya on October 30, 1937, in Pastura, a village in eastern New Mexico. The family moved to Santa Rosa, New Mexico, soon after Anaya's birth. Anaya was the youngest of four brothers, and he had six sisters

Rudolfo Anaya (© *ZUMA Wire Service | Alamy*)

(three siblings were from his parents' previous marriages). The family spoke Spanish, and Anaya spoke Spanish exclusively as a child until the age of six. The family moved again in 1952 to Albuquerque, where the fifteen-year-old Anaya attended a public school, graduating in 1956. After graduation, he attended Browning Business School for two years and then enrolled in the University of New Mexico, from which he received a bachelor of arts degree in 1963. For five years, until 1968, he taught English in Albuquerque's public schools. He married Patricia Lawless in 1966 and received a master's degree in English from the University of New Mexico in 1968. He also acquired a master's degree in guidance and counseling from the same university in 1972, after which he was appointed director of counseling at the university.

Anaya's first novel, *Bless Me, Ultima*, a coming-of-age story that reflects his Mexican American heritage, was published in 1972. It received the Premio Quinto Sol National Chicano Literary Award and established Anaya's

literary reputation. In 1974, he began teaching in the department of English at the University of New Mexico. Two more novels followed in the 1970s: *Heart of Aztlan* (1976), which draws on Aztec myths and legends, and *Tortuga* (1979). The latter won an American Book Award from the Before Columbus Foundation in 1980. The novella *The Legend of La Llorona*, a fictional exploration of the life of La Malinche, the consort of Hernán Cortés, the Spaniard who led the conquest of Mexico in the sixteenth century, was published in 1984. *Lord of the Dawn: The Legend of Quetzalcóatl*, about the deity worshipped in Mexico before the conquest, followed in 1987. In the meantime, Anaya had published his first collection of short stories, *The Silence of the Llano*, in 1982 and an epic poem, *The Adventures of Juan Chicaspatas*, in 1985. The story "In Search of Epifano" was published in *Voces: An Anthology of Nuevo Mexicano Writers* in 1987 and was reprinted in Anaya's second short-story collection, *The Man Who Could Fly and Other Stories*, in 2006.

Anaya's next novel, *Alburquerque* (1992), received the PEN Center West Fiction Award the following year, which was also the year Anaya retired from teaching. He continued to write, and the novels *Zia Summer* and *Rio Grande Fall* followed in 1995 and 1996, respectively, and *Jalamanta: A Message from the Desert* also came out in 1996. As of 2013, Anaya's most recent novel was *Randy Lopez Goes Home* (2011). Anaya has also written ten children's books; a travel journal; six plays, including *Matachines* (1992); and nonfiction essays, thirteen of which appeared in *The Anaya Reader* in 1995.

Anaya has received many awards and fellowships. They include an honorary doctorate from the University of Albuquerque (1981); the New Mexico Governor's Public Service Award (1978 and 1980); the New Mexico Governor's Award for Excellence and Achievement in Literature (1980); the President's National Salute to American Poets and Writers (1980); and a Kellogg Foundation Fellowship (1983–1985).

PLOT SUMMARY

The unnamed protagonist of "In Search of Epifano" is a woman who is nearly eighty years old. In the oppressive heat of summer, she is driving in her Jeep from the Sonoran Desert in Southern

California into the Mexican desert, heading for the land of the Tarahumaras. The Tarahumaras are Native Americans who live in northwestern Mexico. The woman knows she will always be welcomed there.

The Jeep is not in good condition and has already broken down once, which delayed her by several days. The narrator mentions that the woman has Mexican blood. Her great-grandfather Epifano was Mexican, and he had traveled north to Chihuahua (a state in northern Mexico) and built a large ranch there. She carries pictures of him and his family. As she drives on she is hot but feels fully alive in the desert setting. It is not the first time she has been there. But she is worried by the Jeep, which is not performing well. The Mexican garage mechanic had warned her about it. She had stayed at a hotel while he repaired the vehicle, and she had dreamed of Mexico and its atmosphere. Now she rests and dreams again and this time hears the voice of Epifano. She sees his eyes and remembers him. Everyone else in the family had forgotten about him and had forgotten their Mexican roots. But she has not forgotten.

She drives along a dirt road in the desert while vultures fly overhead. She thinks back over her life. She had married young, but the marriage had not been satisfying. She took up hobbies such as painting and travel and began to realize that she and her husband were not suited to each other. Recalling her wedding, she remembers that she saw an Indian standing at the back of the chapel. He was only there for a moment, and she was not even sure if she was just imagining his presence. But she did not forget him and wondered if he was a messenger from her great-grandfather. During her marriage she fulfilled her duty and bore a son and a daughter. But her husband never understood her, and in her dreams she still heard the voice of Epifano. Eventually she left her husband, and she developed a habit of driving south each spring toward the Mexican desert. Her goal each year was to drive farther south and eventually to reach the place where Epifano's ranch had once stood.

She finally reaches her goal in the evening and drinks from a desert spring. There is nothing much left of Epifano's ranch, but she can discern where the foundation had been and the shape of the corrals. She feels sad. Then she hears a noise and turns, thinking it is an animal, but instead she

sees a tall Indian man. She tells him that she came searching for Epifano. He understands, and she sees in his bright blue eyes her great-grandfather. Then she sees more moving shadows and realizes they are women of the desert, who are about to form a circle and enact an old ceremony. She no longer feels sad. Instead, she feels as if a new light is penetrating her entire being.

CHARACTERS

Epifano

Epifano is the great-grandfather of the old woman. He was a Mexican, and he had moved north to Chihuahua, presumably as a young man, to build a ranch and to mine. He was, it appears, extremely successful; the ranch in the desert was a big one, and he built up quite a reputation. His great-granddaughter heard stories about him and his big ranch, and he became a revered figure in her life, even though she had never met him in person. She carries around with her a photograph of Epifano, pictured with his wife and sons. He seems to be a living presence in her life, and in her dreams she hears his voice. Epifano appears to have had a large family, and over the years they spread north from the ranch, reaching the United States and settling there. At the end of the story, Epifano appears as if in a vision to his great-granddaughter. He is tall, with bright blue eyes, and he wears paint, "as they did in the old days when they ran the game of the pelota up and down las montaas of the Caon de Cobre." (*Pelota* is a Spanish word meaning "ball.") He says nothing, but she believes that he knew she was going to come.

Garage Mechanic

The garage mechanic is the man who repairs the old woman's Jeep when it breaks down in Mexico. He tells her that in spite of the repair, the vehicle is not in good condition. He is concerned about her driving alone in the desert and advises her to return home. She ignores his advice and thinks he is just making excuses for the poor quality of his work.

Indian

The Indian is a mysterious figure. The woman thinks she sees him standing in the back of the chapel during her wedding ceremony. His appearance identifies him as a Tarahumara Indian from northwest Mexico. She looks into his eyes, and a moment later he disappears. She does not know whether he was real or she imagined him. She thinks he may be a messenger from Epifano.

Old Woman

The protagonist is an unnamed woman who is nearly eighty years old. She is a Mexican American whose family appears to have lived in Southern California for perhaps one or two generations. Her great-grandfather Epifano was Mexican. Some details of the course of this woman's life can be gleaned from the story. She seems to have had a fairly conventional but not a satisfying life. She married young, and from her description it seems that it was too young. She did not have much self-knowledge. She thought she was in love and seems to have been confident that her ambitious husband was the right choice. But over the years she realized that he was not a passionate man, and he could not fulfill her at any level of her life. To try to compensate for this lack she took to artistic pursuits and to travel. But that did not fill the void in her life. Realizing that her life lacked authenticity, that it was a sham, she left her husband. Although it appears that she was born and raised in California, she decided to leave that life behind. She seems to feel that she belongs not in the United States but in Mexico, where her family came from. Something about her ancestral heritage calls to her, and she drives into the Mexican desert to try to find some kind of connection with her great-grandfather. It is as if in her marriage she unknowingly departed from her ethnic and cultural roots, and she is driven to rediscover them late in life. The protagonist is clearly a very determined, independent kind of woman. She is not afraid to drive alone in an old vehicle into the hot desert. She knows what she is seeking. She is not prepared for her life to end without making one last effort to reconnect with her roots.

THEMES

Questing

The woman whose story is told is on a quest to rediscover the fullness of her being, which she associates with reconnecting to her ethnic heritage. The woman appears to be an American citizen whose family, which came to the United States a few generations earlier from Mexico,

has assimilated into Anglo-American culture and has forgotten its ancestral roots in Mexico. The woman has been disappointed in the most important area of her life. She married young, and the marriage was not happy. No details are given about the ethnicity of the man she married, but it seems likely that he was either not of Mexican descent or, if he was, paid no attention to his heritage. The key word about him is that he was ambitious, which suggests that he wanted to get on in the world, which would have meant identifying with Anglo rather than Mexican culture. Whatever the cause, the woman was unfulfilled in her marriage, and she left her husband. Over the years she began to realize that she had been ignoring the Mexican blood in her. She had become disconnected from her ethnic heritage, which she comes to identify as the deepest aspect of her being. She is helped in this by her memory of the Indian man she saw, whether in the flesh or in her imagination, at the back of the church during her wedding ceremony. The anonymous man, she comes to realize, is the link to her ethnic ancestry, the thread that she must chase back to its source.

The quest she embarks upon is to rediscover this connection to the Mexican element in her ancestry, which exists inside her but has long been buried. She remembers this, if no one else in her family does. The quest is a hard one physically, since she has to undertake an arduous drive alone in an unreliable vehicle into the desert. She must show courage, persistence, and overcome obstacles. But her quest ends with success. Because of her imaginative ability to enter into the spirit of the desert, she is rewarded with a vision of her Mexican ancestor, her great-grandfather, who welcomes her. As a result she feels a fulfillment of her being that she never had before as a wife and mother who had been cut off from her ethnic heritage.

Loneliness

Not counting Epifano, who appears only as a kind of vision; the woman's husband, who is very briefly described in a flashback; the garage mechanic, who plays a very minor role; and the Indian, who may not even be real, the old woman is the sole character in the story. She is a very isolated figure. She drives alone from California into the Mexican desert, where she finds more solitude ("sitting alone in the wide desert"). There is little doubt that she is lonely and has been for many years, perhaps most of

TOPICS FOR FURTHER STUDY

- Read either "Absalom" or "Children of the Desert," both short stories by Anaya, and write an essay in which you compare and contrast them with "In Search of Epifano." What elements do the stories have in common? How do they differ?

- Read *My Land Sings: Stories from the Rio Grande* (1999), written by Anaya and illustrated by Amy Córdova, which contains ten stories for young readers. Five are by Anaya and the remainder are his retellings of traditional tales. All the stories reflect Native American and Catholic-influenced Hispanic folklore of the Rio Grande valley in New Mexico. Pick one story and post a review of it on a blog, in which you write about why you liked or disliked the story and in what ways it is typical of Anaya's work. If you see any similarities to "In Search of Epifano" in theme, setting, or style, note that as well. Invite your friends to comment on your review, and also comment on theirs.

- Write a short story in which a young protagonist encounters something concerning his or her religious or cultural tradition that moves or changes the person in some way. The protagonist can be of any religion or ethnicity.

- In 2012, the school district of Tucson, Arizona, which has a high percentage of Mexican American students, suspended its Mexican American courses. The Arizona state legislature declared them illegal, saying they were too political and included bias against white people. With two other students, conduct Internet research on the history of this controversy. Consult at least six online news articles from mainstream sources. Then give a class presentation in which you describe the issues and the latest developments. Start your research with this January 2013 report from the *Huffington Post*: http://www.huffingtonpost.com/2013/01/09/mexican-american-studies-may-return-tucson-board_n_2441896.html.

her life. She was lonely even when she was married, since there was no deep communication between her and her husband. She has a son and a daughter, but they do not appear in the story, which may suggest that she was not close to them, either. When she realized her marriage had failed, she took up the solitary activity of painting, which helped to assuage the emptiness and lack of meaning in her life. She also traveled—alone.

The woman's drive to the desert for what turns out to be her visionary encounter with her ancestor can be seen as a quest to overcome this lifetime of loneliness and isolation. When it comes, that moment of heightened imagination stimulated by the desert environment also reveals a circle of women who are about to perform a traditional ceremony of some kind. The old woman obviously feels that in the spirit she is part of that women's circle. The circle of Indian women forms the counterpart, the antidote, to what the woman has referred to earlier as the "circle of pretend," that is, the inauthentic nature of her life while she was married. Given her ability to respond to the ancient traditions of the culture she is reclaiming for herself, it seems likely that the old woman has found a way to alleviate some of the loneliness she experiences in ordinary, day-to-day life.

STYLE

Setting

As with many Anaya novels and short stories, the setting is distinctive and important, almost a character in its own right. The setting in this story is the desert of northwestern Mexico. As might be expected, the desert is dry, dusty, oppressively hot, and unpopulated. There is seemingly unending solitude in the desert. More than once there are hints of death, as when the woman feels so many aches and pains that she thinks she may die before she ever reaches Epifano's ranch. Also, she sees vultures circling overhead. (Vultures are universal symbols of death because they feed on scavenged dead animals.) However, there is water in the desert too, as shown when the woman slakes her thirst at a desert spring. The image of life-giving water in the desert provides the bridge from the negative implications of the desert to its positive attributes. The spring is a metaphor

The old woman drives into the desert, looking for her ancestor. (© Brian Weed | ShutterStock.com)

for the new life that will pour into the old woman when she has her visionary encounter with Epifano. In keeping with traditional Native American ways of relating to the earth, there is a sacredness to the desert. The old woman feels it. She is drawn to the desert for this reason. She feels the pull of it when in her artwork she makes sketches of the desert. There is something pure about the desert that allows her to connect with the deepest essence of her being: "In the desert the voices were clear." She feels fully alive there, in contrast to the deadness and sterility she felt while living in the Anglo world in California. She is leaving her old life behind and coming into a new one, which, paradoxically, is also an old one because it partakes of the shared vision of the ancient people of Mexico and their traditional ways.

Symbols

The journey the protagonist undertakes is both an outer, real-world journey and an inner journey that involves symbolic elements. At the literal level the woman drives south in her Jeep to the Mexican desert. But the purpose of the outer journey is to effect an inner journey within the mind and heart of the traveler. She wants to get

beyond the superficial, empty life she has led and get in touch with the essence of who she is. The inner journey is marked by a symbolic event, in which she gains a vision of her ancestor Epifano and also of the circle of women. They symbolize the Mexican heritage that her family has forgotten but which she so earnestly desires to reconnect with. In this aspect of the story the outer world blends with the symbolic, mythic or imaginative world; there is a fluidity between the real—the actual—and what the woman is able to perceive through the visionary, mythic imagination that she discovers in the desert.

This symbolic element also occurs earlier in the story, when as a young woman the protagonist sees an Indian man at the back of the church during the wedding ceremony. The Indian is likely a symbolic rather than literal figure who represents a call or message from the Mexican aspect of her heritage. At the time she does not recognize its importance and ignores her Mexican heritage, which leads to dire consequences for her happiness.

Another symbolic element occurs at the end of the story. As with the journey, it involves a contrast between the inner and outer. When the old woman finally encounters Epifano, it is dusk; night is starting to fall in the desert. But her inner world presents a marked contrast; as she sees Epifano and the circle of women, "in the dying light of the sun a blinding flash filled her being. Like desire, or like an arrow from the bow of the Indian, the light filled her and she quivered." The light that suddenly illuminates her does not come from outside her; it is symbolic of her own newly fulfilled being.

HISTORICAL CONTEXT

The Chicano Movement

Large-scale immigration from Mexico to the United States began in the early twentieth century. Mexican Americans, or Chicanos, lived mostly in rural areas, but after World War II there was a drift toward the cities. During this time, living standards of Mexican Americans were below those of the general population, and Mexican Americans were often subject to discrimination. As a result of the civil rights movement that produced many gains for African Americans in the 1950s and 1960s, Mexican Americans also began to organize to improve their situation.

In the 1960s, the Chicano movement tackled economic and civil rights issues by aiming at securing better housing and jobs. In 1962, a Mexican American named César Chávez organized the National Farm Workers Association (NFWA), a farmworkers' union in California, where Mexican American agricultural workers earned very low wages. The Chicano movement also sparked an explosion of literary activity among Mexican Americans. Chicano writers emphasized the need for social and political action to provide equal opportunities for Chicanos. Many of the prominent Chicano writers of this period were poets who drew on the oral traditions of their culture to inspire their communities. Anaya was a part of this movement. Writing in 1986 in his essay "At a Crossroads," he describes the Chicano movement as "the most important artistic movement of our time." He traces its origins to the dismay felt by Mexican Americans who felt that they "were losing many of their traditional ways" as a result of the postwar movement to the cities. They felt the need to "renew their sense of identity."

Mexican American Literature

Although Mexican American literature dates back to the middle of the nineteenth century, it was not then part of the mainstream literary culture of the United States. When Anaya was growing up in New Mexico in the 1930s and 1940s, only one Chicano work, Josephina Niggli's *Mexican Village* (1945), reached a general readership. This slowly began to change after the Chicano movement began in the 1960s. Several publishing houses were formed to give Mexican American writers an opportunity to present their work. These included Quinto Sol, in Berkeley, California, which instituted a national award for Chicano literature, the Premio Quinto Sol (Fifth Sun Award). The award included a cash prize and publication of the winning entry. The first winner was the novel *Y no se lo tragó la tierra* (*And the Earth Did Not Devour Him*) (1970), by Tomás Rivera (1935–1984), who was to become one of the best-known Chicano writers. This novel is about Mexican American migrant workers and includes the theme of the search for cultural identity. In 1972, Quinto Sol published Anaya's *Bless Me, Ultima*, which has become the most widely read of all Mexican American novels. Rolando Hinojosa (1929–) became known for his novel *Estampas del valle y otras obras* (1973), which won the third Premio Quinto Sol award in 1972. (The title means "Sketches of the valley and other works," but this book has yet to receive an English translation.)

During the 1980s, Mexican American literature continued to grow, aided by the establishment of Arte Público Press in Houston, Texas, in 1979, which published works by Hispanic authors, many of them Mexican American. During this period Chicano poets such as José Montoya (1932–) and Gary Soto (1952–) made their mark. Soto, in particular, managed to reach a mainstream readership with his poetry volumes *Where Sparrows Work Hard* (1981) and *Black Hair* (1985). The 1980s also saw the emergence of work by Mexican American female writers (Chicanas). These writers included Lorna Dee Cervantes (1954–), whose poetry collection *Emplumada* (1981) won an American Book Award; Denise Chavez, who published her collection of short stories *The Last of the Menu Girls* in 1986; and Sandra Cisneros (1952–). Cisneros wrote the novel *The House on Mango Street* (1984), about growing up Chicana in Chicago, and the short-story collection *Woman Hollering Creek and Other Stories* (1991). Both

COMPARE
&
CONTRAST

- **1980s:** From 1980 to 1990 the Mexican American population nearly doubles. In 1990, approximately 13.5 million people identify themselves as Mexican Americans. Mexican Americans remain low on the socioeconomic scale when compared with the general population and other immigrant groups. Much of this is due to low educational attainment; in 1990, 44 percent have a high-school education or higher. The low high-school graduation rate is due in part to language difficulties, as many Mexican Americans have only limited proficiency in English.

  Today: The growth of the Mexican American population is slower than in previous decades. In 2010, there are 31.8 million Mexican Americans, composing 63 percent of the US Hispanic population and 10 percent of the total US population. Mexican Americans still have the lowest level of formal education of any immigrant group as well as lower levels of English proficiency. Second-generation Mexican Americans have higher educational levels, although they still lag behind other immigrant groups.

- **1980s:** In the 1970s and 1980s there is a sharp rise in the number of illegal immigrants to the United States from Mexico. In the 1980s, an estimated 2 to 3 million illegal Mexican immigrants live in the United States, mostly in the Southwest. The rise is caused by the fact that the United States eliminates most legal immigration from Mexico during this period, but the demand for low-skill workers persists. A lack of jobs in Mexico ensures that impoverished Mexicans continue to cross the border to find work. A US-Mexico free trade agreement is passed with the aim of creating jobs in Mexico, thus reducing the need for Mexicans to come illegally to the United States in search of work. In the United States, fears about illegal immigration lead to calls for tighter restrictions on legal and illegal immigration, and many states pass laws designating English as the sole official language.

  Today: In 2010, about 6.5 million Mexican immigrants are in the United States illegally. This figure amounts to 52 percent of all Mexican immigrants. Of the nation's 11.2 million illegal immigrants from all parts of the world, the majority (58 percent) are from Mexico. Political efforts to allow illegal Mexican immigrants to legalize their status and to pursue a path toward US citizenship are frustrated by a bitterly divided Congress.

- **1980s:** With new publishing opportunities and their increased willingness to use their own cultural heritage as subjects and themes, many new Mexican American writers are establishing names for themselves. Anaya publishes *The Legend of La Llorona* in 1984 and *Lord of the Dawn: The Legend of Quetzalcóatl* in 1987. Sandra Cisneros, Gary Soto, Denise Chavez, José Montoya, and Lorna Dee Cervantes all publish during this decade. Alejandro Morales publishes the novel *Death of an Anglo* in 1988. Jimmy Santiago Baca's semiautobiographical verse epic *Martin and Meditations on the South Valley* (1987), receives an American Book Award in 1988 and the Hispanic Heritage Award in 1989.

  Today: In addition to many established writers from the 1980s and earlier who continue to publish, leading Mexican American writers include Dagoberto Gilb, author of the novel *The Flowers* (2008) and *Before the End, After the Beginning: Stories* (2011); Benjamin Alire Sáenz, author of the novels *In Perfect Light* (2005) and *Names on a Map* (2008); and Helena Maria Viramontes, author of *Their Dogs Came with Them* (2007).

works won a wide readership, establishing Cisneros as the leading Chicana writer of the late twentieth century and beyond. These three Chicana writers challenged the values of the patriarchal societies in which they were raised while also affirming their distinctive Mexican American heritage.

Multiculturalism Slow to Take Root

The cause of Mexican American literature, as well as that of other minority groups in the United States, was advanced by the growth of multiculturalism in the 1980s, in particular a multicultural approach to education, which sought to promote in schools an understanding of ethnic diversity. However, in some places the movement found it hard to gain a foothold and faced opposition from traditionalists, who continued to favor a curriculum based largely on Anglo-American literature—literature by white, usually male, authors who wrote from within the dominant culture in the United States. Anaya expressed impatience with the slow progress of multiculturalism as applied to Mexican Americans in his essay "On the Education of Hispanic Children," which was published in the *Albuquerque Journal* in May 1991. He noted that the dropout rate among Mexican American school students in the southwestern United States was extremely high. He argued that the reason for this high rate was that Mexican American students did not find their own culture reflected in the curriculum. As a result, rather than feeling intellectually and emotionally engaged at school, they felt shamed for being different and thus had no interest in their studies. Anaya called for diversity in education that would involve teaching different languages and also the histories of communities and cultures other than the dominant Anglo culture:

> We must not allow our children to feel shame simply because of their cultural background. It is not shameful to be different; rather it is part of the beauty of the cultural diversity of this country. We must insist that quality education for our children in this country include a reflection of their language and history.

Anaya reemphasized this message in a talk titled "The Censorship of Neglect," which he gave at the Secondary Section of the National Council of Teachers of English annual convention in Seattle, Washington, later that year, in November 1991. The talk was published in *The Anaya Reader* in 1995. Anaya wrote that for too

After she finds her great-grandfather, the old woman sees a bright light. (© Fenton | ShutterStock.com)

long the school curriculum had been controlled by teachers, publishers, and politicians operating with a narrow view of what literature consists of and what sort of literature should be taught in schools. "These groups represent the status quo and call themselves 'universalists,'" Anaya wrote. He argued that the term *universalist* was for them a misnomer, since the effect of preserving the status quo is to keep ethnic literature out of the curriculum. "Chicano literature, in a country that has over fifteen million Mexican-Americans, is still virtually unknown in the classroom." The challenge, he continued, was to "incorporate into the curriculum all the voices of our country." To do otherwise amounted to censorship by neglect and meant that Chicanos were not free to teach and learn their own cultural traditions.

CRITICAL OVERVIEW

When "In Search of Epifano" appeared in Anaya's short-story collection *The Man Who Could Fly and Other Stories* in 2006, nineteen years after its first publication, the reviewer for *Publishers Weekly* noted that the story shows "death as a benign figure, representing not only inevitability but also the resolution of a deep-seated desire unquenchable by anything on earth." The reviewer also comments on Anaya's "elegiac, deceptively simple prose, captivating in its aspiration and achievement."

César A. González-T., in his introduction to *The Anaya Reader*, writes that stories such as "Children of the Desert" and "In Search of Epifano" "speak of our human inquisition for that divine beauty 'ever ancient, ever new' in one another." Mario Materassi considers the story at some length in his essay "The Desert and the Seed: Three Stories by Rudolfo Anaya." He notes that the story takes place in three different time frames, and he likens the structure of the story to "three concentric circles." The story is dominated by the "comprehensive icon" of the desert, around which centers an "array of life-negating elements." However, the "archetypical function of the desert as death-dealing is repudiated, and 'Epifano' results in a life-giving message."

CRITICISM

Bryan Aubrey

Aubrey holds a PhD in English. In the following essay, he explores Anaya's interest in the relationship between people and their environment and his quest for universal meaning in "In Search of Epifano" through the use of symbolic and mythic elements.

Rudolfo Anaya has talked in interviews and written extensively about his craft as a writer. In one essay he wrote in 1977, "The Writer's Landscape: Epiphany in Landscape," he makes several points that might well be applied to his short story "In Search of Epifano." Anaya wrote:

> My interest in writing is to explore the magic in realism and in that sense my immediate landscape and my relationship to my region is... the "taking off point." It is the place where imagination and the image-laden memory begin their work, and the three forces—place, imagination and memory—are inextricably wound together in my work.

The deep relationship between people—and in fiction, characters—to their landscape is of vital interest to Anaya. He went on to write in his essay:

> This kinship to the environment... creates the metaphor and the epiphany in landscape. On one pole of the metaphor stands man, on the other is the raw, majestic and awe-inspiring landscape of the southwest: the epiphany is the natural response to that landscape, a coming together of these two forces.

> THE OLD WOMAN MAY BE A PARTICULAR WOMAN ON A PARTICULAR JOURNEY, BUT SHE ALSO SEEMS TO REPRESENT ALL MEXICAN AMERICANS WHO ARE IMPOVERISHED BY THE FACT THAT THEY HAVE FORGOTTEN THE TRADITIONAL WAYS ASSOCIATED WITH THEIR ETHNICITY AND CULTURE."

There in a nutshell is the story of "In Search of Epifano." The deeply unfulfilled old woman finally finds what she is looking for when she drives into the Mexican desert and absorbs the power of that landscape. It is the desert landscape that stimulates the longing in her soul; something about it calls to her in a way that nothing else had been able to, and she is rewarded with an epiphany of the sort that Anaya describes above. An epiphany can range from a moment of deep insight or realization to the appearance either in reality or symbolically of a divine or especially significant being. In "In Search of Epifano," the epiphany is the old woman's perception at sunset in the desert of the presence of her great-grandfather Epifano and also a circle of Indian women. It is her sensitivity to the environment that she has entered, her awareness of its power, that allows her to have this vision, which offers her the connection with her ancient heritage that she has been so earnestly seeking.

Anaya likes to give his stories universal meaning by incorporating symbolic and mythic elements into them. He states in his essay "The New World Man," "the depth of the universal element is that which allows us to communicate across national or ethnic boundaries." It is noticeable in "In Search of Epifano" that the protagonist is unnamed, which tends to universalize her. The old woman may be a particular woman on a particular journey, but she also seems to represent all Mexican Americans who are impoverished by the fact that they have forgotten the traditional ways associated with their ethnicity and culture. Epifano is also a representative figure, a pure example of the indigenous Indians who lived their lives in close harmony with the earth.

WHAT DO I READ NEXT?

- *Bless Me, Ultima* (1972), Anaya's first novel, remains his most popular work. It is a coming-of-age story set in the kind of small-town New Mexico that Anaya grew up in after World War II. Ultima is an elderly *curandera*, or traditional Native American healer, who acts as spiritual mentor for the young boy Antonio (Tony), who narrates the story.

- *Randy Lopez Goes Home* (2011), by Anaya, is a novel about a Mexican immigrant to the United States who has found success there but still feels something is missing in his life. He returns to his ancestral home in Mexico to reconnect with his past, including his godparents and a former teacher. In this spiritual quest he also encounters spirits such as coyote, Death, and the devil, with whom he has conversations about life's purpose and meaning.

- *Growing Up Chicana/o* (1995), edited and with an introduction by Tiffany A. Lopez and with a foreword by Anaya, contains twenty stories about growing up Mexican American in the United States. Authors include such well-known figures as Sandra Cisneros and Gary Soto as well as lesser-known writers such as Gerald Haslem, Alicia Gaspar de Alba, and Rosa Elena Yzquierdo. The anthology makes an excellent introduction to Chicano life and literature.

- *A Gathering of Flowers: Stories about Being Young in America* (1992), edited by Joyce Carol Thomas, is a collection aimed at teenage readers. It contains eleven short stories from a variety of different cultures within the United States. Cultures represented include Chicano (in a story by Gary Soto), Native American, Chinese, Japanese, and African American as well as Anglo.

- *Mexicanos: A History of Mexicans in the United States* (2009), by Manuel G. Gonzales, surveys more than two centuries of Mexican American history. Gonzales analyzes how the culture of the Mexican immigrants was shaped by their Indian and Spanish ancestry as well as Catholicism. Gonzales assesses the impact Mexican Americans have had on American society. He discusses the successes and failures of the Chicano movement and does justice to the range of groups within the Mexican American community, from radical to conservative. This revised and updated edition takes account of recent scholarship in the field.

- A landmark work of Chicana literature, Sandra Cisneros's *The House on Mango Street* (1984) tells in a series of poetic vignettes the coming-of-age story of Esperanza Cordero, a young girl growing up in the impoverished Hispanic community in Chicago that includes Chicanos and Puerto Ricans.

- *Bordering Fires: The Vintage Book of Contemporary Mexican and Chicana and Chicano Literature* (2006), edited by Cristina García, contains poems, essays, short stories, and excerpts from novels. The collection begins with four early Chicano writers and then presents work from established contemporary figures such as Octavio Paz, Elena Poniatowska, Richard Rodriguez, Jimmy Santiago Baca, and Sandra Cisneros, as well as newer writers such as Coral Bracho.

- "New Mexico" is an essay by the English novelist, short-story writer, poet, and essayist D. H. Lawrence, who lived in Taos, New Mexico, during the 1920s. In the essay, Lawrence describes the remarkable effect the desert landscape had on him and reflects on the religion and ceremonies of the Indians, which impressed him deeply. Where the New Mexican landscape permeates the work of Anaya, Lawrence's essay provides interesting insight into the effect of that landscape on a white European who had never before encountered it. The essay can be found in *Mornings in Mexico and Other Essays* (2009), edited by Virginia Crosswhite Hyde. The book also contains other pieces by Lawrence on Mexico and the American Southwest.

Further on the topic of universalism, there are elements in "In Search of Epifano" that recall the "monomyth" described by mythologist Joseph Campbell in his book *The Hero with a Thousand Faces*. Campbell believes that many myths, from many different cultures, exhibit the same basic pattern: a hero receives a call to embark on an adventure, a quest that will take him outside the usual parameters of his life. At first he refuses the call, but he then receives help from a supernatural figure who may provide protection in the form of an amulet that the hero is to carry with him. The hero then crosses a threshold into a "zone of magnified power" where transformation becomes possible; he undergoes trials, encounters what Campbell calls the "Queen Goddess of the World," and is also reconciled with a powerful father figure. Realizing the essential divinity of his own nature, the hero then returns to society enriched and enlightened by his experience and ready to teach others what he has learned.

In Anaya's story, the hero is not a man but a woman. She receives her call to adventure quite early in her life, in the appearance of the Indian at the wedding ceremony, which is a call to remember the indigenous Indian element of her Mexican American heritage. She ignores this call, but it does not go away, and the inner promptings from deep within her psyche (which act in the same way as the supernatural helpers in the monomyth) cause her to take up painting, including desert landscapes, and to travel south into the desert. She also carries with her the equivalent of the amulet given by the helper in the monomyth. This is the family photo album that contains a picture of Epifano, which ensures that she will not forget her task. She also hears the voice of Epifano, which draws her further into her quest. In that sense, Epifano might himself be thought of as a supernatural helper.

The desert is the zone of magnified power, as found in the monomyth, which has the ability, if the old woman will allow herself fully to awaken to it, to restore to her the fullness of her being. The physical trials she undergoes are many, including the discomforts of driving long hours in the desert and the adverse effects of the hot, dry weather. There is even a version of what Campbell describes as the "threshold guardian" that exists at the entrance to the zone of magnified power, who will try to repel the adventurer. The threshold guardian in the story comes in the rather unlikely form of the garage mechanic, who advises the old woman to return home because continuing to drive in the desert in an unreliable vehicle is too dangerous. Showing her courage, the woman ignores him, as the hero must.

The woman's reward is to encounter both male and female figures who if not supernatural are larger than life in the sense that they represent an entire culture. Their acceptance of her—Epifano recognizes her and had been expecting her, and the circle of women forms around her—represents her oneness with these archetypal figures from her cultural tradition. Armed, nourished, and strengthened by this knowledge of who she really is, she is ready to return and become an embodiment of the archetype Carl Jung called the "wise old woman." At the practical level, she will bring to her community—as Anaya earnestly desires Mexican Americans do—a revival of knowledge of the traditions of the past that are unrelated to the Anglo world but correspond closely with their true cultural roots. As Anaya wrote in his essay "Mythical Dimensions/Political Reality":

> We who value the earth as a creative force must renew our faith in the values of the old communities, the ceremonies of relationship, the dances and fiestas, the harmony in our way of life, and the mythic force we can tap to create beauty and peace.

What Anaya wanted to inspire in readers with "In Search of Epifano," as well as with much of his other work, was a desire to learn about this old way of life, which, as he explains in "Mythical Dimensions/Political Reality," is so different from the materialistic life in the cities, or at their margins, that has become the lot of the majority of the Mexican Americans in the Southwest since the drift to the cities began after World War II.

It should also be noted in this connection that Anaya's work beginning in the late 1980s tended to emphasize one aspect of the Mexican American tradition over another. The Mexican aspect of the Chicano heritage is twofold. It is Indian and Hispanic, the result of the Spanish conquest of Mexico in the sixteenth century. Anaya notes in "The New World Man" that it has been more common for Mexican Americans to identify with their Spanish heritage, but this has resulted in neglect of their indigenous Native American origins. In "In Search of Epifano," both Spanish and Native American elements are present, but it is the latter that dominate.

Anaya's protagonist fears her artwork is all that she will leave behind. (© Voronin76 | ShutterStock.com)

Source: Bryan Aubrey, Critical Essay on "In Search of Epifano," in *Short Stories for Students*, Gale, Cengage Learning, 2014.

Margarite Fernández Olmos

In the following excerpt, Olmos explains Anaya's use of myth and the importance of setting in his work.

In a 1980 interview, Rudolfo Anaya reflected on the idea of the existence of a "distinctive perspective" within Chicano writing: "All literature, and certainly Chicano literature, reflects, in its more formal aspects, the mythos of the people, and the writings speak to the underlying philosophical assumptions which form the particular worldview of a culture." By "formal aspects" Anaya is not simply referring to style and technique but, rather, to an author's perspective, which should be "guided by culture, history, language, native mythology" (Bruce-Novoa, *Chicano Authors*). This sense of an author's moral responsibility, of social and cultural commitment, is not unique to Chicano literature, of course, but it does reflect its early origins in the United States. Rudolfo Anaya's writings, and *Bless Me, Ultima* in particular, have played an important role in the development of the Chicano literary movement, which has deep historical roots in U.S. culture. . . .

SETTING

Anaya's earliest memories as a boy growing up in rural New Mexico had a profound impact on his writing. He has often commented on the influence of nature and landscape on his creative sensibility: the landscape of the Southwest is described by Anaya as a power that touched his "primal memory," allowing him to discover the "essential symbols" of his writing. Setting is therefore more than simply a point of reference: "place, imagination and memory . . . are inextricably wound together in my work" ("Writer's Landscape").

Anaya has expressed a spiritual kinship with the majestic environment of his region of the United States; nature, for Anaya, creates an "epiphany," an enlightenment or illumination, that he believes can produce profound changes in those who are open to being a part of it. He credits his ability to respond to *la tierra* (the land) to the elders of his community, who taught him to be conscious of and in harmony with his environment: "When the entire sense of the landscape—characters, emotion, experience, detail

The Spanish elements are primarily linguistic, in the use of Spanish terms integrated into the narrative without quotation marks or italics ("the dull peaks of las montaas met the dull blue of the sky," for example). But the force of the story is all Indian. It is the Indian lands that the old woman heads for; the mysterious figure at the wedding is Indian, not Hispanic; and Epifano, when he manifests at the end of the story, shows himself to be Indian, too, decked out in traditional Indian fashion. The emphasis on the Indian rather than the Hispanic was no doubt deliberate on Anaya's part, in accord with how his thinking was developing. In "The New World Man," which was first published in 1989, he wrote that he had come to identify with his Native American rather than Hispanic identity: "I declare my independence of consciousness from the Iberian Peninsula. I have found that the symbolic content that best describes my nature comes from the people and earth of the Americas." Hence proceeds the power of the Native American message in "In Search of Epifano."

and story—permeates [the writer's] craft, the reader will respond, and that response is the beginning of a new epiphany" ("Writer's Landscape").

MYTHS AND ARCHETYPES

In addition to the unity of setting (all three novels take place in New Mexico), the inclusion of autobiographical details, and the repetition of several characters and mystical motifs, the novels of Anaya's initial trilogy also share his affinity for dream sequences and archetypal figures. Critics have found it useful to refer to the theories of psychiatrist Carl G. Jung regarding myths, archetypes, and a collective unconscious in understanding Anaya's use of dream sequences, particularly in *Bless Me, Ultima* and *Tortuga*.

A myth can be defined as a tale that portrays in symbolic language the origins of a culture. Classical myths are legendary or traditional stories that were created and passed down by generations to explain how natural phenomena came into existence or how human activity originated. Occasionally they embody deeper concepts and human feelings. The ancient poets and writers were born into cultures with established mythologies or collections of such tales; Anglo writers have both recurred to those ancient established mythologies and, though less frequently, created their own. The poet William Blake, for example, felt the need to create his own mythological system, combining elements of Christianity with his own spiritual ideas and those of other cultures. D. H. Lawrence blended elements of Christianity with the pre-Columbian myth of the deity Quetzalcóatl as material for his novel *The Plumed Serpent* (1926). Some authors strive for a universal myth that will embody the experiences of all human beings. The novel *Moby-Dick* (1851) by Herman Melville, for example, is referred to as a myth precisely because it symbolizes a primal conflict—the struggle between man and the forces of nature—that stems from an idea universal to all people. For Jung the stuff of myth lies in what he called the "collective unconscious" of the human race.

The Swiss psychiatrist Carl Gustav Jung (1875–1961) was a student of Sigmund Freud and his theories regarding the unconscious broadened those of his mentor. Jung demonstrated close parallels between ancient myths and psychotic fantasies; human motivation, he felt, had to be understood in terms of a larger

creative energy. In *Psychology of the Unconscious* (1912) he proposed the idea that the unconscious is composed of two dimensions: the personal, which would include the mental and material life of the individual, and the collective unconscious, inherited feelings, thoughts, and memories shared by members of a culture or universally by all humans. The collective unconscious is made up of what Jung called "archetypes," or primordial images that appear in dreams and fantasies. These primordial images might find expression in characteristic forms—the divine child, the Earth Mother, the wise old man, and so forth—that are frequently the themes of religion, fairy tales and mythologies.

Some of these archetypes make their way into Rudolfo Anaya's frequent dream sequences and mythic symbols. In *Bless Me, Ultima* and *Tortuga* in particular, dreams reveal crucial stages in the internal evolution of the characters; they are woven into the framework of all three novels of the trilogy. Anaya's novels were also among the initial Chicano writings that recaptured a sacred mythic vision from pre-Columbian (dating to before Columbus's arrival in America), pre-Christian traditions and successfully incorporated this worldview into contemporary fiction. Precisely this mythic quality of *Bless Me, Ultima*, however, is what led to some of its most strident criticism.

Although universally praised for its unique story and subtle beauty, it should be recalled that *Bless Me, Ultima* was first published during a very politicized era in U.S. society; thus a political critique of the novel soon surfaced. Detractors, usually Marxist critics, observed that the work lacked a bold political message and concentrated instead on less important themes of myth and symbolism. Specifically, they felt that the focus of progressive Chicano literature should be critical analysis of capitalism and the ways in which that economic system exploits the working class. Anaya's novel, they claim, reverts to an illusory and romanticized vision of the past rather than pressing for social change in the present. What have been perceived by some as the work's shortcomings are perceived by others as its strengths. Many believe that *Bless Me, Ultima* transcends the narrow perceptions of what has been characterized as "ethnic" or "regionalist" literature and is a timeless tale that goes beyond a strictly Mexican-American experience to reflect a more universal experience, thereby becoming Anaya's most enduring legacy to American letters. . . .

Source: Margarite Fernández Olmos, "Rudolfo A. Anaya and the Chicano Literary Tradition," in *Rudolfo A. Anaya: A Critical Companion*, edited by Kathleen Gregory Klein, Greenwood Press, 1999, pp. 13, 18–21.

SOURCES

Anaya, Rudolfo, "At a Crossroads," "Mythical Dimensions/Political Reality," and "The Censorship of Neglect," in *The Anaya Reader*, Warner Books, 1995, pp. 335–36, 346, 407, 410, 412.

———, "In Search of Epifano," in *Voces: An Anthology of Nuevo Mexicano Writers*, edited by Rudolfo Anaya, El Norte Publications, 1987, pp. 222–26.

———, "The New World Man," in *The Anaya Reader*, Warner Books, 1995, pp. 361–62; originally published in *Before Columbus Review*, Fall/Winter 1989, Nos. 2–3.

———, "On the Education of Hispanic Children," in *The Anaya Reader*, Warner Books, 1995, p. 402; originally published in *Albuquerque Journal*, May 12, 1991.

———, "The Writer's Landscape: Epiphany in Landscape," in *Latin American Literary Review*, Vol. 5, No. 10, Spring 1977, pp. 98–99.

Brick, Kate, A. E. Challinor, and Marc R. Rosenblum, "Mexican and Central American Immigrants in the United States," Migration Policy Institute, June 2011, www.migrationpolicy.org/pubs/MexCentAmimmigrants. pdf (accessed January 9, 2013).

Campbell, Joseph, *The Hero with a Thousand Faces*, 2nd ed., Princeton University Press, 1973, pp. 77, 109.

Candelaria, Cordelia, *Dictionary of Literary Biography*, Vol. 82, *Chicano Writers, First Series*, edited by Francisco A. Lomelí and Carl R. Shirley, Gale Research, 1989, pp. 24–35.

González-T., César A., Foreword to *The Anaya Reader*, by Rudolfo Anaya, Warner Books, 1995, p. xxii.

Materassi, Mario, "The Desert and the Seed: Three Stories by Rudolfo Anaya," in *Journal of the Southwest*, Vol. 49, No. 4, Winter 2007, pp. 574–75.

"The Mexican-American Boom: Births Overtake Immigration," Pew Hispanic Center website, July 14, 2011, http://www.pewhispanic.org/2011/07/14/the-mexican-american-boom-brbirths-overtake-immigration/ (accessed January 9, 2013).

Olmos, Margarite Fernández, *Rudolfo A. Anaya: A Critical Companion*, Greenwood Press, 1999, pp. 1–11.

Paredes, Raymund, "Teaching Chicano Literature: An Historical Approach," in *Heath Anthology of American Literature Newsletter*, No. 10, Fall 1993, http://www9.georgetown.edu/faculty/bassr/tamlit/newsletter/paredes.html (accessed January 4, 2013).

Review of *The Man Who Could Fly and Other Stories*, in *Publishers Weekly*, January 30, 2006, http://www.publishersweekly.com/978-0-8061-3738-4 (accessed January 2, 2013).

Valdivieso, Rafael, "Demographic Trends of the Mexican-American Population: Implications for Schools," EricDigests.org, September 1990, http://www.ericdigests.org/pre-9217/trends.htm (accessed January 4, 2013).

FURTHER READING

Baeza, Abelardo, *Man of Aztlan: A Biography of Rudolfo Anaya*, Eakin Press, 2001.
    This is a short (eighty-five-page) biography of Anaya.

Dick, Bruce, and Silvio Sirias, eds., *Conversations with Rudolfo Anaya*, University Press of Mississippi, 1998.
    This book contains fifteen previously published interviews with Anaya, covering a period from 1976 to 1997.

González-T., César A., ed., *Rudolfo A. Anaya: Focus on Criticism*, Lalo Press, 1990.
    This collection of criticism contains fifteen articles about different aspects of Anaya's work, an autobiography, a twenty-four-page bibliography on Anaya, three appendices, and an index.

Tatum, Charles M., *Chicano and Chicana Literature: Otra voz del pueblo*, University of Arizona Press, 2006.
    Tatum surveys the entire history of Mexican American literature, from the earliest Spanish documents in the sixteenth century, to the growth of fiction and poetry in the nineteenth and twentieth centuries, the Chicano movement of the 1960s and early 1970s, and the post-Chicano movement. He examines the work of Anaya, Sandra Cisneros, Luis Alberto Urrea, and others.

———, *Chicano Popular Culture: Que hable el pueblo*, University of Arizona Press, 2001.
    This book is an overview of Chicano popular culture, including four centuries of music; three decades of films; newspapers, radio, and television; literature, including fiction, poetry, and theater over the preceding thirty years; and fiestas, celebrations, and art. Tatum also discusses different theories of popular culture.

Vasallo, Paul, ed., *The Magic of Words: Rudolfo Anaya and His Writings*, rev. ed., University of New Mexico Press, 1987.
    This short (eighty-three-page) book contains three essays that discuss Anaya's early works, as well as an essay by Anaya in which he discusses his love of books and some of the literary influences on his work.

SUGGESTED SEARCH TERMS

Rudolfo Anaya

In Search of Epifano

Mexican American history

Chicano OR Chicana

Chicano movement

Mexican immigration AND United States

New Mexico AND immigration

Spanish conquest of Mexico

multiculturalism

The Kiss

ANTON CHEKHOV

1887

Anton Chekhov's story "The Kiss" ("Potseluy" in Russian) was first published in 1887. It first appeared in English in a translation by R. E. C. Long in 1908 in *The Kiss and Other Stories*. Chekhov is considered one of the masters of the short story, and he had a huge influence on the development of the genre over the course of the twentieth century. "The Kiss" is one of his most famous tales. Like many of Chekhov's stories, the emphasis is not on plot or action but more on character, feeling, and mood. At a social gathering at the home of an army general, a shy, unattractive army officer finds himself momentarily alone in a dark room, where he is kissed on the cheek by an unknown woman who thinks he is someone else. The incident ignites in the officer a lot of intense romantic daydreams, setting him up to come back to earth with a jolt.

The story can be found in *The Kiss and Other Stories*, translated by Ronald Wilks and published in 1982, and in *The Essential Tales of Chekhov*, translated by Constance Garnett and published in 2000. This entry uses the version in *The Portable Chekhov* (1968). The story also can be found online, as made available by Project Gutenberg of Australia at http://gutenberg.net.au/ebooks07/0700881.txt and at Cornell University's e-book and text archive at http://archive.org/details/cu31924026700827 (in the Long translation).

Anton Chekhov (© Hulton Archive / Stringer / Getty Images)

AUTHOR BIOGRAPHY

The renowned Russian playwright and short-story writer Anton Pavlovich Chekhov was born on January 17, 1860, in the port city of Taganrog, in southern Russia. He was the third of six children born to Pavel Egorovich Chekhov and Evgenia Iakovlevna Morozova. Chekhov's grandfather had been a serf; his father was a merchant who owned a general store, where Chekhov and his older brothers worked when they were children. In 1876, his father's business failed, and his father moved the family to Moscow, leaving Anton behind to finish school in Taganrog.

In 1879, Chekhov moved to Moscow and began medical studies at Moscow University. He published his first short story, in a comic journal, in 1880. In 1884, he graduated and began to practice as a doctor in Moscow, publishing his first collection of stories in the same year. In that year also, he showed the first signs of the tuberculosis that was to lead to his early death.

Chekhov wrote "The Kiss" in 1887, and his short-story collection *In the Twilight* was published that year. Also in 1887, the first

performance of Chekhov's play *Ivanov* took place in Moscow. Chekhov was becoming well known in literary circles, and he was given the Academy of Science's Pushkin Award for literary achievement in 1888.

In 1892, Chekhov bought a country estate at Melikhovo, fifty miles south of Moscow, where he lived with his family until 1899. In the late 1880s and early 1890s, he traveled extensively in Russia and western Europe, visiting Vienna, Venice, Florence, Rome, and Paris. In 1890, he made the long journey to the island of Sakhalin, a penal colony off Russia's Pacific coast, to compile a report about the prison population there. His book *The Island of Sakhalin* was published in 1895, which was also the year he first met the great Russian writer Leo Tolstoy. The previous year, with his health deteriorating, Chekhov had traveled in the Crimea and southern Europe.

Several years later, in March 1897, he had a severe pulmonary hemorrhage and was diagnosed with tuberculosis. He spent much of that year and the following year in Nice, on the French Riviera, having been advised that a warmer climate would be better for his health. The following year, continuing ill health forced him to give up practicing medicine. He settled in Yalta, in the Crimea, in southern Ukraine.

In the meantime, Chekhov had been establishing his name as a dramatist. The *Seagull* premiered in Saint Petersburg in 1896. It was unsuccessful, but a production two years later in Moscow was very well received. *Uncle Vanya* was first performed in 1899, *The Three Sisters* in 1901, the same year Chekhov married the actress Olga Knipper. *The Cherry Orchard* was first performed in 1904. Chekhov's last story, "The Betrothed," was published in 1903. In May 1904, Chekhov traveled to a health resort in Baden-weiler, Germany, where he died on July 2, 1904.

PLOT SUMMARY

In "The Kiss," on an evening in May, an artillery brigade stays for the night in the village of Mestechki, on their way to camp. A messenger arrives on horseback, telling the officers that they have been invited for tea at the home of Lieutenant-General von Rabbeck. The officers are not pleased with the invitation, because they remember an incident from the previous year

MEDIA ADAPTATIONS

- "The Kiss" is one of eight Chekhov stories available as an audiobook published by Commuter's Library in 1993. Read by Richard Setlok, the collection, with a running time of two hours and fifteen minutes, also includes "Not Wanted," "Anyuta," "A Misfortune," "Expensive Lessons," "The Head of the Family," "The Trousseau," and "The Helpmate."

when a retired army officer invited them to tea; he talked so much and would not let them go, even though they were tired and wanted to go to bed. But the invitation from the general cannot be refused, so the officers make their way to his large house, which is half a mile from the village.

Von Rabbeck and his wife greet the nineteen men cordially when they arrive, but they think that the general has invited them only because he feels under an obligation to do so. The house is already crowded with family and neighbors. About a dozen people are gathered in the dining room, and when the officers enter, they feel awkward. The officer named Ryabovich, who is shy, feels particularly uncomfortable in this social setting. He is struck by the confidence and zest with which the other people in the room socialize with one another. He likes the family, even though he thinks they are insincere.

After tea, the officers enter the drawing room, where many women are gathered. Someone starts to play the piano, and dancing begins. Lieutenant Lobytko, who is confident with the ladies, dances with a young lady in a lilac dress. Ryabovich does not know how to dance, so he just watches, feeling regretful that he cannot join in.

Von Rabbeck's son invites two officers to play a game of billiards. Ryabovich, who has nothing else to do, follows them. The game takes place in a small room in another part of the house. Ryabovich, who does not know how

to play billiards, just watches. After a while he becomes bored and leaves the room. He intends to go back to the drawing room, but he gets lost and ends up entering a completely dark room. He hears footsteps, and then a woman comes up to him, puts her arms around him, and kisses him on the cheek. Then she gives a little shriek and pulls back. She leaves the room quickly.

Stunned with surprise, Ryabovich returns to the drawing room. At first he is embarrassed and thinks everyone must know what has just happened; then he realizes that this is not so, and he feels exhilarated by the fact that for the first time in his life he has been kissed by a woman. He becomes friendly and sociable, and as he eats supper he tries to understand the unusual incident. He decides that the woman must have arranged to meet a man in the darkened room for a romantic encounter and simply mistook Ryabovich for that man. He looks around at the women sitting at the table, wondering which one it could have been. He looks at the attractive young woman in the lilac dress and hopes it was her. Then he notices a girl in a black dress and hopes it was her. He looks at other women, wondering, but concludes that it is difficult to know who the woman might have been.

After supper the officers leave. They are all in good spirits. When they get back to their quarters, Ryabovich, Lobytko, and Lieutenant Merzlyakov prepare for bed. Ryabovich can still feel the sensation of being kissed. As he relives the incident, he feels joyful, and as he goes to sleep, he feels happy.

When he wakes in the morning he still feels full of joy. He hears the voice of Lebedetzky, the commander of Ryabovich's battery, shouting at his sergeant. The sergeant reports on some of the small incidents that have taken place with the men. Lebedetzky looks in on the three officers, Ryabovich, Lobytko, and Lieutenant Merzlyakov, and says good morning to them. Soon, the brigade is on its way. Ryabovich feels sad as they pass the house where the unknown woman kissed him and leave the village behind. He daydreams about her, imagining the two of them married with children.

The general of the brigade drives by in a carriage, and Ryabovich and other officers ride up to him. The general makes a few criticisms and a weak joke and moves on. Ryabovich convinces himself that his daydreaming is normal;

everyone at some point marries and has children, and this will happen for him, too. The brigade ends its march in the evening, and Ryabovich, Lobytko, and Merzlyakov have supper in their tent. Ryabovich drinks three glasses of beer and then tells his companions about what happened to him at the general's house. Merzlyakov is not interested, and Lobytko tells a story of his own, which is probably a lie.

As the days go by, Ryabovich continues to remember the incident, and he acts like a man who is in love. At the end of August, he leaves camp with two batteries of the brigade. When they approach the village where von Rabbeck and his family lives, he is excited. He expects to be invited back, but no messenger comes. Anxious, he walks through the village alone and reaches von Rabbeck's garden gate. But there are no lights and no sounds. He walks away and comes to a river, where he watches the rippling water. He no longer has any hope of meeting the woman again, and life seems pointless and aimless to him. His own life seems wretched. When he returns to camp, his comrades are not there. A servant tells him that they were invited to visit von Rabbeck. Ryabovich feels a moment of joy, but then he is angry at the situation he is in and decides not to go to the general's house.

CHARACTERS

Lebedetzky
Lebedetzky is the commander of Ryabovich's battery. He is short-sighted, with a red beard.

Lieutenant Lobytko
Lieutenant Lobytko is one of the officers who visit Lieutenant-General von Rabbeck's house. He is a contrast to Ryabovich. The twenty-five-year-old Lobytko is tall, confident, and sociable. He talks a lot and likes to drink beer. He is also successful with women and looks forward to meeting women at the general's house. He chats with the fair girl in the black dress and dances with the young lady in the lilac dress. Later, when Ryabovich tells him and Merzlyakov about the incident in the dark room, Lobytko, who is known to be a liar, recites a story of his own about meeting a woman on a train.

Lieutenant Merzlyakov
Lieutenant Merzlyakov is one of Ryabovich's comrades. He is a quiet, well-educated man who spends much time reading a literary journal titled the *Messenger of Europe*. He does not take much notice when Ryabovich tells him and Lobytko about his encounter with the unknown woman.

Lieutenant-General von Rabbeck
Lieutenant-General von Rabbeck is a local landowner who invites the officers of the artillery brigade to visit him as they are passing through the village. Von Rabbeck is a handsome man of about sixty and appears to be retired from the army, since he greets his guests in civilian dress. He is courteous but is not overjoyed to see the nineteen officers he has invited. The house is already full with family guests, and he issued the invitation solely because he felt obliged to do so. Nonetheless, he does his best to entertain his guests and keep them happy.

Lieutenant-General von Rabbeck's Son
Von Rabbeck's son is tall with a red mustache. At the social gathering he talks loudly in English. He dances a waltz with a young lady and then invites two officers who are not dancing to another room for a game of billiards.

Lieutenant-General von Rabbeck's Wife
The wife of the general is a tall and graceful woman who resembles the Empress Eugénie (the wife of Louis-Napoléon Bonaparte, known as Napoléon III of France). However, like her husband, she receives the officers as guests only because she is obliged to do so; she does not really want them there. Nevertheless, she is a skillful hostess who knows how to entertain her guests.

Ryabovich
Ryabovich is the main character in the story. He is one of the army officers who visit the general's house. Ryabovich is small and round-shouldered. He wears glasses, has "lynx-like whiskers," and is not physically attractive. He is also shy and socially awkward. He feels uncomfortable at the general's house and cannot assert himself in the way that the others do. He is timid. Unused to socializing, he seems to have few skills in that area. He does not dance, and he

is mournful as he watches the others doing so, aware of his own inadequacy. The only games he knows how to play are card games, so he cannot participate in the game of billiards that some of the officers are playing. He just stands and watches. Not surprisingly, he is not experienced with women either. When, in the darkened room, an unknown woman puts her arms around him and kisses him, it is the first time that such a thing has happened to him. As he goes back to the drawing room, at first he feels confused and ashamed, but those feelings are quickly replaced by a kind of exaltation and joy. As he falls asleep that night, "his last thought was that someone had caressed him and made him happy—that something extraordinary, foolish, but joyful and delightful, had come into his life." In later days he pictures himself with the young woman and even marrying her. But eventually he is brought back to earth with the realization that he is not likely ever to see her again.

Young Blonde in Black Dress

The young blonde in the black dress attracts the attention of Lobytko, although she does not appear to be very interested in him. After the incident in which Ryabovich is kissed by an unknown woman, Ryabovich for a while hopes that it was she. Comparing her favorably to the woman in the lilac dress, he thinks, "She was younger, simpler, and more genuine, had a charming brow, and drank very daintily out of her wineglass." Later he thinks admiringly of her "candid eyes."

Young Lady in Lilac Dress

The young lady in the lilac dress is one of the guests at the von Rabbeck house. Ryabovich notices her as she takes part in a lively discussion about military matters with other guests. She argues forcefully that the artillery personnel have it much easier than the cavalry and the infantry, even though she knows little about the subject. Ryabovich notices the insincerity of her smile. Later, she is invited to dance by Lobytko. Ryabovich thinks she is attractive for "she had beautiful shoulders and arms, a clever face, and a delightful voice," although he does not care for what he thinks is her artificial laugh.

THEMES

Isolation

The main psychological interest of "The Kiss" centers on the character of Ryabovich, the army officer. As long as he is engaged in routine army activity or talking with his comrades, he seems to fit in reasonably well, but when he attends the social gathering at the house of Lieutenant-General von Rabbeck, his limitations are shown in sharp relief. He simply does not fit in well in a social gathering. He is shy, timid, and self-conscious. At first he is so confused at being thrust into this social situation that he is almost unable to function and feels only "alarm and a desire to hide his head." This is shyness in full measure and is completely disabling for him. In this respect, Ryabovich, who may well be an accomplished soldier, comes across more like an adolescent who has yet to learn basic social skills. His unprepossessing appearance adds to his predicament, since, as the narrator states, it appears to convey the message "I am the shyest, most modest, and most undistinguished officer in the whole brigade!"

Ryabovich suffers from what would now be called low self-esteem, and it is this that leads to his isolation. It prevents him from enjoying dancing, playing billiards, or mixing easily with others in a social situation. So isolated is Ryabovich that he has never kissed or been kissed by a woman. As the game of life is played out in front of him in the general's house, he is an uncomfortable spectator, part of a group yet feeling separate from it, unable to do the things that the other people do so easily. It is because he is so isolated that he reacts in such an extreme way when he is unexpectedly kissed by the unknown woman. Even when the kiss ignites his dormant feelings and makes him happy and sociable, he remains isolated. His inner world has changed from fear and inhibition to daydreams of love, but these are in their way just as isolating, because they are not based in any firm reality and lead inevitably to disillusionment.

Romantic Love

The theme of romantic love might also be referred to as the power that lies in a kiss. The sensual touch of a woman is all it takes for this young, inexperienced army officer to be

TOPICS FOR FURTHER STUDY

- Research shyness online, starting with the Shyness Research Institute at http://www.ius.edu/shyness/. What kind of strategies can be used to overcome shyness? Consult *Don't Be Shy* (2005), by Claude Clement and Melissa Daly, a book aimed at preteens and teens. With another student, give a class presentation in which you present your findings.

- Write a short story featuring a shy person who has an interaction with the opposite sex that changes him or her in some manner. Post your short story on a blog to share with your classmates. Allow your classmates to comment, and then integrate their feedback into your story.

- Make a video recording of yourself reading "The Kiss" and upload it to YouTube. For inspiration, listen to the famous British actor Kenneth Branagh reading Chekhov's "Oh! The Public," available at http://www.youtube.com/watch?v = q6Zd0gFS4FM.

- Read another story by Chekhov and write an essay in which you compare and contrast it to "The Kiss." Suggestions include "The Grasshopper," "Gooseberries," and "The Lady with the Little Dog."

transported into a different, more exalted and thrilling state of mind. It is an experience quite unlike anything he has ever had in his life. It animates his being in ways that eluded him before, and he forgets all about his shyness and awkwardness. He wants to dance, to talk, to run into the garden. He converses easily with the hostess, smiling broadly the whole time. It is as if he has been transformed into an altogether different person. Even though he does not know who the woman was and knows the whole incident was a mistake, he falls in love with her, or at least the image of her he has formed in his

mind. The memory of the incident lives on for him, like the taste of a fine meal or wine, and it feeds the deeper needs of his being: his needs for love and intimacy, for the prospect of a wife and family of his own. Once started, his romantic imagination knows no bounds. He daydreams about the future he will have with this woman whose name he does not know and whom he is unlikely to meet again—and he likely would not know her if he did meet her again, since he never saw her face.

Such is the way the romantic imagination in a shy, isolated young man constructs so much—a passionate, lasting love—on the basis of so little—a kiss in the dark that was never even intended for him. It is an outpouring of intense and irrational feeling in a man who previously held himself well in check, and it is in marked contrast to the dull, mechanical routines of army life that he knows so well. This is emphasized in the story when the brigade moves on the next day; Ryabovich understands exactly why the army moves in the formation and manner that it does. This bores him now, because his mind has been taken over by the antithesis of tedious routine, the astonishing excitement of a man whose mind is in turmoil because of the touch of a woman. Romantic love, the sphere of intense, unpredictable feeling, is thus contrasted with the dull, unimaginative world of the soldier riding with his horses and cannon in a perfect, orderly procession in which everything is under firm control.

Disillusionment

Since the incident that sparks Ryabovich's intoxicated state of feeling is so brief and insubstantial, it is not the least surprising that he comes down to earth with a bump. Reality intrudes on his romantic fantasies when, on the way back from camp some months later with a portion of the brigade, he returns to the village where the general lives. He allows his hopes to build, but when there is no invitation from the general, he realizes in a moment of bitter frustration that he will never see the woman again. His disillusionment is such that he seems to end up in a worse condition than he was before the encounter with her. He thinks there is no purpose in the world. The way things happen is just pointless. Disappointed in love—even though the entire experience was wholly a construction of his own mind—he

Uniforms of Russian soldiers in the late nineteenth century (© *Hein Nouwens | ShutterStock.com*)

reaches a despairing conclusion about life as a whole. Ryabovich has moved from isolation to an imagined communion with a loved object—the woman—to a disillusionment that leaves him even more isolated from other people than he was before, in two respects. First, he now believes that life is pointless, a cruel joke that no one can understand, and second, just a little while later he decides to remain by himself and not go to the general's house, despite the fact that the long-desired invitation was, in fact, made.

STYLE

River Image
The river that flows near the general's house features three times in the story, but with very different effects. The first occurrence of the image is a positive one. The officers are returning from their evening at the general's house, and they take a path that leads by the river. It is nighttime, and the reflection of the stars can be seen in the water; they are broken up, which

indicates that the river "was flowing rapidly." The flowing river forms part of the tranquil, harmonious evening scene, which is in keeping with the mellow, contented mood of the officers.

The image of the river recurs later, in a similarly positive fashion, when the brigade leaves the village. Ryabovich is still intoxicated with the memory of the kiss. As he looks back at the village, he sees the river bathed in sunlight: "the river with its bright green banks, with the blue sky reflected in it and glints of silver in the sunshine here and there, was very beautiful."

The third occurrence of the image, however, shows a dramatic change. Before, the river was part of the harmony and beauty of nature. Now, as Ryabovich gazes at it, having lost hope that he will ever see the woman again, the river tells him a different story. As he looks down on it,

> the river ran rapidly and with a faintly audible gurgle round the piles of the bathing cabin. The red moon was reflected near the left bank; little ripples ran over the reflection, stretching it out, breaking it into bits, and seemed trying to carry it away.

The image has acquired an ominous tone that it did not have in the first instance. It is as if the water is tugging at the reflected moon, doing it violence, wrenching it out of shape and taking it captive. The image reflects the more pessimistic frame of mind that is now afflicting Ryabovich. The harmony of nature has been broken. And as Ryabovich continues to gaze at the river, his observation and thoughts about the natural cycle of water lead him to his final, nihilistic conclusion:

> The water was running, he knew not where or why, just as it did in May. At that time it had flowed into a great river, from the great river into the sea; then it had risen in vapor, turned into rain, and perhaps the very same water was running now before Ryabovich's eyes again.... What for? Why?

Nature continues in an unending cycle, but for Ryabovich in his disappointment it has taken on a negative slant. The river that formerly was beautiful has become a symbol of the pointlessness of life; life is an "unintelligible, aimless jest." Thus the imagery of the river can be seen as an expression of the changing mood of the character.

The Modern Short Story
This story departs from the type of short story that was more common in the late nineteenth century, which depended on well-developed plot and character for its effects. Chekhov pioneered a new type of story in which plot is minimal. Instead, the focus, while the story is still realistic, is on mood and atmosphere. According to Charles E. May in "Chekhov and the Modern Short Story," Chekhov's

> freedom from the literary conventions of the highly plotted and formalized story marked the beginnings of a new or "modern" kind of short fiction that combined the specific detail of realism with the poetic lyricism of romanticism.

May identified some of the characteristics of this new type of story as "character as mood rather than . . . realistic depiction; story as minimal lyricized sketch rather than as elaborately plotted tale"; the importance of an atmosphere that is in part created by the mind and feelings of the protagonist; and an understanding of reality as shaped not so much by objective truth but by individual point of view. All these elements are present in "The Kiss."

HISTORICAL CONTEXT

Chekhov at Voskresensk and Babkino
For some of the characters and for the countryside setting of "The Kiss," Chekhov drew on the places where he lived and visited in the early and mid-1880s. In 1880, his brother obtained a teaching position at the small town of Voskresensk, which was about thirty-five miles west of Moscow. Chekhov would visit Voskresensk, where he met not only members of the medical profession but also the officers of a battalion stationed there. Chekhov befriended the officers and went for walks with them.

In the mid-1880s, Chekhov spent his summers at Babkino, a village about three miles from Voskresensk. As Rosamund Bartlett notes in *Chekhov: Scenes from a Life*, he and his family rented a dacha there, and they also stayed sometimes at the estate of their friends, the Kiselyov family, which lay on the banks of the river Istra. Chekhov wrote to his editor Nikolai Leikin, as quoted by Bartlett:

> The estate is very beautiful, it stands on a steep bank . . . The river is down below, full of fish, beyond the river is an enormous forest . . . I love being in the countryside in the beginning of May . . . It's fun to watch the leaves coming out, and hear the nightingales begin to sing.

COMPARE
&
CONTRAST

- **Late 19th century:** Russia is in the process of modernization, attempting to catch up with the development of western European countries such as Great Britain and France. Rapid industrialization takes place, although the population is still largely rural. Education becomes more widespread, and literacy rates improve. The government expands, creating a sizable bureaucracy under the authoritarian rule of Czar Alexander III (reigned 1881–1894).

  Today: Russia maintains the appearance of being a democratic nation and holds regular national elections, but it is a largely authoritarian state firmly under the rule of the central government. However, unlike in the era of Communism, Russia has a market-based economy and is integrated into the world economy. In 2011, Russia is the leading oil producer in the world.

- **Late 19th century:** In the last two decades of the century, Fyodor Dostoyevsky publishes *The Brothers Karamazov* (1880), and Leo Tolstoy publishes two novellas, *The Death of Ivan Ilyich* (1886) and *The Kreutzer Sonata* (1889), and his final novel, *Resurrection* (1899).

  Today: Popular Russian writers whose work has been translated into English include Lyudmila Ulitskaya, author of *The Funeral Party* (2002) and *Daniel Stein, Interpreter* (2011); Viktor Pelevin, who wrote *Buddha's Little Finger* (2001) and *The Blue Lantern: Stories* (2000); Oksana Robski, author of *Casual* (2006); and Yuri Buida, author of the novel *The Zero Train* (2007).

- **Late 19th century:** As a result of military reforms during the rule of Czar Alexander II (reigned 1855–1881), military service becomes compulsory for all classes of society in 1874. Other reforms include the abolition of corporal punishment in the military.

  Today: Male Russian citizens are registered for the draft at age seventeen and must serve one year in the military, although they cannot be sent to combat zones before they have had six months of training. However, 61 percent of draft-age Russian males receive deferments. Military expenditure in Russia amounts to 3.9 percent of gross domestic product (GDP), ranking the nation 25th in the world in that measure. (The United States ranks 23rd, with 4.06 percent of GDP spent on defense programs.)

It is not difficult to see in this description some of the elements of the setting that went into "The Kiss," written in 1887, the last summer that Chekhov stayed in Babkino. During these summers Chekhov would sit by the river and fish or go out walking in the woods to hunt for mushrooms. In the evenings he and his family would spend evenings with the Kiselyovs in the main house on the estate. As Bartlett notes, "The months spent in the Moscow countryside were fundamental to Chekhov's creativity in the middle of the 1880s, inspiring an increasing number of poetic stories."

The Golden Age of Russian Literature

The period of Czar Alexander II's reign (1855–1881) is sometimes referred to as the golden age of Russian literature, especially the realistic novel. The three best-known novelists of the period were Leo Tolstoy (1828–1910), Fyodor Dostoyevsky (1821–1881), and Ivan Turgenev (1818–1883). Of these three, the greatest was Tolstoy, especially as evidenced in his novels *War and Peace* (1869) and *Anna Karenina* (1877). Dostoyevsky's work during this period included *Crime and Punishment* (1866) and *The Brothers Karamazov* (1880). Turgenev is

Ryabovich receives a kiss by mistake when he attends a party at an officer's estate. *(© formiktopus /* *ShutterStock.com)*

known principally for his novel *Fathers and Sons* (1862). All these authors also wrote short fiction. Earlier in the century, Mikhail Lermontov (1814–1841), known principally for his novel *A Hero of Our Time* (1839), also wrote short stories, as did Nikolai Leskov (1831–1895).

The work of these authors was part of Chekhov's literary heritage when he began his literary career in the 1880s. By then the golden age was almost over. Dostoyevsky and Turgenev died when Chekhov was in his early twenties,

and, according to D. S. Mirsky in *A History of Russian Literature*, "the younger generation had...nothing to show to compare with the work of their fathers." The sole survivor of the golden age into Chekhov's artistic maturity was Tolstoy, whose work changed dramatically after 1880 following his conversion to Christianity. Chekhov met Tolstoy in 1895, and the two men became friends, although Chekhov's work was not much influenced by that of his older contemporary, whom many regard as the greatest novelist of all time.

CRITICAL OVERVIEW

"The Kiss" has a reputation as one of Chekhov's finest stories. In *A New Life of Anton Chekhov*, Ronald Hingley lists it as one of Chekhov's three best stories from the period 1880–1887. (The others are "Typhus" and "The Schoolmaster.") In these stories, as well as in much of Chekhov's best work, "precious little happens," Hingley writes. "It was not 'what happens,' or even 'what does not happen,'" he goes on, "but 'how it felt' which more and more constituted the essence of Chekhov's stories." In *Chekhov: A Spirit Set Free*, V. S. Pritchett praises the story for the manner in which Chekhov gives insight into military life while "yet avoiding tedious documentation." He "put a regiment on duty plainly before us as human beings." Pritchett concludes of Ryabovich that "it seems likely, given his dullness and the routine of military life, that his isolation will be lasting. He will be locked in himself." Ralph Lindheim, in "Chekhov's Major Themes," writes that "the hero's pained awareness of his diminished and limited existence leads him against his better instincts to isolate himself from life, to protect himself against the recurrence of illusion and the inevitability of disappointment."

Donald Rayfield, in *Understanding Chekhov: A Critical Study of Chekhov's Prose and Drama*, argues that "The Kiss" is one of the stories in which Chekhov tries to "disperse the various lies that cloud human vision." One such lie is what Rayfield calls the "social and sexual lie, the lubricant of human contact." In the story, Ryabovich ends up being "tortured by speculations about the kiss. Hitherto merely shy and self-conscious in society, he becomes obsessed." Rayfield also notes that the story was admired by army officers, and he praises its "feeling for the sensitivities of an all-male world," which Chekhov likely picked up while getting to know the men of the artillery battalion stationed at Voskresensk.

For Ronald L. Johnson, in *Anton Chekhov: A Study of the Short Fiction*, Chekhov's achievement in this story lies first in making Ryabovich's experience "so vividly convincing, so his mundane life swells with emotional richness," and second in "illustrating the humanness in his terrible disappointment when he achieves 'true' perspective on his dreams." Ian Almond, in "Chekhovian Overtones in Early Joyce: Some Brief Remarks on 'Araby' and 'The Kiss,'" sees a similarity between Chekhov's story and James Joyce's story "Araby." Almond argues that both stories

> parody the traditional form of the moral tale, in which the main characters cherish a foolish fancy, suffer a delusion but through such disappointment arrive at some profounder understanding of truth which they had been hitherto blind to.... The "truth" finally arrived at by the protagonist is far from comforting, reassuring or morally uplifting.

CRITICISM

Bryan Aubrey
Aubrey holds a PhD in English. In the following essay, he examines "The Kiss" as a study in shyness.

A wide variety of characters appear in the stories of Anton Chekhov, and in "The Kiss" he presents his readers with a portrait of a man who is largely defined by his dominant personality trait, his shyness. The army officer Ryabovich is a shy man, and the story shows how his mood and feelings are affected by this shyness, with largely negative results as far as his happiness is concerned. As with many Chekhov stories, there is not a great deal of action in "The Kiss." Although it is a substantial story of nearly eight thousand words, it would not be difficult to summarize the action in a sentence or two. Indeed, Ryabovich finds this out for himself when he confides in his two comrades the story of what happened to him in the general's house. He thinks beforehand that it will take a long time to tell them about the incident, but in fact, to his disappointment, the story is all over in just a few moments. He cannot convey what the kiss meant to his inner life—how it affected his emotions, how it changed his perception of himself—when his audience consists of a mostly silent intellectual who is more interested in reading his magazine and a womanizer who merely laughs at an innocuous tale of a random kiss and invents a more racy story of his own on the spot. "The Kiss," therefore, is not about outer events; it explores the more subtle, hidden realm of human feeling and emotion in a particular type of man.

The Shyness Research Institute of Indiana University Southeast defines shyness as "a syndrome...characterized by social anxiety and behavioral inhibition resulting from the feeling that others are evaluating you." Shyness produces a number of physiological reactions, including

WHAT DO I READ NEXT?

- "The Lady with the Little Dog" is a very well-known short story by Chekhov, first published in 1899. In marked contrast to "The Kiss," in which a romance takes place only in the mind of the protagonist, in this story a man and woman embark on what they expect will be a fleeting affair, but it proves to be much more durable than either could have imagined. The story can be found in *The Lady with the Little Dog and Other Stories* (2002), translated by Ronald Wilks.

- Like Chekhov, Katherine Mansfield was an acknowledged master of the short story. Writing in the early twentieth century, Mansfield admired Chekhov and was a friend of other literary giants of the era, such as D. H. Lawrence and Virginia Woolf. She died in 1923 at the age of thirty-four, leaving a body of work that is still admired and read today. *The Garden Party and Other Stories* (2008), edited by Lorna Sage, contains fifteen of Mansfield's finest stories.

- *The Plays of Anton Chekhov* (1997) includes *The Seagull, Uncle Vanya, Three Sisters, The Cherry Orchard*, and eight other plays by Chekhov, translated by Paul Schmidt. The translations, by a Russian-language scholar who also acted in many Chekhov plays, has been widely praised. Since Chekhov's reputation rests on his plays as well as his short stories, a knowledge of the plays is essential for understanding the range of his achievement.

- *The Best Short Stories of Fyodor Dostoevsky* (2001), translated by David Magarshack, contains seven stories by the great nineteenth-century Russian writer, including "Notes from the Underground," which is often regarded as the first work of existential literature.

- *The Death of Ivan Ilyich and Other Stories* (2010), translated by Richard Pevear and Larissa Volokhonsky, is a collection of eleven short stories by Leo Tolstoy, one of Russia's greatest authors. Chekhov met Tolstoy in August 1895, and the two men remained friends until Chekhov's death. Although Chekhov rejected Tolstoy's teachings concerning Christian pacifism, he greatly admired the older writer's novels *War and Peace* and *Anna Karenina*. This collection of stories is an accessible introduction to Tolstoy's work in this genre.

- *Other Voices, Other Vistas: Short Stories from Africa, China, India, Japan, and Latin America* (2002), edited by Barbara H. Solomon, is an anthology of contemporary fiction divided into five sections, each representing a geographical region and containing five stories. Among the twenty-five writers represented are Chinua Achebe and Nadine Gordimer (Africa), Wang Anyi and Ding Ling (China), Anita Desai and Ruth Prawer Jhabvala (India), Kobo Abe and Sawako Ariyoshi (Japan), and Jorge Luis Borges and Isabel Allende (Latin America).

- *Eternal Spring: A Young Adult Short Story Collection* (2012) includes thirteen stories that explore what happens in the lives of teenagers when love comes calling in the springtime. Although the time and place differ markedly from Chekhov's exploration of a springtime romantic fantasy in "The Kiss," the emotions felt by Ryabovich are not so removed from what these teens go through when romantic feelings arise. One story ("1:30, Tour Eiffel," by Jennifer McAndrews) even revolves, like "The Kiss," around a kiss in the dark. Many of the authors of these stories have won prestigious literary awards.

- *A Life in Letters* (2004), edited by Rosamund Bartlett, is a selection of Chekhov's letters, translated by Antony Phillips. Of the thousands of letters Chekhov wrote, this selection includes letters to his family, to publishers and theater directors, and to his wife. The letters provide a fascinating window into Chekhov's day-to-day thoughts and concerns.

THE TOUCH OF A WOMAN, THE IRRATIONAL
FEELING IT GENERATES IN RYABOVICH THAT
PERHAPS EVEN HE CAN BE LOVED, TRANSFORMS
HIM. HIS JOY COMPLETELY ERASES HIS EARLIER,
AND CUSTOMARY, FEELING OF SEPARATENESS."

"anxiety, muscle tension, increased heart rate, upset stomach." The condition "reflects the excessive sense of self-consciousness…negative self-appraisal…[and] irrational belief system (e.g., Nobody at the party will find me interesting) characteristic of the way that shy people think about themselves." Shyness results in "behavioral inhibition (e.g., not speaking to others at a party) and social avoidance (e.g., avoiding eye contact or standing in the corner during a group discussion)." Shyness is not uncommon. In a survey mentioned by the Shyness Research Institute, 40 percent of respondents reported it as a characteristic of their personality. Only 7 percent of Americans report that they have never experienced shyness. In coping with shyness, many people consult psychotherapists, and some are prescribed drugs that lessen the anxiety shy people feel in certain social situations. Some shy people withdraw from social contact. If a shy person happens also to be introverted, he or she may be content to spend large amounts of time alone, but many shy people want and need to socialize but are too self-conscious to do so without anxiety and distress.

In "The Kiss," Ryabovich exhibits many of the characteristics that are typical of shy people. Chekhov has captured the type with a remarkable degree of accuracy. It is typical of shy people, for example, to feel anxious when first entering a room full of people at a social event. Ryabovich feels not only anxious but indeed alarmed. A shy person may feel an impulse just to run away, to turn around and leave the room, or at least to find some quiet corner to hide in. Ryabovich wants to hide his head. As he sits at the table he cannot look anyone in the face. He does not want to see or be seen because he might then have to engage in a social interaction, which it appears he has never learned to do with

comfort and ease. He is afflicted by feelings of confusion and disorientation, which also may happen to shy people who are suddenly confronted with a situation that is outside their normal experience and comfort zone.

Shy people may be particularly conscious of their own appearance and judge themselves harshly. Ryabovich is no exception in this regard. He is acutely aware that he is not, to put it mildly, the most handsome man in the room. Unfortunately, he overheard a conversation between two women, either at this party or on another occasion, that confirmed him in this low opinion of himself. One of the women referred to his "undistinguished appearance."

Some shy people may attempt to overcome their handicap by forcing themselves to be sociable, while others may just passively accept their condition. Ryabovich belongs in the latter category. He has known for years that he is timid and seems to accept that he is also uninteresting. He used to envy the social skills of others, particularly those of his companions who possessed "boldness and swagger," but over the years he has grown used to his condition, so that when he looks at his fellow officers "dancing or loudly talking, he no longer envied them, but only felt touched and mournful." This is not the only passage that mentions people talking loudly. Von Rabbeck's son is described in this way, too, but it is likely that the description represents the way Ryabovich is perceiving the situation. A shy person lacking confidence may speak more softly than others and think that others are talking loudly even if they are not. A similar perception may apply when a shy person observes the social skills of others, as when Ryabovich is struck by the "extraordinary boldness of his new acquaintances." Again, that is likely his impression only; the men and women he observes are probably just behaving as people normally do in a lively social situation.

In short, in social situations, shy people, like Ryabovich in the story, feel different from others, set apart from them, as if they are not connected to what is going on around them. It can seem as if there is some mysterious wall that separates them from other people in the room and a feeling that others sense this and give them a wide berth because of it. Sometimes shy people are too nervous or timid even to speak. Tellingly, Ryabovich is not shown

The kiss becomes a hugely significant moment in Ryabovich's mind. (© coka | ShutterStock.com)

saying a single word to anyone until after the surprise kiss. He simply watches others. He is an observer. He does not join in because he does not know how to. And after a while he ends up (in the room where the men are playing billiards) feeling that he is just in the way. This is a man who is at the mercy of a personality trait that does not serve him well but which he has been unable to overcome.

Until, that is, the kiss. This chance encounter, so small and meaningless in any objective consideration, seems to work on him like some magical, instant cure, an antidote to shyness. The touch of a woman, the irrational feeling it generates in Ryabovich that perhaps even he can be loved, transforms him. His joy completely erases his earlier, and customary, feeling of separateness. He is shown talking in an animated and friendly way to the hostess, for example, which are the first words attributed directly to him in the story. When he reflects on his new dreams of love, he thinks of other military men he knows, none of them attractive, who nonetheless have been in love and are now married, and he has what for him is a revelatory moment. He feels

normal, like other men, not set apart from them. "I am the same as everyone else," he realizes. And, as he reflects further, "the thought that he was an ordinary person and that his life was ordinary delighted him and gave him courage." This is an interesting reversal of what might more often be the case, in which people take delight in feeling in some way unique or special. Not Ryabovich. As a shy person, he has found a way of being just ordinary, and that is fine by him. Indeed, it represents a small triumph.

Alas, Ryabovich finds out that it is not so easy to escape or change one's own nature, especially when the escape route is made up of a series of illusions and fanciful ideas. When the layers of illusion crumble—and they crumble very quickly once the process starts—this army officer finds that more than a kiss in the dark and the fragrance of a woman are needed to make him other than he really is. And because he gave in to the sweet illusion of romantic love, in what were in truth almost comic circumstances, he ends up feeling bitter about not only the poverty of his own life but also the absurdity, the meaninglessness, of life itself.

Source: Bryan Aubrey, Critical Essay on "The Kiss," in *Short Stories for Students*, Gale, Cengage Learning, 2014.

Ronald L. Johnson

In the following excerpt, Johnson discusses "The Kiss" in the context of Chekhov's other short stories about love.

In the three-year period from 1885 to 1887, between the ages of twenty-five to twenty-eight, Chekhov made the transition from being primarily a writer of comic entertainment to a serious artist who wrote, not parody and comic sketches, but realistic stories about a wide range of subjects. Some of these stories—such masterpieces as "Misery," "Easter Eve," and "The Kiss"—are now commonly anthologized. Stories such as these not only marked a breakthrough in Russian literature in terms of form and conciseness, but also set the standard in literature for what was to become the traditional form of the short story. In his study of Chekhov's fiction, Karl Kramer aptly terms this traditional form one of "moral revelation," a concept that, as Kramer notes, Northrop Frye uses in conjunction with his analysis of the development of the realistic novel (Kramer, 11–27). It is easy to undervalue Chekhov's development of artistic techniques in these stories since they have become so commonplace in stories by subsequent writers.

With Chekhov's increasing interest in the serious realistic story came an expansion in his publishing outlets, with new editors in turn spurring him on in this direction. His stories not only became more realistic, but he was allowed more length, until he was regularly writing stories of three to six thousand words, often more. This transition was not abrupt, but gradual. Chekhov continued to contribute pieces regularly to the entertainment magazines until late in 1887, although by January of that year, he was disgusted with the entertainment magazine and wanted "to turn out something bigger, or not write at all" (Yarmolinsky, 44).

One of the more important events in changing Chekhov's attitude toward writing serious fiction during this period was a letter he received from Dmitry Grigorovich (1822–1899), a literary lion of the age. In 1886, Grigorovich wrote a letter in response to the more serious stories Chekhov was publishing, in particular to "The Huntsman," in which he termed Chekhov a major talent and urged him to abandon his practice of working toward a press deadline so he could commit himself more completely to his stories. In his reply, Chekhov pledged to change his approach to writing, to commit himself as a literary artist. Chekhov vowed to spend more time with his stories, instead of simply dashing them off and sending them to an editor. Although he could not immediately change his working habits for financial reasons, gradually he positioned himself to attempt more ambitious work with deliberate care.

. . . The events in "The Kiss" (Garnett) revolve around the emotions of an ordinary man, a "little man," the quintessential Chekhovian hero. Ryabovitch, an artillery officer of common feelings and intelligence, is physically small in stature with sloping shoulders, spectacles, and lynxlike whiskers; his appearance suggests he is the "most undistinguished officer in the whole brigade." One evening at a party, Ryabovitch accidentally wanders into a dark room where an unknown woman clasps him in her arms and passionately kisses him. When the woman realizes he is not the man with whom she had an appointed rendezvous, she flees, her face unseen, and Ryabovitch experiences a new sensation, wanting "to dance, to talk, to run into the garden, to laugh out loud." He forgets his undistinguished appearance, and searches for the woman.

Although Ryabovitch cannot identify the woman, later at his quarters the thought of the kiss gives him an "intense groundless joy." He feels something "extraordinary, foolish, but joyful and delightful" has come into his life. When the brigade marches away to another district, he clings to this new agreeable thought to fight the boredom of his life. Ryabovitch considers himself an ordinary person, but now because of his dreams of a relationship with the woman, this ordinariness of his life "delighted him and gave him courage." At summer's end, Ryabovitch is assigned back to the district where the party occurred. But as he passes the house where the party was held, he feels his dreams were all simply imaginings, and nothing will ever come of them. At this point, the whole world seems an "unintelligible, aimless jest"; his own life in particular "struck him as extraordinarily meager, poverty-stricken, and colorless." Chekhov's artistic achievement in "The Kiss" lies first in making this common imagining of a "little man" so vividly convincing, so his mundane life swells with emotional richness; and second, in illustrating the humanness in his terrible disappointment when he achieves "true" perspective on his dreams. Ironically, the imagined experience leaves the "little man" finally poorer in spirit....

Source: Ronald L. Johnson, "The Artist Emerges, 1885–1887," in *Anton Chekhov: A Study of the Short Fiction*, edited by Gordon Weaver, Twayne Publishers, 1993, pp. 17–18, 24–26.

Joseph L. Conrad

In the following excerpt, Conrad explains the significance of the garden as a romantic landscape in "The Kiss."

Anton Chekhov's short stories are not usually considered in terms of literary romanticism, yet many aspects associated with traditional romantic fiction can be found in his prose. In the three stories under consideration Chekhov did not merely adopt the conventions of romanticism: he began by including certain typical features, and then used them to produce situations that are more realistic, and certainly more in keeping with his own time, than those found in tales of the 1830s. A brief review of the essential characteristics of traditional romantic prose may be helpful before proceeding to discussion of those elements as found in "Verochka," "The Kiss," and "The Black Monk."

Romantic tales focus the reader's interest on an unusual event and its impact on the hero's psychology. That event occurs at a time in the hero's life when he finds himself in conflict with his environment. In the exemplary *Novellen* of the German romantic movement, the natural world is marked by a certain duality: temporal and spatial, organized and chaotic, spiritual and physical. It is a place where the egocentric protagonist searches for an unattainable ideal (cf. landscapes in the major works of Ludwig Tieck, Friedrich Novalis, E. T. A. Hoffmann, and Joseph von Eichendorff). But the vision of that ideal (e.g., Novalis's "blaue Blume," truth, eternal beauty, and/or ultimate perception of one's "true self"), is to be fleeting at best. The hero's search for an alternative to stifling routine brings him to reflection that results in understanding of his situation, however short-lived that understanding may be. Other important aspects of traditional romanticism include an interest in history (primarily the medieval period), distant lands, supernatural phenomena (especially the devil), and an integral role played by music.

> THE LEITMOTIV 'STRANGE,' FOUND FIRST IN THE UNUSUAL INVITATION AND THE UNDISCIPLINED HORSE, FIGURES PROMINENTLY IN RIABOVICH'S IMAGINATION AS HE LONGS FOR A REPEAT INVITATION."

Central to most romantic works is an unusual landscape that is often represented by a garden filled with exotic flora. Its description emphasizes the hero's sensory perceptions. Nature's components such as trees and bushes, birds and animals, the moon and stars, and even murky mists are described by verbs and adverbs normally restricted to human actions. In this way natural phenomena and supernatural or demonic forces are personified, thus making the unusual event seem more personal, for both the protagonist and the reader.

... A second stage in Chekhov's use of the romantic heritage can be illustrated by "The Kiss" ("Potselui"; December 1887), where the contrast between the real and the ideal is central. In this story there is regular interaction between the routine details of military life and the hero's fanciful imagination, which is stimulated by sensory perceptions associated with the garden. As we will see, the garden itself is brought inside, both inside the drawing room and inside the mind of the protagonist, Staff-Captain Riabovich.

The opening lines establish a properly realistic background; they read like a military report indicating the precise date (20 May) and time of evening (8:00 P.M.) when Riabovich's artillery brigade arrives at its bivouac. Yet no sooner has this specific information been given than the scene undergoes a transformation: "A rider in civilian dress, on a strange horse (*strannaia loshad'*) appeared from behind a church... the horse approached not directly but sideways, as it were, making little dancing movements as if it were being lashed on the legs." The horseman delivers a formal invitation to tea from retired general von Rabbek, and in a moment the rider and his strange horse disappear behind the church. "The devil knows what that means!"

some of the officers exclaim. Though the officers may not be aware of the danger of invoking the devil by name, readers familiar with romantic literature may be certain that something extraordinary is about to take place.

The scene itself, with its unexpected arrival of the strange horseman, suggests an apparition such as are found in romantic tales from the 1830s. In every way it challenges the regulated nature of military life: the rider is in civilian dress, his strange horse seems undisciplined, and they both appear and disappear "from behind the church." The role of the church is at first puzzling; it is mentioned six times at the beginning, once in the middle, and four times at the end of the story. In a sense, it functions as a frame. And if we think of the dual nature of the church as a place of religious awe and simultaneously dark and mysterious, we may surmise that Chekhov intended it to occupy a place more significant than that of a mere landmark. The rider appears from behind the church, just as pagan forces lurk behind the fervor associated with charismatic believers. Thus the church may be either an ambiguous shield or a source of the mysterious rider.

In a similar way, the landscape is initially undistinguished but soon becomes suggestive of danger. The officers are told that they can reach von Rabbek's estate by one of two paths: "a lower one, going down behind the church to the river and then along the bank to the garden itself... or the upper one—straight from the church along the road which... leads to the master's barns." That the landscape seems to betray a kind of dual personality is suggested by its description: "At the first barn the road divided in two: one branch went straight ahead and disappeared in the evening mist, the other went to the right, to the master's house.... Stone barns with red roofs, heavy and sullen-looking, very like barracks in a district town, stretched along both sides of the road."

At the general's house, even the mild, unassuming Riabovich notices that appearances are more important than reality (cf. the romantic concern with *Schein vs. Sein*). To be sure, the general and his wife follow the formal conventions of gracious hosts. But when she engages the guests in polite conversation, her "beautiful majestic smile" vanishes instantly from her face each time she turns away from them. Moreover, there is an air of something foreign about each:

von Rabbek bears a strange, un-Russian surname and his wife is likened to "Empress Eugénie." Further distortions of the ordinary occur: a group of men in the dining room are "wrapped in a haze of cigar smoke," and "some sort of thin young man with red whiskers" (red hair and whiskers are associated with the devil in traditional European folklore) is talking loudly in English, but with a continental accent (*kartavja*).

Riabovich, who considers himself to be "the shyest, most modest, and most colorless (*bestsvetny*) officer in the whole brigade!" begins to observe the others. The result is anything but positive: the drawingroom, the unfamiliar faces, the crystal decanters of brandy, and the steam from the glasses "become fused into one huge impression planting anxiety (*trevoga*) in Riabovich and a desire to hide his head." (Though he does not realize it, this attack of anxiety is a warning of what is to come.) Recovering his mental equilibrium, he singles out a young lady in a lilac dress, only to note an insincere smile that appears and disappears on her face as she ardently discusses something alien (*chuzhdo*) to her. The narrator tells us that "the more Riabovich looked and listened, the more he liked this insincere, but excellently disciplined family." The lack of sincerity seems to capture his fancy and makes him susceptible to the exciting emotional experience he is about to have.

That experience is prepared by unusual sensory perceptions linking the world outside to that within the drawing room: piano music, a melancholy waltz, flows from the room out the open windows, and the smell of young poplar leaves, roses, and lilacs floats inside. Transplanted into the drawingroom, the aromas of the garden become linked in Riabovich's perception with the women: the various scents seem to come "not from the garden, but from the women's faces and their gowns." References to the lilac blossoms and the "young lady in lilac" (*baryshnia v sirenevom*) recur often (twelve times) as a leitmotiv maintaining the connection between nature, the lilacs in the garden, their intoxicating scent intruding into the rooms, and the sexual stimulation provided by the unknown woman's perfume.

Sensuous nature reappears just before Riabovich is to experience the kiss that initiates his idyllic summer dreams and eventual despair. As he wanders through a darkened room he notices that the smells of poplar, lilac, and roses are coming through the open windows there as well. At this moment he hears hasty steps and the rustle of a dress; a woman's heavy-breathing voice whispers "Finally!" and he feels "two soft, perfumed...feminine arms" embrace him. A warm cheek touches his and a kiss resounds. This description emphasizes Riabovich's sensory perceptions; three of five senses are represented: aural, olfactory, and tactile; a fourth, visual perception is partly present (he sees light from the next room through a crack in the door). The final phrase (*razdalsia zvuk potseluia*) seems an almost bizarre expression for the culmination of a passionate embrace. And its effect is equally strange and magical for it leaves a fifth sensation, that of taste, as a light, mint-flavored, and pleasant chill on his cheek, which signals the beginning of the struggle between fantasy and reality within his mind and soul.

That Riabovich does not yet understand the event's significance is revealed by his mistaken thought: "This adventure (*prikliuchenie*) bore a mysterious and romantic (*romanicheski*) character, but it was not difficult to explain." Yet despite careful scrutiny of each female present, Riabovich cannot identify the mystery woman; rather he creates a composite figure and then begins his idealized, imaginary life with her. Thus, as in the romantic tradition, Riabovich's situation is transformed from the ordinary to the extraordinary; his is an experience that changes his life permanently.

The landscape description as the officers leave the party seems ominous:

> ... They went along the path which descended to the river and then ran along the edge of the water, bending around the shoreline bushes, pools, and the willows hanging above the water. The riverbank and path were barely visible, and the opposite bank was completely drowned in darkness. Here and there on the dark water were reflections of stars; they trembled and became scattered—and this was the only way that one could guess that the water ran swiftly. It was quiet. On the other bank sleepy sandpipers were moaning (*stonali*) but on this side, in one of the bushes,...a nightingale began to pour forth its call loudly. The officers stood next to the bush, touched it, but the nightingale kept on singing.

The threatening dark, the rushing water, the pitiful sound of the birds on the other side of the river, accompanied by the nightingale's insistent call (a warning sign in Slavic and European folklore), should give Riabovich reason for concern.

He does not take notice of them, however; and the remainder of the story pulses between his romantic imagination and military routine.

The leitmotiv "strange," found first in the unusual invitation and the undisciplined horse, figures prominently in Riabovich's imagination as he longs for a repeat invitation. It returns to close the episode. When the unit passes by the von Rabbek estate once again, the river and its banks are the same as before, but there is no aroma of the trees and bushes; even the warning call of the nightingale is missing. The garden's former magic has evaporated, and Riabovich now thinks that it would indeed be strange if he were to meet his unknown woman again. As he approaches the river and watches the rivulets extend the moon's reflection and break it into pieces, his mood of resignation turns to one of despair. Watching the river's constant flow, he now recognizes the contrast between cyclical nature and individual human existence, which is destined never to be repeated. Summarizing his romantic experience and life itself, he exclaims: "How stupid. How stupid." This judgment demonstrates that his existential dilemma is significantly more profound than that of Verochka's Ognev, for Riabovich now perceives his life as "unusually barren, miserable, and colorless...." Here the reader may remember his self-characterization as "colorless" (*bestsvetny*), a description that has a secondary suggestion of "flowerless." Riabovich has been unable to find his ideal, the unknown woman with whom he has spent the summer in imaginary wedded bliss. Was she perhaps the young lady in the lilac dress? If so, then he is indeed without his crowning flower....

Source: Joseph L. Conrad, "Vestiges of Romantic Gardens and Folklore Devils in Chekhov's 'Verochka,' 'The Kiss,' and 'The Black Monk,'" in *Critical Essays on Anton Chekhov,* edited by Thomas A. Eekman, G. K. Hall, 1989, pp. 78–79, 81–84.

SOURCES

Almond, Ian, "Chekhovian Overtones in Early Joyce: Some Brief Remarks on 'Araby' and 'The Kiss,'" in *Orbis Litterarum,* Vol. 56, 2001, pp. 367–77, http://www.academia.edu/409223/Chekhovian_Overtones_In_Early_Joyce_Some_Brief_Remarks_on_Araby_and_The_Kiss (accessed December 31, 2012).

"Are There Different Types of Shyness?," Shyness Research Institute, Indiana University Southeast website, 2012, http://ius.edu/shyness/faq/are-there-different-types-of-shyness.html (accessed December 31, 2012).

Bartlett, Rosamund, *Chekhov: Scenes from a Life*, Free Press, 2004, pp. 102, 110.

Chekhov, Anton, "The Kiss," in *The Portable Chekhov*, edited by Avrahm Yarmolinsky, Viking Press, 1968, pp. 156–80.

———, *Letters of Anton Chekhov*, edited by Simon Karlinsky, translated by Michael Henry Heim, Harper & Row, 1973, p. 212.

Finke, Michael, "Anton Pavlovich Chekhov," in *Dictionary of Literary Biography*, Vol. 277, *Russian Literature in the Age of Realism*, edited by Alyssa Dinega Gillespie, Thomson Gale, 2003, pp. 54–79.

Fisher, Ralph T., Jr., "Chekhov's Russia: A Historian's View," in *A Chekhov Companion*, edited by Toby W. Clyman, Greenwood Press, 1985, pp. 3–16.

"Five Popular Modern Russian Writers," in *Telegraph*, April 24, 2009, http://www.telegraph.co.uk/sponsored/russianow/5214172/Five-popular-modern-Russian-writers.html (accessed December 31, 2012).

Hingley, Ronald, *A New Life of Anton Chekhov*, Knopf, 1976, p. 87.

Johnson, Ronald L., *Anton Chekhov: A Study of the Short Fiction*, Twayne Publishers, 1993, pp. 26–27.

Lindheim, Ralph, "Chekhov's Major Themes," in *A Chekhov Companion*, edited by Toby W. Clyman, Greenwood Press, 1985, p. 60.

May, Charles E., "Chekhov and the Modern Short Story," in *A Chekhov Companion*, edited by Toby W. Clyman, Greenwood Press, 1985, p. 147.

Mirsky, D. S., *A History of Russian Literature*, edited by Francis J. Whitfield, Knopf, 1973, p. 294.

Pritchett, V. S., *Chekhov: A Spirit Set Free*, Random House, 1988, pp. 42, 45.

Radzinsky, Edvard, *Alexander II: The Last Great Tsar*, translated by Antonina W. Bouis, Simon and Schuster, 2005, p. 150.

Rayfield, Donald, *Understanding Chekhov: A Critical Study of Chekhov's Prose and Drama*, University of Wisconsin Press, 1999, p. 61.

"Russia," *The World Factbook*, CIA website, 2012, https://www.cia.gov/library/publications/the-world-factbook/geos/rs.html (accessed December 31, 2012).

FURTHER READING

Emerson, Caryl, ed., *The Cambridge Introduction to Russian Literature*, Cambridge University Press, 2008.
> This is an introduction to the richness of Russian literature from its earliest days to the end of the twentieth century.

Martin, David W., "Chekhov and the Modern Short Story in English," in *Neophilologus*, Vol. 71, No. 1, April 1987, pp. 129–43.
> Martin discusses Chekhov as a major figure in the development of the modern short story, with emphasis on how his work has been received in the English-speaking world.

Rayfield, Donald, *Anton Chekhov: A Life*, Faber and Faber, 2009.
> Originally published in 1998, this book has been hailed by reviewers as the definitive biography of Chekhov. Rayfield delves deeply into primary material, some of which appears new because it was suppressed during the years of Communist rule in the Soviet Union.

Rosen, Nathan, "The Life Force in Chekhov's 'The Kiss,'" in *Ulbandus Review*, Vol. 2, No. 1, Fall 1979, pp. 175–85.
> By analyzing the whole story, Rosen shows how Chekhov prepares the reader for the story's resolution. According to Rosen, the kiss awakens Ryabovich's formerly repressed life, to the extent that he identifies his new life with that lived by the von Rabbecks, but he is shattered when he does not receive another invitation to the general's house.

SUGGESTED SEARCH TERMS

Anton Chekhov

Chekhov AND short stories

The Kiss AND Chekhov

golden age Russian literature

shyness

social anxiety disorder

social phobia

Alexander II AND military reforms

Lob's Girl

JOAN AIKEN

1981

The short story "Lob's Girl," written by acclaimed British children's author Joan Aiken, first appeared in her collection *A Whisper in the Night: Tales of Terror and Suspense*, published in 1981. The heartwarming tale of a dog's undying love for and devotion to a young girl, "Lob's Girl" takes place in a small fishing village in Cornwall, England, the home of the Pengelly family. Aiken uses the relationship between Lob, a German shepherd, and the young Sandy Pengelly over the course of nine years to explore themes of loyalty, identity, maturation, and a love so strong it survives beyond death.

Aiken is the author of hundreds of children's stories and novels as well as adult literature; she is perhaps best known for the Wolves Chronicles, a series which begins with the novel *The Wolves of Willoughby Chase* (1962). In addition to *A Whisper in the Night*, "Lob's Girl" can be found in the collection *Where the Red Fern Grows* (McDougal Littell Literature Connections, 1997).

AUTHOR BIOGRAPHY

Joan Delano Aiken was born in Rye, Sussex, England, on September 4, 1924. Her father, Conrad Aiken, was an American Pulitzer Prize–winning poet who served as poet laureate of the United States from 1950 to 1952. Her mother, Jessie McDonald Aiken, was born in

The Pengelly family lives in a Cornish fishing village. (© ian woolcock | ShutterStock.com)

Canada. Her parents married in 1912 and moved to England in 1921. They had three children: John, born in 1913, Jane, born in 1917, and Joan, the youngest. When Joan was five years old her parents divorced. Later that same year, her mother married English writer Martin Armstrong, and she and Joan moved in with him. Taught at home by her mother, Joan developed a love of books and storytelling and was already writing stories at the age of seven. She regaled her younger brother David Armstrong (born in 1931) with her tales during walks through the countryside.

When she was twelve, Aiken was sent to a boarding school for girls in Oxford. However, in 1939 the advent of World War II forced the closure of the school. After failing her university entrance exam in 1940, Aiken instead got a job at the British Broadcasting Corporation (BBC); in 1941 one of her stories was read on the air during the BBC Children's Hour. In 1943, while working at the United Nations Information Office,

Aiken met and fell in love with journalist Ron Brown. The couple married in 1944. In 1949 their first child, John Sebastian, was born. Aiken left her job to stay home with John but continued to work on her stories. In 1951 she and Brown had a second child, Elizabeth Delano.

Aiken's first story collection, *All You've Ever Wanted*, was published in 1953. This happy event was overshadowed by sad news: her husband was diagnosed with tuberculosis the same year, and because he was unable to work, the family left their home and moved in with Aiken's uncle, who had a farm in Suffolk. In 1955 Brown succumbed to tuberculosis, leaving Aiken with two young children to support.

While Brown's death was obviously a tragic event in Aiken's life, it was also instrumental in her development as a writer. Needing to support her family, Aiken took a job with a popular short-story magazine, *Argosy*, headquartered in

London. Her task was to read and critique short-story submissions sent to the magazine. Later, to supplement her income, she also contributed her own articles and stories. By examining dozens of stories daily she gained valuable insight into what makes a good story, what to avoid, and how to engage the reader.

In light of her success with short stories, Aiken decided to attempt a novel, motivated in part by the desire to better provide for her two children. She had attempted a children's novel at seventeen, which she now revised and submitted for publication. The novel, *The Kingdom and the Cave*, was published in 1960. It was her second book, however, that firmly established Aiken as a children's novelist: *The Wolves of Willoughby Chase*, published in 1962, was the first of a collection of novels later dubbed the Wolves Chronicles. The imaginative books are set in an alternate British history in which the Stuarts still reign in the nineteenth century. (In reality the reign of the Stuarts ended in the early eighteenth century, when the Hanoverians claimed the throne.) Hungry wolves terrorize the English countryside, and the young heroines are equally terrorized by an evil governess, Mrs. Slighcarp. The success of *The Wolves of Willoughby Chase* finally allowed Aiken to work from home as a full-time writer. *Wolves* was followed by a sequel, *Black Hearts in Battersea*, in 1964 and then by *Nightbirds on Nantucket* in 1966. A prequel titled *The Whispering Mountain* was released in 1968.

In the early 1970s Aiken introduced in her fiction Arabel and Mortimer, a young girl and her eccentric pet raven. The two characters appear in numerous works, many illustrated by Quentin Blake. These tales, more lighthearted than the Wolves Chronicles, have been compared to the stories of Roald Dahl for their quirky and unpredictable humor. The 1970s were a time of great change in Aiken's personal life. Her mother passed away in 1970, followed by the death of her father in 1973. On a more positive note, one of her most admired children's novels, *Midnight Is a Place*, was released in 1974 (and would be named a New York Times Outstanding Book for that year). During Aiken's frequent visits to New York to meet with agents and publishers, she met American painter Julius Goldstein, whom she married in 1976.

In the late 1970s Aiken began a series of adult historical novels set in the town of Petworth, England, where she was living at the time. The first of these is *The Lightning Tree* (1980), published in the United States as *The Weeping Ash*. She also wrote several novels featuring characters from Jane Austen's works. By this time in her career, she was a well-known and highly regarded author and often lectured on writing. She was asked to create a guide to writing children's literature, which resulted in the book *The Way to Write for Children* (1982). In 1981 she released the short-story collection *A Whisper in the Night*, which includes the story "Lob's Girl."

Aiken continued to write throughout the next two decades. Remarkably prolific, Aiken wrote well over a hundred books in her lifetime, including novels, short-story collections, and picture books for younger children. She was fond of tales of the supernatural and wrote several collections of ghost stories; she claimed that her house in Petworth was haunted. In 1999 she was named a member of the Order of the British Empire by Queen Elizabeth for her services to children's literature. Just before her death in 2004 she finished the last book in the Wolves Chronicles series, *The Witch of Clatteringshaws*, which was published posthumously in 2005. In the introduction to *The Monkey's Wedding and Other Stories*, a collection of Aiken's released in 2011, her daughter Lizza Aiken describes her mother as "a storyteller of wonderful skill."

PLOT SUMMARY

"Lob's Girl" is the story of Sandy Pengelly, a young girl living in a fishing village in Cornwall, England, and her dog Lob. As the story's title indicates, it is Lob who lays claim to Sandy early in the story, rather than the other way around. The story begins with five-year-old Sandy, her twin siblings Tim and Tess, and her older brother Don enjoying a day at the beach. Sandy is lying on the beach when Lob, a German shepherd, flies into her, covering her with sand. Lob's owner, a businessman on holiday from Liverpool, apologizes and allows Sandy to play with Lob for a while before he returns to his hotel.

Later that evening, the Pengellys hear a crash in the kitchen and run to see what has happened. Lob has somehow found his way from his owner's hotel to the Pengelly house and jumped in through the kitchen window, where Mrs. Pengelly was cooling some Christmas puddings. Sandy's father tells her to return Lob to his owner at the hotel.

The next day the children see Lob again at the beach; he is overjoyed to see them. Sandy and the other children play with him for most of the day.

Sandy learns that Lob's owner is leaving the next morning to return to Liverpool. She sneaks to the train station to watch Lob leave on the train; Lob is dejected and wails mournfully as the train departs.

A week later, the Pengelly family is enjoying a quiet evening at home when, once again, they hear a crash in the kitchen. Once again, it is Lob entering through the window. The dog, longing for Sandy and her siblings, has walked over four hundred miles from Liverpool to Cornwall. They feed him, bathe his tired feet, and call his owner in Liverpool, who must take the train to Cornwall to retrieve him. However, ten days later, Lob returns again, after a second four-hundred-mile journey to be with the Pengellys.

Lob's owner asks the Pengellys if they would like to keep him. "Think of the train fares I'll be saving," he points out. Mr. Pengelly agrees; Sandy and the other children are overjoyed.

Lob lives happily with the Pengellys for nine years. He is devoted to Sandy and follows her everywhere, sleeping next to her bed every night. One evening, when Sandy is fourteen, her mother asks her to go keep her aunt company, because her uncle is gone on a fishing trip. She takes Lob with her. On the way to her aunt's house, Sandy is hit by a speeding truck coming down a steep hill. Fortunately, a doctor drives by shortly afterward, and an ambulance is summoned. Sandy, seriously injured, is taken to a hospital in Plymouth, as the village hospital does not handle such serious cases.

Many anxious hours follow for the Pengelly family; Sandy has fallen into a coma, and the doctors fear her life is in danger if she does not awaken from it soon. Hospital workers notice that a forlorn, wet dog has stationed himself outside the hospital and is repeatedly attempting to get inside. He is turned away each time, until Granny Pearce, Sandy's grandmother, arrives at the hospital for a visit. She recognizes Lob and insists he be allowed to visit Sandy. The doctors explain that this is against hospital regulations, but Granny Pearce stands firm. Finally, due to the desperate nature of Sandy's condition, they

relent and allow Lob to visit. At the sound of Lob's mournful whine, Sandy stirs from her coma and reaches for Lob's head. The doctors are amazed.

Granny Pearce leads Lob back out of the hospital again, and he runs off. She asks Sandy's father why it did not occur to him to bring Lob to see Sandy earlier. Mr. Pengelly tells her that the dog that just visited Sandy could not possibly have been Lob; Lob was killed in the truck accident, and Sandy's brother rowed out with him and buried him at sea. Still, no one can explain the presence of the German shepherd at the hospital, who left a trail of wet footprints down the hospital stairs.

CHARACTERS

Mr. Dodsworth

Mr. Dodsworth, a Liverpool businessman on holiday in Cornwall (a popular vacation destination in England), is described as "a gray-haired man with a limp." It is easy to see why the energetic and playful Lob would prefer the company of Sandy and the twins.

Uncle Will Hoskins

Sandy takes Lob to visit her aunt Rebecca because Rebecca's husband, Will Hoskins, is out fishing.

Lob

Lob is a German shepherd (also called an Alsatian) who falls in love with Sandy at first sight. Both Lob and Sandy are young when they meet; Lob's owner apologizes for his rambunctious behavior by saying "he's only young," and Sandy is just five years old when the story begins. Lob becomes a symbol for Sandy's childhood, in that over the nine years covered by the story, "Lob changed less than Sandy." The word *lob* means to throw or toss, as Sandy tosses a stick for Lob when she first meets him. Another, more archaic meaning of the word is a heavy, hanging object—like the cement block Sandy's brother Don ties around his neck to bury him at sea after he is killed in the crash.

Lob's love and devotion to Sandy support her in her years of growing up. His devotion to her is so strong, in fact, that even after he has died, his spirit cannot rest until he is assured that she will survive.

Granny Pearce

Granny Pearce is Sandy's grandmother. She does not appear until late in the story but plays an important role. A determined old woman with a steely will, it is Granny Pearce who insists that Lob be allowed to see Sandy in the hospital, and she will not take no for an answer.

Bert Pengelly

Like many Cornish men, Bert Pengelly is a fisherman. And like most fishermen, he is a man of modest means; when considering whether to adopt Lob from Mr. Dodsworth, he asks, "Is he a big eater?" A loving father with a playful sense of humor (when they hear Lob's crash from the kitchen and his wife exclaims, "My Christmas puddings!" he replies, "Did you put TNT in them, then?"), Bert is devastated when Sandy is injured by the speeding truck.

Don Pengelly

Don is Sandy's older brother. Twelve when the story begins, he is already going out fishing with his father. By the end of the story, he is twenty-one and "a full-fledged fisherman." Don's adulthood means that Sandy is next in line to come of age. It is Don who rows out in a boat to bury Lob at sea.

Jean Pengelly

Jean Pengelly is Sandy's mother, a practical, strong woman who cares for the family on her own when her husband is away fishing. She is industrious and domestic, making both a supply of Christmas puddings and blackberry jelly in the first week of the story.

Sandy Pengelly

Sandy's real name is Alexandra; she was named after a portrait of a queen that hung in her grandmother's house (most likely Queen Alexandra of England, wife of Edward VII, known for her great beauty). Her namesake, and the fact that Lob singles her out from the beginning as his favorite ("there was never any question who came first with him"), indicate that Sandy is somehow special, and that special things will be happening to her in the course of the story.

Her nickname, however, is also appropriate to her character, because it ties her both to the land where she lives and to Lob. When Sandy first meets Lob, the first thing he does is run into her and cover her with sand. When he runs after the stick she throws for him, he is described as "a

sand-colored bullet." In a way, both Sandy and Lob are "sandy"; Lob's devotion and unconditional love guide Sandy through her adolescent years, which are key to defining one's identity. He becomes a part of her.

Sandy's full name ties her closely to her Cornish home. The daughter of a fisherman, she lives near the sea (and sand). Pengelly is a typically Cornish name; many Cornish surnames begin with "Pen-" or "Tre-," and there is even a small village called Pengelly on the Cornish coast.

When Sandy emerges from her coma at the end of the story, she enters a new phase of her life, which she will have to negotiate without Lob, her companion. She has left her childhood behind.

Tim and Tess Pengelly

Sandy's younger brother and sister, these twins are three years old at the story's beginning and twelve at the end.

Aunt Rebecca

Rebecca, also called Becky, is Sandy's aunt. Sandy is on her way to visit her with Lob when she is struck by the speeding truck.

Dr. Travers

Dr. Travers is traveling through the fishing village where the Pengellys live when he discovers Sandy just after the accident. He stops Sandy's bleeding and sends his wife to call for an ambulance.

THEMES

Loyalty

Lob's devotion to Sandy is a major theme in the story. Twice he walks over four hundred miles to be with her, and he even returns from the dead to save her life. The time that Sandy spends with Lob—from age five to age fourteen—coincides with a time of great growth for a child, both emotionally and physically. At five, she has reached the age when she is just gaining some small measure of autonomy from her parents (in the first scene she is supervising her younger siblings at the beach), and by the end of the story, at fourteen, she is on the cusp of adulthood. Lob's loyalty is a constant throughout this period.

TOPICS FOR FURTHER STUDY

- To get to his beloved Sandy, Lob walks from Liverpool to Cornwall twice. Find or draw a map and chart a course that Lob might have taken to get to Sandy. What sights might he have seen along the way? What other towns and cities might he have passed through? To go along with your map, either write a short narrative of the dog's experiences, or create a photojournal with captions, using images drawn from print and/or electronic sources.

- Aiken uses the literary device of foreshadowing throughout this short story, hinting at but not revealing events to come. Try writing a short story of your own using this technique. Think of a climactic or dramatic event (like Sandy's accident) that will occur later in your story, and try to foreshadow that event earlier on. Read the story to your class and see how many of your classmates are able to predict what happens based on your early clues.

- Research the Cornish fishing industry using print and online sources, and write a history of the industry. Include such details as the most common fish coming from the area, the biggest ports in the area, and the amount of fish caught and sold in Cornwall on a yearly basis.

- Read *Hachiko Waits* (2008), by Lesléa Newman. The book is based on the true story of Hachi, the dog of a Japanese professor, who waits every day for his owner to get off the train on his way home from work in Tokyo. When the professor dies of a stroke while at work, Hachi continues to return to the train station every day for years. Write an essay comparing Hachi's story with "Lob's Girl."

- Aiken skips over nine years of Sandy and Lob's life in the course of the story. Imagine some of the events that might have occurred in the Pengellys' lives during this time—some of the adventures that Lob and Sandy might have had. Write a short story using Sandy, Lob, and the rest of the Pengelly family as the main characters. Share your story on a blog and allow your classmates to comment.

Lob's constancy is in contrast to other dramatic changes and uncertainties throughout the story. Don, just twelve when the story begins, is a grown man and working fisherman by the end, and the twins go from three to twelve. The stability of Sandy's happy home life is at the mercy of her father's occupation as a fisherman; as Aiken's narrator points out, "If your father is a fisherman, he will never be home at the same time from one week to the next." The vagaries of the weather can make it a dangerous occupation as well; the night that Sandy is hit by the truck, "The wind was howling through the shrouds of boats drawn up on the Hard." The word *shrouds* sets an ominous expectation of deadly events to come, and the truck accident that follows serves as yet another reminder of life's unpredictability. Through it all—the maturing of the Pengelly children, the unpredictable nature of their life as a fishing family— Lob is a reassuring constant. The narrator points out that Lob changes little over the years: "There was a touch of gray on his nose, but he was still a handsome dog." Lob is so loyal and reliable that even death cannot keep him from Sandy's side.

Coming of Age

The story takes Sandy from age five to age fourteen, from early childhood to adolescence. When the story begins, Sandy is looking after her twin brother and sister. Years later, she is charged with keeping her adult aunt company while her uncle is gone fishing. In the latter scenario, the

Sandy meets Lob when she is five. *(© Pavzyuk Svitlana/ ShutterStock.com)*

reader sees a glimpse of changes to come: the adults in Sandy's life are aging, and soon she will be an adult herself, caring for them.

Lob appears in Sandy's life at a time when a child is no longer exclusively dependent on her mother and father, and is able to make friends, go to school, and begin the journey toward independence. He guides her through this journey, and by the end, his work is done. Sandy is an independent young woman who can navigate the uncertainties of life without him. He comes back to life just long enough to be sure that she will survive, then disappears.

STYLE

Foreshadowing

Foreshadowing is a literary device in which the author uses certain words or images to hint at events to come in the story, without actually revealing these events or spoiling the suspense. Aiken makes use of foreshadowing several times in "Lob's Girl." For instance, early in the story, her narrator describes the road approaching the Pengellys' fishing village as "a narrow, steep, twisting hillroad . . . guarded by a notice." Later she makes note of the sign again as Dr. and Mrs. Travers are nearing the village in their car, when Mrs. Travers remarks, "What a narrow, dangerous hill!" She also explains that the Pengellys have loud music on in the house after Sandy leaves for Aunt Becky's, and so they do not hear a truck "hurtle down the hill and crash against the post office wall." At this point, the reader has not yet been told that Sandy has been hit by the truck but is anticipating that something has gone wrong.

Another instance of foreshadowing occurs when Lob and Granny Pearce are in the hospital lobby waiting for Lob to be allowed to visit Sandy. The narrator relates that Lob keeps shaking his head, "as if to dislodge something heavy that was tied around his neck." Later the reader learns that Lob died in the crash, and Don took his body out to sea and "sank the dog with a lump of concrete tied to his collar." Lob's return from the dead to reach Sandy is also foreshadowed by his remarkable determination to reach Sandy earlier in the story, when he twice walks over four hundred miles from Liverpool to Cornwall to be with her.

Setting

The setting of "Lob's Girl" is important to the story. Cornwall, located at the southern end of England, is a popular British vacation destination due to its warmer climate, many beaches, and charming seaside villages. Despite its popularity, much of Cornwall is very rural (even today). Historically, fishing, mining, and tourism have been the major segments of the Cornish economy.

The Pengellys live in a small fishing village where everyone knows everyone else. Every male character whom the reader meets living in the village is a fisherman (Bert Pengelly, Don Pengelly, Aunt Becky's husband), as the only characters with other occupations are outsiders (Mr. Dodsworth, Dr. Travers). The sea, therefore, is central to the lives of the Pengelly family. Sandy meets Lob at the beach, and later, after his death, his body is buried at sea. The only hotel in the area is called the "Fisherman's Arms." And the reason why Sandy is on her way to visit her aunt Rebecca when the accident occurs is because "Uncle Will Hoskins has gone out trawling," and her aunt is by herself.

By contrast, Lob's original owner, Mr. Dodsworth, is from Liverpool, a major port city and the third-largest city in England. Very diverse, with many different ethnicities and occupations, Liverpool could hardly be more different from Cornwall and the Pengellys' tiny fishing village.

The Supernatural

Aiken is known for her ghost stories and tales of the supernatural; the short-story collection that contains "Lob's Girl," titled *A Whisper in the Night*, is subtitled *Tales of Terror and Suspense*. While "Lob's Girl" would hardly be described as terrifying, the supernatural twist at the end does provide an unexpected chill in what is, up to that point, a heartwarming story about a girl and her dog. Aiken leaves it up to the reader to determine whether or not Lob really returned from beyond his watery grave. While all evidence seems to indicate that the dog at the hospital is Lob, the one person who could be expected to definitely identify him (Sandy) is barely conscious. Lob is soaking wet, but because it is raining, the reader cannot be sure if this is because Lob has returned from his burial at sea, or because the dog has been sitting in the rain. So while Aiken certainly seems to want the reader to believe that Lob (or Lob's ghost) has returned from the beyond, she leaves enough details ambiguous to give the conclusion an air of mystery.

HISTORICAL CONTEXT

Cornwall

Although Cornwall is a popular tourist destination in England due to its warmer climate and beautiful scenery, by the 1980s (when this story was first released) the area had been in economic decline for some time, and it continues to be one of the poorer areas of the United Kingdom. For centuries Cornwall's economy has been tied to the land; tin and copper mining, fishing, agriculture, and tourism have historically been its largest industries. However, as these traditional industries declined, so did the Cornish economy. Its geographic isolation from the rest of Britain has also made it more difficult for Cornwall to

benefit from the resources of more prosperous locations in the north.

The peak of Cornish mining was in the nineteenth century; the industry experienced a complete collapse in the 1980s. The fishing industry, though it has declined as well due to international competition and European fishing quotas, has fared better than mining, and Cornish fish are highly regarded by the culinary community. In "Lob's Girl," Bert and Don Pengelly are fishermen and live in a fishing village. Their modest means are illustrated by Bert Pengelly's apprehension about adding a dog to the family; he is concerned first that Mr. Dodsworth will want some compensation for the pedigreed dog, and second that the dog will eat more than the Pengellys can afford.

The paradox of modern Cornwall is that while longtime residents working in traditional Cornish industries are economically challenged, it has become a favorite place for wealthier Britons to establish second homes or retire, and also a favorite destination for artists, due to the stunning natural beauty of the area and the quality of light. A bit of this contrast is seen in Mr. Dodsworth and the Pengellys. A Liverpool businessman with a pedigreed dog who takes a holiday in Cornwall every summer, Mr. Dodsworth is clearly wealthier than the Pengellys, who never leave Cornwall and rarely leave their small village. When they must go to Plymouth to be with Sandy at the hospital, it is an unusual event, and they are unsure even where they will stay; Bert tells Aunt Rebecca, "We may get a bed with Jean's mother in Plymouth."

The 1980s

Just two years before this story was first published, Margaret Thatcher was named the first female prime minister of Great Britain, becoming a symbol of new possibilities for women in the United Kingdom (and for the futures of young girls like Sandy Pengelly). Aiken was a single working mother in the 1950s, a time when working women were in the minority and the media depicted the ideal family as a working father, stay-at-home mother, and two to three children. Aiken often wrote tales featuring independent and brave girls facing daunting circumstances.

In 1981, the year this story was published, IBM released its first personal computers. This was long before the advent of the Internet, which first appeared in the 1990s—and has made

COMPARE
&
CONTRAST

- **1980s:** Cell phones are not yet in common use, and the first personal computers have just been introduced.

  Today: Dr. Travers would have no problem calling for help for Sandy today; he would simply use his cell phone, and could even probably give the hospital his exact location using a GPS app.

- **1980s:** The 1980s see a number of firsts for women in both Great Britain and the United States: Margaret Thatcher serves as the first female prime minister of England, Sandra Day O'Connor becomes the first woman judge to sit on the US Supreme Court, and Sally Ride becomes the first American woman astronaut. However, women still face discrimination in both business and politics.

  Today: Women continue to make strides toward equality. As of 2013, there are three female judges on the US Supreme Court: Ruth Bader Ginsburg, Sonia Sotomayor, and Elena Kagan. British businesswoman Angela Knight is the chief executive officer of the British Bankers' Association, and Baroness Brenda Hale is a justice of the British Supreme Court and was the first Englishwoman to become a law lord.

- **1980s:** The Cornish mining industry, which has been in decline for many years, finally collapses.

  Today: The last of the Cornish mines closed in the 1990s; as of 2013, there is talk of attempting to retrieve from Cornish beaches deposits of tin, which was washed out of the old mines, but this is being opposed by environmentalists and surfing enthusiasts. Surfing is now a major attraction for the tourism industry in Cornwall.

---

communicating with people worldwide far easier—such that Cornwall, physically isolated by its rurality and geography, was even more isolated then than now. Cell phones were not yet common either, as is illustrated in the story when Mrs. Travers must run to the nearest house to call for an ambulance for Sandy after the accident.

Because Cornwall is such a rural area, one that has changed far less over the years than have other areas of Great Britain, and because the story is such a personal one, centering mainly on timeless themes such as love and loyalty, the historical context has less of an impact in this tale than it does in some others. (For instance, *The Wolves of Willoughby Chase* is set in a fictional alternate history of Britain which is key to the story.) Political and cultural trends would have had little effect on Lob's loving devotion to Sandy, and hers to him. In fact, one of the themes of the story is that Lob's devotion is unchangeable and indestructible, even in the face of death.

CRITICAL OVERVIEW

Joan Aiken is a highly regarded children's author; her seemingly inexhaustible imagination draws admiration even from those critics who have issues with other elements of her work. The first novel in her Wolves Chronicles, *The Wolves of Willoughby Chase*, was her first work to draw real critical acclaim. A reviewer from *Time* magazine calls it an "incomparable melodrama," and Aileen Pippett of the *New York Times Book Review* praises Aiken's sense of humor, encouraging readers to "share Miss Aiken's evident enjoyment in concocting a good yarn."

Aiken is well known for her ghostly tales of the supernatural. Critic Edward Blishen, in a review of *A Whisper in the Night* in the *Times Literary Supplement*, writes, "No one I can think of turns out more agreeable little horrid tales." He does not specifically mention "Lob's Girl" in the review but does praise the collection as a whole, comparing Aiken to Hans Christian Andersen.

Sandy first meets Lob on the beach. (© Lukrecja | ShutterStock.com)

Blishen is not the only critic to compare Aiken to a classic author. Multiple critics have compared Aiken's novels set in the nineteenth century to those of Charles Dickens. The review in *Time* magazine claims that Aiken "writes about children in distress better than anyone since Dickens," and Pippett compares the travails of Aiken's characters to those of Oliver Twist.

While critics generally agree that Aiken is inventive and imaginative, paradoxically, some find her plots lacking in originality. Anne Rose, in reviewing critical responses to Aiken's work, writes that critics Patricia Craig and Mary Cadogan "believe there is nothing original about her plots" but also points out that Aiken adds inventive details and twists to refresh recycled story lines. A complaint from American critics is that some of Aiken's children's stories contain too much British slang or dialect, making them difficult for young American readers to understand.

These complaints aside, most critics appreciate Aiken's skill as a seasoned writer. Anne Rose, writing in 1989, points out that "recent reviews of Aiken's children's writing are almost consistently favorable." Diana C. Hirsch of *School Library*

Journal cites Aiken's "uncanny skill at bringing to life the past," and a *Publishers Weekly* reviewer, writing about Aiken's novel *The Haunting of Lamb House*, describes her writing as "masterly." In such a prolific career, Aiken has naturally received some unfavorable responses to her work, but overall her writing, especially her writing for children, is highly admired as original, witty, and wildly imaginative.

CRITICISM

Laura Pryor

Pryor has a master's degree in English and over twenty-five years' experience as a professional writer. In the following essay, she compares "Lob's Girl" to another Aiken short story, "Second Thoughts," which features a dissatisfied vicar reincarnated as a cat.

Animals abound in Joan Aiken's writing. Lob, the German shepherd in "Lob's Girl," is an unusually conventional pet, by Aiken standards. Her Arabel and Mortimer series, for example, stars a large black raven (Mortimer) who

WHAT DO I READ NEXT?

- Aiken's best-known series, the Wolves Chronicles, begins with the novel *The Wolves of Willoughby Chase* (1962). The novel is set in a fictional nineteenth-century England and features two young cousins, Bonnie and Sylvia, and their friend Simon the goose-boy—who is the main character in the next book in the series, *Black Hearts in Battersea* (1964).

- "Lob's Girl," despite its mysterious ending, is one of Aiken's more realistic short stories. For a sampling of some of her more fantastical tales, try *The Monkey's Wedding and Other Stories*, a collection released in 2011, which includes six stories never before published. In this imaginative volume, Aiken tells of a sailor who brings home a mermaid in a jar, a woman stranded on an island of talking mice, a saintly vicar who dies and is reincarnated as a wicked black cat, and many others. It includes an introduction by her daughter, Lizza Aiken.

- Phyllis Reynolds Naylor's Newbery Medal–winning novel *Shiloh* (1992) tells the story of eleven-year-old Marty Preston, who finds an abused beagle near his West Virginia home. He discovers that the dog is being mistreated by his owner, Judd Travers, one of the Prestons' neighbors. Torn between the law (which obligates him to return the dog to Travers) and his compassion for the dog, Marty must make difficult choices throughout the novel to protect him.

- William H. Armstrong's 1969 novel *Sounder*, winner of the Newbery Award in 1970, tells the story of an African American boy in the late nineteenth-century South. His sharecropping father struggles to provide for the family, and Sounder, their coonhound, does his part by tracking animals the family can eat and sell. After the father is sent to prison for stealing a hog and Soun-

der is shot, the boy is suddenly thrust into adulthood, trying to support his family, care for the injured Sounder, and bring his father back home.

- In *Winterdance: The Fine Madness of Running the Iditarod* (1995), popular children's author Gary Paulsen (author of *Hatchet* and *Dogsong*) gives his nonfiction, firsthand account of running the 1,150-mile Iditarod sled dog race in Alaska. Paulsen's inexperience leads to both dramatic and hilarious consequences throughout this entertaining book.

- Daphne du Maurier's classic novel *Rebecca* (1938) does not feature loyal dogs or happy fishing families, but like "Lob's Girl," it is set on the Cornish coast, and like many of Aiken's novels, it is an eerie mystery tale. When a young bride comes to her new home, an estate called Manderley, she is greeted by a sinister housekeeper who is still loyal to, and somewhat obsessed with, the husband's deceased first wife. The mystery of what happened to the first Mrs. de Winter gradually unfolds to a dramatic conclusion.

- Daphne du Maurier also wrote the text for *Vanishing Cornwall* (1981), a beautiful pictorial exploration of Cornwall, where du Maurier lived for most of her life (she died in 1989). The photos and fond descriptions by du Maurier provide an excellent portrait of the area where "Lob's Girl" takes place.

- Aiken's father, Conrad Aiken, was an acclaimed poet and winner of the Pulitzer Prize in 1930 and the National Book Award in 1954. Some of his best work is featured in his *Selected Poems* (2003), which includes a foreword by literary critic Harold Bloom.

likes to chew up the family's stairs and answers the telephone by squawking "Nevermore!" into the receiver. Another of her stories, titled "Honeymaroon," features a rather unintelligent woman stranded on an island of very intelligent mice, who teach her to communicate with them. Unlike Lob, many of Aiken's animals behave much like humans: they talk, they plot, and they sometimes behave very badly. One such animal is Blackie (formerly the vicar Paul Dawson) in Aiken's short story "Second Thoughts."

Blackie shares some similarities with Lob, the most significant being supernatural qualities. Just as Lob returns from the grave to be with Sandy, Blackie is actually the reincarnation of the recently deceased Paul Dawson, the village vicar. Unlike the spirit of Lob, however, Blackie/Paul behaves very differently after death than before. According to little Miss Pellett, one of the village women, Paul Dawson was "a saint, . . . a regular saint." As a cat, however, he fraternizes with the disreputable Mr. Monks, drinks beer, eats rats, and raids the village henhouses. Before Paul died, he told his sister, "If I had my life to live again, I'd live it differently." He certainly keeps to that promise. Another of the village women seems to be closer to the truth in her opinion that "vicars were a poor lot of hypocrites."

Aside from the supernatural similarity, there would seem to be little connection between loyal, steadfast Lob and the surly, hypocritical Blackie. While the characters themselves have little in common, the two stories do share similar themes.

In "Second Thoughts," Paul Dawson, as a vicar, was a model citizen. He never thought of himself, helped everyone in the village, and, according to his maid, barely ate enough "to keep a bird alive." Yet on his deathbed he wished he had lived differently. He returns as a black cat that the church sexton describes as "the devil 'imself." The religious imagery in the story is overt; at one point Miss Pellett sprinkles water on the cat in an attempt to baptize him, but naturally, as a cat, he does not appreciate the gesture. "What the devil do you think you're doing?" he says. Paul Dawson has gone from a man of the cloth to the worst sort of pagan: a black cat with "thirteen families of kittens." The vicar who once ate barely enough to keep a bird alive is now a voracious consumer of the village's hens, seen by Miss Pellett "slinking furtively

> **WHILE BLACKIE THE CAT APPEARS TO BE THE DEVIL, IN MANY WAYS LOB BEARS A STRIKING RESEMBLANCE TO JESUS CHRIST."**

along the wall with a struggling, shrieking bird in his jaws."

The religious implications of "Lob's Girl" are not as obvious but are still present. While Blackie the cat appears to be the devil, in many ways Lob bears a striking resemblance to Jesus Christ. First of all, he is a *shepherd*, as Jesus is often figuratively designated. His ability to find his way from Liverpool to the Pengellys' home in Cornwall, over four hundred miles on foot, is nothing short of miraculous. Upon his arrival at the Pengellys' home, Mrs. Pengelly washes his feet and applies disinfectant. The washing of feet is a common practice in the Bible; in the book of Luke an unnamed woman washes Jesus's feet with her tears, and in the book of John, Jesus washes the feet of his disciples to demonstrate his love for them. Unlike Blackie, who objects to even the small amount of water that Miss Pellett sprinkles on him, Lob enjoys the feet washing, and at the end of the story when he arrives at the hospital, he is soaking wet.

The Pengellys' occupation is significant as well. Fishing and fishermen appear over and over again in the Bible, and the fish is a common Christian symbol. Jesus instructs his disciples (who were fishermen) to become "fishers of men." Mr. Pengelly tells Mr. Dodsworth that if Lob comes to live with them, "he'll have to learn to eat a lot of fish." (In contrast, Blackie the cat is not satisfied with the sardines Miss Pellett offers him, preferring to kill and eat the villagers' chickens.)

The most significant similarity between Lob and Jesus, of course, is that both rise from the dead. Both are secured in their "tombs" with a heavy object; Jesus, by a boulder that seals his tomb, Lob, by a cement block hung around his neck, which is meant to keep him at the bottom of the ocean. When Jesus returns, he delivers the message of everlasting life. Lob, similarly, brings Sandy back to life from her coma. As with Jesus, Lob's touch heals Sandy.

Lob can be viewed as a part of Sandy: he rarely leaves her side, and Aiken writes early in the story that Lob "gave himself" to her. If we go so far as to say that Lob is a manifestation of Sandy's soul—the kingdom of God within—then we see that Sandy's soul is consistent with her outward behavior. She is a kind and loving girl, devoted to her family and her pet, and Lob is a mirror of this devotion and love. In contrast, if Blackie represents the soul, the true inner self of Paul Dawson, then Dawson was clearly living a lie as the village vicar. Aiken hints, through comments by the village women, that Dawson's piety and virtue were only a facade, a role that he played throughout his life, and not born of real goodness. The villagers pointed their vicar out to strangers with pride because "he was an impressive figure, tall, with white hair, and the face of an ascetic." Mrs. Maddison's dissatisfaction with the new replacement vicar is based not on his lack of compassion or virtue but on his outward appearance; she remarks of Dawson, "At least he looked like a vicar.... This new one looks more like a plumber if you ask me."

Now, transformed into a cat, Dawson no longer looks or acts like a vicar. When Miss Pellett discovers that Blackie the cat is actually Paul Dawson the vicar, he is unimpressed by her detective work. "Anyone might have guessed it, if they'd taken the trouble to look," he tells her. In other words, if anyone had bothered to look beyond Dawson's facade of holiness, they would have seen the blackness within.

Unlike Lob, who keeps returning to Sandy and the Pengellys out of love and devotion, Blackie resists all of Miss Pellett's attempts to help him and put him on "the true path," despite the fact that she saves him from death at the hands of an angry farmer, pays to replace the chickens he has killed, and feeds him sardines. He has little regard for the village women who admired him as a vicar, referring to them as "you old hens," indicating that he feels as little for them as for the chickens he steals from their neighbors.

Aiken is not the first author to portray dogs as loyal and noble, in contrast to wicked and deceitful cats. The 2001 kids' movie *Cats & Dogs* features an evil cat who plots to take over the world, but is defeated, of course, by dogs. The evil James Bond villain Ernst Stavro Blofeld is always shown stroking the white cat in his lap.

In contrast, Lassie and Rin Tin Tin were loyal heroes who regularly saved hapless humans from their travails.

In these two stories by Aiken, we see the ultimate contrast: a dog so good he evokes comparison to Christ himself, and a cat so evil he is the devil incarnate (or perhaps, in this case, the devil reincarnate). Fortunately, in Aiken's hands, both animals provide readers with entertainment and food for thought.

Source: Laura Pryor, Critical Essay on "Lob's Girl," in *Short Stories for Students*, Gale, Cengage Learning, 2014.

James Crossley
In the following review, Crossley praises Aiken's work as engaging and imaginative.

I intended to read Joan Aiken's retrospective collection methodically, one story at a time, but that's not what happened. The night I picked it up I couldn't sleep because I'd been stung by a bee hours earlier, and so I wound up finishing the whole thing. Worth it, even if it meant suffering a whole swarm of bees—it's wonderful. Aiken started publishing in 1955 and continued as a working writer until her death in 2004. She was part of a storytelling tradition that predates MFA programs and quiet epiphanies, and she concerned herself with a snappier brand of narrative entertainment. The results prove that careful attention to craft raises it to the level of art. Her stories draw on folk and fairy-tale traditions but add a good deal of irony to freshen the taste, similar to the approach of John Collier. In one, a sailor brings home a mermaid in a jar; in another, a saintly vicar passes away lamenting his wasted life, followed closely by the appearance of a talking black cat who shocks the town with his irreverence. My favorites feature young couples in conflict or love with each other, including "Spur of the Moment," "Red-Hot Favorite" and "Octopi in the Sky." They're exceedingly witty and imaginative, and so lively I couldn't believe how economical they are. The magical elements they share make them quite literally charming. Maybe it was the medicine talking, but I've decided the only proper way to express my appreciation is to open a pub and name it after "The Paper Queen." Not sure how that's going to work out, but I may give it a try.

Source: James Crossley, Review of *The Monkey's Wedding and Other Stories*, in *Review of Contemporary Fiction*, Vol. 31, No. 3, Fall 2011, pp. 246–47.

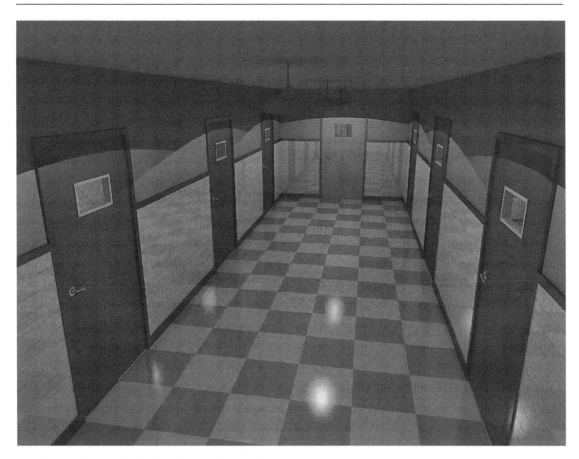

Sandy is taken to the hospital after the accident. (© SSSCCC / ShutterStock.com)

Joan Aiken

In the following essay, Aiken explains what she believes is important for children to find in stories.

A children's book—a *good* children's book—is not something that can be dashed off to schedule, turned off a production belt like a piece of factory goods. It should not be anything with an axe to grind, propaganda for something, a hidden sales-message. It should not be perfunctory, meaningless, flat, coy, or second-rate.

Children have huge needs. There may be disastrous gaps in their education, their environment, their upbringing. Not every child lives in a happy, well-organised home or family. And any child, however fortunate, may have some need which reading will help to fill. Should writers feel any moral responsibility about this? Can they do anything to fill these gaps?

Librarians—who tend, bless them, to look on books as a commodity, rather as bakers do bread, or chemists cosmetics—are apt to approach writers and say, 'Couldn't you write a book about such-and-such, it would be so useful.'

This is putting the cart before the horse. Books should not be written to order in this way. But of course it can do no harm for the alert writer to keep scanning the scene, to be aware of contemporary problems, if possible to study them at close quarters, so that, perhaps unconsciously, his mind may begin to work and churn and create ideas on current issues. A good children's writer may be particularly well-equipped to do this. I have said that a children's writer is a kind of lunatic or poet. Poets are the sensitive points in a civilisation. They can't help being aware of problems, and their writing can't help reflecting this awareness.

But beware! If you deliberately produce a book in order to point out some wrong that needs righting, you will produce a tract. The book will be journalism. It won't be nourishing.

The *story* is the main thing, and you should keep that in mind first, last, and all the time.

Beware, too, of over-simplification. There is a current fashion for suggesting that everything is very easy, if it is properly explained. Sex is simple, just a case of understanding about hormones and genes and contraception. Science is simple. Even old age and death are simple. If the sixth form are taken to visit a few geriatric wards, they will have it all taped in no time.

I can hardly state strongly enough what a mistake I think this is, to tell children that they will find a solution to every problem they are likely to encounter. First, it is a flat lie. Second, if they believe these optimistic assurances, they will end up as schizophrenics. Third, if they don't believe what they are told, it will make them mistrustful and cynical.

So it is the writer's duty to demonstrate to children that the world is *not* a simple place. Far from it. The world is an infinitely rich, strange, confusing, wonderful, cruel, mysterious, beautiful, inexplicable riddle. We too are a riddle. We don't know where we come from or where we are going, we are surrounded by layers of meaning that we can only dimly apprehend, however much we try to learn.

And how much more enjoyable it is for children—how much more it accords with their own observations and instinctive certainties—to be told this, than to be told that the world is a flat, tidy, orderly place, with everything mapped out and accounted for by computer, with no unexplored regions left; that somewhere, neatly waiting, each person has an identity, like a parcel left at the post-office to be collected; that the naughty bear who doesn't like playing with other bears has only to be invited to a party, and he will soon change his ways.

Children need to get from the stories they read a sense of their own inner existence, and the archetypal links that connect them with the unexplored past; of the similarity in patterns between large and small, old and new; they need to receive something that extends beyond ordinary reality.

Stories ought not to be just little bits of fantasy that are used to wile away an idle hour; from the beginning of the human race stories have been used—by priests, by bards, by medicine men—as magic instruments of healing, of teaching, as a means of helping people come to terms with the fact that they continually have to face insoluble problems and unbearable realities.

> SHE IS SOMETHING MORE THAN A 'MERE' ENTERTAINER, FOR THE SHEER IMAGINATIVE STRETCH OF HER WORK MUST IN ITSELF HAVE SOME LIBERATING EFFECT; THE CHILD WHO READS THESE NOVELS MUST EXPERIENCE SOME WIDENING OF ITS OWN IMAGINATIVE RANGE."

A story should give a child some kind of glimpse or vision or key or intimation that things are not necessarily what they seem.

Of course it may be said, with some justice, that children don't need Coleridge's *Kubla Khan* or Poe's *Tales of Mystery and Imagination* to get such a feeling; they can get it from reading what seems to their parents the most abysmal trash—or, from a table with a blanket thrown over it.

But this is no argument against your trying to introduce into *your* story as much as you possibly can in the way of richness and interestingness and layers of meaning.

Your vision doesn't have to be beautiful. It just has to be your own—your own glimpse, your own angle. It may be a rusty bridge, a mousetrap, a dragon lost in a supermarket, a box of buttons, a wayside railway station. It may not be a thing, but a situation—a bird stuck inside an organ pipe, a crinolined lady in a revolving door, a person who tells his fortune every day by switching on the radio just long enough to hear one word.

What do you do then?

That must wait till the next chapter.

Source: Joan Aiken, "What Should a Children's Writer Write—and Not Write?," in *The Way to Write for Children*, St. Martin's Press, 1982, pp. 15–17.

John Rowe Townsend
In the following essay, Townsend lists Aiken's merits as a very original, if lightweight, writer.

Joan Aiken is one of the liveliest and most exuberant of today's writers for children. She is also one of the hardest to assess, for she has few points of resemblance to anyone else. She is an original, a writer who has marked out a special territory of her own.

For children at least, her appeal is primarily as a storyteller of great pace and resource. But she is a storyteller whose invention is peculiarly uninhibited; her plots are so wild and whirling, her disregard for probability so outrageous as to be highly enjoyable to some tastes while much less acceptable to others. At the same time, she is a humorist of individual flavour; and humour, too, is notoriously a matter of taste. If therefore, as I do, one responds wholeheartedly to her work, the response tends to be personal and spontaneous, appreciative rather than critical, and not easily susceptible to analysis.

Up to 1970, Miss Aiken has written—in addition to books for adults—four novels for children and four collections of short stories. The novels are all based on a single curious premise: that the Hanoverian succession to the throne of England never happened. It is the realm of unhistory, with Good King James III as the reigning monarch and the Hanoverians plotting to overthrow him in favour of Bonnie Prince Georgie:

My Bonnie lies over the North Sea
My Bonnie lies over in Hanover,
My Bonnie lies over the North Sea,
Oh why won't they bring that young man over?

The time is the early nineteenth century, and there are wolves and wild boar in the remoter parts of Britain; the wolves were driven by hard winters in Russia and northern Europe to migrate through the recently opened Channel Tunnel. Clearly, in such circumstances, anything can happen. There is no out-and-out magic in these stories, but the merest of lip service is paid to the laws of nature. A railway passenger has no difficulty in stabbing a wolf with a sliver of glass from a carriage window, or an inventor in devising a cannon that will fire across the Atlantic.

The first three novels—*The Wolves of Willoughby Chase*, *Black Hearts in Battersea*, and *Night Birds on Nantucket*—are loosely linked together and have characters in common. In the first, which is set in the frozen north of England, two small girls, left in the care of a wicked governess, are put into a brutally and parsimoniously run charity school, but duly escape to take part in the defeat of villainy. The second book is a story of deep, dark Hanoverian plotting, centred upon the London seat of the Duke of Battersea. In the third, the scene shifts to the eastern seaboard of America, from which Hanoverians are planning to blow up St James's Palace, complete with His Stuart Majesty. The fourth book, *The Whispering Mountain*, stands somewhat apart; it is set in the same imaginary period but has a Welsh background and concerns the recovery of a lost and legendary golden harp.

These are stories of eye-defeating speed and complexity which carry the reader breathlessly onward from page to page. There is no time to stop and consider probabilities; and indeed any writer of a rapid-action adventure story, even without the open licence which Joan Aiken has written for herself, faces less exacting standards of probability than does the realistic novelist. The two kinds of book run in different gears, and episodes are acceptable in one that would be quite unconvincing in the other. Yet a price must be paid for the high-speed storyteller's freedom of action, and it is in portrayal of character. Character development in depth is a process of slow unfolding; the tempo is not the same. Miss Aiken commonly draws her characters with a few swift strokes; sometimes hardly draws them at all. When Miss Slighcarp, the newly-arrived governess in *The Wolves of Willoughby Chase*, snatches up a heavy marble hairbrush and strikes a savage blow at the maid who innocently picked up her private papers, we immediately know all we need to know about her. Both she and her brother—who appears in *Night Birds on Nantucket*—are double-dyed villains, and that is that.

Joan Aiken is, in fact, a caricaturist and a mimic. She catches a likeness and presents it in exaggerated form so that it is clear and recognizable—in the way in which a cartoonist's figures are clear and recognizable—by the exploitation of a salient feature. Because she works in words, the salient feature is usually a way of speech. Again and again her minor characters are defined by their idiosyncrasies of language. In *The Whispering Mountain* two Cockney rogues, Bilk and Prigman, speak entirely in thieves' cant:

'Watch out, Bilk, you silly cullion! Don't raise such a garboil, or we'll have half the mace-mongers in town on our tail.'

And there is an Oriental potentate, the Seljuk of Rum, who seems to have learned his English from a thesaurus:

'Doubtless you are wishing me at Jericho, Timbuktu, the ends of the earth, so I shall hasten to be off, take my departure, make myself few and far between, ho, ho! I have had a most pleasant, famous natter, gossip, conversazione with your good papa.'

Then, in *Night Birds on Nantucket*, there is the innocent inventor of the transatlantic cannon, Professor Axeltree Breadno, with his fractured middle-European English:

> 'Aha, konigsbang! Is soon blowing up London...Monsterbang, grosseboom...Is shooting up palast—Sint Jim's Palast, not?'

All this is, of course, shamelessly overdone; but it is not merely verbal high jinks, it is a kind of cartooning in words.

With Miss Aiken's gift for mimicry and caricature goes a tendency to burlesque. It would be misleading to describe her novels as parodies of earlier fiction, but there are elements of parody in them nonetheless. *The Wolves of Willoughby Chase* and *Black Hearts in Battersea* can be seen in one light as comic Victorian melodramas. *Night Birds on Nantucket* has in it something of a light, and light-hearted, skit on *Moby Dick*, for one of its main characters, Captain Casket, is the strange, sad skipper of a New Bedford whaler, obsessed with the pursuit of the pink whale Rosie. And *The Whispering Mountain* looks suspiciously like a send-up of all those children's stories in which elaborate riddles from the past are ingeniously unravelled.

There is a high Dickensian colour about the first two books which reminds one that Dickens, too, was, among other things, a mimic and a caricaturist. Although Joan Aiken does not for a moment attempt to be a writer of comparable weight, it seems clear that Dickens has been a major source of inspiration. Possibly he is master and victim at once, since much of his work could be described as Victorian melodrama and is part of the material she seems to be parodying. Mrs Brisket and her charity school in *The Wolves of Willoughby Chase* and the Twite household in *Black Hearts in Battersea* could have come straight from the Dickens stockpot. It is a curious literary relationship.

Miss Aiken has, in fact, several Dickensian qualities whose appearance is not restricted to the first two books. Like Dickens, she loves to work with a crowded canvas and can always find room for more figures, more detail, more action. Like him, she can evoke the physical presence of places and people; like his, though on a slighter scale, her more successful characters can be basically 'flat' and yet memorable, vivid, larger than life. And where she has the time or inclination to use more than her few quick strokes she can produce portraits of impressive power. Here is

the bad Lord Malyn, villain of *The Whispering Mountain*:

> He was a tall man, not yet much past middle age. Seen close to, almost everything about him appeared pale—his fine thin lips were colourless, so was his skin. His hair looked as if it had been bleached by weather or ill-health. His long delicate hands were whiter than the lace ruffles which fell over them. Only his eyes had colour—they were a deep, clear, burning yellow, like the eyes of a tiger, dark-rimmed, with pupils small as peppercorns. He held a long, slender but heavy piece of gold chain, and played with it, pouring it from one hand to the other...It was an odd characteristic of Lord Malyn that, although he always appeared fatigued, he never seemed able to keep still, but was in continual, languid, restless motion; whereas Mr Hughes, with a sailor's economy of effort, moved only when it was needful, and then in a brisk, neat, finished manner.

From one point of view it is disappointing that we never really learn any more of Lord Malyn than we know after reading this; his part in the book is purely functional. But in this splendid portrait he is not only present in the flesh; we have the sense of a complicated man underneath.

Miss Aiken's young heroes and heroines are not particularly interesting. Some of her child characters, like Sylvia and Bonnie in *The Wolves of Willoughby Chase* and Dutiful Penitence in *Night Birds on Nantucket*, are little more than 'types.' The incredibly resourceful Owen of *The Whispering Mountain* appears to be a caricature of the standard juvenile hero; one cannot really care about him or doubt that he will come out on top. But Dido Twite, the sharp, shrewish, knowing child who appears first in *Black Hearts in Battersea*, then in *Night Birds on Nantucket*, is different. Gradually one comes to realize that, besides the Cockney perkiness which is immediately obvious, she has a heart and a genuine individuality. It is as though the author had come to care for her as she went along, and had breathed life into her. She is the most rounded and the most successful of Miss Aiken's child characters.

Joan Aiken is, I think, essentially a lightweight writer; and there is nothing wrong with that. Lightweights of quality are scarce. She is something more than a 'mere' entertainer, for the sheer imaginative stretch of her work must in itself have some liberating effect; the child who reads these novels must experience some widening of its own imaginative range. But I can see no moral or psychological complexities in her books; nor do they try to convey any view of life more subtle than that of the ordinary decent person. Good is good and bad is bad, and there is never any doubt which is which. And, reassuringly, good always triumphs in the end.

I cannot find any clear line of development in the first three novels, though there are differences of flavour. *The Wolves of Willoughby Chase* has a deliberate artlessness which the later books seem less concerned to maintain. *Black Hearts in Battersea* is the funniest of the books, and has some of the most splendid incidental details. (The eccentric fourth Duke of Battersea, we learn, spent a lifetime building Battersea Castle in pink granite in the shape of a half-open rose. When at last it was complete, he drove out to survey the effect. "'It looks like a cod cutlet covered in shrimp sauce," he said, drove home, took to his bed, and died.') *Night Birds on Nantucket* seems slightly less satisfactory, perhaps because Miss Aiken, in spite of her American and Canadian ancestry, is a very English writer, and her work does not quite transplant successfully. But she always has a trick or two in hand. Unpretentious but pleasant verses are a feature of this book, and she shows that she can turn a neat stanza:

> Oh fierce is the Ocean and wild is the Sound,
> But the isle of Nantucket is where I am bound.
> Sweet isle of Nantucket, where grapes are so red
> And the light flashes nightly on Sankaty Head.

The Whispering Mountain takes the proliferation of character and action as far, one would think, as it can go. It is so crowded that even an attentive reader forgets who all the people are and cannot grasp all that is happening. It is a feast; but possibly enough would have been as good. I feel that Miss Aiken will have to thin down the mixture a little. But if she does it will certainly not be through any shortage of ideas. Besides her novels she has written four books of short stories for children—*All You've Ever Wanted* (1953), *More Than You Bargained For* (1955), *A Small Pinch of Weather* (1969), and, for younger children, *A Necklace of Raindrops* (1968)—all of which make reckless use, in a chapter or even in a single page, of enough material to last many writers through a whole book.

Where extravagance is of the essence, it is hard to draw the line beyond which a writer is to be regarded as *too* extravagant. To say that Joan Aiken often develops an idea or situation beyond reasonable limits, makes her characters behave absurdly, and indulges in wild excesses of word-play is not necessarily to make an adverse criticism. It could be retorted that these are exactly the things she sets out to do and that make her work what it is. And if the snaffle and the curb are not much in evidence, at least there is no doubt about the presence of the horse. Energy, speed, inventiveness, a gift for mimicry, a total command over words and, not least, a reckless audacity: it all adds up to a formidable array of qualities, and indicates why Joan Aiken can get away with ventures that the majority of sensible authors would never even attempt.

Source: John Rowe Townsend, "Joan Aiken," in *A Sense of Story: Essays on Contemporary Writers for Children*, J. B. Lippincott, 1971, pp. 17–23.

SOURCES

Aiken, Joan, "Lob's Girl," in *A Whisper in the Night: Tales of Terror and Suspense*, Laurel-Leaf Books, 1988, pp. 1–15.

———, "Second Thoughts," in *The Monkey's Wedding and Other Stories*, Small Beer Press, 2011, pp. 29–39.

Aiken, Lizza, "The Making of a Storyteller," in *The Monkey's Wedding and Other Stories*, Small Beer Press, 2011, pp. iii–viii.

"Biographies of Current Justices of the Supreme Court," Supreme Court of the United States website, http://www.supremecourt.gov/about/biographies.aspx (accessed March 6, 2013).

Blishen, Edward, Review of *A Whisper in the Night*, in *Times Literary Supplement*, July 23, 1982, p. 788.

Hirsch, Diana C., Review of *The Haunting of Lamb House*, in *School Library Journal*, Vol. 39, No. 5, May 1993, p. 141.

"An Industrial History of Cornwall," Cornwall Guide website, http://www.cornwalls.co.uk/history/industrial/ (accessed March 6, 2013).

McNamer, Elizabeth, "Cast Your Nets: Fishing at the Time of Jesus," in *Scripture from Scratch*, July 2004, http://www.americancatholic.org/newsletters/sfs/an0704.asp (accessed March 6, 2013).

Morris, Stephen, "Surfers Oppose Cornwall Mining Plans," in *Guardian* (London, England), February 8, 2013, http://www.guardian.co.uk/environment/2013/feb/08/surfers-cornwall-mining-plans (accessed March 6, 2013).

"100 Most Powerful Women in Britain: Business, Academia and Politics," in *Telegraph* (London, England), November 23, 2010, http://www.telegraph.co.uk/finance/newsbysector/8135038/100-most-powerful-women-in-Britain-Business-Academia-and-Politics.html (accessed March 6, 2013).

Pippett, Aileen, Review of *The Wolves of Willoughby Chase*, in *New York Times Book Review*, October 6, 1963, p. 42.

Review of *The Haunting of Lamb House*, in *Publishers Weekly*, Vol. 239, No. 49, November 9, 1992, p. 74.

Review of *Midnight Is a Place*, in *Time*, December 24, 1974, p. 71.

Rose, Anne, "Profile: Joan Aiken," in *Language Arts*, Vol. 66, No. 7, November 1989, pp. 784–90.

Willett, Joanie, "Why Is Cornwall So Poor? Narrative, Perception and Identity," PhD diss., University of Exeter, 2006, pp. 1–12.

FURTHER READING

Aiken, Joan, *The Way to Write for Children: An Introduction to the Craft of Writing Children's Literature*, St. Martin's Press, 1998.

>   Originally published in 1982, this affable guide to writing for children begins by asking the reader if one wishes to write *for* children or *about* children and describing the key difference between the two. From there Aiken explores plot, character development, and writing for different media (television, theater) and offers a helpful assortment of dos and don'ts for connecting with child readers.

Austen, Jane, *Pride and Prejudice*, W. W. Norton, 2000.

>   A Norton Critical Edition of Austen's 1813 classic, this volume includes biographical sketches of Austen, samples of her earliest writing, literary criticism of the novel, and even an interview with actor Colin Firth, who portrayed Mr. Darcy in the BBC television adaptation of the novel. Aiken was a great fan of Austen and wrote several novels using charac-
ters from Austen's works, continuing their stories.

Bradbury, Ray, *Bradbury Stories: 100 of His Most Celebrated Tales*, William Morrow, 2003.

>   One of the writers Aiken worked with in her years at *Argosy* magazine was the famed short-story writer Ray Bradbury, who died in 2011 at the age of ninety-one. Like Aiken, Bradbury was a prolific writer, one who turned out such acclaimed works as the novel *Fahrenheit 451* (1953) and the short-story collections *The Martian Chronicles* (1950) and *The Illustrated Man* (1951). Bradbury was known for his stories in the fantasy, science-fiction, horror, and mystery genres.

Guran, Paula, ed., *The Year's Best Dark Fantasy and Horror: 2012*, Prime Books, 2012.

>   This collection of eerie short stories includes tales from Stephen King, Charles de Lint, and Aiken, among others. Though Aiken died in 2004, the story included in this collection, titled "Hair," was released in 2011 in the posthumous collection *The Monkey's Wedding*. It tells of a young man, widowed shortly after his marriage, who comes to the disturbing home of his mother-in-law (whom he has never met) to return a lock of his wife's hair.

SUGGESTED SEARCH TERMS

Joan Aiken

Lob's Girl

A Whisper in the Night AND Aiken

Joan Aiken AND supernatural

Joan Aiken AND short stories

Joan Aiken AND Conrad Aiken

Joan Aiken AND Cornwall

Joan Aiken AND animals

Cornwall AND fishing

The Rain Horse

TED HUGHES

1960

"The Rain Horse" is a psychologically charged tale by English author Ted Hughes about an episode that occurs when a young man makes a nostalgic return to the countryside he ranged as a youth. In his introduction to his collection *Difficulties of a Bridegroom*, Hughes classes "The Rain Horse" as autobiographical in inspiration. Thus, the protagonist is readily perceived as a stand-in for the author himself—except the circumstances of the protagonist are mostly glossed over within the story, leaving the specifics of his background all but irrelevant to the immediate action. The reader is told little beyond the fact that the young man is wearing a new grey suit.

Decked out in this suit, which is getting unfortunately muddied by the sodden ground, the man is disappointed when he arrives at the hilltop overlooking the farmland he knew so well to find that it looks familiar but stirs no emotions; it does not really know him anymore. He turns to leave—but out of the corner of his eye spots a black horse running along through the rain in the field ahead. When the horse reaches a distant crest of the same hill and shows a curious profile while crossing over, the man is awestruck, sensing an uncommon significance in the horse. What proceeds to happen proves his impression right. "The Rain Horse" was written in 1958 and published first in *Harper's* in January 1960 and then in several other periodicals. The story was included in Hughes's volume of verse and short fiction *Wodwo* in 1967 as well as in *Difficulties of a Bridegroom* in 1995.

Ted Hughes (© Nils Jorgensen / Rex Features / Alamy)

AUTHOR BIOGRAPHY

Edward James Hughes was born on August 17, 1930, in Mytholmroyd, West Yorkshire, England, as the youngest of three children. Mytholmroyd is located in the well-saturated Calder Valley in the midst of moors and farmland, while more broadly Yorkshire is known as a rural, working-class region. Hughes has related that he was always fascinated by animals, with his activities ranging from playing with toy animals, to drawing and making models of animals, to retrieving the rats, weasels, rabbits, magpies, and owls that his brother shot while hunting. Yorkshire's West Riding dialect would come to characterize Hughes's poems, which offer a unique combination of literary ambition and proletarian speech patterns, reflecting the concision and directness borne of honest, hardworking communities. When Hughes was seven, the family moved to Mexborough, South Yorkshire, where he attended school with the children of railwaymen and miners.

Hughes was writing poems by age fifteen, much of them—like those about Zulu warfare and the Wild West—inspired by his colonialist forebear Rudyard Kipling. His talents were nurtured by a succession of supportive English teachers. After winning a scholarship to attend Cambridge University, Hughes first completed two years of National Service with the Royal Air Force. His service began in 1949, when he worked at a radio station as a wireless mechanic, in which capacity he mostly read Shakespeare. He then enrolled in Cambridge's Pembroke College, ultimately focusing on archaeology and anthropology instead of English and graduating in 1954. He published his first poem in the Cambridge periodical *Granta* that year. While working variously as a rose gardener, steelworks night watchman, zoo attendant, and teacher over the next couple years, he continued publishing verse, gaining attention for his visceral poem "The Jaguar" in particular.

In 1956 Hughes met the American poetic talent Sylvia Plath, whose fame would far exceed that of Hughes in the United States. They married just four months after meeting and moved to the United States in 1957, the year Hughes's first collection, *The Hawk in the Rain*, was published. Plath thrived in America, but Hughes, teaching at the University of Massachusetts, Amherst, felt he was losing his poetic inspiration; they moved back to England in late 1959, and their daughter, Frieda, was born in early 1960. This was the year Hughes's first short story, "The Rain Horse," was published in *Harper's* as well as *London* magazine and *Introduction*. It was also broadcast on BBC Radio. The couple had a son in 1962, but that year, in light of Hughes's acquaintance-ships with other women, Plath insisted they separate. In 1963, though Hughes had thought they were starting to reconcile, Plath committed suicide. American audiences in particular would long blame Hughes for the literary shooting star's early death, even calling him a murderer at his public readings. Incidentally, the woman who loomed largest over Plath's suicide, Assia Wevill, also killed herself—along with her and Hughes's young daughter—after some seven years of involvement with him. In 1970, Hughes married Carol Orchard, with whom he remained for the rest of his life.

Through and beyond these tragedies, Hughes published a prolific number of volumes, including dozens of chapbooks, full poetry collections, radio and stage plays, and children's books, in addition to edited volumes, librettos, essays, stories, and translations. His children's book *The Iron Giant* would be adapted as an animated film in 1999. Hughes was named to the Order of the British Empire in 1977, and he served as poet laureate of Great Britain for fourteen years, from 1984 until his death from liver cancer on October 28, 1998. He is memorialized in the prestigious Poets' Corner in Westminster Abbey.

PLOT SUMMARY

The opening of "The Rain Horse" introduces a young man who finds a rainstorm coming on as he crests a hill. After crossing the muddy countryside on foot, he is concerned about having come too far and having soiled his shoes and grey suit. After an absence of twelve years, he has returned to the valley of farmland he grew up playing in. He is disappointed not to feel much of anything upon reaching it.

Full of anxiety, he considers how best to proceed: ahead a mile past the farm, where the road loops, or back the two cross-country miles he has walked. Deterred by the thought of having to interact with the farmer, he turns back—but just then notices a black horse dashing across the farmland toward the hill. The horse crosses over a crest in the hill some three hundred yards off, showing a leopard-like form that frightens and confounds the man. As the rain intensifies, he turns again to head back down the hill and across the countryside, soon reaching the top of an expanse of woods. Seeing no decent shelter there, he crosses the hillside, jogging through a field to another stretch of woods, where a leaning oak provides some protection from the intensifying rain.

Crouching down, the man grows absorbed in the scene despite the chilly rain and even wishes the rain would never stop. Upon shivering, he recalls the horse. He turns back toward the crest of the hill the horse had crossed, above the wood he is huddling in: at the top of the wood, the horse is standing still and staring at him. Baffled by the horse's alert behavior—since horses in the rain usually wait it out sedately—he grows unnerved. At this he considers himself foolish—but then the horse crashes through the wood toward him, and he lunges away at the last moment and scampers back up the hill through

the wood. Falling down, he rolls in a panic, but the horse is nowhere in sight.

Angry now, he blames the horse's behavior on the rain and heads toward the farm after all. Approaching and starting to slip through the hawthorn hedge at the hilltop, he realizes that the horse is awaiting him in the first sloping field, and he quickly backs down and away. Even more disturbed now by the horse's behavior, he heads down into the wood again and proceeds back the way he came, along under the crest of the hill. Reaching the edge of an open field, he creeps back up to the crest of the hill to peer through the hedge toward where he last saw the horse—but the horse has gotten ahead of him and from close along the hedge thunders his way, leaving the man to rush headlong down through the wood. When he reaches a clearing of bracken (ferns), stones, and rabbit holes, he realizes he is alone again.

The man sits on the ground, his hair and clothes soaked through and his trousers ripped. Certain now that the horse is deliberately attacking him, he gathers two goose-egg-sized stones and heads to the bottom of the wood, planning to cross a meadow and follow a river along a three-mile loop back to the road. But through the dense hawthorn trees at the bottom of the wood, he sees the horse, looking across the meadow toward the river. Hoping to elude the horse at last, the man reverses direction again, intending to head back through the clearing of ferns, out the other side of the wood, and on toward the farm.

It is much darker now, the rain still getting heavier, veritably flooding the land. The man starts running, and then he hears the horse running, too, as it crosses the clearing behind him. Roaring out, the man flings one stone and causes the horse to rear up and shy to the side. He flings another stone and appears to hit the horse, which now rushes back down through the hawthorns.

Proceeding beyond the woodside, the man gathers more stones, feeling powerful, as though he could have killed the horse. He sees it now twenty yards off in the middle of the sloping field before him. He yells, throws, and misses the horse. He throws stones and misses for several minutes, until his shoulder aches, and when he rests, the horse plunges toward him. He throws again and now succeeds in striking the horse, which stumbles. He throws and strikes again, and the horse now rushes away down the hill, cantering back up the hill at the far side of the field, shaking its head and at one point pawing its ear with its hoof. The man yells once more to put the horse in its place, and the horse stops and watches idly as the man climbs and crests the hill.

The man feels freezing cold. Gathering an armload of stones, he lumbers down across the muddy fields toward the farm. Halfway through the first of three fields, he sees the horse back at the crest of the hill. He trudges along, burdened by the mud, his soaked clothes, and his armload of stones, his breathing labored. Halfway through the last field, he sees the horse still back at the crest of the hill.

Reaching a gate at the farm, the man drops his stones and is once more absorbed in the rain, even imagining lying down in the mud. Scanning the hilltop behind him, he cannot see the horse anymore. Gaining the shelter of a shed, he sits atop a drum of gasoline and recalls the familiar scene inside. In pain, having already slipped beyond the visceral experience of the ordeal

with the horse, he begins shedding his garments and squeezing out the water—but then he stops, somehow feeling as if an important part of his brain has been excised.

CHARACTERS

Horse

Although the man dominates the exposition of Hughes's story as the protagonist and only human being, the horse looms larger as a character, both literally and figuratively. The man is baffled by the horse's aggressive behavior, which can perhaps be explained only by attributing to the horse a degree of personality, or at least territoriality: offended or upset by the man's presence on what the horse seems to consider its home ground, the horse does everything it can to drive the man away. Yet more than simply pushing the man away, the horse quite cunningly attacks the man, who imagines the horse must be clairvoyant since it repeatedly appears just ahead of him no matter which way he turns and proceeds. The blackness of the horse contributes to its shading as a mysterious, perhaps evil creature with access to supernatural or mystical powers.

Despite the horse's ferocity, the man proves victorious in the end, as he succeeds in pelting the horse with enough stones to leave it subdued at a distance, enabling him to finally escape to the farm. While the reader can only guess about the horse's designs in attacking the man, it seems clear why the horse finally lets the man go: after being struck by stones several times, the horse apparently fears physical injury enough to leave the man be—as if the man knocked some sense into the maddened horse, so to speak. Yet the horse is so effectively personified that there also seems to be an act of will behind the horse's decision to finally let the man go, as if it is not simply afraid but is content to have thoroughly spooked the man and got under his skin. That is, even though the man gets away, the horse has successfully defended its territory, and in the psychological contest that has taken place, the horse may recognize itself as the winner.

Man

The young man who finds himself mired in the midst of the countryside after trekking too far overland seems, in most respects, to be an ordinary civilized person. As would any man who has paid decent money for a respectable suit and pair of shoes, he is concerned about ruining those items. Though it must have been cloudy, he presumably did not anticipate the rain or else underestimated the time it would take for him to cross the muddy rural landscape. Either way, he is left in the uncomfortable situation of wanting to sink into nostalgia over his childhood stomping grounds but being too beset by anxiety over his circumstances to do so. Indeed, he gives up on the idea of reconnecting with the environs and turns to head back—at which point he sees the horse.

The man's interactions with the horse govern the remainder of the story. As the only other cognizant being the man encounters, the horse becomes and remains the center of his attention even before it attacks him. Crouching beneath an oak, the man loses himself in the rain for a while, but at length he must tend to his thoughts of the horse. He then sees the horse again watching him and tries to ignore it, but the horse launches its attack, and from then on the man expends all his energy trying to deduce the horse's state of mind and escape. Meanwhile, he grows conflicted about his own emotional state: he is roused to significant fear, but rationally he has trouble believing that his fear is justified; he feels silly being so afraid. But after the horse charges toward him several times, he caters to his fear and arms himself with stones.

By now the man's original purpose for visiting the area has been entirely forgotten—he thinks no longer of lingering over his nostalgia but only of escaping the terrifying horse. He at last succeeds, and the reader might expect him to be relieved and contented by this success. But the daze in which the man remains and especially the final line of the story reveal that he has somehow not won but lost—he has lost not only the contest with the horse, despite his escape, but also an entire portion of his brain. This line suggests that the man is reading his own experience symbolically—as most everyone does in registering an experience through one's intuitive emotions, which attach value to experiences in ways other than those assigned by rational consideration, as based instead on impressions. In physical terms, he has won a successful retreat from the battle with the horse, which was all he wanted, but emotionally, impressionistically, somehow he has lost. The reader too, then, is directed to consider the man's experiences on an impressionistic/symbolic plane.

THEMES

Nostalgia

Hughes's story begins by fronting the minor theme of nostalgia, a theme that seems relatively inconsequential once the horse comes into the picture. But the theme is significant in providing the framework for the tale. The protagonist has quite a specific purpose in visiting the valley: having spent some eight years roaming the farmland there as a youth, he wants simply to view the valley and sink into his nostalgia—to enjoy the scene retrospectively, perhaps remembering little incidents and adventures. But his expectations are vague at best: "he had expected something, some pleasure, some meaningful sensation, he didn't quite know what." And the sentiments he desires never come; though he tries to awaken those sentiments by looking more closely at everything, he remains indifferent to the scene. This seems to be the case because, as the narration states, he has changed—he has been civilized. Part of what civilization instills in a person is a constant anxious concern for one's circumstances, and the man's present circumstances are less than ideal. In a word, there is too much to worry about. A child can play out in the rain with the utmost delight, but an adult may be unable to suppress concerns about getting wet and cold and ruining clothes. That is, the adult cannot relax enough to have fun. Where the man in Hughes's story wants to have fun only in his mind, to mentally wander through the past, the demanding present does not allow it.

Nature

There is a sense of duality to the roles played by elements of nature within "The Rain Horse," the title of which highlights the two major elements confronted by the man. The rain, to begin with, is an obstacle and a nuisance, fueling the mud that slows his progress and ruins his shoes, disrupting his attempts at nostalgic reverie, and leaving him soaked and eventually chilled to the bone. For the most part, the rain is an antagonist. Yet the rain also soothes the man, once he gains the shelter of the oak tree, helping him sink "into a state of comfort that was all but trance" and leaving him wanting the rain "to go on for ever." In fact, now he grows anxious not when the rain intensifies, but when it seems to be slowing down. Thus, when the man's interests (enjoying his nostalgia, staying warm and dry) are

TOPICS FOR FURTHER STUDY

- Write a short story in which the protagonist encounters an animal in unique circumstances and ends up being mystified by the animal's behavior for some reason, leading to a crisis of sorts or a moment of illumination.

- In various respects, Hughes's story has the surreal qualities of a dream. Consult two or three sources on the meaning of dreams—such as Sigmund Freud's *The Interpretation of Dreams* (1900), James Albert Hall's *Jungian Dream Interpretation: A Handbook of Theory and Practice* (1983), or Lauren David Peden's *Mystical Arts: Dream Interpretation* (2001)—to analyze "The Rain Horse" as if the action taking place were a dream. In a paper, relate what each of your sources says about what the rain, the horse, the muddy countryside, and other elements of the story might represent. Conclude by discussing how and why the sources offer contrasting interpretations and whether analyzing the episode as a dream is useful for understanding the story. Post your paper on a blog and allow your classmates to comment and discuss.

- Read the story "My Wonder Horse," by Sabine R. Ulibarrí, available in his volume *Tierra Amarilla: Stories of New Mexico* (1971), translated from the Spanish by Thelma Campbell Nason. In this story, a fifteen-year-old boy dreams of encountering and perhaps even capturing a legendary white horse. Write an essay in which you compare this story with Hughes's "The Rain Horse," commenting on the significance of the horse both in the literal circumstances and symbolically, the role the horse plays in the protagonist's life, the narrative treatment of the themes, the literary style, and other noteworthy aspects of the tales.

- Either write a research paper or assemble a multimedia presentation on the history of the relationship between humans and horses, focusing on whatever countries, cultures, or traditions you choose. For a research paper, consult at least two print sources and be sure to cite accurately; for a presentation, construct a time line, and download drawings, photographs, and maps that illustrate commentary you provide.

---

contrary to the rain, he resents it, but when the rain itself—in its sounds and the way it drips from twigs—becomes what he is interested in, his relationship to the rain inverts.

The man's interactions with the horse echo his interactions with the rain to a certain extent. At first, as with the rain, the man tries to remain stoically indifferent to the horse, despite its potentially threatening nature. As the horse intensifies its affronts, the man gradually loses his composure. With the rain, the point when he loses his composure—when he shelters under the oak—is the point when he has the liberty to actually appreciate the rain. But the man never attains such an appreciation for the horse, as the animal is simply too threatening. Relatively

speaking, the rain proves a passive agent of nature that the man can bear and appreciate, but the horse is an active agent that the man cannot be at peace with and which necessarily rouses the man's defenses.

Irrationalism

Throughout the man's ordeal with the horse, he shies away from his emotional responses and insists upon seeking a rational explanation for the horse's behavior. His initial emotional reaction to the horse's appearing momentarily leopard-like is an "unpleasantly strange" one, and when he later recalls this moment, he immediately "tried to dismiss the thought," replacing it with the rational notion that "horses wander about the countryside often enough." When,

The protagonist returns to the farm where he grew up after being away for twelve years. *(© MaxyM /*
ShutterStock.com)

crouching under the oak, he sees the horse staring him down and grows unsettled, the narration
affirms his thought that "this was absurd," referring to his own state of alarm. As such, "he took
control of himself," meaning he shrugs off his
gut feelings in favor of a rational mind-set that
denies the possibility that the horse could have
any designs toward him. When the horse indeed
attacks him, he grows furious—not necessarily
at the horse alone, but at himself for being so
spooked. Again rationalizing the situation, he
figures the horse must be insane, perhaps owing
to an "abscess on its brain." In all of these rationalizations, the man denies the horse any agency
of its own; he refuses to consider the animal as a
creature acting out of free will or intelligent
interests. It is simply a dumb animal. And the
man is literally embarrassed by his responses to
it: "He was ashamed to find himself acting so
inanely, ducking and creeping about in this way
just to keep out of sight of a horse."

Yet the man's rationalizations prove consistently wrongheaded. By the end of the story, the
reader is likely convinced that the horse does
have agency, it does have designs, and it is not
insane. Had the man approached the idea of the
horse not from a rationalist mind-set but from
an intuitive mind-set—had he given credence to
the possibility of an emotional relationship with
the animal—the situation might have turned out
differently. Perhaps had he engaged in supposedly irrational behavior like simply talking to the
animal, treating it as a fellow creature and spirit,
the horse might have seen him as an ally and
declined to attack him.

Primitivism

Ultimately, through its subordination of the protagonist's attempts at self-centered nostalgia, its
attribution of superior power to elements of
nature, and its implicit refutation of the value of
rationalism, "The Rain Horse" is, like much of
Hughes's greater body of work, an homage to
primitivism—to a precivilized appreciation for
and relationship to the natural world. In his
essay "Hughes and Animals," Chen Hong detects
the author's primitivist leanings in "his criticism

of humans," who are deemed inferior to animals "in terms of energy and completeness of being." This perspective is said to stem from Hughes's "trust in the physical reality of the animal world, from which he came to develop a faith in the material essence of all the energies in the universe." Hughes was much interested in shamanism, in the indigenous relationship between the chosen or self-selected man and the realm of animal spirits, ancestral spirits, and the divine. The shaman would often gain his relationship with the spirit world through a specific animal spirit, perhaps encountered in a dream or during a vision quest, which would become his sacred totem animal—belief in which "is basically a primitive attitude," as Hong notes.

In Hughes's poems as well as in his stories, animals often appear in totemic guises—in dreams or in the course of singular circumstances, offering guidance or direction or simply embodying natural power. In this sense, "The Rain Horse" is readily linked with Hughes's poems "The Horses" and "A Dream of Horses." In "The Horses," a man crosses a frost-laden predawn landscape to happen upon a group of ten horses standing as still as statues, at which point the sun rises; the narrator explicitly likens the transcendent experience to a dream. In "A Dream of Horses," a group of grooms—the poem is narrated by this collective *we*—dream of the land being overrun by thunderous horses, an immersive scene that makes the grooms yearn to be trampled to death. In other words, the grooms accept the horses as their totem animals. As Hong states, in words that apply to both poems, "The horse as a shamanic totem is thus extremely effective in making the men drop their consciousness to enter and stay in the divine world of animals." With the protagonist of "The Rain Horse," the effect is inverted: instead of welcoming the spirit of the horse, the man discounts and ignores it. In doing so, he denies the possibility of a shamanic connection with nature and thus denies his own primitive side.

STYLE

Psychological Drama

Hughes's story is readily identified as a psychological drama, a classification reflected in several aspects of the narrative. To begin with, the protagonist is the only human being who appears,

such that the story is devoid of interaction between persons. Naturally, then, a great deal of the plot advancement, beyond the basic action, consists of the evolution of the protagonist's psychological state. The reader is told not simply what the protagonist does but moreover precisely what he is thinking, how he mentally responds to what takes place, and why he decides to act as he does. Some of the narration can be understood as directly communicating the protagonists's thoughts; for example, the young man, not the narrative voice, makes the judgment "This was absurd" regarding his response to the horse, though the thought goes unattributed. In effect, the reader is placed inside the man's head, experiencing the action as fully as if the story were written in the first person, if not more fully (since the self-consciousness of a first-person narrator can actually function as a barrier between the reader and the narrator's unfiltered thoughts). Through the intimate third-person narration, the reader is encouraged to sympathetically experience precisely what the man does. This encouragement is furthered by two additional facets of the style: the surrealism and the symbolism.

Surrealism

"The Rain Horse" is mostly grounded in a realistic world and setting, but the action is tweaked just far enough into the realm of improbability to push the style beyond ordinary realism. Specifically, the actions of the horse produce the sense, in both the protagonist and the reader, that it must be exceptionally intelligent, possessive of dark powers, or perhaps divine. Surmising that the horse might be insane, the man also explicitly wonders if it might be clairvoyant, that is, if it could see the future. In the last couple of meetings between horse and man, the man is no longer surprised to find the horse once again appearing suddenly ahead of him; he has come to expect it to operate beyond the bounds of ordinary reality. Less extreme in pushing those boundaries than magical realism (which can be seen to open a gulf between reader and characters in forcing the reader's willing suspension of disbelief in the characters' world), surrealism leaves the protagonist and reader alike uncertain as to whether what is occurring is being properly perceived or whether one is perhaps losing one's grip on reality. This state of piqued immediacy is linked with the experience of recognition of totem animals; in the words of Alan Bleakley (cited in Hong), Hughes presents human existence "through the medium of animal life, as a sur-reality...where biological, psychological and conceptual animals come to overlap, to fuse." This reference to the fusion of the several possible senses of an animal points to the role of the rain horse as both character and symbol.

Symbolism

Hughes's story makes for a riveting read if taken strictly on a literal level—interpreting the action as no more than action, faithfully reported—but the reader is apt to be left with the sense that the horse is more than just a horse, especially in light of the final line of the poem, which punctuates the story by expressing the psychological loss that the man has somehow just experienced. If he had only been confronting a horse as a horse, he would have lost little more than the cost of his shoes and suit. But just as a person in reality can be affected by an extraordinary interaction on a sentimental level that does not necessarily corre-spond with a rational interpretation of the expe-rience, the protagonist of Hughes's story absorbs his experience with the horse on a sym-bolic level, and the reader is urged to follow suit.

As most critics who have approached the story affirm, the horse is readily understood as representing the young man's own primitive or instinctual self. Out in the farmland in near per-fect isolation, the horse appears before him, beg-ging to be noticed—as if the rural environs and drumming rain have served to withdraw the man's psyche from his civilized existence. He has the chance to commune with his primitive self, to commune with a totem animal that would allow him a connection with the divine unself-conscious world that animals inhabit. The man declines the chance, however; to the best of his ability, he ignores the horse and marches away—he sup-presses his instincts, repeatedly deferring to his rationalizations. But the instinctual self resists; deep down in this civilized man the primal self yearns to breach the surface, and the horse charges the man. For a spell the man becomes ruled by this inner self, beginning at the point when he heaves two rocks at the horse, which he finds "had set the blood beating in his head and given him a savage energy. He could have killed the horse at that moment." This is not to suggest that the man would have had to kill the horse to fully access his primal self, but it does acknowl-edge that the primal self is not entirely virtuous or safe; the primal self is that which is capable of tapping into a vicious energy to kill for the sake of

necessity—food or survival—as animals and primitive man evolved to do. Rather than sug-gesting that the man should have catered to this raw energy, the story suggests that the man should have harnessed it, so to speak; once he subdued the horse, he might have seized the chance to make peace with it. Instead, the man threatens the horse for good measure as he makes his getaway. He has declined the totem animal's advances and thus definitively turned away from his primal self.

Hughes offered comments bearing direct relevance to the symbolic level of "The Rain Horse" in an interview with Ekbert Faas. Responding to a question about how modern-day society addresses "the problem of violence," Hughes pointed out that human communities' indigenous religious rituals and dogma allowed people to connect with their primal selves, and thus with the "bigger energy" of the universe, in safe and sanctioned ways. In modern society, however, where so much of religion has been sanitized or discredited by science, "force of any kind frightens our rationalist, humanist style of outlook." Hughes elaborates:

> In the old world God and divine power were invoked at any cost—life seemed worthless without them. In the present world we dare not invoke them—we wouldn't know how to use them or stop them destroying us. We have settled for the minimum practical energy and illumination—anything bigger introduces problems, the demons get hold of it. That is the psychological stupidity, the ineptitude, of the rigidly rationalist outlook—it's a form of hubris, and we're paying the traditional price. If you refuse the energy, you are living a kind of death....

HISTORICAL CONTEXT

Britain after World War II

"The Rain Horse" has only tenuous connections with the historical period in which it was written and takes place, largely because the events of the story are entirely insulated from historical cir-cumstances. The reader does not learn anything about what is going on in the world, not even through the protagonist's employment. None-theless, Hughes has classed the story as autobio-graphical, and he relates in the foreword to *Difficulties of a Bridegroom* that it is set "on a farm in South Yorkshire which was my constant

COMPARE
&
CONTRAST

- **1950s:** With school attendance in England angling upward, industrial employment opportunities leveling off, and white-collar employment growing, increasing numbers of people advance into higher income brackets, enabling more widespread ownership of cars and travel.

  Today: Travel and ownership of cars are commonplace, but employment opportunities have become limited and educational expectations ever higher. As such, the British government seeks to limit immigration from outside the European Union, in part to limit public spending and contain the unemployment rate.

- **1950s:** The latest trend in British literature is dubbed "the Movement," with authors like Kingsley Amis and John Holloway seeking to restore strict poetic standards by shying away from romantic hyperbole, grand theoretical constructs, and forays into mysticism. Hughes diverges from these writers.

  Today: As some view lingering British literary heavyweights like Salman Rushdie, Ian McEwan, and Julian Barnes as being past

  their prime and overrated—leaning heavily on irony and cynicism dolled up in precise language—newer literary voices, like Kazuo Ishiguro and Zadie Smith, are taking center stage. In the London *Times*'s list of the fifty best British writers since 1945, Hughes is ranked fourth, behind only Philip Larkin, George Orwell, and William Golding.

- **1950s:** Though Queen Elizabeth II's coronation in 1953 boosts the nation's morale, Great Britain begins to see its colonies claim independence, is dominated by America in international relations, and must cope with no longer being the world's leading nation.

  Today: With many people thrilled about the impending birth of the child of Prince William and his wife, the Duchess of Cambridge (née Catherine Middleton), in 2013, Britons seek to maintain morale while the country, highly affected by a double-dip recession begun in 2008, endures governmental austerity, being mired in debt, and losing its top-notch credit rating.

---

playground between 1938 and about 1944." Thus, since the story's protagonist's return takes place twelve years after he left the rural region, the story can be read as taking place in the mid-1950s. This was a time of class evolution in British society, with material progress following World War II allowing increasing numbers of sons and daughters of working-class families to attain middle-class, white-collar jobs. Indeed, manual employment declined through the late 1950s, while white-collar employment increased.

Yet a person's rise to a higher income bracket did not necessarily correspond to a shift to middle-class, bourgeois attitudes favoring materialism and conservative complacency. C. J. Bartlett, in *A History of Postwar Britain,*

1945–1974, speaks of "a new 'central' class . . . straddling the old divide between manual and white-collar worker." Hughes's protagonist in "The Rain Horse" can be viewed as signifying this central class, having progressed from the rural environs of his youth to employment that, judging from his important grey suit, should be understood as white collar. And he experiences conflict with regard to sentimental and material concerns, as he wishes to connect with his rural homeland but has difficulty in part owing to anxiety over the state of his garments.

British Literature after World War II

Hughes merits contextualization among his literary contemporaries, with some of whom he shared an outlook or a sensibility. English poetry by the 1950s was skewing away from both the sentimental indulgences of romanticism and the intellectual acrobatics of modernism in favor of the subdued appreciation of common life—the aesthetic of "the Movement," made explicit in Robert Conquest's introduction to the 1967 collection *New Lines*. Among writers who allied with the Movement were the so-called angry young men—such as Kingsley Amis and John Osborne—who deplored all that was seen as pretentious, materialist, and superficial about the era. In Bartlett's words, such writers "shocked, amused, or inspired according to the taste of their readers and audiences." But part of the program of such writers was to eschew poetic attempts to reach toward a higher plane of existence or the realms of mysticism (hallmarks of romanticism). Thus Hughes, whose verse and prose alike reflect romantic sensibilities, is not readily considered such an "angry" writer. Rather, as Annie Schofield notes in "Hughes and the Movement," Hughes's intent was "to submit himself to the necessary discipline to hear and proclaim a message of spiritual renewal in a decadent age."

Regardless of his intents, Hughes certainly startled and even shocked many of his readers, especially with images from the predatory world of wild animals, which led many to label and sometimes dismiss his writings as violent. With the release of his first collection, *The Hawk in the Rain*, in 1957, Edwin Muir (cited in Bentley), in view of this poetic violence, characterized Hughes as "quite outside the currents of his time." Amis, even while exuding negativity about the pretentious aspects of society, was considered a writer who, like Philip Larkin, adhered to what has been called "the Gentility Principle" (cited in Bentley), whereby life remains orderly, people polite and decent, and their emotions controllable. With Hughes's forays into the primeval animal world, gentility was often thrown to the wayside.

Hughes also differentiated himself from most of his contemporaries in producing poetry and prose that, rather than tending toward genteel ideals of precious literary elocution, drew heavily on the syntax, sense, and tone of the rural Yorkshire dialect of his youth. One of the few poets who shared Hughes's grounding in dialect was Tony Harrison, also a Yorkshire native. Hughes's uncommon syntax and grammar (that is, uncommon in literature for being

The horse behaves unnaturally, charging at the protagonist and disappearing suddenly. (© Tyler Olson / ShutterStock.com)

rooted in the syntax and grammar of the common people) can be detected in "The Rain Horse"—but the American reader, lacking awareness of the sound of Yorkshire speech, may come away from the story with an impression of the narrator's verbal patterns as merely stilted or peculiar. This gap in dialectic understanding may have had something to do with the fact that Hughes remained unappreciated by many American critics throughout his life.

CRITICAL OVERVIEW

Hughes is primarily approached as a poet, such that his occasional stories have elicited less critical commentary. In reviewing his 1967 verse-and-story collection *Wodwo* for the *Kenyon Review*, Robin Skelton observes that the stories within "all describe moments of dark illumination when the protagonists glimpse or come face to face with their shadow selves." The volume as a whole is said to present "numerous troubled and troubling creatures watching us and affecting us." In an *English Studies* review, Michael Thorpe calls the stories in *Wodwo* "excellent," though he expresses that the combination of poetry and prose "reads less effectively than it might sound." He concludes, "Nevertheless, there is more life in Hughes than in most of our 'living' poets put together and consequently more hope of his future achievement." In a *Poetry* review, Hayden Carruth calls *Wodwo* "a mixed book . . . because the quality, or rather the authenticity, of the writing fluctuates considerably." The reviewer concedes, however, that his "taste may be too contrary . . . , or too jaded, to respond to" Hughes adequately. Carruth considers "The Rain Horse" and one other story "the best pieces in the book" and concludes that *Wodwo* "is a book that most readers will wish to judge for themselves."

The stories of *Wodwo* were given more focus upon being reprinted in the 1995 volume *Difficulties of a Bridegroom: Collected Short Stories*, which contains only stories—which Hughes himself, in the foreword, concedes he views as merely "an accompaniment to my poems." Andy Solomon, writing for the *New York Times*, finds that the stories "succeed in conveying gripping incidents, brightened by the poet's shimmering imagery." He notes that in "The Rain Horse" and the other tales set in South Yorkshire, "landscapes are evoked with a Wordsworthian appetite, shadowed by menacing images of violence." In *World Literature Today*, Sudeep Sen considers Hughes's collection "a quiet and startling book."

Writing for *Booklist*, Bonnie Smothers admires the "tremendous depth and mythic power" displayed in Hughes's stories. She finds "The Rain Horse" to be positively "overwhelming," a story that "possesses beautiful timelessness, the effortless mythmaking of a master poet." A reviewer for *Publishers Weekly* judges that among the "taut, intense" stories of *Difficulties of a Bridegroom*, "The Rain Horse" is one of the "most neatly constructed" tales. The reviewer concludes, "Though Hughes is not a natural raconteur, these stories . . . show how effectively he can concentrate his talent for forceful images into compelling narratives."

Thematically "The Rain Horse" has been recognized as representative of Hughes's greater body of work, especially as seen in his earlier verse. Chen Hong, in "Hughes and Animals," refers specifically to the poem "A Dream of Horses" but also speaks to "The Rain Horse" when (citing the words of Neil Roberts) he sees the poem as indicative of Hughes's broader theme of "the usurpation or invasion of the world that the rational intellect has constructed, by a power that is represented as greater and ultimately more real." Keith Sagar, in *The Art of Ted Hughes*, notes that the story "is distinctively Hughes" in presenting a chance for communion with an animal spirit that signifies access to one's own primitive consciousness. David Porter, in "Beasts/Shamans/Baskin: The Contemporary Aesthetics of Ted Hughes," sums up that "we come upon ourselves in Hughes's animals."

CRITICISM

Michael Allen Holmes

Holmes is a writer with existential interests. In the following essay, he considers evidence in "The Rain Horse" suggesting that the protagonist would benefit from a Zen mind-set.

Almost nothing is said of or by the protagonist of Ted Hughes's story "The Rain Horse" indicating what spiritual or religious perspective, if any, he might have. No conspicuous religious symbols appear, such as in the form of jewelry or a feature of the landscape, to suggest the symbols that permanently occupy his mind. None of his comments contain any reference, whether straightforward or sarcastic, to a divinity such as Christianity's God. There is not even a mention of the day of the week, which would at least offer a clue as to when the protagonist is not attending a religious service. In one contrapositive hint, the reader might expect that, were the protagonist a monotheist (believing in one God), he would at some point conceive of the horse as carrying out God's will—but he never does. Considering the story as autobiographical in nature, the reader may examine Hughes's own religious inclinations to shed light on his protagonist. In fact, while Hughes drew on Christian myth in his poetry, he made his aversion to the religion clear. As stated by Michael Sweeting in "Hughes and Shamanism," he considered Christianity "the

WHAT DO I READ NEXT?

- The reader intrigued by "The Rain Horse" might next turn in Hughes's oeuvre to his translation *Tales from Ovid* (1997), which includes two dozen selections from Ovid's classical-era *Metamorphoses*. The stories in the latter half of *Tales from Ovid* focus on the fates of protagonists who fail to accept the power of nature and the gods.

- Hughes regarded Robert Graves's nonfiction volume *The White Goddess: A Historical Grammar of Poetic Myth* (1948), which foregrounds goddess reverence and the poet's need to worship a (perhaps ever-changing) muse, as something of a manifesto with regard to his poetic and personal lives alike.

- A work seen as an influence on Hughes's creation of "The Rain Horse" is D. H. Lawrence's novel *The Rainbow* (1915), which concludes with a scene where the protagonist Ursula encounters a group of horses. Hughes is known to have read *The Rainbow* at about the age of eighteen while encamped in a tent in a field where, in the course of a downpour during the night, horses repeatedly charged across the field around his tent.

- In turn, Lawrence's *Fantasia of the Unconscious* (1922), a continuation of his *Psychoanalysis and the Unconscious* (1921)—both exploring psychology and science from an amateur historical perspective—features a passage midway through in which horses are considered as sensually powerful dream objects.

- Another short story that features isolation, a muddy landscape, and psychological uncertainty and which pushes the boundaries of realism is Chicana author Diana García's "The Flat of the Land," published in the anthology *Pieces of the Heart: New Chicano Fiction* (1993), edited by Gary Soto.

- Among the authors Hughes cited as important influences is Dylan Thomas, whose World War II–inflected poetry collection *Deaths and Entrances* (1946) was viewed by Hughes for a time as a sacred book of sorts.

- Barbara Anne Porte's young-adult collection *Beauty and the Serpent: Thirteen Tales of Unnatural Animals* (2008) uses the framework of an exotic school librarian telling eerie stories to rule breakers, depicting singular interactions between the human and animal worlds.

---

worn-out religious machinery of a worn-out culture"; in the words of Leonard M. Scigaj in *The Poetry of Ted Hughes*, he judged that the religion "represses instinctual life."

In drawing on shamanic lore and practice in his poetry and stories, Hughes was explicitly seeking to spiritually reconnect modern humankind with primitive tradition and the natural world. In "The Rain Horse," the protagonist proves far from capable of engaging in any kind of spiritual relationship with the natural world through the untamed horse. But perhaps the reverse would be possible: perhaps he could manage to establish a spiritual connection with

the horse through the greater natural world. Arguably such a connection with the world is precisely what the protagonist needs. One means of his gaining such a connection would be through the precepts and practices of Zen Buddhism.

The mature Hughes was himself no stranger to Zen Buddhism as well as other Eastern spiritual philosophies. Scigaj cites the author's store of "Oriental and occult sources" as including "Zen Buddhism, the Hindu Upanishads, Chinese Taoism, the Tibetan *Bardo Thödol*, the disciplines of yoga, cabbalistic doctrine and alchemical lore, South Indian *vacanas*, and Sufi

> WHAT THE MAN LACKS IS THE MENTAL
> CAPACITY TO TAKE THAT STATE OF SUSPENSION
> WITH HIM WHEREVER HE GOES—TO APPROACH THE
> PARTICULARS OF HIS LIFE WHILE REMAINING AS
> DETACHED FROM THEM AS HE IS WHEN HE LOSES
> HIMSELF IN THE RAIN."

and Japanese fables." The Bardo Thödol is also known as the Tibetan Book of the Dead, which represents the conjunction of Buddhism and the primitive shamanism native to Tibet. Hughes became intimately familiar with this book when he worked on a libretto version when invited to do so in 1960 by the Chinese composer Chou Wen-chung (for a project that lapsed into obscurity). Zen Buddhism is a similar outgrowth of the Buddha's teachings, one that evolved when the line of patriarchs migrated into China and saw Buddhist philosophy fused with that of Taoism, which holds the elusive Tao, or Way, as the original motive sphere and energy of the universe. Connection with this original energy through meditative practices that ideally lead toward enlightenment is at the heart of the Zen tradition.

Part of the goal of Zen meditation is to cultivate an unceasing appreciation for the present moment. To attain such an appreciation, the Zen practitioner must be capable of draining all conceptual formulations from his mind, since actively *thinking* precludes actively *being* and *doing*. In the words of Vietnamese Zen master Thich Nhat Hanh, "*The world of Zen is the world of pure experience without concepts.*" It is precisely the world of concepts that is giving the protagonist of "The Rain Horse" trouble as the story opens. One extension of the world of concepts is the world of emotions, which often dominate people's behavior. Pleasant emotions may be sought despite moral costs, while unpleasant emotions may be avoided despite the potential for inner growth. Hughes's protagonist is acutely aware of his emotional state in visiting the valley of his youth because he has high expectations: he wants to delight in feelings of nostalgia, to draw on the past to gain pleasure in the present. But the

delight he expects never surfaces, largely because of the anxiety caused by the rain and the state of his clothes. But another factor may be the deliberate nature of his attempt; he is not so much *feeling* as he is *trying* to feel. He is not connecting himself with true reality but with the facsimile of reality he has projected through his expectations. As such, he does not succeed. Thus in a sense, the quest for past-centered nostalgia is equated with a failure to appreciate the reality of the present.

Where he is not focused on the past, Hughes's protagonist instead tends to focus on the future. Part of his concern for the future revolves around his shoes and clothes. It is hard to say, of course, at what point a soiled garment will prove impossible to get fully clean, such that this matter is weighing on the man's mind from the beginning of the story. By the second paragraph he has already concluded that "he had come too far." He is soon overcome by boredom and "then, suddenly, impatience, with a whole exasperated swarm of little anxieties about his shoes, and the spitting rain and his new suit and that sky and the two-mile trudge through the mud to the road." His anxiety over the future is also reflected in how he declines to take the shortcut past the farm because the idea of encountering the farmer, "to be embarrassingly remembered or shouted at as a trespasser," deters him.

Nhat Hanh speaks to the protagonist's troubles in these regards in *The Heart of the Buddha's Teaching: Transforming Suffering into Peace, Joy, and Liberation.* In words that speak directly to Hughes's character, he states, "Anxiety, the illness of our time, comes primarily from our inability to dwell in the present moment." Nhat Hanh points out that letting go of one's anxieties, and thus ceding control over fate to the universe, is essential to peace of mind. He declares, "Letting go gives us freedom, and freedom is the only condition for happiness. If, in our heart, we still cling to anything—anger, anxiety, or possessions—we cannot be free." The man in "The Rain Horse," one may surmise, would respond positively to such suggestions; he is clearly frustrated with his own mental constrictions but seems unaware of what to do about them. Nhat Hanh advises, "Do not lose yourself in the past. Do not lose yourself in the future. Do not get caught in your anger, worries, or fears. Come back to the present moment, and touch life deeply."

At more than one point Hughes's protagonist does manage to grow absorbed in the present and touch life deeply, namely, when he immerses himself in the experience of the rainstorm. Beyond just enjoying the sound and sight of the rain—while temporarily inuring himself to its chilly feel—the man finds his powers of perception so fully engaged by the sense-inundating storm that he slips away from his ordinary rational consciousness: "As long as it lasted he was suspended from life and time." But he remains aware that this state of suspension attained in stillness will dissipate as soon as he tends to his material circumstances, such that "he didn't want to return to his sodden shoes and his possibly ruined suit and the walk back over the land of mud." That is, what the man lacks is the mental capacity to take that state of suspension with him wherever he goes—to approach the particulars of his life while remaining as detached from them as he is when he loses himself in the rain.

What would potentially grant him this capacity would be devotion to Zen meditation, the very aim of which is to bring the student closer and closer to the transcendent experience of satori and the state of enlightenment. There, material concerns and daily anxieties are effectively abolished. The enlightened individual is still capable of negotiating the ups and downs of daily life, but affronts are not experienced as affronts, insults not as insults; fate brings what fate will—whether through the elements, accidents, other people, or any other agents—and the individual is no more than a leaf riding on the winds of fate for as long as the air allows. Physical circumstances of all kinds can thus be perceived as incidental and ephemeral and borne with pacific acceptance. As Eugen Herrigel notes in *The Method of Zen*, such acceptance of the elements is fostered through training in Zen monasteries, whereby "the change in the seasons makes no difference; the coldest and the hottest times of the day are preferred." Similarly Nhat Hanh, explaining in *Zen Keys* how whatever the present is must be accepted, remarks, "The sea is either calm or stormy. If you want a calm sea, you cannot get it by suppressing the stormy sea. You must wait for the same sea to become calm."

Herrigel, a German who underwent training with a Japanese Zen master for six years, also refers to the appreciation for nature and animals that is fostered by the Zen mind-set. One of the essential traits of the Zen master is the accomplishment of a universal compassion, whereby one fully communes with and accepts—and thus in essence loves—all aspects of the world around him, including all creatures and even inanimate objects. In Herrigel's words, the adept "lets everything and everybody have a share in his rich capacity for loving, without counting on any love in return." Further, "He embraces in these feelings everything that lives and breathes, including animals and plants, and he does not shut out even the least among them." Herrigel finds that the idealization of such a universal compassion "would explain why the Japanese love of nature is bound up with Zen," as exemplified in, for example, the profound Japanese appreciation for flowers. Offering a contrast to the Zen tradition, Hughes noted in his own prose how Christianity shaped modern culture to distance humankind from this instinctive compassion and appreciation for nature. In his 1970 review of Max Nicholson's volume *The Environmental Revolution* (cited in Scigaj), Hughes takes Reformed Christianity and Old Testament Puritanism to task, remarking, "The fundamental guiding ideas of our Western Civilization . . . are based on the assumption that the earth is a heap of raw materials given to man by God for his exclusive profit and use." He continues:

> The result has been to exile man from Mother Nature—from both inner and outer nature. The story of the mind exiled from Nature is the story of Western Man. It is the story of his progressively more desperate search for mechanical and rational and symbolic securities, which will substitute for the spirit-confidence of the Nature he has lost.

The passages from these various authors confirm that what the protagonist of "The Rain Horse" lacks—the ability to consciously unify himself with nature, not just the rain but also the horse, and not just momentarily but permanently—is an ability that can be fostered through adherence to the philosophy and practices of Zen Buddhism.

Yet the grey-suited man's episode with the horse seems to expose a fault line in Zen, as one question lingers: What can one do when one's life is threatened but act in un-Zenlike ways? The man arguably brought the horse's wrath upon himself through his dismissive attitude toward it; had he approached the horse from a standpoint colored by Buddhist compassion, the horse likely would have sensed this and acted much differently. But

Throughout "The Rain Horse," the weather is relentless, soaking the protagonist with heavy rain.
(© chaoss | ShutterStock.com)

once the man has made his mistake, once the horse is deliberately attacking, his aggression seems to prove necessary. In his introduction to *The Method of Zen*, Herrigel relates an anecdote about how he experienced an earthquake in Japan and was rushing out the door in a panic when he realized his companion, a Zen Buddhist, "was sitting there unmoved, hands folded, eyes nearly closed, as though none of it concerned him." Herrigel admires and aspires to the exceptional composure of his companion; but in "The Rain Horse," had the protagonist attempted to manifest such composure, he likely would have been trampled to death. When his life is threatened, naturally, he resorts to a violent response, heaving rock after rock at the horse until his strikes overturn the dynamic between the two. However un-Zenlike this aggressive outburst may be, the physical intensity of the episode actually helps bring the man into unity with nature. For a spell, the man taps into his primitive energies and, in effect, becomes a fellow animal. As Hughes told interviewer Ekbert Faas, "Any form of violence—any form of vehement activity—invokes the bigger energy, the elemental

power circuit of the Universe." Having gained an acute awareness of the energy contained within this universal circuit, the young man is perhaps more primed than ever to set aside his anxieties and anger alike in order to approach this energy instead through the unceasingly compassionate channel of Zen Buddhism.

Source: Michael Allen Holmes, Critical Essay on "The Rain Horse," in *Short Stories for Students*, Gale, Cengage Learning, 2014.

Susan Bassnett

In the following excerpt, Bassnett discusses the effects of Hughes's British background on his work.

In 1979 Hughes published *Remains of Elmet*, subtitled 'A Pennine Sequence' in an edition illustrated with photographs by Fay Godwin. The book is dedicated to his mother Edith and in his prefatory note, Hughes explains the impulses that lay behind its creation. He generously attributes his inspiration to Fay Godwin, suggesting that her photographs of the Yorkshire landscape moved him to write poems to

THE MYSTERY OF BEING BRITISH AND WHAT THAT MIGHT SIGNIFY TO HIM IS CONTINUALLY BEING EXPLORED BY TED HUGHES."

accompany them, though he had in fact always been inspired by the landscapes of his childhood as can be seen even in his first collection of poems. He made three subsequent versions of the sequence of poems, the last simply entitled *Elmet* in 1994.

In the preface, he also traces the history of that particular Yorkshire valley, a history that goes back into ancient times. As with his philosophy of language, that connects his own Yorkshire speech with Middle English, so Hughes draws links between the contemporary and the past, stressing the individualism of the local people. The Calder Valley 'was the last ditch of Elmet, the last British Celtic kingdom to fall to the Angles.' The inhabitants of the valley are therefore the descendants of a warrior race, a Celtic tribe who resisted invaders to the end. That fierce heritage lived on: Hughes relates how for centuries the valley was a lawless place, until the Industrial Revolution in the eighteenth century transformed it into a hub of textile production. In the post-industrial age that Hughes inhabits, all those histories are unravelling:

> Throughout my lifetime, since 1930, I have watched the mills of the region and their attendant chapels die. Within the last fifteen years the end has come. They are now virtually dead, and the population of the valley and the hillsides, so rooted for so long, is changing rapidly.

The starting point then is loss: the death of a way of life, the end of a long period of proud resistance, the dispersal of a population that carries traces of its ancient heritage within. Yet critics such as Ann Skea and Keith Sagar have drawn attention to the prevalence of images of light in this collection, Sagar going so far as to suggest that these poems show the distance that Hughes has 'travelled from the world of blood to the world of light.' Violence has been replaced with elegy, with a lament for a vanishing world.

A sense of mourning pervades this collection. In 'Walls at Alcomden,' stone walls built

by 'exhilarated men' have crumbled—'here is the hulk, every rib shattered,' and only 'a few crazed sheep' are left. Farms are dead in 'Shackleton Hill,' the land is 'naked now as a wound' in 'Wadsworth Moor.' Farms are like 'melting corpses' in 'The Sheep Went on Being Dead,' and hikers have replaced the mill-workers and farmers who kept the valley alive. In 'Remains of Elmet' that same message is reinforced by a string of images that personify the man-made constructions in landscape, representing them as grotesquely voracious creatures. The farms are 'stony masticators,' eating each other, while 'the sunk mill-towns' devour everything that comes into contact with them. Through the remains of the ruined world come 'tourists, to pick among crumbling, loose molars / And empty sockets.' This final image returns us to the opening image where Hughes envisions the Calder Valley as a great gullet, created aeons ago in the 'death-struggle of the glacier.' Formed violently in the Ice Age, the valley has continued to devour all with which it comes into contact.

. . . The tension between a changing world and the fixity of landscape runs right through Hughes's writing. He uses geological imagery to convey the idea of sedimented layers, of one world pressing down on another, burying earlier ones. In 'The Ancient Briton Lay under His Rock' he writes about himself as a boy, digging with his friends to try and find the long-dead mythical ancient hunter whose stories are still told in the valley. A poem in *Earth-Numb* (1979), 'Here Is the Cathedral' is underpinned by the image of buried civilizations. A Roman bath house is being excavated from beneath the cathedral itself, and during the excavation, generations of other dead are emerging, the bones of people who died of plague, families buried together, now being picked over by archaeologists. Around the cathedral is tarmac, where lines of cars are parked. The contrast between the modern world and the ancient one is subtly drawn, with the string of images allowing readers to make their own connections. Then the mood changes: the focus of the poem shifts to an incident at the door of the cathedral. The poet gives some loose change to a grubby wino, then watches as he is evicted from the cathedral by a 'pink-scrubbed, brass-eyed Christian knight.' The message of the poem is plain: the coming of Christianity has done nothing to change man's basic brutality. The layers of dead being unearthed have nothing to say, except to reinforce the sad truth that cruelty and unkindness remain strong in the world.

It would be wrong to see Hughes's vision of humanity as unwaveringly bleak, however. Besides the imagery of geological and archaeological layers upon which new generations tread, is another image, that of genetic continuity. In 'For Billy Holt,' in *Remains of Elmet*, traces of a Viking heritage can be seen 'anchored in nose and chin.' Earlier, in *Wodwo*, 'The Warriors of the North' sketches the coming of the Vikings and their gradual transformation into 'the iron arteries of Calvin.' The indomitable sense of resistance of the ancient Britons who held the Calder Valley against all comers and the savage strength of the Norsemen can be traced in the genetic fabric of the present. Other continuities are also observed. An uncollected poem about the poet's mother 'Edith' (*CP 700*) published in *The Listener* in 1985, depicts her walking over the moors as she approaches seventy, still dreaming dreams of freedom. She is described as a 'belated, errant, furious Brontë figment,' and this conscious linking of Hughes's mother and a character from a Brontë novel continues a thread that is developed in *Remains of Elmet*, that of a literary continuity, a connection between writers across time. 'Top Withens,' 'Haworth Parsonage,' 'Emily Brontë' all develop the Brontë link, an obvious one in terms of simple geography, given the closeness of Haworth to Hughes's childhood home, and linked also to his relationship with Sylvia Plath, when the explicit comparison between Hughes and Heathcliffe had first been made. 'Wuthering Heights" in *Birthday Letters* brings all these threads together: the visit of Hughes and Plath to Yorkshire and their walk over the moors through Brontë country, the differences between what they each saw and how they responded, the difference between the fate of 'dour Emily' trapped in her small Yorkshire community and able only to leave it through her imagination and that of Sylvia Plath, bearer at that time of a 'huge / Mortgage of hope.' Looking back, he sees Plath through a series of photographic images, sitting in a tree, leaning against a stone wall. She is depicted as an elemental creature, the wind and the clouds come to look at her, even the grass 'took idiot notice of you.' The great promise of a brilliant future that Plath and Hughes shared when they first went to Yorkshire together is contrasted with the confined life of Emily Brontë, and the sadness of the loss that promise pervades the poem. Just as the novel,

Wuthering Heights ends with a description of the landscape, where possibly the ghost of Heathcliffe and Cathy still walk, so this poem concludes with the same landscape, but with a hopeful final image: perhaps Emily's ghost, 'trying to hear your words' looked on, feeling a sudden surge of envy that is 'gradually quelled in understanding.' The fame of both women will endure, each of them in different ways as part of the same landscape now.

One of the most memorable poems in *Remains of Elmet* is 'Heptonstall Cemetery.' In this short poem, Hughes lists the names of his beloved dead—Thomas, Walter, Edith, Esther and Sylvia, 'living feathers' on the wings of 'a family of dark swans' that fly on towards the Atlantic, towards the mythical Western lands. It is a beautiful imagist poem, that brings together the physical reality of the graves in the cemetery with the metamorphosis of the dead into birds. Significantly, these birds are not carrion-eaters, not crows, not savage birds, of the kind that peopled Hughes's earlier poetry, they are strong, lovely birds capable of beating through storm-clouds. Diane Middlebrook sees this poem as important, suggesting that the inclusion of Plath's name indicates a process that he was going through as he worked on editing her poems, journals and stories for publication:

> Gradually, he was drawing his mother and Sylvia Plath together as composite influences in the history of his vocation.

The mystery of being British and what that might signify to him is continually being explored by Ted Hughes. He articulates his sense of identity in different ways—through the enduring nature of the land, both the Yorkshire of his youth and the Devon of his later years, through its stones, grass, and soil, through the layers of civilization that are buried in the earth, through the genetic continuity that is still discernible in the faces of ordinary men and women, through shared memories, through history, whether ancient or more recent, a history of religion, conflict, pain and survival, through the connections between writers, through story-telling, through symbolic associations. *Remains of Elmet* may not be one of Hughes's best-known collections, but it is significant, for it brings together many of the themes he had been exploring earlier in his writing, and through its elegiac quality establishes other themes that he would follow later.

Source: Susan Bassnett, "'Being British Is the Mystery': Hughes and His English Roots," in *Ted Hughes*, Northcote House Publishers, 2009, pp. 48–49, 61–64.

Sudeep Sen

In the following review, Sen praises Hughes's talents as a poet and a writer of both fiction and nonfiction prose.

For anyone who is a modern poetry enthusiast, particularly in the work of Ted Hughes, the last twelve months or so have been a virtual feast. First, *Winter Pollen*, a book of "occasional prose," appeared, then the much-awaited *New Selected Poems 1957–1994* (see the Verse subsection above), and most recently the volume of collected short stories *Difficulties of a Bridegroom*. A total of almost one thousand printed pages of the poet's selected works corroborates Sean O'Brien's comment in the *Sunday Times*: "It demonstrates anew that he is one of the bare handful of important English poets to emerge since the Second World War."

Winter Pollen is a substantial book, one that contains forty-five prose pieces ranging from reviews and essays to broadcasts. Its subjects include such literary figures as Shakespeare, Coleridge, T. S. Eliot, Emily Dickinson, Isaac Bashevis Singer, and Sylvia Plath (five illuminating pieces); other writers discussed include Vasko Popa, Janos Pilinszky, Keith Douglas, and Laura Riding. Perhaps the two most outstanding pieces in the book (both written in 1993 and hitherto unpublished) appear at the very end: "Myths, Metres, Rhythms" and "The Snake in the Oak." For these two pieces alone, the book is worth acquiring; the fact that there are other gems makes its possession imperative. Mention must be made of William Scammell, who has edited the collection incisively and intelligently with a poet's exactitude and care.

Difficulties of a Bridegroom, which contains nine stories, is a quiet and startling book. In the foreword Hughes writes, "These nine pieces hang together, in my mind, as an accompaniment to my poems." In fact, six of them are taken from his 1967 collection *Wodwo* and other writings. Except for "The Head" (1978) and "The Deadfall" (1993), all the items are dated between 1954 and 1962. The foreword is an important document in itself, as it provides a valuable insight into the thoughts and peculiarities of inspiration and process of Hughes's writing. For instance, the first piece, "O'Kelly's Angel," was written a year after he left the university in 1954 as "a joke of sorts" about one of his closest friends. Three of them—"Sunday," "The Rain Horse," and "The Harvesting"—were part of a planned series about his boyhood in Yorkshire. For me, however, the most fascinating of the lot is "The Wound," a story which was later adapted as a radio play. It incorporates the whole subconsciousness of dream, with metaphors arising out of fragmented images of memory, as well as effects from film and drama, and eventually it has to do as much with reason as with unreason.

Hughes was born in 1930. He was appointed Poet Laureate in 1984. Eleven years hence, we see him still writing, weaving various genres into intricate patterns, poetry and prose interlocking in a manner that "places him firmly in the great tradition of poet-critics whose practical and theoretical meditations make up the canon of classic English literary criticism, from Sidney Campion and Johnson down to Yeats, Pound, Eliot, Auden and Empson" (Scammell). In the words of the Nobel laureate Derek Walcott, "The poetry of Ted Hughes has brought us, in the most exact sense, closer to nature, its complete workings, than any English poet we can think of, including Clare and Hardy.... It is poetry of exultation." When one views Hughes as an artist, however, it is difficult not to conclude that his essential center remains poetry, and that poetry feeds everything that is essential in life.

Source: Sudeep Sen, Review of *Difficulties of a Bridegroom: Collected Short Stories*, in *World Literature Today*, Vol. 70, No. 2, Spring 1996, p. 414.

SOURCES

Alberge, Dalya, "Feted British Authors Are Limited, Arrogant and Self-Satisfied, Says Leading Academic," in *Guardian* (London, England), July 28, 2010, http://www.guardian.co.uk/books/2010/jul/28/gabriel-josipovici-dismisses-english-authors (accessed February 24, 2013).

Bartlett, C. J., *A History of Postwar Britain, 1945–1974*, Longman, pp. 146–53.

Bentley, Paul, "The Debates about Hughes," in *The Cambridge Companion to Ted Hughes*, edited by Terry Gifford, Cambridge University Press, 2011, pp. 27–39.

Carruth, Hayden, Review of *Wodwo*, in *Poetry*, Vol. 112, No. 6, September 1968, pp. 422–23.

Collins, Warwick, "The 50 Best British Writers since 1945?," in *Public Poems*, January 15, 2008, http://www.publicpoems.com/2008/01/times-books-section-under-editorship-of.html (accessed February 24, 2013).

Faas, Ekbert, *Ted Hughes: The Unaccommodated Universe; With Selected Critical Writings by Ted Hughes and Two Interviews*, Black Sparrow Press, 1980, pp. 86–87, 197–208.

Hasan, Mehdi, "In UK's Heated Debate over Immigration, Ministers Avoid Using the A-Word," in *Huffington Post*, February 2, 2013, http://www.huffingtonpost.co.uk/2013/02/01/uk-immigration-debate_n_2598786.html (accessed February 24, 2013).

Herrigel, Eugen, *The Method of Zen*, translated by R. F. C. Hull, Vintage Books, pp. 11, 33, 94–95, 119.

Hong, Chen, "Hughes and Animals," in *The Cambridge Companion to Ted Hughes*, edited by Terry Gifford, Cambridge University Press, 2011, pp. 40–52.

Hughes, Ted, "A Dream of Horses," in *Lupercal*, Faber and Faber, 1960, pp. 21–22.

———, Foreword and "The Rain Horse," in *Difficulties of a Bridegroom: Collected Short Stories*, Picador USA, 1995, pp. ix–xi, 67–78.

———, "The Horses," in *The Hawk in the Rain*, Faber, 1968, pp. 15–16.

———, "Myth and Education," in *Critical Essays on Ted Hughes*, edited by Leonard M. Scigaj, G. K. Hall, 1992, pp. 255–68.

Jenkins, Simon, *A Short History of England: The Glorious Story of a Rowdy Nation*, PublicAffairs, 2011, pp. 314–16, 348–50.

Moulin, Joanny, "The Problem of Biography," in *The Cambridge Companion to Ted Hughes*, edited by Terry Gifford, Cambridge University Press, 2011, pp. 14–26.

Nhat Hanh, Thich, *The Heart of the Buddha's Teaching: Transforming Suffering into Peace, Joy, and Liberation; The Four Noble Truths, the Noble Eightfold Path, and Other Basic Buddhist Teachings*, Broadway Books, 1998, pp. 78, 81.

———, *Zen Keys*, Doubleday, 1995, pp. 84, 88.

O'Neill, Sean, and Sandra Berwick, "'Towering' Poet Laureate Ted Hughes Dies of Cancer," in *Independent.ie*, October 30, 1998, http://www.independent.ie/world-news/towering-poet-laureate-ted-hughes-dies-of-cancer-26172579.html (accessed February 25, 2013).

Porter, David, "Beasts/Shamans/Baskin: The Contemporary Aesthetics of Ted Hughes," in *Critical Essays on Ted Hughes*, edited by Leonard M. Scigaj, G. K. Hall, 1992, pp. 49–66.

Review of *Difficulties of a Bridegroom*, in *Publishers Weekly*, Vol. 243, No. 36, September 2, 1996, p. 111.

Sagar, Keith, *The Art of Ted Hughes*, 2nd ed., Cambridge University Press, 1978, pp. 19–20, 78–85, 232–33, 258.

Schofield, Annie, "Hughes and the Movement," in *The Achievement of Ted Hughes*, edited by Keith Sagar, University of Georgia Press, 1983, pp. 22–36.

Scigaj, Leonard M., *The Poetry of Ted Hughes: Form and Imagination*, University of Iowa Press, 1986, pp. 19–20, 85–121.

Sen, Sudeep, Review of *Difficulties of a Bridegroom: Collected Short Stories*, in *World Literature Today*, Vol. 70, No. 2, Spring 1996, p. 414.

Skelton, Robin, "Leaders and Others: Some New British Poetry," in *Kenyon Review*, Vol. 30, No. 5, 1968, pp. 689–96.

Smothers, Bonnie, Review of *Difficulties of a Bridegroom*, in *Booklist*, Vol. 93, No. 3, October 1, 1996, p. 321.

Solomon, Andy, Review of *Difficulties of a Bridegroom*, in *New York Times*, October 13, 1996, http://www.nytimes.com/1996/10/13/books/books-in-brief-fiction-740993.html (accessed February 22, 2013).

Sweeting, Michael, "Hughes and Shamanism," in *The Achievement of Ted Hughes*, edited by Keith Sagar, University of Georgia Press, 1983, pp. 70–90.

Thorpe, Michael, Review of *Wodwo*, in *English Studies*, Vol. 49, No. 3, June 1968, p. 278.

"UK Loses Top AAA Credit Rating for First Time since 1978," BBC News website, February 23, 2013, http://www.bbc.co.uk/news/business-21554311 (accessed February 24, 2013).

FURTHER READING

Horn, Gabriel, *Contemplations of a Primal Mind*, University Press of Florida, 1996.
> In this book, Native American author Horn draws from his own experiences to praise the importance of connecting with the natural world and laments how modern society fails to appreciate the sacredness of nature.

Howkins, Alun, *The Death of Rural England: A Social History of the Countryside since 1900*, Routledge, 2003.
> This volume focuses on how the relationship between Britons and their rural homelands, with regard to work as well as leisure, evolved over the course of the twentieth century.

Roberts, Neil, *Ted Hughes: A Literary Life*, Palgrave Macmillan, 2006.
> Drawing heavily from manuscripts contained in the voluminous Hughes collections held at Emory University and the British Library, Roberts's critical biography examines how Hughes's life and relationships—especially that with Plath—are reflected in his writings.

Skipper, Lesley, *Understanding Horse Behavior: An Innovative Approach to Equine Psychology and Successful Training*, Skyhorse Publishing, 2007.
> Although the lay reader may be less interested in the finer points with regard to training horses, the passages discussing horses' emotional and intellectual lives will enlighten any animal enthusiast.

SUGGESTED SEARCH TERMS

Ted Hughes AND The Rain Horse

Ted Hughes AND Wodwo

Ted Hughes AND Difficulties of a Bridegroom

Ted Hughes AND the Movement

Ted Hughes AND British literature

Ted Hughes AND British poetry

horse AND short story

rain AND short story

Ted Hughes AND primitivism

Sylvia Plath AND Ted Hughes

Rose-Johnny

BARBARA KINGSOLVER

1987

Barbara Kingsolver's "Rose-Johnny" was her first literary publication. The short story, published in 1987, is about a strange woman with a mysterious past in a small Appalachian farm community. Reputed to be "half-man and half-woman," Rose-Johnny is believed to be a lesbian in a time (the 1950s) and place (Kentucky) where such an identity left one marginalized and considered dangerous. The ignorant gossip about the woman is dispelled and the truth uncovered when a young farm girl, Georgeann, befriends her.

So began Kingsolver's stellar career as a feminist fiction writer, journalist, essayist, poet, and political activist. The author of fourteen books by the early 2010s, Kingsolver's characters and stories come from her wide experiences in Appalachia, the Southwest, Africa, the Caribbean, and the Canary Islands, and they include Native Americans, Hispanics, African Americans, Spanish, South Americans, Africans, and poor and middle-class white Americans who are workers, farmers, mothers, and children. Women and their challenges are her special focus. Community is depicted as important for solving social problems. Known as an idealist for presenting solutions to world problems in her fiction, Kingsolver also tries to live by her own philosophy—for instance, living off the land on her own organic farm. She has won many literary honors, including being short-listed for the Pulitzer Prize for *The Poisonwood Bible* (1998), and she was

Barbara Kingsolver *(© Alastair Grant | Staff | AFP | Getty Images)*

presented with the National Humanities Medal by President Bill Clinton in 2000. "Rose-Johnny" is included in Kingsolver's collection *Homeland and Other Stories* (1989) as well as *New Stories from the South: The Year's Best, 1988* (1988) and *The Kentucky Anthology: Two Hundred Years of Writing in the Bluegrass State* (2005).

AUTHOR BIOGRAPHY

Barbara Ellen Kingsolver was born on April 8, 1955, in Annapolis, Maryland, to Dr. Wendell R. Kingsolver, a navy physician, and Virginia Lee Henry Kingsolver. She was a middle child with an older brother, Rob, who became chairman of the Biology Department at Kentucky Weslyan College, and a younger sister, Ann, who would be an anthropology professor at the University of California, Santa Cruz. The children grew up in the outdoors in the Appalachian foothills in Carlisle, in eastern Kentucky.

Kingsolver took refuge in books and in nature. The parents taught the children the importance of social service to humanity. In grade school, Kingsolver spent two years in a village in the Congo where her father was posted as a public health doctor. This became the personal background for her novel *The Poisonwood Bible*. Her father also practiced medicine in a convent hospital in Saint Lucia, in the Caribbean, the setting for her story "Jump-Up Day" (in *Homeland and Other Stories*).

Kingsolver learned about gender and race at Nicholas County High School, in Kentucky, where segregation was the norm and girls took home economics while boys took shop. In 1973, Kingsolver entered De Pauw University, in Indiana, on a music scholarship. In college, she read Karl Marx and became a political activist, espousing the antiwar cause, feminism, and environmentalism. She changed her major to zoology with an English minor and graduated magna cum laude in 1977. For two years after, she studied in Athens and Paris and lived in European communes.

In 1979, Kingsolver became a graduate student at the University of Arizona in the field of ecology. She was headed for a doctorate but grew dissatisfied with academia. While serving as a graduate assistant and technical writer, she began her career in journalism, publishing articles on human rights and environmental issues. In 1985, she married University of Arizona chemistry professor Joseph Hoffmann. "Rose-Johnny" was her first literary piece. It was published in the *Virginia Quarterly Review* in 1987, the same year she gave birth to her daughter Camille and sold her first novel, *The Bean Trees*, published in 1988.

In 1989, Kingsolver published a nonfiction study of mostly Hispanic and Native American women who helped local miners, called *Holding the Line: Women in the Great Arizona Mine Strike of 1983*, as well as the collection *Homeland and Other Stories*, which includes "Rose-Johnny." In 1990, her novel *Animal Dreams* conveyed her outrage at the covert American wars in Central America. In 1991, to protest the Gulf War, Kingsolver and her daughter moved to the Canary Islands. Her marriage was breaking up; she divorced Hoffmann in 1993. In the same year *Pigs in Heaven*, the sequel to *The Bean Trees*, came out. In 1994, she married

Steve Hopp, an environmentalist, and with him had another daughter, Lily, in 1996. Kingsolver's varied body of work, including her first collection of essays, *High Tide in Tucson* (1995); her novel about the Congo, *The Poisonwood Bible* (1998); *Prodigal Summer* (2000); her second collection of essays, *Small Wonder* (2002); *Last Stand: America's Virgin Lands* (2002); *Animal, Vegetable, Miracle: A Year of Food Life* (2007); *The Lacuna* (2009); and *Flight Behavior* (2012), has established her as a major award-winning authority on the environment and social justice.

PLOT SUMMARY

The narration in "Rose-Johnny" is from the first-person point of view of a ten-year-old country girl, Georgeann Bowles. She describes an odd character in her rural Appalachian town of Walnut Knobs: Rose-Johnny. The mothers of the town warn children against Rose-Johnny as a terrible person to be avoided, like a legendary figure from myth, half man and half woman. She has a man's haircut and wears a man's boots. However, Georgeann is not frightened upon seeing her or encountering her, because she thinks it gives her a secret power to have done or known something her older sister, Mary Etta, has not. Normally Georgeann has to follow in Mary Etta's footsteps, never having her own clothes or experiences. Still, her first encounter with Rose-Johnny becomes a secret that for nearly a year she must keep to herself. This creates agitation in her.

Rose-Johnny is odd, but she wears a dress like any other woman. She works in the feed store where Georgeann is sent to buy chicken feed one day during haying time. Georgeann is too small to help with haying, when workers have to lift bales and throw them on the truck beds, or with setting tobacco plants in the spring. Mary Etta teases and scolds her younger sister by calling her lazy, so Georgeann is proud to be given the task of buying the feed after school with a quarter she is given. She gets a ride with Aunt Minnie, who teaches first grade. Aunt Minnie has a 1951 Dodge, one of the newest cars among their relations. Aunt Minnie waits in the car while Georgeann goes into the feed store. Rose-Johnny is in the back feeding baby chicks, while her father, Lester Wall, the owner of the store, is in front talking to some men.

Georgeann is surprised when Rose-Johnny comes to the counter to wait on her. She thinks Rose-Johnny looks like someone's mother. The girl orders five pounds of laying mash (feed for eggs laying hens), and Rose-Johnny weighs it for her. One of the men in the store tells Georgeann that her mother is wasting money, because chickens will just eat corn. Georgeann explains to the men that laying mash has oyster shells mixed in with corn and is exactly what she needs. The men start hassling Rose-Johnny about the purported oyster shells in the mash. She is quiet and gives the girl her bag.

Outside the store, one of the men, obviously a farmer, gives Georgeann a quarter to replace the one she spent and tells her to give a message to her father: he should never send daughters to Wall's store, only sons. She replies that her father only has two daughters, and they tell her that her father should come himself. In the car, Georgeann asks Aunt Minnie why girls cannot go into Wall's store. Aunt Minnie says she cannot explain until Georgeann is older. It is because Rose-Johnny is a "Lebanese."

At home, Georgeann does chores and at dinner notices that Mary Etta is pale from helping with haying and cannot speak or eat much. When her mother urges her to finish her potatoes, Mary Etta complains that she is not growing anymore. She has had the same dress size for over a year. Georgeann is distressed, thinking it means she will not inherit any more dresses from her sister.

Georgeann tells a lie to her father as she gives him the quarter the man gave her. She says Mr. Wall gave her the mash for nothing because Rose-Johnny was sick and he needed help, so she helped him out. She continues the lie, saying that Mr. Wall has said she could work in exchange for feed in the future. Her father looks at her suspiciously, as if he knows she is lying, but he does not contradict her. Georgeann is bursting to tell all this to Mary Etta but restrains herself and only tells her doll, Miss Regina, at bedtime.

Georgeann looks up the word *Lebanese* in Aunt Minnie's Bible dictionary, and it says the Lebanese are a seafaring people who built ships from cedar trees. She cannot connect this information with Rose-Johnny and does not believe that growing up will solve the mystery. Next week when she goes back for mash, she follows Rose-Johnny to the back of the store and asks her if she came from over the sea. Rose-Johnny laughs and says she was born in Slate Holler. Georgeann asks if that is where she gets "osters" (oysters). Rose-Johnny laughs again. When she rings up the sale, Georgeann puts on an act and says that she is too poor to pay, and her daddy asked if she could do some work in exchange. Rose-Johnny says bless her heart, she will find something for her to do.

Georgeann begins to work with Rose-Johnny for the chicken feed. Mr. Wall is never in the store; Rose-Johnny does everything, including keeping the accounts and ordering. Mr. Wall and Rose-Johnny have an apartment in the back where he stays all day. Georgeann learns everything about the store—how to feed and water the ducks and chickens, how to weigh and mix mash. Georgeann thinks Rose-Johnny is the smartest, most competent person she has ever met. She knows all the customers, though she rarely speaks to them, especially the men, who bring a change over her face when they harass her. Rose-Johnny tells Georgeann the histories of the men, such as Ed Charney, who abuses his wife and mule, and Bud Mattox, the father of all the Mattox boys in school. Black children come to the store after hours, and Rose-Johnny opens for them. She knows all their

names, such as Cleota, who is the eldest, and teaches them to Georgeann, telling her she must call them by name, even in public. She also charges them less for the feed.

Georgeann always worries her lie will be found out, although she enjoys being with Rose-Johnny every day after school. Georgeann confesses to her doll to assuage her guilt. Every night Mary Etta brushes her long hair hoping to stop it from turning gray early like their mother's. Georgeann starts to cry because she believes that something bad will happen because of the lie, and it will happen to her sister. Mary Etta soothes her.

Rose-Johnny falls sick, and Georgeann feels guilty, worrying that it is because of her. She goes into the apartment to visit and smells whiskey in the cold, bare rooms. Rose-Johnny is in bed, but her face lights up when she sees Georgeann, who throws herself on Rose-Johnny's bosom and cries, confessing her lie to her and saying she is sorry for the illness. She can hear the wheezing in Rose-Johnny's chest. Rose-Johnny comforts her.

Weeks pass, and Rose-Johnny does not get better. Mr. Wall needs Georgeann's help because she is the only one besides Rose-Johnny who knows how to run the store. Georgeann is now eleven, and Mary Etta is sixteen. Georgeann waits on Cleota, and she knows how to treat the sick chicks, when Mr. Wall does not.

People begin to talk about the situation. Georgeann knows all the rumors about how Rose-Johnny's daddy is a colored man and how she is a lesbian. Georgeann knows all these rumors are false because she knows the woman herself. She reads to her in bed. Georgeann asks if Rose-Johnny's daddy, Mr. Wall, makes her cut her hair. Rose-Johnny teases and says yes, he is a very mean man. Georgeann then knows it is not the truth.

At school one of the Mattox boys, Roy, calls Georgeann names and gets in a fight with her, giving her a bloody nose. She bites his arm very hard. She tells the other children that Rose-Johnny is not a pervert and that she loves her. Another boy calls Georgeann a pervert. When she goes to the store that day, it is locked, and Mr. Wall will not let her in. She tells him what happened through the glass. The next day she is allowed in. Rose-Johnny can hardly talk. She says Mr. Wall is her grandfather, not her daddy. Georgeann says the colored man must be her daddy then.

Rose-Johnny tells her story. Her father was white, but when he died, her mama loved a man who was brown, and they had a sweet baby named Johnny. She has a drink of what Georgeann thinks is her medicine and continues her story: some of the townspeople lynched her mama's lover and drowned the baby in Jackson Crick when it was frozen. The men then sexually assaulted the mother and promised to do as much to little Rose when she was old enough. Rose-Johnny says triumphantly that they did not do anything to her because of what her mama did: she cut off Rose's hair and said that from now on, she had to be Rose and Johnny both, and then she went to the creek where they put the baby and drowned herself. Georgeann sits with her friend for a long time in silent sympathy.

This is the last time she sees Rose-Johnny. A month later the store is boarded up. Some say she died, and some say she moved with Mr. Wall to the Blue Ridge.

When Georgeann gets home the night Rose-Johnny told her story, her mother is standing in the door. She runs out and hugs Georgeann, saying her daddy is looking for her in the truck. Some men tried to hurt Mary Etta, and Mr. and Mrs. Bowles were afraid they were going to hurt Georgeann.

Georgeann finds Mary Etta in bed crying. She has marks on her neck. Her good dress is torn in half at the bodice. Georgeann says she will mend it for her. Mary Etta says it cannot be mended. Some men with masks attacked her. She thinks it was the Mattoxes. Mary Etta screamed, and Mr. Dorsey came along the road just then and helped her. The men kept asking her if she was the Bowles girl. Georgeann believes they were looking for her, and she goes to bed and will not speak or eat, out of guilt. She cuts off her own hair and Miss Regina's. She calls herself George-Etta, and she calls her doll Rose-Johnny. Their father lets the girls stay home from school that month and set tobacco plants. It takes all summer for Georgeann's hair to grow out.

CHARACTERS

Georgeann Bowles

Georgeann Bowles is the first-person narrator of the story. She is ten years old, the younger daughter of a poor tobacco farmer. She has spunk and curiosity, and this is what leads her to tell a lie in order to work in Rose-Johnny's store. She tells Rose-Johnny she has no money to pay for the feed and must work it off. Her father lets her get away with the lie because it helps the family. Georgeann does not understand why Rose-Johnny is an outcast or why she is cruelly harassed by the townspeople. Georgeann feels guilt about her lie, thinking it causes Rose-Johnny's illness and the attack on her sister, Mary Etta. Georgeann recounts how she learned about human values and prejudice by sticking up for Rose-Johnny. When she tells her classmates she loves Rose-Johnny, they call her a pervert, thinking she is learning to be a lesbian. Georgeann simply sees Rose-Johnny as a good human being and a friend. She becomes Georgeann's role model.

Mary Etta Bowles

Mary Etta, Georgeann's older sister, is concerned her looks are being ruined by her heavy farmwork. She wants to look at dress patterns in town but has to pick potato bugs off the vine or plant tobacco that stains her hands. At sixteen, she is already turning gray from exhaustion and malnutrition. She teases her younger sister for being lazy because Georgeann does not have to work as hard. Mary Etta is sexually assaulted on the road by a gang of masked men she believes includes the Mattoxes.

Mr. Bowles

Mr. Bowles is a poor Appalachian tobacco farmer who has a farm near Walnut Knobs, Kentucky. His only concern is to make a living to support his family. He complains of having no sons to help on the family farm; he relies on his daughters and wife, who are clearly exhausted doing so much hard labor, such as baling hay, day after day.

Mrs. Bowles

Mrs. Bowles is careworn and has grayed prematurely. She raises potatoes and chickens and sells eggs to supplement the family income. She is the younger sister of Aunt Minnie but looks older.

Ed Charney, Sr.

Ed Charney is one of the local farmers who insults Rose-Johnny. He also abuses his mule and his wife.

Cleota

Cleota is the oldest of the African American children who shop at Wall's store after hours. Rose-Johnny gives them a special price on all items and insists that Georgann call Cleota by her right name, along with her companions, Venise, Anita, Little-Roy, and James.

Mr. Dorsey

Mr. Dorsey is a neighbor who hears Mary Etta's screams and saves her from her attackers on the road.

Baby Johnny

Baby Johnny was Rose-Johnny's half brother, a baby of mixed race killed by vigilantes after they lynch the baby's father. Rose-Johnny takes his name in his memory.

Bud Mattox

Bud Mattox is one of the ignorant farmers who harasses Rose-Johnny in her store. He gives Georgeann a quarter and a message to her father not to let her shop there anymore. He makes it sound dangerous for a girl to be around Rose-Johnny, supposedly because she is a lesbian. It is implied that he and/or his children are among the gang of males with masks on who sexually assault Mary Etta Bowles.

Roy Mattox

Roy Mattox is a schoolmate of Georgeann's who calls her names because of her friendship with Rose-Johnny. She gets in a fight with him and bites his arm. This starts a family feud, with the Mattox males going after the Bowles daughters.

Aunt Minnie

Aunt Minnie is the older sister of Mrs. Bowles, but everyone thinks she is younger because she is single and fixes herself up. She teaches first grade at the local school and gives Georgeann rides in her 1951 Dodge, one of the newer cars in the area. Aunt Minnie utters a malapropism when she tells Georgeann that Rose-Johnny is a Lebanese.

Miss Regina

Miss Regina is Georgeann's doll and confidante. Georgeann tells Miss Regina about her secret friendship with Rose-Johnny. Miss Regina was a present from her grandmother, a blonde doll with a pretty dress representing traditional female roles at the time, like a Barbie doll. After Rose-Johnny leaves town, Georgeann cuts Miss Regina's hair and renames her Rose-Johnny.

Rose-Johnny

Rose-Johnny is the central character of the story, an ostracized woman in a small Appalachian town who runs a feed store. She is competent, kind, compassionate, and fair-minded, a contrast to the bigoted and ignorant country folk she lives among. She is thought to be a lesbian (or Lebanese, as they call her) because she has traits of both male and female behavior, with a man's crew cut and boots but also a woman's dress. Rose-Johnny runs the feed store, doing the accounts and taking care of the livestock. She is smart, knowing how to mix feed and garden seeds so the farmers will be successful.

Eventually, it is revealed why she is unfairly persecuted. In the past, her widowed mother took a second amour, an African American man, and had a baby. He was lynched, and Baby Johnny was drowned. The mother was raped and committed suicide but first cut the hair of her little girl, Rose, and told her she must be Rose-Johnny now. Her supposedly lesbian identity has protected her from the kind of assault Mary Etta suffers, but it has also made her an outcast or marginal figure. Rose-Johnny falls ill with something like pneumonia as events come to a head when the townspeople interfere with her friendship with Georgeann. Rose-Johnny disappears with her grandfather, and Georgeann hopes she has not died but has opened a store somewhere in the Blue Ridge.

Lester Wall

Lester Wall is the owner of his feed store and supposedly Rose-Johnny's father. In fact, he turns out to be her maternal grandfather and is completely unable to run the store. He has memory loss from either dementia or drinking. He relies on Georgeann to run the store when Rose-Johnny gets sick. He takes Rose-Johnny away and closes the store after the incident with Mary Etta.

THEMES

Racism

Kingsolver's story takes place in southern Appalachia in the 1950s, before the successes of the civil rights movement. Racism is the norm in this unprogressive town. Rose-Johnny has to serve the black farmers after hours by themselves because Jim Crow laws (segregation) are in effect. Blacks may not mix with the white customers. Miscegenation, or mixed racial marriage, is not

TOPICS FOR FURTHER STUDY

- James Still's *Way Down Yonder on Troublesome Creek: Appalachian Riddles and Rusties* (1974) presents old riddles of the region. Create a web page or wiki on riddles from various cultures, such as Native American, Indian, and African. Share findings with the class for discussion. How do riddles preserve folk wisdom and culture?

- Read *The Scarlet Letter*, by Nathaniel Hawthorne, and compare and contrast Hester with Rose-Johnny as a deviate from sexual norms in society. Write a short essay on how these marginal figures contribute to their communities in spite of their rejection.

- Research the history of mixed-race marriage in the United States. Where has it been illegal and what were the consequences? Trace the gradual acceptance of interracial love and friendship in the history of films and show clips to the class in a presentation.

- Read Anzia Yezierska's *The Breadgivers* (1925). The book's heroine, Sara Smolinsky, is a young Jewish Polish immigrant girl in the slums of Manhattan. How does Sara, as an outsider, try to grow up to become an insider in American culture? Does she succeed? Write a paper on the topic, citing other stories of outsiders who become insiders for comparison.

- Research Appalachian ballads, legends, and tall tales. Share a PowerPoint presentation on such stories with the class and include visuals. Does "Rose-Johnny" have any of the flavor of these sorts of stories?

tolerated. By local mob thinking, though not by law, the informal union of Rose-Johnny's white mother with a black man is punishable by lynching. The killing of the baby of mixed birth is extreme but in the direction of the sort of racist crimes overlooked by the law before the 1960s. Walnut Knobs is an isolated mountain town apparently without legal or moral restraints on racism. The Ku Klux Klan is suggested when the men attack Mary Etta with masks on their faces, as if to punish any family fraternizing with blacks or those who are liberal or sexually different, like Rose-Johnny.

Rose-Johnny defies the racism of the town by serving the black population and charging them less for the same merchandise. She makes a point of treating the children with dignity, calling them by name and insisting that Georgeann do the same, even in public. Rose-Johnny is persecuted for being different in her behavior. As an outsider, she sympathizes with other outsiders. She has taken the name of her murdered biracial half brother, Johnny, and is motherly to the black children. Many believe that her father was black, and to an extent she has become regarded as black by association.

Sexism

Women are not treated with respect in Walnut Knobs. This is a time before the women's movement when women of any class had few rights or options. Stereotypes are the accepted norm here. A female is a wife, daughter, mother, or, in Aunt Minnie's case, spinster schoolteacher, rather than a person. In this poor community, women have little education, marry young, and work themselves into old age quickly. Georgeann mentions that her mother's hair has grayed prematurely, and Mary Etta's hair is already starting to turn gray, though she is only sixteen. Georgeann and Mary Etta are farm girls, and because the Bowles family has no sons, the daughters have to help out as best they can. It is obvious that Mary Etta is suffering from malnutrition and exhausted because of the heavy physical labor. Her future is grim: probably an early marriage to a farmer and more exhausting work and childbearing.

Georgeann's grandmother gives her a doll called Miss Regina, a glamorous, blonde doll with a pretty dress, the equivalent of a Barbie doll, another stereotype, but a female fate that seems appealing to these poor girls. The level of education they receive is represented by Aunt Minnie, who does not have a complete dictionary but only a Bible dictionary. Aunt Minnie's ignorant malapropism for lesbian, "Lebanese," underscores that she is conservative and not especially broad-minded. Georgeann is a curious and spunky girl who has little outlet for her

Georgeann helps care for the chickens at home and at Wall's store. *(© joyfuldesigns / ShutterStock.com)*

spirit, and that is why she is attracted to Rose-Johnny's larger worldview.

Sexism is clearly represented in the fate of Rose-Johnny. She is persecuted as a lesbian, although there is no evidence she is one. Her mother, who was raped, devised for her the protective mask of being both boy and girl, little Rose and her dead brother, Johnny, together. Indeed, she is described as being androgynous, half man and half woman. She wears a dress but a man's haircut and boots. Her maleness is represented in her competence in running a business in her grandfather's name. Her femaleness is represented in her motherliness to Georgeann and the black children and her kindness to the animals and plants. When the men in the store taunt her, Rose-Johnny is silent and morose.

The threat for blacks out of line is lynching. The threat for women out of line is rape. The lynching mob raped Rose-Johnny's mother, and they threatened to do the same to Rose-Johnny when she was of age. Her reputed lesbianism is her protection, but it makes her an outcast. The men warn Georgeann that no little girls should go near her, as if for fear of contamination. Georgeann and her sister also suffer by association with Rose-Johnny, both being attacked and

called names by the Mattox clan. Mary Etta's sexual assault and beating are injuries that cannot be mended, she implies to her sister. She evokes the lifelong trauma many women experience from rape and violence.

Love

In spite of all odds, Kingsolver shows, love can blossom anywhere. Here it is shown in an unlikely friendship between an outcast woman and a poor farm girl. Georgeann does not believe the rumors about Rose-Johnny. She decides to investigate for herself and finds her to be gentle, wise, fun, and loving. Rose-Johnny is the only one in town who shows Georgeann attention and respect. She teaches the child how to run the store, and they enjoy each other's company. Georgeann has to keep the friendship secret, and it produces a strain and terrible guilt, because she knows she is breaking social rules, although she does not know why. When she is called names at school and people repeat terrible things about Rose-Johnny, Georgeann stands up for her and says she loves her. The more she protests her love, the more the town thinks she is speaking of a perversion. Kingsolver does a good job showing that love has no boundaries and is so precious to life that people are willing to be ostracized for it. The friendship with Rose-Johnny becomes central to Georgeann's life, symbolized by her cutting her doll's hair and renaming it Rose-Johnny.

STYLE

Modern Short Story

The modern short story gained popularity in the nineteenth century with the stories of Nathaniel Hawthorne, Edgar Allan Poe, Nikolai Gogol, and Guy de Maupassant. They gave the short narrative its modern form as a compressed story with a unified plot striving for a single effect. "Rose-Johnny," for instance, is unified around the single event in Georgeann's life of her friendship with Rose-Johnny and the effects of that relationship on the town. The modern short story generally concerns the everyday world of realistic events and settings, although some authors use fantastic and symbolic effects. The short story is a highly polished form, with surprise turns and philosophical implications, where the character has a revelation, usually near the end of the story. Georgeann's revelation is a positive one—that a person is not always what other people think.

Although Kingsolver is known more for her novels, her short fiction, collected in *Homeland and Other Stories*, is acknowledged to be well crafted. Her prose rhythm is often poetic and suggestive, and her characters are memorable, with dialogue reflecting dialect and place. Kingsolver draws on mythic elements from different traditions but is primarily a realistic author, concerned with spelling out social and political realities. Her characters face tough times and often brutality but must find a way through suffering to assert their basic humanity. Like the classic realistic writers, Kingsolver presents a moral point of view in her stories, with characters having to make ethical choices. There is no ambiguity or doubt as to which side Kingsolver is on with the issues she presents. She is for the larger, more inclusive humanitarian view.

Southern Gothic Fiction

The gothic story, or supernatural mystery story, which took its name from the spooky Gothic mansions of its settings, originated in eighteenth- and nineteenth-century Europe and was adapted to fiction that takes place in the southern United States. The style may include old mansions, threats of violence, grotesque characters, death or a murder mystery, the theme of decay, an appeal to the supernatural, a spiritual or moral dimension, and a haunting past with family secrets, omens, and prophesies. William Faulkner, Flannery O'Connor, Eudora Welty, Carson McCullers, Harper Lee, and Truman Capote are among the writers of this genre.

Harper Lee's *To Kill a Mockingbird*, for instance, has similarities to "Rose-Johnny" in that it contains racism, a town mystery, and a marginal social figure, Boo Radley, a mysterious recluse who is the subject of gossip but who heroically saves the Finch children. Scout, the feisty tomboy heroine, like Georgeann, must assert a moral view against a background of racist ignorance. Atticus Finch, the liberal white lawyer in Lee's story, is mirrored in function by Rose-Johnny, who has the largest, most liberal point of view in town and teaches it to Georgeann. However, as with much southern gothic fiction, death, alienation, and tragedy form the background of Kingsolver's plot.

Appalachian Literature

Appalachian literature is considered a branch of southern literature. Kingsolver grew up in Kentucky in the Appalachian region of the United States, and this area is the setting of much of her fiction, as concerned with both social and ecological conditions. In this story, the Bowles family, like the others in the area, are poor tobacco farmers who can barely make a living. The children are ill fed and poorly clothed, living in an isolated place without any vision of a larger world. It is a place of superstition and prejudice and family feuding, as when the Mattox men take on the Bowles family after their children fight in school.

Appalachian literature has its classics that find echoes in Kingsolver's setting. Davy Crockett's *A Narrative of the Life of Davy Crockett* (1834) sets the tone for depicting the wilderness of the mountainous area, its local color, and tall tales. James Still's *River of Earth* (1940) dramatizes the conflict of a family trying to live off the land or having to go into the coal mines. Harriet Simpson Arnow's *The Dollmaker* (1954), about a poor Kentucky family, became popular in its film version, starring Jane Fonda. Other famous Appalachian authors include James Agee (*A Death in the Family*, 1957); Wendell Berry, from Kentucky (*The Broken Ground*, 1964); Thomas Wolfe, from North Carolina (*Look Homeward, Angel*, 1929); and Rachel Carson, from Pennsylvania (*Silent Spring*, 1962). Writers in this region tend to focus on local color, social conditions, and saving the environment.

Feminism

Kingsolver encountered feminist ideas and literature in college, such as Betty Friedan's *The Feminine Mystique* (1963). She admires feminist writers Virginia Woolf, Doris Lessing, and Ursula LeGuin. Her fiction contains feminist themes, showing the sexist behavior of society as unfair and backward. She portrays strong female characters who have to deal with injustice and obstacles, which they overcome. "Rose-Johnny" depicts the condition of women in the 1950s in the United States, a particularly conservative time when women had few opportunities. Rose-Johnny escapes the stereotype in both her appearance and her occupation at the feed store. She looks and acts like a man in this rural town, so she is ostracized, yet Georgeann Bowles finds her to be an admirable role model of courage, independence, and knowledge of how to do practical work outside the home. Rose-Johnny has created her own life, however odd it may seem.

HISTORICAL CONTEXT

Appalachia

"Rose-Johnny" is set in the Appalachian region. Appalachia is a region in the eastern United States associated with the Appalachian mountain range as it runs through southern New York, Pennsylvania, Ohio, Maryland, Kentucky, Alabama, Mississippi, Georgia, North Carolina, South Carolina, Tennessee, Virginia, and West Virginia. This rugged land became known as a distinctive region in the nineteenth century through such legends as Davy Crockett, Daniel Boone, and railroad worker John Henry, with various tall tales about frontier heroes and distinctive country music derived from African American blues and Scottish fiddling. The region still boasts an oral culture of storytelling. Indian tribes such as the Cherokee left their influence as well. They were removed from their ancestral lands in

Georgia and the Carolinas and forced to walk the Trail of Tears in 1838–1839 to Arkansas. The small Eastern Band of Cherokees stayed in Appalachia. Kingsolver, like the narrator of "Homeland," has some Cherokee blood.

The regional stereotypes include an undereducated population, the making of illegal liquor, poverty, mountain shacks, family feuds, isolated backwaters, and hardy mountain people who belong to a past era. Kingsolver grew up in Carlisle, Kentucky, a small town in the Appalachian foothills, where her father was the town doctor. She saw firsthand the poverty, racial prejudice, and social conservatism. Most of the farmers in the area were poor, with tobacco the main crop, as it is for the Bowles family. The other means of income in the area traditionally came from mining and timber. Because much of Appalachia borders on the Deep South, it overlaps with southern culture, and many of the states were part of the Confederacy during the Civil War. The racism and terrorism of the Ku Klux Klan are evoked in "Rose-Johnny," and Kingsolver has said she became aware of the issues of segregation in her high school in Nicholas County, Kentucky. "Rose-Johnny" is set in this area in the 1950s, while it still retained its distinctive backwater characteristics. In her essays, Kingsolver notes the discrepancy between the poor Appalachian farmers and miners and the rich Blue Grass country adjacent, where swimming pools were built for horses.

Besides the negative stereotypes, Appalachia has produced an admirable recognizable culture, on which Kingsolver's story draws. The world of country ballads, tall tales, folk art, oral history, strange and colorful characters, and tragic stories with heroic figures informs the fabric of this story, although Kingsolver tells it embedded in a realistic foreground. The tragic demise of Rose-Johnny's family could be a ballad, but lynching and racial crimes are also historically real for this area. The odd character of Rose-Johnny as an androgyne is reminiscent of tall tales and the supernatural, but Kingsolver also uses her to bring up the issue of lesbianism as a marginal and misunderstood social identity.

Lynching and Racism

Reconstruction (1865–1877) is the period after the Civil War in which the United States tried to restructure American society by abolishing slavery and amending the Constitution (with the

COMPARE
&
CONTRAST

- **1950s:** Middle-class women are encouraged not to have higher education and careers but to stay home and take care of the house and children. A schoolteacher is often a single woman like Aunt Minnie. Poor women like Mrs. Bowles are largely prevented by social and economic conditions and lack of education from bettering their situations.

  Today: Women of all economic backgrounds are urged to finish high school and go to college. Many families require incomes from both parents to meet expenses. Even mothers at home are expected to have a career or part-time work to fall back on.

- **1950s:** African Americans before the civil rights movement are subjected to Jim Crow laws in the South and in Appalachia. Even in northern cities, they have a difficult time getting an education and anything but menial work.

  Today: African Americans are enfranchised and part of the middle and upper classes,

with college educations, careers, social status, and entrepreneurial opportunity, although they still have to battle prejudice and economic inequality in various ways.

- **1950s:** Appalachia is an isolated and limited part of the country compared to the rest of the United States. Poverty is a concern, with many tobacco farmers and coal miners unable to make a decent living.

  Today: After President Lyndon Johnson declared war on poverty in Appalachia in 1965, more attention and development were extended to the region. Today, with technology, communication, larger cities, diversified industry, a tourism sector, and a vibrant culture of literature, art, and music, Appalachian people have many more opportunities and are no longer isolated from the rest of the country by their geography and history.

Thirteenth, Fourteenth, and Fifteenth Amendments) to give civil rights to four million former slaves. By 1877, however, white supremacists in the South had reasserted their power and states' rights to enact "Jim Crow" laws that instituted segregation of the races and deprived blacks of their civil liberties. Blacks were forbidden from mixing with whites and had their own churches, communities, schools, movie theaters, and stores. Many states had miscegenation laws forbidding interracial marriage. Full citizenship for African Americans had to wait until the civil rights movement in the 1960s.

The terrorism of the Ku Klux Klan and other hate groups in the late nineteenth and early twentieth centuries was largely countenanced by both southern and northern whites. There were hundreds of lynchings with virtually no legal recourse. They were still not uncommon in the 1940s and 1950s, when the story takes

place, up until the civil rights movement of the 1960s brought public outrage to this illegal and immoral practice.

Political Activism

Kingsolver was in college during the anti–Vietnam War demonstrations of the early 1970s. She has reported that she never forgot the thrill of the success of that activism and that she consciously writes stories that elicit a political response. In "Rose-Johnny," she brings up the economic woes of the Appalachian people, with their dependence on tobacco and mining, industries that exploit the workers. Land is used for tobacco instead of food, and the Bowles children are starving, reduced to little more than potatoes to fill in their diet. Kingsolver wrote a journalistic exposé of an Arizona mining strike in her book *Holding the Line* (1989).

Georgeann meets Rose-Johnny at Wall's feed store. *(© Stanley Carter | ShutterStock.com)*

Kingsolver has described her philosophy as basically Marxist—that is, aware of class differences and struggles and the exploitation of workers and minorities. She points out the economic aggression of big corporations and favors grassroots organizations and local autonomy. "Rose-Johnny" also touches on racism and sexism. Rose-Johnny is a successful businesswoman but an outcast in her community. Lesbianism is criticized by society, while sexual violence is excused. Kingsolver takes not only a feminist position in this story, but an ecofeminist position. Ecofeminists believe that women, with their community values and knowledge of interconnectedness, have an important place in saving the environment. Rose-Johnny is credited with caring for the land. She is a fertile Mother Nature figure, responsible for the success of gardens and farms in the area. Kingsolver describes the importance of returning the land to subsistence farming in *Animal, Vegetable, Miracle* (2007). Kingsolver's books and essays demonstrate that she not only writes about political convictions; she tries to show how to live them.

CRITICAL OVERVIEW

"Rose-Johnny" was Barbara Kingsolver's first publication, appearing in the *Virginia Quarterly Review* in the winter 1987 issue. It appears in *New Stories from the South: The Year's Best, 1988* and is included in the collection *Homeland and Other Stories* (1989), which won an American Library Association award. This story is frequently noted by reviewers as one of the memorable ones in the collection. In *Library Journal*, Timothy Zindel says the collected short stories are "enhanced by real wisdom and generous warmth." Although he does not find Kingsolver an "innovator," he feels her "voice is sure and her narrative skill accomplished." Russell Banks, in the *New York Times*, finds the stories "extraordinarily fine" and thinks the author has a "Chekhovian tenderness toward her characters." Her characters "struggle to make sense of what has happened to them" and with "moral toughness" try to find meaning in a difficult world.

Kingsolver's career actually took off with the publication of her longer fiction. *The Bean*

Trees in 1988 immediately won praise from critics and readers. Jack Butler in the *New York Times Book Review* notes that Kingsolver's fiction is both poetic and realistic. He singles out the success of the character Taylor Greer, a strong Appalachian woman whose backwoods voice the author admitted almost took over her writing. Butler feels the only flaws in the book are a manipulation of the plot and her making Greer too perfect.

Kingsolver's 1990 novel *Animal Dreams* won the Edward Abbey Ecofiction Award in 1991. In terms of artistry, however, critic Jane Smiley for the *New York Times Book Review* feels the author took on too many social issues to pull together into one novel. The character of Taylor Greer reappears in *Pigs in Heaven* (1993), and reviewers such as Joan Merrill Gerber for the *Los Angeles Times* were happy to see Taylor appear on the Oprah Winfrey show in the book. Gerber notes that the novel is constructed like a talk show on the important issues, with each character standing for a different position. Maureen Ryan, in her article "Kingsolver's Lowfat Fiction" in the *Journal of American Culture* in 1995, agrees that Kingsolver's work is charming, popular, and successful but questions whether it should be called serious literature. She praises Kingsolver for tackling the important social issues of the day but feels Kingsolver offers feel-good sentimental solutions that make readers think there are easy fixes.

It was the publication of *The Poisonwood Bible* in 1998, short-listed for the Pulitzer, that made Kingsolver into an international author of postcolonial status. The *New York Times Magazine* treats the novel as having major importance through Sarah Kerr's review "The Novel as Indictment." Héloïse Meire wrote a feminist essay placing it within a historical dialogue about Africa: "Women, a Dark Continent? *The Poisonwood Bible* as a Feminist Response to Conrad's *Heart of Darkness*."

In the twenty-first century, Kingsolver is increasing her popularity as an ecofeminist with essays and fiction about the environment. Often studied as a regional writer, she has roots in both Appalachia and the Southwest. Most readers do not seem to mind her self-professed idealism and assurance that problems can be solved with a little love, tolerance, and social action. In her introduction to 2010's *Seeds of Change: Critical Essays on Barbara Kingsolver*, Priscilla Leder

concludes that "Kingsolver's work reconsiders and reimagines the discourses of our culture to reveal possibilities for a better world."

CRITICISM

Susan K. Andersen

Andersen holds a PhD in literature. In the following essay, she examines Kingsolver's depiction of a new kind of everyday heroism that stands up to social prejudice in "Rose-Johnny."

Homeland and Other Stories, including "Rose-Johnny," is a collection of tales by Barbara Kingsolver about women who try to find a home or place for themselves. In the title story, "Homeland," Gloria St. Clair recounts a childhood memory of her Cherokee great-grandmother, who wants only to see the place she grew up before she dies. She does not fit in with her mostly white Appalachian descendants in a coal-mining town, but when she sees the Cherokees of Tennessee making their living by dressing up for tourists, she is ready to go, for her time and place are past. Although her people have been destroyed, she leaves her Cherokee stories to her great-granddaughter to cherish.

In "Covered Bridges," Lena and her husband have to come to terms with the fact that they cannot have children. In "Stone Dreams," the narrator has an affair to get out of a stifling marriage. "Islands on the Moon" concerns an estranged mother and daughter finding something in common when they both become pregnant. The stories concern ordinary women who must deal with obstacles or even, in the case of Rose-Johnny, tragedy. In her essay "Small Wonder," written after the 9/11 attacks in 2001, Kingsolver says we live in fearsome times where we as humans are challenged by hatred and violence and trauma that at the same time furnish us with "huge opportunities" to reinvent ourselves. Kingsolver delivers portraits of strong women who become heroes in ordinary ways, just in the acts of loving and surviving.

The author states in her essay "The Spaces Between," in *High Tide in Tucson: Essays from Now or Never*, that she is attracted as a writer to "the places where disparate points of view rub together—the spaces between." Different points of view of the main character are juxtaposed in "Rose-Johnny" to highlight a woman's difficult choice to live on the margins of society as the

KINGSOLVER DELIVERS PORTRAITS OF
STRONG WOMEN WHO BECOME HEROES IN
ORDINARY WAYS, JUST IN THE ACTS OF LOVING AND
SURVIVING."

town's supposedly lesbian androgyne, "half man and half woman." In the Appalachian farm town of Walnut Knobs in the 1950s, ten-year-old Georgeann Bowles has already accumulated the town gossip on the odd woman running the feed store, who calls herself Rose-Johnny. Georgeann is a curious child who wants to find out things for herself. When she meets Rose-Johnny, with her man's haircut and boots and woman's dress, Georgeann is surprised that she is ordinary; she does not find Rose-Johnny to be the monstrous Lebanese or lesbian her aunt warns her about. Using Georgeann's innocent first-person point of view as she becomes friends with Rose-Johnny, the author is able to show how society constructs identities and forces people to live in them. The town prejudice and persecution of the woman have nothing to do with who she is. The friendship between Georgeann and Rose-Johnny brings out the depth, strength, and heroism of both characters for being themselves against all odds.

Georgeann is the naive narrator who lets on more than she understands. She does not necessarily comprehend her hard life, for she has nothing to compare it to. For instance, she complains that she has to wear her sister's hand-me-downs and that she is too little to help with haying, jealous that Mary Etta gets to do it. We soon get the impression, however, that sixteen-year-old Mary Etta is exhausted doing the work of a man when she is too tired to speak at dinner. Her hair is already graying, and she has not grown at all in the last year on the diet of potatoes her mother gives her. The men in town speak of Bowles's hard luck, having only daughters. Georgeann for the moment is freed from the family hardship, still having her own world of fantasy with her doll, Miss Regina. She slips through the cracks of adult care with her lively curiosity. When she has a chance for an

adventure, to work with Rose-Johnny in her store, she exults that she has a secret that gives her a certain power, outside the ordinary life of her family. She joins the ostracized woman in a rich world of their own. The adventure soon becomes something that shapes her character and calls for courage when she has to stand up for Rose-Johnny, explaining to her classmates, "I love her." Ironically, the town outcast becomes her role model.

Georgeann cannot see anything wrong with Rose-Johnny. She is kind and teaches Georgeann many things about the store, about raising chickens, and about the feed and garden seeds. She sees that Rose-Johnny is not a drudge, like Georgeann's mother and sister on the farm, but an independent businesswoman who likes her work and contributes to the town's prosperity through her competent knowledge of farming methods. She is fair and compassionate, teaching Georgeann to see the town's African American children as people. On the other hand, Rose-Johnny pays a price, for the male customers who come into the store are cruel to her and make snide remarks. The look on her face shows what a heavy burden she bears by being the town scapegoat.

Georgeann subjects herself to the same harassment by associating with the woman, and that makes the reader wonder what makes little Georgeann different. She seems to have her own mind. Like Rose-Johnny, she also has an androgynous name, a combination of "George" and "Ann." Rose-Johnny strikes a chord in her. They respect one another. Rose-Johnny's androgynous appearance seems like lesbian behavior to the townspeople, but the androgyne figure in traditional literature is a symbol of balance, wholeness, and power. One of Kingsolver's favorite feminist science-fiction writers, Ursula LeGuin, explores the theme of androgyny in *The Left Hand of Darkness* (1969). When Georgeann says she loves Rose-Johnny, people assume it is some kind of sexual lesbian relationship rather than a human connection. They have preconceived ideas. Georgeann finally finds out what those hateful ideas are after she gets in a fight with Roy Mattox.

"Rose-Johnny" has something in common with the southern gothic style that Kingsolver grew up admiring in such writers as William Faulkner, Flannery O'Connor, Eudora Welty, and Carson McCullers. Such stories often take place in the South where there is a town mystery

WHAT DO I READ NEXT?

- *The Absolutely True Diary of a Part-Time Indian* (2007), by Sherman Alexie, is a young-adult book dealing with racism, poverty, and tradition. A winner of the National Book Award, the novel is a semiautobiographical story about a young Indian who decides to leave the reservation for a white high school and has to negotiate being an outsider.

- Kingsolver's *The Bean Trees* (1988) introduces Appalachian heroine Taylor Greer, with her country accent, traveling from Kentucky to Tucson, Arizona. She picks up an orphaned Native American child called Turtle on the way.

- Ursula LeGuin's *The Left Hand of Darkness* (1969) is an award-winning feminist science-fiction novel about the androgynous planet Gethen, where there is no war because there is no male dominance.

- *The Heart Is a Lonely Hunter* (1940), by Carson McCullers, is a novel about a deaf man, John Singer, and the people he meets in a mill town in Georgia in the 1930s. McCullers writes about the rejected and the oppressed of society.

- *Fair and Tender Ladies* (1988), by popular Appalachian author Lee Smith, is an epistolary novel in the voice of Ivy Rowe, a poor woman who cannot escape her hard farm life. She shows the changes of Appalachia over the seven decades of her life.

- James Still, an important Appalachian author, writes about his boyhood in the young-adult tale *Sporty Creek: A Novel about an Appalachian Boyhood* (1977). Still includes folklore and tales in his realistic storytelling about Kentucky.

- "A Worn Path" (1941) is a short story by Eudora Welty about the difficulties of an elderly African American woman named Phoenix Jackson, who walks through the woods into Natchez, Mississippi, to buy medicine for her grandson, who has accidentally swallowed lye. The story demonstrates the power of her love to make her take the almost impossible journey each time.

- Richard B. Drake's *A History of Appalachia* (2003) brings together the elements of the region, including folk traditions, the environment, the roles of African Americans and women, and a complete social history of this mostly rural area. Corporate exploitation through coal mining and strip mining, as well as technology, have modernized the area with urbanization.

---

based on a past tragedy, including elements like racism, violence, rigid social codes, and a thwarted love affair. Rose-Johnny is the remains of such a mystery that Walnut Knobs would like to cover up. She defiantly stays in her place despite her mother's lover being lynched, her half brother being murdered, and her mother committing suicide. "Rose-Johnny" explores the familiar legacy of southern storytelling. Kingsolver, however, is more concerned with issues of social injustice than with the psychological probing of the collective past. She shows the ugliness of the town's ignorance but focuses more on how the two women overcome that ignorance. As a feminist and political activist, Kingsolver asks, what do people do in such situations of blatant injustice?

In "Letter to My Mother," in *Small Wonder: Essays*, Kingsolver tells of her own experience of acquaintance rape when she was in college. In a gesture similar to Rose-Johnny's, she cut off her long dark hair and wore a combat helmet and military jacket to become more unattractive. She became a feminist and activist. Kingsolver appeals as a writer in part because, as Mary Ellen Snodgrass comments in *Barbara Kingsolver:*

A Literary Companion, she is "a master writer blessed with moral vision." She is interested not merely in political outcomes but in human outcomes. In the essay "Flying," also in *Small Wonder*, Kingsolver comments, "There can be no greater spiritual accomplishment than to come through brutal trials and then look back and see that mean times did not render us mean spirits." In "Small Wonder," contemplating the 9/11 events and whether she should hate the perpetrators of the attack on the Twin Towers, she concludes, "It's the same struggle for each of us, and the same path out: the utterly simple, infinitely wise, ultimately defiant act of loving one thing and then another, loving our way back to life."

Kingsolver demonstrates such wisdom in the unlikely friendship of Georgeann Bowles and Rose-Johnny. Despite the darkness around the edges of their lives, their mutual love is the central shining light that changes the life of Georgeann ever after. When Rose-Johnny is forced out of town, Georgeann cuts off her own hair in an act of identification and calls herself George-Etta to take on the guilt of her sister's sexual assault, much as Rose-Johnny included her brother's memory in her own name. Georgeann makes Miss Regina, the formerly glamorous doll, into Rose-Johnny. Thus, the reader knows, this was a defining moment in the formation of her moral character. Rose-Johnny's example is the door that leads out of limitation and defeat and narrow-mindedness.

Kingsolver's stories are filled with the horrors of sexual and child abuse, murder, political intrigue, war, colonial and economic exploitation, genocide, acts of violence, the destruction of nature, and ecological crimes. In her essay "In Case You Ever Want to Go Home Again," in the collection *High Tide in Tucson*, Kingsolver comments on her writing. She explains she "cannot look away from the painful things." In "Careful What You Let in the Door" in the same volume, she discusses the place of violence in literature. She admits that violence in literature can promote violence as entertainment if done sensationally. She does not like women to be portrayed as vulnerable victims. Classical tragedy as in Shakespeare, she shows, is about human suffering, but it does not dwell on violence, only on its consequences. If Kingsolver shows violence, she says, she is trying to work out "the connection of events with their consequences." "Rose-Johnny," like Greek and Shakespearean tragedy, puts the violence off-stage. We hear about the lynching and murders, but they are summarized in a sentence or two rather than portrayed in detail. We are left to contemplate the consequences of those acts.

In her defense of fiction in "What Good Is a Story?" in *Small Wonder*, the author writes, "The business of fiction is to probe the tender spots of an imperfect world." Fiction helps the reader to understand and sympathize with other lives, a first step in doing something to solve the world's inequity. Art can change life, she claims in the essay "Jabberwocky" from *High Tide in Tucson*. In an interview with Robin Epstein in the *Progressive*, Kingsolver points out that she is trying to write about a new kind of heroism, not the heroism of the popular superheroes, but ordinary heroism of everyday life through endurance, dignity, and love. Survival itself can be heroic, she says. In the story "Rose-Johnny," Georgeann's Appalachian farm family is hungry but determined, Rose-Johnny survives hate crimes, and Georgeann is brave enough to stand up for her.

Kingsolver feels that her background in both literature and science helps her to show the way out of social injustice through a larger picture of nature and the human place in it. She told Donna Perry in an interview in *Backtalk: Women Writers Speak Out* that biology is her religion, because it demonstrates unifying principles such as the interrelatedness of all things. In the essay "A Fist in the Eye of God" in *Small Wonder*, Kingsolver speaks of Darwin's theory that genetic variety is important to survival and evolution. Similarly, she maintains, cultural diversity is necessary for our survival, an inherent moral in every story she writes. A culture with a low tolerance for difference, such as the town in "Rose-Johnny," is reducing its own chance for survival and growth. Georgeann Bowles did not look at Rose-Johnny for her odd appearance or reputation but admired her because of what she gave. Georgeann says she was "the secret witness" of the care Rose-Johnny took to create the seed packages that gave rise to all the gardens in the community. The source of the town's moral right, Rose-Johnny is not a label like lesbian or Lebanese: "Rose-Johnny was simply herself."

Source: Susan K. Andersen, Critical Essay on "Rose-Johnny," in *Short Stories for Students*, Gale, Cengage Learning, 2014.

Georgeann's Aunt Minnie drives a 1951 Dodge. *(© aodaodaodaod | ShutterStock.com)*

Mary Ellen Snodgrass

In the following essay, Snodgrass discusses Kingsolver's use of strong, varied female characters.

In Kingsolver's writings, female strength emerges in women like Sugar Hornbuckle, Alice Greer, Lou Ann Ruiz, Annawake Fourkiller, Mama Tataba and her Kilangan sisters, Deanna Wolfe, Rose-Johnny, and Mattie the tire dealer, all of whom endure and fight for self and community. Examples are as disparate as the innkeeper Mrs. Hoge at the Broken Arrow Motor Lodge in *The Bean Trees* (1988), hard-hatted female mine workers in Kingsolver's documentary *Holding the Line: Women in the Great Arizona Mine Strike of 1983* (1989), a suspected lesbian and her friend Georgeann in the story "Rose-Johnny" (1989), the forest ranger in *Prodigal Summer* (2000), and Great Mam in *Homeland and Other Stories* (1989), the Cherokee matriarch who "was like an old pine, whose accumulated years cause one to ponder how long it has stood, not how soon it will fall." Kingsolver rejects a pervasive misperception about women: "A woman without a man—a condition of 'manlessness'—is defined as alone. But a single mother is less alone than the average housewife" (Karbo, p. 9). The author's ability to overturn erroneous stereotypes informs her fiction, enabling her female characters with an inborn courage and feistiness.

The redoubtable female in Kingsolver's writings is capable of bonding with other women to empower the circle and energize its members according to the needs of the moment. They batter themselves and their hopes against age-old double standards that keep females powerless, disenfranchised, and, in some cases, hopeless. Taylor Greer, protagonist in *The Bean Trees*, thinks of women as homey dispensers of food and consolation. When Estevan, a Mayan refugee, reports his wife's near-suicide from an overdose of baby aspirin, Taylor offers him food and a beer and muses, "From my earliest memory, times of crisis seemed to end up with women in the kitchen preparing food for men." She identifies the ritual as "good solid female traditions."

In a choice between the roles of wife and parent, Kingsolver characterizes motherhood as the height of womanly attainment. Most

KINGSOLVER EXALTS NETWORKING AMONG FEMALE CHARACTERS, A METHOD ATTESTING TO COMMONALITIES IN WOMEN'S LIVES."

maintain a tight-lipped empathy with their daughters, particularly Alice Greer in *The Bean Trees* (1988), who "always said barefoot and pregnant was not [Taylor's] style." When Taylor faces her first predicament—the abrupt receipt of a homeless, parentless Cherokee child through her car window—she stops at the first motel in which a woman works. The instinct for woman-to-woman empathy is unfailing. The aid of Mrs. Hoge, innkeeper at the Broken Arrow Motor Lodge, suffices to get Taylor and the child through Christmas.

Poet Clive Matson praised the author's hard-shell females for their moral conviction and righteous energy, forces that keep them alive and thriving. Taylor's toughness arises in her response to Lou Ann Ruiz's description of the door to Fanny Heaven with a doorknob at the crotch of a painted female figure, "like a woman is something you shove on and walk right through." Instead of feeling put down, she advises her roommate, "You got to get pissed off." When faced with endangerment to the Mayan couple, Taylor remarks on woman's place in rescue scenarios: "More often than not . . . the woman carried the man through the tragedy. The man and the grandma and all the kids." Through Taylor, the author champions the bulwark matriarch, women like John Steinbeck's Ma Joad in *The Grapes of Wrath* (1939) and the rebel Pilar in Ernest Hemingway's *For Whom the Bell Tolls* (1940).

Kingsolver exalts networking among female characters, a method attesting to commonalities in women's lives. Because no single person, no single plan of action, and no formal behavior code or personal philosophy is any matriarchal community's salvation, each member must depend on make-it-up-as-you-go logic and teamwork. Mattie teaches Taylor that small children must have liquids to ward off dehydration in Tucson's desert climate. Taylor shares Turtle with Esperanza to begin the healing process that

will carry her Mayan friend through the loss of her little girl Ismene to a political nightmare. Edna Poppy relies on the sound of the attacker and a wide swath with her cane to rescue Turtle. Perhaps the most rewarded by female invincibility is Lou Ann Ruiz, who finds in herself parallels to Taylor's resolve and self-respect.

For *Holding the Line: Women in the Great Arizona Mine Strike of 1983* (1989), the author sifted and weighed the experiences of female citizens of copper-mining communities. Her first inkling of gender bias lay in a perusal of mining folklore that marginalized women as jinxes who allegedly could cause a cave-in just by their presence in the shaft. Their worse evil lay in violating the men-only dictum of "the devil's domain." The women who fought management's devaluation of labor obtained "a new perspective on a power structure in which they were lodged like gravel in a tire." The sturdiest among them encountered racial profiling, false arrest, corporate conspiracy with police, and the tear-gassing of a liquor store. Annie Jones, head of a women's auxiliary in Ajo, modeled female strength against coercion with a feisty motto: "We come back fighting every time they try to slap us down."

Kingsolver's self-assured women draw critical complaint for their smugness, e.g., Sugar Hornbuckle's thought that "A woman knows she can walk away from a pot to tend something else and the pot will go on boiling; if she couldn't, this world would end at once." Within a few paragraphs, the author can't resist describing Cherokee matrons as having "The obstinate practicality [that] pierces and fortifies these families like the steel rods buried in walls of powdery concrete." Less bristly is Alice Greer's generous compliment to Cash Stillwater's self-effacing ways: "Modesty makes women fall in love faster than all the cock-a-doodling in the world."

Pigs in Heaven perpetuates Kingsolver's theme of female solidarity during perplexing and threatening times, as demonstrated by the women at the stomp dance who converse in Cherokee sprinkled with three English terms— permapress, gall-bladder, and Crisco—each an answer to a domestic quandary. In an attempt to locate Sugar Marie Boss Hornbuckle, a beloved cousin, Alice Greer comes upon the familiar dead end of searching for a woman who may have remarried and changed her surname. Through Alice, the author speaks an observation on the shift: "Isn't that the dumbest thing, how the wife ends up getting filed under the husband? The husband is not the most reliable thing for your friends to try and keep track of." The witty complaint implies the displacement of women from historical data by the custom of cloaking them under a new family name.

Extolled by critic Henry Aay are Kingsolver's strong set of female figures in *Animal Dreams* (1990), a work of ecofiction grounded in cultural anthropology. The author takes particular delight in self-reliant Latinas like Doña Althea and Viola Domingos, who are willing to fight the Black Mountain mining firm for clean water in Grace, Arizona. Kingsolver noted in "Lush Language," a 1993 book review for the *Los Angeles Times*, that Mexicans produced "a culture whose pantheon includes the Virgin Mary, Pancho Villa, and Aztec goddesses." The two-out-of-three logic gives women the lion's share, a source of courage that emboldens and consoles them in difficult times.

In the novel, the author pictures a Latina circle of fighting matriarchs under the unlikely moniker of the Stitch and Bitch Club. As the art dealer Sean Rideheart explains, the women of Grace brought to the lifeless ores of the canyon a unique "economic identity" comprised of "embroidery and peacocks and fruit trees and piñatas and children." While selling feathered piñatas in Tucson's upscale area, they link up with Jessie, a bag lady, who offers her shopping cart as transportation. The first day's sale goes so well that the women up their stock to five hundred piñatas, each accompanied by a broadside explaining the town's endangerment by threatened water rights. When Hallie disappears in Nicaragua, the clubwomen turn their efforts to a letter-writing campaign sending a thousand messages to members of Congress and the media. In both instances, they refuse to be stymied by fear or female political powerlessness. When the Black Mountain Mining company backs down from its leaching operation and its plans to dam the river, the twenty-two activists triumph at the thing they do best—preserving the natural resources of their homeland to nurture both family and nature. Codi Noline ponders how "mountains could be moved," in this case, by having the community declared a national treasure on the historic registry.

Womanhood takes on new angles in *The Poisonwood Bible* (1998), in which female roles and dress in the Congo are more stringently one-sidedly gender-based than in the white world. Leah Price views Kilangan girls her own age already married and bearing babies. She recognizes the change from youth by the torpor in their eyes, which "look happy and sad at the same time, but unexcited by anything.... *Married* eyes." She deduces that, while little boys continue climbing trees and playing army, "little girls were running the country," a veiled comment on the value of African women in a land where men value them like dray labor.

To five-year-old Ruth May Price, Leah's little sister, the lesson of African womanhood is embodied in Mama Mwanza, a Congolese woman who arouses compassion because she survives a catastrophic roof fire and learns to scoot around using her hands for leverage. In deplorable condition, she still must feed and tend seven or eight children and a demanding father. Laden with a laundry basket on her head, she follows the other women of Kilanga village to the river to attend to the wash. In the direst situations, her ability to organize family labor and delegate authority proves beneficial to the Mwanzas' survival as well as to starving neighbors whom she surreptitiously aids with gifts of food. Ironically, she is more Christlike in extending kindness than is the Reverend Nathan Price, who comes to the Congo to save heathens like her.

Nathan's wife, Orleanna Price, herself a discounted and devalued wife and mother, pictures Congolese women as the tall-stalked lilies who bear blooms on their heads in the form of "manioc-root bundles the size of crumpled horses." Their gathering, pounding, drying, and boiling of manioc into a tasteless blob called fufu contrasts the "thirty-minute production [of a meal] in the land of General Electric." Their travail parallels Orleanna's thankless chores of keeping the Price family fed, dressed, and safe against the onslaught of everyday ills and dangers, such as the spread of hookworm and *kakakaka* (enteritis) and a fall from a tree that requires setting of a broken arm bone. Her wifeliness seems perpetually aimed at some threat to life and health which arises from life at the jungle's rim.

Because Orleanna hovers on the edge of her husband's good graces, she must watch her tongue above all for the danger of arousing Nathan's ire. As an outlet for anger, wordlessly, she slams plates and pots at dinner. She comes close to rebuking his thinking about human bodies by reminding him that black women "do a hateful lot of work in a day...like we use *things* at home." To herself, she admits, "I was his instrument, his animal. Nothing more." Surprisingly, Mama Tataba, the housekeeper, stands up to Nathan's bullying and quits her job. The example presages Orleanna's last straw and her departure from Kilanga with two of her girls in tow.

When the idealism of missionary work in Kilanga unravels, Orleanna is the only voice accusing Belgian King Baudouin I of enriching himself on the misery of black Africans. She stands out among the gathering of four white adults as the one thinking resident who foresees chaos after the Belgians leave the Congolese to run their own nation, school, bureaucracies, and military. In contrast to Nathan, who dismisses local people as know-nothings on a par with sheep and chickens, Orleanna rejoices that the Underdowns charter a plane to evacuate the Prices on June 28, 1960. When the plane leaves without her, she takes to her bed. Thirty years later, she "[tries] to wear the marks of the boot on my back as gracefully as the Congo wears hers," the author's subtextual overlay of wifely servitude on colonialism.

In contrast to Orleanna, her married daughter Leah Ngemba is Kingsolver's image of woman as sanctuary. Grown deep and compassionate from decades of coping with Mobutu's atrocities, she makes a new nest for her family in Sanza Pombo, Angola. At a cooperative farm, she welcomes women and children fleeing the madness that Zaire has become for its peasants. With the wisdom of a survivor, she lets the silent women acclimate to safety, then listens to "the accounting of places and people they've lost." The stories of transient women's travails vary only in the details. In place of pain, "Mama Ngemba" offers them lessons in sanitation and nutrition, but realizes that life on the run has stripped these refugees of family stability and denied them hope of anything better than brief respites.

In naturalist Deanna Wolfe in *Prodigal Summer*, Kingsolver removes the woman from the nuclear family and resituates her in the natural family. Wisps of commentary about a former marriage ending in divorce indicate that Deanna was unable to adapt to the urban stereotype of wife, in part because she is scholarly and maintains a fast gait rather than a wifely stroll. She summarizes the split as "an older husband facing his own age badly and suddenly critical of

a wife past forty." In her estimate, femininity is "a test like some witch trial she was preordained to fail." Thus "discarded," she withdrew to the mountains, trailing her husband's surname like a male scent mark. She wastes no time in brooding and accepts the divorce as one stage of her education in the price of independence.

For those women immersed in the womanly arts, Kingsolver makes her standard obeisance, spoken through widower Garnett S. Walker, III, who admits that "God's world and the better part of daily life were full of mysteries known only to women." Unlike Deanna, Lusa Maluf Landowski, a widowed farm wife, fights her battles in the confines of the Widener kitchen. Alienated by her husband's siblings who think of the appliances and cabinets as their mother's, Lusa believes that a kitchen ghost "stirs up fights," both with Cole and his five sisters. During late-summer canning chores, she receives a womanly gift from Cole's youngest sister Jewel, who imparts guidance on how to fathom her four jealous sisters. Searching for an appropriate compliment to Lusa's dedicated gardening and preserving fruits and vegetables, Jewel compares her to Mother Widener, an appropriate choice of paragons of womanhood. Jewel concludes, "You should be real proud of yourself," a suggestion that women must reward themselves for their labors.

Source: Mary Ellen Snodgrass, "Women," in *Barbara Kingsolver: A Literary Companion*, McFarland, 2004, pp. 203–207.

Mary Jean DeMarr

In the following excerpt, DeMarr highlights how Kingsolver explores issues of prejudice in "Rose-Johnny."

...After the publication of *Holding the Line*, her first foray into extended examination of a place and group of people, and *The Bean Trees*, her almost-accidental first novel, Kingsolver decided to turn her hand to another genre, that of the short story. Her goal was to gain more versatility, to practice using a variety of voices, to create characters and situations different from those she had already invented. *Holding the Line* is a study of actuality. *The Bean Trees*, while in no real sense autobiographical, makes use of some aspects of her own experience and uses a narrative voice much like the Kentucky idiom which had been Kingsolver's own. *Homeland and Other Stories*, published in 1989 and winner of the 1990 American Library Award, is a collection of twelve short stories which range in setting from her familiar Southwest and the Kentucky of her childhood, which had briefly appeared in her first novel, to the Indiana of her college years, to California, and to the island of St. Lucia in the Windward Islands. Kentucky is particularly important, serving as the setting for several of the stories. Although the settings are varied, the sharpness of focus on place is as strong as in this author's longer fiction. While including major themes familiar from Kingsolver's novels, themes, like settings, are more varied here. Some stories are closely related to materials used in other works, as, for instance, "Homeland" in its use of the Kentucky background and Cherokee ancestry given to Taylor Greer in *The Bean Trees* and "Why I Am a Danger to the Public," which deals with a copper-mining strike much like the one Kingsolver covered in *Holding the Line* and a spunky female protagonist like some of those she came to know and admire while working on that book. Kingsolver has called the story a "collection of things that didn't quite happen but could have, and I sort of wish had" (Ross 288).

. . . "Rose-Johnny," another Kentucky story making use of poor and uneducated people, is perhaps Kingsolver's best-known effort in short fiction. It was her first published short story, appearing in *The Virginia Quarterly Review* in 1987 and later reprinted in *Homeland*. It is unusual for Kingsolver in having been inspired by a character rather than by a question or theme (Ross 288). Like "Homeland" and *The Bean Trees*, it is told by a young Kentucky girl who lacks education but has courage and grit. This narrator, Georgeann Bowles, at ten and eleven over the course of the story, is younger than the others, and since she does not understand many events at the time they occur, she may be seen as a naive narrator. Since her understanding of events and people is partial because of her inexperience, the reader knows more than she does. The narrative centers around her curiosity about the title character, an eccentric and controversial inhabitant of her village, her relationship with Rose-Johnny, and finally revelations about Rose-Johnny's history which explain her odd behavior and appearance.

What is most obvious about Rose-Johnny, who keeps the village store owned by her father, Mr. Wall, is her mannish appearance. On her first encounter with Rose-Johnny, an errand into the store, Georgeann is frightened by the odd, even threatening, behavior of two men. They tell her not to come into the store again and return the quarter charged for her purchase. Puzzled, she asks her aunt, who as a first-grade teacher is the most educated member of the Bowles family, about it. Aunt Minnie, in the custom of elders trying to protect youngsters from unpleasant information or themselves from having to instruct them in unpleasant facts, tells her that Rose-Johnny is a "Lebanese" and that she will understand all about it when she is older. That Aunt Minnie is confusing two words, "Lesbian" and "Lebanese," is clear to the reader but not to Georgeann, who knows neither of these terms and is even more puzzled after she looks up "Lebanese" in a Bible dictionary, apparently the only reference work at hand. More confusion follows, but Georgeann establishes a relationship with Rose-Johnny as she begins working for her in the store, trading work for supplies. That this relationship is built on a lie to her parents bothers her, but not enough so that she confesses it.

Running parallel to the theme of Rose-Johnny's assumed lesbianism is her demonstrated concern for some African American children of the community. This is a strictly segregated town, in which the black youngsters must wait outside the store and come in to make their small purchases only after it is officially closed. Rose-Johnny is kind to the children, calls each of them by name, and insists that Georgeann also learn and use their names. Rose-Johnny, unlike the rest of the villagers, grants these children individual human dignity. Later, when Rose-Johnny is ill and Georgeann works alone in the store, she learns that Rose-Johnny had been charging the African American children much less than the listed prices. Not understanding the sexual politics of the village and its fear of homosexuality, Georgeann does comprehend something of the racial politics and realizes that there are complexities in Rose-Johnny's life that she does not understand. She also realizes that no one will tell her whatever the truth about Rose-Johnny may be.

The truth is revealed after Georgeann is in a fight at school because she defends Rose-Johnny from the cruel slurs of a schoolmate. A tragic and complicated tale of death and miscegenation (intermarriage between members of two different races) explains why Rose-Johnny has a particular affection for African Americans and a concern for children. It also explains her mannish haircut and her hyphenated name. Originally named Rose, she had been given the boy's haircut and the name of her little brother in order that she might be a living continuation of him, both Rose and Johnny. After this revelation, Rose-Johnny disappears, and Georgeann never learns whether she is dead or living somewhere else, as rumor has it.

But that is not the end of the story. Georgeann, who had lived a lie throughout her relationship with Rose-Johnny, is determined to tell all the truth she can about the enigmatic character and the effects of her own actions. Her sister is beaten up, and Georgeann is certain that she was the intended victim and that her connection with Rose-Johnny was the motivation. In pain and anger, she attempts to become more like Rose-Johnny, cutting off her hair and that of her doll to resemble Rose-Johnny's mannish cut and changing her name to George-Etta, so as to emphasize its combination of masculine and feminine parts and also to combine her own name with that of her sister, Mary Etta, who had been victimized in her stead. "Rose-Johnny" is a powerful and insightful story, and both Georgeann and Rose-Johnny are fully rounded, believable, and likeable characters. . . .

Source: Mary Jean DeMarr, "Politics and Genres," in *Barbara Kingsolver: A Critical Companion*, Greenwood Press, 1999, pp. 28–29, 32–33.

SOURCES

Banks, Russell, "Distant as a Cherokee Childhood," in *New York Times Book Review*, June 11, 1989, p. 16.

Butler, Jack, "She Hung the Moon and Plugged in All the Stars," in *New York Times Book Review*, April 10, 1988, p. 15.

DeMarr, Mary Jean, *Barbara Kingsolver: A Critical Companion*, Greenwood Press, 1999, pp. 3–4, 13, 20–21, 28–36.

Epstein, Robin, "The *Progressive* Interview: Barbara Kingsolver," in *Progressive*, February 1996, pp. 33–37.

Gerber, Joan Merrill, "Those Ideas in the Air," in *Los Angeles Times*, October 31, 1993, pp. 10, 12.

Kerr, Sarah, "The Novel as Indictment," in *New York Times Magazine*, October 11, 1998, pp. 53–55.

Kingsolver, Barbara, "In Case You Ever Want to Go Home Again," "The Spaces Between," "Jabberwocky," and "Careful What You Let in the Door," in *High Tide in*

Tucson: Essays from Now or Never, Harper Perennial, 2003, pp. 43, 154, 230, 253.

———, "Rose-Johnny," in *Homeland and Other Stories*, Harper Perennial, 1993, pp. 203–26.

———, "Small Wonder," "A Fist in the Eye of God," "Letter to My Mother," "Flying," and "What Good Is a Story?," in *Small Wonder: Essays*, Harper Perennial, 2003, pp. 9, 19, 93–108, 160–75, 193, 213.

Leder, Priscilla, ed., Introduction to *Seeds of Change: Critical Essays on Barbara Kingsolver*, University of Tennessee Press, 2010, p. 22.

Meire, Héloïse, "Women, a Dark Continent? *The Poisonwood Bible* as a Feminist Response to Conrad's *Heart of Darkness*," in *Seeds of Change: Critical Essays on Barbara Kingsolver*, edited by Priscilla Leder, University of Tennessee Press, 2010, pp. 71–86.

Perry, Donna, *Backtalk: Women Writers Speak Out; Interviews*, Rutgers University Press, 1993, pp. 143–69.

Ryan, Maureen, "Barbara Kingsolver's Lowfat Fiction," in *Journal of American Culture*, Vol. 18, No. 4, Winter 1995, pp. 77–82.

Smiley, Jane, "In One Small Town, the Weight of the World," in *New York Times Book Review*, September 2, 1990, p. 2.

Snodgrass, Mary Ellen, *Barbara Kingsolver: A Literary Companion*, McFarland, 2004, p. 3.

Zindel, Timothy L., Review of *Homeland and Other Stories*, in *Library Journal*, May 15, 1989, p. 90.

FURTHER READING

Awiakta, Marilou, *Selu: Seeking the Corn-Mother's Wisdom*, Fulcrum, 1993.
    Awiakta presents Cherokee/Appalachian essays, poems, and myths about the land. She includes discussion of modern problems from both scientific and Native American points of view.

Garin, Marita, ed., *Southern Appalachian Poetry: An Anthology of Works by 37 Poets*, McFarland, 2008.
    This anthology includes poems from James Still, Louise McNeill, Robert Morgan, Fred Chappell, Charles Wright, and others. The poems display the narrative tradition, dialect, syntax, and rhythm associated with Appalachian literature. Essays and notes explain the background for use in Appalachian studies.

Kentoff, Maureen, "To Live Deliberately: Feminist Theory in Action in *High Tide in Tucson*," in *Seeds of Change: Critical Essays on Barbara Kingsolver*, edited by Priscilla Leder, University of Tennessee Press, 2010, pp. 47–69.
    In reviewing Kingsolver's collection of essays *High Tide in Tucson*, Kentoff shows the author as a modern feminist Thoreau who tries to live her own ideals.

Kingsolver, Barbara, *Another America/Otra America*, Spanish translations by Rebeca Cartes, Seal Press, 1992.
> Kingsolver presents her feminist poetry with a Spanish translation on each facing page. She includes political and personal topics.

Warren, Karen J., ed., *Ecofeminism: Women, Culture, Nature*, Indiana University Press, 1997.
> Kingsolver is known as an ecofeminist. These essays define ecofeminism in its many approaches and show how it is being used in academic disciplines and in social activism for the environment and social justice.

Zilak, James P., ed., *Appalachian Legacy: Economic Opportunity after the War on Poverty*, Brookings Institution Press, 2012.
> Zilak is a noted scholar on poverty at the University of Kentucky. In the articles collected in this volume, economists discuss the legacy of President Lyndon Johnson's war on poverty through the Appalachian Regional Development Act of 1965.

SUGGESTED SEARCH TERMS

Barbara Kingsolver

Rose-Johnny

Homeland and Other Stories

androgyne

Appalachia

Appalachian literature

short story

southern gothic

ecofeminism

lynching

miscegenation

Ku Klux Klan

Saint Helene

ALICE HOFFMAN

2005

Alice Hoffman's "Saint Helene" is a moving portrayal of a young woman gripped by guilt and depression. Shelby was the driver in an accident that rendered her best friend, Helene, comatose five years earlier. Helene has since become a figure of mythic significance to Middleborough, the town where she and Shelby reside. She is known to accomplish miracles, and people from around the country pilgrimage to touch her hand. Shelby, meanwhile, has become a recluse, unable to come to terms with the tragedy.

With her characteristic use of mythology and mysticism, Hoffman explores the weight of the past, the effects of alienation, the power of human connection, and the role of myth in everyday life—all through the story of this struggling young woman. As these qualities run throughout Hoffman's vast body of work, "Saint Helene" offers a fine introduction to her style. Originally published in the winter 2005–2006 edition of *Ploughshares*, the story can be found in the seventh edition of *Literature: Reading, Reacting, Writing*, by Laurie G. Kirszner and Stephen R. Mandell, published in 2009. Readers should be advised that mellow drug use features prominently in "Saint Helene."

AUTHOR BIOGRAPHY

Hoffman was born in New York City on March 16, 1952, and grew up in Valley Stream, on Long Island. Her parents divorced when she was eight,

Alice Hoffman (© *Bloomberg | Getty Images*)

and she took solace from an unhappy home life in books, among them the Grimms' fairy tales and the works of Ray Bradbury. "Reading was a complete salvation for me," Hoffman told Elfrieda Abbe in an interview for the *Writer*. "I just felt like it was a window to alternative universes and ones I'd rather be in than the one I was experiencing," she added; "I felt like I had parallel lives. I had the life I was living, and I had the life I was reading. I preferred the life I was reading."

At age seventeen, she landed her first job at the Doubleday factory in Garden City; discovering quickly that she had no taste for the daily grind, she quit by lunchtime on her first day. She attended Adelphi University, where she received a BA in English and anthropology in 1973. Her short stories earned her an Edith Mirrielees Fellowship to the Stanford University Creative Writing Center. There she became a protégé of the writer Albert J. Guérard, who, along with his

wife, the writer Maclin Bocock Guérard, encouraged Hoffman to publish her first short story in *Fiction* magazine. When an editor asked if she had a novel, she developed the story into *Property Of*, her first novel, which was published in 1977. Hoffman was just twenty-one and still a student when she wrote it. In 1975, she received an MA in creative writing from Stanford.

A prolific author, Hoffman has published more than twenty novels as well as several young-adult novels, children's books, and short-story collections. Frequently classified as magic realism, a genre that brings elements of magic or the supernatural into an otherwise ordinary world, her work often features women struggling to come into their own. Their experiences are often touched by legend or myth, and symbolism abounds. Hoffman also makes regular use of fairy-tale elements. While many of Hoffman's novels have been *New York Times* best sellers, her most well-known works are *Practical Magic* (1995), which was adapted as a feature film starring Sandra Bullock and Nicole Kidman in 1998, and *Here on Earth* (1997), which was an Oprah's Book Club selection. Her preteen novel *Aquamarine* (2001) was also adapted as a film, starring Sara Paxton, in 2006. In 2011, Hoffman released her highly anticipated historical novel *The Dovekeepers*, about women of the Jewish resistance in the Roman siege of Masada. Her work has been published in more than twenty languages.

Hoffman has also contributed short fiction and nonfiction to periodicals, including the *New York Times, Boston Globe Magazine, Kenyon Review, Los Angeles Times, Architectural Digest, Harvard Review*, and *Ploughshares*. "Saint Helene" first appeared in the winter 2005–2006 edition of *Ploughshares*. Hoffman has also written two other stories about Shelby Richmond: "Dirty White Dogs," published in the summer 2007 edition of *Prairie Schooner*, and "Changeling," published in the spring 2007 edition of *Kenyon Review*.

After receiving treatment for breast cancer at Mount Auburn Hospital in Cambridge, Massachusetts, Hoffman helped found the Hoffman Breast Center there. She lives in Boston, Massachusetts, with her husband, the writer Tom Martin, and two sons.

PLOT SUMMARY

Set in the month of February, "Saint Helene" opens with the image of a snowy Route 23 dotted with "little globes of light," paper bags filled with sand and candles. Hoffman notes that the globes line only one side of the road, the side "which slopes off when a driver least expects it." She begins to set up the central myth of the story by stating that the candles burn much longer than they should, "part of the miracle."

The globes are made by Middleborough High School teachers and students, many of whom never knew Helene Boyd. On the night of the anniversary of the crash, girls of all stripes close themselves into their bedrooms and give thanks that they are not Helene. The next day they all come together, "even the ones who hate each other," and remove the candles.

The only one who does not participate in the commemoration activities is Shelby Richmond. Shelby graduated five years earlier, as Helene would have if not for the accident. The two girls had planned to attend New York University together, but neither did. Shelby's parents paid the first semester's tuition and lost it because Shelby never went. She was hospitalized when she stopped talking, but she resumed when she realized that talking was the only way to be able to go home and be left alone. Shelby is the only person in town who has not been to see Helene, who resides in a hospital bed in the sunroom of her parents' house. Instead, Shelby takes shelter in the isolation of the basement, shaves her head, and pays her "penance"—living a comatose existence like her best friend's.

Her only companion is Ben Mink, an old high-school acquaintance who "has fallen upon hard times" and sells weed to her. The two mostly sit in silence in the park, but sometimes they will share a joint and talk. One day Ben asks Shelby if she believes the legend that touching Helene's hand can cure sickness. Startled by his boldness, Shelby responds, "I believe in tragedy." After a brief but charged exchange, Shelby tells Ben not to get personal with her. At the same time, Shelby realizes that she has spoken more to Ben than to anyone else in her life.

In the basement, Shelby remembers old times talking about true love with Helene. She recalls the night of the accident, how Helene laughed as the car spun around, how Helene had begged Shelby to drive her to her ex-boyfriend's house to see whether Chris was out with another girl. Shelby never told anyone she did not want to go out that night. She once walked by Chris's house, and his mother came out. Shelby ran off and then slept for eighteen hours, until her mother finally woke her by pouring cold water on her.

One day Shelby's mother, Sue, happens to drive by Helene's house. Outside is a line of people, many having traveled from other states to see Helene. The porch is filled with bouquets. Sue parks and walks up to the house and is moved to tears. She joins others crying, and two of her neighbors, with whom she is not particularly friendly, embrace her. When Sue returns home, she goes down into the basement, which she never does anymore. She is surprised by how she finds Shelby, looking like a baby wrapped in a blanket and watching *American*

Idol, something she never would have been interested in before. When Sue suggests that they go to the Boyds' house, saying that "something's happening" there, Shelby becomes aggressive, firing off rhetorical questions implying that Helene, who "wouldn't even sneeze in public," would be mortified by the attention she is getting. Sue says that maybe the miracle is that Helene likes getting to help people. When Shelby fires back that she knows Helene better than anyone, Sue shuts her down by saying that Shelby and Helene would not know each other anymore. "You're nothing like you were," Sue says.

When Shelby next calls Ben, he informs her that he is out of weed. She asks him if she is different from how she was in high school, and he tells her that she is totally different, like a strange sister of her former self. He, on the other hand, is just a predictable extension of his "loser self."

Desperate to escape reality, Shelby decides to hunt for prescription drugs in her parents' medicine cabinet and then runs into her father in the living room. She joins him as he watches the televised talent show. When he will not tell her where her mother is, Shelby guesses that she has gone to the Boyds'. Her father suggests that there might be some truth to the legend, and Shelby responds, "Don't make me vomit." "You'd have to be alive to do that," her father retorts. Shelby takes the medication she has found and goes outside. Her mother pulls up and finds her on the porch, counting stars in the freezing cold. Sue tells Shelby that it is peaceful at Helene's house, that Helene is peaceful, and that "it wasn't anyone's fault." Shelby surprises herself by sobbing. She tells Sue she thinks she has lost her soul.

Shelby calls Ben again, and this time he has some weed for her. They make a plan to meet, and Shelby heads out into the cold. She has trouble breathing. Ben is waiting at the bus station, and she pays for the weed with money stolen from her parents. Ben tells her that he will be leaving soon. He asks her not to laugh, but she doubles over when he says that he is going to pharmacy school. He teases Shelby by pointing out that she used to be in an antidrug club at school and says that he likes her better now. She asks where a lost soul goes, and he suggests they go find it. "Let's just walk by," he

says, and they walk toward the Boyds' house. It is easier to do than she had thought.

They arrive at Helene's house, which is dark and quiet, and Ben pulls Shelby toward Helene's window. Ben confesses that he used to spy on Helene from the window and begins to cry. He divulges that he was "crazy about her," and both he and Shelby laugh. She tells him that Helene was in love with Chris, that Ben would not have had a chance with her, and the news is a relief to him. They lean into one another. Ben asks Shelby if she wants to look, but she tells Ben to do so. He steps onto a window well cover, hoisting himself up to look through Helene's window and staying for a minute before coming back down. Shelby asks how Helene is, and Ben says that she looks like someone from a fairy tale, that she is all in white, her hair trails the floor, and she looks peaceful. Ben says that she was always beautiful but that Shelby had more personality and a great laugh. Shelby remarks that she has indeed become her own evil twin, but Ben says he likes her better this way. He says that when he gets a job, he is getting an indestructible Volvo. "You'd be safe with me," he tells her.

Shelby asks if she should look, and Ben says that it is up to her but adds, "That's not her in there." They resume their banter, and Ben makes clear his affection for Shelby. She laughs and then begins to sob. Then they get up to leave. The narrator notes that Shelby could have looked, could have crawled into the room, could have touched Helene's hand and "begged her for something, the way people did on a regular basis, greedy for a miracle. Instead, she followed Ben." Shelby and Ben continue to tease each other, and the narrator reveals that Ben did not actually open his eyes at Helene's window. Instead, he chose to preserve the image of Helene that he held in his memory, just as he would preserve his memory of this night and the girl beside him now.

CHARACTERS

Diana Boyd

Helene's mother, Diana Boyd, does not appear in the story, but her presence is felt by virtue of her absence. Jack Harry watches to see whether she changes the candles on the road, but she does not. She has positioned Helene in the sunroom of the house and has allowed her hair to go uncut for five years. The Boyds' house is regularly bombarded with lines of miracle-seeking visitors, presumably with Diana's permission. Given the parallels that Hoffman draws between Shelby and Helene, and having witnessed Sue and Shelby's relationship, the reader is left to wonder how Diana relates to her comatose daughter. Does she believe or perpetuate the myth? Or is she, like Sue, just a heartbroken mother trying to get through the day?

Helene Boyd

Helene, Shelby's best friend and the story's title character, was rendered comatose in a car accident five years before the story begins. Although the reader never sees her, Helene's presence is deeply felt throughout the story. The entire community commemorates the night of the accident, and the high-school girls thank their stars they are not her. At the same time, while she is not conscious, she is one of the most powerful figures in the community. She is reputed to accomplish miracles and so draws pilgrims seeking healing and journalists looking for a sensational story. The description of her that Ben fabricates at the end of the story aligns with the fairy-tale image she is said to have. Her hair trails the floor, and she is dressed all in white. Readers can imagine her almost glowing in the light of the sunroom.

The title, "Saint Helene," alludes to her miracles, as one of the abilities of some saints of the Catholic Church is the performance of miracles. However, the title can also be read ironically, to suggest that the community has overblown her goodness because of the tragedy. Shelby knows that Helene "wasn't all pure and good. She mistrusted people. She gossiped." In a way, Helene shares responsibility for what happened, as she dragged Shelby out on a night when she did not feel like driving in order to spy on her ex-boyfriend. Shelby also states that Helene was very private and that she would be mortified by all of the attention she is getting. As Sue and Ben make clear, however, this beatified Helene is not the same Helene that she was in the past. Rather, she has become larger, more transcendent.

Helene serves as both a mythic figure and a foil to Shelby. Shelby believes they are living parallel lives, but Helene is peaceful, where Shelby is tormented. Helene lives in the light of the sunroom, Shelby in the darkness of the basement and the night. While Helene resembles Rapunzel, her flowing hair evidence of her vitality, Shelby resembles a cancer patient or a baby, with a bald head and large eyes. Through such contrasts, Hoffman makes Helene seems more alive than Shelby.

Pat Harrington

Pat Harrington is one of the neighbors who hugs Sue Richmond outside the Boyds' house. (The other is Martha Lee.) Hoffman says that it is unclear whether Pat and Martha do so because Sue is crying, because they pity her for being Shelby's mother, or because they are recalling her making a scene the night of the accident, before she knew that Shelby was okay. In any case, this moment plays a key role in Sue's healing.

Jack Harry

Jack Harry works at the Arco station across from the site of the accident. Hoffman says that he used to watch for Helene's mother to replace the candles along the highway, eager to reveal a hoax. Now he "doesn't even want to catch Helene's mother at anything." On the anniversary of the accident, he wonders about how many other things there are in the world that are beyond his comprehension.

High-School Girls

Girls from Middleborough High School who never knew Helene participate in the commemoration activities. Hoffman highlights the tragedy of Helene's situation by remarking that girls with all sorts of problems—"the fat, the unbeautiful, the lonely, the sorrowful, the lost," and even the snobs—are all grateful that they are not in her place. Yet Helene is so significant that they all come together, even the enemies, to gather the commemoration candles.

Martha Lee

Martha Lee is the other neighbor who hugs Sue Richmond outside the Boyds' house.

Ben Mink

Ben is Shelby's marijuana dealer and the one person who is able to break through to her. He is funny, forthright, and open, qualities that seem to make Shelby more comfortable with him. Moreover, he brings out these qualities in her. She seems most alive when she is with him, and he plays a critical role in leading her through the grieving process. He accompanies her to Helene's house, pretends to look through the window, and reassures Shelby that while she looks beautifully otherworldly, the friend she knew is gone. In the end, rather than have her own moment with Helene, Shelby follows him.

Ben and Shelby did not run in the same circles in high school; he describes himself as having been a "loser" whose course in life has developed predictably. However, he is ambitious. He is planning to attend pharmacy school, and he hopes to one day afford a Volvo that would protect Shelby in any accident. He teasingly flirts with Shelby but in the process expresses genuine affection for her. When they talk about how Shelby used to be, he states twice that he likes her "better this way." One wonders whether he is attracted to her brokenness and whether he likes playing the role of the protector. Perhaps he relates to her antipathy; when she states that he did not like her in high school, he says, "Well, I didn't like anyone, so don't think you were special."

Ben and Shelby are also connected by the fact that they both loved Helene and that they both harbor guilt related to her. Having spied on her through her window, Ben determines that "he'd been a pervert, and he had a pervert's remorse." He shares his grief openly and does not hide his tears from Shelby.

Dan Richmond

Dan Richmond is Shelby's father. He appears in just one scene in the story, when Shelby, having just stolen Ativan from his medicine cabinet, finds him watching television in the living room. Shelby is known for not saying much, and while it may be an attempt to cover her theft, she tries to initiate conversation with her father several times. He mostly responds sarcastically. His statement that maybe there is truth to what people say about Helene suggests that he is an open-minded person. But when Shelby responds with hostility, saying, "Don't make me vomit," he delivers a poignant dig: "You'd have to be alive to do that." This blunt statement surprises Shelby, and one wonders whether his intent is to shock her into feeling something. It is also reminiscent of Sue's seemingly harsh assertion to Shelby, "You're nothing like you were." Shelby notices that Dan looks old, suggesting that the stress of recent years has worn and aged him.

Shelby Richmond

The protagonist of "Saint Helene," Shelby was the driver in the accident that rendered her best friend, Helene, comatose five years earlier. Having emerged with only a hairline fracture, Shelby must live with the guilt of surviving with her body and mind intact. Wracked with depression, she shuts down, confining herself to the basement, avoiding other people, and numbing her own feelings and pain through drug use. Shelby has been diagnosed with major depression, but she believes that "she is paying her penance... stopping her life, matching her breathing to be the counterpart of the slow intake of air of a girl in a coma." When she talks to her only friend, Ben, she practices self-mortification, digging her house key into her flesh, producing blood that is "strictly penance."

Hoffman paints Shelby as something of a shadow of a person, in Ben's words a "weird... sister" of her former self. The narrator qualifies descriptions of Shelby that might convey happiness or desire: "She wants—if that is not too strong a word"; "She smiled, or at least Ben thought she did." When Shelby leaves the house, she layers on winter clothes that make her "shapeless, anonymous." Rather than making her look tough, her shaved head makes her look vulnerable, like a baby to her mother, like a cancer patient to the outside world. She lives a dreamy, almost comatose existence. When her mother pours cold water on her to wake her up, all she does is say, "*Don't.*" She does not even move.

Shelby's primary objective is to escape her own pain. When Ben runs out of drugs and Shelby is forced to endure emotional exchanges with her parents, she becomes desperate and steals prescription antianxiety medication from her parents. Yet even the drugs cannot separate her from the accident. Sometimes when she smokes too much she sees Helene on the basement stairs and tries to tell her not to fall. When she smokes she can "actually feel her brain waves shift.... Pseudo-coma. Drift of snow." This image calls to mind snowdrifts along Route 23.

Shelby is finally able to begin coming to terms with her grief through a budding relationship with Ben. By gradually allowing him into her life, she is able to feel again. She laughs and jokes when she is with him; he seems to puts her at ease—a fact that at first causes her to try to put him off. But she wonders about his thoughts and feelings and soon is able to give voice to her own feelings, telling her mother that she thinks she has lost her soul. Ironically, by giving voice to that fear, she is able to find it, walking with Ben to Helene's house shortly after. There, at the site that most terrifies her, her soul resurfaces as she cries and laughs in the cold with Ben, talking about how Ben had feelings for Helene, feelings that he now has for Shelby. Because he looks through the window and tells Shelby that she looks peaceful but "that's not her in there," Shelby decides not to look. It is unclear whether she has attained the resolution she needs, but when Hoffman describes her "walking into the center of the cold night, looking straight ahead," one senses that Shelby is finally moving forward, walking toward a future.

Sue Richmond

Sue Richmond is Shelby's mother. She makes a habit of avoiding the Boyds' house when running errands, suggesting that she, too, has been traumatized by the accident as well as its effects on Shelby. Perhaps she carries some of the same guilt of surviving that Shelby does, only she is guilty because she did not lose a daughter, whereas Diana did. When Sue accidentally ends up at the Boyds' house, she is moved and her grief tumbles out. Hoffman writes that "she felt something inside her cracking apart, and all of a sudden she felt vulnerable in some odd way." She is not alone in this moment; a crowd of others joins her in vulnerability, crying peacefully. Drawing a parallel to Shelby, Hoffman writes that Sue is not friendly, but she approaches her neighbors and allows them to embrace her. It seems that the experience at Helene's house is healing for Sue, lending credence to the "miracle." She wants Shelby to have that experience, too.

Hoffman suggests that Sue has become increasingly estranged from Shelby. She avoids the basement. In the past she would have asked if Shelby was smoking down there, but now she says nothing. To Sue's surprise, Shelby looks like she did as a baby. Perhaps Sue has ceased to see her daughter as vulnerable, seeing her instead as a hardened, jaded person. Hoffman says that a sound in Shelby's voice is the "thing that Sue Richmond feared more than anything in the world. Almost more." It is unclear what that "sound" is—perhaps rage, hatred, or emptiness—but it is clear that Sue is afraid of what her daughter has become or is becoming. She gives voice to this fear, telling Shelby that Helene would no longer know her: "You're nothing like you were."

Sue also demonstrates gentleness with Shelby. When she returns home from another visit to the Boyds' house to find Shelby sitting out in the cold, she joins Shelby and reassures her: "It wasn't anyone's fault." That this statement produces a sob from Shelby makes the reader wonder whether Sue has never said this before or whether Shelby is only just now open to hearing it. Sue tries to assure Shelby that she cannot lose her soul, but Shelby highlights the distance between them when she says, "You have no idea what can happen, Mom." At the same time, calling her "Mom" reinforces an intimate connection.

Chris Wilson

Chris Wilson is Helene's ex-boyfriend. Helene was in love with him and begged Shelby to drive her by his house on the night of the accident so that she could see whether he was out with another girl. Unlike Shelby, who puts her life on hold, Chris goes on to Cornell and then moves to Boston. Shelby walks by his house several times after the accident. His house seems to serve as a kind of proxy for the house that Shelby cannot bring herself to visit, the one where Helene resides.

Chris Wilson's Mother

On one occasion when Shelby is walking past the Wilsons' house, Chris's mother comes out and calls to Shelby. Hoffman suggests that the two women have a shared pain, that Chris's mother "had trouble sleeping, too." Hoffman says that "she was probably kind-hearted" and concerned about Shelby, but Shelby runs away from her.

THEMES

Guilt

"Saint Helene" poignantly demonstrates the potentially crippling power of guilt. Guilt has transformed Shelby psychologically and physically. She lives her life as if she is a prisoner serving out a sentence. She has ceased even to buy clothes; her shoes are crumbling. She practices self-mortification, producing blood as penance. She says that she shaves her head so that people will treat her gently, like a cancer patient, but this seems instead like another way of paying penance, as a prisoner or a monk would. Moreover, it singles her out wherever she goes. She can never escape the reminders of what she did.

TOPICS FOR FURTHER STUDY

- "Saint Helene" depicts a number of rituals that the town enacts each year to honor the memory of the accident. Research different ways that communities have commemorated tragedy and create a digital slideshow depicting these rituals. Include different cultures from around the world.

- In "Saint Helene," the reader never encounters Helene's perspective. How do you imagine Helene experiences life? Is she aware of her surroundings, or is her mind in another realm? What would she have to say to Shelby? Write a brief account as if you were Helene and set up a writers' workshop with your classmates. What do they find most moving or surprising in your account? What do you find most notable about theirs?

- Create a book club within your class, and read John Green's young-adult novel *The Fault in Our Stars* (2012), about a teen with terminal cancer and her relationship with a handsome young cancer survivor. Lead a discussion in which you compare Green's protagonist, Hazel, with Shelby. What do they have in common? How do they differ? How does her relationship with Augustus compare with Shelby's relationship with Ben?

- Shelby is diagnosed with major depression. Research depression and create a website dedicated to depression awareness. What are the types of depression, signs and symptoms of the disease, and treatments associated with it? What are some guidelines for friends and family members of depressed individuals? Include statistics of teen depression and celebrities who have depression. Be sure to use credible sources and cite them.

Shelby clearly takes full responsibility for what happened, and the weight of it is crushing. When she reflects on the fact that Helene had begged her to go out that night, "it sounds corny, a lame excuse; it feels like a lie, even to herself." She attempts to escape the pain of her guilt by getting high, but it is when she has smoked too much that she thinks she sees Helene on the stairs and tries to stop her from falling. Helene disappears, and Shelby's guilt remains.

Alienation

Perhaps more powerful than guilt in "Saint Helene" is its pernicious side effect—alienation. At the outset Hoffman highlights Shelby's separateness: while all the girls in the community, "even the ones who hate each other," gather to commemorate Helene, Shelby is "the one person who is never included." As the story progresses, the reader deduces that this is not because Shelby would be unwelcome, but rather she refuses to participate. Because she cannot forgive herself, Shelby retreats from all society, including her family. She hides in the basement and leaves the house only to go to the 7-Eleven and to buy drugs. She ran away from Chris Wilson's mother, though her intention was likely to offer comfort.

Shelby's seclusion may seem like another attempt to punish herself, but it is more likely an attempt to protect herself from additional pain. Interacting with others could throw into relief Helene's condition, highlighting the injustice and deepening Shelby's guilt. It may also force her to begin to give voice to her feelings, a difficult but necessary step in the mourning process. No doubt she fears that no one else could understand how she feels. Even as she and her mother begin to connect, she tells Sue, "You have no idea what can happen, Mom."

Sadly, Shelby's seclusion only worsens her pain. The great irony is that, while Shelby believes she is "stopping her life" in order to match her friend's, Helene has become the center of the community. Although she cannot communicate, at least through traditional means, her house is a vibrant hub of life, activity, and community.

Healing

Hoffman's primary message in "Saint Helene" may be the healing power of human connection and memory. While it is rumored that people journey to Helene's house for physical healing, Sue finds emotional healing there by connecting with others in a moment of vulnerability. The connection is deepened because they remember

Shelby's packed trunk stays in the front hall for a long time before her parents accept that she will not be leaving for college. (© Feng Yu | ShutterStock.com)

her reaction on the night of the accident. Although Shelby's journey is more difficult, ultimately she is able to find healing in the same way. With his humor and frankness, Ben Mink is able to pierce her isolation. Shelby also endures difficult conversations with her parents in which they pointedly state how different she has become. At the same time, she is able to release some of her anger and outrage, feelings that, from a psychological perspective, are often a cover for sadness. Readers see that sadness surface when Shelby says, "I think I lost my soul."

Ultimately, her connection with Ben gives her the courage to go look for it at Helene's house. The two tease each other, reminisce about Helene and about the people they used to be, and connect over the fact that Ben also loved Helene. Critically, Ben shares his feelings for Shelby, affirms that he likes who she is now, and even demonstrates a desire to protect her. Feeling safe with Ben, Shelby is finally able to grieve, a crucial step in the process of healing.

STYLE

Mysticism and Mythology

Hoffman makes extensive use of mysticism in her works, and "Saint Helene" is no exception. Literary mysticism involves the use of mysterious supernatural elements. In "Saint Helene," these elements come in the form of the miracles that Helene is reputed to perform. The sense of mysticism is heightened throughout by the use of religious images, such as the candles that burn longer than they should, an allusion, or reference, to the Jewish Hanukkah story. Similarly, the sacrificial blood that Shelby produces by digging into her flesh with her house key brings to mind the sacrificial blood of Jesus, who is said to have paid for the sins of the world. It is noteworthy that in the Catholic tradition, Saint Helen, also called Saint Helena, is rumored to have found pieces of the cross on which Jesus was crucified, its authenticity shown when a dying woman was healed by touching it. Some reported that Saint Helen also found the nails used in the Crucifixion and that these, too, had miraculous powers.

Legends surround Helene, who becomes a figure of mythic proportions to the community. In this context, *myth* does not mean falsehood; rather, literary myth draws on traditional stories that use supernatural elements to explain some aspect of life, in this case healing. Mythic figures are often larger than life, mysterious, and symbolic. Helene's mythic stature is evident in the fact that, despite being unconscious, she draws throngs of people to her bedside to find healing. Her fairy-tale image and the fact that she is never actually seen in the story help sustain the myth.

Hoffman frequently makes use of magic realism, a literary genre that infuses ordinary worlds with supernatural or fantastical elements or events. However, it should be noted that "Saint Helene" does not properly fall into this category. In magic realism, the narrator and characters find the fantastical elements unremarkable; they proceed as if they are natural occurrences. In "Saint Helene," the fantastical elements are considered out of the ordinary, and Shelby actively challenges their existence.

Symbolism

Often used to explain or represent a natural occurrence, myths frequently make use of symbols, concrete objects that represent something abstract. One symbol that appears in "Saint Helene" is the snow globe. At the story's opening, Hoffman hints that things in this world are amiss by describing snow falling outside globes of light—the opposite of a snow globe, in which snow falls inside. By contrast, when Shelby dreams of the way things used to be before the accident, "the whole world was open and blue and shining, a globe no more complicated than a Christmas ball." During the accident, things whirl and turn "Christmas globe blue," and then, readers assume, the globe breaks. The globe is used in an interesting way; whereas a Christmas globe would usually represent a fantasy world, here it represents normal life. Its opposite is the world Shelby inhabits now, a world of myth and, for Shelby, tragic darkness.

HISTORICAL CONTEXT

Written and set in the present day, "Saint Helene" speaks to contemporary culture in a number of interesting ways. The image of a community shaken by tragedy is all too familiar for modern readers. In 2009, *USA Today*

reported on killings at a total of fifty schools since 1983. At the time of this story's writing in 2005, the horrors of a shooting at Columbine High School in Colorado in 1999 still reverberated across the United States. The shootings, in which two teens killed twelve other students and one teacher and injured twenty-four before taking their own lives, was the subject of filmmaker Michael Moore's 2002 documentary *Bowling for Columbine*. Sadly, the occurrence of such tragedies has not waned. In the years after the publication of "Saint Helene," communities across the United States have had to bear the likes of the Sandy Hook Elementary School shooting in Newtown, Connecticut, as well as mass shootings at a political event in Tucson, Arizona; a Sikh temple in Milwaukee, Wisconsin; and a movie theater in Aurora, Colorado, among others. Moreover, an increasing number of natural disasters have wracked communities across the globe. Thus Hoffman's portrayal of a community united in mourning and commemoration is likely to resonate with many readers.

Teen driving safety, the source of the conflict in Hoffman's story, has also been a topic of concern in the early twenty-first century. The Centers for Disease Control and Prevention reports that in 2010 car accidents resulted in the deaths of about 2,700 teens aged sixteen to nineteen in the United States. Almost 282,000 were treated in emergency rooms for injuries suffered in motor-vehicle crashes. Per mile driven, teens in this age range were three times more likely than other drivers to be in a fatal crash. Notably, the likelihood of an accident increases dramatically when there is another teen in the car, according to a study by the Automobile Association of America's Foundation for Traffic Safety, cited in *Traffic Injury Prevention*. Since the mid-1990s, every state has adopted three-stage graduated licensing laws. The restrictions (depending on the stage) affect, for example, teens' ability to drive with passengers younger than twenty-one and curtail or ban nighttime driving.

"Saint Helene" explores yet another issue of public interest: teen depression and drug use. Whereas in the past, depressed teens were often dismissed as being difficult, it is now known that clinical depression is common among teenagers. According to the National Institute of Mental Health, 11 percent of adolescents will have a depressive disorder by age eighteen. As reported in *Science Daily* in 2008, the White

Helene's death affected the entire high school community. (© *Michael-John Wolfe | ShutterStock.com*)

House Office of National Drug Control Policy found that more than two million teens felt depressed at some point during the year of the study and that those teens were more than twice as likely to have used marijuana or other illicit drugs during that period. They were also more than twice as likely to abuse or experience dependence on marijuana. While some depressed teens use marijuana to "self-medicate," the study showed that marijuana use can not only cause depression but indeed worsen it, increasing the occurrence of suicidal thoughts and the likelihood that more serious mental health conditions will develop.

CRITICAL OVERVIEW

As of 2013, no reviews treating "Saint Helene" were available. However, the story is emblematic of Hoffman's style, which has won her both a mainstream fan base and critical acclaim.

Indeed, hers is a household name. While not wholly uncritical of Hoffman's works, reviewers have praised her skilled writing and captivating use of mysticism. "Hoffman casts her spell with graceful, polished writing," states Abbe in her piece for the *Writer*; "She moves agilely through different points of view, travels back and forth in time, creates memorable characters, and tells a great story."

In a *New York Times* review of Hoffman's novel *The Story Sisters*, Chelsea Cain writes that the author "has a child's dreamy eye, in the best possible sense." Cain explains: "To her, the stuff grown-ups don't see anymore looms huge and important. . . . She invents a realm where that sense of the fictive doesn't go away, where imagination and reality bleed together." In a statement that might have easily been written about "Saint Helene," Abbe writes that Hoffman

> judiciously uses bits of magic realism to reveal what Bruno Bettelheim called "the inner turmoils of our soul," and to show a way toward healing. Perhaps it is that healing quality that draws so many readers to Hoffman's writing.

Donna Seaman echoes these sentiments in her *Booklist* review of *Here on Earth*, writing that Hoffman's emotional intelligence and the "bruised tenderness of her prose lift her . . . into a luminous realm where the souls of her poignant characters open like moonflowers."

CRITICISM

Andrea Betts

Betts is a freelance writer specializing in literature. In the following essay, she explores the difficulties posed by the ending of "Saint Helene" and offers possible explanations.

One of the most challenging aspects of reading "Saint Helene" is deciding how to feel about the ending. The reader wants to see Shelby come face to face with Helene and to find redemption in the encounter. More than that, the reader wants to see Helene herself, as if in seeing her one might better discern the truth or untruth of the legend. The reader is, like Shelby, somehow reassured by Ben's description of her but soon learns what Shelby does not: that Ben did not open his eyes. While one can accept Alice Hoffman's conclusion that "some things were best remembered the way you wanted to remember them," this is

WHAT DO I READ NEXT?

- "Dirty White Dogs," Hoffman's sequel to "Saint Helene," depicts Ben and Shelby's life in New York City. It can be found in the summer 2007 edition of *Prairie Schooner*, pp. 11–19.

- A third story featuring Shelby Richmond, "Changeling," follows Shelby after her relationship with Ben has ended. "Changeling" was published in the spring 2007 edition of *Kenyon Review*, pp. 123–30.

- Hoffman's best-known work, *Practical Magic* (1995), is a novel about two sisters, Sally and Gillian Owens, whose gifts of sorcery are marred by a deadly curse.

- Published in her collection *The Latin Deli: Telling the Lives of Barrio Women* (1993), Judith Ortiz Cofer's short story "American History" tells of another alienated young woman, Elena, a Puerto Rican immigrant who relieves the pain of her solitude by fantasizing about her neighbor, Eugene.

- Walter Dean Myers's young-adult novel *Dope Sick* (2009) employs magic realism in telling of a seventeen-year-old African American drug addict's redemption.

- The Argentinian writer Jorge Luis Borges is known as one of the founders of magic realism, a genre in which Hoffman frequently writes. His short story "The Secret Miracle," originally published in 1943, involves the supernatural and the manipulation of time. It can be found in his *Collected Fictions* (1998).

- The noted psychologist Elisabeth Kübler-Ross developed the concept that there are five distinct phases to the grieving process. She and coauthor David Kessler describe them in *On Grief and Grieving* (2005).

somehow cold comfort when a potentially powerful encounter was within reach. As it is, the ending leaves readers breathless. Like the

> AS IT IS, THE ENDING LEAVES READERS BREATHLESS. LIKE THE HIGH-SCHOOL GIRLS WHO NEVER KNEW HELENE, THEIR 'FINGERS DUSTED WITH SAND' AFTER GATHERING THE STILL-BURNING CANDLES, READERS HAVE TOUCHED ONLY FAIRY DUST."

high-school girls who never knew Helene, their "fingers dusted with sand" after gathering the still-burning candles, readers have touched only fairy dust.

So why is it that Shelby does not look? Why does Ben not look, and why does he lie about it? And why are readers, too, denied a glimpse of Helene?

Through difficult conversations with her parents and reminiscing with Ben, Shelby has begun to take down her barriers, and this stage of the healing process culminates at Helene's house. It would seem that the connection she feels to Ben is what empowers her to go looking for her soul there. Given how she ran away from Chris Wilson's mother and how vehemently she responded to her mother's suggestion that she visit Helene, her willingness to go there with Ben takes readers by surprise. When he admits that he spied on Helene and that he had loved her, he begins to cry. While this act of open vulnerability unnerves Shelby—"Pull yourself together," she says to him—it also makes it a safe place for her to do the same.

When Ben steps up to look through the window, the difficulty of the moment for Shelby is clear. She sits with "knees pulled up, head spinning, her hands covering her eyes." She uncovers them only when he rejoins her. He confirms the legend, reassuring her that Helene looks peaceful, like someone from a fairy tale. But the conversation quickly shifts to Shelby. Ben tells her how he remembers her being full of personality, with a memorable laugh, and the remark spurs Shelby to reflect on how she is now. But Ben affirms that he likes her "better this way"; talks about how he would be able to protect her with the Volvo he plans to buy; and, in his playful way, makes clear his feelings for her. It is in this safe atmosphere that she poses the critical question to him. She has been freezing, "her skull...so cold she felt it might shatter," and her breath is "damp and hot" as she asks, "Should I look?"

For readers wanting to see Shelby fully come into her own, this is something of a disappointment. Should she not answer this question herself? Instead, she invites Ben's input and then weighs his assertion that "that's not her in there." Surprisingly, the very next thing Shelby says has to do with Ben's stalking. One wonders whether she might think that looking in on Helene now would be like stalking, revealing something she is not meant to see. Ben again shifts the attention from Helene to Shelby, stating that he is now stalking her.

When her laugh turns to "something else," it is plainly a moment, maybe *the* moment, of true emotional release for Shelby. The passage that follows this moment is perhaps the most troubling. "Shelby could have looked," Hoffman writes, and then she proceeds to state a number of other courses Shelby could have taken.

> She could have stepped onto the window well sill, held her gloved hand up to the glass, climbed into the room, gotten down on her knees, touched Helene's warm hand, and begged for something, the way people did on a regular basis, greedy for a miracle.

By yoking together all of these courses of action, Hoffman suggests they are equivalent. Looking would be the same as begging, "greedy for a miracle." To the reader, this rings untrue, and indeed Hoffman as narrator seems to be speaking directly to readers, addressing our desire for a moment of encounter between the two girls. But Hoffman is unequivocal. "Instead she followed Ben."

What is Hoffman trying to say? One answer may be that, as human connection enables Shelby to release her grief, it is also the path forward to redemption. Ben's presence, playful manner, and affection for Shelby make it possible for her to bear this experience, indeed for her to have it in the first place. Shelby's fragility is evident when she asks Ben whether she should look, and yet she is most alive at this moment, her breath warm and wet. It is her connection with this tender, imperfect man, the intimacy that results from asking the most difficult question aloud, that enables her to ask it at all.

The frequent shifts of focus from Helene to Shelby also suggest that this moment is more about Shelby than Helene. By stating that Shelby "could have looked," Hoffman implies that she consciously decides not to. Would she really benefit from seeing her friend transformed, whether for the better or for the worse? Or does Shelby need to, emotionally speaking, lay her friend to rest? One presumes that what she might have begged for is forgiveness. Quite possibly it is not Helene's forgiveness that Shelby needs, but her own. It seems as if Ben's words "that's not her in there" allow Shelby to acknowledge that her friend is gone and to move forward with newfound strength, "walking into the center of the cold night, looking straight ahead."

And yet these explanations do not quite satisfy. It still seems as if there is something more to it. One recalls the healing that Sue Richmond experienced at Helene's house, her assertion that Helene enjoys helping others and that "maybe that's the miracle." Perhaps this is the answer: Shelby experiences healing without having to experience that painful moment of crisis—coming face to face with the result of her crime—before she is ready to do so. She receives a degree of forgiveness, readers hope, without having to ask it. Given the extent of Shelby's guilt and self-judgment, this would indeed be miraculous. Even the name *Helene* sounds remarkably like *healing*. Hoffman is intentionally ambiguous about Shelby's state of mind at the story's conclusion, but her tone connotes a sense of hopefulness. Whether or not Shelby feels her penance has been paid, there is a kernel of redemption that the reader hopes will grow in her. It may even bring her back to Helene in time.

These theories may provide readers some sense of resolution over the story's puzzling climax, but the issue of why Ben keeps his eyes closed remains. Hoffman's conclusion, that "some things were best remembered the way you wanted to remember them," resonates, and yet one suspects there must be another reason. Approaching Helene's window reminds Ben of the last time he was there, spying on her. His shame emerges in tears: "He hadn't even known how bad he felt. He'd been a pervert, and he had a pervert's remorse." The reader gets the sense that, to Ben, looking in on Helene now might be yet another kind of invasion. Perhaps in keeping his eyes closed this time, Ben is able to atone for that sin of the past.

But why lie about it? Consider that he steps up to the window at Shelby's request. His description of Helene is just the kind that would reassure her. And he quickly turns his talk to Shelby, her personality and laugh, how he would be able to protect her. As the story closes, his attentions are set not on Helene but on "this road, these stars, this girl right beside him." No doubt a visit to the home of the comatose girl he used to love is momentous for him—so much so that it produces tears—and yet Ben is concerned with Shelby. By saying "that's not her in there," it is as if he knows what she needs to hear. On one hand, the reader wants Shelby to find her own redemption, but on the other, this grand gesture of protection—that someone could so love this apparently unlovable young woman—seems yet another miracle. The everyday kind no doubt, but a miracle nonetheless.

In such an ambiguous scene, much is left to speculation, and the line between miracle and the mundane becomes blurry. Of course, because neither Ben nor Shelby looks through the window, the reader, too, is denied a view. Helene remains wrapped in legend, and the truth evades us. The myth is upheld. The scene as Ben and Shelby walk away—and the feelings it evokes in readers—brings to mind the opening scene, in which we are told that Jack Harry used to watch to see whether Helene's mother was involved in a con but now simply wonders how many things exist that he will never understand. In keeping the myth and the truth just out of reach, Hoffman seems to suggest that they are equally ephemeral; neither can be fully grasped. But, more than that, maybe they are indistinguishable. Maybe myth is a deeper truth, a spiritual one that cannot be verified or dispelled and which leaves only ethereal traces of a greater mystery of life, loss, and the miraculous workings of the human heart. Perhaps the greatest magic of "Saint Helene," then, is not how it works upon Shelby but how it works upon readers, leaving them weightless, swept up in the wonder of the unexplained and unexplainable.

Source: Andrea Betts, Critical Essay on "Saint Helene," in *Short Stories for Students*, Gale, Cengage Learning, 2014.

On the anniversary of her death, Helene's mother lights luminary bags. (© Geoffrey Kuchera / ShutterStock.com)

Maryanne O'Hara
In the following essay, O'Hara describes the simplicity of Hoffman's life and writing.

Alice Hoffman is a prolific writer with a bent toward the magical and luminous, and it's easy to imagine her at some fantastical loom, spinning tales of daily life turned to myth. In the real world, though, she works quietly and consistently out of an old Victorian house near Boston that she shares with her husband, two sons, and three dogs.

One early *New York Times* review said her work had "the quality of folk tale—of amazing events calmly recounted." Countless reviews since then speak of her skill in fusing the mysterious with the practical, the dark with the optimistic. In her novel *The River King*, she describes a great flood that consumes an entire town: "Whole chimneys floated down Main Street, with some of them still issuing forth smoke." It's the kind of matter-of-fact, Hoffman-esque

"THE REAL WORLD, LIKE LIFE IN HOFFMAN'S FICTIONS, IS UNCERTAIN AND WONDROUS AND GENERALLY RESISTANT TO OUR ATTEMPTS TO CONTROL IT."

line that makes a reader do a double-take. Could such a thing really happen? Does it matter?

Hoffman doesn't think so. She is endlessly surprised when people make a fuss over the uncanny aspects of her fiction, and points to pregnancy as a prime example of the fact that life itself is magical. "Magic in fiction is a long tradition," she says. "One of the reasons we like fables and fairy tales is that they're emotionally true, and page-turners at the same time."

Her strong reader base might say that statement summarizes her own work. She is the best-selling author of fifteen novels, one book of short fiction, and five books for children; she also wrote, with her husband, Tom Martin, an average of two screenplays a year for twenty-five years, so it's surprising to hear that this hard-working author grew up with no real ambitions, thinking she might perhaps cut hair for a living. "I'd have cut a lot of hair," she says wryly. "I always have to be doing something—have four things going at once."

Born in 1952 in New York, she grew up in a working-class Long Island town, positioned, as she says, to be a lifelong observer. Her parents divorced when she was eight, at a time when parents did not divorce, and her mother worked at a time when mothers did not work. Though both her parents had attended college, they were the only people in her neighborhood who had, and Hoffman never really considered college as an option for herself. Certainly she did not expect to make words a career. Though she was always writing, she says, "I was a secret writer." So what got her writing for the rest of the world?

Her first job, at age seventeen, was a push in the right direction. She worked, ironically, at the Doubleday factory—publisher of her most recent novel, *The Probable Future*. "I stayed till lunch and then quit" she says. One morning was enough to show her that eight hours a day in a

world where you had to ask permission to go to the bathroom wasn't for her. There is still some wonder in her voice when she says, "I think it was the first time I ever really thought." At the same time, most of the friends she'd grown up with were drowning in serious heroin addictions. "A lot of people were lost." She didn't want to be one of them.

She enrolled in night school at Adelphi University. She's not sure that she would have stayed in college if she'd had to abide by "a lot of rules and regulations. But it was the sixties. One year it was Kent State, and we never finished the semester." She took writing classes and had the good fortune to study with excellent teachers who encouraged her. She left with a degree in English and anthropology, and applied to the Stanford University Creative Writing Center. Not only was she accepted, she was offered, out of the blue, a Mirrielees fellowship. At Stanford, she met Albert Guerard, who became her mentor. Guerard and his wife, the writer Maclin Bocock Guerard, helped her publish her first story in the literary magazine *Fiction*. Legendary editor Ted Solotaroff then beckoned—did she have a novel? She quickly began to write one. *Property Of* was published in 1977 when she was twenty-five years old.

Hoffman has enjoyed early and continued success. Her work has been published in more than twenty translations and one hundred foreign editions. Her novels have repeatedly received mention as notable books of the year by the *New York Times*, the *Los Angeles Times*, *Library Journal*, and other periodicals. *Practical Magic* was made into a film starring Nicole Kidman. *Here on Earth* was chosen by Oprah's Book Club. *At Risk*, a novel about a family coping with a child with AIDS, is on the reading lists of numerous secondary schools and universities.

Yet she says, "I really struggle every time. I have terrible self-doubt. I've had periods where I've had writer's block and then I haven't, and I feel like I've had periods where I've had to learn to write all over again. It took me a long time to be able to tell anyone I was a writer.

And the glamour doesn't attract her. "How do you become a writer if you're interested in all that? Because if you want to be a writer, you want to be alone in a room."

She spends a lot of time alone in a room. But she calls her life normal, and like all normal lives, hers has not been without hardship. For years, she struggled with phobias. It is impossible to read *Illumination Night* and not feel that you know what it is to suffocate in the bell jar of agoraphobia. Hoffman intersperses third-person narrative with relentless second-person panic, as in this passage of agoraphobic Vonny attempting to board a plane:

> Her legs will not move. Her skin is cold. She is not quite sure why but she knows that if she walks into the plane she will die.
> Your heart is beating much faster than a human heart.

A believer in writing as an act of healing, Hoffman helps her characters find ways to heal, too. By the end of the book, Vonny begins to come out the other side:

> When your safe place begins to feel dangerous it can mean your pattern of phobias is breaking down. This can be a sign of recovery...one morning you go out and drive back and forth in the driveway. By the time you have made your third run down the driveway you have stopped asking yourself why you have to start all over again. You are simply a woman practicing the art of real life.

Real life is hard life in Hoffman's books, which tend to feature outsiders—strong women, single women, struggling women, children facing danger. Even though she has enjoyed a long marriage and raised two children, she continues to mull on themes that have long preoccupied her. This is natural, she believes. "Very often what you're writing about is what you've experienced as a child."

In *Illumination Night*, she wrote: "It is terrifying how people can misjudge each other." Years later, *Turtle Moon*'s Lucy reflects: "It hits her, all in a rush, that she may have not been the only one who was unhappy in their marriage—a possibility she has never once considered before." And most recently, *The Blue Diary* depicts a contented married couple suddenly exposed to the fact that the husband committed a brutal rape fifteen years before. All beg the question: can a person ever completely know another?

"I think it's much easier to know your dog," Hoffman says, quite seriously. In *Turtle Moon*, an embittered young boy bonds with a dog. When Hoffman writes, "No one has ever known him the way this dog does," you believe her.

It's a line that recognizes that life is uncertain, a fact which was made poignantly clear to Hoffman in 1998 when she learned, after a prolonged period of illnesses and deaths in her family, that she herself had breast cancer. In a 2000 *New York Times* article entitled "Sustained by Fiction While Facing Life's Facts," she writes of her reaction to the news: "I was certain my doctor was phoning to tell me the biopsy had come back negative. I was absolutely sure of it, but then she said, 'Alice, I'm sorry.' I could hear the concern and sadness in her voice, and I understood that some things are true no matter how and when you're told."

More than ever, she found that writing sustained her during her months of treatment. "When I became too ill to sit up for long, I moved a futon into my office and went from desk to bed, back and forth until the line between dreaming and writing was nothing more than a thin, translucent thread."

She has been healthy since those twilight months of treatment ended. In recent years, she has written for younger readers. She sees a lot of mother-daughter duos at readings, and decided she wanted to write to both generations, because "what you read when you're twelve stays with you in such a deep way."

She also wanted to include her younger son in her writing life, so they wrote a book together. "He's been able to experience the whole process, and how incredibly long it takes," she says. *Moondog*, by Alice Hoffman and Wolfe Martin, will be published by Scholastic on Halloween 2004.

Besides writing? "What else is there to do? I walk with a friend every morning. I go to the beach, the Cape. Mostly I work, and I always feel like there's not enough time. I always feel like I'm so lucky to be a writer."

That feeling of luck translates into a desire to give back. Years ago, she donated her advance from *At Risk* to AIDS research and funding for People with AIDS. After September 11, she wrote *Green Angel*, a kind of apocalyptic fairy tale for young adults. Proceeds benefit the New York Women's Foundation. Proceeds from *Local Girls*, a collection of interrelated stories, benefit breast cancer.

"I've been lucky," she says. "And I feel like fiction needs to matter in the real world."

The real world, like life in Hoffman's fictions, is uncertain and wondrous and generally resistant to our attempts to control it. But Hoffman herself increasingly embraces all of her worlds. Recently an elderly driver hit the gas instead of the brake and crashed into Hoffman's backyard. "And I thought, Well, this is a message," she says. "Here's someone telling you something. You might as well live."

Source: Maryanne O'Hara, "About Alice Hoffman: A Profile," in *Ploughshares*, Vol. 29, Nos. 2–3, Fall 2003, p. 194.

Barbara Ann Schapiro

In the following excerpt, Schapiro discusses desire and loss in one of Hoffman's novels, themes that are also important in "Saint Helene."

Alice Hoffman's novel *Seventh Heaven* is, above all, about desire. By desire I mean not only the erotic but also a more general condition of being and feeling. The condition is generated by absence; loss or lack is the seed of desire. I am associating desire, therefore, with a yearning or striving for *presence*—presence as an experiential state that involves both self and other. The yearning for the presence of an other also contains the wish to recapture one's own existential presence or fullness of being. Desire seeks to restore what has been lost, denied, or split off from one's being so that one may be more fully present, more fully alive.

Hoffman's novel is specifically about the pain, as well as the potential joys, bound up with the condition of desire, and the difficulty of awakening to it. Desire is painful because it involves recognition, or at least an unconscious connection, with the absence or loss—and the accompanying fear and anger—at its source. *Seventh Heaven* depicts a whole community—a fictitious suburb of Long Island in 1959—that has insulated itself from desire. Into this community moves a young divorced mother—Nora Silk—who disrupts its surface order and calm but ultimately revives its inner life. Nora becomes the agent of desire, and the fact that she is a mother is, as I will discuss, psychologically significant. Nora is also associated with witchcraft and voodoo. The house she moves into is said to be haunted, and running throughout this novel, as in many of Hoffman's other works, is a magical, mystical element. A child reads minds, a ghost appears, and inner wishes have external, material effects. In the middle of the novel, when the inhabitants of the community find themselves "overcome with desire,

> HOFFMAN MAKES THE FALSENESS, THE FLIMSINESS OF THE SUBURBAN FACADE QUITE OBVIOUS. COMPLIANCE, CONFORMITY, AND A NEATLY KEPT LAWN CANNOT, OF COURSE, STAVE OFF THE REALITY OF LOSS—OF DEATH—OR OF 'BAD,' DANGEROUS, AND VIOLENT PASSIONS."

a desire that made everything ache, fingers and elbows and toes," that desire is accompanied by an atmosphere of fog, disorientation, and the presence of ghosts: "People stared at each other from their driveways and wondered what they were doing on this street, and the ghosts whispered in their ears, egging them on, and things began to happen for no reason at all."

Our earliest experience of desire originates in an irrational or prerational realm. Desire also generates creative activity, particularly the creation of illusions. Thus the irrational and the illusory, as Hoffman's work imaginatively conveys, are indeed entangled with desire. Her novel playfully taps a deep level of psychodynamic functioning. Illusions are created out of desire and can provide a route back to it. If desire comprehends the intense and painful truth of inner experience, then one can, paradoxically, access truth via illusion. *Seventh Heaven* shows how illusions can actually promote honest, creative, and healthy living.

The positive role of illusion in psychic life is also a central concern of D. W. Winnicott's theoretical writing. Winnicott uses the term "illusion" at various times, as Thomas Ogden has noted, to refer to two quite different phenomena: "The first is the illusion of the subjective object (more accurately described as the illusion of the invisible subject and object), where the mother's empathic responsiveness protects the infant from premature awareness of the self and of the other." This is the illusion of oneness and omnipotence or, in Winnicott's words, the illusion that mother's "breast is part of the infant. It is, as it were, under the baby's magical control" (PR). The mother's task is gradually to disillusion the infant, making possible the second, more developmentally advanced form of illusion—the illusion found in playing, in the making of transitional objects or symbols. Transitional objects such as teddy bears occupy an intermediate, illusory, or "potential" space between internal fantasy and external reality. They represent a form of illusion, as Ogden explains, in which "the experience of oneness with the mother and separateness from her coexist in a dialectical opposition." This form of illusion is created out of desire: it arises out of necessary frustration, out of imperfect or incomplete maternal adaptation to infantile need.

Thus desire generates creative illusion or symbol making. As Ogden states, "Symbols are required only when there is desire." Lacan's ideas about the relationship of desire to the creation of the symbolic realm are quite similar to Winnicott's here. The crucial difference between the two theorists, however, is that for Lacan, the symbolic alienates us from the intensity of inner experience, while for Winnicott, the symbolic provides the very route back to that intensity. Creative illusions keep us in touch with a passionate inner reality. The potential space of symbolic play, Winnicott argues, "constitutes the greater part of the infant's experience, and throughout life is retained in the intense experiencing that belongs to the arts and to religion and to imaginative living, and to creative scientific work" (PR). Winnicott also emphasizes the paradoxical reality, or, in Ogden's terms, the "dialectical opposition," of the transitional realm of illusion. The inability to maintain this paradoxical state of illusion can in fact have pathological results: "What emerges from these considerations is the further idea that paradox accepted can have positive value. The resolution of paradox leads to a defence organization which in the adult one can encounter as true and false self organization" (PR).

The suburban community as a whole in *Seventh Heaven* can be understood metaphorically as an expression of Winnicott's "false" self. The false self is a compliant, social self that protects—or in pathology, engulfs—an underlying "true" self. The true self refers to a basic "sensorimotor aliveness" (Winnicott, *Maturational Processes* 149), to a spontaneous, authentic expression of core being. The false self can defend against the helpless dependency, the neediness and frustrations, of early emotional life. It is an ideal, "good" self that denies the painful, "bad" feelings of separation, anger, and hostility. Hoffman's depiction of American suburbia in the fifties reflects this type of defensive structure: built on the principles of compliance and conformity, suburbia projects an ideal of the good life that denies the existence of separateness and difference, of loss and pain—indeed, of any passion at all. The following description of the subdivision also typifies Hoffman's playful "transitional" style: it is at once fantastic and naturalistic, exaggerated beyond our sense of ordinary reality, yet plainly and factually asserted.

> Each house in the subdivision was the same, and for the longest time husbands pulled into the wrong driveways after work; children wandered into the wrong houses for cookies and milk; young mothers who took their babies out for walks in their new carriages found themselves wandering past identical houses, on identical streets, lost until twilight, when the ice-cream man's truck appeared, and they could follow the sound of his bell, which traced his reliable route past their doorsteps.

Hoffman makes the falseness, the flimsiness of the suburban facade quite obvious. Compliance, conformity, and a neatly kept lawn cannot, of course, stave off the reality of loss—of death—or of "bad," dangerous, and violent passions. The main street in the subdivision is significantly named Hemlock Street, and on the other side of the parkway intersecting the area protrudes Dead Man's Hill. Though the children are told "Good night, sleep tight," they are aware of monsters in closets and under trees. "They never told their parents or whispered to each other. Sometimes the monsters reappeared on paper in school, drawn with crayons and colored pencils; they had purple hair and large yellow eyes, and you could tell they didn't believe in good nights or sleeping tight." The novel is also framed by two incidental accounts of abusive families. In an early chapter entitled "Sleep Tight," the detective Joe Hennessy is called to a house where neighbors had made anonymous complaints. He discovers a battered wife—her "legs were purple with bruises"—and a little girl who kept her room perfectly neat and "was doing a good job of faking sleep." The wife refuses to make a complaint, and a few weeks later Hennessy discovers that the family has silently left town. Toward the end of the novel, Hennessy is called to a home where a boy has stabbed his father to death. He learns that the father had consistently beaten the boy, but neither the neighbors nor his fellow policemen want to hear the story. The boy is dismissed as crazy, "off his rocker," and quickly carted off to the state mental hospital.

Though the hollow, fraudulent nature of fifties suburban life is hardly an original theme in contemporary art and literature, Hoffman's perspective is distinguished by its affectionate attitude. Her portrayal of suburbia's deceptive facade is suffused with compassion for the vulnerabilities and fears that prompted its construction. Her perspective does not project the same sense of impending disintegration, the sort of explosive violence, that lurks beneath the placid surface lives of, for instance, Ann Beattie's aging fifties children. Nor does it convey the menace and malignancy harbored within a David Lynch vision of suburban life. The type of death or loss that most haunts Hoffman's suburban characters is a deadness within, a loss of inner vitality, expressed through images of ice, entrapment, and constriction. The novel is dedicated to the memory of Houdini, the escape artist whose magical feats of release dominate the imagination of Nora Silk's son Billy. The deadliness of Dead Man's Hill is specifically associated with that of frozen entrapment: "The sunlight reflecting off the ice would make you so dizzy you'd just lie there after your sled overturned, and then in a panic you'd get up as quickly as you could, terrified, convinced that if you didn't move soon the ice would freeze you into place, and that's the way they'd find you, sometime in the spring, deep within the thaw of Dead Man's Hill."

Only through a painful reawakening to desire, the novel suggests, can one escape this frozen, deathlike state that constricts and isolates the self. In the middle of the novel, Joe Hennessy's wife, Ellen, feels "something she didn't want and didn't understand surface within her. It was the desire, and it hit her hard, and she was so furious about all those years when she had never wanted anything that she grew colder each day, until she was a perfect piece of ice and Joe Hennessy couldn't touch her, he couldn't even be in the same room with her." The agent of desire in this suburban community, as stated before, is Nora Silk. Though she is represented as possessing a vivacious, irrepressible spirit, she also comes significantly weighted with associations of loss, death, and abandonment. She is, first of all, divorced, a word so threatening to the wives of the

neighborhood that "no one had to say it, but the word was there, it had entered their vocabularies and now hung above them, a cloud over their coffee cups." She moves into the house of Mr. Olivera, the first person in the neighborhood to have died and therefore "violated the pact," the unspoken agreement to keep up appearances. Furthermore, we learn that Nora is parentless and was raised in an isolated, run-down house by a misanthropic grandfather who practiced voodoo. The spirit of desire she embodies, in other words, is directly related to her history of ruptured human connections, of absence and loss....

Source: Barbara Ann Schapiro, "Desire and the Uses of Illusion: Alice Hoffman's *Seventh Heaven*," in *Literature and the Relational Self*, edited by Jeffrey Berman, New York University Press, 1994, pp. 160–64.

SOURCES

Abbe, Elfrieda, "Writing Her Way into the Story," interview with Alice Hoffman, in *Writer*, Vol. 122, No. 7, July 2009, p. 18.

"Biography," Alice Hoffman website, http://alicehoffman.com/bio/biography/ (accessed February 10, 2013).

Cain, Chelsea, "Fairest of Them All," in *New York Times Book Review*, June 7, 2009, p. 14.

Cochran, Kate, "Alice Hoffman," in *Dictionary of Literary Biography*, Vol. 292, *Twenty-First-Century American Novelists*, edited by Lisa Abney and Suzanne Disheroon-Green, Thomson Gale, 2004, pp. 164–72.

"Depression in Children and Adolescents Fact Sheet," National Institute of Mental Health website, http://www.nimh.nih.gov/health/publications/depression-in-children-and-adolescents/depression_children_adolescents_508_ln.pdf (accessed February 15, 2013).

Drijvers, Jan Willem, *Helena Augusta*, Brill, 1992, pp. 106, 111.

Hoffman, Alice, "Saint Helene," in *Ploughshares*, Vol. 31, No. 4, Winter 2005–2006, pp. 84–95.

"Mapping School Violence," in *USA Today*, April 12, 2009, http://usatoday30.usatoday.com/news/nation/graphic-school-killings.htm (accessed February 15, 2013).

"Massacre at Virginia Tech," NBCNews.com, April 26, 2007, http://www.nbcnews.com/id/18138369/ (accessed February 15, 2013).

Pearson, Michael, "Gunman Turns 'Batman' Screening into Real-Life 'Horror Film,'" CNN.com, July 20, 2012, http://www.cnn.com/2012/07/20/us/colorado-theater-shooting (accessed February 17, 2013).

Rodriguez, Cindy Y., "Intern's Memoir Recalls Giffords Shooting," CNN.com, February 6, 2013, http://www.cnn.com/2013/02/05/living/daniel-hernandez-giffords-book/index.html (accessed February 15, 2013).

Seaman, Donna, Review of *Here on Earth*, in *Booklist*, Vol. 93, No. 21, July 1997, p. 1774.

"Teen Drivers: Fact Sheet," Centers for Disease Control and Prevention website, October 2, 2012, http://www.cdc.gov/motorvehiclesafety/teen_drivers/teendrivers_factsheet.html (accessed February 15, 2013).

"Teen 'Self Medication' for Depression Leads to More Serious Mental Illness, New Report Reveals," in *Science Daily*, May 10, 2008, http://www.sciencedaily.com/releases/2008/05/080509105348.htm (accessed February 15, 2013).

Tefft, Brian C., Allan F. Williams, and Jurek G. Grabowski, "Teen Driver Risk in Relation to Age and Number of Passengers, United States, 2007–2010," in *Traffic Injury Prevention*, Vol. 13, No. 3, 2013, pp. 283–92.

Toppo, Greg, "10 Years Later, the Real Story behind Columbine," in *USA Today*, April 14, 2009, http://usatoday30.usatoday.com/news/nation/2009-04-13-columbine-myths_N.htm (accessed February 15, 2013).

FURTHER READING

Hoffman, Alice, *Green Heart*, Scholastic Paperbacks, 2012.
> Hoffman's young-adult novel tells of a teen who is haunted by loss and the past but finds healing through mysterious encounters in her garden.

Paley, Grace, *The Collected Stories*, Farrar, Straus and Giroux, 2007.
> Hoffman has said that she was influenced by the writings of Grace Paley. A finalist for the National Book Award, this collection features numerous poignant stories of struggling women.

Pullman, Philip, *Fairy Tales from the Brothers Grimm: A New English Version*, Viking, 2012.
> As a child, Hoffman read the fairy tales of the brothers Grimm. Pullman offers retellings of these classics along with critical commentary.

Walsh, Ann, ed., *Dark Times*, Ronsdale Press, 2005.
> The result of a contest in Canada, this anthology of short stories features young people experiencing grief and loss.

SUGGESTED SEARCH TERMS

Alice Hoffman

Alice Hoffman AND Saint Helene

Alice Hoffman AND short stories

Alice Hoffman AND myth

Alice Hoffman AND alienation

Alice Hoffman AND Shelby

magic realism

Alice Hoffman AND symbolism

Tiny, Smiling Daddy

MARY GAITSKILL

1997

The story that Mary Gaitskill tells in "Tiny, Smiling Daddy" is woven from familiar elements that most modern readers have faced at one time or another. It concerns a father, Stew, who is mired in his old-fashioned views of the world and finds it difficult to come to grips with the fact that his daughter is gay, and a daughter, Kitty, who copes with her father's rejection by publishing her thoughts where the whole world can see them. She publishes her thoughts in a magazine, but the urge toward self-revelation that the story addresses relates to the ways people today discuss their lives on Twitter, Facebook, and other forms of social media.

Finding out about the article drives Stew down a path of contemplation that is not normal for him, because he is not a very reflective person. He thinks about his daughter's life with him, how he found out about her orientation, and how he responded to it, and readers are left waiting to see whether he will ever reach a point of regret for driving her away.

"Tiny, Smiling Daddy" was published in Gaitskill's 1997 second short-story collection, *Because They Wanted To*. Since its publication, the author has come to be recognized as one of America's preeminent working fiction writers, nominated for major awards and regularly included in anthologies and "best story" collections.

Mary Gaitskill (© *Ulf Andersen | Getty Images*)

AUTHOR BIOGRAPHY

Gaitskill was born on November 11, 1954, in Lexington, Kentucky. Her father was a college teacher, her mother a homemaker. Her childhood was spent in a suburb of Detroit. It was not a happy childhood: she ran away from home for a while, living on her own in New York City at the age of sixteen, supporting herself as an exotic dancer. At the age of eighteen she decided to become a writer and went back to school. She attended the University of Michigan, where she won the coveted Hopwood Award for her writing and earned a bachelor of arts degree in 1981.

In 1988 her first book was published, the short-story collection *Bad Behavior*, which earned her national attention. With this book, critics formed an expectation for Gaitskill's writings that would continue through the coming years, seeing her as a writer of tension and sexual insecurity. One of the stories from *Bad Behavior*, "Secretary," about a working woman who allows herself to become a sexual object to her boss, was adapted as a movie in 2002. Gaitskill followed that collection with the novel *Two Girls, Fat and Thin* in 1991 and then *Because They Wanted To*, the collection that includes "Tiny, Smiling Daddy," in 1997. By the time of her later works, such as the 2005 novel *Veronica* (a finalist for the National Book Award) and the collection *Don't Cry: Stories*, published in 2009, she was already accepted as one of the country's premier writers.

Throughout her writing career, Gaitskill has taught English at various colleges, mostly along the East Coast. She married the writer Peter Trachtenberg a few days after the terror attacks of September 11, 2001. The couple considered adopting children but ended up deciding to become mentors for two young children through the Fresh Air Fund. Separated from Trachtenberg in 2010, Gaitskill lives in upstate New York.

PLOT SUMMARY

"Tiny, Smiling Daddy" begins when an older retired man, Stew, receives a phone call in the middle of the day as he sits in a chair, dozing. At the other end of the line is his friend Norm. Norm has called to ask what Stew thinks of the article that Kitty, Stew's daughter, has published in *Self*, a national magazine. It was brought to Norm's attention by his own daughter. The subject of Kitty's article is her relationship with Stew, but once Norm finds out that Stew does not know about this publication, he quickly gets off the line.

After hanging up, Stew thinks about his life with Kitty. He does not think that the article she has written could be flattering to him. As he ponders, he indulges in a nervous habit of stroking the hairs inside his nose. He remembers how Kitty, when she was a little girl, found that habit funny but also how he tried to amuse her with it when she was around the age of fourteen, and she left the room in disgust. This was the first of many times that Stew felt his daughter rejected him.

He considers going to the store to buy a copy of *Self*. He lives outside the downtown area, and his wife, Marsha, is out with the car. He would have to walk to the store. The day is very hot, and the walk would exhaust him. He rules out phoning Kitty, assuming that she would probably be defensive. He thinks that she should know how this kind of public exposure of their personal life would embarrass him, given how much he was embarrassed when she came out as a lesbian when she was sixteen.

Listening to a radio broadcast of the opera *La bohéme*, Stew thinks about how Kitty changed as a young woman. She was a happy child, but as she became a teenager she grew increasingly glum and sullen. Other children picked on her. In Stew's eyes, she made herself ugly, hiding her natural beauty. She was an angry teen, lashing out at her parents. Stew recalls overhearing her when she was fifteen telling one of her friends that her mother was "stupid," which surprised him because Marsha and Kitty had a very strong, loving relationship when she was young. He recalls his anger at the way Kitty treated her mother in those days. He felt that she was an ungrateful, spoiled child who behaved as if she were a victim, even though they had given her a good life.

When Marsha returns home, Stew immediately takes the car keys from her and races out to the store to buy the magazine. Driving there, he thinks of all of the copies of *Self* magazine in circulation and becomes increasingly self-conscious and angry about the idea that millions of strangers and his neighbors will see it and mock him. He recalls when Kitty came out as a lesbian. Children at her high school picked on her and bullied her. She wrote strange poetry. When Marsha read the books and magazines Kitty was reading, she thought they were bad for her, glorifying prostitution, so she threw them in the garbage. In the ensuing heated argument, Stew, trying to defend his wife, ended up hitting Kitty. Marsha tried to separate them, and he turned his anger on her; then Kitty tried to defend her mother. For months they lived on, trying to establish a semblance of normality, but it was always broken when Stew remembered that Kitty was an avowed lesbian.

Kitty ran away from home at age sixteen. The police found her living with an older woman named Dolores and brought her home. She was put into a psychiatric hospital, at Marsha's insistence, but Stew did not like the doctors there and had her released. When high school was finished, she moved out of their house, with her parents' approval. After that, Stew and Marsha saw much less of Kitty as she moved from one place to the next. She lived for a while in Detroit with a woman named George and worked with special needs children, coming

home every few weeks with her laundry. When she moved to San Francisco, they found out only because of a postcard she sent them. Unsure of what she was doing, wondering about how she was surviving in the big city, and suspicious that she might be involved in drugs and the sex business, Stew stayed up nights worrying about her.

When she was twenty-two she came home for Christmas. She no longer had the more outlandish hairstyle and piercings that she had had in her most rebellious years, and she tried to have a pleasant holiday with her parents, but Stew continued to focus on her sexual orientation. Although he did not fight with her, he felt that her life in San Francisco, stable and surrounded with friends, was still one that he considered terrible. He felt that she was a stranger and could not understand how his daughter had come to be the way she was.

Back in the present, Stew arrives at the drugstore and goes to the magazine rack to find *Self*. The article by Kitty is printed in a column titled "Speak Easy," with a brief biographical sentence that lists her profession as "ceramic artist." He skims the article. In it, Kitty discusses the emotional rift between herself and her father. Gaitskill gives a few sentences from Kitty's article, to show her writing style. She talks about the trouble she has in talking to her father. She suspects that he may love her but that he has trouble showing his love because she is gay. Stew buys the magazine and takes it to his car. As he reads, he becomes increasingly aware of other people around him, and he grows more and more defensive.

The article makes Stew remember his own childhood. He once was given advice that told him he had the power to view the world in any way he wanted to view it. His uncle suggested that he close his eyes tight, and when he opened them, he would see whatever he wanted to see in front of him. When Stew tried this, he saw a mysterious whitish ball floating before him. Years later he suggested the same exercise to young Kitty, and the image that came up before her mind was rich and colorful, containing flowers and palm trees and dolphins and mermaids. The lack of his own imagination, contrasted with the fullness of Kitty's, made him defensive, and he dismissed her response to this mental exercise as stupid.

He recalls another memory of childhood, of coming home at sundown on a summer night. He remembers feeling the beauty of that night and being sad that it would end soon, when he arrived home. That night he was aware of life as a balance of sorrow and happiness, and he told himself that this was a memory that he should bring up whenever he feels that time is passing too quickly.

As soon as Stew arrives home, Marsha can tell that something is bothering him. He does not tell her about Kitty's article but instead complains about his discontentedness with life in general and with his wife and daughter in particular. He mentions the fact that Norm called to tell him about the magazine article. Marsha's response is not about Kitty's article; she is surprised that Norm would have told him about it. Marsha offers to rub Stew's shoulders. As she massages him, Stew's anger fades. He feels sorry for Kitty and regrets how harshly he treated her as a teenager.

His memory goes to his father, who, Stew thinks, was much more distant to him than he ever was to Kitty. When he was young, Stew had admired his father. He remembers staring at his face; his father, noticing, swore at him and told him to stop looking at him. He remembers his large, brutish father coming home sweaty from work, alert and suspicious, ready for trouble from the world.

A phrase from Kitty's article comes to mind, where she mentioned that one must look for "the good parent in yourself." In his mind, Stew sarcastically dismisses such soft-hearted psychological jargon. His father's death was final and absolute, he thinks: he does not have a "tiny, smiling daddy" that he carries around with him.

Marsha, sensing his mood change, finishes rubbing his back. Stew looks across the room, at where once was the chair that Kitty was sitting in when she came out to her parents. He remembers cursing her upon hearing that she was a lesbian, telling her to leave his house and that he would hate her until the day he died. He remembers how Kitty cried. Marsha removes her hands from his back and moves away from him, to a different piece of furniture, reinforcing the isolation that will always be a part of Stew's life.

CHARACTERS

Dolores

Dolores is mentioned just once in the story. She is a bodybuilder with whom Kitty moved in after running away from home at age sixteen. The police found Kitty living with her and brought her home.

George

George is the woman Kitty moves in with as soon as she graduates from high school. They share an apartment in Detroit until Kitty moves away to San Francisco.

Norm Pissaro

Norm is Stew Thorne's friend. He phones at the beginning of the story to tell Stew about the article Kitty has published. Norm takes pains to make clear that he does not think the article says anything explicitly bad about Stew; he phoned because he does not understand the point of the article, and he thought that Stew might be able to explain why Kitty would write and publish it. Once he finds out that Stew does not even know about this very public discussion of his family life, Norm gets off the phone as soon as he can; although they are friends, Norm clearly knows about Stew's angry disposition.

Kitty Thorne

At the time of the story, Kitty is twenty-eight years old and lives in South Carolina. She has had a complex relationship with her parents, particularly her father, Stew, one that has made her life so chaotic that Stew can barely accept the fact that she has grown into a stable, mature woman. Much of "Tiny, Smiling Daddy" chronicles Kitty's life as seen by Stew. He remembers her approvingly as "his beautiful, happy little girl" but is mystified about how she changed from that to "a glum, weird teenager that other kids picked on." Because her sexual orientation took her in a direction that Stew did not approve of, he felt that something had gone wrong with her. He does not see that he was responsible for much of her mental anguish when he harshly rejected her because she is gay.

Without her parents' support, Kitty has been left to struggle to find a life of her own, sometimes making mistakes along the way. Her efforts to establish and understand her individuality made her an outcast in her rural Michigan high school, driving her to dress and act in ways that her parents found offensive. When she did come out to them about her sexual orientation, her parents rejected her, though the story does not reveal until near the very end the absolute and vicious language that her father used to tell Kitty that he would thus never love her.

In trying to find herself, Kitty has gone through several phases. During her rebellious phase, she criticized her parents, ran away from home, and then, when she was old enough, left home legally. When she moved to San Francisco, she found a community of gay women like herself. During this phase, she developed enough self-assurance to come home for a week at Christmas. Living in South Carolina, she seems to have found a life that she is comfortable with on her own, away from the support of San Francisco's strong gay community. The article she publishes shows that Kitty is hurt about her family relationship, but she is also hopeful about it and curious as to how she can make it better. Stew's focus on the turmoil of her life makes it difficult for him to see how she has come to terms with who she is.

Marsha Thorne

Marsha is a conciliator, the voice of reason who is trapped between her husband and her daughter as they blame each other for their problems. A good example of this occurred when Kitty ran away from home at age sixteen: Gaitskill makes clear that it was Marsha's idea to react by getting Kitty psychiatric help and that it was Stew's idea to have Kitty pulled out of the psychiatric hospital.

Caught in the middle, Marsha is derided by both sides. When Kitty had her rebellious phase in her teens, Stew overheard her telling a friend that Marsha is neither kind nor intelligent. Stew, for his part, takes out his frustrations on Marsha, blaming her for things that are essentially beyond her control, like his loneliness.

Like many traditional wives, Marsha accepts her husband's anger without speaking up for herself. She does what she can to avert inciting him any further. When she sees that he is not going to calm down about the article Kitty has written, she does not talk to him about it; instead, she offers to massage his shoulders. Stew accepts her offer without thanking her, as if it is only to be expected. He thanks her non-verbally, by touching her hand, which could be a sign that their love is so clear to them both that words are not necessary. Marsha's relationship with Stew is not actually a close, loving one, though, which is indicated in the story's final gesture, as she draws away from him and moves to another part of the room.

Stew Thorne

Stew is a man whose narrow understanding of the world was established in his youth, through observing and admiring a cold and cruel father. In his childhood he established expectations about gender roles that have blocked his ability to form healthy relationships with his wife and daughter. Ultimately, the story reveals that his problems go beyond the social norms of his time, showing that self-isolation has always been a part of his personality.

Stew thinks nothing of dominating his wife, Marsha. When she is out with the car at a time that he wants to use it, he blames her, although there is no way she could have known his wishes. He continually takes his frustration with the world out on her. Still, he sees himself as Marsha's protector, viewing his disappointment in Kitty, his daughter, as a disappointment in the way that Kitty has ceased to be Marsha's close friend, a role he knows he cannot fulfill himself.

Because Kitty has stopped being the kind of docile girl he thinks a female should be, Stew turns against her. He eventually recalls driving her to tears when he cursed her out about being gay, but he does not see himself as having been wrong for driving his daughter away from him so cruelly. Though Stew thinks of his bad relationship with Kitty as being her fault, caused by the sexual orientation he believes she has chosen, the story gives readers enough evidence to see that his problem harks back to his relationship with his father. Stew looked up to his father, who at least once verbally abused him; he patterns his own masculinity after his father's distance. When Kitty picks up similar masculine traits from her own father, as she tries to find out what being a lesbian means, Stew is angered and disgusted.

Although the article written by Kitty causes Stew to focus his attention on her sexual orientation, his real problem is the alienation that he has imposed upon himself by copying the pattern of his father. He is horrified that the article publicly exposes him. While going to buy the magazine, before even reading what Kitty has written, he thinks that he has not typically been

> so aware of this unpleasant sense of disconnection between him and everyone else, but he had the feeling that it had been there all along, underneath what he thought about most of the time.

Stew Thorne's Father

One strong clue about why Stew is the way he is toward his daughter is the behavior of his father, whom he reminisces about late in the story. He has vague memories of his father, who died when Stew was young. Although the images of his father paint an unattractive picture—he is described as a hairy, sweaty man who swore at his son without provocation—Stew still thinks that their relationship was not as bad as the way Kitty makes her relationship with her own father sound in the article she wrote.

Stew Thorne's Uncle

While listening to the radio, Stew recalls an uncle, who is mentioned in only one paragraph and is not given a name in this story. When he was young—about nine or ten—his uncle gave Stew a mind exercise. The uncle told him to blink ten times and close his eyes, as a way of enabling young Stew to imagine seeing anything he wants to see. Stew's result was drab and unimaginative, in stark contrast to Kitty's result when she tried the same exercise at the same age.

THEMES

Father-Child Relationships

"Tiny, Smiling Daddy" starts out with the premise that the relationship between Kitty and Stew is being discussed publically, in a magazine article. As the story progresses, it becomes increasingly apparent that Stew has very good reason to fear public exposure. His history of anger and cruelty toward his daughter becomes more and more evident. He was physically abusive, punching her when he saw what kind of literature she was reading, and he was verbally cruel, turning her joke about being "white trash" into a direct insult. Although it is clear that most of his anger stems from his own homophobia, the story does mention more than once that Stew resented the way that Kitty let her "beauty" be hidden as she grew up, as she was trying on one identity after another. Much of his resentment seems to stem from this.

Later in the story, Gaitskill shows readers another significant father-child relationship, the one that Stew had with his own father. Stew does not seem to resent his father's coldness toward him, apparently accepting it as the natural course of events. It becomes clear, however, that his father's behavior is a key to how Stew has treated his daughter, regardless of her sexual orientation. The story even gives Stew and his father similar harsh wording as they are dismissive of their offspring, showing that Stew believes such cruelty to be not only acceptable but actually proper parental behavior. As the title of the story suggests, he turns his back on the idea of a happy parent with mocking derision.

Lesbianism

In this story, Kitty goes through several different lifestyles while trying to find a social identity that will fit her sexual orientation. In high school, when she first realizes that she is a lesbian, she becomes involved with a very masculine woman named Dolores, who lifts weights and has a tattoo of a woman, indicating that Kitty associates lesbianism with women who act like men. After she leaves home to live with a woman named George in Detroit, she moves to San Francisco, where she is able to live among varied lesbians instead of being limited to the narrow role models she could find while growing up in rural Michigan. At this point in her life, she is just learning to incorporate her sexual identity into her lifestyle, describing for her parents activities that have as much to do with art as they have to do with being a lesbian. This leads her, by the end of the story, to living in South Carolina. No society of other lesbians or any particular romantic interest is mentioned, but Kitty's identity is well secured at this phase in her life; she does not need to seek out what it means to be a lesbian anymore. Her article about her relationship with her father mentions her sexual orientation, but it does so in passing. Although Stew cannot let her orientation go, Kitty knows that it is just one factor playing into the trouble between them.

Gender Roles

Much of the animosity between Stew and Kitty stems from the way in which she offends his old-fashioned sense of traditional gender roles. He resents her for turning her back on the beauty that he saw in her when she was young because he believes that it is a woman's role to be beautiful. He became even more resentful toward his daughter when he heard her insulting Marsha to a friend. It may just have been a child's attempt to sound cool by distancing herself from the parent

TOPICS FOR FURTHER STUDY

- Read Lauren Myracle's acclaimed 2003 young-adult novel *Kissing Kate*, about two girls who find that their friendship might be romantic love. The novel details emotional complications of understanding sexual orientation that are only hinted at in "Tiny, Smiling Daddy." After reading the book, write a paper in which you discuss five things that you think Stew from Gaitskill's story might say he learned if he read the book, and explain how these insights would make him view his daughter differently.

- In this story, Stew objects to the implication that he is supposed to be a "tiny, smiling daddy," automatically accepting anything his daughter does with cheer. Look through advertisements, TV shows, and movies for signs that American culture encourages a gruff, stoic stance like the one Stew tries to present to the world. Put together a montage of scenes (perhaps five to ten minutes in length) to show viewers how Stew's attitude might be instilled by the world around him.

- One of the most powerful scenes in this story is when Stew remembers his father's dismissing him flatly. Research modern psychological theories about family relations and write a short essay, citing sources, that explains whether or not you think fathers are a stronger influence on daughters than their mothers are.

- Find an article in a print or online magazine in which the writer explains his or her relationship with a parent. Write a short story from the perspective of the parent, explaining how he or she reacted upon reading the article.

- Many ethnic cultures have more stringent views of homosexuality than does American culture at large. Examine a culture that you are familiar with. Write an explanation, based on research and any personal experience you may have, that explains whether Stew Thorne would have been more harsh or more forgiving to his daughter, Kitty, if he had been from that culture.

- Edmund White's book *A Boy's Own Story: A Novel* (1982), about growing up gay in the repressive 1950s, is considered a literary classic. Read White's book about the hardships he faced. Make a chart that tracks societal attitudes toward homosexuality through three time frames: the 1950s, the 1990s of Gaitskill's story, and today.

who is most like her, but Stew became defensive toward his wife, not realizing that Marsha does not need her relationship with Kitty defended.

Marsha plays into his expectations about gender roles as they age together, quietly accepting his anger and offering him a soothing massage rather than insisting that he listen to reason. But Kitty's emerging sexual orientation offends Stew's narrow sense of gender roles throughout the story, leading him to focus on every masculine trait she has acquired as she matured and making him more and more angry that she is not the girl that he had hoped she would grow up to be.

Stew's relationship with his own father is skewed by traditional gender roles. His memories of his father focus on his masculinity, all knuckles and body hair and muscles. When his father cursed at him, Stew seems to have accepted the verbal abuse as being the kind of harshness a boy should expect. His father hurt him, but he cannot admit that because it is not masculine to admit being hurt. He bottles up his anger because he believes that to be what a man is supposed to do.

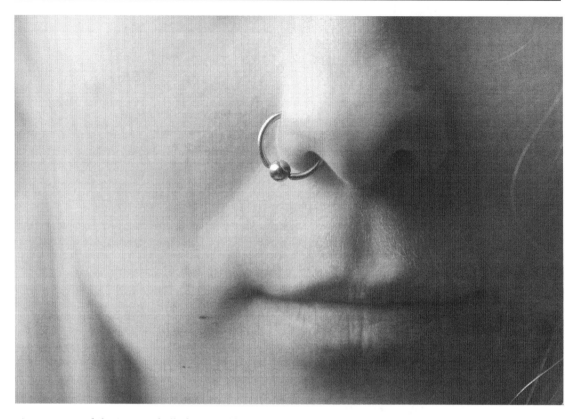

As a young adult, Kitty rebelled against her parents, dying her hair and piercing her nose.
(© ollyy | ShutterStock.com)

STYLE

Flashback

Parts of this story take place in the present, starting with Stew's receiving his friend's phone call about the magazine article and going through to the moment Marsha massages his shoulders to calm him. Much of the action, though, takes place in the past. Gaitskill manages to fit years of familial interaction into the course of this short story, taking Kitty from her youth through her adulthood, revealing different stages of her life through Stew's memories.

Some events from particular times and places are told in flashback scenes. This is always the case when exact words are quoted in dialogue, such as when Stew remembers overhearing Kitty and a friend talking about Marsha or when he relates his specific cutting remark to her. There are other places, however, where Gaitskill does not offer a true flashback but just Stew's general impressions, as when he generalizes about the good relationship Kitty had

with her mother, saying things like "When Kitty was seven, she and her mother had special times" without showing a specific moment between them. This kind of vague generalization says more about Stew's attitude than it does about what really went on then; if it were a true flashback, readers could watch the characters interacting with one another and form an independent judgment about the kind of relationship they had.

Limited Point of View

Gaitskill controls the information that the reader has about Stew's life, doling it out slowly, to make readers question what they are told. She does this by limiting the narrative to events that have happened in Stew's life as they are filtered through his thoughts. With this kind of focus, readers do not know at the start what is in the article that Kitty wrote, because they are exposed to Stew before he has obtained a copy of the magazine. They formulate an opinion of him from the things that he thinks. From the very first paragraph of the story, readers can see that he is opinionated and angry.

COMPARE
&
CONTRAST

- **Late 1990s:** High schools are tolerant of students who pick on each other's differences, which can make students who are less popular secretive and defensive.

  Today: Bullying still occurs among schoolchildren, but administrators are more aware of its causes and effects, and more systems are in place to provide support for students who are bullied.

- **Late 1990s:** Magazines about personal fulfillment, like *Self*, *Allure*, and *Cosmopolitan*, offer writers a way of making money while publicly exploring the complications of their personal lives.

  Today: Blogs and social media give anyone who is not a professional writer the unpaid chance to write about their past.

- **Late 1990s:** The quickest way for a person to get a magazine is to visit the nearest library or store that has a magazine stand.

  Today: Even the diminishing number of magazines that still offer a print edition are available online.

- **Late 1990s:** A gay woman in rural Michigan might gravitate to an open-minded city like San Francisco to live in a community of other gay women.

  Today: Gay culture is familiar most everywhere. According to Richard Florida, one in seven gay people lives in a rural area of the country, and Ann Arbor, Michigan, is among the country's twenty "gayest cities" (a list still topped by San Francisco).

- **Late 1990s:** The same year that Gaitskill's story "Tiny, Smiling Daddy" is published, the comedian Ellen DeGeneres is lauded for taking a chance on destroying her television career when she comes out publicly as a lesbian.

  Today: The sexual orientation of film and television actors is sometimes a subject of gossip, but openly gay actors are accepted in all kinds of starring and supporting roles.

Readers also get to judge how honest Stew is by the way he interacts with his friend Norm, who seems almost fearful in the way he apologetically asks Stew about the article, and by the way that he interacts with his wife, Marsha, who is so accustomed to his bad moods that she responds to Stew's anger by quickly offering to soothe him.

Because readers know the situation only from Stew's point of view, they are naturally inclined to sympathize with his interpretation of past events. Gaitskill chisels away at this natural sympathy, as in the scene where Stew rejects Kitty with extreme, almost psychotic language, trying to bully her in the way that he was earlier seen bullying Norm and Marsha. By the end, he is no longer a sympathetic figure, just a man who is locked in the same cycle of anger that consumed his brutish father.

HISTORICAL CONTEXT

Literary Iconoclasm
When "Tiny, Smiling Daddy" was published in 1997, literary fiction was not quite accustomed to explicit portrayals of human sexuality, according to William Deresiewicz. Writing in the *Nation*, Deresiewicz points out that Gaitskill became widely known with her first three books (*Bad Behavior* in 1988, *Two Girls, Fat and Thin* in 1991, and *Because They Wanted To* in 1997) as a writer who was willing to tackle subjects that had previously been avoided by the mainstream. Sexuality, and especially violent or nonstandard sexuality, had previously been left to disreputable publishers of genre fiction.

Gaitskill's writing was recognized for the talent that produced it but also for the author's willingness to explore facets of culture that made some readers uneasy, including rape, masochism, pornography, and prostitution. Although Gaitskill acquired a reputation for writing about "dark" subjects, she moved on with later works, affirming that it was her skill, not her subject matter, that led to her success as a writer. Still, her works about currents of human sexuality that were rarely discussed intellectually led the way for such writers as Melanie Abrams, Susie Bright, Chuck Palahniuk, and Catherine Millet, all of whom write about complex variations on human sexuality in novels and memoirs that are acknowledged as literary. Sexuality is also more openly examined in popular culture on cable television, where programs like *Californication* and *Girls* examine subjects that would once have been considered the province of Gaitskill.

Gay Rights

When this story was published in 1997, the struggle for gay equality had achieved many notable advances, but there was an antigay element fighting against it that had a strong grip on mainstream society. Matters had come a long way from the days when homosexuality was criminalized, but it was still viewed with suspicion. Although there were activists working to assure the rights of gays and lesbians, the political establishment lacked the will to solidify such rights into the laws of the United States.

The culture had changed markedly in the previous decades. One of the most significant turning points in the history of gay rights in America, often considered the single most important moment in the struggle for equality, occurred on June 28, 1969, with the infamous Stonewall riots in New York City. At the time, homosexual behavior was considered a psychological abnormality, listed as a sociopathic personality disturbance by the American Psychiatric Association. Police forces, even in a place as progressive as New York City, regularly arrested gay people under arcane laws that prohibited homosexuality. When the police raided the Stonewall Inn, a gay bar in Greenwich Village, that night in 1969, however, the patrons stood up and fought back; people came from around the neighborhood to join the fight, reaching a crowd of up to two thousand rioters. The fighting in the streets continued over the next four days and brought worldwide attention to the fight of gay Americans to attain equality.

Phone conversations are important in Gaitskill's story, showing distance between people and the difficulties of communicating.
(© olivier | ShutterStock.com)

After that, the struggle for social recognition for same-sex couples became increasingly open, though there was still widespread disagreement about the rights that gays and lesbians should have in American society. In 1993, for instance, President Bill Clinton signed a law enacting the "Don't Ask, Don't Tell" policy, which was seen as a compromise benefiting both sides. It permitted gay people to serve in the military, but only if their sexuality was kept a secret. That law was overturned in 2011.

When other countries started recognizing gay couples and conferring marriage or partnership rights to them, opponents moved to prevent similar laws from taking hold in the United States, culminating in the passage of the Defense of Marriage Act in 1996, the year before Gaitskill's story's publication. The act restricts federal marriage benefits to opposite-sex couples only and stipulates that states are not required to recognize same-sex marriages or domestic partnerships sanctioned by other states. Although Vermont introduced civil unions as early as 2000, it was not until 2004 that Massachusetts became the first state to recognize same-sex marriages; slowly, other states have followed. There have been constant challenges to same-sex marriage, indicating that society still views homosexuality as a controversial issue.

of the only stories from the book discussed in a short review by R. L. Pela in the *Advocate*, an influential gay publication. After generalizing that the stories could be "occasionally repetitive" though they were also "among the brightest, most urgent new fiction on the shelf," Pela uses this story as an example of Gaitskill's work, deeming it "a tense tale of love and betrayal that's worth [the book's] cover price."

CRITICAL OVERVIEW

"Tiny, Smiling Daddy" comes from Gaitskill's third book, *Because They Wanted To*, which was her second collection of short stories. By the time of its publication, she had gained a reputation for writing frankly about sexual experiences. This particular story was considered to be on the tame side of the stories in the collection because it does not talk explicitly about sexuality, but it was also thought by critics to be one of the book's best.

One sign of Gaitskill's literary eminence at the time that this story was published was the glowing review that it received in the *New York Times*, one of the country's most influential newspapers. *New Yorker* editor Craig Seligman, writing in the *Times*, notes the author's progression over her earlier work:

> The new stories dig deeper . . . attempting less on the surface but turning up more underneath it; compared with the subtly twisted characters in this collection, a lot of her earlier ones look like complex cartoons.

Seligman ends his review by saying, "A lot of these stories are just about perfect," though he regrets that their perfection of form might make it difficult for readers to fully appreciate them.

Amy Sickels, writing about *Because They Wanted To* for the *Literary Review*, captures the virtues that led to almost universal praise for Gaitskill when she notes that as much as readers would like to pull away from uncomfortable subjects, the author

> pushes us in with her hard-edged prose, tough realism, and perplexed characters, and we leave the book feeling as if we would never want to know any of these people, yet at the same time, we're sure we already do.

Most reviews of the story collection singled out "Tiny, Smiling Daddy" as being noteworthy in its focus on character. It was, for instance, one

CRITICISM

David Kelly

Kelly is an instructor of literature and creative writing. In the following essay, he discusses how the most captivating characters in "Tiny, Smiling Daddy," Stew and Kitty, are actually the least significant to the story's point.

On the surface, Mary Gaitskill's short story "Tiny, Smiling Daddy" seems to be about one of two things. The most obvious interpretation of the story is that it is about a rough, angry man with traditional homophobic values who has been locked in a battle of wills with his equally strong-willed daughter throughout her later lifetime. In this view, Kitty, having reached maturity, has found a way to live comfortably in the world whether she wins her father's approval or not. A second reading of the story would be that it presents a one-sided battle: Stew, the father, sits sulking and isolated in his house, angry that Kitty has moved on beyond his circle of influence. He keeps cursing her, stewing because he is egotistical enough to read her sexual identity as a personal insult, while Kitty, in another part of the country, carries on with what she has to do to get over her life with him. In one of these views, it is a story about two people; the other sees it as the story of one person.

Both of these interpretations are drawn from the influence of the powerful, iconic characters of Stew and Kitty. It is clearly Stew's story—the narrative stays with him for every word, recording his thoughts and observations, even when he himself is not clear about what he thinks. By publishing an article about her life of parental rejection in a national magazine, Kitty may be a symbol of healing, or she may be exacting revenge on Stew by tattling—bringing his offenses to the attention of people beyond the boundaries of the home he obsessively rules.

WHAT DO I READ NEXT?

- Gaitskill's first novel, *Two Girls, Fat and Thin*, is a social comedy that applies the author's sharp, ironic view and terse writing skills to subjects as diverse as body image, gender, sexual identity, and Ayn Rand. It was published in 1991.

- In the short story "Because They Wanted To," the title story from the collection that includes "Tiny, Smiling Daddy," a sixteen-year-old girl runs away from home, as Kitty does in this story and as Gaitskill did in real life. She is taken in as a nanny by a woman with three children and, at a young age, ends up being a mother figure. The book was published in 1997.

- Dr. Michael C. LaSala's book *Coming Out, Coming Home: Helping Families Adjust to a Gay or Lesbian Child*, first published in 2010, can help readers understand the characters in this story and both the bad and the good choices they make.

- Christopher Yuan explains what it is like to come out as gay to parents in a traditional Chinese American family in his memoir *Out of a Far Country: A Gay Son's Journey to God; A Broken Mother's Search for Hope*, cowritten with his mother, Angela Yuan. Published in 2011, this tale gives readers a sense of how another culture handles the situation faced by the Thornes in the book.

- Matthew Sharpe's interview with Gaitskill for *BOMB* magazine in the spring of 2009 shows how the author coped with her early fame in the 1980s and 1990s and how she has matured. It was published online at http://bombsite.com/issues/107/articles/3265.

- To understand the article that Kitty wrote for *Self*, which uses such terminology from the self-help movement as finding the "good parent in yourself," readers might look at a book like Jane Middelton-Moz's *Children of Trauma: Rediscovering Your Discarded Self*, published in 1989. Middleton-Moz uses stories of adults who, like Kitty, are trying to come to grips with difficult situations that derailed their lives when they were young.

- Short-story writer Lorrie Moore often covers subjects similar to those Gaitskill writes about, but with a kinder, softer sense of absurd humor. One of her most frequently anthologized stories, "How to Talk to Your Mother (Notes)," for example, comprises short sections which take place in reverse chronology, starting in the 1980s and ending in the 1930s. It is this kind of playfulness with serious intent that makes Moore a favorite of readers. The story was first published in Moore's 1985 collection *Self-Help*.

Either way, she is exacting a revenge that every rejected child hopes to have one day.

As interesting as both of these characters are—standing as intertwined icons in an age when homosexuality is making itself known and accepted—the whole point of Gaitskill's story is that neither of them is actually all that important. In making clumsy claims for the attention of those around them, they have each rendered themselves irrelevant.

To find out what any story is truly about, it often helps to look to its ending. In the same way

as one would go to the right side of an equation to work out what is supposed to happen on the left side of the equal sign, it is relevant to find out what the author feels to be the story's fulfillment in order to understand the significance of the various parts. The most interesting moment of a story is not necessarily its climax. In "Tiny, Smiling Daddy," the most gripping moment comes when Stew recalls the awful words he used to throw his daughter out of the home she grew up in: "I don't care if I'm on my deathbed, I'll still have the energy to spit in your face." The

READERS WILL FIND KITTY TO BE THE MOST INTERESTING CHARACTER ON THE PAGE AND STEW THE MOST INFURIATING ONE, AND GAITSKILL USES THESE EMOTIONAL RESPONSES, ALONG WITH CAREFUL NARRATIVE STRUCTURE, TO COMMENT ON FATE AND THE SEARCH TO KNOW ONESELF."

statement is so hypercharged that it is likely to leave an impression on anyone who reads it. It is a demented sentiment—the man would defy death itself to insult and humiliate not just another human being, but his own daughter!

In the context of this story, however, that line's function is not terribly remarkable. By the time it comes around, it is already history. Readers will have known from the start that Stew is and always has been angry and crude, the kind of man whose idea of a cute joke involved taunting his young daughter with his nose hairs. And the fact that he once actually struck her is revealed about halfway through the story. Stew's threat to never forgive, using the gross image of spitting to make his attitude clear, would disgust any reasonable reader, but the power of language, thought, and imagery does not make this the story's climax.

There are two other events at the end of the story that are more significant in changing readers' understanding of Stew, Kitty, and their lives with each other, and their significance to the arc of the story makes either of them likely candidates for being read as the story's climax. First, Gaitskill gives her readers a glimpse of the twisted relationship between Stew and his own father, which clearly set the standard for the way Stew would later treat his own child. Young Stew's emotions about his father are filled with soft emulation, captured in a sentence that uses words like "godlike" and "admiration." But the boy's warmth is shredded by the father's dismissive "Stop staring at me, you little shit." It is a sentiment so cruel that Stew's own threat to rise from his deathbed and spit in his daughter's face, coming a page later in the story, is weak in comparison, vicious though it is. Also, Stew's father's response comes without context, forcing readers

to think about where it fits into the story, while Stew's insult to Kitty is something that the story has been working toward all along. His own line about spitting in his daughter's face is vicious, but it shows that Stew has gained or lost little understanding over the course of his own long life.

His insult to Kitty is the most powerful moment among the story's many flashbacks. The most powerful moment that occurs within the time frame of the story, not in flashback, is presented in the final sentence. Gaitskill could have ended the story with Stew's wife, Marsha, massaging his back and with Stew then reaching behind to pat her hand; that would have shown him to be a man who has trouble expressing his love face to face but who nonetheless tries to acknowledge the kindness of another human being's touch. This would take the readers beyond their basic understanding of Stew as a man who cursed his daughter and promised to curse her for the rest of his life. But the story adds to that action by then including Marsha's simple gesture of moving away from him.

Marsha is not the kind of person to stand up and openly disagree with her husband, or they would not still be together in middle age. By focusing on Marsha's motion away from him, leaving that gesture to linger in readers' minds like the resonant tolling of a bell as the story comes to a close, Gaitskill makes the emptiness of Stew's life the focus of the story. He is isolated at home before Marsha arrives; when she comes home, she goes through the motions of pretending to care for him but then moves from him as soon as she can.

From youth to middle age, Stew's life is bracketed by these two scenes. His father's cold rejection of him establishes the attitude of iron-jawed machismo that he has adapted as his own, and Marsha's silent rejection of him shows the results that his coldness is bound to leave. Stew's conflict with his daughter, his decision to reject her, and his fear of being found out are almost irrelevant when viewed in this context. Readers of the story might argue about what he thinks he is doing, whether he actually feels that he is going to help Kitty return to the beautiful child she once was by refusing to acknowledge who she has grown up to be, or if he is indeed so egotistical that he is acting out of revulsion and hurt feelings. It does not matter. Once Stew accepted his father's bitterness as his own, whatever he does is bound to lead him to abandonment in his old age. Specific incidents with nose hairs, psychiatric wards,

Stew feels guilty when he remembers how his rejection of Kitty made her feel. *(© Jpaget | RF Photos | ShutterStock.com)*

holiday reunions, and magazine publications are stops along the way, but the outcome is inevitable.

Because Kitty is not frozen in her view of life in the way that Stew is, readers might think that the story is really about her and her adventure through life. Throughout the story's flashbacks she is unmoored, floating around and trying to find an appropriate response to her father's attitude toward her. She would, in fact, be an interesting subject for a short story, but she is not the focus of this one. In "Tiny, Smiling Daddy," Kitty appears only in those flashbacks. The filter of Stew's memory leaves out much about her that would be important for readers to know about a story's protagonist; what is told *is* fascinating, but it is not enough to hold a story together. While Stew's decision to reject his daughter might seem inevitable, given his past, Kitty's decision to write a magazine article about her father is anything but inevitable. Readers might see this as Gaitskill's comment on the way that a father's egotism trickles down to his child, since the very title of the magazine, *Self*, implies Kitty's interest in herself and her

personal growth overall. Although that growth may be unique and interesting, it is not present enough to be the story's focus.

Arguably the villain and hero of this story, if one were to use such basic terms, are, respectively, Stew's unnamed father (who gives him the idea that it is okay to reject his child) and Marsha (who knows better than to think that a man like Stew can ever really have a close relationship). These are not the characters one notices most. Readers will find Kitty to be the most interesting character on the page and Stew the most infuriating one, and Gaitskill uses these emotional responses, along with careful narrative structure, to comment on fate and the search to know oneself. The characters readers want to focus on and see more are not the characters who move the story along: that honor belongs to the supplemental but important characters who have defined Stew's life from its beginning to the story's end.

Source: David Kelly, Critical Essay on "Tiny, Smiling Daddy," in *Short Stories for Students*, Gale, Cengage Learning, 2014.

Sarah Anne Johnson

In the following interview excerpt, Gaitskill answers questions about her writing process, including some of her thoughts behind "Tiny Smiling Daddy."

Many of the writers I've interviewed were inspired to write by their early interest in reading. What drew you to writing fiction, and what did you do to develop your craft?

It's really hard to say what draws you to writing. Early reading had a lot to do with it. Even before I read or was able to read much, my mother read to us, so I had a very strong concept of stories. When I was six, when I first learned how to write, one of the first things I did was try to write a story.

Did you go to a writing program?

No. When I was in school, there were very few writing programs. I remember hearing about Iowa, but I had no interest in it. Now it's become something that people feel they have to do, which I think is very unfortunate. I taught myself to write by reading and writing a lot and by not showing it to people constantly. That's the thing about the writing program that bothers me, this idea that you need to show it immediately to a group of twelve people. They're not going to have a deep understanding of your work even if they spend the entire two years with you. It's very difficult to have a deep understanding of another person's work. It's a very intimate thing, how a story is working on the inside. It's very difficult to comment on that. All you can comment on is the outside.

I've worked very alone and very privately. In the past I occasionally showed things to people, and they almost never liked it. When I was younger, I was aware of writing groups, but I never wanted to do that, and I think it was good that I didn't. You really are alone when you write, and these groups give you the illusion that you're doing it with other people, and you really can't be.

Do you think the group detracts from finding your own way?

Not for everybody. Some people feed off the energy of a group—these people are typically the people who dominate the group. Ultimately, I think even they need to get out of the group at some point, but for a time it can be inspiring for that type of personality.

> "YOU'RE INFLUENCED BY ALMOST ANYTHING YOU ABSORB. YOU LEARN FROM VERY HIGH-QUALITY WRITERS, BUT THE LEARNING DOESN'T TAKE PLACE ON A RATIONAL LEVEL."

You've said that some of your favorite books are classics such as Ulysses *by James Joyce,* Lolita *and* Pale Fire *by Vladimir Nabokov, and the stories of Anton Chekhov. How does the work of other writers influence you, and how do you use your reading life to inform your writing life?*

I don't know the answer to that. I don't think that anyone does. Influence is completely indiscriminant. It's an unconscious process. I'm sure that I have been influenced in various ways by writers that I've loved, but I also think I've been influenced by writers I've read very casually. I've been influenced by trashy writers as well as by really great writers. I've been influenced by music, by things I hear on the news, by newspapers, movies, cartoons. You're influenced by almost anything you absorb. You learn from very high-quality writers, but the learning doesn't take place on a rational level. Someone can point out how a writer is doing something, and you can copy it, but it doesn't work. If you're a really good copier, all you're going to wind up with is a weak version of the superior writer's idea.

What reading great writers can give you, especially if you reread them, is better apprehension of depth, which, again, is not a rational process.

Myla Goldberg also cited Pale Fire *as an influential book in that it experimented with form and was about the unreliability of memory. What draws you to the book?*

Its beauty mostly, its ridiculousness, its comedy, its poignancy in the sense that it's a story of misdirected love. It's about the sense of a beautiful dream world that shimmers under a prosaic and dull reality, and trying to find a bridge to that world through love or an ideal or a poem. There's a section that I always read to students which is about a minor character. She's the girl that the narrator was forced to marry.

She's not important at all. She shows up in one or two sections. He must marry her for social reasons even though he's not interested in women, generally. He won't have sex with her, and she doesn't understand why not, and she becomes more and more despairing. There's this gorgeous section where he remembers the first time he told her that he didn't love her. She sinks down on the grass, and he immediately changes the subject. He says that, in spite of his lack of love and interest in her in life, his dream life made "extraordinary amends." In his dream life, his love for her exceeded in passion and tenor anything he ever experienced with anyone else. It's that strange misconnection with an imaginary connection underneath that's poignant and very true to human experience.

You've written short stories, novels, nonfiction articles, and essays. Do you feel more comfortable in one form or another? Rick Moody said that when he writes nonfiction he can then go back to writing fiction and feel refreshed.

There was a period of time when I really enjoyed writing essays. I haven't been interested in them lately. Something that really annoys me is when people try to interpret my fiction through what I've said in my essays, because they come from totally different places. One critic laboriously tried to unravel my fiction using things I'd said in disparate essays on a variety of subjects. At one point he said that I insist, through my fiction, on a fully sexualized society. I certainly don't need to insist on any such thing. We're already there, regardless of what I say about it.

An essay is a much more rational medium. I can say much more directly what I mean and hope that there's a minimum of misinterpretation. Usually people can understand essays better than they can fiction because it's a more direct expression of rational opinion. The relative simplicity of that is sometimes a relief. Also, I think it develops your skills even though it's a different form. Any kind of writing that you do is in some way developing your skills. You have to express yourself clearly in an essay just as you do in fiction, though the clarity takes a different form.

Novels and stories occur for every writer in different ways. Edwidge Danticat told me, "The stories sometimes come in one line or one scene.. ..I've had many stories where I had ten pages and nothing was happening, and I put those away and

picked them up much later." How do your novels or stories come to you?

Similarly to what she was saying. I sometimes get an idea for a book or story with an image, or a single event, or a personality. *Veronica* was more about a personality through which I connected to the subjects of illness and mortality and beauty. It was a crude juxtaposition that had a lot of power for me—and I'm not using the word "crude" in a negative sense here. The novel I'm working on now started with an image of the weather being embodied in human form. I have no idea what it has to do with the book in rational terms. Before that, I was thinking of the book in terms of characters and how these characters would come into play with each other. But I didn't sit down to write until I got this image of the weather as people.

When you gather stories together for a book, do you see them differently? Do you make changes to accommodate the book?

I do see them differently. When they get into relationship with one another, they take on a different meaning. Thus far I haven't made that many changes to accommodate a book, only one, really, which was in the last collection of stories. I took out one story because it repeated the circumstances of another story too closely, and it was the weaker one.

When you're working on stories, are you thinking about the collection?

What happens is that I start out just writing stories, but at some point when I have five or six of them, I do start thinking in terms of a collection. Then it can change, because I start thinking about how these ideas work together or how they might be varied.

How do you arrive at an order for stories in a collection?

To me, the story that follows the previous story ideally is a story that further develops a theme or emotional tone in the previous story or turns a corner somehow.

Because They Wanted To opens with "Tiny, Smiling Daddy," a story about a man thinking back on his ambivalent relationship with his lesbian daughter. What drew you to exploring this father's point of view?

That was a story that took a long time. I wrote it originally when I was writing the stories that went into *Bad Behavior*. The original version wasn't as developed. In that draft, the

daughter hadn't written anything—there was a phone call that triggered him thinking about her, which was much less dramatic. I don't remember why I chose to write it from his point of view. In general, I think it can give a story a very interesting energy if you write from a point of view that you're not naturally sympathetic with or that's somewhat foreign to you. I tell my students, if you're going to write a story from your real life, what can make it interesting is to write it from the point of view of someone besides yourself, ideally, a person you didn't like.

The story ends when he remembers how Kitty told him she was a lesbian, and he screamed, "You mean nothing to me. You walk out that door, it doesn't matter. And if you come back in, I'm going to spit in your face." His wife was consoling him, but she slides away from him on the couch, and he is left with the violent words in his head. What makes for a strong ending to a short story?

That one works because you get a feeling of remorse, but because of all the other thoughts he's had, his feelings are more complicated than that. He's someone who would have difficulty expressing them even to himself. He's had these feelings and thoughts, but they've created a lot of confusion for him. At the end, it's allowed for him to see the contradiction between what he's said and what he actually feels.

In general, I'm not sure I can tell you what I think constitutes a good ending. I think often it's an ending in which the story is cracked open. I just assigned Flannery O'Connor's "Everything That Rises Must Converge," where you're seeing these very nasty, rigidly defined characters act out their personalities again and again. At the end, a woman is knocked down and has a stroke, and the son falls apart. They are cracked open; they can't hold onto their characters anymore. There's a huge outpouring of emotion and dark mystery that's an intense contrast to the repetition and rigidity that went before.

Another good ending is a scene that contrasts what the characters are saying and doing with what they really feel, or an ending where you finally get all the information about what's been going on with the characters and it opens up at the end. Or one in which the scope of the story is dramatically changed, and you suddenly have an apprehension of another world totally outside that of the story which may supersede the story—the end of "Signs and Symbols"

by Nabokov might be described that way, or Chekhov's "Gusev."

Some writers write the entire first draft of a novel and then go back and revise, while others work through each page until it's perfect, taking their time reaching the end. Ann Patchett was the only writer I've interviewed who thinks a book out in her head and then sits down to write it out in a couple of drafts. What is your process like for writing and revising a novel?

I definitely don't think it all out in advance. I wish I could. Usually I get a basic idea. Sometimes the idea is more or less fully formed, like with *Veronica*. With *Two Girls* or the one I'm working on now, I have an idea for the ending. Typically, I have a basic situation and a thought for an ending, but I don't have any idea how to get there. I'll make notes in the margin about things I want to happen somewhere in the novel. Occasionally I'll write a scene without knowing where it belongs, but I know I want it there somewhere. That happened repeatedly with *Veronica....*

Source: Sarah Anne Johnson, "Mary Gaitskill: 'I've Worked Very Privately and Alone,'" in *The Very Telling: Conversations with American Writers*, University Press of New England, 2006, pp. 30–34.

E. J. Graff

In the following excerpt, Graff describes Gaitskill's characters as emotionally disconnected.

Long ago I realized that women (if I might generalize without a license) read and write fiction about sexual drama because that's where we navigate the tidal clash of our own and others' desires. It's along these dangerous shoals that fiction writers Amy Bloom and Mary Gaitskill made their high-profile debuts during the past decade.

Gaitskill's *Bad Behavior* turned a flat, glaring light on bottom-dwelling women and men. In her stunning novel, *Two Girls, Fat and Thin*, her skillful exploration of childhood viciousness and adult emotional and sexual desperation ended with a surprising moment of redemption.

. . . While Bloom's characters' strong emotions give them a morality all their own, Mary Gaitskill's specialize in a gray disconnection that makes their sexual encounters aimlessly amoral. These stories read like a verbal cross between the artwork of Nan Goldin and Bruce Naumann: false intimacy mixed with cruelty, numbed tedium and anxiety, interrupted by unhappy sex with strangers. One story gives a clear clue to Gaitskill's world, describing a billboard in which the model's

> eyes were fixated, wounded, deprived. At the same time, her eyes were flat, her body was slender, almost starved, giving her delicate beauty the strange, arrested sensuality of unsatisfied want.... The photograph loomed over the toiling shoppers like a totem of sexualized pathology, a vision of feeling and unfeeling chafing together. It was a picture made for people who can't bear to feel and yet still need to feel. It was a picture by people sophisticated enough to fetishize their disability publicly. It was a very good advertisement for a product called Obsession.

The best stories render such feeling/unfeeling incisively, in a way that left me with the writer's envious awe: You can do that? In "Tiny, Smiling Daddy" (may it be anthologized endlessly), a suburban father is stunned to learn that his daughter has published an essay about him in the magazine *Self*, written in bathetic self-help prose. "[H]e felt helplessness move through his body the way a swimmer feels a large sea creature pass beneath him. How could she have done this to him?" As he drives to the drugstore and reads the essay, he angrily recalls her shape-shifting life, from lovely and loved child to miserable adolescent to angry, muscular leather dyke to lipsticked and pierced urban sophisticate. No one escapes the story's chilly judgment: not the daughter who gets backhanded revenge on her father via public confession; not the self-help culture that substitutes nonsense concepts for emotion; and certainly not the sputtering father who finally remembers (as much with renewed anger as regret) responding to his daughter's coming out with "I don't care if I'm on my deathbed, I'll still have the energy to spit in your face."

Equally breathtaking is "The Girl on the Plane," a conversation between two flawed people: a woman who offers her alcoholism and unhappy past as a casual conversational gambit, relying on AA meeting conventions in a wildly inappropriate setting, and her male seatmate, startled into remembering a murky and disgusting group sexual encounter which he, in return, confesses as rape. Gaitskill's detailed look at both the ex-college boy and the unstable girl he remembers goes far beyond the simplistic divisions of "she asked for it" and "no means no" into a world where everybody's choices are wrong.

For Gaitskill, what invests us squirms at the more aggressive end of Freud's emotional spectrum: suppressed rage and hatred are waiting to arise at any moment. Margot, a thirtyish social worker in "Orchid," remembers the time one of her college roommates "watched her with bemusement and, Margot thought, perverse, furtive attraction enlivened by a little hot streak of disgust"—a combination Gaitskill characters find especially alluring. In the title story, the main character's stepmother owns a shop that tattoos women's faces to look constantly made up. "'I fixed it so I wouldn't have to wash my face off at night,' she said. She said it with brisk self-deprecation, as if her face, everybody's face, was a vaguely ridiculous thing that could come off at any moment. She also said it with pride that she'd acknowledged the problem and then gone right in there to fix it."

Gaitskill's method might be called experience recollected in distress. Nothing happens in the present—nothing, that is, except discussions over coffee, drinks, dinner, or sex, all trying to make sense of the past. That works well in such stories as "Tiny, Smiling Daddy" and "The Girl on the Plane"—stories in which the narrators despise the idea of self-review, even while groping their way through memory toward some sense of responsibility. But it can become deadly when lacking narrative distance. In "The Dentist," for instance, a woman is unable to accept with gratitude a fairly simple kindness. She constantly re-hashes the situation with her unstable friends (minutely, tediously, inaccurately, in conversations that remind me of the pointless "processing" I'll do anything to avoid) until she makes her poor dentist the object of a bizarre fetish, in a kind of *Fatal Attraction* told from Glenn Close's point of view. Here Gaitskill's talent at rendering fleeting, sour emotions begins to feel suffocating and paralyzed, like being trapped in someone else's depression without a window. The book's title reads as a (surely intentional) mockery: Because they wanted to what? No one here knows.

Bloom and Gaitskill, two brazen and clear-eyed writers, have more in common than the writing of uneven books about women in sexual extremity. They've also written work that fits what I've lately heard called "post-queer." Gaitskill's women pursue both women and men with no particular differentiation; Elizabeth Taube's loves could all be fairly called queer.

Recently the *New Yorker* rather self-importantly declared that there was a new genre of writing about bad sex. In its pantheon stood Mary Gaitskill; Amy Bloom might well have been in the picture. What both tell us is that every unhappy act of human intercourse—sexual or otherwise—is unhappy in its own way; that faced with life's impossible questions about how to make reasonable contact with other human beings, loneliness can look cozy. Or as Bloom's Elizabeth thinks near her novel's end, "it may really be too hard and too late, not even desirable, after such long familiar cold, to be known, and heard, and seen."

Source: E. J. Graff, Review of *Because They Wanted To: Stories*, in *Women's Review of Books*, Vol. 14, No. 8, May 1997, pp. 7–8.

SOURCES

Bellafante, Ginia, "Can a Writer of Malaise Find Happiness in Acclaim?," in *New York Times*, October 30, 2005, http://www.nytimes.com/2005/10/30/fashion/sundaystyles/30Gaitskill.html?pagewanted=all&_r=0 (accessed February 14, 2013).

Deresiewicz, William, "When the Whip Comes Down: On Mary Gaitskill," in *Nation*, May 11, 2009, http://www.thenation.com/article/when-whip-comes-down-mary-gaitskill?page=0,0 (accessed February 10, 2013).

Florida, Richard, "America's Top 20 Gayest Cities," in *Daily Beast*, July 19, 2010, http://www.thedailybeast.com/articles/2010/07/20/the-20-gayest-cities-in-america.html (accessed February 14, 2013).

Gaitskill, Mary, "Tiny, Smiling Daddy," in *Because They Wanted To: Stories*, Simon & Schuster, 1997, pp. 11–24.

"Gay Rights Timeline," in *Time*, 2012, http://www.time.com/time/interactive/0,31813,1904681,00.html (accessed February 14, 2013).

Pela, R. L., "Bisexual Scenes," in *Advocate*, No. 728, 1997, p. 59.

Seligman, Craig, "Carnal Knowledge," in *New York Times*, February 9, 1997, http://www.nytimes.com/1997/02/09/books/carnal-knowledge.html?pagewanted=all&src=pm (accessed January 31, 2013).

Sickels, Amy, Review of *Because They Wanted To*, in *Literary Review*, Vol. 42, No. 2, 1999, p. 349.

Singleton, Dave, "40 Years Later: A Look Back at the Turning Point for Gay Rights," in *AARP Bulletin*, June 2009, http://www.aarp.org/politics-society/rights/info-06-2009/stonewall_riots_40_years_later_.html (accessed February 14, 2013).

FURTHER READING

de Zengotita, Thomas, *Mediated: How the Media Shapes Your World and the Way You Live in It*, Bloomsbury, 2006.

> The author takes a psychological approach to the ways in which modern life is understood through the prism of the media, giving insight into the way being published in the "Speak Easy" column of a magazine called *Self* may be the thing that Kitty needs, as a way to cope with her difficult past.

Gaitskill, Mary, "On Not Being a Victim: Sex, Rape, and the Trouble with Following Rules," in *Harper's*, March 1, 1994, p. 35.

> Gaitskill's discussion of the complexities of acquaintance rape and date rape draws from her real-life experiences and gives insight into the kind of life she may have imagined for Kitty, who is left to face the world without her parents' support.

Griffin, Carolyn Welch, Marian J. Wirth, and Arthur G. Wirth, *Beyond Acceptance: Parents of Lesbians & Gays Talk about Their Experiences*, St. Martin's Griffin, 1996.

> The experiences recounted in this book give parents an idea of how to deal with unexpected news about their children's sexual orientation. Readers can apply these lessons to understanding what makes Stew Thorne such a complex character.

Nussbaum, Emily, "Mary, Mary, Less Contrary," in *New York*, November 14, 2005, pp. 40–43.

> This profile of Gaitskill late in the writer's career focuses on how the obsessions that characterized her early writing have mellowed with time.

"Q&A: Mary Gaitskill on Vampires and Dick Cheney," in *Flavorwire*, March 22, 2010, http://flavorwire.com/78896/qa-mary-gaitskill-on-vampires-and-dick-cheney.

> Of the many interviews with Gaitskill available on the Internet, this is one of the most frank and the most perceptive.

SUGGESTED SEARCH TERMS

Mary Gaitskill

Tiny, Smiling Daddy

Tiny, Smiling Daddy AND gay life

Gaitskill AND fathers

Gaitskill AND short story

Tiny, Smiling Daddy AND isolation

Gaitskill AND Because They Wanted To

Tiny, Smiling Daddy AND parent

A Tree. A Rock. A Cloud

CARSON MCCULLERS

1942

"A Tree. A Rock. A Cloud," by Carson McCullers, is a brief story set in a small twenty-four-hour café. When a twelve-year-old paperboy stops in before dawn for a cup of coffee, he is beckoned by an older man nursing a beer. The man tells the boy, whom he has never met, that he loves him, and then tells him the story of his unfortunate marriage. He also explains that he has developed a "science" to teach himself to practice and understand love. The other customers ignore or laugh at the man, and the boy does not know what to think of him.

"A Tree. A Rock. A Cloud" was first published in the November 1942 issue of *Harper's Bazaar* and became one of the best known and widely anthologized of McCullers's short stories. Like much of the author's work, it is set in a small southern town and features characters who are isolated and searching. It is frequently included on high-school reading lists, and questions about the mysterious man's ideas about love—and whether the author is herself endorsing them—are the subjects of many high-school writing assignments. The story is included in the collection *The Ballad of the Sad Café: The Novels and Stories of Carson McCullers*, issued in 1951, as well as her *Collected Stories*, published in 1987.

Carson McCullers (© *Leonard McCombe | Getty Images*)

AUTHOR BIOGRAPHY

Lulu Carson Smith was born on February 19, 1917, in Columbus, Georgia. Both of her parents could trace their family trees back through the South for several generations, and even though the author—who adopted her middle name as her first name when she was about thirteen— lived for extended periods in New York, New Hampshire, and Europe later in her life, she claimed that the South would always be a part of her and of her writing. As a child, she was passionate about playing the piano, practicing up to eight hours a day and intending to become a concert pianist. By the time she was seventeen, however, she gave up her ambition to be a great musician and focused her energies on writing.

In 1934, she moved alone to New York City, working during the day and studying fiction writing at Columbia University at night. Almost right away she had two stories accepted for publication in the magazine *Story*. She frequently had to travel back home to Georgia because of illness; she had been ill with pneumonia and

rheumatic fever as a teenager, and her heart seemed to have been permanently weakened as a result. In 1936, she met Reeves McCullers, whom she married in 1937. Reeves was in the military and was also a writer; like his wife, he was also a heavy drinker. The couple had a tumultuous life together and apart, divorcing in 1942 and remarrying in 1945. Both Carson and Reeves were conflicted about their sexuality, and they were about to divorce a second time when Reeves committed suicide in 1953. During these years, McCullers also endured several strokes, which left her temporarily blind, paralyzed, and unable to speak. Severely depressed, she attempted suicide in 1948.

In spite of her personal struggles, McCullers was remarkably successful as an artist. By the time she was thirty, she had published four well-received novels, including *The Heart Is a Lonely Hunter* (1940) and *The Member of the Wedding* (1946); had published several short stories, including "A Tree. A Rock. A Cloud" (1942); had won a Guggenheim Fellowship and a grant from the Academy of Arts and Letters; and had been invited to spend time at prestigious writers' retreats. She also wrote poetry and essays, although her novels are considered her most important works. She was well known and popular in trendy literary circles, and she was financially successful as well. In 1950, she adapted *The Member of the Wedding* as a play; it ran on Broadway for more than five hundred performances and won several awards. During her last years, McCullers wrote comparatively little new material, in large part because she suffered from breast cancer, depression, a fractured hip that required several surgeries, and her lifelong heart condition. She suffered another stroke, fell into a coma, and died on September 29, 1967, in Nyack, New York.

PLOT SUMMARY

As "A Tree. A Rock. A Cloud" begins, a twelve-year-old paperboy enters an all-night café near the streetcar line of a southern city. The boy has almost finished delivering his newspapers and has stopped in before sunrise on a rainy morning for a cup of coffee. It is a café he visits regularly; he knows the owner, Leo, and recognizes the workmen who sit at the counter. In one corner, though, there is a man whom he does not know,

MEDIA ADAPTATIONS

- *A Tree, a Rock, a Cloud* was adapted as a short film starring Dana Andrews, and produced and directed by Rex Victor Goff. It was issued by Phoenix Films in 1978.

- The story, along with several others, is available on the MP3 audiobook *The Ballad of the Sad Café*, published by Audible in 2013.

hunched over a mug of beer. As the boy is leaving, the man calls him over. He puts a hand on the boy's shoulder, cups his chin in his other hand and says, "I love you."

The workmen laugh at this, and the boy is embarrassed. The man apologizes and invites the boy to sit with him. He takes two rumpled photographs from his pocket and shows them to the boy, explaining that the woman in them was his wife. In answer to the boy's question, he says that she is not dead, but gone; she left him less than two years after they were married. He was a railroad engineer; he believed that he was a good provider and that they were a happy couple, but he came home one day to find that she had left with another man. That was eleven years before the story begins.

As the man talks, the boy and Leo exchange glances, and Leo taunts the man, who seems not to notice. The man urgently explains to the boy that he has since made a science of love and he wants the boy to learn about it. For his first fifty years, he says, he thought he understood love, but when he was fifty-one and met the woman who would become his wife he found that he had not understood love until that moment. The feelings he had for the woman, whom he called Dodo, were new and powerful, and made him feel complete for the first time. They married only three days later. He was devastated when she left him and traveled across the country for two years looking for her in every city she had ever mentioned. He never saw her again. But in the third year, he explains, his memories of her

grew fainter, and although he often caught himself thinking of her at random moments, he could not call up her memory at will. He turned to liquor and fornication and other sins, but could not shake the feeling that his wife was chasing and tormenting him.

In the fifth year, he says, he found peace and began his science. On a rainy day in Portland he suddenly felt at peace as he came to a new understanding of love. According to his new theory, when a man loves for the first time, he should not try to love a woman, because this would be to start with the grandest and most difficult object of love. Instead, he says, men should start small; they should first love "A tree. A rock. A cloud." He began to find objects, take them home, and love them. He explains how he once loved a goldfish. Leo interrupts him, yelling "Shut up!" but the man continues telling his story. He says that he has been practicing his science for six years, and now he is able to love everything and everybody—except for a woman. He is not yet ready for that last step, he confesses. The man gets up and leaves the café, but not before he tells the boy one more time, "Remember I love you."

The boy does not know what to make of this encounter. He asks Leo if the man was drunk or on drugs, and Leo says no. Leo will not say whether or not he thinks the man is crazy. Not knowing what else to do, the boy concludes the story by saying, "He sure has done a lot of traveling."

CHARACTERS

The Boy

The boy, who is twelve years old and never named, enters the café to have coffee and warm up before he finishes delivering his newspapers. He is drawn into a one-sided conversation with the old man, who tells him about his science of love. The boy wears a leather jacket and an aviator cap, and he pulls one flap away from his ear when he enters the café. He is small and childlike and does not know how to respond to the old man's declaration of love or his story about finding his science. A few times, he looks to Leo or the men at the counter for help, but they only laugh at the old man and ignore the boy's pleading looks. The boy does not know how to handle this strange situation; he is uncomfortable with the man but does not understand what he is saying and does not wish to anger or hurt him. When the old man leaves, the boy sits quietly for a time before asking Leo if the man was drunk or on drugs or crazy, but Leo will not help him. Trying not to show his confusion, the boy fixes his cap and gets ready to leave, saying, "He sure has done a lot of traveling."

Dodo
Dodo is the name the old man called his wife, but it seems likely that this is not her real name. She was from Tulsa and claimed to be thirty, the man reports, and she married him three days after they met. According to the man's counting, she left him for another man after "one year, nine months, three days, and two nights."

Leo
Leo, the owner, cook, and server at the all-night streetcar café, is described as a "bitter and stingy man." He serves beer all night and breakfast in the morning, and although he has regular customers he does not chat with them in a friendly way. He does not offer free refills of coffee, and he is said to be stingier the longer he knows a customer. After refusing to pour the twelve-year-old boy a beer, as the man requests, Leo listens to the old man talking to the boy and occasionally interrupts with mocking comments about the man's story. He is busy throughout the old man's narration, fixing himself a bacon sandwich, pouring coffee, taking money. When the old man gets to the part of his story where he buys a goldfish, Leo shouts "Shut up!" at him and seems agitated through the rest of the story. Leo has run the café for fourteen years and is used to the crazy stories of the men who pass through; he refuses to help the boy understand the old man's story.

The Old Man
The old man, "with a big nose and faded orange hair," is sitting in a corner of the café nursing a beer when the boy comes in. He calls the boy over to him and tells the boy that he loves him. Most of the rest of the story is taken up with his telling the boy the story of his youth, his marriage, his abandonment by his wife, and his new-found science of love. He is so insistent about what he is saying that the boy thinks he must be drunk or crazy. The man was a railroad engineer, and was perhaps typical of a wandering

railroad man, until he fell in love with a woman when he was fifty-one years old. She left him after less than two years, and he has spent the eleven years since then searching—at first for the woman, and then for a scientific understanding of love. He believes he has now found it, and he is eager to share it with the boy. He tells the boy that the reason men are often unhappy is that they learn about love in the wrong order; instead of loving a woman first, a man should learn to love simpler things, such as "A tree. A rock. A cloud." This is the way to peace. When the man finishes telling the boy about his science, he again says that he loves him, and he leaves, looking old and frail but happy.

Soldiers
Among the men sitting at the counter of the café when the boy enters are two soldiers. They are not named and do not speak, except to join in the laughter when the old man tells the boy he loves him. The soldiers, who are drinking beer, pay and leave as the sun is coming up.

Spinners
As the boy enters the café, he notices three spinners siting at the counter eating their breakfast. Spinners are manual laborers at a cotton mill, and these three are regular customers at the café. They do not speak and are not named; one of them signals for a refill on his coffee while the old man is speaking. When the mill whistle blows for the beginning of the six o'clock shift, the three men leave.

THEMES

Love
Clearly, the main idea of the old man's long speech—and of the whole of "A Tree. A Rock. A Cloud"—is love, and how it can be lost and acquired. This comes up near the beginning of the story, when the old man calls the boy over, places his hand on his shoulder, and says, "I love you." Like the boy, the reader does not know what to make of this declaration, coming as it does from a man drinking a beer in the predawn hours, sitting alone and speaking to a young boy he does not know. But the man assures his listeners that he is serious, that what he is saying is important, that, for him, love "is a science."

TOPICS FOR FURTHER STUDY

- All of the characters in the café in "A Tree. A Rock. A Cloud" are male. How might the story be different if it were about a twelve-year-old girl coming into a café full of women? Write a script for an all-female version of the story. With a group of colleagues, do a reader's theater presentation of your play, or make a video.

- Research the work a spinner would have done in a textile mill in the 1930s or 1940s. Prepare a PowerPoint presentation with historical photos and share it with your class.

- Imagine the action of "A Tree. A Rock. A Cloud" as it might be narrated by one of the other characters in the story—perhaps Leo, or one of the soldiers or spinners. Write a monologue in your chosen character's voice as he tells his friends what occurred in the café.

- Read one of the recent young-adult novels that are set largely in diners or cafés: Newbery Honor Book *Hope Was Here* (2000), by Joan Bauer, Sarah Dessen's *Along for the Ride* (2009), or another book your teacher or librarian may suggest. Write an essay or a poem in which you explore the reasons all-night diners are attractive to lonely or isolated people, using what you have learned from your reading.

- Research some of the American artists who have painted scenes of diners or cafés, and lead your class in a discussion of whether the artists depict these settings in similar ways. You may want to consider Edward Hopper's paintings *Nighthawks* (1942) and *Automat* (1927), Norman Rockwell's paintings *The Runaway* (1958) and *After the Prom* (1957), Josh Ellingson's comic art *The Collaboration Diner* (2003), the photos of John Baeder, and other works. Compile your conclusions in an essay or a blog.

For the first fifty years of his life, the man says, he had a feeling "laying around loose" in him; although he had experienced many things, he had never truly loved. At fifty-one he met the woman who would become his wife, and looking back after studying his science for years he can still say, "I loved her. I thought also that she loved me." The fact that the old man says this early on in his story raises the expectation that his lesson is going to be about recognizing love, not about living it—it is his wife's love that is called into question here, not his own. He does not say, "I thought I loved her." The woman came into his life, and for the first time he felt complete: "Nothing lay around loose in me any more but was finished up by her." Is this love? Is this what the old man wants the boy to understand? When his wife left, he experienced his loss of her as "a kind of mania," followed by an emptiness, followed by a new kind of mania that turned him into a drinking and fornicating "sick mortal," followed by peace.

It was in this stage of peace that the man discovered his science. Over the next six years, he developed the idea that in order to experience "the most dangerous and sacred experience in God's earth," men should work their way up from loving small, uncomplicated things: "A tree. A rock. A cloud." A goldfish. A bird. A twelve-year-old boy in an all-night café. But although the old man calls himself "a master" after years of pursuing his science, and he experiences "a beautiful light" when he loves a bird or a stranger, he is "not quite ready yet" to love a woman again. One has to believe that the man, who must be nearing sixty-five years of age and who travels alone, never will experience that kind of love again, because he is not putting himself into a position to experience it. Still, as the man leaves the café, his last words to the boy are "Remember I love you."

Like any rational attempt to tackle human feeling, the old man's science of love raises more questions than it answers. His science seems to have brought him some peace after the sorrow and humiliation of being abandoned by the woman he loved, to give him a way to move through the day and feel connected to the world. But whether what he feels for the goldfish and the boy can properly be called love is a question that the boy, if not the reader, is too young to contemplate.

The paper boy goes into a streetcar cafe for a cup of coffee and meets the old man. *(© Jason Keith Heydorn /*
ShutterStock.com)

Isolation

If the old man in "A Tree. A Rock. A Cloud" is
searching for love, what he finds instead is isolation. In the world of this story, no one is truly
connected to anyone else. The young boy works
alone in the predawn hours, and although he often
finds some company in the café, on this particular
morning "Leo did not look into his face and none
of the men were talking." When the boy is greeted
by the old man he looks to the other men for
guidance in how to respond, but there is no help
from the men who "had gone back to their beer or
their breakfast and did not notice him." He is
alone in a room full of people. Leo, too, isolates
himself from even his regular customers, refusing
the traditional ways that café owners build familiarity and intimacy: the narrator comments that
"the better Leo knew his customers the stingier he
treated them." The old man was married once,
after years of not knowing love, but even during
his marriage, he says, he did not know his wife's

real age or realize that she was unsatisfied with
their life together. Afterward, wandering alone for
eleven years since his wife deserted him, he made a
"science" of isolation, calling it a science of love.
Just after his wife left, he tried to fill the empty
space inside him with the casual company of other
people ("I boozed. I fornicated."). But that period
was "terrible"; it was "miserable." Though he
would not formulate it this way himself, the old
man finally found what he calls the peace of "a
queer and beautiful blankness" by isolating himself from other people. He turns the force of his
feelings first toward inanimate objects like "A tree.
A rock. A cloud," and gradually works his way up
to a goldfish and then to people with whom he
does not really have to connect—"a street full of
people" or "a traveler on the road." In loving
"everything . . . and anybody" he is really loving
nothing and no one; only in remaining isolated,
in keeping the objects of his love as strangers, can
he find the peace that comes from not risking hurt.

The man's interaction with the boy is a clear example of what kind of connection this type of love offers, and it is no real connection at all. The man twice declares his love; he puts his hand on the boy's shoulder, and he explains his science as patiently as he can. But the boy does not understand a thing that the man says and can only conclude when the man is gone, "He sure has done a lot of traveling." The man and the boy wander into each other's lives, share a few minutes of conversation, and separate as isolated as they were before.

STYLE

Third-Person Point of View

A story's *point of view* refers to the vantage point from which the narrator presents information to the reader. In "A Tree. A Rock. A Cloud," the point of view is third person limited: *third person* because the narrator is outside the story, referring to all of the characters as "he" or "they," and *limited* because the narrator is limited in what she or he knows. (An omniscient narrator would know what all of the characters are thinking.) The narrator can see into the thoughts of only one character—the boy—and presents only a few small glimpses of even the boy's internal activity. Because of the story's third-person point of view, it is more difficult for a reader to know what to make of the old man's strange "science." Like a movie camera, the narrator presents the old man from outside; readers see his actions and hear his words, but do not know what the old man is thinking or if even he believes what he is saying. Leo, the café owner, clearly does not agree with or approve of the old man's "science," as he demonstrates with a series of angry exclamations and gestures. But readers do not know the reasons for Leo's reactions. Leo presents, in an oblique way, a challenge to the old man's words, but the narrator does not take sides; the narrative voice simply records what the characters say and do.

Only the boy is given something of an internal voice through the narrator's brief references to his reactions. For the most part, the narrator tells only what the boy says and does, but occasionally there is also a sense of the boy's thoughts and feelings. When the old man announces his love for the boy, the boy "shrank back uneasily" and "did not know what to do." As the old man tells his story, the narrator comments, "The boy did not know what to think of the man." At the end of the story, the boy makes "the only comment that seemed safe to him, the only remark that could not be laughed down and despised." If the narrator had commented likewise on the old man's motivation—or on his sanity or sobriety—it would have steered the reader toward a more solid interpretation of the man's "science." But because the story does not reveal anything of the man's internal life, nor of that of any adult character in the café, the reader is left only with the man's words and actions and with an understanding that these words are confusing to a twelve-year-old boy. The point of view helps the story leave open the question of whether the old man is wise or foolish—a central question of the story.

Setting

Setting refers to the time and place in which a story takes place. Depending on the story in question, setting might have a large or small effect on readers' understanding. "A Tree. A Rock. A Cloud" is set in an all-night café in a city in the American South. Cafés and diners—especially those that stay open all night—are places that have a special position in American literature and art, providing what another writer, Ernest Hemingway, referred to as a "clean, well-lighted place" where wandering and lonely people find small moments of comfort. In McCullers's story, Leo's café is a place of refuge for the old man, who has spent years traveling around the United States investigating his science of love. He seems to have no friends, no family, and nowhere he has to be. The boy is also drawn to the café: "After the raw, empty street, the café seemed friendly and bright." On a typical morning, the boy can find someone to greet him and chat with him there. It is the kind of place where strangers meet and share a few minutes of conversation and human contact. The location of the story is important: it is hard to imagine many others places where an old man and a twelve-year-old boy who do not know each other would find themselves together.

The story seems to be set in the early 1940s, when McCullers published it. The clues are the soldiers sitting at the counter, perhaps on leave from their duties in World War II; the spinners having breakfast before their shift at a nearby cotton mill, pointing to the days when the textile industry in the South was strong; and the boy's

COMPARE & CONTRAST

- **1940s:** The United States is involved in World War II in the first half of the decade. In 1945, the year the war ends, there are more than 12 million active-duty military personnel.

  Today: The United States is no longer fighting a war in Iraq and is winding down a war in Afghanistan that began in 2001. In September 2011, there are fewer than 1.5 million active-duty personnel.

- **1940s:** Hundreds of thousands of people hold jobs as spinners and do other types of work in textile mills across the southern United States.

  Today: Most of the textile mills in the southern United States have been shut down, as cheaper labor has driven most textile work to China, India, Mexico, and elsewhere.

- **1940s:** Teenage or preteen boys delivering newspapers on foot or on bicycles are a common sight in American cities and neighborhoods. A paper route is considered a good way for a boy to make money.

  Today: Instead of young boys, approximately 81 percent of America's newspaper carriers are adults who deliver the newspapers from their cars, according to the Associated Press.

occupation of newsboy and his aviator cap, both common in the 1940s. But the year the action takes place is less important to this story than its location. The story's focus is tightly on the old man and the boy, and there is little or nothing that they say to each other that could not be heard in the twenty-first century. People are still lonely, still searching for love, and children are still puzzled by the lessons their elders try to teach them. The café provides a place for these characters to come together, but once they meet their conversation is timeless.

Southern Writers and the Grotesque

McCullers was one of several prominent female writers in the American South during the middle of the twentieth century. Others included Harper Lee, Flannery O'Connor, Eudora Welty, Zora Neale Hurston, and Katherine Anne Porter. These writers are often discussed as a group, as their writing demonstrates some commonalities, including the use of southern dialect, an awareness of southern race relations, and clear southern settings. Another prominent feature of much of the work coming out of the midcentury South was the presence of strange characters, often with physical disabilities or deformities, who summoned up

feelings of both disgust and pity in readers. Fiction that featured these characters was commonly labeled "grotesque" or "gothic," and critics came to expect it, as Flannery O'Connor noted in her influential 1960 lecture "Some Aspects of the Grotesque in Southern Fiction." McCullers drew on this regional tradition, especially in her novels: *The Heart Is a Lonely Hunter* (1940) features a deaf-mute character and another who is unattractive and mentally ill; the protagonist in *Reflections in a Golden Eye* (1941) is impotent, sexually confused, and addicted to drugs. Writers of the grotesque believe that including these suffering or distorted characters—perpetual outsiders—makes it possible for fiction to more faithfully represent the world as it is.

McCullers clearly belongs to this group of southern writers when one considers her whole body of work, although "A Tree. A Rock. A Cloud," published the year after *Reflections in a Golden Eye*, does not highlight these similarities. Robert Phillips, in "Freaking Out: The Short Stories of Carson McCullers," argues that the author shaded her use of the grotesque in her short fiction, focusing on what she described as "spiritual isolation" rather than physical isolation. He writes, "For whatever reason, there is less physical abnormality in the stories. Instead of mutes and dwarfs, what we generally encounter here are people isolated by circumstances rather than physical appearance or malady." The character of the old man in "A Tree. A Rock. A Cloud" clearly fits into this group, a model for the way McCullers worked with an influential tradition while making the approach her own.

HISTORICAL CONTEXT

World War II

McCullers published "A Tree. A Rock. A Cloud" in *Harper's Bazaar* in 1942, while the United States was engaged in World War II. The conflict had begun in 1939, when France and Great Britain declared war on Germany after Germany invaded Poland, but the United States did not enter the expanding war until 1941, after the Japanese attacked the US naval base at Pearl Harbor, Hawaii. The United States fought alongside the Allied nations, including France, Great Britain, the Soviet Union, and many others; opposing them were the Axis powers, including Germany, Italy, and Japan. The conflict was truly global, fought across Europe and in the Pacific Ocean, in Asia, and in North Africa. By the time peace was declared in 1945, between fifty million and seventy million people worldwide had been killed as a result of the war, including more than four hundred thousand Americans. McCullers's husband, James Reeves McCullers, was an army corporal when they met in 1937, and he served in the Second Ranger Battalion in Europe during the war. In all, more than sixteen million Americans served in the military during the war, and soldiers on leave, such as the two sitting in Leo's café in the story, were a common sight in the country.

The American Literary Landscape

In many ways, the Second World War's impact on daily life was, for many Americans, surprisingly limited, especially in the beginning. This was so in large part because, other than the attack on Pearl Harbor, there was no fighting on US or Canadian soil. The midcentury urban landscape provided many opportunities for artists to interact and draw inspiration from each other, often ignoring the war, and although McCullers was a southerner to her core, during

The old man explains how he learned to love again, starting with little things like a goldfish.

(© Elena Sherengovskaya | ShutterStock.com)

the first half of the 1940s she spent most of her time in New York, completely immersed in the artistic scene there. She was an artist in residence at the prestigious Yaddo artists' retreat in Saratoga Springs, New York, at least five times, was a resident artist at the Bread Loaf Writers' Conference in Middlebury, Vermont, and won a 1942 Guggenheim Fellowship to support herself as she wrote. In New York City, she socialized with famous writers including Truman Capote and Tennessee Williams, and for a time she shared a large communal home with the writers Richard Wright and W. H. Auden, the striptease dancer Gypsy Rose Lee, and others. The house, called February House, was one of the most important gathering places for artists in New York. McCullers was often ill—sometimes seriously so—and always went back to Georgia to recover before returning to New York, where she was able to live a kind of passionate and profligate life she could never have lived in Columbus, Georgia.

Another feature of the midcentury literary landscape that influenced McCullers's success was the importance of the short story. Until the 1980s, many popular magazines, including the *New Yorker, Harper's Bazaar, Redbook, Mademoiselle, Saturday Evening Post,* and *Ladies' Home Journal* regularly published high-quality short fiction, and writers often rose to prominence—and earned book contracts for their novels—by having short stories published in influential magazines. Volumes of short stories, including McCullers's own *Ballad of the Sad Café* (1951), were published by popular presses and became best sellers. In 1951 and 1952, the NBC radio network ran a program called *NBC Presents: Short Story,* featuring half-hour adaptations of short stories by prominent writers. Toward the end of the century, after McCullers's career, the short story remained a proving ground for writers but became less important among readers. The *Saturday Evening Post, Colliers,* and other large-circulation magazines that had published short fiction at midcentury cut back or ceased publication, and major publishers found that it no longer made economic sense to release short-story collections by little-known writers. With a few notable exceptions, most of the short fiction published in the United States came to appear in small literary magazines or in collections issued by university or scholarly presses, reaching smaller audiences.

CRITICAL OVERVIEW

When "A Tree. A Rock. A Cloud" was published in 1942, McCullers was already a best-selling author. The story, appearing in the influential *Harper's Bazaar,* drew more attention than short stories often do, and it was included in the collection *O. Henry Memorial Award Prize Stories of 1942.* Early critical analysis of the story focused on noting similarities between the story and other works, including McCullers's own novels. Frank Baldanza, in a 1958 article in the *Georgia Review,* compares the story to Ernest Hemingway's "The Killers." In his 1966 critical biography *The Ballad of Carson McCullers,* Oliver Evans gives an extensive analysis in which he compares the story to another work by Hemingway, "The Snows of Kilimanjaro," before concluding that "the most perfect analogue" to the story is Samuel Taylor Coleridge's 1798 poem "The Rime of the Ancient Mariner."

"The theme of both," he writes, "is salvation through love." An extended essay on this idea appeared in 1975 in the *South Central Bulletin,* in which Mary Dell Fletcher treats the short story as an updated version of Coleridge's poem. Unlike the ancient mariner, she writes, the old man in McCullers's story does not "end on a note of hope" but rather tries "to explain the nature of love to a world that is embarrassed by such emotions and which feels far safer in negating them." From 1978, in an essay appearing in the *Southwest Review,* Robert Phillips also notes that the old man resembles Coleridge's famous character. Phillips writes, "Like Coleridge's ancient mariner, [the old man] is forever having to unburden himself upon strangers." Margaret B. McDowell, author of the Twayne volume on McCullers, is representative of those who find McCullers working out in her short fiction ideas she also develops elsewhere. McDowell sees "A Tree. A Rock. A Cloud" as an attempt to wrestle with the same themes as she does in her poem "The Twisted Trinity"; other critics see echoes of the story in *The Ballad of the Sad Café.*

Most critics, including Phillips, have taken the old man's lessons about love at face value, accepting his words as an articulation of the author's own beliefs. For Evans, the lesson of the story "is that there is a science of love which can be learned." But Virginia Spencer Carr observes in *Understanding Carson McCullers* that the old man's "sterile formula has led him to love things that cannot love back." She concludes, "The reader feels intuitively that the dissolute tramp will never be ready for the final step" in his own plan to experience real love. This is also McDowell's view. She writes that "the encounter provides no indication that the tramp has learned to love, to see the need for commitment to another person, or to inspire love."

By the late twentieth century, McCullers's reputation had faded. Several of her short stories, including "A Tree. A Rock. A Cloud," were frequently included in high-school anthologies and curricula, but critics and the book-buying public had largely moved on. In 1987, Michiko Kakutani reviewed a new edition of the short stories for the *New York Times,* remarking that "one is struck by just how old-fashioned most of them are." Joyce Carol Oates, in a 1999 review for the *London Review of Books,* notes McCullers's declining reputation, observing that

"McCullers may be perceived in some quarters as a writer of young adult classics whose work has not transcended its era." And in the words of Elizabeth Bennett, reviewing a new biography of McCullers for the *Pittsburgh Post-Gazette* in 2001, McCullers has become "a once-famous literary figure often dismissed today as a minor regional writer." Nonetheless, in 2004 McCullers's novel *The Heart Is a Lonely Hunter* (1940) was chosen by Oprah Winfrey as an Oprah's Book Club selection.

CRITICISM

Cynthia A. Bily

Bily teaches English at Macomb Community College in Michigan. In the following essay, she explores a contrarian view of the character Leo in "A Tree. A Rock. A Cloud."

The most prolific speaker in "A Tree. A Rock. A Cloud" is, of course, the old man, who describes for a twelve-year-old newsboy his science of love. The story is nearly a dramatic monologue; in a story running just over 3,200 words, the old man speaks more than 1,200 of them, telling the boy the story of his search first for his runaway wife and then for a way to understand and experience love. The boy often responds to the man's questions and prompts with one-word answers like "Dead?" or "Huh?" or "No." He speaks twenty times, for a total of only ninety words. The third important character in the story is Leo, owner of the all-night café, who is not part of the conversation between the old man and the boy but who interrupts the old man's story frequently to challenge or mock it. As the boy and Leo listen to the man's story, their responses inform the reader's attitude toward the man. Does Carson McCullers present the man's science as wise and profound or as sad and drunken nonsense? The answer is found in the responses of the boy and of Leo. Of the three characters at the heart of the story, Leo is the only one with a clear vision, and what he sees is the emptiness of the old man's "science."

Throughout the story, the narrator emphasizes the boy's innocence and naivety. The boy is only twelve; he has a "pink little ear" and "round child eyes"; he wears an aviator cap to look like a war hero. As the man speaks, the boy does not know how to respond; he does "not know what to do." He stares at the man's photograph, but

> LEO MAY BE ANGRY, BUT HE IS STEADY, RELIABLE; THE BOY KNOWS WHAT LEO IS AND COUNTS ON HIM—OR WANTS TO COUNT ON HIM."

there is nothing to see. He hears the man "uneasily" and "cautiously," and he wants to leave, but there is something about the old man "that held the boy and would not let him go away." "The boy did not know what to think of the man," the narrator says, "and his child's face was uncertain with mingled curiosity and doubt." Nearly every question the boys asks, nearly every guess he makes, is wrongheaded: the man's wife is not dead; her name, says the man, "is immaterial"; it is immaterial to the man what part of the country he was in when he lived through his lowest period. The boy's last words—the last line of the story—show that he has not understood anything the man has been getting at: "He sure has done a lot of traveling."

The innocent boy knows that he is out of his depth in this encounter, and he frequently looks to Leo for guidance (as readers might be wise to do also). That is part of the reason he comes into the café in the first place. Even though Leo is introduced as "a bitter and stingy man," he is a source of comfort to the boy. The café itself seems "friendly and bright," and the narrator points out the rarity when "this morning Leo did not look into his face." The boy's first reaction when the old man says "I love you" is to look "over the counter at Leo," and as the man continues his story the boy tries to catch Leo's eye. But Leo turns away, and what follows is a subtle struggle between the old man and Leo over the boy.

While Leo does not look at the boy, the old man "grasped the boy's chin and turned his face slowly from one side to the other" before announcing his love, and as he tells his story, "the man did not take his eyes from the boy's face." The old man wants to buy a beer for the boy; Leo pours coffee instead and curtly tells the man, "He is a minor." Leo interrupts the man's story several times—always speaking to the man, not to the boy—and the man tells him, "I was not speaking to you." Turning back to the boy he

WHAT DO I READ NEXT?

- The novella *The Ballad of the Sad Café* (1951), by McCullers, is the story of Miss Amelia, a woman in a small southern town who turns her father's store into a café after she meets a strange man claiming to be her cousin. In its exploration of loneliness and love, this novella is often paired with "A Tree. A Rock. A Cloud" in critics' discussions of the author's style and thematic concerns.

- The main character of McCullers's novel *The Member of the Wedding* (1946) is Frankie, a twelve-year-old girl who is unsure of her place in the world. Her mother has died, her father is emotionally unavailable, and her older brother is about to be married, leaving Frankie lonely and confused. She has no one to feel close to except the family's African American housekeeper and her six-year-old cousin. *The Member of the Wedding* was adapted as a play by McCullers for production in 1950, and the play version is also available in many libraries.

- *The Signet Classic Book of Southern Short Stories* (1991), edited by Dorothy Abbott and Susan Koppelman, collects thirty-four stories created by important writers from the American South between 1829 and 1973.

Writers include McCullers and contemporaries Flannery O'Connor, Truman Capote, Eudora Welty, and Ernest J. Gaines.

- Christopher Paul Curtis's young-adult novel *Bud, Not Buddy* (2000) depicts a ten-year-old African American orphan living in Flint, Michigan, in 1936. Like the young boy in "A Tree. A Rock. A Cloud," Bud is alone in a world in which adults—in Bud's case, a group of traveling musicians—are both attractive and mystifying.

- *Sacred Groves and Ravaged Gardens: The Fiction of Eudora Welty, Carson McCullers, and Flannery O'Connor* (1985), by Louise Hutchings Westling, examines how McCullers and two other women writers from the American South drew on and rejected the roles traditionally given to women in southern culture.

- Roger Scruton's *Spinoza: A Very Short Introduction* (2002) is, as the title suggests, a brief and accessible introduction to the Jewish Dutch philosopher Baruch Spinoza (1632–1677), whose ideas about love, solitude, and nature were important to McCullers.

---

says, "Let's not pay any attention to him, O.K.?" Leo interrupts again, and the man says again, "Don't listen to him." At the next interruption the man waves his hand "as though fanning away flies" and keeps his eyes "concentrated and fixed on the shallow little face of the paper boy." The two men compete for the boy's attention, while the boy is trapped between them, "small and listening and still." Finally, the old man grabs the boy "by the collar of his leather jacket" and holds on until the boy breaks the spell by asking, "Have you fallen in love with a woman again?" At this question, the man lets go of the boy's collar,

turns his face away, and departs, leaving the boy and Leo alone.

What, as the critic Oliver Evans asks, is the role of Leo in this story? For Evans, the answer is clear:

> That he is intended as a foil to the tramp is obvious enough, so that we associate him with the principle of hatred rather than of love. It is no accident that he is "stingy"; his penury contrasts with the lavishness of the tramp's love—while the latter "can love anything," Leo can love nothing. That is why he is "bitter," whereas the tramp seems "very happy."

Similarly, Robert Phillips argues that Leo's reactions highlight the wisdom of the old man's science. Phillips explains,

> That McCullers sides with him [the old man] is made clear by the actions she attributes to Leo, the café owner. Leo not only treats his regular customers stingily, but also does not love himself enough to nourish his body adequately. He grudges himself a bun.

Both critics argue that Leo's unpleasant and rude behavior demonstrates that he lacks the human feeling that would enable him to understand the old man's ideas; he is rude and angry, and therefore a poor judge of what it takes to love and be loved.

But there is another way to look at Leo, especially as he relates to the boy. He may be "bitter and stingy," but he does run a business that puts him in daily contact with down-and-out folks, and Leo's café is "friendly and bright." He is gruff with his regular customers, but he does *have* regular customers, who ask for refills that they know will not be free, and who perhaps know that Leo's bark is the meanest thing about him. Phillips makes a good point when he says that Leo is "bitter," but he is not completely correct to call the old man "very happy." At the beginning and the end of the story the man is said to look happy, but in between he is described as "serious and sad," "sad," "excited," "bright and tremulous and old," "grave," "earnest and bright and wild," and "shrunken and seedy and frail." There may be flashes of happiness, but they are impermanent, not rising from a place of love or deep understanding. And, of course, the man has never dared love a woman since Dodo. Leo may be angry, but he is steady, reliable; the boy knows what Leo is and counts on him—or wants to count on him.

Leo, in turn, wants to protect the boy from the man's foolishness. But he is a man with a reputation to protect, and he cannot be seen showing tenderness or concern in front of his regular customers. He looks after the boy in the only way he can: by making sarcastic and rude comments to disrupt the man's story, and to help the clueless boy see through the man's wishful thinking. Leo's diction in his outbursts is hard to pin down. Sometimes he seems more formal than one would expect ("Prominent transient drowns in beer"), while at other times he uses colorful slang ("floozie," "frazzled old rascal," "draggle-tailed old Romeo"). This artificiality underscores that the interruptions are calculated, that Leo is aware of how he sounds to the man, to the boy, and to the other customers. His anger increases as the man's story goes on, but Leo is unwilling to show his anger, other than the moment when he "balled up a dishcloth he was holding and threw it down hard on the floor."

Only when the cotton spinners and the soldiers leave, and Leo, the man, and the boy are alone, is Leo free to show how he really feels about the old man's attempts to take control of the boy. "'Aw shut up!' screamed Leo suddenly. 'Shut up! Shut up!'" Why does he suddenly react with such ferocity? Evans explains the outburst as

> a cry of rage. Had he thought the tramp's claim merely an idle boast, he would not have expressed himself so strongly. It is not because he doubts the tramp's story but because he believes it that he reacts as he does.

But while the man's story is probably true, the science is clearly not—the man's story does not demonstrate the path to understanding or experiencing love. And Leo is not a man to be taken in by such shallow revelations. "Leo had run a night café for fourteen years," the narrator points out, "and he held himself to be a critic of craziness. There were the town characters and also the transients who roamed in from the night. He knew the manias of all of them." Leo can see what McCullers wants the reader to see: that for all his talk of science and love, the old man is alone, sad, giving his love to trees, rocks, clouds, goldfish, and twelve-year-old boys, none of whom return his love or even understand a thing that he says.

Leo finally shouts at the old man because he has been bottling up his anger and jealousy since the man began drawing the boy in, but he was not about to show it in front of the others. Leo is fond of the boy and resented losing him, even for a short while, to the old man—an echo of the man's losing his wife to another man. Like the old man, Leo has limits to how great a risk he is willing to take. The old man is "not quite ready yet" to risk loving a woman; Leo is not able to show honest affection for the boy. Unlike the old man, though, Leo is able to feel a kind of love for the boy and to intercede for him; Leo does not dedicate his energy to loving inanimate objects, but to running a café, a refuge from the "mild, gray, endless rain."

Leo, the bitter owner of the café, constantly interrupts the conversation. (© *Warren Goldswain / ShutterStock.com*)

The old man's departure does not immediately restore harmony between Leo and the boy. The boy thinks quietly, and when he speaks again it is "without looking at Leo." Leo does not give him the answers he wants, and the boy finally does look up, "and his flat little face was desperate, his voice urgent and shrill." Still Leo will not reach out to the boy. Instead of answering his questions, he "tightened his pale face and was silent." And now the boy demonstrates that he has learned a lesson from the old man and from Leo—he has learned to play it safe. Not sure what to say next, "he made the only comment that seemed safe to him, the only remark that could not be laughed down and despised." Leo and the old man have shown the boy two approaches to life. Which approach is better? Is it better to love as the old man does, with brief flashes of happiness when he tells complete strangers that he loves them? Or is it better to be like Leo, angry and rude but surrounded every day by a small community of regulars? The boy is only twelve, and he will have many more opportunities to observe and think about what kind of man he wants to become.

Source: Cynthia A. Bily, Critical Essay on "A Tree. A Rock. A Cloud," in *Short Stories for Students*, Gale, Cengage Learning, 2014.

Jan Whitt

In the following excerpt, Whitt describes McCullers as a southern writer who instills her work with a strong sense of place.

. . . The literature of the South is, of course, especially rich in its suggestion that place matters; that it may be possible to come home again; that whether one flees to New York, as did Carson McCullers, or locates oneself in the community in which one grew up, as did Flannery O'Connor and Eudora Welty, one's geographic center matters very much indeed.

Since this collection is designed not only for the scholars who read voraciously and who seek to pass along to their students a love of narrative but also for readers outside academia who value literature, this introduction is just that: an introduction to the life and work of Carson McCullers. Camera in hand, I once traveled with my husband, a devotee of Southern literature, to

> WHAT THE READER OF MCCULLERS' WORK REMEMBERS IS THE POWER OF A REGION CHARACTERIZED BY A BELIEF IN THE HETEROSEXUAL NUCLEAR FAMILY, A RELIANCE ON RELIGION, THE RUGGED INDIVIDUALITY BORN OF AN AGRARIAN ECONOMY, AND THE MEMORY OF THE CIVIL WAR AND OF AN END TO SLAVERY."

meet McCullers biographer Virginia Spencer Carr in Atlanta before making our way to Columbus, Georgia, McCullers' birthplace. We wandered through the Linwood Cemetery; stood reverently outside 1519 Stark Avenue, McCullers' childhood home; found the home of the "Mother of the Blues," Gertrude Pridgett ("Ma") Rainey; remembered as we walked past the First Baptist Church that McCullers attended services there at her grandmother's insistence; saw the old Columbus Public Library where McCullers first read the classics; sat in the gazebo on the playground of Wynnton School and walked up the front steps of Columbus High School; and stood outside the *Columbus Ledger-Enquirer* newspaper building, where McCullers had an internship in 1935. Not long afterwards on an October morning, I traveled to McCullers' grave site in Nyack, New York, and sat in the leaves in the cemetery overlooking the Hudson River, as many others have done.

For those who love Southern literature, these are not minor reminiscences. A sense of place both grounds and torments Southern writers from William Faulkner to William Styron to Robert Penn Warren to Thomas Wolfe. Regionalism is not optional. To better understand McCullers, one need only travel to Georgia on a sultry summer day and wander through downtown or through a local mill or cross a bridge into Phenix City, Alabama.

Georgia is a region McCullers both longed for and avoided. She was born in Columbus, Georgia, Feb. 19, 1917, the daughter of Lamar and Marguerite Smith. The ambivalence she felt toward her homeland is revealed in "The Flowering Dream: Notes on Writing": "People ask me why I don't go back to the South more often. But the South is a very emotional experience for me, fraught with all the memories of my childhood. When I go back South I always get into arguments, so that a visit to Columbus in Georgia is a stirring up of love and antagonism" (*Mortgaged*). McCullers even once told a friend that she needed to "go home periodically to renew [her] sense of horror" (*Collected*).

Yet McCullers often spoke lovingly and tenderly of Georgia summers and childhood Christmas seasons, and she was heir to a rich and dramatic regional history that enlivened her fiction. "Down in the South it will be early evening," she reminisced during a New Year's Eve in London. "Quiet, orange firelight will flicker on kitchen walls, and in the cupboards there will be the hog-jowl and the black-eyed peas to bring good fortune in the coming year" (*Mortgaged*). In "How I Began to Write," McCullers describes the sitting-rooms of her "old Georgia home" in which she and her brother and sister performed homemade dramatic productions: "In summertime the rooms were stifling until the time for curtain, and the clock was silenced by sounds of yard-boy whistling and distant radios" (*Mortgaged*).

McCullers may often have fled the South, but as she wrote, "the voices reheard from childhood have a truer pitch" (*Mortgaged*), and as a child she explored the Georgia woods and imagined stories while sitting under an awning of trees beside her home. Although McCullers was quick to remember the "vacant, broiling" afternoons of August and quick to describe the "heat-shimmered air" (*Mortgaged*), she drew on locale in all her novels. "When I work from within a different locale from the South," McCullers wrote, "I have to wonder what time the flowers are in bloom—and what flowers?" (*Mortgaged*).

Today, the Chattahoochee River still winds through Columbus, Georgia, beside the old mill buildings, some of which are being converted into residential lofts. Downtown slumbers during summer afternoons, traffic edging down the streets. Columbus is changed from the days when McCullers roamed its streets or crossed the bridge into Phenix City, Alabama, also known alluringly as "Sin City." For example, the downtown area has a riverwalk, a performing arts center, and bustling nightlife. Columbus State University has moved its art, theater, and music complex to downtown, making it a popular place for college students.

Although Columbus was idyllic and secure for the novelist often in her career, thoughts of New York City provided an adolescent McCullers with an escape from the dreary dullness of her early Georgia days. "I longed for wanderings," McCullers wrote. "I longed especially for New York. The firelight on the walnut folding doors would sadden me, and the tedious sound of the old swan clock. I dreamed of the distant city of skyscrapers and snow" (*Mortgaged*). Descriptions of small-town Southern life appear in much of McCullers' fiction, including *The Ballad of the Sad Café* and *The Member of the Wedding*. "There is absolutely nothing to do in the town," writes McCullers in *The Ballad of the Sad Café*. "Walk around the millpond, stand kicking at a rotten stump, figure out what you can do with the old wagon wheel by the side of the road near the church. The soul rots with boredom."

McCullers loved the cold and snow of the North; no wonder, then, that she describes Southern cotton mill towns as "dreary," their "summers white with glare and fiery hot" (*Ballad*). In *The Member of the Wedding*, McCullers records the thoughts of her young protagonist, Frankie: "The long and flowering spring was over and the summer in the town was ugly and lonesome and very hot. Every day she wanted more and more to leave the town: to light out for South America or Hollywood or New York City" (*Member*). Even though Frankie, 12, wants to "tear down this whole town" (*Member*), ultimately, she cannot escape it. When McCullers describes Frankie's longings, she, of course, reveals her own. "But although she packed her suitcases many times," McCullers writes, "she could never decide to which of these places she ought to go, or how she would get there by herself" (*Member*).

The poverty and racism of Georgia during McCullers' youth seemed to McCullers incongruous with the affluence of many white town leaders and with the prevalent religious beliefs of the region, respectively, and McCullers battled many of the attitudes that were a part of the fabric of Columbus life. Christian ministers proclaimed human equality and the unmerited love of God, but the founding families of Columbus often upheld a class system and promoted racial hatred. In her essay "The Russian Realists

and Southern Literature," McCullers analyzes Southern society and its "spiritual inconsistencies." She writes: "The 'cruelty' of which the Southerners have been accused is at bottom only a sort of naiveté, an acceptance of spiritual inconsistencies without asking the reason why, without attempting to propose an answer. Undeniably, there is an infantile quality about this clarity of vision and rejection of responsibility" (*Mortgaged*).

Compassion for the millworkers of her hometown poured out of McCullers' pen in *The Heart Is a Lonely Hunter*. She knew too well the affluence and apathy of many of the wealthy families in neighborhoods near her home. The poverty and desperation that McCullers saw in the townspeople exist today—as they do in towns and metropolitan areas across America—and hopelessness tinges the words of the unemployed who sit on their front porches or walk along dirt streets pushing grocery carts filled with their belongings.

Although McCullers felt smothered by her homeland and fled repeatedly to New York, she was influenced by Southern custom and was weaned on Southern attitudes. Graced with a Southern name, Lula Carson Smith, McCullers revealed small-town Southern living with all its Protestant shadowings in her novels and short stories. The racism and economic inequality of Columbus affected her all her life, and the early Protestant education McCullers received through the First Baptist Church of Columbus appears often in the fictional worlds she created.

What the reader of McCullers' work remembers is the power of a region characterized by a belief in the heterosexual nuclear family, a reliance on religion, the rugged individuality born of an agrarian economy, and the memory of the Civil War and of an end to slavery. Although to live in the South for McCullers and her characters might be to "rot in boredom," there was "ever an ambivalent pull, for home was also a balm that soothed, healed, enveloped, protected," writes Carr.

McCullers the writer never entirely left the people and the locale she knew best. Whether she described the terrain; the soldiers of nearby Fort Benning, Georgia; or the mind of an adolescent, McCullers relied on what she understood about the South she loved and hated. She exchanged the provincial people with whom she grew up for the cosmopolitan, artistic people of New York; she traded the anonymity of Columbus for the excitement of friendships with the famous. She associated with Edward Albee, W. H. Auden, Leonard Bernstein, Elizabeth Bowen, Truman Capote, Aaron Copeland, Salvador Dali, Isak Dinesen, Gypsy Rose Lee, Marilyn Monroe, Edith Sitwell, Tennessee Williams, and others. But in spite of the New York life she made for herself, McCullers remained a native of Columbus, married twice to a Southerner, Reeves McCullers of Alabama. She wrote of the climate, landmarks, and mindset of Georgia. A Southern expatriate, McCullers inherited many of the attitudes, beliefs, and dreams that were born in her earlier home.

McCullers described humankind as exiled heirs in "Father, Upon Thy Image We Are Spanned." Drawing upon her religious training, she identified men and women as descendents of Adam and Eve, banished from the Garden of Eden. McCullers deliberately exiled herself from the South, although she continued to love her homeland—often against her will. . . .

Source: Jan Whitt, ed., "The Exiled Heir: An Introduction to Carson McCullers and Her Work," in *Reflections in a Critical Eye: Essays on Carson McCullers*, University Press of America, 2008, pp. xiv–xviii.

Robert Phillips

In the following excerpt, Phillips examines how McCullers uses freakish characters to illustrate social isolation.

The work of Carson McCullers is whole cloth. Few writers have maintained such a consistent vision. Moreover, few writers have such a clear conception of their preoccupations and themes. In "The Flowering Dream: Notes on Writing" (included in *The Mortgaged Heart*, edited by Margarita G. Smith) McCullers wrote:

> Spiritual isolation is the basis of most of my themes. My first book was concerned with this, almost entirely, and all of my books since, in one way or another. Love, and especially love of a person who is incapable of receiving it, is at the heart of my selection of grotesque figures to write about—people whose physical incapacity is a symbol of their spiritual incapacity to love or receive love—their spiritual isolation.

There, in one paragraph, McCullers answered satisfactorily all the queries raised concerning *why* in her novels she wrote almost exclusively of grotesques. Elsewhere, in "A Personal Preface"

> THIS INABILITY TO ADJUST TO PHYSICAL CHANGE SIGNALS A STATE OF SPIRITUAL ISOLATION IN SEVERAL OF THE BEST STORIES BY MCCULLERS, INCLUDING 'THE SOJOURNER' AND 'A TREE. A ROCK. A CLOUD,' AS WELL AS THE MORE SUPERFICIAL 'ART AND MR. MAHONEY.'"

to her second play, *The Square Root of Wonderful*, she again stated, "I suppose my central theme is the theme of spiritual isolation. Certainly I have always felt alone."

Now if we take the lady at her word, and I believe we should, this theme of spiritual isolation is the cornerstone to her house of fiction. One of the smallest rooms of that house is the region of her short stories. While there already is a considerable body of criticism concerning her four novels and the fifth novella, very little has been said about her shorter fiction—particularly the fourteen stories published in the posthumous collection, *The Mortgaged Heart*. Which is a pity, because of the total of nineteen stories to be found there and in the earlier omnibus collection, *The Ballad of the Sad Café*, several are quite superb fiction. Certainly all are typical McCullers, with this exception: they are all less likely to be labeled "Gothic" or "grotesque" when compared to her novels. For whatever reason, there is less physical abnormality in the stories. Instead of mutes and dwarfs, what we generally encounter here are people isolated by circumstance rather than physical appearance or malady. Instead of freaks we find an inner freaking-out.

What does Carson McCullers mean by "spiritual isolation"? I have taken the phrase to mean, simply, personal dissociation—the feeling of being severed from society, disunited from others, lonely, separate, different, apart. Certainly that state characterizes Frankie Addams of *The Member of the Wedding*, one of McCullers's more "normal" characters, just as it does Cousin Lymon of the *Ballad*, a more "abnormal" one. Obviously the term "spiritual isolation" applies to the freaked-out as well as to the freaks.

. . . Bridging the generation gap between the author's younger and older short story protagonists is the eighteen-year-old university student in the early tale "Court in the West Eighties." This is a character who neither acts nor is acted upon, but merely records the scenes about her in an apartment house which serves as a microcosm of the macrocosm. She seems to make a God figure of one inhabitant, a serene, red-headed man: "The sun made a haze of light around his bright hair that was almost like a sort of halo." He is perhaps an early precursor of John Singer of *The Heart Is a Lonely Hunter*. He is also a demiurge, looking on unfeelingly while a young jobless couple living across the court slowly starve. McCullers injects a potent symbol into the story in the form of a balloon man—that is, a man made of balloons, bearing a silly grin and hanging perpetually from one apartment window. He is an effigy mocking mankind and man's helplessness. In the world of McCullers's imagination we are all dangling, hanged men.

In McCullers's stories portraying adults confronting adult problems—or rather not confronting them, since most either freak out or flee the situation rather than face it—the characters are occasionally absolutely normal in appearance. Later, however, they are rendered symbolically grotesque, as in "Instant of the Hour After," a mood piece in which a young married couple's love for one another is inexplicably destroying them. In the story's chief symbol they are seen as two figures in a bottle—small, perfect, yet white and exhausted, like "fleshly specimens in a laboratory." This image is quite akin to that of the pickled fetus in "The Orphanage." The story also predates the conflict of the later and vastly superior "A Domestic Dilemma."

In "A Domestic Dilemma," the isolated character is a housewife, physically transplanted from Alabama to New York. Unable to adjust to the changes involved in the move or to make friends, she seeks escape through drinking. Without the artifice of alcohol her interior life is insufficient. Just as the son in "The Haunted Boy" lives in fear that his crazy mother may again harm herself, so too this suburban housewife's husband is haunted by her earlier drunken accident with one of the children and by the possibility that it could happen again. A threat of undefined disaster underlies his days. Far worse is his fear that her daily drunken behavior is causing invisible psychic damage to the two children—damage which can only increase as the immunity of incomprehension passes. In this, my personal favorite of her shorter fiction, McCullers explores love/hate relationships in marriage and what she calls "the immense complexity of love."

This inability to adjust to physical change signals a state of spiritual isolation in several of the best stories by McCullers, including "The Sojourner" and "A Tree. A Rock. A Cloud," as well as the more superficial "Art and Mr. Mahoney."

"The Sojourner" is a meditation on what McCullers terms "the improvisation of human existence." Some people adjust to life's variations, some do not. John Ferris, this story's protagonist, has not adjusted to the anxieties of transience and solitude brought about by his divorce. On the other hand, his former wife has adjusted, and he makes the discovery of his own emotional poverty during a visit to her and her new family. It is as traumatic for him as the *wunderkind*'s discovery of her own shortcomings. He perceives immediately that his ex-wife has created a rich new life for herself, with two children and a second husband. He, by contrast, has put down no roots. Recently even his father has died, reminding him of wasted years and death, cancelling out the past in a life which has no present or future. Physically he is an expatriate from America; emotionally he is an expatriate from the human heart. At the end he is vowing to reach out, to create a meaningful relationship with his mistress's son, an act he may or may not be able to accomplish.

The disintegration of a marriage also creates another dis-integrated soul in "A Tree. A Rock. A Cloud." The story relates the encounter in a café of a twelve-year-old boy and an old cuckold. It is not so much a plotted story as the plodded meditations of the old man on the nature of love—surely one of Mrs. McCullers's favorite topics. Love here is expounded as a condition which must be achieved through small steps. Rather than presuming to begin one's love life with a woman—what the old man (and McCullers) calls "the most dangerous and sacred experience in God's earth"—we should instead begin in very small ways, loving tiny inanimate objects first: a tree, a rock, a cloud. Only when we can relate to the minimal can we hope to possess the maximal.

That the old man's experience of losing his wife has stunted him emotionally is undeniable. His science of love can be taken as mere justification of his remaining womanless. Like Coleridge's ancient mariner, he is forever having to unburden himself upon strangers. But there is something more to be said for his love-science. That McCullers sides with him is made clear by the actions she attributes to Leo, the café owner. Leo not only treats his regular customers stingily, but also does not love himself enough to nourish his body adequately. He grudges himself a bun. But then, in McCullers's love affairs, everyone seems to be grudging their buns.

The twelve-year-old paperboy listener, drinking his coffee in a café of adults drinking their beer, is another McCullers alien. He is as out of his element in the café as Ferris is in Paris. The paperboy is further endowed with a physical difference. One shoulder is lower than the other, from the weight of the paper sack. This qualifies him as a freak in a café which prefigures Miss Amelia's place, in the *Ballad*, as a place of fellowship and understanding. . . .

Source: Robert Phillips, "Freaking Out: The Short Stories of Carson McCullers," in *Critical Essays on Carson McCullers*, edited by Beverly Lyon Clark and Melvin J. Friedman, G. K. Hall, 1996, pp. 172–77.

Virginia Spencer Carr
In the following excerpt, Carr discusses aspects of McCullers's fiction, including how she portrays unrequited love throughout much of her work.

McCullers was a much-acclaimed author and playwright both in America and abroad when her omnibus edition, *"The Ballad of the Sad Café": The Novels and Short Stories of Carson McCullers*, appeared a few weeks after *The Member of the Wedding* closed its long and successful run on Broadway. Although all of the stories (with the exception of "A Domestic Dilemma") had appeared in such magazines as the *New Yorker*, *Mademoiselle*, and *Harper's Bazaar*, they had never before been brought together in a single volume. Thus, with her three novels, a novella, and six short stories published in a single volume, McCullers was able to reach new readers. Reviewers and scholars alike praised her mastery of the short story and continued to commend her skill as a novelist.

. . . In tale after tale, regardless of its date of composition, the conflicts depicted by McCullers are intensified by the "immense complexity of love," a phrase that the author coined for one of her most successful short stories, "A Domestic Dilemma." Such love may be between a husband and his wife, an adolescent piano pupil and her teacher, a simple boy and a male cousin he idolizes, a "haunted" youth and his suicidal mother, a seemingly indifferent mother and her tubercular daughter, a jockey and his injured friend, a young girl "in love with a wedding" (or enamored of a Brazilian pen pal who never writes back), an Amazonian woman and a hunchback dwarf, and countless other fictional potential conjoinings that never quite materialize. Most of the latent love relationships in McCullers's short fiction never reach maturity, and for good reason. As her narrator expressed it in *The Ballad of the Sad Café* (and evident, as well, throughout her writings), "The value and quality of any love is determined solely by the lover himself," and such myopic vision by its very nature destines one's love to go unnoticed or bitterly unrequited.

To McCullers, a lover was always vulnerable unless he loved someone—or some thing—from whom he expected nothing in return. In "A Tree. A Rock. A Cloud," a beery tramp confides to a pink-eared newspaper boy, a stranger to him, his "science of love," which he conceived after being abandoned by his wife. The tramp's sterile formula has led him to love things that cannot love back—first, a goldfish, then a tree, a rock, a cloud. But he invites the catcalls of mill workers in the all-night café in which he accosts the child and tells him: "Son! Hey Son! . . . I love you." Despite his declaration, the tramp knows that he can walk out alone into the predawn silence and never see his so-called "beloved" again. Loving a woman is the "last step" to his science, he tells the boy. "I go cautious. And I am not quite ready yet." The reader feels intuitively that the dissolute tramp will never be ready for the final step. He will not risk again his vulnerability to *eros*.

Whereas all of McCullers's novels are set in the South, only six of her short stories—"A Tree. A Rock. A Cloud," "Art and Mr. Mahoney," "The Haunted Boy," "The March," and two apprentice pieces, "Breath from the Sky" and "The Aliens"—make such a setting explicit. At least ten of her stories have obvious settings in the North, and three of her earliest stories ("Sucker," "Like That," and "The Orphanage") have settings that could be anywhere (although the characters, dialogue, and events offer a kind of southern authenticity to the setting, which could well be McCullers's hometown in Georgia or the fictional towns in which *The Heart Is a Lonely Hunter* and *The Member of the Wedding* are set). Her characters who do, in fact, live in the North are often transplanted southerners whose home region remains a memory of pain and anguish.

Despite the acclaim of McCullers's short fiction over the years, little criticism was devoted to the work as a whole until 1978, when Robert Phillips's excellent critical discussion, "Freaking Out: The Short Stories of Carson McCullers" added a new dimension to McCullers scholarship. Phillips demonstrated that most of the characters in her short stories behave quite normally on the surface, yet suffer an "inner freaking-out." Though they exhibit none of the vagaries or physical grotesqueries common to the characters in her longer works, they are immobilized as "spiritual isolates of circumstance."

Another significant characteristic unique to the short stories is the way in which McCullers transformed her personal reality into fiction. Whereas readers who know something of McCullers's girlhood in Georgia (or who knew the author personally) can recognize readily the autobiographical elements in the novels—especially in her depiction of Mick Kelly, Frankie Addams, and Jester Clane—the self-portraits in her short fiction are more cleverly disguised. On the other hand, McCullers's husband appears almost full cloth in three of the short stories: "Instant of the Hour After," "Who Has Seen the Wind?" and "A Domestic Dilemma." In the novels, Reeves McCullers can be recognized only in the characterization of Jake Blount.

The most prevalent theme in the novels—rejection or unrequited love—repeats itself, as one might expect, in her short fiction. McCullers's characters must learn again and again the lesson of *eros*, just as their creator herself had to learn it many times—and to live with it—over the years. . . .

Source: Virginia Spencer Carr, "The Short Fiction," in *Understanding Carson McCullers*, University of South Carolina Press, 1989, pp. 127–31.

SOURCES

"Active Duty Military Personnel, 1940–2011," Infoplease.com, http://www.infoplease.com/ipa/A0004598.html (accessed January 17, 2013).

Baldanza, Frank, "Plato in Dixie," in *Georgia Review*, Vol. 12, No. 1, Summer 1958, pp. 151–67.

Bennett, Elizabeth, Review of *Carson McCullers: A Life*, in *Pittsburgh Post-Gazette*, March 4, 2001, http://old.post-gazette.com/books/reviews/20010304review716.asp (accessed January 23, 2013).

Carr, Virginia Spencer, *Understanding Carson McCullers*, University of South Carolina Press, 1989, p. 129.

Drye, Willie, "In the U.S. South, Textile Mills Gone but Not Forgotten," in *National Geographic News*, October 19, 2004, http://news.nationalgeographic.com/news/2004/10/1019_041019_textile_mills.html (accessed January 17, 2013).

Evans, Oliver, "Trees, Rocks, and Clouds," in *The Ballad of Carson McCullers: A Biography*, Coward-McCann, 1966, pp. 88–96.

Fletcher, Mary Dell, "Carson McCullers' 'Ancient Mariner,'" in *South Central Bulletin*, Vol. 35, No. 4, Winter 1975, pp. 123–25.

Hemingway, Ernest, "A Clean, Well-Lighted Place," in *The Snows of Kilimanjaro and Other Stories*, Scribner, 1999, pp. 29–33.

Kakutani, Michiko, "Books of the Times," in *New York Times*, July 14, 1987, p. C20.

McCullers, Carson, "A Tree. A Rock. A Cloud," in *The Ballad of the Sad Café and Other Stories*, Mariner, 2005, pp. 143–52.

McDowell, Margaret B., "Development of the Writer and Her Theory of Fiction" and "'A Tree, a Rock, a Cloud,'" in *Carson McCullers*, Twayne's United States Authors Series, No. 354, Twayne Publishers, 1980, pp. 15–25, 129–31.

"NBC Short Story," Internet Archive, http://archive.org/details/NBC_short_story (accessed January 31, 2013).

Oates, Joyce Carol, "You Are the We of Me," in *London Review of Books*, Vol. 21, No. 17, September 2, 1999, pp. 15–16.

O'Connor, Flannery, "Some Aspects of the Grotesque in Southern Fiction," in *Mystery and Manners: Occasional Prose*, Macmillan, 1969, pp. 36–50.

"Oprah's Book Club: The Complete List," Oprah.com, http://www.oprah.com/book-list/Oprahs-Book-Club-The-Complete-List/2 (accessed February 1, 2013).

Phillips, Robert, "Freaking Out: The Short Stories of Carson McCullers," in *Southwest Review*, No. 63, Winter 1978, pp. 65–73.

Stokesbury, James L., *A Short History of World War II*, William Morrow, 1980, pp. 15–20, 175–83, 378–80.

"While You Were Sleeping, the Paperboy Grew Up," NBCNews.com, April 25, 2006, http://www.msnbc.msn.com/id/12485231/ (accessed January 17, 2013).

FURTHER READING

Bloom, Harold, ed., *Carson McCullers*, Bloom's Modern Critical Views, Chelsea House, 1986.
This volume collects twelve critical essays, demonstrating the central questions that critics raise about McCullers's work. Bloom's introduction addresses McCullers's place in the literary canon, and the essays are supplemented with a chronology of the author's life and an extensive—though no longer current—bibliography.

———, ed., *Carson McCullers*, rev. ed., Bloom's Modern Critical Views, Bloom's Literary Criticism, 2009.
The ten essays in this new edition of Bloom's collection show the bold new directions that criticism of McCullers's work has taken since the 1980s. Several of the essays address the author's queer fiction, queer identity, and gender ambiguity, and two deal with race and "racial uncertainty." Like the earlier edition, this volume includes a chronology of the author's life and an extensive bibliography.

Carr, Virginia Spencer, *The Lonely Hunter: A Biography of Carson McCullers*, Doubleday, 1975.
This long and definitive biography of McCullers captures the author's eccentricity and abandon, demonstrating such qualities without overplaying the similarities between McCullers's life and some of the most important characters in her fiction. Carr illuminates the force of McCullers's personality as she explores the author's sexuality, illnesses, friendships, family, and talent.

McCullers, Carson, *Illumination and Night Glare: The Unfinished Biography of Carson McCullers*, edited by Carlos L. Dews, University of Wisconsin Press, 1999.
This biography was pieced together and edited from memories and comments that McCullers, in poor health, dictated to various assistants after she was paralyzed by a stroke in 1967. The result is episodic and uneven but offers striking moments of personal revelation.

Sickels, Robert C., *The 1940s*, Greenwood Press, 2004.
Part of the American Popular Culture through History series, this book describe the lives of average citizens in the United States as the Great Depression ended and World War II began. Also included are a time line, a cost comparison, and a list of suggested readings.

Whitt, Jan, ed., *Reflections in a Critical Eye: Essays on Carson McCullers*, University Press of America, 2008.
This collections begins with an introduction by the editor that gives a broad overview of McCullers's life and work. The other nine critical essays deal with gender roles and same-sex relationships, alcohol, politics, and McCullers's place in the tradition of southern women writing nonfiction prose.

SUGGESTED SEARCH TERMS

Carson McCullers

A Tree. A Rock. A Cloud

A Tree. A Rock. A Cloud AND McCullers

McCullers AND rock

McCullers AND Spinoza

McCullers AND grotesque

McCullers AND love

southern women writers

Under Reconstruction

MORI ŌGAI

1910

One of the first modern Japanese stories, "Under Reconstruction," by Mori Ōgai, was first published in 1910 as "Fushinchu." Written by a well-traveled army doctor about his home country at a time of great change in Japan's history, "Under Reconstruction" perfectly captures the uneasy transition of an ancient, secluded nation into modern times. Today, inarguably, Japan is an influential world power at the frontier of technological development and with many important cultural exports. But as recently as 1867, Japanese borders had just opened up to outside and particularly Western influence, as a result of the downfall of the feudal system and a new emperor who admired European forms of government. "Under Reconstruction" alludes to this larger national narrative through a small personal crisis between a Japanese government official, Watanabe, and his former lover, a German singer on tour. They meet in a restaurant undergoing reconstruction. Half reflecting traditional Japanese aesthetics, half attempting westernized decor, the restaurant, like both Watanabe and Japan, is making an awkward effort to bridge the gulf between traditions and modernity. "Under Reconstruction" can be found in *Modern Japanese Stories: An Anthology* (1962), edited by Ivan Morris, as well as Ōgai's *Youth and Other Stories* (1994).

Mori Ōgai (© *INTERFOTO | Alamy*)

AUTHOR BIOGRAPHY

Mori Ōgai was born Mori Rintaro on February 17, 1862, in Tsuwano, Japan. The eldest son in a family of doctors who had served the feudal lord for over ten generations, Ōgai was raised in the setting and value system of the samurai, and indeed his family, as personal doctors to the lord of the Tsuwano domain, held a separate but comparable position of honor alongside the samurai class.

With the dissolution of the feudal system in Japan in 1870, Ōgai moved in 1871 to Tokyo to continue his studies to become a doctor. He graduated from Tokyo University School of Medicine in 1881 when he was only nineteen years old. Already fluent in Chinese and Dutch, Ōgai joined the army as a doctor that same year and traveled to Germany to observe their methods of modern medicine. From a young age Ōgai excelled in medicine, yet he nurtured a passion for literature and writing. He was first published in a newspaper the year of his graduation, but his family discouraged him from choosing writing as an occupation.

Germany's effect on Ōgai was immediate and lasting. He devoted himself to translating the German classics to Japanese, effectively introducing Japanese readers to Western works. When he returned to Japan, a German woman—his lover—followed him. Ōgai's family and the military authorities arranged for her to be sent home without the scandal of an affair with a foreign woman costing Ōgai his reputation and bureaucratic status. The heartbreak provided Ōgai with years of writing material.

Home from his studies, Ōgai set about enacting what he had learned from the German model of Western medicine in Japan. Along with contributing two new magazines on the subject to the medical field, *Hygienics Journal* (established in 1880) and *New Medical Journal* (in 1881), he published works of fiction in the fashion of Western modernism, blending Japanese imagery and settings with Western writing techniques and philosophies. He rose steadily in the ranks of the army until being appointed army medical commissioner and chief of the Bureau of Medical Affairs in 1907.

The culmination of his military career triggered an era of success in Ōgai's literary ambitions. He published "Under Reconstruction" (1910) and his popular novel *The Wild Geese* (1911–1913) during this time, in addition to founding a literary journal, and rose to even greater literary fame. As a novelist, he was powerful enough to criticize government censorship of one of his novels, though as a government employee this was strictly forbidden.

He grew older without fear of death, a reflection of his childhood upbringing in the samurai tradition. Appointed the director of the Imperial Museum and Archives as well as the Imperial Art Academy in 1917 and 1919, respectively, he enjoyed the success that both the military and literary paths of his life had brought him. However, his final wish was to be buried without military honors with a grave marker saying only his birth name: Mori Rintaro. He died of tuberculosis on July 8, 1922.

PLOT SUMMARY

As "Under Reconstruction" opens, Councillor Watanabe, arriving in Tokyo by train after a heavy rain, passes the kabuki theater (referring to a traditional style of Japanese drama) on his way toward a restaurant where he has reserved a table. Struggling to find the place, called the Seiyoken Hotel, he shares the deserted streets of Tokyo with a group of men in Western-style clothes, a woman in a kimono, and a rickshaw. When he reaches his destination, the sign is written out horizontally, as opposed to vertically. The building is awkwardly shaped, and scaffolding obscures a large section of its wall facing the canal.

Watanabe enters the Seiyoken Hotel to find very wide, empty hallways. Guests are meant to keep their shoes on inside the building—a serious break from Japanese tradition. Watanabe thoroughly cleans his shoes before walking any farther. He notices the loud sounds of the saws and hammers of the workers remodeling the building. When no one comes to greet him, he sets out down the hallway alone. A bored-looking man leaning against the wall snaps into action when Watanabe mentions he has made a reservation. Watanabe realizes that, with the heavy reconstruction, the hotel is not popular. The waiter brings him to a dining room on the second floor, assuring Watanabe that the construction workers will leave at precisely five o'clock.

The dining room is overloaded with too many chairs per small table and an enormous sofa out of proportion with the delicate houseplants placed beside it. The waiter leads him to a second, smaller dining room with a table set prettily for two. A large, fresh bouquet serves as the centerpiece. Watanabe is satisfied with the private table and waits for his dining companion in the larger room. As promised, the construction stops at exactly five o'clock. Watanabe lights a cigar. He is surprised at himself for his calm state of mind as he waits for his guest, as if the guest could be anyone and Watanabe would not care. He smokes and gazes out the window at the quiet city below.

He moves to the sofa to study the room's curious decor. Strangely assembled pictures and Japanese texts seem dwarfed by the height of the walls on which they are displayed. Watanabe, disappointed, thinks, "And this is meant to be the land of art."

Still, he enjoys simply sitting and feeling good until noises in the hall announce the arrival of his guest. She is a German woman wearing long gloves and a hat. She is dressed all in gray and carries an umbrella. Watanabe forces himself to smile in greeting as he rises from the sofa.

She takes off her veil to reveal large brown eyes with deep shadows. The waiter who showed her in does not immediately leave the two alone. She greets Watanabe in German, and he takes her gloved hand, dismissing the waiter until dinner is ready. Once the waiter leaves, she collapses casually on the sofa, and he draws a chair up beside her. He explains that the hotel is so quiet because it is under reconstruction. She says she came to Japan two days before and was surprised to run into Watanabe on the street yesterday.

She hesitantly explains that she was touring in Russia as a singer and is now touring Japan with a man named Kosinsky—her piano accompanist. Watanabe does not waste time in accusing her of being in a relationship with this man. He seems to know Kosinsky by name from his shared past with the woman. She brushes off Watanabe's idea, though she mentions that she and Kosinsky are staying in the same hotel—and do "have a good time together" now and then. Watanabe, seeming jealous of this new man, says he does not want to meet him.

After Japan, the German singer plans to tour America. She has heard that finding work as an entertainer in Japan is hard. Watanabe admits that Japan is backward and, like the Seiyoken Hotel, under reconstruction. She teases him for admitting that his own country is struggling to be modern—especially since he is a government employee. He swears that he is an honorable worker but that tonight is an exception. She takes off her glove, holds his hand, and asks if he wants a kiss.

Watanabe scoffs at the idea: "We are in Japan," he says. Suddenly the waiter bursts through the door to announce dinner, and Watanabe repeats his remark. They move to their private dining room and take a seat at the table. However, the experience is anything but private. There are too many waiters for so small a room. They bumble around, annoying Watanabe and his guest as they try to dine.

The German woman says that the waiters are just as bad at her own hotel; this reminds Watanabe of Kosinsky's presence in her life. He says it must be difficult for her and Kosinsky when the waiters barge in without knocking. The German woman again denies that she and Kosinsky are an item. Their conversation goes nowhere as they eat.

Finally the woman asks if Watanabe is jealous. She is immediately embarrassed because, despite her intent to tease him, the question came out with a serious tone. She remembers their closeness when they were together in Germany. They would fight but make up and faced each other happily over many dinner tables. Watanabe, in response to her question, lifts his champagne glass in a toast in German to Kosinsky. She raises her own glass but hides her other hand under the table as it violently shakes.

At eight thirty that evening, a car drives the German woman back to her hotel. She sits alone in the backseat with her face hidden behind her veil.

CHARACTERS

The German Woman

The German woman is a professional singer touring the world with her accompanist. In Tokyo she has run into her former lover, Watanabe, whom she knew in Germany. The two have made dinner plans. Though she is excited to reconnect, flirting and asking if she can kiss him, Watanabe's jealousy and suspicion of Kosinsky get in the way of any lightheartedness. Wistful for a time when they were in love, she returns to her hotel alone after dinner.

Kosinsky

Kosinsky is a Polish pianist who is touring with the German woman. Watanabe knows of him by name from his time in Germany and evidently disapproves. Though the German woman denies any substance to their relationship, Watanabe understands that Kosinsky is her new lover. Kosinsky does not appear in the story in person, but his presence in the German woman's life strains the dinner conversation painfully.

Waiters

The waiters at the Seiyoken Hotel, as if lost in the absence of customers, are overbearing in their service.

Councillor Watanabe

Watanabe is a Japanese government official who has spent time abroad in Germany. He meets his former lover—a German singer—in a Japanese hotel for dinner. A formal man with a dry sense of humor, he is not forthcoming with his feelings toward his old lover, and the two do not reconnect with any success.

Watanabe is struck by the similarity of the hotel to his home country. Both are under reconstruction, that is, becoming westernized. Watanabe, though himself westernized by his time abroad, firmly reminds the woman when she attempts to flirt openly, "We are in Japan." Jealous of her traveling companion, Kosinsky, Watanabe holds a grudge that prevents himself and the German woman from enjoying their brief time together at dinner.

THEMES

Cultural Identity

The issue of cultural identity is so important to "Under Reconstruction" that within its few pages the reader hears of a Pole, a German, and of course the Japanese, as well as about America and Russia. The characters are world travelers: he was once a Japanese man in Germany, she is now a German woman in Japan. The mix of cultures even extends into the setting: the Seiyoken Hotel is in the process of adapting Western customs, such as horizontal writing and shoes inside the building, in what was once a traditionally Japanese restaurant. The result of this global intermingling is a set of uncomfortable gaps in understanding. The Seiyoken seems to have been modernized in no particular pattern—the proportions are warped between delicate Japanese paintings and an enormous sofa, in a dining room with small tables and a large number of chairs. Yet the setting fits the two lovers, who are themselves trying to meet halfway between East and West and finding difficulty bridging the gulf.

Watanabe is particularly uncomfortable and even seems ashamed at his country's misguided attempts to be Western, openly admitting that the country is "backward." While he has seen a Western country firsthand, most in Japan have not. This has made the country's westernization more of a guessing process. With the German woman in Japan, Watanabe is at his most self-conscious with regard to his country's lack of modernization, mourning the decor of the restaurant and the incompetence of the waiters. Still, the German woman brings out a kind of defensive pride in Watanabe for his "backward" country. He admonishes the woman for flirting openly with the ominous phrase "We are in Japan." With Watanabe defensive and embarrassed at his own

TOPICS FOR FURTHER STUDY

- Write a short story from either the German woman's or Kosinsky's first-person point of view. What do they think of Councillor Watanabe? What do they think of each other? Put yourself in either character's shoes and be creative!

- Using online search skills, find and print a map of the Ueno district of Tokyo, Japan, where "Under Reconstruction" takes place. How many miles is Tokyo from your home? What was the weather like there today? Write the answers to these and other such questions on the back of your map, along with an explanation of how and where you found them online. Using your map, write a short scene from the German woman's perspective as she travels to her meeting with Watanabe. What are her hopes or fears about the rendezvous? What does she notice about the scenery on her route to the hotel?

- Read the young-adult novel *When You Were Here* (2013), by Daisy Whitney. After finishing the book, compose a response comparing Danny's first visit to Tokyo to the German woman's. What impressions does Danny have, and how is his situation different from that of the singer in "Under Reconstruction"? Write an essay in which you address these questions and discuss any other significant similarities or differences between the two characters who visit Japan.

- Create a travel blog about Tokyo and plan a future trip you will take there. Post a minimum of five times about sights and activities you have researched online, include new foods you would like to try, and any interesting information you discover about the city. If possible, visit two classmates' similar blogs, and leave well-thought-out responses to two of their posts.

homeland and the German woman misunderstanding the implications that an affair with a foreigner would have on Watanabe's career, the two cannot bridge the cultural gap in Japan as they did in Germany. The hotel as well as the country of Japan are in transition, navigating somewhat blindly. The first meeting of cultures is a fragile occasion, and complications and misunderstandings are inevitable

Jealousy

Before the arrival of the German woman, Watanabe reflects with wonder at his calm state of mind. Meeting an old lover might be a nerve-racking event fueled by excitement and nervous energy, but Watanabe feels none of this toward the German woman, as if he has let their relationship pass completely from his mind. Not until the mention of Kosinsky does Watanabe show any strong emotion. Despite his earlier nonchalance toward the woman, he appears to be overcome by jealousy at the thought of her with another man. His jealousy reflects his defensive attitude toward his country. While the German woman and the Polish pianist travel the world together, he is stuck at home guiding the somewhat ridiculous process of catching an ancient, secluded country up to modern times as quickly as possible. When the German woman complains of a lack of work in Japan, Watanabe ironically points out that like the hotel, the country itself is being rebuilt. His dry sense of humor adds sharp edges to the brief dialogue that he has with his former lover. There is a great sadness behind his jokes and false smiles at her. Watanabe believes himself to be a cultured man. But meeting the German woman in such an awkward restaurant, during such a confusing point in Japan's process of revising its cultural identity, is humiliating to the proud, educated man, who believes himself equal to Kosinsky in worldliness.

Despite the overall subtlety of the characters' exchanges, Watanabe's jealousy is the dominant force of the story, driving the overall negative-intone conversations between the two. Talk never drifts far from his bitter feelings toward Kosinsky or disparaging remarks about the hotel, and fond memories of Germany appear only as private thoughts, never spoken. While they have crossed borders, languages, and cultures to find one another not only once in Germany but also again in Japan, the power of jealousy proves greater than the momentum produced by their having overcome these enormous barriers.

"Under Reconstruction" takes place when Japan was beginning to shift from traditional to modern. (© *deepblue-photographer | ShutterStock.com*)

STYLE

Suspense

Ōgai uses suspense—the audience's anticipation of events to come—to make a short encounter at a restaurant into a dramatic crisis in the emotional lives of the two characters. A large part of the story describes Watanabe simply waiting for the arrival of some unknown person, yet tension is built through Ōgai's use of setting. The strange mismatches in the decor and furniture foreshadow the mismatch between the councillor and the German singer. Nothing seems to fit right in the Seiyoken Hotel, with an empty entryway and a surprised host waiter, the workers hammering loudly outside, the walls too large for the small paintings, too many chairs at each tiny table, and the emptiness of the restaurant at dinner time. These strange details keep the audience guessing, building suspense as to why Watanabe would come to such a place. But the Seiyoken perfectly represents the mismatched couple.

Once the two are finally together, the startling waiters interrupt their private moments and prevent an honest conversation. Romantic tension is built by delaying audience satisfaction. Naturally, an audience wants to see two lovers reunite happily. Yet if the two were to meet, close their emotional distance immediately, and leave together without incident, the story would not be compelling to read. Instead Ōgai places enormous obstacles in the way; for example, the two speak in German, as if to avoid causing a scandal. Prevented from communicating effectively and continually blocked by Watanabe's jealousy of Kosinsky, there is no hope of their passion for each other reigniting. In the story's climax, the German woman can no longer take the tension and asks, "Aren't you jealous—even a little?" To this Watanabe, after a suspenseful pause in which the woman remembers their good times together in the past, only lifts his glass in a cruel toast to Kosinsky. By building tension over the course of several pages and keeping the audience from what they want (the reunification of the two lovers), Ōgai finally allows a single direct question to be asked as to the state of the lovers' feelings. Watanabe's response leaves no question: their relationship is over.

Metaphor

Metaphor, the direct comparison of two unlike things, is used in "Under Reconstruction" to equate the awkwardly transitioning restaurant to the country of Japan as it undergoes modernization. Watanabe uses the phrase "under reconstruction" to describe both the restaurant and the country to his German guest. When an author uses a small part to symbolize a much larger entity, it is called *synecdoche*. The Seiyoken Hotel is a synecdoche of Japan: it is a small part of Japan and yet symbolic of the whole of Japan in its momentary cultural confusion as it tries to catch up to the Western world. Without a clear idea of what it meant to become modern, Japan set out to modernize itself with all possible speed. This resulted in the confusion of cultural identity seen in the Seiyoken Hotel. Unsure which traditions to hold on to and which to discard, the hotel has picked randomly: keeping shoes on inside a building is considered modern, and writing horizontally instead of vertically is modern, but Buddhist texts and delicate hothouse grape plants are still on display. None of this, Ōgai seems to say, does any real work toward modernizing a country. It only broadens the cultural confusion and disconnect between Japan and a modern reality. This is why, gazing at the terribly mismatched decor, Watanabe sighs that Japan was once a country that prided itself on art.

The metaphor of the story, made explicit by Watanabe, is that the Seiyoken's confusion is symbolic of Japan's confusion. Without a plan, without grace or even forethought, the country is moving clumsily forward with reconstruction. Both the Seiyoken and Japan are seen as unpopular in the story due to this awkward transitioning period: the restaurant is empty during what could be a dinner rush, and the country has few opportunities for a traveling German singer. Real efforts at modernization are needed to bring the country and hotel into the world scene, rather than surface-level makeovers and a strange hybrid of Eastern and Western cultures. The fate of Japan is the fate of the Seiyoken Hotel in "Under Reconstruction." Will the hotel find an appealing balance between Japanese tradition and modern aesthetics and culture? Or will the shallow application of Western decor and clumsy adaptation of Western behavior turn visitors away from what was once a proud and elegant civilization?

HISTORICAL CONTEXT

Meiji Restoration

When Emperor Meiji took power in Japan in 1867, a drastic shift in the country's ideological perspective took place. Before Meiji, feudalism persisted as the economic and social structure of Japan, but after Meiji took power he eliminated the feudal domains in favor of a new government mimicking those of European countries. Morris writes in his introduction to *Modern Japanese Stories*, "The political structure was completely reorganized and . . . in the effort to become 'modern,' countless old customs, habits, and heritages were scrapped."

The Meiji Restoration, as it would be called, was marked by rapid westernization. Using Germany as their model, the Japanese set to work reordering their entire way of life. It is in this time period that "Under Reconstruction" takes place—a time of friendly Japanese and German relations, a time of awkward reconfiguring, and a time when traditions were crumbling. Watanabe, it can be assumed, traveled to Germany as a government official to observe their methods for modernizing the country, just as Ōgai journeyed to Germany as an army doctor. This accounts for the acute disappointment Watanabe feels toward the hotel's efforts at modernization: he is well versed in the reality of European customs and finds the Seiyoken Hotel's attempts to mimic them unsuccessful. The German woman, in turn, is disappointed in Japan's lack of work for a foreign entertainer. The effects of the Meiji Restoration can be seen immediately when Watanabe first gets off the train: he shares the streets with men dressed in Western style contrasted by a woman in a traditional kimono. Japan at the time of Meiji was truly under reconstruction and bound to suffer some growing pains along the way. Ōgai captures this moment of uncertainty with the careful disarray of the Seiyoken Hotel.

Modernization

The rush to modernize during the Meiji Restoration affected all areas of life, from new medicine to new government to new art forms. Ōgai

COMPARE
&
CONTRAST

- **1910:** Literature, specifically fiction, in Japan is seen as entertainment, not as a serious form of art. Writing is not considered an honorable career for someone born into a well-respected family, like Ōgai. Ōgai makes great progress introducing Japan to world literature and the concept of fiction as an art form with relevant insights toward human interaction.

  Today: Japanese literature is thriving, with many active and talented authors representing their country on the global scene. Many authors' works are translated immediately after publication. The exchange of literature between Japan and other countries is rampant.

- **1910:** It is considered extremely inappropriate for Japanese citizens to marry foreigners. A Japanese official like Watanabe would be expected to abstain from an affair with a German woman at the risk of losing his position and reputation. This is why Watanabe so strictly scolds the German woman when she flirtatiously asks about a kiss.

  Today: Tokyo is a global city attracting innumerable visitors and world ambassadors. Intermarriage is no longer cause for scandal and demotion.

- **1910:** Many businesses, like the Seiyoken Hotel, follow the national example and attempt to modernize, blending Eastern and Western design and philosophy with varying success. One contributing factor to the clumsiness of the westernization process is that few among the general Japanese population have actually seen a Western country in person, Ōgai being an exception.

  Today: With borders wide open, Japan has modernized, leading the world in technology in particular. Despite the late-blooming nation's fitful first attempts at modernization, as depicted in "Under Reconstruction," Japan has come into its own modernity—keeping in place many Japanese traditions while updating others beyond recognition.

---

led the Japanese literary world in modernization through translating Western literature and writing Western-style literature himself. At the time of modernization, fiction was only considered valuable as entertainment. Ōgai, through his exposure to European literature, felt that fiction could do more than entertain. Michael R. Reich writes in *Six Lives, Six Deaths: Portraits from Modern Japan*, "Ōgai did not merely record minute details of daily existence but sought to express his personal philosophy of life."

In modernizing fiction in Japan, Ōgai inspired generations of authors to follow his example. While Japanese fiction had long held a backseat to poetry, Ōgai introduced short stories, like "Under Reconstruction," which read very similarly to Western short stories in both depth and technique. Modern aspects of "Under Reconstruction" include the introduction of new themes in Japanese literature, such as world travel, foreign influence, disillusionment with the government, and cultural identity. The depiction of the Seiyoken's uneven progress toward westernization serves as Ōgai's critique of those who would westernize Japan out of fashion: a logical, well-laid plan is needed behind the dramatic changes that must occur in order to bring the feudal country up to date with Europe. To Meiji Japan, modernization meant westernization—but after the initial awkward period of adapting a foreign culture, Japan would eventually discover its own unique and successful style of modernism, imitating others no longer.

Watanabe reunites with an old friend in a hotel that is under construction. *(© OlegD | ShutterStock.com)*

CRITICAL OVERVIEW

Ōgai is a cherished and still deeply respected author of the Meiji Restoration, responsible for bringing Western literature to Japan. Succeeding authors are aware of the great debt owed Ōgai for his influence in spurring the expansion of the Japanese literary palate and the legitimization of fiction as a respectable art form. Ōgai brought modern literature to Japan through both his own writings and his translations of German literature to Japanese, at a time when few foreign works besides Chinese texts were translated for Japanese audiences.

Reich writes of Ōgai's influence and style, "He is one of the few people in the Meiji period who might be called a genius...a writer of exceptional prose which blended an exquisite aesthetic sensibility with a cool, clinical logic." Ōgai's treatment of the Seiyoken Hotel is an example of his aesthetic sensibility—with his sharp eye for details and imbalances in the mood of his setting, he equates the strange experience of the Seiyoken with the zeitgeist of Japan at the time of transition. As a world traveler himself, Ōgai had an intimate knowledge of Western countries (in particular Germany) when few Japanese had traveled abroad, and thus he understood how misguided, blind attempts at westernization, such as those efforts to modernize the Seiyoken, did more harm than good to the country's hope of becoming an equal to those it wanted to imitate. Insight into Ōgai's life fills out his short stories, which were often drawn from his experiences, as Morris explains: "It is because Mori Ōgai knew Europe so well himself that he was able, as in this story, to describe the pseudo-Westernization of his own country with such penetration."

Referring to "Under Reconstruction," Roy Starrs, in *Japan's Competing Modernities*, remarks, "It is a beautifully written, understated story of faded love.... But the story also works brilliantly on another level—as Ōgai's image of the uneasy mixture of Eastern and Western culture in late Meiji Japan." The double narrative of "Under Reconstruction," as both a love story and a metaphor, has impressed critics since its publication. With a delicate touch, Ōgai manages in a few pages to summarize the state of an entire nation.

CRITICISM

Amy Lynn Miller

Miller attended the University of Cincinnati and now resides in New Orleans, Louisiana. In the following essay, she examines Ōgai's equation of the Seiyoken Hotel to Meiji Japan in "Under Reconstruction."

One of Mori Ōgai's greatest accomplishments as the modernizer of Japanese fiction is his mastery of modernism itself. Ōgai's writing blends beautiful imagery and phrasemaking with cold dialogue and unsatisfying human relationships. The realism of "Under Reconstruction" is so honest as to be brutal. The two former lovers will not have a happy ending for reasons as diverse as the presence of another man in the singer's life, the Japanese cultural taboo of becoming romantically involved with foreigners, and even the ineptitude of tactless waiters. Ōgai's attention to his characters' every shift in emotion creates an expansive volume of meaning within the small space of this very short story. Much is implied without being spoken, much is said with body language instead of words. Tension is built, and a climax is reached before being simply brushed aside with the lifting of a champagne glass in a bitter toast. All of this occurs as Ōgai simultaneously paints a portrait of his home country struggling to modernize through the images of the poorly decorated hotel. Michael R. Reich writes in *Six Lives, Six Deaths: Portraits from Modern Japan*,

> Like most Meiji thinkers, Ōgai chose the conflict between Western and Japanese cultural traditions as his central theme. Yet he was one of few Meiji intellectuals who was deeply grounded in both the European and traditional Japanese world.

This dual existence allowed Ōgai powerful insights into the two cultures he straddled. Ōgai has masterful control of his narrative despite the staggering depth of its subject matter, proof that he not only understood modernism but also had mastered the style. By taking a closer look at what is implied rather than stated directly—what is shown rather than told—the reader can perceive how "Under Reconstruction" unfolds its short narrative into a long and complex tale of a love expired and a country on the verge.

Introducing the anthology *Modern Japanese Stories*, Ivan Morris notes, "One of the earliest writers to attempt to produce in Japanese the

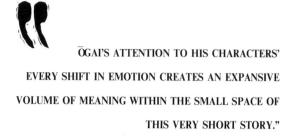

> ŌGAI'S ATTENTION TO HIS CHARACTERS'
> EVERY SHIFT IN EMOTION CREATES AN EXPANSIVE
> VOLUME OF MEANING WITHIN THE SMALL SPACE OF
> THIS VERY SHORT STORY."

type of story that was current in Europe was Mori Ōgai, who...did so much to familiarize Japanese readers with Western literary forms." Japanese literature, seen at the time as only entertainment, was often fantastical and rarely carried with it a larger message. "Under Reconstruction," however, has a clear beginning, middle, and end, with well-developed characters and a plot grounded in reality. The stability of this short story is a result of Ōgai's immersion in European literature from his time in Germany. Ōgai, Reich writes, "conceived of literature in Western terms, as a cognitive means of interpreting human existence, which differed greatly from the traditional Japanese idea of literature as entertainment." The sad love story between Watanabe and the German woman is told through subtle dialogue as the two attempt to conceal their true feelings. Instead of an honest and direct approach to the state of their affair, the two lovers must speak in German to avoid being understood by the waiters, and they are interrupted at their closest approach to an intimate moment—when the German woman asks to kiss Watanabe. Certainly the woman is more relaxed and open than Watanabe, whose emotions are held so severely in check that his jealousy over Kosinsky can escape only through sarcasm. For example, when she sees they will be dining together in a private room, she attempts to get a rise out of Watanabe: "'They've given us a *chambre separée*,' she said, laughing. 'How exciting!' She straightened her back and looked directly at Watanabe as if to see how he would react."

By pointing out their private dining room with so much energy, the woman is hoping to bring up the status of their affair. In Japan, the relationship would cause a scandal for Watanabe as a government official, and so a private dining room would have been necessary if not for the

WHAT DO I READ NEXT?

- *The Wild Geese* (1911–1913), Ōgai's most popular work, tells the story of a poverty-stricken woman during the time of the decline of the feudal state and the transitional period of the Meiji Restoration. Told with great skill and sympathy for the position of women at the time, *The Wild Geese* was written during the same period of productivity in Ōgai's career that saw "Under Reconstruction" published, after he had attained the highest medical position possible in the Japanese military hierarchy.

- *Sakamoto Ryoma and the Meiji Restoration* (1961), by Marius B. Jansen, tells the story of the Meiji Restoration with a focus on Sakamoto Ryoma, a samurai and folk legend in Japanese history for his role in the dissolution of the feudal domains and re-creation of Japan in the image of the West.

- *I Live in Tokyo* (2001), by Mari Takabayashi, is a month-by-month introduction to the culture of Tokyo with informative illustrations for young adults. Highlighting a festival or event that marks each month in Tokyo, the book introduces readers to the sights, sounds, and smells of the metropolis as well as to common Japanese practices.

- In *Sandalwood Death* (2013), a translation of Mo Yan's *Tan xiang xing* (2001), characters struggle in China during the Boxer Rebellion, a fight against the spreading Western influence of the early twentieth century. Families and lovers are torn apart in this emotional appeal to reason amid nationalistic madness.

- *The Sound of Waves* (1956), a translation of Yukio Mishima's *Shiosai* (1954), is a novel about young love on a small fishing island off the coast of Japan. Isolated and extremely traditional, the village erupts in rumors when a poor fisher boy and the daughter of a wealthy shipowner fall in love. Though on the mainland westernization has taken hold in the form of movie houses and trains, on the island the ancient past is preserved, and the gods still take notice of the fisher boy's prayers.

- *Snow Country* (1956), a translation of *Yukiguni* (1941), by Yasunari Kawabata, tells the story of an affair between a wealthy Tokyo sophisticate and a county geisha who works for the hot spring resorts of a snowed-in mountain town. With dialogue as subtle as Ōgai's, Kawabata's lovers cannot face the truth of their fragile relationship without also facing its inevitable demise.

---

emptiness of the restaurant. But Watanabe's reaction gives the woman no information about his thoughts toward their future: "'I'm sure it's quite by chance,' he said calmly." Of course, it is not by chance at all but by Watanabe's request that the two are dining privately. This is one of many implied meanings behind the former lovers' short exchanges of dialogue. What seems on the surface to be light conversation is turned through Ōgai's skillful control to a painful realization on the part of the lovers that they cannot and will not continue their relationship. When the German woman finally confronts Watanabe, asking if he is jealous, she is ashamed to find the words come out seriously instead of in the teasing, lighthearted tone she had wanted to assume. That she is ashamed to have spoken honestly, and that he answers in the most dishonest way possible—not admitting to his feelings but instead raising a toast to Kosinsky's health—show the extent to which both lovers are willing to lie in order to appear as casual and calm as they do, sitting across a table from one another facing their relationship's end.

In *Japan's Competing Modernities*, Roy Starrs writes, "Fiction may take on metaphorical or symbolic overtones and thus encompass very large areas of meaning within even the smallest areas of text." In "Under Reconstruction," the use of synecdoche equates the story's setting, the Seiyoken Hotel, with Japan. While the lovers' drama unfolds, a cultural crisis is also explained through the minute details of the setting: walls out of proportion with tiny plants, a giant sofa dwarfing a dining room crowded with few tables and too many chairs, horizontal writing on an entrance sign, and shoes left on inside a building. Morris writes, "The Seiyoken Hotel . . . represents in microcosm the results of the country's efforts at rapid Westernization." The results are mixed: with the hotel under reconstruction, no guests are coming to stay, and the lovers are the only diners during what would perhaps normally be a dinner rush. The German woman says that she has heard there is no work for entertainers in Japan, and Watanabe is obliged to repeat a point he made earlier about the hotel: "It's still under reconstruction, you see."

Both hotel and country are unpopular with visitors during a time of such radical transformation. Morris notes, "Japan, . . . isolated from the mainstream of Western development, tried in the period of a few decades to absorb everything from the outside that would turn her into a modern nineteenth-century state." The Meiji Restoration, during which the story is set, was marked by the rush to westernize Japan at all costs. The hotel serves as a symbol for this dramatic cultural shift. Under heavy construction, the decor a mash-up of East and West, shoes worn inside and no guests to be found, the Seiyoken is nothing short of a disaster. Morris describes the hotel's attempts at modernization as "clumsy and, for those familiar with the West, somewhat ludicrous."

This, too, is Ōgai's point: modernization must be completed through a plan and not by simply grabbing whatever one can of Western cultures and mimicking them without understanding. Just as Watanabe does not fully understand the relationship between Kosinsky and the woman yet holds on to his jealousy, the hotel does not understand westernization yet continues to grasp at this or that Western custom in hopes that it will ring authentic. The relationship is destroyed as a result of this self-blinding misunderstanding. Starrs writes, "The very

awkwardness of their meeting, the result not just of lapsed time but of culture clash, echoes the awkwardness of Japan's encounter with the West." Himself modernized by his time in Germany, Watanabe is sensitive to his home country's struggles to understand what modern means. Privileged in his ability to interact with the West on his own terms, he seems to draw into himself out of allegiance to his "backward" country when the German woman's presence in his homeland threatens his pride in Japan. Though a modern man, Watanabe is first and foremost a Japanese man, and the emasculating effects of his lover touring Japan with a stranger and a hotel bowing down blindly to Western ideas is too much for him to bear. To keep his pride he must, in a display of samurai-like emotional control, raise his glass in a toast to another man, thus rejecting the German woman and all the European scandal she would bring to his home in Japan.

Ōgai creates a metaphorical link between the Seiyoken Hotel and Japan, and Watanabe too is a part of the metaphor. A witness to both East and West, he does not seem to care much for one or the other until his pride is attacked with the introduction of Kosinsky. His warning to the German woman, "We are in Japan," serves as a way to confirm his cultural identity at a time and in a place where to be Japanese was a confusing existence. No one understood this dichotomy better than Ōgai himself. A man of both East and West, he worked throughout his life to navigate between identities as a writer and doctor, as a lover and worker, as a westernized Japanese man in Japan as it struggled to westernize. Ōgai, Reich writes, "thus personified Meiji society. He and Meiji Japan balanced between two cultures." Understanding both cultures, he was able to produce in "Under Reconstruction" a perfect example of cultural misunderstanding.

Source: Amy Lynn Miller, Critical Essay on "Under Reconstruction," in *Short Stories for Students*, Gale, Cengage Learning, 2014.

Sidney DeVere Brown

In the following review, Brown describes Ōgai's work as exquisitely styled and points out that many of his stories have patriotic themes.

Thomas Rimer's contribution to *Youth and Other Stories* lies in collecting Mori Ōgai's short pieces from obscure places and commissioning translations of others, as well as bringing Ōgai's third and last novel before the

Watanabe's old friend wears a hat with a veil, suggesting that she has something to hide. (© Trudy Wilkerson /
ShutterStock.com)

English-reading public. The two literary lions
of early twentieth-century Japan were Natsume
Soseki (1867–1916) and Mori Ōgai (1862–
1922). We have long had admirable translations of Soseki's major works, including his
classic *Kokoro* (1914); now Ōgai's are available
for comparison, particularly the novel *Youth*
(1910–11).

Soseki studied in England, and his work in
the English tradition has attracted more translators and critics than has Ōgai, whose career as
a foreign student was lived out in Germany and
who wrote in the less accessible German tradition. Represented here are two periods of feverish activity: 1890–91, a time of experiment just
after his return from the University of Berlin;
and 1909–15, when Ōgai, a military bureaucrat
in medicine, paused in midcareer to take stock of
the restrictive society which had developed
around him and thwarted his ambitions.

His exquisite short stories are here, not only
"The Dancing Girl" (1890) and "Under Reconstruction" (1909), autobiographical statements
of his attraction to German women and ultimate
rejection of them, but also the less familiar
humorous tale "The Gold Coin," about a thirsty
thief who felt obliged to steal something besides
liquor to uphold his honor as a burglar. He
filched a fake gold coin, to the amusement of
the owner on the thief's apprehension, and was
let off with a warning; but the carousing servant
who nailed him in the early morning hours on
returning from a night on the town was severely
disciplined.

Righteous indignation is a more common
stance for the author who called himself "the
eternal malcontent." "The Tower of Silence"
(1910), though set in an unnamed country, is a
parody on Japanese thought control in the Meiji
era (1868–1912). Crows fed on the bodies atop
the tower, executed for espousing "subversive
doctrines," socialism, anarchism, and even sexual desire, derived from "dangerous western
books." Dim-witted censors could not distin-
guish between exposition of these ideas and
advocacy of them.

Throughout, Ōgai reminds us that he was a medical scientist and a patriot. German associates might be skeptical that Japanese researchers would ever play a role in conquering diseases. To the German who said "Never," Ōgai replied, "Not yet." A kind of medical naturalism which pervades these stories reveals how far Japan had to go. Key characters died of whooping cough, tuberculosis, typhus, and other diseases. Ill health was a fact of life in Meiji Japan, though a doctor may have emphasized it unduly in his stories.

The novel *Youth* reveals that Ōgai was a doctor alive to the more general world of European thought, as were those in his literary circle who talked incessantly of Ibsen, Hauptmann, Nietzsche, Goethe, and many lesser-known writers and philosophers. The novel is an important source for intellectual history but probably lacks the universal appeal of Soseki's *Kokoro. Youth* is specific to time and place, and much less dramatic. A cast of young and middle-aged women stirred the young man's emerging sexual consciousness, but when the widow of a famous writer seemed to be on the verge of starting an affair, the young man said good-bye and returned to his room to buckle down to his oft-postponed writing. The denouement is as unlikely as any in all literature. Certainly it lacks the dramatic climax of Soseki's *Kokoro* with its suicides.

We are deeply indebted to Rimer and his brilliant corps of translators—which includes Richard Bowring, Ivan Morris, Karen Brazell, and John Dower, among others—for making Ōgai come alive for the English-reading public.

Source: Sidney DeVere Brown, Review of *Youth and Other Stories*, in *World Literature Today*, Vol. 69, No. 1, Winter 1995, p. 228.

J. Thomas Rimer

In the following excerpt, Rimer explains why Ōgai's works should appeal to Western audiences.

Despite a lasting reputation in Japan, Mori Ōgai has yet to achieve any satisfactory reception in the West. Natsume Soseki, the only writer of Ōgai's generation to share his stature, has been widely translated and admired, but Ōgai remains a shadowy figure, austere, even obscure. It often happens, of course, that the work of certain writers cannot be sufficiently understood outside their own cultures. Some towering figures never earn anything like their rightful reputation through translation. One thinks of the

French playwright and poet Paul Claudel, whose Catholicism and expansive style have so far prevented any effective linguistic adaptations into an English-speaking, Protestant culture.

Nevertheless, there is much in Ōgai that might well appeal to a Western reader. The nature of his mental world, unlike that of a number of his contemporaries, was overwhelmingly cosmopolitan; indeed, he spent a great deal of time throughout his career translating into Japanese such diverse writers as Goethe (Ōgai's version of *Faust* is still the standard), Ibsen, Strindberg, and Hofmannsthal. In a very real sense the stories presented in this volume can be considered "translations" by Ōgai of historical Japanese and Chinese materials into contemporary terms. Our difficulties in approaching his art may lie elsewhere.

They may originate, for example, in the relatively narrow boundaries set down around the word "literature" in the Anglo-American tradition. For the French, Pascal and Montaigne are literary figures. We might feel more comfortable calling them philosophers. The combination of personal introspection and abstract concepts found in their writings seems somehow outside the scope of our own decorums. They seem both too direct and too obscure. Men like Goethe and Voltaire were permitted sufficient scope within their literary traditions to expand easily from the world of narrative to the world of ideas in their writings. Ōgai, drawing on his own heritage in Chinese and Japanese, was able to do the same. His early training in the Confucian classics, reinforced by his later studies of German literature and culture, gave him a strong sense of the high importance of literature and of the possibility—indeed the necessity—of its use as a means to convey philosophical ideas. Ōgai's work contains little that is "popular." His seriousness of purpose provides from the first a hurdle to those readers who turn to fiction, oriental or occidental, merely for pleasant entertainment. Nevertheless, these stories, read carefully, reveal a depth and precision of observation that goes far beyond the usual kind of romantic fantasy that so often constitutes "historical fiction" in the West.

Our decision to translate a number of Mori Ōgai's historical stories was made in the hope that, by putting the works into a form accessible to the English-speaking reader, we might induce him to share our conviction that there is much to be admired in Ōgai's trenchant observations and deep understanding of human nature, even though the stories operate in a series of peculiar historical situations. Other, earlier works of Ōgai are somewhat simpler and more accessible, but surely the Japanese critics are correct when they single out the works of Ōgai's later years as the very finest and most subtle he produced.

Hasegawa Izumi, a leading Japanese scholar on Ōgai, writes of these later works that

> ... here one sees Ōgai at his best as a writer, for every phase in his development as an artist and a man is reflected in them: the youth growing up within the fatally limited confines of modern Japanese society; the young man undergoing a thorough process of Westernization; and finally, the aging giant adopting a characteristically Oriental approach to life which is best described as the philosophy of resignation.

Whether such praise is warranted the reader will ultimately have to decide for himself. Forming judgments on the basis of translated material is hazardous, of course, but if the brilliant precision and striking style of Ōgai's prose cannot be adequately reproduced in English, at least the organization of his artistic material and the general thrust of his thought can be made available.

... Another important technique of Ōgai is his personal assumption of the role of narrator. Ōgai the writer and the man is never far from his reader; he constantly comments, shapes the narrative before the reader's eyes, speculates on the motives for the actions he is in the process of describing. The process may seem at first somewhat troubling, even occasionally didactic. Some of the reasons for the technique, of course, are inherent in the speculative, contemplative nature of the works Ōgai wished to create. Intellectual awareness requires objectivity, and aesthetic distance permits the reader to contemplate what he has read and generalize from it. Ōgai wants more than a personal, emotional response. Bertholt Brecht, in describing his celebrated "alienation effect," wrote that his object was ". . . not just to arouse moral objections to certain circumstances of life but to discover means for their elimination." Ōgai, in his own way, is attempting a similar effort in his Apollonian meditation.

The direct presentation to the reader of the working out of the author's own mental processes was a style of writing quite new in Japan at that time. Kato Shuichi has written that in Ōgai's late stories.

> ... the form is original, almost a new genre, namely a "biography in progress," in which the

author describes not only the life of the persons concerned but also the author's own intellectual process of writing a biography—his sorrow for lost documents, his joy at others discovered, his reasoning about available materials, his imagination, his insight. . . .

Ōgai's sense of objectivity is chiefly conveyed through the tone of his language, which is terse, brilliant, and precise. Ōgai's style has always received unstinted praise from Japanese critics and writers. He has been admired by such diverse talents as Nagai Kafu and Mishima Yukio. Ōgai may have developed his ability to create his kind of lucid precise Japanese because, like his brilliant predecessor, the novelist Futabatei Shimei, he took an interest in the spoken language. Futabatei, a generation before Ōgai, had virtually created the modern literary language (classical Japanese having been considered unsuited for the composition of modern works) by making translations into a precise and flexible Japanese from stories of Turgenev. Futabatei knew spoken and written Russian well. Ōgai made the same use of his German. One often has the feeling there is not a word wasted in an Ōgai text; and although unfortunately the same cannot be said about the present translations, they have been made as faithful to the general tone of his language as the translators have been able.

Source: J. Thomas Rimer, "The Historical Literature of Mori Ōgai: An Introduction," in *The Historical Fiction of Mori Ōgai*, edited by David A. Dilworth and J. Thomas Rimer, University of Hawai'i Press, 1991, pp. 1–2, 9–11.

SOURCES

Morris, Ivan, ed., Introduction to *Modern Japanese Stories: An Anthology*, Tuttle Publishing, 1962, pp. 9–37.

Ōgai, Mori, "Under Reconstruction," translated by Ivan Morris, in *Modern Japanese Stories: An Anthology*, edited by Ivan Morris, Tuttle Publishing, 1962, pp. 37–44.

Reich, Michael R., "Mori Ōgai (1862–1922): 'Neither Fearing nor Yearning for Death,'" in *Six Lives, Six Deaths: Portraits from Modern Japan*, by Robert Jay Lifton, Kato Shuichi, and Michael R. Reich, Yale University Press, 1979, pp. 67–109.

Starrs, Roy, "Writing the National Narrative: Changing Attitudes toward Nation-Building among Japanese Writers, 1900–1930," in *Japan's Competing Modernities: Issues in Culture and Democracy, 1900–1930*, edited by Sharon A. Minichiello, University of Hawai'i Press, 1998, pp. 206–10.

FURTHER READING

Keene, Donald, ed., *Modern Japanese Literature: From 1868 to the Present Day*, Grove Press, 1989.

This influential anthology collects works of the most admired Japanese authors who have written modern fiction, following the trail Ōgai blazed. From the Meiji Restoration beginning in 1868 to working authors of the late twentieth century, Keene has selected careful translations of the best short stories accompanied by brief introductions to each writer and his work. Included are examples of modern Japanese poetry and haiku.

Ōgai, Mori, *The Historical Fiction of Mori Ōgai*, edited by David A. Dilworth and J. Thomas Rimer, University of Hawai'i Press, 1991.

Considered his best work, Ōgai's historical fiction, written late in his career, was a reflection of his newly found passion for Japanese traditions. After devoting much of his life to modernizing Japanese literature, Ōgai turned to Japan's feudal past to explore samurai history and culture, preserving oral legends for generations to come.

Starrs, Roy, *Modernism and Japanese Culture*, Palgrave Macmillan, 2011.

Starrs offers a history of Japan's relationship with modernity, considering the Meiji Restoration through the world wars and beyond. Offering a mix of facts and insights into the Japanese approach to modernism, Starrs traces the cultural shifts that led the isolated island on the path toward becoming the world power it is today.

Swale, Alistair, *The Meiji Restoration: Monarchism, Mass Communication and Conservative Revolution*, Palgrave Macmillan, 2009.

The Meiji Restoration saw the collapse of an ancient economic system and the rise of a European model of government in its place. A remarkable event in Japanese history, the rebuilding and expansion of the once-secluded nation is the subject of Swale's text. Paying specific attention to Japanese thought and cultural attitudes toward change, Swale examines how such a massive reconstruction of values and methods took place and the extent to which the country succeeded.

SUGGESTED SEARCH TERMS

Mori Ōgai

Under Reconstruction AND Mori Ōgai

modern Japanese literature

Meiji Restoration AND literature

Seiyoken Hotel AND Mori Ōgai

German AND Japanese literature

Ivan Morris AND Mori Ōgai

Japanese literature AND Mori Ōgai

What Means Switch

GISH JEN

1990

In a 1993 interview with Martha Satz, author Gish Jen admitted a desire to be "wicked." When asked to explain what she meant by the word, Jen said,

> It means writing about the things we're not supposed to write about. For example in "What Means Switch" I'm pretty close to the edge. People are uncomfortable when one starts writing about the Jews and the Japanese.... It's dangerous but as a writer you have to get up the nerve to write about the things that are dangerous.

Indeed, in the short story "What Means Switch," Jen fearlessly tackles the controversial issues of personal cultural identity, racial stereotypes, and the budding romantic interest and social complications of eighth graders.

The topics proved challenging enough for Jen to continue exploring them: the story first appeared in the *Atlantic* magazine in 1990, and Jen later expanded it into a full-length novel, *Mona in the Promised Land* (1996). The short story can be found in the young-adult collection *Who Do You Think You Are? Stories of Friends and Enemies* (edited by Hazel Rochman and Darlene Z. McCampbell) and in *Growing Up Asian American: An Anthology* (edited by Maria Hong), both published in 1993.

AUTHOR BIOGRAPHY

Jen was born in 1955 in Scarsdale, New York. Her parents had immigrated from China before Jen was born. Her father was a professor of

Gish Jen *(© Steve Liss | Time & Life Pictures | Getty Images)*

engineering, and her mother was an elementary-school teacher. "Gish" is a nickname; Jen's given name is Lillian. The nickname came from silent-movie actress Lillian Gish.

Jen grew up in Yonkers and Scarsdale, New York. She had three brothers, all of whom became successful businessmen, and one sister, who became a doctor. Jen was expected to embark upon a similar professional career and went to Harvard University, intending to study law or medicine. While there, she took a poetry class, which she loved. Her professor saw her talent and encouraged her to pursue a career in

a field related to literature. Jen explained to Satz, "I'm the daughter of immigrants—it never even crossed my mind for one minute that I might become a poet." Instead of trying her hand at writing, she worked for a year at a publishing job that her professor helped arrange for her after she graduated from Harvard with a degree in English, but the job was not satisfying.

Jen enrolled at Stanford University, intending to get her master's in business administration, but her heart was not in the work. Her grades in business classes suffered while she took writing classes that she thoroughly enjoyed.

While at Stanford she met her future husband, David O'Connor, who helped her study for exams in an effort to improve her grades. Finally, Jen took a leave of absence from Stanford and was accepted at the prestigious Iowa Writers' Workshop.

After Jen earned her master's degree from the University of Iowa in 1983, she and O'Connor were married. They lived for a few years in California before settling in Cambridge, Massachusetts. Jen lacked confidence in her abilities as a writer and applied for a job as a secretary. However, before she accepted such a job, she received a fellowship from Radcliffe College's Bunting Institute, which gives financial support to promising writers. With this encouragement, she kept writing.

"What Means Switch" was first published in 1990 in the *Atlantic*, and Jen published her first novel, *Typical American*, in 1991. It was named by the *New York Times* a notable book of the year and was a finalist for the National Book Critics Circle Award. Jen expanded her story "What Means Switch" into a full-length novel, *Mona in the Promised Land* (1996), which was also a *New York Times* notable book. In addition, the *Los Angeles Times* named it one of the ten best books of 1996. Jen has written short stories and essays that have been published in the *New York Times* and the *New Yorker* magazine. Her short-story collection *Who's Irish?* was published in 1999. Jen still lives in Cambridge with her husband, her son, Luke, and her daughter, Paloma.

PLOT SUMMARY

"What Means Switch" is narrated in the first person, which means the narrator, Mona Chang, refers to herself as "I" and the story is told from her point of view. The story opens with Mona describing the family's decision to move from Yonkers to Scarsdale, a wealthier neighborhood with good schools. Their house is at a sharp curve in the road, which sometimes causes drivers to lose control and drive up into the yard. When the car tires damage their grass and flowers, Mona's mother is polite, letting the drivers use the telephone and waving their apologies away.

Mona explains that social classes in her new school are divided based on one's knowledge of

and experience with romantic activity. Mona begins to think she will never be popular unless she finds a boyfriend, but then she blurts out to Barbara Gugelstein that she knows karate. When Barbara is impressed, Mona begins to realize that her Chinese heritage, instead of making her a social outsider, can give her an exotic appeal. She shows off her few words of Chinese and acts as if she is an expert on Chinese cuisine, though in truth she prefers to eat frozen turkey pot pies.

Mona settles in at the new school, "ad-libbing [her] way through eighth grade," until another Asian student enrolls at the school. Mona has a moment of panic: he might uncover her secrets and let her classmates figure out how ordinary she is. It turns out he is Japanese, not Chinese, and he was not born in the United States like Mona. His name is Sherman.

Mona's classmates immediately assume that she and Sherman will be friends, simply because they are both of Asian descent. The girls send Mona notes, telling her, "He has a crush on you already." Their teacher, Mrs. Mandeville, takes the notes away, but she does not have a chance to read them aloud—her usual policy—before the bell rings and class is over.

Mrs. Mandeville introduces Mona to Sherman; his mother wanted him in a class with "any other Orientals." From then on, Sherman tags along after Mona, much to Mona's embarrassment. Sherman does not know how to fit in. He has a notebook with a fluffy kitten on it, and when Mona suggests he get a cooler notebook, he misunderstands and buys her a matching one instead. Because Sherman and Mona are together so much, the other students assume that they are a couple, and Mona says little to correct this impression. She begins to think that maybe they are in love, since everyone else seems to think they are an item.

The boys from Sherman's gym class discover that he knows judo, and this impresses them. Sherman is no longer a social outcast, and he stops sitting at the girls' table with Mona during lunch. He continues to bring Mona small presents such as flowers and oranges.

Sherman tells Mona a little about his life back in Japan. She is surprised to learn that Tokyo only recently got electricity everywhere. Mona explains that she is American because she was born in the United States but that Sherman could also become American. She tells him, "You only have to learn some rules and speeches." Sherman insists that he is Japanese.

Sherman draws some pictures that reflect stereotypical ideas: an American who looks like John Wayne; a Jewish person who "looks like the Wicked Witch of the West, only male"; and Japanese and Chinese people, both of whom look like Sherman. He draws a picture of a Japanese flag and puts it on the Changs' refrigerator to demonstrate how in school in Japan, they bow to show respect to the flag. Mrs. Chang is angry when she sees this. She yanks the picture of the flag down and tells Sherman that it is time for him to go home. After he leaves, Mrs. Chang explains her extreme reaction to the Japanese flag: Japan and China were enemies in World War II.

Barbara presses Mona for information about whether she and Sherman are friends or something more. Mona does not know how to answer because she does not know herself. Mona feels as if she is losing ground in terms of her popularity at school. Danielle Meyers used to hang out with Mona and Barbara but spends more time with other girls now, and Mona thinks that it is because of her own lack of success with Sherman.

Mona begins to hint to Barbara and the other girls that she has more experience with boys than she truly does. She notes, "The more I intimate that Sherman and I are hot and heavy, the more it seems we actually are." She develops a crush on him.

Gradually Sherman begins to show Mona physical affection. First their shoulders touch, then they link pinkie fingers, and then they finally hold hands. When the school year ends and Sherman is about to return to Japan, he asks Mona to marry him. She is surprised: she is only thirteen years old. He wants her to come to live in Japan someday. He kisses her cheek.

Sherman's mother comes to pick him up at Mona's house and accidentally drives up onto the lawn. Mona's mother assures Mrs. Matsumoto that it is "no trouble." Mrs. Chang invites Mrs. Matsumoto in for tea. Mr. Matsumoto comes in a taxi to meet her and Sherman.

Sherman and Mona sneak out into the backyard for a private good-bye. He kisses her neck and hugs her. They discuss again whether one of them could "switch," and Mona thinks Sherman

should be the one to change because "the way you do everything is weird." Sherman argues that she only wants a boyfriend to become popular and then uses judo to flip her onto the grass. After Sherman has gone back to Japan, Mona writes him a letter, but he makes it clear that their relationship is over.

Mona remembers that she did not tell Barbara how she and Sherman parted. She also never let her parents know what happened. She did not go inside when her mother called her, telling her to come and say a formal good-bye to Mr. and Mrs. Matsumoto. Mona recalls how after the Matsumotos left, her family resumed discussing whether or not they should build a low brick wall as protection against the cars that tear up the lawn.

CHARACTERS

Callie Chang
Callie is Mona's sister. Like Mona, she wants to present a certain image to her friends at school, so they agree to keep certain details of their life at home secret, like their enjoyment of frozen pot pies. Mona calls Callie "the liar in the family," but Mona herself also lies to impress her friends.

Mona Chang
Mona is the main character of the story and its narrator. Like many young teenagers, Mona feels that she does not completely fit in with her classmates. She fears that many of them have more experience with boys, and her Chinese heritage makes her feel like even more of an outsider. She tries to turn this into a positive thing: claiming to know karate to impress her friends and throwing out the few words of Chinese that she knows: "'*Be-yeh fa-foon . . . Shee-veh. Ji nu.*' Meaning, 'Stop acting crazy. Rice gruel. Soy sauce.'" The girls in Mona's class seem to assume that Sherman will become her boyfriend simply because they are both of Asian descent. Mona convinces herself that she does indeed love Sherman, though by the end of the story, she realizes that she never truly knew or understood him.

Mr. Chang
Mr. Chang is Mona's father. He does not play a large role in the story. His desire to buy a house in Scarsdale shows his wish to fit in and to improve his position in society.

Mrs. Chang

Mrs. Chang is Mona's mother. Like her husband, she sees their move to a new town as a way to fit into mainstream American society, but she also clings to old-world traditions. Part of the reason the family moves is because Scarsdale is on "a list of the top ten schools nationwide," yet Mrs. Chang also tells Mona, "No good for a girl be too smart anyway." Mrs. Chang is extremely polite, even when people, including Mrs. Matsumoto, drive across the lawn, which is near a treacherous turn in the road. However, when Sherman puts a drawing of the Japanese flag on the Changs' refrigerator, Mrs. Chang becomes angry, remembering how the Chinese were treated by the Japanese during World War II.

Barbara Gugelstein

Barbara is Mona's best friend. They seem to have fun together, though Mona feels the need to present a certain image to Barbara: worldly in her experience with boys and exotically different with her Chinese heritage. Mona's relationship with Sherman blossoms in part because of peer pressure from Barbara and the other girls in Mona's class.

Andy Kaplan

Andy is another student in Mona's class. Her friend Barbara has a crush on him.

Mrs. Mandeville

Mrs. Mandeville is Mona's teacher. Mona gives the impression that she is strict, because her "policy is to read all notes aloud" when she confiscates them in class.

Mr. Matsumoto

Mr. Matsumoto is Sherman's father. Mona describes him as a "heavy-browed business man, friendly but brisk." Sherman tells Mona that his father once accidentally burned him with a cigarette when he was drunk and afterward bowed to his wife in apology. He comes to the Changs' house in a taxi after his wife accidentally drives up onto their lawn.

Mrs. Matsumoto

Mrs. Matsumoto is Sherman's mother. When she enrolled Sherman in school in Scarsdale, she asked if he might be placed in a class with another Asian student. When she comes to pick Sherman up at the Changs' house, she accidentally drives up onto the lawn. She and Mona's mother "negotiate ferociously" after the accident, with Mrs. Matsumoto wanting to pay for the damage and Mrs. Chang insisting that it is "no trouble."

Sherman Matsumoto

Sherman is a student in Mona's class who has temporarily come to the United States from Japan. His mother specifically asked if he could be put into a class with another Asian student. Sherman does not speak English very well, and he does not fit in socially at first, carrying a notebook with a fluffy kitten on it. After the other boys learn that Sherman knows judo, however, he earns more respect. He and Mona start an awkward courtship that ends in frustration just before he leaves to go back to Japan.

Danielle Meyers

Danielle is a classmate of Mona's, but she does not seem to be a true friend. Her willingness to talk to Mona seems to depend on how much experience Mona has with boys.

Real Estate Broker

The real estate broker who helps the Chang family find their house in Scarsdale hints that because many of the people who live in the neighborhood are wealthy and Jewish, the Changs might not fit in.

Amy Weinstein

Amy is one of Mona's friends at school.

THEMES

Cultural Identity

Throughout "What Means Switch," Jen plays with the theme of cultural identity. At first, Mona seems to see her Chinese heritage only as a tool to make her more interesting to her classmates. She lies and claims to know karate. When her friends' mothers ask her "to taste-test their Chinese cooking," she pretends to be an expert on Chinese cuisine, but in actuality she prefers frozen pot pies to her mother's oxtail soup, which both she and her sister find gross. Mona hopes that her background will be viewed positively as exotic rather than weird in a bad way.

Although Mona's heritage is Chinese, she is completely American. When Sherman asks her questions, she realizes "they're not topics I ever

TOPICS FOR FURTHER STUDY

- Read *Mona in the Promised Land*, which Jen wrote by expanding on the events and themes in "What Means Switch." In the novel, Mona struggles to define her cultural identity, converting from Catholicism to Judaism. Think of some other things Mona could have "switched" to, such as becoming very active in sports or charity work, learning more about her Chinese heritage, or joining the drama club. Write a short story to show what might have happened if Mona had made another choice, portraying the reactions of her family and friends.

- "What Means Switch" appears in various short-story collections, including *Growing Up Asian American: An Anthology* (1993), edited by Maria Hong. Choose a story from this book, or find another story elsewhere in which characters try to define themselves both in terms of their ethnic heritage and as Americans. Write a paper that compares Mona's experience with that of a character in your selected story.

- Jen is praised for her use of humor to tackle serious issues. In the novel *The Jumping Tree*, René Saldaña Jr. does much the same thing. The book tells the story of first-person narrator Rey Castanada, a middle-school student who lives in a small Texas town. After reading Saldaña's novel, imagine that Rey and Mona meet. What would they think of one another? What would they talk about? Write a dialogue between the two characters and film it with a partner. Post the video online, and ask your classmates to offer feedback.

- Research international relations between Japan and China before and during World War II to understand why Mona's mother was angry to see Sherman's drawing of a Japanese flag on her refrigerator. Make a time line listing and describing the major historical events.

discussed before. Do I like it here? Of course I like it here. I was born here." She also takes for granted the typically American assumption that people can create their own identities, choosing what they want to be. She tries to explain this idea to Sherman, telling him, "You could become American.... Like I could become Jewish, if I wanted to. I'd just have to switch, that's all." Sherman does not seem to understand: he insists that he is Japanese. His cultural identity is firmly fixed.

Those of the older generation in the story also seem to have a more static idea of their cultural identity. Mona's parents have assimilated to some extent, but only according to their specific idea about what it is to be American. For example, they are proud of their financial success. To them, something like a citizenship test is abstract, but buying a house in a good neighborhood where their daughters can get a good education feels like successfully achieving the American dream.

Social Class

Anyone who has ever eaten lunch in a school cafeteria has seen evidence of the intricate system of social class, which Jen clearly understands. With Mona's efforts to be accepted at her new school, "What Means Switch" delves into the complicated subject of junior-high and high-school popularity. Mona's first indication of what might make her popular comes when others are impressed with her knowledge, however vague that knowledge may be, about "virgins and nonvirgins." However, she quickly realizes that she "need[s] to find somebody to kiss" if she wants to keep her social position. Experience with boys is a major factor in a girl's popularity, as Jen shows with Danielle Meyers's changing level of interest in Mona, which is based on how serious she believes Mona's relationship with Sherman to be.

Mona also uses her Chinese heritage to gain social standing. Her classmates are impressed with her knowledge of Chinese language and cooking, and Mona tells her friend Barbara that she knows karate, though she only saw something about it on television. When Sherman arrives and Mona imagines he is Chinese, she fears that his superior knowledge might rob her of the social position she has managed to gain.

Sherman, however, starts out farther down the social ladder than Mona. He does not speak enough English to impress anyone, and he carries a notebook with a fluffy cat, complete with a bow on each ear, on the cover. It is far from cool for anyone, but especially for a boy, to have such a notebook. Mona is embarrassed on his behalf. Although she wishes to be popular, Mona is willing to risk her hard-won social status and be kind to Sherman. "After all, the kid's so new," she reasons; "I think I ought to have a heart." He soon gives her a notebook that matches his own—her kitten has pink bows instead of blue—but Mona tries to keep it hidden. She is too nice to hurt his feelings, but Jen makes clear how nerve-racking it is for Mona to carry Sherman's gift by highlighting Mona's relief that "for a livelong day nobody notices" the notebook. Jen understands that even a small thing can get a student forced out of one's social class in school.

Love

In this story Jen humorously but realistically portrays the trials of first love. Mona and Sherman have a sweetly awkward kind of courtship. It starts perhaps more because their classmates seem to expect it to happen than from any real attraction. From the moment Sherman enters the classroom, the other girls send Mona notes, claiming, "He has a crush on you already." Mona receives so many notes on the subject that she thinks, "I could use a secretary." Throughout the story, Mona's friend Barbara asks for details about Sherman, and Mona is at a loss to explain, because she herself does not understand what is going on. She says, "We don't kiss and we don't exactly have fantastic conversations," since Sherman does not speak English very well.

Once Mona's shoulder brushes Sherman's, and she claims it is "at least equivalent to first base" because she "felt as though I'd turned into one huge shoulder." However, it seems her excitement is more from her desire to gain experience with boys than from any real attraction to Sherman. Later, when their shoulders brush again, Mona compares them to "a pair of bleachers, pushed together but not quite matched up." This is far from a romantic metaphor, and it stresses that they are not quite connecting. Still later, when Mona and Sherman progress to actual hugs and kisses, Mona is unmoved. Even while Sherman is kissing her, she realizes that she is "not much in danger of wrecking my life on the shoals of passion; his unmoving hand feels more like a growth than a boyfriend."

The protagonist of "What Means Switch" is Mona, an average teenage girl of Chinese heritage. (© szefei / ShutterStock.com)

By the end of the story, Mona realizes she did not truly know Sherman very well. However, early romantic relationships are important in terms of what people learn about themselves rather than simply what they discover about someone else, and in this, Jen presents a very true and touching portrayal of first love.

STYLE

First-Person Narrator

Mona is the first-person narrator of "What Means Switch." This means that she refers to herself as "I" and the story is told from her point of view. Because the events are related by a single character rather than an impartial, omniscient narrator, readers should keep in mind that the perspective is limited: the things that Mona says may be biased or incorrect. Jen's choice of a first-person narrator for the story was appropriate. It gives the narration a kind of uncertainty that reflects one of the important themes in the story: Mona's uncertainty about her own identity.

Foreshadowing

Foreshadowing is a literary tool authors can use to hint early in a story about what will happen later. In "What Means Switch," Jen uses Sherman's knowledge of judo to foreshadow the climax of the story. The first hint the reader has of the importance of martial arts in the story is Mona's lie that she knows karate. Then Mona hears from the boys in Sherman's gym class that he knows judo. The fact that Mona does not figure this out for herself illustrates that she does not know him well and indicates how little effort she makes to learn more about him. The other boys start calling Sherman "Mister Judo" with "real respect," making it a central part of his character. Jen mentions martial arts throughout the story to hint at its importance in the final confrontation between Mona and Sherman. He uses his knowledge of judo to flip her, turning her into "a flailing confusion of soft human parts." The physical flip represents her understanding of the situation being turned upside down, and Mona realizes that her ideas about Sherman are wrong.

HISTORICAL CONTEXT

Multiculturalism

Multiculturalism is defined as the preservation of different cultural identities within a unified society. It can be considered in contrast to the idea of America as a great "melting pot," where some bits of individual cultures might be retained and added to the mainstream culture but where, for the most part, people are assimilated.

As a development in culture and education, multiculturalism arose out of the civil rights movement in the 1960s. As all Americans—men and women, people of all races and backgrounds—began to demand equal rights politically and socially, there was a push to recognize the value of cultures other than the mainstream, dominant, largely white European American culture. This led to the inclusion of elements of various cultures in school curricula, increasing the

diversity of what is studied and enhancing students' understanding of the world around them. Throughout the 1970s, and even more in the 1980s and 1990s, school systems began to include points of view and voices that had been previously ignored, especially in history and literature.

There was opposition to this trend. Some claimed that the word "multiculturalism" was used inconsistently until it became almost meaningless. Others argued that ethnic cultures were disappearing in the United States and that it was a natural outcome, not to be fought. Still others feared that concentrating on cultural differences would dissolve the common culture that binds the country together. There were also those who supported a middle-of-the-road approach: teaching children the more traditional, mainstream curriculum but including aspects of other cultures. It was hoped that this approach would increase universal knowledge and interests, including various heritages, without losing the shared culture. At the start of the twenty-first century, the controversy over this issue has still not been resolved.

In literature, multiculturalist writers are those whose work is concerned with issues specifically related to race, ethnicity, and culture. This does not mean, however, that any author who happens to belong to a racial, ethnic, or cultural minority is necessarily a multiculturalist. To be considered so, a writer's work must focus largely on these themes and issues.

In various interviews, Jen has explained her mixed feelings about multiculturalism. She herself has benefited from the interest in the work of ethnic minorities: she started writing when there was a trend in the publishing world to promote the work of Asian American authors, especially women. However, although the multicultural trend in the late twentieth century likely helped her work get published and recognized, Jen does not feel that it is a completely positive development.

Jen explained her thoughts in her interview with Satz in 1993. While Jen feels that multiculturalism "has added questions to the lists with which we approach literature and . . . has been an enormous contribution to our understanding," she also sees evidence of the negative effects: "readers reading a minority writer now assume that these new concerns are the ones you must be addressing." Jen fears that the true depth of literature will be ignored, that interpretations

COMPARE & CONTRAST

- **1980s:** Starting after World War II and continuing well into the 1980s, teachers and linguists research and refine the best methods for teaching English as a second language (often called ESL). Many ESL programs are launched as a result of the Immigration Reform and Control Act of 1986, which allows certain groups of undocumented immigrants to maintain permanent residence in the United States if they follow a strict application process and receive instruction in English. Because these programs are designed to help adults gain US citizenship, they merge civics and history lessons with instruction in language. However, many teenage students, like Sherman, are simply put into classrooms without any additional instruction and expected to learn English as well as they can.

  Today: ESL instruction continues to be important in the United States, where as many as one in five kids speaks a language other than English at home. Many of the methods developed in the 1980s are still used today to teach ESL, but some schools have set up programs providing instruction in students' native languages (most commonly Spanish) as well as English. Some critics object that this practice allows students to stay dependent on their first language rather than learning English.

- **1980s:** Stories by Asian American authors start to become popular, especially those by women, largely because of the success and popularity of works like Maxine Hong Kingston's *Woman Warrior* (1976) and Amy Tan's *Joy Luck Club* (1989). Stories about immigration and the children of immigrants are well represented, and there are many novels of historical fiction. Most of the literature portrays the experiences of Asians from China and Japan.

  Today: Literature by Asian Americans shows more cultural diversity and addresses a wider range of themes. Although issues specifically related to cultural heritage are still addressed, general social issues are equally important. Japanese *manga* (and spinoffs such as Korean *manwha*) and graphic novels are hugely popular.

- **1980s:** The 1990 US census shows Chinese Americans to be the tenth-largest immigrant group. Many immigrants from China settle in California and New York.

  Today: Chinese immigrants are the third-largest US immigrant group, after those born in Mexico and the Philippines. Although almost half of Chinese immigrants to the United States live in California and New York, more are choosing to settle in other states, such as Wyoming and Nebraska, where the Chinese American population was previously relatively low.

---

of an author's work may very well be limited if that author happens to fit under a convenient cultural or ethnic label.

Jen has experienced this problem herself, as she explained to Yuko Matsukawa in *MELUS*. Jen was told by some people who had read one of her books that "it was a book about preserving one's heritage." She resented what she felt was a "knee-jerk reaction" on the part of these readers and saw their interpretation as being restricted because they read the work only through the lens of multiculturalism. These readers seemed to think,

> You're an ethnic writer, so you must be writing about "people striving to preserve their heritage." I'm not saying that on some level there isn't some kind of tug about what to retain and what to take on but that wasn't what the book was all about.

Mona feels peer pressure when her friends whisper about her and Sherman. *(© Sergey Mironov | ShutterStock.com)*

While Jen feels that multiculturalism in literature has been a wonderful advance overall, allowing different voices to be heard and prompting new and interesting questions to be asked, she does not want to be limited by it in what she writes or in how readers see her work. She is not alone in this feeling; in the literary world, there has been some angry backlash from writers who do not want to be limited by being categorized. Jen, as a Chinese American author, does write about issues specific to being Chinese American. However, she also addresses issues that apply to all Americans, or to all families, or to all humans, and readers' interpretation and enjoyment of her work should not be limited by labels. Multiculturalism is about diversity, and that should include diversity of thought and intent within the work of an individual author.

CRITICAL OVERVIEW

Because "What Means Switch" was published fairly early in Jen's career and because short stories rarely get much individual critical attention, it is difficult to find comments about this story specifically. When Jen expanded the story into the novel *Mona in the Promised Land*, however, it received very positive reviews, as have Jen's other books.

Several critics appreciate Jen's ability to authentically capture the characteristic rhythm of speech of Asian Americans, especially those for whom English is not a first language, without resorting to caricature. For example, the *Globe & Mail*'s Charles Foran applauds the voices Jen gives her characters: "Like Maxine Hong Kingston, . . . Gish Jen is all ears to both the new things members of 'half-half' families say about themselves and where they live, and how they express those things."

In *Interactions*, Esra Sahtiyanci Oztarhan praises Jen's work as "humorous stories about serious issues like racism and identity quest of Chinese Americans," executed with "irresistible charm." Yahlin Chang agrees, writing in a review in *Newsweek* that Jen "dissolves cultural and ethnic conflicts in the acid of comedy."

This is not to say that Jen's books are all for the sake of inconsequential humor. Foran admits that Jen makes use of "old-country secrets and abiding sweet-sour mamas," which he calls typical "concerns of the Chinese-American novel." However, he feels that "Jen, a genuinely funny writer, is too smart and unsentimental not to press the material in a fresh direction." David Gates, in a review of Jen's short-story collection *Who's Irish?*, explains that "Jen's performance isn't a series of one-liners, but an elaborate balancing act: Chinese and American, painful and funny." She is not writing only to amuse, Gates believes, but instead "uses her ever-ready wit to provide ironic distance from genuinely dark places."

Perhaps Marina Heung, in the *Women's Review of Books*, best sums it up: "True to her satiric mode, Jen takes delight in the incongruities brewed when different races and classes are mixing to create unexpected affinities and tensions." Critics agree that Jen uses humor deftly to tackle these difficult and complex issues.

CRITICISM

Kristen Sarlin Greenberg

Greenberg is a freelance writer and editor with a background in literature and philosophy. In the following essay, she examines Jen's exploration of perception and identity in "What Means Switch."

From the opening line of "What Means Switch," Gish Jen makes it clear that perception will be important to the story. The first thing Mona tells us about herself is that she comes from a "nice Chinese family." She wants it to be clear that she is from a good family and that she is a good girl. She mentions the fact that she has gotten "almost straight A's her whole life" and that her "sister, Callie, is the liar in the family," not Mona herself. Mona seems to understand that being perceived as a good girl from a nice family will work in her favor in most situations.

Mona is somewhat concerned, however, about her Chinese heritage. She understands that, in the largely Jewish population of Scarsdale, New York, others will notice immediately that she is Chinese American, and she is afraid that it will make her an outsider. She does her best to control how her classmates perceive her. She lies to her friend Barbara, claiming to know karate. She shows off the Chinese words she knows, and Barbara is "impressed." Barbara

> WHEN MONA AND SHERMAN FIRST DISCUSSED THE IDEA OF MAKING A 'SWITCH,' SHE WAS WILLING TO CHANGE. NOW, HOWEVER, MONA SAYS, 'I THINK YOU SHOULD SWITCH.'"

does not know that the only words Mona knows are for things like "rice gruel" and "soy sauce." Food becomes important as Mona's friends' mothers try to imitate authentic Chinese cooking, asking Mona to taste it and give her opinion. Mona feels the need to exaggerate: the fact that her mother remembers eating "sliced tomatoes with sugar on top" in China is simply not interesting enough to share with her classmates. However, "the fact that somewhere in China, somebody eats or has eaten or once ate living monkey brains—now that's conversation."

Mona also exaggerates and hedges around the truth to change her friends' perceptions regarding her experience with boys. When Barbara says she thinks Mona and Sherman are "just friends," Mona answers vaguely and "mysteriously" because this "is how Danielle Meyers talks; everything's secret, she only lets out so much." Danielle is popular and, Mona thinks, experienced with boys. Danielle loses interest in Mona when she stops talking about her relationship with Sherman, and Mona is afraid to lose whatever popularity she has gained at her new school. Not only are her classmates' perceptions important in terms of popularity, they are the main reason Mona gets together with Sherman in the first place. Her classmates seem to expect it, simply because Mona and Sherman are both Asian.

As Mona works to change others' perceptions of her identity, she seems to alter her actual identity, adapting it to suit her circumstances. For example, her classmates expect her to be Sherman's girlfriend, and she gradually develops a crush on him. It is a complicated idea of identity that Jen is presenting in this short story. According to Marina Heung in the *Women's Review of Books*, "Jen seems to be telling us that identity is a slippery concept because the social rituals by which we define ourselves are

WHAT DO I READ NEXT?

- Jen's first novel, *Typical American* (1991), tells the story of Mona's Chang's father from 1947, when he came to the United States to get his doctorate, to the time when he is a husband and father. Jen explores the crux of the immigrant experience: how to preserve tradition while finding a place in one's new home.

- The popular graphic novel *American Born Chinese* (2006), by Gene Luen Yang, tackles some of the same issues often explored in Jen's work: belonging, identity, friendship, racism, and what it means to be an American. Yang weaves three story lines together into a book that is both provocative and funny.

- *Cuba 15* (2003), by Nancy Osa, is the story of Violet Paz as she plans her *quinceañera*. Like Mona, Violet considers herself American but must figure out how she feels about her ethnic heritage while dealing with the stresses of day-to-day life: school, friends, and parental expectations.

- Sherman Alexie's 2007 young-adult novel *The Absolutely True Diary of a Part-Time*

Indian follows Junior as he leaves the Spokane reservation where he grew up to attend a mostly white high school in another town. Junior, treated like an outsider by his new classmates and criticized as a traitor by friends he left behind, struggles to find his place.

- *IraqiGirl: Diary of a Teenage Girl in Iraq* (2009) is a record of the personal blog of fifteen-year-old Hadiya (IraqiGirl is a pseudonym). She is a teenage girl like any other, but as her country comes under military occupation, she witnesses firsthand the consequences of war: strict curfews, families fleeing from their homes, and death. She tells her story with brave honesty and maintains a sense of humor.

- In *The Namesake* (2003), Jhumpa Lahiri tells the story of two generations of an Indian American family. Through the characters of Gogol Ganguli and his parents, Lahiri explores the themes of family, tradition, finding one's identity, and parental expectation.

---

constantly changing and adapting to circumstances." For Mona, identity is not an unchanging thing. She wants her classmates to think her more experienced with boys than she truly is, for example, but she would likely be horrified if her parents thought that. Mona presents different aspects of herself to different people.

In *Critique: Studies in Contemporary Fiction*, Fu-jen Chen explains that one might be able to change one's identity not only between different aspects of oneself but also between broader social categories. Chen believes that Jen's idea of creating one's own identity, rather than accepting a "consistent inherited identity, . . . suggests that identity is merely performative and always open to the possibility of 'crossing'—

passing as a member not only of a given race, but of any given culture."

This notion of change is highlighted in the discussion between Mona and Sherman in the Changs' kitchen. Sherman asks Mona if she is American, and she laughs: "'Sure I'm American,' I say. 'Everybody who's born here is American, and also some people who convert from what they were before. You could become American.'" Sherman asserts that he is Japanese, but Mona does not see the problem. She is certain that she herself could change into anything she wanted. She would "just have to switch, that's all." Where Mona is open to change, Sherman cannot see it as a possibility. His sees his own identity as more fixed.

Mona's parents also seem to have more fixed ideas about identity. Like Mona, they worry about the perceptions of others. They contemplate putting up a low brick wall to protect their lawn and flowers from drivers who veer off the curving road in front of their house, but they worry: "What will the neighbors say?" However, where Mona sees the perceptions of others only as an indicator of her popularity and firmly believes that she can change and adjust these perceptions at will, for her parents the opinions of the neighbors become a measure of how successful they have been at becoming truly American. Mr. and Mrs. Chang do not want to change any more than they already have, according to Chen: "What their children celebrate—an incessant movement or a freedom to perform various identities endlessly—designates, for the immigrant generation, a horrible experience of endless displacement and a denial of their American citizenship."

For the Changs, economic success is closely linked to their idea of the American dream. In an interview with Martha Satz in the *Southwest Review*, Jen explained:

> People think you set foot in America and you become American instantly. For the characters in my book, it takes a while to become American and it's not so much becoming a citizen that makes them feel American, it's something like buying a house.

Mr. and Mrs. Chang have achieved their definition of success, which makes them feel more like true Americans.

There is a possible negative side effect to this view of success and this definition of being American, as explained by Siham Arfaroui in *Interactions*: "The mobility of the Chang family to a Jewish neighbourhood in suburban New York already imposes the incarceration of a model minority mentality." The phrase "model minority" is sometimes used to describe an ethnic, racial, or religious group that is perceived to achieve a high degree of success and is thought of as a model for other minorities to imitate. The notion of a model minority comes from the same assumptions that created the stereotype of the overachieving Asian student who gets stellar grades while also excelling at music or sports or both. Although these ideas are positive, they are still stereotypes and therefore limiting. Arfaroui describes this way of thinking as "incarceration" because it can make people feel trapped and pressured to behave in a certain way. In "What Means Switch," Jen alludes to the idea of a model minority with both the Changs' new house and Mona's

mention of her good grades, but she is too talented and aware a writer to allow this stereotypical image of Chinese Americans to take over. Her characters are complicated and complete.

The final interaction between Mona and Sherman is another interesting example of how Jen explores ideas of identity and perception. Sherman asks Mona to marry him even though they are only thirteen, and is said to tell Mona, "more or less, *You will need to study how to switch*." When she refuses, he turns her upside down—flipping her over using his skills in judo. The literal, physical flip echoes the turnaround in her perceptions of Sherman. Mona realizes that she did not really know him; she made assumptions about him and never bothered to assess them as they compared with reality. Mona says that afterward her "brain aches as though it's been shoved to some new place in my skull," which in a way it has, with her new perception of Sherman as well as her new understanding of herself.

With this last interaction Mona starts to assert herself and the identity that she is in the process of creating. When Mona and Sherman first discussed the idea of making a "switch," she was willing to change. Now, however, Mona says, "I think you should switch." She is no longer willing to change herself just to get a boyfriend or because she is worried about what others think of her. When she writes Sherman a letter after he returns to Japan, she backs away from this assertiveness, claiming "I was just trying to be entertaining." However, when Sherman rejects her in his answering letter, Mona throws away the mementos she saved from her time with him with very little regret. She moves on.

At the very end of the story, Mona says, "If I could, I'd switch everything to be different." However, she recognizes that she cannot do that, and perhaps she does not know what changes she would make—she is still young and does not yet know what her identity will be. Instead, she decides to join her family, thinking she "might as well sit here at the table for a while, discussing what I know how to discuss. I nod and listen. . . ." Perhaps that is not a bad situation for a young woman to be in as she makes decisions about who she wants to be. She will listen to her parents, respecting her heritage, but will reserve the right to create her own identity and make her own changes.

Source: Kristen Sarlin Greenberg, Critical Essay on "What Means Switch," in *Short Stories for Students*, Gale, Cengage Learning, 2014.

"What Means Switch" explores the excitement and frustration of Mona's first experience with romance. *(© nathapol HPS | ShutterStock.com)*

Esra Sahtiyanci Oztarhan

In the following review, Oztarhan discusses Jen's work as an exploration of what it means to be American.

Mona in the Promised Land is Asian American writer Gish Jen's novel about the identity quest of a Chinese American girl heroine Mona. The story takes place in early 1970's where Mona lives in a Jewish suburbia in Scarshill, NY, with her China born parents and her American born sister. The novel centers on the conversion of Mona into Judaism, thus reconstructs notions such as nationalism, assimilation, multiculturalism and identity that are the common themes of immigrant literature. Jen's novel brings new approaches to these notions by her choice of a young protagonist and her humorous style.

All the novels of Gish Jen are humorous stories about serious issues like racism and identity quest of Chinese Americans. Her first novel *Typical American* (1991) follows the lives of Ralph Chang, his sister and his sister's roommate who later becomes his wife. The novel is a

satirical account of the family's various efforts of fulfilling the American dream, of becoming a "typical American" and the obstacles they face. The first line of the novel makes it clear that "it's an American story" in which the characters try to adapt to the American Dream while trying to hang on to their Chinese roots. Jen has also written a collection of short stories entitled *Who's Irish?* (1999), about the immigrant experiences of Chinese Americans, but also of Jewish Americans, African Americans, Irish Americans, etc.

Her latest book of 2004, *Love Wife*, explores similar issues such as being Chinese American in white mainstream society by portraying a racially mixed family. The family consists of Carnegie Wang, his WASP wife, whom Carnegie's mother refers to as "Blondie," their two adopted children and one biological son. Their family life is disturbed by the arrival of a Chinese cousin, who is arranged by Carnegie's mother to work as a nanny to the children. It becomes quite clear early on, however, that Carnegie's mother brings the Chinese cousin into the family with the intention of presenting "an ideal wife" for her son. The Chinese cousin not only disturbs the relations of the couple as a "love wife," she also brings with her stories and traditions of China. Thus she enables the characters', mainly Carnegie's rediscovery of his Chinese roots. Jen's novel discusses concepts like what is real, what is constructed or what is natural, which will construct the basic problematic themes in her other novels as well.

Mona in the Promised Land is the continuation of her literary tradition of exploring the Chinese American experience in contemporary United States. The novel is the story of the Chinese American family Changs (who came to America in her first novel *Typical American*) that is told through the eyes of their daughter Mona. Mona is a typical adolescent having problems with her family and her peer group, who finds herself being converted to Judaism amidst these cultural controversies. The novel is a good example of ethnic bildungsroman with a clearly defined identity search. The bildung of the novel is reached when Mona, the rebellious adolescent, comes to a final reconciliation with her mother, and by so doing with her ancestry and roots and, paradoxically enough, it is precisely through Jewish rituals and conversion that Mona comes to understand her Chineseness. It is stated in the novel as such: "Now that she is Jewish, she feels more of a Chinese than ever"; or she says: "The more Jewish you become, the more Chinese you'll be." Gish Jen, therefore succeeded in portraying the pain of finding oneself in adolescence as a communal representation for the larger identity quest struggle of Chinese American immigrants as a whole. Therefore Jen defends the irresistible charm of returning to one's roots in coping with the racist and multicultural atmosphere of United States.

The novel apart from being an adolescent narrative, just like any immigrant story, reflects the in between situation of Chinese American

Mona split between the Chinese and the American cultures. Jen depicts Mona's uneasiness as being like "a sore thumb...sticking out by herself." Being born and raised in America, she is under constant pressure from her parents who are still tied to their Chinese roots. She is also surrounded by her peer group, which pushes her to be like "an American girl." Mona has to find her own identity as opposed to her hyphenated one determined by the dominant culture, free from the identity her parents and peer group design for her. In this sense, Gish Jen's novel has so many common features with the Asian American women's fiction of 70's and 80's like Kingston, Ng and Tan's works. These works of Chinese American women with Jen's focus on the situation of the Chinese daughters born in United States torn between their parent's world and the new world. These novels reflect the ongoing generation struggle between "the swan feather mothers" and "Coca Cola daughters" so to say.

At the same time, Jen brings a fresh insight to Asian American women literature in the 1990s to "what it means to be an Asian American girl in 70's." Her novel is quite revolutionary by portraying a purely postmodern identity model for the new immigrants. It is Mona's solution to be torn between two cultures. As Mona summarizes by saying: "American means being whatever you want, and I happened to pick being Jewish." Mona with her new chosen identity of a "Catholic Chinese Jew" differs from the hybrid characters of the earlier literary examples. In her depiction of Mona's active claiming of Judaism, Jen criticizes the American Dream in the earlier immigrant literature by choosing to portray a character who claims fluid identities. The new American experiment is about the naturalness of choices. A possible reason why Jen used conversion to Judaism in the novel is because in the United States, the Chinese are called the "New Jews." That is because they seem to be the living proof of the American Dream, the "model minority." And it is exactly what Jen criticizes in her novel.

Mona's choice of changing her identity is a practical reflection of Homi Bhabha's "third space" concept of immigrant experience. It is defined as an empowering position, which enables the subject to choose among the various possibilities. Thus, Mona being in the third space, being neither a pure Chinese nor a typical American, feels free to choose whichever she likes. Belonging to neither culture is not a disempowering situation, but an interplay of identity for Mona. She tells her friends that she "just have to switch and that's all." From time to time when her exoticism attracts attention in class, she acts as if she knows Chinese and Chinese civilization. She tells her friends that: "[S]he knows karate... she can make her hands like steel by thinking hard... she knows how to get pregnant by tea... she knows Chinese." But in fact all she knows in Chinese is how to say: "Stop acting crazy. Rice gruel. Soy sauce" which becomes enough to impress her friends. And from time to time she can reject her Chinese culture and roots entirely when she felt being oppressed by Chinese traditions. Mona converts to Judaism, because she believes it to be about "ask, ask, instead of just obey, obey" which is exactly the opposite of what she always hears at home about being the oppressed minority. These identity switches are predominant throughout the whole novel in other characters as well like her Jewish friends who decide to be a WASP, and back again at their convenience. Also for example her sister decides to become more Chinese than her parents all of a sudden. Mona's boyfriend joining the black power although he is white is another example of identity switch in the novel. This postmodern sense of unfixed identity is a criticism to Orientalist discourses and essentialist theories.

Jen changes the standard notion of Americanness, Jewishness and Chineseness completely by her work. Being a Chinese American women writer herself, she deconstructs all existing stereotypes. That is to say she criticizes the model minority myth of the previous generations. Some critics like Frank Chin label the works of Kingston, Ng and Tan as a continuation of the Western myth of "the model minority." In this respect Jen unlike the previous Asian American women writers subverts this existing tradition. Gish Jen intentionally creates unconventional and unrepresentative characters in her novel to reinvent Chinese Americanness to the same extent as she reenacts her Americanness. Jen says: "This book is not a denial of my heritage, but [America] is the place where I grew up. This is my country; this is what I know. And, in this book, I lay claim to that." In the same interview of the *Asian Week*, Jen confesses that she created her own definition of American. She says: "It is not something that you come into [and] particularly does not involve abandoning where you came from. I think of Americanness as a

preoccupation with identity. It is the hallmark of the New World because we live in a society where you are not only who your parents were, and you don't already know what your children will be. That is not to say that I am blond and eat apple pie, but any definition that finds me less American—well, all I can say is that something is wrong with the definition." This reaction against essentialist definitions of identity brings out one of the best examples of a protagonist with a fluid identity in *Mona in the Promised Land*.

Despite its many strengths, there are a number of small weaknesses in the novel, like the plot being a bit erratic. The coming of age story of Mona ends too quickly at the end of the novel. The final bildung of reconciliation with her mother and her marriage are mentioned at the last two or three pages of the book before we understand how she grew up that fast. However, *Mona in the Promised Land* is an important and timely novel on postmodern identity. It opens new horizons in the minds of the reader in bringing forward brand new definitions to Asian American identity. Jen's criticism of Oriental identity and stereotypes provides new meanings to contemporary Chinese American and contemporary immigrant fiction. Moreover the story of Mona—often very humorous—offers new dimensions to many concepts of American culture like assimilation and discrimination. Academicians who are interested in ethnic studies, Asian American literature, identity theory, girl studies and contemporary women's literature can find Gish Jen's *Mona in the Promised Land* worth reading to witness the experiences of the new immigrants like Mona.

Source: Esra Sahtiyanci Oztarhan, Review of *Mona in the Promised Land*, in *Interactions*, Vol. 15, No. 2, Fall 2006, pp. 165–68.

Sarah Anne Johnson

In the following interview excerpt, Jen talks about her resistance to being pigeonholed as an Asian American author.

. . . *You are such a quintessentially American writer in that you turn what it means to be American on its head and redefine it altogether. You first did this in* Typical American, *where you depict the Chang family pursuing the American dream and struggling with homesickness, assimilation, racism, and greed. When you're writing, are you aware of making these points, or do they rise out of character?*

" I THINK THE FACT THAT PEOPLE FIND THE

BOOK SO FUNNY IS PROOF THAT IT IS A CHALLENGE

TO IDEAS THAT ARE HELD RIGHT NOW IN OUR

CULTURE."

They rise out of character, and I bring it up a little bit. That would be the analytical part. I try to stay ahead of the critics, and see what I wrote myself. That said, no novel can be written by sitting down and saying, "Now I'm going to turn ideas about the American dream on their head." You better have a lot of cappuccino before you start that one. I write about these nerves, and some of these nerves have to do with how American I am. The whole question of whether an Asian-American is an American or a foreigner has been with me my whole life, even after *Who's Irish?* came out.

Does it make you angry?

I have to say that I mostly think it's ridiculous. It's so ridiculous that it's hard to be angry. It'd be like being angry at a child. The level of ignorance can be so unbelievable, but I see it as a kind of amiable irritant. When *Who's Irish?* came out, the first line of one of my reviews referred to the collection as a series of stories about America as seen by foreigners. I thought, this is 1999! What can you do but laugh? If I didn't feel the weight of the culture and educated people behind me, I'm sure I'd be furious, but that's not the case.

When I wrote *Typical American,* I was aware that to call a book about Chinese-Americans *Typical American* was provocative, and that felt good. I don't know if that's anger, or what that is. It's a desire to set something straight at some level, sure, and there's a measure of defiance in it. The world is full of nonsense; if you can use it more than it uses you, for a writer, it's a gift.

Typical American is told in the third-person personal point of view looking over the shoulder of Ralph Chang. How did you decide on this point of view?

I think that because people were so convinced that I must be writing immigrant autobiography, I instinctively shied away from first person.

Do you find it more or less difficult to inhabit characters of the opposite sex? Are there inherent challenges in this?

I don't find it difficult.

Ralph's assimilation begins with his renaming from Y. Fang Chang to the American Ralph Chang by a secretary at the Foreign Student Affairs Office. While this is a common experience for many immigrants, it's ironic that upon entrance into America, where people hope to find a new freedom, they must first give away an essential part of themselves—their name!

There are many ironies in this book, and that certainly is one of them. I have to say that Ralph finds, ironically, a kind of freedom in his new name. For many people the new name might not be freeing, but in Ralph's case it is. One of the many things that, in hindsight, I was trying to do was to complicate the immigrant story. There isn't one story; there are millions of stories. Some people come and find restriction here, and some people come and find liberty. Sometimes that liberty is what we think it is, and sometimes it's a totally different kind of liberty. For Ralph, it's liberty from his family. "Goodbye, Dad!" That was probably 90 percent of it for him.

You describe that point in the immigration experience at which Ralph is no longer Chinese, and not yet an American. Ralph ". . . refused to be made an American citizen. He thumbed his nose at the relief act meant to help him, as though to claim his home was China was to make China indeed his home. And wasn't it still? Even if his place in it was fading like a picture hung too long in a barbershop—even if he didn't know where his family was anymore?" There seems to be resistance to claim a home in either China or America.

That's pretty common, don't you think? We often imagine that everybody comes here and is dying to become American. I actually think that most people are not dying to become American, even the ones who are not unhappy to be partaking of the American feast, and that's not everyone either. We don't read that much about the people who go home, and that's a lot of people. As for the ones who stay here, a lot of them are quite ambivalent for a long time, if not forever.

In Typical American, *the Changs eventually adopt the culture and values that they originally despised. Do you think this is an inevitable result of assimilation?*

One irony of *Typical American* is that "typical American" is something they call other people, but by the end of the novel, they are the kind of people that others might call "typical American." It's not like they've whole-hog adopted every facet of American culture. They've simply availed themselves of the freedom here in a way that makes them think hard about who they are now; they spend much more time thinking about their identities than they would have if they'd stayed in China.

Typical American *begins, "It's an American story: . . ." And yet, many critics labeled you as an Asian-American writer, which seems to me reductive. In fact, your work seeks to redefine what it means to be American. Was* Mona in the Promised Land *written in any way as a response to those early classifications?*

I suppose I wanted to complicate people's ideas about ethnicity in general, and how better to do that than to write about the invention of ethnicity?

I do struggle with the Asian-American thing. I don't mind it being used as a description of me, but I do mind it being used as a definition of me. Frank McCourt is an Irish-American writer who writes about Irish things. And yet sometimes he's "Irish-American writer Frank McCourt," and sometimes he's simply "writer Frank McCourt," or more often "best-selling writer Frank McCourt." The term "Irish-American" is somehow detachable from "writer" in a way that "Asian-American" is not.

That said, I'm happy to report that in many places now I am seen as someone who writes about the American dream.

In this novel you expand your territory from the Chinese immigrant experience in Typical American *to explore a larger canvas of characters with a variety of backgrounds including WASP, Jewish, African-American, and Chinese immigrants. How do you discover and define your territory as a writer?*

I write about whatever I'm interested in. I didn't for a minute wonder if I had the right to write about other groups, but I did think I needed to do my homework if I was going to. I knew that if I got one thing wrong, I would get

called on it. But that's as it should be. I think anyone writing about anything should get it all right.

As Mona in the Promised Land *progresses, each character becomes less fixed in her or his cultural identity. Mona even converts to Judaism, and her friends call her Changowitz. What interests you about the fluidity of ethnic or cultural identity?*

It is a kind of reclaiming of a reality that threatens to be lost. There is a way in which someone like me is always in danger of being frozen into an ethnic mold. I think the fact that people find the book so funny is proof that it is a challenge to ideas that are held right now in our culture. Is an Irish-American turning Jewish funny? But for a Chinese-American to turn Jewish, now that's funny!

You also capture a range of voices and inflections from New York Jewish to African-American to Chinese-American with apparent ease. Are there any pitfalls to watch for in rendering these voices?

You try to listen to the way that people really talk. If you do, it's not that complicated. I have no advice to the young writer, other than to *pay attention.*

The title story of Who's Irish? *is narrated in pidgin English by a Chinese grandmother. Did you have any concerns about writing a story in this voice?*

People have suggested that the way to gain freedom as a writer is to use a pseudonym, but for the ethnic writer, freedom actually comes with having a name and creating your own context. If I had written that story twenty years ago and sent it to the *New Yorker*, I guarantee that I would've gotten a little slip back saying "please try again when your English is better." I don't think they would've assumed the voice was artifice. Today they get the story and it says Gish Jen on it, and they know I speak English.

I've seen this again and again. If I didn't have a name of some sort, I wouldn't have been able to publish a book called *Who's Irish?* with no subtitle. As it was, nobody at my publishing house said we have to subtitle this "Stories about Asian-Americans."

One of my greatest satisfactions as a writer has been earning myself a context different than the one supplied to me by our culture. . . .

Source: Sarah Anne Johnson, "Gish Jen: Writing Off into the Darkness," in *Conversations with American Women Writers*, University Press of New England, 2004, pp. 91–95.

Andrew Furman

In the following excerpt, Furman explores Jen's treatment of immigrant cultural identity versus assimilation.

. . . To be sure, the Changs raise their daughters to be Americans, sans hyphenation. The rub is that the very definition of American identity has become slippery in the years since, say, Abraham Cahan and Anzia Yezierska were penning their immigrant novels. This has a good deal to do with the demographic rise of "minorities" in America. At the beginning of the twenty-first century, the very word, "minorities," seems a misnomer. For we are now, as the novelist Shawn Wong and others have observed, a nation of minorities (Wong 230). Consequently, the "mainstream" American experience becomes more and more difficult these days to pin down. The white Anglo-Saxon Protestant cohort in this country seems ever on the decline, both demographically and (one might as well say it) culturally. As the literary critic Stephen Sumida perceptively notes, "the repositioning of 'minority' literatures and literary studies at the 'center' of American literary history and criticism . . . [is] actively underway" (804). That the multicultural approach currently prevails at our universities bespeaks primarily the shared sense of duty on the part of academics to rescue minority fiction from years of historical neglect; however, a concomitant derision toward the culture of an increasingly embattled mainstream manifests itself in our cultural conversation as well. To wit, in Jen's first novel, *Typical American* (1991), the Changs define mainstream America by a seemingly inexhaustible string of unsavory descriptors (e.g., "no consideration for others," "no manners," "no shame") that often follow the phrase "typical American."

It should come as little surprise, amid such a zeitgeist, that Jen's characters cling to whatever cultural identity might distance themselves from the increasingly nebulous, and toothless, "mainstream." The days of cultural homogenizing seem long past in Jen's novel. In fact, a homogenized mainstream identity seems scarcely to exist for Jen's characters even as an option to reject. Instead, a whole host of "minority" identities form a patchwork quilt that one might as well call the American character. Mona must explain to her perplexed mother that to be Jewish is to be American under the current dispensation: "American means being whatever you want, and I happened to pick being Jewish."

One could hardly imagine Abraham Cahan's David Levinsky uttering such sentiments, which is simply to emphasize that to be an American at the turn of the twentieth century had exceedingly little to do with embracing whatever religion or ethnicity one wanted and everything to do with sacrificing that element of one's identity, often at a tremendous spiritual cost. Even in Philip Roth's *Portnoy's Complaint* (1969), set just after World War II, the novel's Jewish American protagonist reads the cultural landscape, from the Christmas carols that bombard him for two straight months a year, to the genteel television families so alien from his own, to the anti-Semitism that keeps his father on one of the lower rungs of the corporate ladder. He gleans enough to know that the distinctively Jewish remains decidedly un-American; thus, Roth depicts his flight from Judaism in all its religious and cultural manifestations. For example, he seeks lurid encounters with shikses like Thereal McCoy (sound it out) since "America is a shikse nestling under your arm" (*PC* 146).

Clearly, a disparate set of civic promises has emerged on the cusp of the twenty-first century during our multicultural moment. As Mona implies above, the freedom to choose one's cultural identity lies at the heart of this new civic promise. Importantly, Mona could have chosen a number of minority cultures through which to forge her own unique American identity. The pervasiveness of Jewish culture in Scarshill and its attractiveness to her convince Mona to appropriate Judaism. But the interplay between Chinese-American and Jewish American culture in Scarshill suggests, above all, the interplay between the plethora of minority cultures in all sorts of combinations and intensities that currently defines our national character. Jen's epigrams are instructive. She chooses to quote both a Japanese-American, David Mura, who reflects upon his immersion in Jewish culture growing up in Skokie, Illinois, and a Mexican-American writer, Richard Rodriguez, who reflects upon his immersion in Chinese culture: "I'm becoming Chinese, I know it."

It is the temerity of Gish Jen's approach, rather than her conception of the American identity, per se, that strikes me as dazzlingly original. Jen's characters brazenly flout their prerogative to adopt or eschew ethnicities at their convenience. On converting to Judaism, Mona blithely observes, "I'd just have to switch, that's all"; her friends, Eloise Ingle and Barbara Gugelstein, switch from Jew to Wasp and back again at their convenience. All the same, it has been some ten years since Werner Sollors, in his landmark study, *Beyond Ethnicity* (1986), noted the dynamic interplay between "consent" and "descent" in the formation of cultural identity in America. "One may say," Sollors argued, "that ethnicity is continuously created anew" (245). So, while Jen dramatically affirms the mosaic of cultural influences that inform (in varying combinations and intensities) our individual American identities, other prominent American voices have beaten her to the punch. . . .

Source: Andrew Furman, "Immigrant Dreams and Civic Promises: (Con-)Testing Identity in Early Jewish American Literature and Gish Jen's *Mona in the Promised Land*," in *MELUS*, Vol. 25, No. 1, Spring 2000, p. 209.

Don Lee

In the following excerpt, Lee explains Jen's desire to complicate the perception of race both in the short story "What Means Switch" and in its expanded novel form, Mona in the Promised Land.

. . . As successful as *Typical American* was, Jen sometimes resented critics who quickly labeled—and diminished—her as an Asian-American writer. Her reaction was to complicate what that meant via her second novel, *Mona in the Promised Land*, which came out in 1996 through Knopf. It surprised everyone. A sequel of sorts, the novel focuses on Ralph and Helen Chang's daughters, Mona and Callie, as they grow up in a Jewish suburb of New York called Scarshill. Mona Chang joins a temple youth group and then, to her parents' dismay, converts, and is thereafter referred to as "Changowitz." Ironically, Mona learns that her rabbi is right in telling her, "The more Jewish you become, the more Chinese you'll be." With the backdrop of Vietnam and the civil rights movement, the novel is a riotous, provocative collision of social, ethnic, and racial issues, populated by a mishmash of characters who are Chinese, Jewish, black, Wasp, and Japanese—a dizzying sendup that challenged readers to redefine ethnicity, and prompted one very confused

journalist to headline her review of the novel "Matzo-Ball Sushi."

Mona in the Promised Land grew out of a short story, "What Means Switch?," that Jen wrote while trying to finish *Typical American*. She had lost her first pregnancy, and didn't know if she'd be able to see her way to the end of the novel. Then she ran into an old high-school acquaintance and was inspired to revisit her teen years in Scarsdale in a short story. "You could feel the intense liberation," she says. At the same time, she jotted down some ideas for a new book in a binder of index cards. "A year or two later," she says, "I looked at one of the cards, and it said, 'Mona turns Jewish.' And I thought, 'Oy! Can't write that,' and I laughed. Then I paid attention. The uncomfortable laughter told me that I'd hit a nerve." . . .

Source: Don Lee, "About Gish Jen," in *Ploughshares*, Vol. 26, Nos. 2–3, Fall 2000, pp. 217–22.

SOURCES

Agatucci, Cora, "Gish Jen," in *Contemporary American Women Fiction Writers: An A-to-Z Guide*, edited by Laurie Champion and Rhonda Austin, Greenwood Press, 2002, pp. 147–53.

Arfaroui, Siham, "A Quest for a 'House with No Walls between the Rooms': An Ethnic Approach to Gish Jen's *Mona in the Promised Land*," in *Interactions*, Vol. 17, No. 1, Spring 2008, p. 15.

Barkan, Elliott R., "Multiculturalism," in *Dictionary of American History*, 3rd ed., edited by Stanley I. Kutler, Vol. 5, Charles Scribner's Sons, 2003, pp. 473–74.

Canion, Erika, Stephanie Johnson, Kristyna Nazar, and Keisha Ritchie, "Gish Jen," in *Voices from the Gaps*, University of Minnesota website, May 5, 2000, http://voices.cla.umn.edu/artistpages/jenGish.php (accessed February 18, 2013).

Chang, Yahlin, Review of *Mona in the Promised Land*, in *Newsweek*, Vol. 128, No. 3, July 15, 1996, p. 56.

Chen, Fu-jen, "Postmodern Hybridity and Performing Identity in Gish Jen and Rebecca Walker," in *Critique: Studies in Contemporary Fiction*, Vol. 50, No. 4, Summer 2009, p. 377.

Foran, Charles, Review of *The Love Wife*, in *Globe & Mail* (Toronto, Ontario, Canada), October 23, 2004, p. D15.

Gates, David, "On Being Hyphenated," in *Newsweek*, Vol. 133, No. 23, June 7, 1999, p. 75.

Heung, Marina, Review of *Mona in the Promised Land*, in *Women's Review of Books*, Vol. 13, No. 12, September 1996, p. 25.

Jen, Gish, "What Means Switch," in *Atlantic*, Vol. 265, No. 5, May 1990, pp. 76–84.

Lee, Don, "About Gish Jen," in *Ploughshares*, Vol. 26, Nos. 2–3, Fall 2000, pp. 217–22.

Matsukawa, Yuko, "*MELUS* Interview: Gish Jen," in *MELUS*, Vol. 18, No. 4, Winter 1993, p. 111.

"Multiculturalism," Post–World War II American Literature and Culture Database, University of California–Berkeley website, http://english.berkeley.edu/Postwar/multiculti.html (accessed February 18, 2013).

Nhan, Doris, "Maryland County Is at the Intersection of Diversity, Culture, and Language," NationalJournal.com, July 17, 2012, http://www.nationaljournal.com/thenextamerica/education/maryland-county-is-at-the-intersection-of-diversity-culture-and-language-20120727 (accessed February 19, 2013).

Oztarhan, Esra Sahtiyanci, Review of *Mona in the Promised Land*, in *Interactions*, Vol. 15, No. 2, Fall 2006, pp. 165–68.

Satz, Martha, "Writing about the Things That Are Dangerous: A Conversation with Gish Jen," in *Southwest Review*, Vol. 78, No. 1, Winter 1993, p. 132.

Terrazas, Aaron Matteo, and Bhavna Devani, "Chinese Immigrants in the United States," Migration Policy Institute website, June 2008, http://www.migrationinformation.org/feature/display.cfm?ID=685 (accessed February 19, 2013).

Terrill, Lynda, "Civics Education for Adult English Language Learners," Center for Adult English Language Acquisition website, November 2000, http://www.cal.org/caela/esl_resources/digests/civics.html (accessed February 19, 2013).

Yokota, Junko, "Asian and Asian American Literature for Adolescents: What's Important for Librarians and Teachers to Know?," in *Voice of Youth Advocates*, August 2010, p. 214.

FURTHER READING

Chang, Iris, *The Chinese in America: A Narrative History*, Viking, 2003.

Chang explores the experiences and accomplishments of Chinese immigrants and their descendants living in the United States over the last 150 years. She includes both general history and the personal stories of people striving for the American dream.

Cisneros, Sandra, *The House on Mango Street*, Arte Público, 1983.

Cisneros's book has become a classic of American Latino literature. Part poetry and part prose, the vignettes are narrated by Esperanza, a young girl living in Chicago with her family. Esperanza searches for her identity as she recounts her adventures and describes her family and her neighborhood.

Hoobler, Thomas, and Dorothy Hoobler, *We Are Americans: Voices of the Immigrant Experience*, Scholastic Nonfiction, 2003.

The Hooblers present an overview of immigration to America from prehistoric times, through the slave trade, to modern times. The book explores why people left home and how their arrival affected the United States. Personal accounts add detail to the broad historical background for a comprehensive picture of this integral part of America's population.

Jen, Gish, *The Love Wife*, Knopf, 2004.

Jen continues to examine what it means to be American and what it means to be a family in this funny, touching novel, which tells the story of a second-generation Chinese American man, his white wife (dubbed "Blondie" by her disapproving mother-in-law), their two adopted Asian daughters, and their biological son.

———, *Who's Irish? Stories*, Vintage, 1999.

In this short-story collection, Jen explores the ambition of immigrants and their efforts at assimilation. She also uses her trademark humor to portray the lack of direction sometimes displayed by the children of immigrants, much to the dismay of their hardworking parents.

SUGGESTED SEARCH TERMS

Gish Jen AND What Means Switch

Gish Jen AND short story

Gish Jen AND interview

Gish Jen AND multiculturalism

Gish Jen AND Chinese American author

stereotypes AND perception

World War II AND Japan AND China

Chinese American AND food

Japan AND etiquette

Glossary of Literary Terms

A

Aestheticism: A literary and artistic movement of the nineteenth century. Followers of the movement believed that art should not be mixed with social, political, or moral teaching. The statement "art for art's sake" is a good summary of aestheticism. The movement had its roots in France, but it gained widespread importance in England in the last half of the nineteenth century, where it helped change the Victorian practice of including moral lessons in literature. Oscar Wilde and Edgar Allan Poe are two of the best-known "aesthetes" of the late nineteenth century.

Allegory: A narrative technique in which characters representing things or abstract ideas are used to convey a message or teach a lesson. Allegory is typically used to teach moral, ethical, or religious lessons but is sometimes used for satiric or political purposes. Many fairy tales are allegories.

Allusion: A reference to a familiar literary or historical person or event, used to make an idea more easily understood. Joyce Carol Oates's story "Where Are You Going, Where Have You Been?" exhibits several allusions to popular music.

Analogy: A comparison of two things made to explain something unfamiliar through its similarities to something familiar, or to prove one point based on the acceptance of another. Similes and metaphors are types of analogies.

Antagonist: The major character in a narrative or drama who works against the hero or protagonist. The Misfit in Flannery O'Connor's story "A Good Man Is Hard to Find" serves as the antagonist for the Grandmother.

Anthology: A collection of similar works of literature, art, or music. Zora Neale Hurston's "The Eatonville Anthology" is a collection of stories that take place in the same town.

Anthropomorphism: The presentation of animals or objects in human shape or with human characteristics. The term is derived from the Greek word for "human form." The fur necklet in Katherine Mansfield's story "Miss Brill" has anthropomorphic characteristics.

Anti-hero: A central character in a work of literature who lacks traditional heroic qualities such as courage, physical prowess, and fortitude. Anti-heroes typically distrust conventional values and are unable to commit themselves to any ideals. They generally feel helpless in a world over which they have no control. Anti-heroes usually accept, and often celebrate, their positions as social outcasts. A well-known anti-hero is Walter Mitty in James Thurber's story "The Secret Life of Walter Mitty."

Archetype: The word archetype is commonly used to describe an original pattern or model from which all other things of the same kind are made. Archetypes are the literary images that grow out of the "collective unconscious," a theory proposed by psychologist Carl Jung. They appear in literature as incidents and plots that repeat basic patterns of life. They may also appear as stereotyped characters. The "schlemiel" of Yiddish literature is an archetype.

Autobiography: A narrative in which an individual tells his or her life story. Examples include Benjamin Franklin's *Autobiography* and Amy Hempel's story "In the Cemetery Where Al Jolson Is Buried," which has autobiographical characteristics even though it is a work of fiction.

Avant-garde: A literary term that describes new writing that rejects traditional approaches to literature in favor of innovations in style or content. Twentieth-century examples of the literary avant-garde include the modernists and the minimalists.

B

Belles-lettres: A French term meaning "fine letters" or" beautiful writing." It is often used as a synonym for literature, typically referring to imaginative and artistic rather than scientific or expository writing. Current usage sometimes restricts the meaning to light or humorous writing and appreciative essays about literature. Lewis Carroll's *Alice in Wonderland* epitomizes the realm of belles-lettres.

Bildungsroman: A German word meaning "novel of development." The *bildungsroman* is a study of the maturation of a youthful character, typically brought about through a series of social or sexual encounters that lead to self-awareness. J. D. Salinger's *Catcher in the Rye* is a *bildungsroman*, and Doris Lessing's story "Through the Tunnel" exhibits characteristics of a *bildungsroman* as well.

Black Aesthetic Movement: A period of artistic and literary development among African Americans in the 1960s and early 1970s. This was the first major African-American artistic movement since the Harlem Renaissance and was closely paralleled by the civil rights and black power movements. The black aesthetic writers attempted to produce works of art that would be meaningful to the black masses. Key figures in black aesthetics included one of its founders, poet and playwright Amiri Baraka, formerly known as Le Roi Jones; poet and essayist Haki R. Madhubuti, formerly Don L. Lee; poet and playwright Sonia Sanchez; and dramatist Ed Bullins. Works representative of the Black Aesthetic Movement include Amiri Baraka's play *Dutchman,* a 1964 Obie award-winner.

Black Humor: Writing that places grotesque elements side by side with humorous ones in an attempt to shock the reader, forcing him or her to laugh at the horrifying reality of a disordered world. "Lamb to the Slaughter," by Roald Dahl, in which a placid housewife murders her husband and serves the murder weapon to the investigating policemen, is an example of black humor.

C

Catharsis: The release or purging of unwanted emotions—specifically fear and pity—brought about by exposure to art. The term was first used by the Greek philosopher Aristotle in his *Poetics* to refer to the desired effect of tragedy on spectators.

Character: Broadly speaking, a person in a literary work. The actions of characters are what constitute the plot of a story, novel, or poem. There are numerous types of characters, ranging from simple, stereotypical figures to intricate, multifaceted ones. "Characterization" is the process by which an author creates vivid, believable characters in a work of art. This may be done in a variety of ways, including (1) direct description of the character by the narrator; (2) the direct presentation of the speech, thoughts, or actions of the character; and (3) the responses of other characters to the character. The term "character" also refers to a form originated by the ancient Greek writer Theophrastus that later became popular in the seventeenth and eighteenth centuries. It is a short essay or sketch of a person who prominently displays a specific attribute or quality, such as miserliness or ambition. "Miss Brill," a story by Katherine Mansfield, is an example of a character sketch.

Classical: In its strictest definition in literary criticism, classicism refers to works of ancient Greek or Roman literature. The term may also be used to describe a literary work of recognized importance (a "classic") from any time period or literature that exhibits the traits of classicism. Examples of later works and authors now described as classical include French literature of the seventeenth century, Western novels of the nineteenth century, and American fiction of the mid-nineteenth century such as that written by James Fenimore Cooper and Mark Twain.

Climax: The turning point in a narrative, the moment when the conflict is at its most intense. Typically, the structure of stories, novels, and plays is one of rising action, in which tension builds to the climax, followed by falling action, in which tension lessens as the story moves to its conclusion.

Comedy: One of two major types of drama, the other being tragedy. Its aim is to amuse, and it typically ends happily. Comedy assumes many forms, such as farce and burlesque, and uses a variety of techniques, from parody to satire. In a restricted sense the term comedy refers only to dramatic presentations, but in general usage it is commonly applied to nondramatic works as well.

Comic Relief: The use of humor to lighten the mood of a serious or tragic story, especially in plays. The technique is very common in Elizabethan works, and can be an integral part of the plot or simply a brief event designed to break the tension of the scene.

Conflict: The conflict in a work of fiction is the issue to be resolved in the story. It usually occurs between two characters, the protagonist and the antagonist, or between the protagonist and society or the protagonist and himself or herself. The conflict in Washington Irving's story "The Devil and Tom Walker" is that the Devil wants Tom Walker's soul but Tom does not want to go to hell.

Criticism: The systematic study and evaluation of literary works, usually based on a specific method or set of principles. An important part of literary studies since ancient times, the practice of criticism has given rise to numerous theories, methods, and "schools," sometimes producing conflicting, even contradictory, interpretations of literature in general as well as of individual works. Even such basic issues as what constitutes a poem or a novel have been the subject of much criticism over

the centuries. Seminal texts of literary criticism include Plato's *Republic,* Aristotle's *Poetics,* Sir Philip Sidney's *The Defence of Poesie,* and John Dryden's *Of Dramatic Poesie.* Contemporary schools of criticism include deconstruction, feminist, psychoanalytic, poststructuralist, new historicist, postcolonialist, and reader-response.

D

Deconstruction: A method of literary criticism characterized by multiple conflicting interpretations of a given work. Deconstructionists consider the impact of the language of a work and suggest that the true meaning of the work is not necessarily the meaning that the author intended.

Deduction: The process of reaching a conclusion through reasoning from general premises to a specific premise. Arthur Conan Doyle's character Sherlock Holmes often used deductive reasoning to solve mysteries.

Denotation: The definition of a word, apart from the impressions or feelings it creates in the reader. The word "apartheid" denotes a political and economic policy of segregation by race, but its connotations—oppression, slavery, inequality—are numerous.

Denouement: A French word meaning "the unknotting." In literature, it denotes the resolution of conflict in fiction or drama. The *denouement* follows the climax and provides an outcome to the primary plot situation as well as an explanation of secondary plot complications. A well-known example of *denouement* is the last scene of the play *As You Like It* by William Shakespeare, in which couples are married, an evildoer repents, the identities of two disguised characters are revealed, and a ruler is restored to power. Also known as "falling action."

Detective Story: A narrative about the solution of a mystery or the identification of a criminal. The conventions of the detective story include the detective's scrupulous use of logic in solving the mystery; incompetent or ineffectual police; a suspect who appears guilty at first but is later proved innocent; and the detective's friend or confidant—often the narrator—whose slowness in interpreting clues emphasizes by contrast the detective's brilliance. Edgar Allan Poe's "Murders in the Rue Morgue" is commonly regarded as the earliest example of this type of story. Other practitioners are Arthur Conan Doyle, Dashiell Hammett, and Agatha Christie.

Dialogue: Dialogue is conversation between people in a literary work. In its most restricted sense, it refers specifically to the speech of characters in a drama. As a specific literary genre, a "dialogue" is a composition in which characters debate an issue or idea.

Didactic: A term used to describe works of literature that aim to teach a moral, religious, political, or practical lesson. Although didactic elements are often found inartistically pleasing works, the term "didactic" usually refers to literature in which the message is more important than the form. The term may also be used to criticize a work that the critic finds "overly didactic," that is, heavy-handed in its delivery of a lesson. An example of didactic literature is John Bunyan's *Pilgrim's Progress.*

Dramatic Irony: Occurs when the reader of a work of literature knows something that a character in the work itself does not know. The irony is in the contrast between the intended meaning of the statements or actions of a character and the additional information understood by the audience.

Dystopia: An imaginary place in a work of fiction where the characters lead dehumanized, fearful lives. George Orwell's *Nineteen Eighty-four,* and Margaret Atwood's *Handmaid's Tale* portray versions of dystopia.

E

Edwardian: Describes cultural conventions identified with the period of the reign of Edward VII of England (1901–1910). Writers of the Edwardian Age typically displayed a strong reaction against the propriety and conservatism of the Victorian Age. Their work often exhibits distrust of authority in religion, politics, and art and expresses strong doubts about the soundness of conventional values. Writers of this era include E. M. Forster, H. G. Wells, and Joseph Conrad.

Empathy: A sense of shared experience, including emotional and physical feelings, with someone or something other than oneself. Empathy is often used to describe the response of a reader to a literary character.

Epilogue: A concluding statement or section of a literary work. In dramas, particularly those of the seventeenth and eighteenth centuries, the epilogue is a closing speech, often in verse, delivered by an actor at the end of a play and spoken directly to the audience.

Epiphany: A sudden revelation of truth inspired by a seemingly trivial incident. The term was widely used by James Joyce in his critical writings, and the stories in Joyce's *Dubliners* are commonly called "epiphanies."

Epistolary Novel: A novel in the form of letters. The form was particularly popular in the eighteenth century. The form can also be applied to short stories, as in Edwidge Danticat's "Children of the Sea."

Epithet: A word or phrase, often disparaging or abusive, that expresses a character trait of someone or something. "The Napoleon of crime" is an epithet applied to Professor Moriarty, arch-rival of Sherlock Holmes in Arthur Conan Doyle's series of detective stories.

Existentialism: A predominantly twentieth-century philosophy concerned with the nature and perception of human existence. There are two major strains of existentialist thought: atheistic and Christian. Followers of atheistic existentialism believe that the individual is alone in a godless universe and that the basic human condition is one of suffering and loneliness. Nevertheless, because there are no fixed values, individuals can create their own characters—indeed, they can shape themselves—through the exercise of free will. The atheistic strain culminates in and is popularly associated with the works of Jean-Paul Sartre. The Christian existentialists, on the other hand, believe that only in God may people find freedom from life's anguish. The two strains hold certain beliefs in common: that existence cannot be fully understood or described through empirical effort; that anguish is a universal element of life; that individuals must bear responsibility for their actions; and that there is no common standard of behavior or perception for religious and ethical matters. Existentialist thought figures prominently in the works of such authors as Franz Kafka, Fyodor Dostoyevsky, and Albert Camus.

Expatriatism: The practice of leaving one's country to live for an extended period in another country. Literary expatriates include Irish author James Joyce who moved to Italy and France, American writers James Baldwin, Ernest Hemingway, Gertrude Stein, and F. Scott Fitzgerald who lived and wrote in Paris, and Polish novelist Joseph Conrad in England.

Exposition: Writing intended to explain the nature of an idea, thing, or theme. Expository writing is often combined with description, narration, or argument.

Expressionism: An indistinct literary term, originally used to describe an early twentieth-century school of German painting. The term applies to almost any mode of unconventional, highly subjective writing that distorts reality in some way. Advocates of Expressionism include Federico Garcia Lorca, Eugene O'Neill, Franz Kafka, and James Joyce.

F

Fable: A prose or verse narrative intended to convey amoral. Animals or inanimate objects with human characteristics often serve as characters in fables. A famous fable is Aesop's "The Tortoise and the Hare."

Fantasy: A literary form related to mythology and folklore. Fantasy literature is typically set in non-existent realms and features supernatural beings. Notable examples of literature with elements of fantasy are Gabriel García Márquez's story "The Handsomest Drowned Man in the World" and Ursula K. Le Guin's "The Ones Who Walk Away from Omelas."

Farce: A type of comedy characterized by broad humor, outlandish incidents, and often vulgar subject matter. Much of the comedy in film and television could more accurately be described as farce.

Fiction: Any story that is the product of imagination rather than a documentation of fact. Characters and events in such narratives may be based in real life but their ultimate form and configuration is a creation of the author.

Figurative Language: A technique in which an author uses figures of speech such as hyperbole, irony, metaphor, or simile for a particular effect. Figurative language is the opposite of literal language, in which every word is truthful, accurate, and free of exaggeration or embellishment.

Flashback: A device used in literature to present action that occurred before the beginning of the story. Flashbacks are often introduced as the dreams or recollections of one or more characters.

Foil: A character in a work of literature whose physical or psychological qualities contrast strongly with, and therefore highlight, the corresponding qualities of another character. In his Sherlock Holmes stories, Arthur Conan Doyle portrayed Dr. Watson as a man of normal habits and intelligence, making him a foil for the eccentric and unusually perceptive Sherlock Holmes.

Folklore: Traditions and myths preserved in a culture or group of people. Typically, these are passed on by word of mouth in various forms—such as legends, songs, and proverbs—or preserved in customs and ceremonies. Washington Irving, in "The Devil and Tom Walker" and many of his other stories, incorporates many elements of the folklore of New England and Germany.

Folktale: A story originating in oral tradition. Folk tales fall into a variety of categories, including legends, ghost stories, fairy tales, fables, and anecdotes based on historical figures and events.

Foreshadowing: A device used in literature to create expectation or to set up an explanation of later developments. Edgar Allan Poe uses foreshadowing to create suspense in "The Fall of the House of Usher" when the narrator comments on the crumbling state of disrepair in which he finds the house.

G

Genre: A category of literary work. Genre may refer to both the content of a given work—tragedy, comedy, horror, science fiction—and to its form, such as poetry, novel, or drama.

Gilded Age: A period in American history during the 1870s and after characterized by political corruption and materialism. A number of important novels of social and political criticism were written during this time. Henry James and Kate Chopin are two writers who were prominent during the Gilded Age.

Gothicism: In literature, works characterized by a taste for medieval or morbid characters and situations. A gothic novel prominently features elements of horror, the supernatural, gloom, and violence: clanking chains, terror, ghosts, medieval castles, and unexplained phenomena. The term "gothic novel" is also applied to novels that lack elements of the traditional Gothic setting but that create a similar atmosphere of terror or dread. The term can also be applied to stories, plays, and poems. Mary Shelley's *Frankenstein* and Joyce Carol Oates's *Bellefleur* are both gothic novels.

Grotesque: In literature, a work that is characterized by exaggeration, deformity, freakishness, and disorder. The grotesque often includes an element of comic absurdity. Examples of the grotesque can be found in the works of Edgar Allan Poe, Flannery O'Connor, Joseph Heller, and Shirley Jackson.

H

Harlem Renaissance: The Harlem Renaissance of the 1920s is generally considered the first significant movement of black writers and artists in the United States. During this period, new and established black writers, many of whom lived in the region of New York City known as Harlem, published more fiction and poetry than ever before, the first influential black literary journals were established, and black authors and artists received their first widespread recognition and serious critical appraisal. Among the major writers associated with this period are Countee Cullen, Langston Hughes, Arna Bontemps, and Zora Neale Hurston.

Hero/Heroine: The principal sympathetic character in a literary work. Heroes and heroines typically exhibit admirable traits: idealism, courage, and integrity, for example. Famous heroes and heroines of literature include Charles Dickens's Oliver Twist, Margaret Mitchell's Scarlett O'Hara, and the anonymous narrator in Ralph Ellison's *Invisible Man.*

Hyperbole: Deliberate exaggeration used to achieve an effect. In William Shakespeare's *Macbeth,* Lady Macbeth hyperbolizes when she says, "All the perfumes of Arabia could not sweeten this little hand."

I

Image: A concrete representation of an object or sensory experience. Typically, such a representation helps evoke the feelings associated with the object or experience itself. Images are either "literal" or "figurative." Literal images are especially concrete and involve little or no extension of the obvious meaning of the words used to express them. Figurative images do not follow the literal meaning of the words exactly. Images in literature are usually visual, but the term "image" can also refer to the representation of any sensory experience.

Imagery: The array of images in a literary work. Also used to convey the author's overall use of figurative language in a work.

In medias res: A Latin term meaning "in the middle of things." It refers to the technique of beginning a story at its midpoint and then using various flashback devices to reveal previous action. This technique originated in such epics as Virgil's *Aeneid.*

Interior Monologue: A narrative technique in which characters' thoughts are revealed in a way that appears to be uncontrolled by the author. The interior monologue typically aims to reveal the inner self of a character. It portrays emotional experiences as they occur at both a conscious and unconscious level. One of the best-known interior monologues in English is the Molly Bloom section at the close of James Joyce's *Ulysses.* Katherine Anne Porter's "The Jilting of Granny Weatherall" is also told in the form of an interior monologue.

Irony: In literary criticism, the effect of language in which the intended meaning is the opposite of what is stated. The title of Jonathan Swift's "A Modest Proposal" is ironic because what Swift proposes in this essay is cannibalism—hardly "modest."

J

Jargon: Language that is used or understood only by a select group of people. Jargon may refer to terminology used in a certain profession, such as computer jargon, or it may refer to any nonsensical language that is not understood by most people. Anthony Burgess's *A Clockwork Orange* and James Thurber's "The Secret Life of Walter Mitty" both use jargon.

K

Knickerbocker Group: An indistinct group of New York writers of the first half of the nineteenth century. Members of the group were linked only by location and a common theme: New York life. Two famous members of the Knickerbocker Group were Washington Irving and William Cullen Bryant. The group's name derives from Irving's *Knickerbocker's History of New York*.

L

Literal Language: An author uses literal language when he or she writes without exaggerating or embellishing the subject matter and without any tools of figurative language. To say "He ran very quickly down the street" is to use literal language, whereas to say "He ran like a hare down the street" would be using figurative language.

Literature: Literature is broadly defined as any written or spoken material, but the term most often refers to creative works. Literature includes poetry, drama, fiction, and many kinds of nonfiction writing, as well as oral, dramatic, and broadcast compositions not necessarily preserved in a written format, such as films and television programs.

Lost Generation: A term first used by Gertrude Stein to describe the post-World War I generation of American writers: men and women haunted by a sense of betrayal and emptiness brought about by the destructiveness of the war. The term is commonly applied to Hart Crane, Ernest Hemingway, F. Scott Fitzgerald, and others.

M

Magic Realism: A form of literature that incorporates fantasy elements or supernatural occurrences into the narrative and accepts them as truth. Gabriel Gárcia Márquez and Laura Esquivel are two writers known for their works of magic realism.

Metaphor: A figure of speech that expresses an idea through the image of another object. Metaphors suggest the essence of the first object by identifying it with certain qualities of the second object. An example is "But soft, what light through yonder window breaks? / It is the east, and Juliet is the sun" in William Shakespeare's *Romeo and Juliet*. Here, Juliet, the first object, is identified with qualities of the second object, the sun.

Minimalism: A literary style characterized by spare, simple prose with few elaborations. In minimalism, the main theme of the work is often never discussed directly. Amy Hempel and Ernest Hemingway are two writers known for their works of minimalism.

Modernism: Modern literary practices. Also, the principles of a literary school that lasted from roughly the beginning of the twentieth century until the end of World War II. Modernism is defined by its rejection of the literary conventions of the nineteenth century and by its opposition to conventional morality, taste, traditions, and economic values. Many writers are associated with the concepts of modernism, including Albert Camus, D. H. Lawrence, Ernest Hemingway, William Faulkner, Eugene O'Neill, and James Joyce.

Monologue: A composition, written or oral, by a single individual. More specifically, a speech given by a single individual in a drama or other public entertainment. It has no set length, although it is usually several or more lines long. "I Stand Here Ironing" by Tillie Olsen is an example of a story written in the form of a monologue.

Mood: The prevailing emotions of a work or of the author in his or her creation of the work. The mood of a work is not always what might be expected based on its subject matter.

Motif: A theme, character type, image, metaphor, or other verbal element that recurs throughout a single work of literature or occurs in a number of different works over a period of time. For example, the color white in Herman Melville's *Moby Dick* is a "specific" motif, while the trials of star-crossed lovers is a "conventional" motif from the literature of all periods.

N

Narration: The telling of a series of events, real or invented. A narration may be either a simple narrative, in which the events are recounted chronologically, or a narrative with a plot, in which the account is given in a style reflecting the author's artistic concept of the story. Narration is sometimes used as a synonym for "storyline."

Narrative: A verse or prose accounting of an event or sequence of events, real or invented.

The term is also used as an adjective in the sense "method of narration." For example, in literary criticism, the expression "narrative technique" usually refers to the way the author structures and presents his or her story. Different narrative forms include diaries, travelogues, novels, ballads, epics, short stories, and other fictional forms.

Narrator: The teller of a story. The narrator may be the author or a character in the story through whom the author speaks. Huckleberry Finn is the narrator of Mark Twain's *The Adventures of Huckleberry Finn.*

Novella: An Italian term meaning "story." This term has been especially used to describe fourteenth-century Italian tales, but it also refers to modern short novels. Modern novellas include Leo Tolstoy's *The Death of Ivan Ilich,* Fyodor Dostoyevsky's *Notes from the Underground,* and Joseph Conrad's *Heart of Darkness.*

O

Oedipus Complex: A son's romantic obsession with his mother. The phrase is derived from the story of the ancient Theban hero Oedipus, who unknowingly killed his father and married his mother, and was popularized by Sigmund Freud's theory of psychoanalysis. Literary occurrences of the Oedipus complex include Sophocles' *Oedipus Rex* and D. H. Lawrence's "The Rocking-Horse Winner."

Onomatopoeia: The use of words whose sounds express or suggest their meaning. In its simplest sense, onomatopoeia may be represented by words that mimic the sounds they denote such as "hiss" or "meow." At a more subtle level, the pattern and rhythm of sounds and rhymes of a line or poem may be onomatopoeic.

Oral Tradition: A process by which songs, ballads, folklore, and other material are transmitted by word of mouth. The tradition of oral transmission predates the written record systems of literate society. Oral transmission preserves material sometimes over generations, although often with variations. Memory plays a large part in the recitation and preservation of orally transmitted material. Native American myths and legends, and African folktales told by plantation slaves are examples of orally transmitted literature.

P

Parable: A story intended to teach a moral lesson or answer an ethical question. Examples of parables are the stories told by Jesus Christ in the New Testament, notably "The Prodigal Son," but parables also are used in Sufism, rabbinic literature, Hasidism, and Zen Buddhism. Isaac Bashevis Singer's story "Gimpel the Fool" exhibits characteristics of a parable.

Paradox: A statement that appears illogical or contradictory at first, but may actually point to an underlying truth. A literary example of a paradox is George Orwell's statement "All animals are equal, but some animals are more equal than others" in *Animal Farm.*

Parody: In literature, this term refers to an imitation of a serious literary work or the signature style of a particular author in a ridiculous manner. Atypical parody adopts the style of the original and applies it to an inappropriate subject for humorous effect. Parody is a form of satire and could be considered the literary equivalent of a caricature or cartoon. Henry Fielding's *Shamela* is a parody of Samuel Richardson's *Pamela.*

Persona: A Latin term meaning "mask." Personae are the characters in a fictional work of literature. The persona generally functions as a mask through which the author tells a story in a voice other than his or her own. A persona is usually either a character in a story who acts as a narrator or an "implied author," a voice created by the author to act as the narrator for himself or herself. The persona in Charlotte Perkins Gilman's story "The Yellow Wallpaper" is the unnamed young mother experiencing a mental breakdown.

Personification: A figure of speech that gives human qualities to abstract ideas, animals, and inanimate objects. To say that "the sun is smiling" is to personify the sun.

Plot: The pattern of events in a narrative or drama. In its simplest sense, the plot guides the author in composing the work and helps the reader follow the work. Typically, plots exhibit causality and unity and have a beginning, a middle, and an end. Sometimes, however, a plot may consist of a series of disconnected events, in which case it is known as an "episodic plot."

Poetic Justice: An outcome in a literary work, not necessarily a poem, in which the good are rewarded and the evil are punished, especially in ways that particularly fit their virtues or crimes. For example, a murderer may himself be murdered, or a thief will find himself penniless.

Poetic License: Distortions of fact and literary convention made by a writer—not always a poet—for the sake of the effect gained. Poetic license is closely related to the concept of "artistic freedom." An author exercises poetic license by saying that a pile of money "reaches as high as a mountain" when the pile is actually only a foot or two high.

Point of View: The narrative perspective from which a literary work is presented to the reader. There are four traditional points of view. The "third person omniscient" gives the reader a "godlike" perspective, unrestricted by time or place, from which to see actions and look into the minds of characters. This allows the author to comment openly on characters and events in the work. The "third person" point of view presents the events of the story from outside of any single character's perception, much like the omniscient point of view, but the reader must understand the action as it takes place and without any special insight into characters' minds or motivations. The "first person" or "personal" point of view relates events as they are perceived by a single character. The main character "tells" the story and may offer opinions about the action and characters which differ from those of the author. Much less common than omniscient, third person, and first person is the "second person" point of view, wherein the author tells the story as if it is happening to the reader. James Thurber employs the omniscient point of view in his short story "The Secret Life of Walter Mitty." Ernest Hemingway's "A Clean, Well-Lighted Place" is a short story told from the third person point of view. Mark Twain's novel *Huckleberry Finn* is presented from the first person viewpoint. Jay McInerney's *Bright Lights, Big City* is an example of a novel which uses the second person point of view.

Pornography: Writing intended to provoke feelings of lust in the reader. Such works are often condemned by critics and teachers, but those which can be shown to have literary value are viewed less harshly. Literary works

that have been described as pornographic include D. H. Lawrence's *Lady Chatterley's Lover* and James Joyce's *Ulysses*.

Post-Aesthetic Movement: An artistic response made by African Americans to the black aesthetic movement of the 1960s and early 1970s. Writers since that time have adopted a somewhat different tone in their work, with less emphasis placed on the disparity between black and white in the United States. In the words of post-aesthetic authors such as Toni Morrison, John Edgar Wideman, and Kristin Hunter, African Americans are portrayed as looking inward for answers to their own questions, rather than always looking to the outside world. Two well-known examples of works produced as part of the post-aesthetic movement are the Pulitzer Prize–winning novels *The Color Purple* by Alice Walker and *Beloved* by Toni Morrison.

Postmodernism: Writing from the 1960s forward characterized by experimentation and application of modernist elements, which include existentialism and alienation. Postmodernists have gone a step further in the rejection of tradition begun with the modernists by also rejecting traditional forms, preferring the anti-novel over the novel and the anti-hero over the hero. Postmodern writers include Thomas Pynchon, Margaret Drabble, and Gabriel Gárcia Márquez.

Prologue: An introductory section of a literary work. It often contains information establishing the situation of the characters or presents information about the setting, time period, or action. In drama, the prologue is spoken by a chorus or by one of the principal characters.

Prose: A literary medium that attempts to mirror the language of everyday speech. It is distinguished from poetry by its use of unmetered, unrhymed language consisting of logically related sentences. Prose is usually grouped into paragraphs that form a cohesive whole such as an essay or a novel. The term is sometimes used to mean an author's general writing.

Protagonist: The central character of a story who serves as a focus for its themes and incidents and as the principal rationale for its development. The protagonist is sometimes referred to in discussions of modern literature as the hero or anti-hero. Well-known protagonists are Hamlet in William Shakespeare's *Hamlet* and Jay Gatsby in F. Scott Fitzgerald's *The Great Gatsby*.

R

Realism: A nineteenth-century European literary movement that sought to portray familiar characters, situations, and settings in a realistic manner. This was done primarily by using an objective narrative point of view and through the buildup of accurate detail. The standard for success of any realistic work depends on how faithfully it transfers common experience into fictional forms. The realistic method may be altered or extended, as in stream of consciousness writing, to record highly subjective experience. Contemporary authors who often write in a realistic way include Nadine Gordimer and Grace Paley.

Resolution: The portion of a story following the climax, in which the conflict is resolved. The resolution of Jane Austen's *Northanger Abbey* is neatly summed up in the following sentence: "Henry and Catherine were married, the bells rang and every body smiled."

Rising Action: The part of a drama where the plot becomes increasingly complicated. Rising action leads up to the climax, or turning point, of a drama. The final "chase scene" of an action film is generally the rising action which culminates in the film's climax.

Roman a clef: A French phrase meaning "novel with a key." It refers to a narrative in which real persons are portrayed under fictitious names. Jack Kerouac, for example, portrayed various friends under fictitious names in the novel *On the Road*. D. H. Lawrence based "The Rocking-Horse Winner" on a family he knew.

Romanticism: This term has two widely accepted meanings. In historical criticism, it refers to a European intellectual and artistic movement of the late eighteenth and early nineteenth centuries that sought greater freedom of personal expression than that allowed by the strict rules of literary form and logic of the eighteenth-century neoclassicists. The Romantics preferred emotional and imaginative expression to rational analysis. They considered the individual to be at the center of all experience and so placed him or her at the center of their art. The Romantics believed that the creative imagination reveals nobler truths—unique feelings and attitudes—than those that could be discovered by logic or by scientific examination. "Romanticism" is also used as a general term to refer to a type of sensibility found in all periods of literary history and usually considered to be in opposition to the principles of classicism. In this sense, Romanticism signifies any work or philosophy in which the exotic or dreamlike figure strongly, or that is devoted to individualistic expression, self-analysis, or a pursuit of a higher realm of knowledge than can be discovered by human reason. Prominent Romantics include Jean-Jacques Rousseau, William Wordsworth, John Keats, Lord Byron, and Johann Wolfgang von Goethe.

S

Satire: A work that uses ridicule, humor, and wit to criticize and provoke change in human nature and institutions. Voltaire's novella *Candide* and Jonathan Swift's essay "A Modest Proposal" are both satires. Flannery O'Connor's portrayal of the family in "A Good Man Is Hard to Find" is a satire of a modern, Southern, American family.

Science Fiction: A type of narrative based upon real or imagined scientific theories and technology. Science fiction is often peopled with alien creatures and set on other planets or in different dimensions. Popular writers of science fiction are Isaac Asimov, Karel Capek, Ray Bradbury, and Ursula K. Le Guin.

Setting: The time, place, and culture in which the action of a narrative takes place. The elements of setting may include geographic location, characters's physical and mental environments, prevailing cultural attitudes, or the historical time in which the action takes place.

Short Story: A fictional prose narrative shorter and more focused than a novella. The short story usually deals with a single episode and often a single character. The "tone," the author's attitude toward his or her subject and audience, is uniform throughout. The short story frequently also lacks *denouement*, ending instead at its climax.

Signifying Monkey: A popular trickster figure in black folklore, with hundreds of tales about this character documented since the 19th century. Henry Louis Gates Jr. examines the history of the signifying monkey in *The Signifying Monkey: Towards a Theory of Afro-American Literary Criticism,* published in 1988.

Simile: A comparison, usually using "like" or "as," of two essentially dissimilar things, as in "coffee as cold as ice" or "He sounded like a broken record." The title of Ernest Hemingway's "Hills Like White Elephants" contains a simile.

Socialist Realism: The Socialist Realism school of literary theory was proposed by Maxim Gorky and established as a dogma by the first Soviet Congress of Writers. It demanded adherence to a communist worldview in works of literature. Its doctrines required an objective viewpoint comprehensible to the working classes and themes of social struggle featuring strong proletarian heroes. Gabriel Gárcia Márquez's stories exhibit some characteristics of Socialist Realism.

Stereotype: A stereotype was originally the name for a duplication made during the printing process; this led to its modern definition as a person or thing that is (or is assumed to be) the same as all others of its type. Common stereotypical characters include the absent-minded professor, the nagging wife, the troublemaking teenager, and the kind-hearted grandmother.

Stream of Consciousness: A narrative technique for rendering the inward experience of a character. This technique is designed to give the impression of an ever-changing series of thoughts, emotions, images, and memories in the spontaneous and seemingly illogical order that they occur in life. The textbook example of stream of consciousness is the last section of James Joyce's *Ulysses.*

Structure: The form taken by a piece of literature. The structure may be made obvious for ease of understanding, as in nonfiction works, or may obscured for artistic purposes, as in some poetry or seemingly "unstructured" prose.

Style: A writer's distinctive manner of arranging words to suit his or her ideas and purpose in writing. The unique imprint of the author's personality upon his or her writing, style is the product of an author's way of arranging ideas and his or her use of diction, different sentence structures, rhythm, figures of speech, rhetorical principles, and other elements of composition.

Suspense: A literary device in which the author maintains the audience's attention through the buildup of events, the outcome of which will soon be revealed. Suspense in William Shakespeare's *Hamlet* is sustained throughout by the question of whether or not the Prince will achieve what he has been instructed to do and of what he intends to do.

Symbol: Something that suggests or stands for something else without losing its original identity. In literature, symbols combine their literal meaning with the suggestion of an abstract concept. Literary symbols are of two types: those that carry complex associations of meaning no matter what their contexts, and those that derive their suggestive meaning from their functions in specific literary works. Examples of symbols are sunshine suggesting happiness, rain suggesting sorrow, and storm clouds suggesting despair.

T

Tale: A story told by a narrator with a simple plot and little character development. Tales are usually relatively short and often carry a simple message. Examples of tales can be found in the works of Saki, Anton Chekhov, Guy de Maupassant, and O. Henry.

Tall Tale: A humorous tale told in a straightforward, credible tone but relating absolutely impossible events or feats of the characters. Such tales were commonly told of frontier adventures during the settlement of the west in the United States. Literary use of tall tales can be found in Washington Irving's *History of New York,* Mark Twain's *Life on the Mississippi,* and in the German R. F. Raspe's *Baron Munchausen's Narratives of His Marvellous Travels and Campaigns in Russia.*

Theme: The main point of a work of literature. The term is used interchangeably with thesis. Many works have multiple themes. One of the themes of Nathaniel Hawthorne's "Young Goodman Brown" is loss of faith.

Tone: The author's attitude toward his or her audience maybe deduced from the tone of the work. A formal tone may create distance or convey politeness, while an informal tone may encourage a friendly, intimate, or intrusive feeling in the reader. The author's attitude toward his or her subject matter may also be deduced from the tone of the words he or she uses in discussing it. The tone of John F. Kennedy's speech which included the appeal to "ask not what your country can do for you" was intended to instill feelings of camaraderie and national pride in listeners.

Tragedy: A drama in prose or poetry about a noble, courageous hero of excellent character who, because of some tragic character flaw, brings ruin upon him- or herself. Tragedy treats its subjects in a dignified and serious manner, using poetic language to help evoke pity and fear and bring about catharsis, a purging of these emotions. The tragic form was practiced extensively by the ancient Greeks. The classical form of tragedy was revived in the sixteenth century; it flourished especially on the Elizabethan stage. In modern times, dramatists have attempted to adapt the form to the needs of modern society by drawing their heroes from the ranks of ordinary men and women and defining the nobility of these heroes in terms of spirit rather than exalted social standing. Some contemporary works that are thought of as tragedies include *The Great Gatsby* by F. Scott Fitzgerald, and *The Sound and the Fury* by William Faulkner.

Tragic Flaw: In a tragedy, the quality within the hero or heroine which leads to his or her downfall. Examples of the tragic flaw include Othello's jealousy and Hamlet's indecisiveness, although most great tragedies defy such simple interpretation.

U

Utopia: A fictional perfect place, such as "paradise" or "heaven." An early literary utopia was described in Plato's *Republic,* and in modern literature, Ursula K. Le Guin depicts a utopia in "The Ones Who Walk Away from Omelas."

V

Victorian: Refers broadly to the reign of Queen Victoria of England (1837-1901) and to anything with qualities typical of that era. For example, the qualities of smug narrow-mindedness, bourgeois materialism, faith in social progress, and priggish morality are often considered Victorian. In literature, the Victorian Period was the great age of the English novel, and the latter part of the era saw the rise of movements such as decadence and symbolism.

Cumulative Author/Title Index

Cumulative
Nationality/Ethnicity Index

African American

Baldwin, James
  The Rockpile: V18
  Sonny's Blues: V2
Bambara, Toni Cade
  Blues Ain't No Mockin Bird:
    V4
  Gorilla, My Love: V21
  The Lesson: V12
  Raymond's Run: V7
Brooks, Gwendolyn
  Home: V35
Butler, Octavia
  Bloodchild: V6
Chesnutt, Charles Waddell
  The Goophered Grapevine: V26
  The Sheriff's Children: V11
Clifton, Lucille
  The Lucky Stone: V34
Collier, Eugenia W.
  Marigolds: V28
  Sweet Potato Pie: V30
Ellison, Ralph
  King of the Bingo Game: V1
Hughes, Langston
  The Blues I'm Playing: V7
  Slave on the Block: V4
  Thank You Ma'm: V29
Hurston, Zora Neale
  Conscience of the Court: V21
  The Eatonville Anthology: V1
  The Gilded Six-Bits: V11
  Spunk: V6
  Sweat: V19
Lee, Andrea
  New African: V37

Marshall, Paule
  To Da-duh, in Memoriam: V15
McPherson, James Alan
  Elbow Room: V23
Myers, Walter Dean
  The Treasure of Lemon Brown:
    V31
Toomer, Jean
  Blood-Burning Moon: V5
Walker, Alice
  Everyday Use: V2
  Roselily: V11
Wideman, John Edgar
  The Beginning of Homewood:
    V12
  Fever: V6
  *What We Cannot Speak About We
    Must Pass Over in Silence:*
    V24
Wright, Richard
  Big Black Good Man: V20
  Bright and Morning Star: V15
  The Man Who Lived Underground:
    V3
  The Man Who Was Almost a Man:
    V9

American

Adams, Alice
  Greyhound People: V21
  The Last Lovely City: V14
Agüeros, Jack
  Dominoes: V13
Aiken, Conrad
  Impulse: V34
  Silent Snow, Secret Snow: V8

Aiken, Joan
  Lob's Girl: V38
  Sonata for Harp and Bicycle: V33
Alexie, Sherman
  *Because My Father Always Said
    He Was the Only Indian Who
    Saw Jimi Hendrix Play "The
    Star-Spangled Banner" at
    Woodstock:* V18
Allen, Woody
  The Kugelmass Episode: V21
Alvarez, Julia
  Daughter of Invention: V31
  Liberty: V27
Anaya, Rudolfo
  In Search of Epifano: V38
Anderson, Sherwood
  Death in the Woods: V10
  The Egg: V37
  Hands: V11
  Sophistication: V4
Asimov, Isaac
  The Machine That Won the War:
    V33
  Nightfall: V17
Baida, Peter
  A Nurse's Story: V25
Baldwin, James
  The Rockpile: V18
  Sonny's Blues: V2
Bambara, Toni Cade
  Blues Ain't No Mockin Bird: V4
  Gorilla, My Love: V21
  The Lesson: V12
  Raymond's Run: V7
Barrett, Andrea
  The English Pupil: V24

Cumulative Nationality/Ethnicity Index

Yamamoto, Hisaye
   The Eskimo Connection: V14
Yates, Richard
   The Canal: V24
Yezierska, Anzia
   America and I: V15
Yolen, Jane
   Suzy and Leah: V29

Antiguan
Kincaid, Jamaica
   Girl: V7
   What I Have Been Doing Lately: V5

Argentinian
Borges, Jorge Luis
   The Aleph: V17
   The Circular Ruins: V26
   The Garden of Forking Paths: V9
   The House of Asterion: V32
   *Pierre Menard, Author of the
      Quixote:* V4
Cortázar, Julio
   Axolotl: V3
   End of the Game: V31
   House Taken Over: V28
   The Night Face Up: V34
   The Pursuer: V20
Valenzuela, Luisa
   The Censors: V29

Asian American
Jen, Gish
   What Means Switch: V38
   The White Umbrella: V34
Kingston, Maxine Hong
   On Discovery: V3
Lee, Don
   The Price of Eggs in China: V25
Tan, Amy
   Rules of the Game: V16
   Two Kinds: V9
Uchida, Yoshiko
   Tears of Autumn: V31
Yamamoto, Hisaye
   The Eskimo Connection: V14

Australian
Malouf, David
   Great Day: V24

Austrian
Kafka, Franz
   A Country Doctor: V33
   A Hunger Artist: V7
   In the Penal Colony: V3
   The Metamorphosis: V12
Stephenson, Carl
   Leiningen Versus the Ants: V32

Bosnian
Hemon, Aleksandar
   Islands: V22

Canadian
Atwood, Margaret
   Happy Endings: V13
   Rape Fantasies: V3
Bellow, Saul
   A Silver Dish: V22
Callaghan, Morley
   All the Years of Her Life: V19
Mistry, Rohinton
   Swimming Lessons: V6
Mukherjee, Bharati
   The Management of Grief: V7
   The Middleman: V24
   The Tenant: V32
Munro, Alice
   Boys and Girls: V5
   Day of the Butterfly: V28
   How I Met My Husband: V36
   Meneseteung: V19
   Walker Brothers Cowboy: V13
Swan, Mary
   The Deep: V23

Chilean
Allende, Isabel
   And of Clay Are We Created: V11
   The Gold of Tomás Vargas: V16
Bombal, María Luisa
   The Tree: V36

Chinese
Dao, Bei
   The Homecoming Stranger: V35
Jie, Zhang
   Love Must Not Be Forgotten: V30
Jin, Ha
   In the Kindergarten: V17
   Saboteur: V32
Yiyun Li
   Immortality: V24

Colombian
García Márquez, Gabriel
   Eyes of a Blue Dog: V21
   *The Handsomest Drowned Man in
      the World:* V1
   Tuesday Siesta: V37
   *A Very Old Man with Enormous
      Wings:* V6
   *The Woman Who Came at Six
      O'Clock:* V16

Cuban
Calvino, Italo
   The Feathered Ogre: V12

Rivera, Beatriz
   African Passions: V15

Czech
Kafka, Franz
   A Country Doctor: V33
   A Hunger Artist: V7
   In the Penal Colony: V3
   The Metamorphosis: V12
Kundera, Milan
   The Hitchhiking Game: V10

Danish
Dinesen, Isak
   Babette's Feast: V20
   The Ring: V6
   The Sailor-Boy's Tale: V13
   Sorrow-Acre: V3
Høeg, Peter
   Journey into a Dark Heart: V18

Dominican
Alvarez, Julia
   Daughter of Invention: V31
   Liberty: V27
Díaz, Junot
   The Sun, the Moon, the Stars: V20

Egyptian
El-Bisatie, Mohamed
   *A Conversation from the Third
      Floor:* V17
Mahfouz, Naguib
   Half a Day: V9
   The Norwegian Rat: V33

English
Aiken, Joan
   Lob's Girl: V38
   Sonata for Harp and Bicycle: V33
Barnes, Julian
   Melon: V24
Bates, H. E.
   The Daffodil Sky: V7
Bowen, Elizabeth
   The Demon Lover: V5
Burton, Richard
   The Arabian Nights: V21
Byatt, A. S.
   Art Work: V26
Carter, Angela
   The Bloody Chamber: V4
   The Erlking: V12
Christie, Agatha
   Wasps' Nest: V34
   The Witness for the Prosecution:
      V31
Clarke, Arthur C.
   Dog Star: V29

Subject/Theme Index